Making Cultural Connections

Readings for Critical Analysis

MARILYN RYE

Rutgers University

BEDFORD BOOKS *of* ST. MARTIN'S PRESS · BOSTON

FOR BEDFORD BOOKS

Publisher: Charles H. Christensen
Associate Publisher/General Manager: Joan E. Feinberg
Managing Editor: Elizabeth M. Schaaf
Developmental Editor: Ellen M. Kuhl
Production Editor: Lori Chong
Copyeditor: Anthony Perriello
Text Design: Claire Seng-Niemoeller
Cover Design: Steve Snider
Cover Art: We Are the People, © Tom Phillips/DACS, London/VAGA, New York 1993

Library of Congress Catalog Card Number: 92–75314

8 7 6 5 4

f e d c b a

For information, write: St. Martin's Press, Inc.
175 Fifth Avenue, New York, NY 10010
Editorial Offices: Bedford Books of St. Martin's Press
29 Winchester Street, Boston, MA 02116

ISBN: 0–312–06782–8

ACKNOWLEDGMENTS

Paula Gunn Allen, "Where I Come from Is Like This." From *The Sacred Hoop* by Paula Gunn Allen. Copyright © 1986 by Paula Gunn Allen. Reprinted by permission of Beacon Press.

James Baldwin, "Whose Child Are You?" From *The Fire Next Time* by James Baldwin. Copyright © 1962, 1963 by James Baldwin. Used by permission of Doubleday, a division of Bantam Doubleday Dell Publishing Group, Inc.

Simone de Beauvoir, "Introduction from *The Second Sex.*" From *The Second Sex* by Simone de Beauvoir, trans. H. M. Parshley. Copyright © 1952 by Alfred A. Knopf, Inc. Reprinted by permission of the publisher.

Raymonde Carroll, "Parents and Children." From *Cultural Misunderstandings: The French-American Experience* by Raymonde Carroll. Copyright © 1988. Reprinted by permission of the University of Chicago Press and the author.

Robert C. Christopher, "The Fruits of Industry." From *The Japanese Mind* by Robert C. Christopher. Copyright © 1983 by Kriscon Corporation. Reprinted by permission of Linden Press, a division of Simon & Schuster, Inc.

Jane Collier, Michelle Z. Rosaldo, and Sylvia Yanagisako, "Is There a Family? New Anthropological Views." This chapter first appeared in *Rethinking the Family: Some Feminist Questions,* eds. Barrie Thorne with Marilyn Yalom (New York: Longman, 1981) and is reprinted in the second edition of this work (Boston: Northeastern University Press, 1992). Reprinted by permission of Marilyn Yalom and Stanford University's Institute for Research on Women and Gender.

Jill Ker Conway, "The Right Country." From *The Road from Coorain* by Jill Ker Conway. Copyright © 1989 by Jill Conway. Reprinted by permission of Alfred A. Knopf, Inc.

Annie Dillard, "The Writing Life." Excerpted from *The Writing Life* by Annie Dillard. Copyright © 1989 by Annie Dillard. Reprinted by permission of HarperCollins Publishers.

Acknowledgments and copyrights are continued at the back of the book on pages 582–583, which constitute an extension of the copyright page.

Preface for Instructors

Cultural Diversity, Critical Thinking, and Composition

MAKING CULTURAL CONNECTIONS is the first of a second generation of cultural readers. The real value of using readings from diverse cultures is the multitude of perspectives they can bring to bear on any topic of discussion, and the way these texts can be used to stimulate critical thinking. This book presents a limited number of texts arranged to throw into relief diverse perspectives on issues that are germane to students' lives. While many of the readings give students a way to study unfamiliar cultural experiences, as well as a chance to understand the experiences they share with members of their own culture, this reader doesn't fit the usual description of the multicultural reader. Its purpose is not to give a representative sample of each culture in order to help students escape a home-grown parochialism, but to use diversity as a way to help students rethink familiar issues with a critical mind.

The Readings

Although the readings are by authors from diverse backgrounds, I deliberately chose not to duplicate the many excellent readers that exist to make students aware of all the other cultures in the world. Instead of using many short selections that give balanced views of many cultures, I wanted to be more selective and use longer readings that could convey how the experience of living in a particular culture shapes ideas and creates a context for human lives.

The selections in *Making Cultural Connections* range from personal narratives from writers like Philip Roth and Annie Dillard to theoretical examinations by David Gilmore and Simone de Beauvoir. Although most of the selections were written by contemporary writers, some are classics that continue to provoke important responses. The selections also represent a range of academic disciplines—anthropology, psychoanalysis, feminist studies, economics, history, and sociology—and fiction. Seeing the various theoretical stances authors use in analyzing their subjects emphasizes this reader's theory that the continual reframing of a subject creates complex discussion. Students responding to this diversity will write papers that become more complex as their writing develops as a cumulative response to a progression of texts.

Because each reading is thematically rich and multifaceted, thematic connections between readings in different chapters emerge quite easily. Despite the arrangement of readings into topics, alert readers will note that each reading has a cluster of themes and that many of these themes reappear frequently throughout the book. In addition to the topic themes and issues of culture, *Making Cultural Connections* focuses on issues of race, class, and gender. Many of the readings show how individuals resist, as well as accept, cultural expectations by challenging norms, crossing boundaries, and investing themselves in a process of self-definition.

Although students are never asked to imitate the texts they read, they will find models for the many different types of discourse they will use to explore a subject. Obviously, one reading will not foster a complete grasp of a text's ideas and ambiguities. Because they are not short readings that can be reduced to one statement of meaning—the proverbial thesis sentence—students have as models of writing works that are rich, puzzling, unruly, enlightening, and unpredictable. Although they will find no formulas for good writing, students will find excellent examples of what good writing is.

The Organization

The thirty essays and eight short stories in *Making Cultural Connections* are organized into eleven topics that encourage students to explore their lives in a continually expanding frame of reference. Students will explore the personal experiences of family life and growing up; the increasingly important role of society in shaping the lives of individuals according to gender roles; their connections to others in the larger culturally defined groups of working environments and communities; the way in which prejudice categorizes and defines social connections; how cultural and imaginative narratives give meaning to individual lives; how individuals reshape their lives, sometimes crossing cultural boundaries as they make choices; the way language shapes knowledge of experience and people's reactions to each other; and, finally, the way contacts between cultures influence the development of each culture.

The Apparatus

Chapter introductions. Each chapter begins with a selection of quotations drawn from the texts that immediately follow. While these quotations should pique students' interest, their most important function is to stimulate preliminary discussion on the topic and to help students generate questions that they seek to answer as they read. We know that experienced learners recall as many associations as possible about the subject at hand, thus relating new ideas to concepts they already understand. We also know that sophisticated readers read to answer questions they formulate before they begin reading. The chapter introductions will also stimulate student interest in the topic by touching on basic themes and questions.

Questions and writing assignments. After each reading are questions entitled "Considerations," designed to focus on important features or difficulties present in a text. The "Invitation to Write" question invites students to write a paper that examines a student's own experience and how it relates to the reading. "Connections" assignments ask students to examine some aspect of the chapter topic as it appears in two readings; these questions often highlight an aspect of an essay that is different from the one explored in the chapter in which it appears. All of these questions can be used as discussion questions or as writing assignments.

Assignment sequences. In "The Writing Life," Annie Dillard defines the act of writing as an act of creation, discovery, construction, and progression. This book is based on a similar understanding of what writing should be. All too often, college students approach writing as an act of imitation. But students *can* learn to see writing and thinking as processes that result in an increasingly complex examination and articulation of their ideas. *Making Cultural Connections* is designed to teach them to do just that.

Through a series of assignments that prompt students to understand the context of their own experiences and those of others, students develop the skills of comparing, contrasting, reframing, and testing that they need to think critically. As they write and rewrite about the ideas they are generating, they will find that they are making increasingly complex arguments and drawing conclusions that refute simplistic and reductive formulations of ideas. And as they move from writing about their experience to writing about other texts, they will become aware of the way framing a subject in cultural and theoretical terms changes discourse from personal to academic writing.

Each of the chapters in this book is built around a sequence of assignments that appears at the end of the chapter. Through each sequence, students will, in turn, examine the topic in terms of his or her own experience; examine a particular text in light of his or her particular experiences; reexamine the topic from a slightly different angle as new texts are added; and, finally, reflect back on the various stances they have taken toward a topic, often by viewing it again through a theoretical frame. The final assignment can test the theoretical frame, ask students to begin to formulate their own theory, and recall all of their earlier attempts to grapple with different aspects of the topic.

The final assignments, which return students to earlier texts and papers, invite students to reinterpret and clarify their ideas. With each rereading, students should become aware of the increasing complexity of the issues they are considering; they should also become more assured in their ability to understand and articulate the problems that generate their discussions. Writing that is structured as a progression helps students develop a repertoire of ideas to explore. Instead of looking around desperately for something to say, students think more about what has already been said.

Although the assignments in this book work together, I have carefully designed the apparatus in *Making Cultural Connections* to be as flexible as possible. Instructors have a great deal of flexibility assigning questions. Many instructors who choose to write their own assignments may turn to them only as models. Some teachers will focus on the writing questions following the readings, using sequences only occasionally. On the other hand, some may prefer to assign only the sequences. There are enough assignments in a chapter to fill a full semester, but an instructor could easily pick and choose from the assignments, using a number of different sequences in the course of semester.

The Instructor's Manual

Resources for Teaching Making Cultural Connections, written by Anca Rosu, does not attempt to give definitive answers to the questions in the text, but rather to suggest some of the issues and difficulties the questions will raise in the classroom. Because many questions are designed to promote discussion and highlight a selection's complexity, we felt it would be reductive to suggest that one "correct" answer exists. The manual also includes some helpful commentary on how to use the assignments in a flexible way.

Acknowledgments

After completing this project, I am more aware than ever that writing is a collaborative act. My interest in developing a reader began when I was an associate director of composition at Rutgers University. I would like to thank all the people who worked with me on a very early version of a reader suited to our basic composition course, particularly Ellen Kreitler, Anca Rosu, Ike Shambelain, Guy Shebat, Kenneth Smith, Colin Wells, and Jonathan Worley. Other colleagues in the writing program who offered suggestions were Maxine Susman and Dawn Skorczewski. I've learned a great deal about how to teach writing from all the writing teachers working in the Rutgers Writing Program and from several fine writing program directors, particularly Martin Gliserman, George Kearns, and Kurt Spellmeyer.

I'd also like to thank all those dedicated readers who offered suggestions and comments on the manuscript at various stages of its development. My excellent readers were Nancy K. Barry, JoAnn Campbell, Karin B. Costello, Toni Empringham, Kathryn Flannery, Stephanie Muller, Kathleen Shine Cain, Irwin Weiser, and Jonathan Worley. In addition to writing the instructor's manual, Anca Rosu wrote the sequence on language and contributed her thoughtful evaluation to the entire manuscript.

The staff at Bedford Books deserves the lion's share of credit for steering this book through to its present form. Karen S. Henry, who was immediately enthusiastic and supportive of my initial proposal, guided the book in its earliest stages. Charles Christensen and Joan Feinberg were committed from the beginning. Ellen Kuhl worked unsparingly to keep the book on course; she was the person I depended on most, and her suggestions and responses were always helpful. Beth Castrodale and Mark Reimold helped clear up many details, and David Gibbs and Beth Chapman prepared the manuscript. I'd also like to thank Anthony Perriello for his copyediting, Kim Chabot for clearing permissions, and Lori Chong and Karen Baart for seeing the book through production.

Above all, I'd like to thank Martin, Jane, Nicholas, and Agatha for their unfailing support.

Contents

4 Defining Men's Lives 171

5 Working in the World 217

The experience convinced Scott that he would never get where he wanted to go as long as he stayed inside a large corporation. He resolved to commit himself only to tasks that would enhance his own career—eventually outside Memorex.

"Had the company been different," he says, "I might have stayed. But there was no reason to. No one really cared what you did. You were penalized for being entrepreneurial. I knew I would get a check whether I sold or not. And no one seemed to share the same goal."

What constitutes the alienation of labor? First, that the work is *external* to the worker, that it is not part of his nature; and that, consequently, he does not fulfill himself in his work but denies himself, has a feeling of misery rather than well-being, does not develop freely his mental and physical energies but is physically exhausted and mentally debased.

No one had been invited to her new pebble-dash house, and the two sisters who called unannounced were left standing on the doorstep, with some flimsy excuse about her distempering the kitchen ceiling. She was determined to remain aloof, and as if to emphasize the point she had venetian blinds fitted.

"We can't afford not to care about other people in a place this small. Our survival, in a way, depends on minimizing privacy because the lack of it draws us into each other's lives, and that's a major resource in a little town where there aren't a thousand entertainments."

Through such reasoning, it has become possible to maintain a self-image of generosity toward, and solidarity with, one's "community" without bearing any responsibility to "them"—the other "community."

And there seemed to be no way whatever to remove this cloud that stood between them and the sun, between them and love and life and power, between them and whatever it was that they wanted. One did not have to be very bright to realize how little one could do to change one's situation; one did not have to be abnormally sensitive to be worn down to a cutting edge by the incessant and gratuitous humiliation and danger one encountered every working day, all day long.

of the night unless we checked twice. She said a mirror could see only my
face, but she could see me inside out even when I was not in the room.

11 Cultures in Contact   533

Introduction
for Students

Making Connections Between
Experience and Texts

THE TITLE *Making Cultural Connections* implies that your own role in using this text will be an active one. Your need to be an active participant in the process of reading and constructing ideas will motivate you as a writer. You will use your writing to explore many of the circumstances and situations of your own life that influence the way you construct your own identity. You will also see how differences in cultures affect and influence this process. As you examine the connections between experience and identity, and between cultures and experience, you will simultaneously be experiencing the transformation of personal knowledge and human experience into theoretical knowledge. In short, you will be making many connections: self to society; individuals to their cultural contexts; experience to texts; personal knowledge to theoretical knowledge; reading to writing; and reading to rereading.

Making Connections Between
Experience and Cultural Contexts

The philosophy behind this book rejects the assumption that students arrive at college without worthwhile knowledge and valuable experience. It rejects the idea that the purpose of college is to provide "what you didn't learn in high school" or to give you the necessary information and a few basic writing skills that will make you employable. College students do not lack experience and information. Usually, however, they haven't learned how to reflect critically upon those experiences and the cultural contexts that have shaped them.

The best way to do this is to understand that our own lives are situated in a particular culture and to explore lives in other cultural contexts. Understanding provides the key to appreciating the richness of cultural diversity and the contexts that shape individual lives, as well as the means to grow beyond the boundaries of one's personal experience. Using this book should help you develop the awareness you need to read critically. It should help you develop the critical thinking skills that are necessary to clarify the difficult and unexpected problems you will meet in college, and after.

The topics in this reader are mostly familiar ones: family, growing up, living in a community, the way work affects our lives, and society's expectations of us as men and women, among others. The readings give you a chance to see how these familiar situations can become unfamiliar in different cultural environments. However, some of the topics, like "Lives in Transition," are not usually found in college readers. In both cases, the writing assignments approach the topics in ways that will ask you to take a new look at the issues involved.

Considering the Texts

The authors I have chosen may be unfamiliar to many of you, but their works are here because they offer a rich range of responses and experiences. Some, like Annie Dillard and Richard Rodriguez, are now well known to college students. Some, like Karl Marx and Simone de Beauvoir, are famous. Many others, like Leonard Kibera or Wakako Yamauchi, are wonderful writers whose work has so far received little attention. You will be among the first to discover the power of their writing. These readings demonstrate how exciting our lives can become when we listen to voices that express the experiences of other cultures and learn to appreciate the complexity and diversity of our own American culture. Although the writers represent different cultures and different aspects of our own culture, as well as what is considered mainstream American life and experience, this book is not a multicultural reader in the typical sense. More selective than most multicultural readers, it does not attempt to survey the world's cultures in any balanced way in order to teach you about the cultures of the authors. Instead, the writing assignments serve to initiate discussions of ideas. Choosing texts written by authors from diverse cultures ensures that you can consider these ideas in the broadest range of contexts.

Critical Reading
and Analysis of Texts

Reading these texts, then, will be an initial step toward appreciating cultural diversity, understanding the contexts that shape individual lives, and learning how to grow beyond the limitations of personal experience.

Many of these texts are difficult and will not be grasped easily after just one reading. You will need to work toward understanding them because the language is complex and the authors' ideas are unfamiliar. Using your own experience to approach these texts can help you develop as a writer and a thinker because it will involve you as a reader. You cannot assume that the texts will reflect your own experience, but you can use your experience as a bridge between the world you know and an unfamiliar text. We know that we respond to new experiences, knowledge, and texts in light of what we already know. We come to every new situation with presuppositions that are ready to be tested against what we find. We know we learn better when we can associate new information with familiar ideas. While our presuppositions may be rejected eventually, they provide an initial way to approach a new subject. Good readers—experienced readers—proceed through a text using a similar method. While inexperienced readers read one sentence at a time, focusing their attention on the words they are reading, experienced readers go beyond the sentence under their eyes. They have expectations about what the author will say next. Drawing on their experiences from their own lives and their experiences of other texts, good readers imagine the possibilities that are open to the author and they try to guess which line of thought the author will develop.

Understanding this process should make clear the structure of questions after each reading and the order of writing assignments in each sequence. After each reading are questions called "Considerations," which help you understand some of the difficulties readers face in understanding each text. These are the types of questions that experienced readers might pose about a text as they read or as their normal expectations are challenged. These questions point to difficulties in reading the text that complicate simple and routine understandings. It will be necessary for you to reread the text to consider how these complications affect your initial responses.

Constructing Knowledge:
Writing Assignments and Sequences

Your teacher may ask you to write responses to the questions after each reading, the sequence assignments, or both. The opportunity to write twice about the same topic, in more depth the second time, will help you become a more thoughtful and articulate writer. Each time you return to a text, you can discuss it with more authority. As you feel more confident in your analyses of other texts, you write about the texts with more confidence and clarity. Your prose will reflect this. If you look back over your papers, you will find that your initial papers are less articulate because the ideas are not as clearly formulated in your mind. As you become more certain of the way you interpret the text, you will find your comprehension reflected in your ability to write about it. The more mastery you have over your ideas, the more control you will have over grammar, syntax, organization, and other mechanics of writing.

You will notice that each writing assignment breaks into two distinct parts. The first part poses the actual topic or question, while the second suggests ways to begin your paper, or ideas that you can discuss in your paper. You should never let yourself feel limited by the suggestions. Follow them when they are helpful, but don't feel restricted by them. You can develop your own plan for your paper's discussion, keeping in mind that you do need to answer the question. Even then, good writers will not be content to limit themselves to the actual question. The best papers usually answer the questions but extend their answers to consider the importance and significance of the conclusions they offer.

"Invitation to Write," your first opportunity to form a written response to a reading, asks you to look at some particular aspect of a text in light of your own experience. As you reread the text to generate ideas for your assignment, you will necessarily be thinking about how the ideas in the text relate to your own experience. Your experience may lead you to expect one way of viewing a topic. Testing the essay against your experience will give you an idea to read against—and may cause you to consider your own experience in a new light.

Considering the text you have just read in light of a second text, as the "Connections" assignments ask, will challenge your assumptions about it, as you consider it again from a different frame of reference. Rereading the text from different angles should help you see it more clearly and understand more of its complexities. Thus the writing assignments following the readings are developed to help you become more proficient readers as well as writers. Sometimes the second writing assignment refers you to other readings in the same chapter. Other times, however, it refers you to readings in other chapters. These connections ask you to look at new issues in familiar texts. For example, "Scott Myers, Entrepreneur" appears in the chapter titled "Working in the World." But a "Connections" question in the chapter "Functions of the Family" links the Myers story to "Is There a Family?" and asks you to consider what it suggests about the relationship between work and family life. These types of connections will help you appreciate the way the readings develop and interconnect several themes. In any particular assignment, you can use ideas from all your readings. Thus, you might want to refer back to "Scott Myers, Entrepreneur" in a paper you are writing in the chapter "Functions of the Family."

The "Assignment Sequences" involve you in a more extensive exploration of the topic under discussion. Like the writing assignments after each reading, they begin by asking you to write about the topic in light of your experience. Sometimes your teacher will ask you to approach the first sequence as a journal assignment. Sometimes he or she will assign it as a formal paper. In either case, turning to your own experience will suggest topics of discussion and will help you pose questions that following assignments may ask you to address.

The second assignment in each sequence asks you to use your personal knowledge to build a bridge to a text. Although you begin with personal knowledge, most of the assignments in a sequence are focused on the texts and your reading of the texts. Many of the questions direct you to focus on specific texts and provide you with quotations from passages that can provide a beginning point for your investigation of that text. You should not limit yourself to that quotation alone; instead, go on to find several more that expand upon its meaning, either through restatement or contradiction. Think about the differences between quotations and how you would explain the differences. The sequence format keeps directing you to additional readings. You will want to consider how key quotations from new readings relate to the quotations you have studied elsewhere. Again you may find reiteration, contradiction, or expansion of an idea.

As you read additional texts to explore a topic from new angles, you will see the value of rereading. You will see how a text can change each time you raise different questions about it. You will experience how rereading makes a text more meaningful without reducing it to one meaning. Rereading prevents us from missing meaning. It allows us to shift our sense of what is important in a text.

The final assignment in a sequence usually asks you to reconsider the subject at hand in light of all the reading, thinking, and writing that led up to it. You end by looking at the subject theoretically, by either testing the theoretical ideas of another against your own ideas or developing a theoretical approach of your own. Traditionally, college composition readers ask students to weigh different theoretical approaches against each other and to pick the best one. These sequences ask you instead to understand that knowledge is not an either-or proposition. Seeing knowledge as the result of a progressive examination of ideas will help you understand that choices are never that clear and that constructions of an issue are never that simple. The assignments in this reader ask you to do more than choose between ideas: They ask you to participate in the processes that construct knowledge, to articulate your own views, and in doing so, to understand the way academic writing evolves from experience, culture, and responses to other texts.

Functions
of the Family

W*hat I'm go'n do and my nan-nane gone? I love her so much.*"
"*Ever'body love her.*"
"*Since my mama died, she been like my mama.*"
"*Shhh," I say. "Don't let her hear you. Make her grieve. You don't want her grieving, now, do you?*"
                                        —ERNEST J. GAINES, *Just Like a Tree*

One aspect of child-rearing Mo and Ellen were sure about was that the child would be both of theirs; they were determined to minimize the primacy of the biological mother as much as possible. "I don't want this to be my *child," Mo said firmly. "It is going to have my last name, and when Ellen has a baby that one will have her last name. But they will be* our *kids and we are going to try to reinforce that in as many ways as we can.*"
                                        —NEIL MILLER, *A Time of Change*

If most modern social scientists have inherited Victorian biases that tend ultimately to support a view uniting women and The Family to an apparently unchanging set of biologically given needs, we have at the same time failed to reckon with the one small area in which Victorian evolutionists were right. They understood, as we do not today, that families—like religions, economies, governments, or courts of law—are not *unchanging but the product of various social forms, that the relationships of spouses and parents to their young are apt to be different things in different social orders.*

—JANE COLLIER, MICHELLE Z. ROSALDO,
and SYLVIA YANAGISAKO, *Is There a
Family? New Anthropological Views*

Every American generation has created its own idea of how the perfect family looks and acts. The perceived model family has changed radically over the last fifty years. Prior to the 1950s, the model family consisted of a large extended family that proved necessary to an agriculturally based economy. In the 1950s, the size and composition of the model family changed. It consisted of two parents, a homemaking mother and a wage-earning father, and two children, one boy and one girl, preferably in that order. At that time, our postwar society was ready to fuel an economic expansion, and a higher per capita income divided among a small family group meant a higher standard of living. During the following two decades, widespread social changes disrupted traditional family structures. Today's model families include working mothers and stay-at-home fathers, exemplifying the changing roles of individuals within the family. Furthermore, single-parent families are now as prevalent as two-parent families, and unrelated individuals are often included in the family circle through a network of emotional and proximate relationships.

The changing composition of the family doesn't necessarily alter all of its functions, however. Understanding family life requires consideration of more than the physical make-up of the family; it requires examination of the similarities among families that exist despite obvious differences. What do individuals seek in a family that makes it an enduring social institution despite radical changes in its own outward form and in society? And, since it is a social institution, how is the family influenced by changes in the surrounding society?

The "family" is a familiar topic. As members and observers of families, most people are familiar with family life. Yet few students look at it in relation to the extended social order. In addition to looking at the impact of the family on individual lives, this chapter asks you to think about the family as a social institution. The readings in this chapter present different ideas about the ties that bind individuals together in a family unit.

Ernest J. Gaines, in the story "Just Like a Tree," enlarges the traditional definition of family to include relationships based on familiarity and affection, regardless of legal, economic, or blood ties. His characters live in extended families that span several generations and several households but are confined to a few square miles of space. Thus the boundaries between family and community get blurred. Neil Miller reports on the way gays and lesbians are freeing the traditional nuclear family from its association with a heterosexual couple and clearly defined gender roles. In "Is There a Family? New Anthropological Views," Jane Collier, Michelle Z. Rosaldo, and Sylvia Yanagisako trace the development of the idea of the nuclear family across two hundred years of anthropological theory and analyze the influence of those ideas on our current ideas of family life. The definitions of family they consider all depend on separate parental roles based on gender.

By looking at theory and experience, these readings will help you think about individual roles in contemporary families and the family's place in contemporary society. From your observations, you can form your own conclusions about why people have recreated and reshaped the institution of the family, instead of replacing it.

ERNEST J. GAINES

Just Like a Tree

Ernest J. Gaines was born in 1933 near Baton Rouge, Louisiana. His early life was hard. With his eight brothers and sisters, he worked on a sugar plantation picking cotton and digging potatoes. When he was fourteen, his mother and stepfather moved the family to California. The years of his childhood remain vivid in Gaines's memory and, in spite of the relocation, he most often returns to the world and characters of rural Louisiana in his novels and short stories. Gaines pays particular attention to the relations between fathers and sons as he believes that "black fathers and sons were separated in Africa in the seventeenth century and have not come back together since. They can eat across the table, but that is not the same as coming together." His first novel, *Catherine Carmier,* was published in 1964; his most famous work, *The Autobiography of Miss Jane Pittman,* was published in 1971 and adapted for television in 1974. Although the television production brought Gaines fame, it also deemphasized the usual thrust of his work, which focuses on the links between individual characters and their community.

His other works include the novels *A Long Day in November* (1971), *In My Father's House* (1978), and *A Gathering of Old Men* (1983). Gaines's most recent novel is *A Lesson Before Dying* (1993).

The following short story first appeared in a collection entitled *Bloodline* (1968). It was later republished in *Memory of Kin: Stories About Family by Black Writers* (1991), edited by Mary Helen Washington. In individual interior monologues, the story captures a small southern African-American community's reaction to the departure of one of its members, Aunt Fe. Although the language of each monologue is clearly indicative of an individual voice, the monologues converge in conveying the feeling of community, almost family, which makes Aunt Fe's departure a sad event for everyone.

5

I shall not;
> *I shall not be moved.*
I shall not;
> *I shall not be moved.*
> *Just like a tree that's*
> *planted 'side the water.*
>> *Oh, I shall not be moved.*

I low' my head little bit, 'cause that wind and fine rain was hitting me in the face, and I can feel Mama pressing close to me to keep me warm. She sitting on one side o' me and Pa sitting on the other side o' me, and Gran'mon in the back o' me in her setting chair. Pa didn't want bring the setting chair, telling Gran'mon there was two boards in that wagon already and she could sit on one of 'em all by herself if she wanted to, but Gran'mon say she was taking her setting chair with her if Pa liked it or not. She say she didn't ride in no wagon on nobody board, and if Pa liked it or not, that setting chair was going.

"Let her take her setting chair," Mama say. "What's wrong with taking her setting chair."

"Ehhh, Lord," Pa say, and picked up the setting chair and took it out to the wagon. "I guess I'll have to bring it back in the house, too, when we come back from there."

Gran'mon went and clambed in the wagon and moved her setting chair back little bit and sat down and folded her arms, waiting for us to get in, too. I got in and knelt down 'side her, but Mama told me to come up there and sit on the board 'side her and Pa so I could stay warm. Soon 's I sat down, Pa hit Mr. Bascom on the back, saying what a trifling thing Mr. Bascom was, and soon 's he got some mo' money he was getting rid o' Mr. Bascom and getting him a horse.

I raise my head to look see how far we is.

"That's it, yonder," I say.

"Stop pointing," Mama say, "and keep your hand in your pocket."

"Where?" Gran'mon say, back there in her setting chair.

"Cross the ditch, yonder," I say.

"Can't see a thing for this rain," Gran'mon say.

"Can't hardly see it," I say. "But you can see the light little bit. That chinaball tree standing in the way."

"Poor soul," Gran'mon say. "Poor soul."

I know Gran'mon was go'n say "poor soul, poor soul," 'cause she had been saying "poor soul, poor soul," ever since she heard Aunt Fe was go'n leave from back there.

Emile

Darn cane crop to finish getting in and only a mule and a half to do it. If I had my way I'd take that shotgun and a load o' buckshots and—but what's the use.

"Get up, Mr. Bascom—please," I say to that little dried-up, long-eared, 15 tobacco-color thing. "Please, come up. Do your share for God sake—if you don't mind. I know it's hard pulling in all that mud, but if you don't do your share, then Big Red'll have to do his and yours, too. So, please, if it ain't asking you too much to—"

"Oh, Emile, shut up," Leola say.

"I can't hit him," I say, "or Mama back there'll hit me. So I have to talk to him. Please, Mr. Bascom, if you don't mind it. For my sake. No, not for mine, for God sake. No, not even for His'n, for Big Red sake. A fellow mule just like yourself is. Please, come up."

"Now, you hear that boy blaspheming God right in front o' me there," Mama say. "Ehhh, Lord—just keep it up. All this bad weather there like this whole world coming apart—a clap o' thunder come there and knock the fool out you. Just keep it up."

Maybe she right, and I stop. I look at Mr. Bascom there doing nothing, and I just give up. That mule know long's Mama's alive he go'n do just what he want to do. He know when Papa was dying he told Mama to look after him, and he know no matter what he do, no matter what he don't do, Mama ain't go'n never let me do him anything. Sometimes I even feel Mama care mo' for Mr. Bascom 'an she care for me her own son.

We come up to the gate and I pull back on the lines. 20

"Whoa up, Big Red," I say. "You don't have to stop, Mr. Bascom. You never started."

I can feel Mama looking at me back there in that setting chair, but she don't say nothing.

"Here," I say to Chuckkie.

He take the lines and I jump down on the ground to open the old beat-up gate. I see Etienne's horse in the yard, and I see Chris new red tractor 'side the house, shining in the rain. When Mama die, I say to myself, Mr. Bascom, you going. Ever'body getting tractors and horses and I'm still stuck with you. You going, brother.

"Can you make it through?" I ask Chuckkie. "That gate ain't too wide." 25

"I can do it," he say.

"Be sure to make Mr. Bascom pull," I say.

"Emile, you better get back up here and drive 'em through," Leola say. "Chuckkie might break up that wagon."

"No, let him stay down there and give orders," Mama say, back there in that setting chair.

"He can do it," I say. "Come on, Chuckkie boy." 30

"Come up, here, mule," Chuckkie say.

And soon 's he say that, Big Red make a lunge for the yard, and Mr. Bascom don't even move, and 'fore I can bat my eyes I hear *pow-wow; sagg-sagg; pow-wow.* But above all that noise, Leola up there screaming her head off. And Mama—not a word; just sitting in that chair, looking at me with her arms still folded.

"Pull Big Red," I say. "Pull Big Red, Chuckkie."

Poor little Chuckkie up there pulling so hard till one of his little arms straight out in back; and Big Red throwing his shoulders and ever'thing else in it, and Mr. Bascom just walking there just 's loose and free, like he's suppose to be there just for his good looks. I move out the way just in time to let the wagon go by me, pulling half o' the fence in the yard behind it. I glance up again, and there's Leola still hollering and trying to jump out, but Mama not saying a word—just sitting there in that setting chair with her arms still folded.

"Whoa," I hear little Chuckkie saying. "Whoa up, now." 35

Somebody open the door and a bunch o' people come out on the gallery.

"What the world—?" Etienne say. "Thought the whole place was coming to pieces there."

"Chuckkie had a little trouble coming in the yard," I say.

"Goodness," Etienne say. "Anybody hurt?"

Mama just sit there about ten seconds, then she say something to herself 40 and start clambing out the wagon.

"Let me help you there, Aunt Lou," Etienne say, coming down the steps.

"I can make it," Mama say. When she get on the ground she look up at Chuckkie. "Hand me my chair there, boy."

Poor little Chuckkie, up there with the lines in one hand, get the chair and hold it to the side, and Etienne catch it just 'fore it hit the ground. Mama start looking at me again, and it look like for at least a' hour she stand there looking at nobody but me. Then she say, "Ehhh, Lord," like that again, and go inside with Leola and the rest o' the people.

I look back at half o' the fence laying there in the yard, and I jump back on the wagon and guide the mules to the side o' the house. After unhitching 'em and tying 'em to the wheels, I look at Chris pretty red tractor again, and me and Chuckkie go inside: I make sure he kick all that mud off his shoes 'fore he go in the house.

Leola

Sitting over there by that fireplace, trying to look joyful when ever'body there 45 know she ain't. But she trying, you know, smiling and bowing when people say something to her. How can she be joyful, I ask you; how can she be? Poor thing, she been here all her life—or the most of it, let's say. 'Fore they moved in this house, they lived in one back in the woods 'bout a mile from here. But for the past twenty-five or thirty years, she been right in this one house. I know ever since I been big enough to know people I been seeing her right here.

Aunt Fe, Aunt Fe, Aunt Fe, Aunt Fe; the name's been 'mongst us just like us own family name. Just like the name o' God. Like the name of town—the city. Aunt Fe, Aunt Fe, Aunt Fe, Aunt Fe.

Poor old thing, how many times I done come here and washed clothes for her when she couldn't do it herself. How many times I done hoed in that garden, ironed her clothes, wrung a chicken neck for her. You count the days in the year and you'll be pretty close. And I didn't mind it a bit. No, I didn't mind it a bit. She there trying to pay me. Proud—Lord, talking 'bout pride. "Here." "No, Aunt Fe, no." "Here, here, you got a child there, you can use it." "No, Aunt Fe. No. No. What would Mama think if she knowed I took money from you? Aunt Fe, Mama would never forgive me. No. I love doing these thing for you. I just wish I could do more."

And there, now, trying to make 'tend she don't mind leaving. Ehhh, Lord.

I hear a bunch o' rattling round in the kitchen and I go back there. I see Louise stirring this big pot o' eggnog.

"Louise," I say.   50

"Leola," she say.

We look at each other and she stir the eggnog again. She know what I'm go'n say next, and she can't even look in my face.

"Louise, I wish there was some other way."

"There's no other way," she say.

"Louise, moving her from here's like moving a tree you been used to in   55
your front yard all your life."

"What else can I do?"

"Oh, Louise, Louise."

"Nothing else but that."

"Louise, what people go'n do without her here?"

She stir the eggnog and don't answer.   60

"Louise, us'll take her in with us."

"You all no kin to Auntie. She go with me."

"And us'll never see her again."

She stir the eggnog. Her husband come back in the kitchen and kiss her on the back o' the neck and then look at me and grin. Right from the start I can see I ain't go'n like that nigger.

"Almost ready, honey?" he say.   65

"Almost."

He go to the safe and get one o' them bottles of whiskey he got in there and come back to the stove.

"No," Louise say. "Everybody don't like whiskey in it. Add the whiskey after you've poured it up."

"Okay, hon."

He kiss her on the back o' the neck again. Still don't like that nigger. Something 'bout him ain't right.

"You one o' the family?" he say.

"Same as one," I say. "And you?"

He don't like the way I say it, and I don't care if he like it or not. He look at me there a second, and then he kiss her on the ear.

"Un-unnn," she say, stirring the pot.

"I love your ear, baby," he say.

"Go in the front room and talk with the people," she say.

He kiss her on the other ear. A nigger do all that front o' public got something to hide. He leave the kitchen. I look at Louise.

"Ain't nothing else I can do," she say.

"You sure, Louise? You positive?"

"I'm positive," she say.

The front door open and Emile and Chuckkie come in. A minute later Washington and Adrieu come in, too. Adrieu come back in the kitchen, and I can see she been crying. Aunt Fe is her godmother, you know.

"How you feel, Adrieu?"

"That weather out there," she say.

"Y'all walked?"

"Yes."

"Us here in the wagon. Y'all can go back with us."

"Y'all the one tore the fence down?" she ask.

"Yes, I guess so. That brother-in-law o' yours in there letting Chuckkie drive that wagon."

"Well, I don't guess it'll matter too much. Nobody go'n be here, anyhow."

And she start crying again. I take her in my arms and pat her on the shoulder, and I look at Louise stirring the eggnog.

"What I'm go'n do and my nan-nane gone? I love her so much."

"Ever'body love her."

"Since my mama died, she been like my mama."

"Shhh," I say. "Don't let her hear you. Make her grieve. You don't want her grieving, now, do you?"

She sniffs there 'gainst my dress few times.

"Oh, Lord," she say. "Lord, have mercy."

"Shhh," I say. "Shhh. That's what life's 'bout."

"That ain't what life's 'bout," she say. "It ain't fair. This been her home all her life. These the people she know. She don't know them people she going to. It ain't fair."

"Shhh, Adrieu," I say. "Now, you saying things that ain't your business."
She cry there some mo'.   100
"Oh, Lord, Lord," she say.
Louise turn from the stove.
"About ready now," she say, going to the middle door. "James, tell everybody to come back and get some."

James

Let me go on back here and show these country niggers how to have a good time. All they know is talk, talk, talk. Talk so much they make me buggy round here. Damn this weather—wind, rain. Must be a million cracks in this old house.

I go to that old beat-up safe in that corner and get that fifth of Mr. Harper   105 (in the South now, got to say Mister), give the seal one swipe, the stopper one jerk, and head back to that old wood stove. (Man, like, these cats are primitive—goodness. You know what I mean? I mean like wood stoves. Don't mention TV, man, these cats here never heard of that.) I start to dump Mr. Harper in the pot and Baby catches my hand again and say not all of them like it. You ever heard of anything like that? I mean a stud's going to drink eggnog, and he's not going to put whiskey in it. I mean he's going to drink it straight. I mean, you ever heard anything like that? Well, I wasn't pressing none of them on Mr. Harper. I mean, me and Mr. Harper get along too well together for me to go around there pressing.

I hold my cup there and let Baby put a few drops of this egg stuff in it, then I jerk my cup back and let Mr. Harper run a while. Couple of these cats come over (some of them aren't so lame) and set their cups, and I let Mr. Harper run for them. Then this cat says he's got 'nough. I let Mr. Harper run for this other stud, and pretty soon he says, "Hold it. Good." Country cat, you know. "Hold it. Good." Real country cat. So I raise the cup to see what Mr. Harper's doing. He's just right. I raise the cup again. Just right, Mr. Harper, just right.

I go to the door with Mr. Harper under my arm and the cup in my hand and I look into the front room where they all are. I mean, there's about ninety-nine of them in there. Old ones, young ones, little ones, big ones, yellow ones, black ones, brown ones—you name them, brother, and they were there. And what for? Brother, I'll tell you what for. Just because me and Baby are taking this old chick out of these sticks. Well, I'll tell you where I'd be at this moment if I was one of them. With that weather out there like it is, I'd be under about five blankets with some little warm belly pressing against mine. Brother, you can bet your hat I wouldn't be here. Man, listen to that thing out there. You can hear that rain beating on that old house like grains of rice, and that wind coming through them cracks like it does in those old Charlie

Chaplin movies. Man, like you know—like *whooo-ee; whooo-ee.* Man, you talking about some weird cats.

I can feel Mr. Harper starting to massage my wig and I bat my eyes twice and look at the old girl over there. She's still sitting in that funny-looking little old rocking chair, and not saying a word to anybody. Just sitting there looking into the fireplace at them two pieces of wood that aren't giving out enough heat to warm a baby, let alone ninety-nine grown people. I mean, you know, like that sleet's falling out there like all get-up-and-go, and them two pieces of wood are lying there just as dead as the rest of these way-out cats.

One of the old cats—I don't know which one he is—Mose, Sam, or something like that—leans over and pokes in the fire a minute, then a little blaze shoots up, and he raises up, too, looking as satisfied as if he'd just sent a rocket into orbit. I mean, these cats are like that. They do these little bitty things, and they feel like they've really done something. Well, back in these sticks, I guess there just isn't nothing big to do.

I feel Mr. Harper touching my skull now—and I notice this little chick 110 passing by me with these two cups of eggnog. She goes over to the fireplace and gives one to each of these old chicks. The one sitting in that setting chair she brought with her from God knows where, and the other cup to the old chick that Baby and I are going to haul from here sometime tomorrow morning. Wait, man, I mean like, you ever heard of anybody going to somebody else's house with a chair? I mean, wouldn't you call that an insult at the basest point? I mean, now, like tell me what you think of that? I mean—dig—here I am at my pad, and in you come with your own stool. I mean, now, like man, you know. I mean that's an insult at the basest point. I mean, you know . . . you know, like way out. . . .

Mr. Harper, what you trying to do, boy?—I mean, *sir.* (Got to watch myself, I'm in the South. Got to keep watching myself.)

This stud touches me on the shoulder and raise his cup and say, "How 'bout a taste?" I know what the stud's talking about, so I let Mr. Harper run for him. But soon 's I let a drop get in, the stud say," "'Nough." I mean I let about two drops get in, and already the stud's got enough. Man, I mean, like you know. I mean these studs are 'way out. I mean like 'way back there.

This stud takes a swig of his eggnog and say, "Ahhh." I mean this real down-home way of saying "Ahhhh." I mean, man, like these studs—I notice this little chick passing by me again, and this time she's crying. I mean weeping, you know. And just because this old ninety-nine-year-old chick's packing up and leaving. I mean, you ever heard of anything like that? I mean, here she is pretty as the day is long and crying because Baby and I are hauling this old chick away. Well, I'd like to make her cry. And I can assure you, brother, it wouldn't be from leaving her.

I turn and look at Baby over there by the stove, pouring eggnog in all these cups. I mean, there're about twenty of these cats lined up there. And I bet you not half of them will take Mr. Harper along. Some way-out cats, man. Some way-out cats.

I go up to Baby and kiss her on the back of the neck and give her a little pat where she likes for me to pat her when we're in the bed. She say, "Uh-uh," but I know she likes it anyhow.

Ben O

I back under the bed and touch the slop jar, and I pull back my leg and back somewhere else, and then I get me a good sight on it. I spin my aggie couple times and sight again and then I shoot. I hit it right square in the middle and it go flying over the fireplace. I crawl over there to get it and I see 'em all over there drinking they eggnog and they didn't even offer me and Chuckkie none. I find my marble on the bricks, and I go back and tell Chuckkie they over there drinking eggnog.

"You want some?" I say.

"I want shoot marble," Chuckkie say. "Yo' shot. Shoot up."

"I want some eggnog," I say.

"Shoot up, Ben O," he say. "I'm getting cold staying in one place so long. You feel that draft?"

"Coming from that crack under that bed," I say.

"Where?" Chuckkie say, looking for the crack.

"Over by that bedpost over there," I say.

"This sure's a beat-up old house," Chuckkie say.

"I want me some eggnog," I say.

"Well, you ain't getting none," Gran'mon say, from the fireplace. "It ain't good for you."

"I can drink eggnog," I say. "How come it ain't good for me? It ain't nothing but eggs and milk. I eat chicken, don't I? I eat beef, don't I?"

Gran'mon don't say nothing.

"I want me some eggnog," I say.

Gran'mon still don't say no more. Nobody else don't say nothing, neither.

"I want me some eggnog," I say.

"You go'n get a eggnog," Gran'mon say. "Just keep that noise up."

"I want me some eggnog," I say, "and I 'tend to get me some eggnog tonight."

Next thing I know, Gran'mon done picked up a chip out o' that corner and done sailed it back there where me and Chuckkie is. I duck just in time, and the chip catch old Chuckkie side the head.

"Hey, who that hitting me?" Chuckkie say.

"Move, and you won't get hit," Gran'mon say.

I laugh at old Chuckkie over there holding his head, and next thing I know here's Chuckkie done haul back there and hit me in my side. I jump up from there and give him two just to show him how it feel, and he jump up and hit me again. Then we grab each other and start tussling on the floor.

"You, Ben O," I hear Gran'mon saying. "You, Ben O, cut that out. Y'all cut that out."

But we don't stop, 'cause neither one o' us want be first. Then I feel somebody pulling us apart.

"What I ought to do is whip both o' you," Mrs. Leola say. "Is that what 140 y'all want?"

"No'm," I say.

"Then shake hand."

Me and Chuckkie shake hand.

"Kiss," Mrs. Leola say.

"No, ma'am," I say. "I ain't kissing no boy. I ain't that crazy." 145

"Kiss him, Chuckkie," she say.

Old Chuckkie kiss me on the jaw.

"Now, kiss him, Ben O."

"I ain't kissing no Chuckkie," I say. "No'm. Uh-uh. You kiss girls."

And the next thing I know, Mama done tipped up back o' me and done 150 whop me on the leg with Daddy belt.

"Kiss Chuckkie," she say.

Chuckkie turn his jaw to me and I kiss him. I almost wipe my mouth. I even feel like spitting.

"Now, come back here and get you some eggnog," Mama say.

"That's right, spoil 'em," Gran'mon say. "Next thing you know, they be drinking from bottles."

"Little eggnog won't hurt 'em, Mama," Mama say. 155

"That's right, never listen," Gran'mon say. "It's you go'n suffer for it. I be dead and gone, me."

Aunt Clo

Be just like wrapping a chain round a tree and jecking and jecking, and then shifting the chain little bit and jecking and jecking some in that direction, and then shifting it some mo' and jecking and jecking in that direction. Jecking and jecking till you get it loose, and then pulling with all your might. Still it might not be loose enough and you have to back the tractor up some and fix the chain round the tree again and start jecking all over. Jeck, jeck, jeck. Then you hear the roots crying, and then you keep on jecking, and then it give, and you jeck some mo', and then it falls. And not till then that you see what you done done. Not till then you see the big hole in the ground and piece of the taproot still way down in it—a piece you won't never get out no matter if you dig till doomsday. Yes, you got the tree—least got it down on the ground, but did you get the taproot? No. No, sir, you didn't get the taproot. You stand there and look down in this hole at it and you grab yo' axe and jump down in it and start chopping at the taproot, but do you get the taproot? No. You don't get the taproot, sir. You never get the taproot. But, sir, I tell you what you do get. You get a big hole in the ground, sir, and you get another big hole in the air where the lovely branches been all these years. Yes, sir, that's what you get. The holes, sir, the holes. Two holes, sir, you can't never fill no matter how hard you try.

So you wrap yo' chain round yo' tree again, sir, and you start dragging it. But the dragging ain't so easy, sir, 'cause she's a heavy old tree—been there a long time, you know—heavy. And you make yo' tractor strain, sir, and the elements work 'gainst you, too, sir, 'cause the elements, they on her side, too, 'cause she part o' the elements, and the elements, they part o' her. So the elements, they do they little share to discourage you—yes, sir, they does. But you will not let the elements stop you. No, sir, you show the elements that they just elements, and man is stronger than elements, and you jeck and jeck on the chain, and soon she start to moving with you, sir, but if you look over yo' shoulder one second you see her leaving a trail—a trail, sir, that can be seen from miles and miles away. You see her trying to hook her little fine branches in different little cracks, in between pickets, round hills o' grass, round anything they might brush 'gainst. But you is a determined man, sir, and you jeck and you jeck, and she keep on grabbing and trying to hold, but you stronger, sir—course you the strongest—and you finally get her out on the pave road. But what you don't notice, sir, is just 'fore she get on the pave road she leave couple her little branches to remind the people that it ain't her that want leave, but you, sir, that think she ought to. So you just drag her and drag her, sir, and the folks that live in the houses 'side the pave road, they come out on they galley and look at her go by, and then they go back in they house and sit by the fire and forget her. So you just go on, sir, and you just go and you go—and for how many days? I don't know. I don't have the least idea. The North to me, sir, is like the elements. It mystify me. But never mind, you finally get there, and then you try to find a place to set her. You look in this corner and you look in that corner, but no corner is good. She kind o' stand in the way no matter where you set her. So finally, sir, you say, "I just stand her up here a little while and see, and if it don't work out, if she keep getting in the way, I guess we'll just have to take her to the dump."

Chris

Just like him, though, standing up there telling them lies when everybody else feeling sad. I don't know what you do without people like him. And, yet, you see him there, he sad just like the rest. But he just got to be funny. Crying on the inside, but still got to be funny.

He didn't steal it, though, didn't steal it a bit. His grandpa was just like   160
him. Mat? Mat Jefferson? Just like that. Mat could make you die laughing.
'Member once at a wake. Who was dead? Yes—Robert Lewis. Robert Lewis
laying up in his coffin dead as a door nail. Everybody sad and droopy. Mat
look at that and start his lying. Soon, half o' the place laughing. Funniest
wake I ever went to, and yet—

Just like now. Look at 'em. Look at 'em laughing. Ten minutes ago you
would 'a' thought you was at a funeral. But look at 'em now. Look at her
there in that little old chair. How long she had it? Fifty years—a hundred? It
ain't a chair no mo', it's little bit o' her. Just like her arm, just like her leg.

You know, I couldn't believe it. I couldn't. Emile passed the house there
the other day, right after the bombing, and I was in my yard digging a water
drain to let the water run out in the ditch. Emile, he stopped the wagon there
'fore the door. Little Chuckkie, he in there with him with that little rain cap
buckled up over his head. I go out to the gate and I say, "Emile, it's the truth?"

"The truth," he say. And just like that he say it. "The truth."

I look at him there, and he looking up the road to keep from looking back
at me. You know, they been pretty close to Aunt Fe ever since they was children coming up. His own mon, Aunt Lou, and Aunt Fe, they been like sisters,
there, together.

Me and him, we talk there little while 'bout the cane cutting, then he say   165
he got to get on to the back. He shake the lines and drive on.

Inside me, my heart feel like it done swole up ten times the size it ought to
be. Water come in my eyes, and I got to 'mit I cried right there. Yes sir, I cried
right there by that front gate.

Louise come in the room and whisper something to Leola, and they go
back in the kitchen. I can hear 'em moving things round back there, still getting things together they go'n be taking along. If they offer me anything, I'd
like that big iron pot out there in the back yard. Good for boiling water when
you killing hog, you know.

You can feel the sadness in the room again. Louise brought it in when she
come in and whispered to Leola. Only, she didn't take it out when her and
Leola left. Every pan they move, every pot they unhook keep telling you she
leaving, she leaving.

Etienne turn over one o' them logs to make the fire pick up some, and I
see that boy, Lionel, speading out his hands over the fire. Watch out, I think
to myself, here come another lie. People, he just getting started.

Anne-Marie Duvall

"You're not going?"   170

"I'm not going," he says, turning over the log with the poker. "And if you
were in your right mind, you wouldn't go, either."

"You just don't understand, do you?"

"Oh, I understand. She cooked for your daddy. She nursed you when your mama died."

"And I'm trying to pay her back with a seventy-nine-cents scarf. Is that too much?"

He is silent, leaning against the mantel, looking down at the fire. The fire throws strange shadows across the big, old room. Father looks down at me from against the wall. His eyes do not say go nor stay. But I know what he would do. 175

"Please go with me, Edward."

"You're wasting your breath."

I look at him a long time, then I get the small package from the coffee table.

"You're still going?"

"I am going." 180

"Don't call for me if you get bogged down anywhere back there."

I look at him and go out to the garage. The sky is black. The clouds are moving fast and low. A fine drizzle is falling, and the wind coming from the swamps blows in my face. I cannot recall a worse night in all my life.

I hurry into the car and drive out of the yard. The house stands big and black in back of me. Am I angry with Edward? No, I'm not angry with Edward. He's right. I should not go out into this kind of weather. But what he does not understand is I must. Father definitely would have gone if he were alive. Grandfather definitely would have gone, also. And, therefore, I must. Why? I cannot answer why. Only, I must go.

As soon as I turn down that old muddy road, I begin to pray. Don't let me go into that ditch, I pray. Don't let me go into that ditch. Please, don't let me go into that ditch.

The lights play on the big old trees along the road. Here and there the lights hit a sagging picket fence. But I know I haven't even started yet. She lives far back into the fields. Why? God, why does she have to live so far back? Why couldn't she have lived closer to the front? But the answer to that is as hard for me as is the answer to everything else. It was ordained before I—before Father—was born—that she should live back there. So why should I try to understand it now? 185

The car slides towards the ditch, and I stop it dead and turn the wheel, and then come back into the road again. Thanks, Father. I know you're with me. Because it was you who said that I must look after her, didn't you? No, you did not say it directly, Father. You said it only with a glance. As Grandfather must have said it to you, and as his father must have said it to him.

But now that she's gone, Father, now what? I know. I know. Aunt Lou, Aunt Clo, and the rest.

The lights shine on the dead, wet grass along the road. There's an old pecan tree, looking dead and all alone. I wish I was a little nigger gal so I could pick pecans and eat them under the big old dead tree.

The car hits a rut, but bounces right out of it. I am frightened for a moment, but then I feel better. The windshield wipers are working well, slapping the water away as fast as it hits the glass. If I make the next half mile all right, the rest of the way will be good. It's not much over a mile now.

That was too bad about that bombing—killing that woman and her two   190
children. That poor woman, poor children. What is the answer? What will happen? What do they want? Do they know what they want? Do they really know what they want? Are they positively sure? Have they any idea? Money to buy a car, is that it? If that is all, I pity them. Oh, how I pity them.

Not much farther. Just around that bend and—there's a water hole. Now what?

I stop the car and just stare out at the water a minute, then I get out to see how deep it is. The cold wind shoots through my body like needles. Lightning comes from towards the swamps and lights up the place. For a split second the night is as bright as day. The next second it is blacker than it has ever been.

I look at the water, and I can see that it's too deep for the car to pass through. I must turn back or I must walk the rest of the way. I stand there a while wondering what to do. Is it worth it all? Can't I simply send the gift by someone tomorrow morning? But will there be someone tomorrow morning? Suppose she leaves without getting it, then what? What then? Father would never forgive me. Neither would Grandfather or Great-grandfather, either. No, they wouldn't.

The lightning flashes again and I look across the field, and I can see the tree in the yard a quarter of a mile away. I have but one choice: I must walk. I get the package out of the car and stuff it in my coat and start out.

I don't make any progress at first, but then I become a little warmer and   195
I find I like walking. The lightning flashes just in time to show up a puddle of water, and I go around it. But there's no light to show up the second puddle, and I fall flat on my face. For a moment I'm completely blind, then I get slowly to my feet and check the package. It's dry, not harmed. I wash the mud off my raincoat, wash my hands, and I start out again.

The house appears in front of me, and as I come into the yard, I can hear the people laughing and talking. Sometimes I think niggers can laugh and joke even if they see somebody beaten to death. I go up on the porch and knock and an old one opens the door for me. I swear, when he sees me he looks as if he's seen a ghost. His mouth drops open, his eyes bulge—I swear.

I go into the old crowded and smelly room, and every one of them looks at me the same way the first one did. All the joking and laughing has ceased. You would think I was the devil in person.

"Done, Lord," I hear her saying over by the fireplace. They move to the side and I can see her sitting in that little rocking chair I bet you she's had since the beginning of time. "Done, Master," she says. "Child, what you doing in weather like this? Y'all move, let her get to that fire. Y'all move. Move, now. Let her warm herself."

They start scattering everywhere.

"I'm not cold, Aunt Fe," I say. "I just brought you something—something small—because you're leaving us. I'm going right back."   200

"Done, Master," she says. Fussing over me just like she's done all her life. "done, Master. Child, you ain't got no business in a place like this. Get close to this fire. Get here. Done, Master."

I move closer, and the fire does feel warm and good.

"Done, Lord," she says.

I take out the package and pass it to her. The other niggers gather around with all kinds of smiles on their faces. Just think of it—a white lady coming through all of this for one old darky. It is all right for them to come from all over the plantation, from all over the area, in all kinds of weather: this is to be expected of them. But a white lady, a white lady. They must think we white people don't have their kind of feelings.

She unwraps the package, her bony little fingers working slowly and de-   205
liberately. When she sees the scarf—the seventy-nine-cents scarf—she brings it to her mouth and kisses it.

"Y'all look," she says. "Y'all look. Ain't it the prettiest little scarf y'all ever did see? Y'all look."

They move around her and look at the scarf. Some of them touch it.

"I go'n put it on right now," she says. "I go'n put it on right now, my lady."

She unfolds it and ties it round her head and looks up at everybody and smiles.

"Thank you, my lady," she says. "Thank you, ma'am, from the bottom   210
of my heart."

"Oh, Aunt Fe," I say, kneeling down beside her. "Oh, Aunt Fe."

But I think about the other niggers there looking down at me, and I get up. But I look into that wrinkled old face again, and I must go back down again. And I lay my head in that bony old lap, and I cry and I cry—I don't know how long. And I feel those old fingers, like death itself, passing over my hair and my neck. I don't know how long I kneel there crying, and when I stop, I get out of there as fast as I can.

Etienne

The boy come in, and soon, right off, they get quiet, blaming the boy. If people could look little farther than the tip of they nose—No, they blame the boy. Not that they ain't behind the boy, what he doing, but they blame him for what she must do. What they don't know is that the boy didn't start it, and the people that bombed the house didn't start it, neither. It started a million years ago. It started when one man envied another man for having a penny mo' 'an he had, and then the man married a woman to help him work the field so he could get much 's the other man, but when the other man saw the man had married a woman to get much 's him, he, himself, he married a woman, too, so he could still have mo'. Then they start having children—not from love; but so the children could help 'em work so they could have mo'. But even with the children one man still had a penny mo' 'an the other, so the other man went and bought him a ox, and the other man did the same—to keep ahead of the other man. And soon the other man had bought him a slave to work the ox so he could get ahead of the other man. But the other man went out and bought him two slaves so he could stay ahead of the other man, and the other man went out and bought him three slaves. And soon they had a thousand slaves apiece, but they still wasn't satisfied. And one day the slaves all rose and kill the masters, but the masters (knowing slaves was men just like they was, and kind o' expected they might do this) organized theyself a good police force, and the police force, they come out and killed the two thousand slaves.

So it's not this boy you see standing here 'fore you, 'cause it happened a million years ago. And this boy here's just doing something the slaves done a million years ago. Just that this boy here ain't doing it they way. 'Stead of raising arms 'gainst the masters, he bow his head.

No, I say, don't blame the boy 'cause she must go. 'Cause when she's dead, and that won't be long after they get her up there, this boy's work will still be going on. She's not the only one that's go'n die from this boy's work. Many mo' of 'em go'n die 'fore it's over with. The whole place—everything. A big wind is rising, and when a big wind rise, the sea stirs, and the drop o' water you see laying on top the sea this day won't be there tomorrow. 'Cause that's what wind do, and that's what life is. She ain't nothing but one little drop o' water laying on top the sea, and what this boy's doing is called the wind . . . and she must be moved. No, don't blame the boy. Go out and blame the wind. No, don't blame him, 'cause tomorrow, what he's doing today, somebody go'n say he ain't done a thing. 'Cause tomorrow will be his time to be turned over just like it's hers today. And after that, be somebody else time to turn over. And it keep going like that till it ain't nothing left to turn—and nobody left to turn it.

"Sure, they bombed the house," he say, "because they want us to stop. But if we stopped today, then what good would we have done? What good? Those who have already died for the cause would have just died in vain."

"Maybe if they had bombed your house you wouldn't be so set on keeping this up."

"If they had killed my mother and my brothers and sisters, I'd press just that much harder. I can see you all point. I can see it very well. But I can't agree with you. You blame me for their being bombed. You blame me for Aunt Fe's leaving. They died for you and for your children. And I love Aunt Fe as much as anybody in here does. Nobody in here loves her more than I do. Not one of you." He looks at her. "Don't you believe me, Aunt Fe?"

She nods— that little white scarf still tied round her head.

"How many times have I eaten in your kitchen, Aunt Fe? A thousand   220
times? How many times have I eaten tea cakes and drank milk on the back steps, Aunt Fe? A thousand times? How many times have I sat at this same fireplace with you, just the two of us, Aunt Fe? Another thousand times—two thousand times? How many times have I chopped wood for you, chopped grass for you, ran to the store for you? Five thousand times? How many times have we walked to church together, Aunt Fe? Gone fishing at the river together—how many times? I've spent as much time in this house as I've spent in my own. I know every crack in the wall. I know every corner. With my eyes shut, I can go anywhere in here without bumping into anything. How many of you can do that? Not many of you." He looks at her. "Aunt Fe?"

She looks at him.

"Do you think I love you, Aunt Fe?"

She nods.

"I love you, Aunt Fe, much as I do my own parents. I'm going to miss you much as I'd miss my own mother if she were to leave me now. I'm going to miss you, Aunt Fe, but I'm not going to stop what I've started. You told me a story once, Aunt Fe, about my great-grandpa. Remember? Remember how he died?"

She looks in the fire and nods.   225

"Remember how they lynched him—chopped him into pieces?"

She nods.

"Just the two of us were sitting here beside the fire when you told me that. I was so angry I felt like killing. But it was you who told me get killing out of my mind. It was you who told me I would only bring harm to myself and sadness to the others if I killed. Do you remember that, Aunt Fe?"

She nods, still looking in the fire.

"You were right. We cannot raise our arms. Because it would mean death   230
for ourselves, as well as for the others. But we will do something else—and that's what we will do." He looks at the people standing round him. "And if they were to bomb my own mother's house tomorrow, I would still go on."

"I'm not saying for you not to go on," Louise says. "That's up to you. I'm just taking Auntie from here before hers is the next house they bomb."

The boy look at Louise, and then at Aunt Fe. He go up to the chair where she sitting.

"Good-bye, Aunt Fe," he say, picking up her hand. The hand done shriveled up to almost nothing. Look like nothing but loose skin's covering the bones. "I'll miss you," he say.

"Good-bye, Emmanuel," she say. She look at him a long time. "God be with you."

He stand there holding the hand a while longer, then he nods his head, and leaves the house. The people stir round little bit, but nobody say anything.

Aunt Lou

They tell her good-bye, and half of 'em leave the house crying, or want cry, but she just sit there 'side the fireplace like she don't mind going at all. When Leola ask me if I'm ready to go, I tell her I'm staying right there till Fe leave that house. I tell her I ain't moving one step till she go out that door. I been knowing her for the past fifty some years now, and I ain't 'bout to leave her on her last night here.

That boy, Chuckkie, want stay with me, but I make him go. He follow his mon and paw out the house and soon I hear that wagon turning round. I hear Emile saying something to Mr. Bascom even 'fore that wagon get out the yard. I tell myself, well, Mr. Bascom, you sure go'n catch it, and me not there to take up for you—and I get up from my chair and go to the door.

"Emile?" I call.

"Whoa," he say.

"You leave that mule 'lone, you hear me?"

"I ain't done Mr. Bascom a thing, Mama," he say.

"Well, you just mind you don't," I say. "I'll sure find out."

"Yes'm," he say. "Come up here Mr. Bascom."

"Now, you hear that boy. Emile?" I say.

"I'm sorry, Mama," he say. "I didn't mean no harm."

They go out in the road, and I go back to the fireplace and sit down again. Louise stir round in the kitchen a few minutes, then she come in the front where we at. Everybody else gone. That husband o' hers, there, got drunk long 'fore midnight, and Emile and them had to put him to bed in the other room.

She come there and stand by the fire.

"I'm dead on my feet," she say.

"Why don't you go to bed," I say. "I'm go'n be here."

"You all won't need anything?"

"They got wood in that corner?"

"Plenty."

"Then we won't need a thing."

She stand there and warm, and then she say good night and go round the other side.

"Well, Fe?" I say.

"I ain't leaving here tomorrow, Lou," she say.

"'Course you is," I say. "Up there ain't that bad."

She shake her head. "No, I ain't going nowhere."

I look at her over in her chair, but I don't say nothing. The fire pops in the fireplace, and I look at the fire again. It's a good little fire—not too big, not too little. Just 'nough there to keep the place warm.

"You want sing, Lou?" she say, after a while. "I feel like singing my 'termination song."   260

"Sure," I say.

She start singing in that little light voice she got there, and I join with her. We sing two choruses, and then she stop.

"My 'termination for Heaven," she say. "Now—now—"

"What's the matter, Fe?" I say.

"Nothing," she say. "I want get in my bed. My gown hanging over there."   265

I get the gown for her and bring it back to the fireplace. She get out of her dress slowly, like she don't even have 'nough strength to do it. I help her on with her gown, and she kneel down there 'side the bed and say her prayers. I sit in my chair and look at the fire again.

She pray there a long time—half out loud, half to herself. I look at her kneeling down there, little like a little old girl. I see her making some kind o' jecking motion there, but I feel she crying 'cause this her last night here, and 'cause she got to go and leave ever'thing behind. I look at the fire.

She pray there ever so long, and then she start to get up. But she can't make it by herself. I go to help her, and when I put my hand on her shoulder, she say, "Lou? Lou?"

I say, "What's the matter, Fe?"

"Lou?" she say. "Lou?"   270

I feel her shaking in my hand with all her might. Shaking, shaking, shaking—like a person with the chill. Then I hear her take a long breath, longest I ever heard anybody take before. Then she ease back on the bed—calm, calm, calm.

"Sleep on, Fe," I tell her. "When you get up there, tell 'em all I ain't far behind."

Considerations

1. What is the significance of Gaines's title "Just Like a Tree"?

2. What other images of relationships and connections appear throughout the story? How do they help define the sense of community of the characters?

3. What is the effect of telling the story from the viewpoints of so many different characters? What, for example, does a character like James add to the story? Why does the author include a character like Emmanuel? How does the structure of the story reflect the sense of community of the characters?

Invitation to Write

The community in Gaines's story is very much like an extended family, although the individuals involved are not blood relatives. Write an essay in which you explore the significance of the community described by Gaines. Consider the way his characters relate to each other and the way their thinking follows similar patterns. Compare this community with your own ideas about what constitutes a community. How important is it in this story for an individual to be part of the community?

Connections

In "Just Like a Tree," Aunt Fe is the symbol of community. The café in William Least Heat-Moon's "The Emma Chase" (p. 282) plays a similar role. Both narratives present an idea about what a community is and relate that idea to a symbol. Write an essay in which you compare the ideas of community that dominate in each case. Consider how both communities express a sense of themselves in choosing a symbol, and determine how important that symbol is in ensuring the communities' survival.

NEIL MILLER

A Time of Change

Neil Miller grew up in Kingston, New York. After graduating from Brown University in 1967, he edited the *Gay Community News,* a Boston paper, from 1975 to 1977. Until recently, Miller was a staff writer for the *Boston Phoenix.* He has also written for the *Boston Globe Sunday Magazine, Boston* magazine, *Glamour, Travel and Leisure,* and *Seven Days.* He has traveled widely in the United States, as well as abroad in Iran and Turkey. For several years he lived in Israel, where he taught high school English to the children of Moroccan and Iraqi immigrants. Before choosing a career as a reporter, he also taught English at a Berlitz school. He now lives in Somerville, Massachusetts.

"A Time of Change" comes from Miller's book *In Search of Gay America* (1989). In order to write this book, Miller traveled extensively in the United States during the 1980s, visiting many different types of gay communities. He wanted to view and assess the enormous changes in the lives of lesbians and gay men, their new roles in their communities, and their communities' attitudes toward them. The essay that follows deals with the issue of family life and parenting among gay people.

WHEN I RETURNED HOME TO BOSTON from my trip through small-town America, it was as if I was returning to the modern gay world. The gay and lesbian March on Washington was scheduled for the following week; organizers were hoping for a turnout of as many as half a million people. The memorial AIDS quilt—the size of two football fields—was on its way from San Francisco to be unveiled at the march. The film version of *Maurice,* E. M. Forster's novel about homosexuality in Edwardian England, was playing to packed houses in Harvard Square.

In the copy of the *New York Native* that I found in the stack of mail on my desk, the ever-controversial AIDS activist Larry Kramer was blaming the "white middle-class male majority" for the AIDS epidemic—and preaching the gospel of sexual conservatism. "The heterosexual majority has for centuries denied us every possible right of human dignity that the Constitution was framed to provide to all," he argued at a symposium sponsored by the New

York Civil Liberties Union. "The right to marry. The right to own property jointly without fear the law would disinherit the surviving partner. The right to hold jobs as an openly gay person. The right to have children. . . . So rightly or wrongly—wrongly, as it turned out—we decided we would make a virtue of the only thing you didn't have control over: our sexuality. Had we possessed these rights you denied us, had we been allowed to live respectably in a community as equals, there would never have been an AIDS. Had we been allowed to marry, we would not have felt the obligation to be promiscuous."

For its part, *GCN* was proudly publishing photographs of five babies born to Boston-area lesbians earlier in the year.

And Mo was seven and a half months pregnant. Mo and her lover, Ellen, are close friends of my friend Katie. Katie and Ellen grew up in the same Cleveland suburb (they met at Girl Scouts) and went to high school together. I had never met Mo or Ellen but Katie kept me closely apprised of developments in their lives. A couple of years ago, they had moved out of the city to suburban Newton—"For the schools," Katie said. Mo had bought a station wagon. Next, I heard that Mo was attempting to get pregnant through artificial insemination. After twelve months of trying, she was finally going to have a baby.

Katie recounted all these events with a mixture of pride and trepidation. She was excited at the prospect of being an "aunt" but was also concerned that her friends were gradually growing more distant—the move to the suburbs, the station wagon, and finally, of course, the baby. She was worried about being left behind. That was a fear that gay people (and childless heterosexuals) often experienced when married friends started raising children; in the past, you could at least have been sure your gay friends wouldn't abandon you for the suburbs, mothers' support groups, and the PTA.

I was aware that the number of gay people—primarily lesbians, but some gay men, too—choosing to become parents had grown dramatically in the past few years, especially in the large urban centers. In Boston, it seemed as if virtually every lesbian in her thirties was either having a baby or thinking about it. Gay men were becoming sperm donors to lesbian friends for at-home insemination (although fear of AIDS was making most lesbian parents-to-be turn to sperm banks and "unknown" donors); some gay men and lesbians were involved in complicated co-parenting arrangements.

A friend told me about spending the weekend at the home of a lesbian couple in Boston. One of the women in the household was trying to become pregnant; a gay man in Los Angeles was providing the sperm and would play a role (albeit a distant one) in raising the child. My friend, who was sleeping on the fold-out couch in the living room, was awakened early Saturday morning by the doorbell. It was Federal Express delivering a package. My friend signed for it, assuming it was a pair of khakis from L. L. Bean or the latest

5

lesbian detective novel. When her hosts came down for breakfast, she learned the package contained a sperm specimen, packed in dry ice for transcontinental shipment.

As much as people joked about "turkey-baster babies" and the "lesbian baby boom," the decision of increasing numbers of gay people to become parents outside of heterosexual norms marked a major change in gay and lesbian life. Coming out no longer meant forgoing the option of having children, as had been assumed in the past. By the late eighties, with the aging of the gay baby-boom generation, parenting had unexpectedly emerged as the cutting edge of gay and lesbian liberation. It was a new stage in the development of self-affirmation and identity. But to reach that point, a specific gay and lesbian community had to achieve a certain degree of cohesion and comfort. As a result, the new parenting was primarily a phenomenon of large cities and the East and West coasts, where gay people had developed the most extensive support systems and felt the most secure. Lesbians and gay men I visited in smaller towns wouldn't consider the possibility of having children (although many had them from previous heterosexual marriages); it would be too exposing, call too much attention to themselves.

Most lesbians I knew who were having babies were open about their sexuality and were politically active. Mo and Ellen were, to some degree, in the closet; their neighbors and their co-workers were unaware of their relationship. According to Katie, they intended to continue to live discreetly after the baby was born. I thought the fact that these suburban, relatively closeted lesbians were having a child might indicate that the lesbian baby boom was extending to more mainstream women.

One Saturday, six weeks before their baby was due, I went to visit Mo and Ellen. They were waiting for a changing table to arrive from Sears and would be home all morning, they told me when I phoned. I headed for the land of Dutch Colonials and station wagons, of well-dressed parents pushing well-scrubbed children through the park in Aprica strollers, of the comfortable, child-centered middle class. Traditionally a Jewish middle-class suburb, Newton was increasingly drawing Boston-area yuppies like Mo and Ellen. 10

I always felt a pang of nostalgia and sadness when I drove to Newton. When I was growing up, my aunt and uncle and my closest cousins lived there. Visiting them was a treat, to be savored weeks in advance. By the time I was in college, my aunt and uncle were in the middle of an acrimonious divorce and my cousins were estranged from them. My relatives had long since moved out of Newton but I couldn't help but think about the breakup of their family every time I went there.

Mo and Ellen's house was a two-story brick fifties-style dwelling located on a main thoroughfare. The interior was decorated with wall-to-wall carpeting, comfortable furniture, and living-room curtains featuring a pattern of ducks; the clock on the mantelpiece was flanked by framed photographs of

Mo and Ellen's families. It was friendly, tasteful, undistinctive—the kind of house where most American middle-class suburban kids have grown up in the past three decades.

Mo and Ellen had been together for more than ten years. They met as sorority sisters at Ohio State. No one in their sorority knew they were involved; they were just best friends who spent all their time together and did their best to hide the truth of their relationship. Later, they found out that most of the officers of the sorority were lesbians and that Mo's former roommate had been having an affair with the woman across the hall.

To me, they seemed quite evenly matched—opinionated, good-humored, a little on the boisterous side. Both looked like they should play rugby or lacrosse. Mo was a tall, dark-haired woman of thirty-one who grew up in rural Ohio. She was dressed in a light blue pullover top and matching running pants; her outfit was a cross between sweats and pajamas. "The latest in lesbian maternity apparel," she joked. She worked as a career counselor at a nearby college but was planning to quit once the baby was born. Ellen, thirty, had long, sandy hair and radiated wholesome good cheer. She was in a management position at a Boston computer company and tended to have a somewhat tough-minded, businesslike way of viewing things. Katie told me she thought Ellen had softened and begun to express more of her emotional side since Mo's pregnancy.

Mo had always wanted to have kids but once she came out she assumed 15 it wasn't a possibility. Still, she wouldn't give up on the idea entirely. She asked her gay brother (of five siblings in her family, three were gay) if he might consider offering his sperm so Ellen could get pregnant. He was appalled at the notion, she said; he told Mo, somewhat self-righteously, that she and Ellen should adopt a handicapped child. Mo and Ellen started attending meetings of the Choosing Children Network, a Boston-area group that offered information and support to lesbians considering parenthood. They began to lean towards adopting a child. At about that time, the administration of Governor Michael Dukakis issued the controversial regulations that effectively barred gays and lesbians from becoming licensed as foster parents. This policy was widely interpreted as applying to adoption as well, and adoption agencies were running scared. Mo would call up adoption agencies and ask if they would accept applications from gay couples. "We'll get back to you," they would tell her, but they rarely did.

With possibilities for adoption apparently closed off, Mo and Ellen decided to try artificial insemination (also called AI or alternative insemination, to make it sound less clinical). They began going to a Boston community-health center that performed the procedure. (Under the clinic's policy the identity of donor and recipient remained unknown to each other; donors waived all rights to any child conceived with their sperm.) Mo and Ellen had to wait three months before beginning insemination; in the meantime, they joined a support group of other lesbians who were trying to get pregnant.

The health center permitted them to choose specific characteristics they wanted in a donor—height, hair and eye color, ethnic background, occupation, and the like. But after months of unsuccessful insemination, Mo found herself caring less and less about whether the donor had blue or brown eyes. "After a while," she said, "I was just concerned with getting pregnant. I really didn't care about anything else." In the end, the father turned out to be a six-foot-three Seventh-Day Adventist of Irish extraction from southern California. The health center gave Mo a letter he wrote telling about himself and why he had become a sperm donor; she and Ellen planned to show the note to the child when it got older.

I asked Mo how her parents felt about her pregnancy. She pointed to two large boxes of baby clothes that her mother had sent a few days before, which were still sitting in the front hall. Her parents had known for many years that Mo was a lesbian; that was nothing new. And Mo's baby would be the first grandchild, a fact which made her parents more accepting than they might have been otherwise.

Still, her parents were uncomfortable. Her mother was especially worried about how to explain the pregnancy to her neighbors in the small town where she lived and where the family was quite prominent. Everyone there knew that Mo was unmarried, and her mother had never acknowledged to a soul— not even to her closest friends—that three of her children were gay. But with the baby on the way, her mother had to say something. She began telling neighbors that her daughter was having a child and bringing it up herself. The father, she said, lived in California and would take no part in raising the baby. That was accurate as far as it went. "The disgrace of illegitimacy is better than the truth in her eyes," noted Mo.

Until the couple decided to have a child, Ellen had never told her parents   20 she was gay. But she was seriously thinking about having a baby herself in a couple of years, "to balance things out," as she put it. When Mo began undergoing insemination, Ellen wrote to her parents and revealed the truth of their relationship. Her parents seemed to have responded well. "They offered us a crib," she said. "My mother is buying Christmas ornaments for my sister's child and our child. My father is wondering what he should call the child and how he should talk about it. They are planning to consider it a grandchild."

Mo's mother was preparing to visit after the birth of the baby, and Ellen's parents would follow a couple of weeks later.

That degree of parental support, however qualified, was not typical of the other lesbians (three couples and a single woman) in their childbirth class, they told me. "The other women in the group have parents who are saying, 'This is not our grandchild. We will have nothing to do with this child,'" Mo noted. "We go to these meetings and feel incredibly lucky."

Interestingly, both Mo's and Ellen's parents had become friends, a bond formed before the parents were aware the two young women were lovers. The parents, who lived a few hours' drive from each other, had much in common. Like their daughters, both sets of parents met when they were students at Ohio State, and were active in their alumni organizations; both were members of the same religious denomination. "If I were a guy or you were a guy, it would be a marriage made in heaven," Mo joked to Ellen. The parents had gone to dinner and the theater together—without their daughters.

After Mo became pregnant, Ellen's parents invited Mo's mother and father to their home, where they discussed the baby. In fact, Ellen's mother had been helping Mo's mother cope with her worries about the situation. "My mother is less inhibited," Ellen explained. "Mo's parents are very uptight about what people think. Mo has been pregnant all this time but her mother only told her own sister-in-law a couple of weeks ago."

The story Mo's mother was giving out to friends and relatives, that "the baby's father lives in California and won't be involved," was identical to what Mo and Ellen were telling people at their jobs, where both kept their relationship a secret. Mo was convinced that her boss would fire her if he learned she was gay; she was planning to leave anyway once the baby was born. People are "one hundred percent more accepting" of a single, heterosexual woman having a baby than a lesbian mother, she maintained. Ellen said that her co-workers were aware she had a female roommate and that the two owned a house together, but apparently made no assumptions beyond that. She had informed the other employees that Mo was pregnant and that she was going to be the birth coach. "They are telling me, 'You are going to be like a father!'" Ellen said. "I think they understand at some level what is going on, even if it is not a conscious level." Still, Ellen was reluctant to come out at work. Acknowledging her sexuality "wouldn't be good for my career," she insisted.

I asked them how they felt about this misrepresentation of their relationship and of the baby's conception. Mo emphasized that her priority was to protect the child as much as possible. If she had to pretend to be heterosexual for the child to have an easier time, she would do so—to some extent, anyway. "Not to a total extent though," she said. "But I am willing to make some accommodations." What accommodations, I asked. She thought that if her child brought a friend home to stay overnight, there was no reason to make her sexuality known. What about school? About parents of other kids? She just wasn't sure. Of course, they would tell the child about their homosexuality when it was old enough. "Some lesbian mothers are really out," Mo said. "I admire that. But I don't know yet just how open to be. Our big worry is how society will react and how to make it easier for the child. If that means playing a game with people we don't care about, I'll play a game. We're not the most militant people. I think I'll be more middle-of-the-road than most other lesbian mothers. That is how we've lived so far."

I thought that Mo and Ellen might be fooling themselves. I had talked to a number of gay parents who emphasized that a child's comfort with a

25

parent's homosexuality was directly proportional to how relaxed the parent seemed about it. I questioned whether the way Mo and Ellen were planning to handle the issue indicated the necessary degree of ease. How, for example, would the child react to having two mothers in Boston but one mother (and an absent father somewhere in California) when it went to visit its grandmother in Ohio?

In the middle of our talk, the doorbell rang. It was Sears, delivering the changing table. We moved to the front hall, and I thought the deliverymen might assume that, as the only male present, I was the expectant father. But Mo and Ellen immediately took charge, and the men never even looked in my direction. They carried the table upstairs to the guest room, and Mo and Ellen enthusiastically unpacked it. Then, Ellen and I lugged the two boxes of baby clothes from Mo's mother upstairs.

When we sat down again, the conversation shifted. One aspect of child-rearing Mo and Ellen were sure about was that the child would be both of theirs; they were determined to minimize the primacy of the biological mother as much as possible. "I don't want this to be *my* child," Mo said firmly. "It is going to have my last name, and when Ellen has a baby that one will have her last name. But they will be *our* kids and we are going to try to reinforce that in as many ways as we can." They had graduated from college without any money or possessions and had shared everything since then, they said. This would extend to the child. Their biggest problem was what to have the child call them. Most lesbian couples they knew used Mommy and the first name of the co-parent. They rejected this formulation because they felt it reinforced the role of the biological mother as primary parent. But they were unsure what to do instead.

As part of Mo's insistence on downplaying the biological tie, she was determined to bottle-feed the baby. Bottle-feeding would give Ellen an equal role in feeding and prevent her from feeling excluded. The other women in their childbirth class were strong proponents of breast-feeding, however. Mo differed from the rest of the class in still another respect; she was willing to entertain the idea of anesthesia if labor proved too painful, an idea that was totally unacceptable to the other mothers-to-be. In their childbirth class they were "the most mainstream," Mo said. But, always worried about appearing overly conservative, she added, "We are talking about mainstream liberal. Don't get us wrong."

Mainstream liberal or just mainstream, Mo and Ellen were nonetheless pioneers of a sort and they knew it. They emphasized that what they were doing would have been unthinkable ten years ago. As gay people, "We have stopped fighting and started living, really," said Ellen.

Shortly after the first of the year, Katie called me up excitedly. Mo was in the hospital, about to go into labor. For the next day or so, I received up-to-the-minute bulletins: contractions had begun; Ellen was there by her side; the doctors thought they might have to induce labor. Finally, Katie telephoned to announce that Mo had had the baby, a girl named Emma Claire.

In February, I went to Florida for a few days to visit my own parents, who now live there most of the year. During my stay, I spent an evening with six gay women in the living room of a ranch-style home in the Miami suburb of Kendall. All the women but one had been married before. As a result of these marriages, they had eleven children among them.

The house belonged to two women in their early forties—Rexine Pippinger, who managed a Radio Shack franchise, and her lover of seven years, Becky Anderson, a pediatric nurse. (The other women had just come by for the evening.) Rexine's two red-headed, freckle-faced teenage sons wandered in and out, bantering affectionately with their mother. The family dog, a little black spaniel, was about to give birth and was pacing nervously. Despite the cozy "Leave It to Beaver" atmosphere, the women had horror stories to tell. They were examples of gay parenting the traditional way—coming to terms with sexuality *after* marriage and childbearing. And the degree of rage in the suburban living room was sometimes frightening.

Four of the five women who had been married had emerged on the losing end of grueling legal battles with their ex-husbands. Becky, the nurse, had lost her house and custody of her two children (now twenty-one and sixteen) in the late seventies, at the height of Anita Bryant's antigay crusade. She wound up taking care of the kids for the next eight years anyway. Her lover, Rexine, initially won custody of her children. Later, her alcoholic ex-husband had sued her for fraud—dragging several of her ex-lovers into court as witnesses. As a result, she lost her children for two years and her house, as well.

Another woman had lost custody and even been denied visitation rights. Her former husband had moved out of state with her two children. Now the ex-husband, his new wife, and the kids had moved back to Miami and she got to see the children. But her oldest daughter was pregnant and unwed; her fourteen year old was having sex with her boyfriend. She got the blame for the kids' actions; everything they were doing was to show *they* were not lesbians, according to their stepmother. "I used to think there was some truth in it until I finally learned to stop laying guilt trips on myself," the woman said.

The one parent who had been spared a custody battle nearly lost her children another way. The previous year, Arlie Brice, a graphic designer in her early thirties, had been living in Jacksonville, Florida, with her lover and her two sons, aged nine and eleven. On the children's school forms, Arlie would scratch out "father" and write "co-parent" instead, putting down her lover's name. Both were members of the PTA and baked brownies for school events. One Saturday when Arlie was at work, she got a call from her lover. An investigator from the State Department of Health and Rehabilitative Services had

35

shown up at their door. Someone had accused them of child abuse. After two weeks of investigation, which proved an "utter terror" for the kids (and their parents), they were cleared of any wrongdoing. Still, once you're reported for child abuse, Arlie noted, "you are on a master computer in Tallahassee, whether the accusation is justified or unjustified. Right now if I wanted to work with kids or be a foster parent, I would be denied."

Their accuser, she found out, was the principal of the public school her children attended. He was a religious fundamentalist. When Arlie confronted him, he admitted he had reported them to state authorities, she said. "I know you love your kids," Arlie quoted the principal as saying. "But you are living a life-style that is wrong." Arlie's only recourse would have been to hire an attorney and, as she put it, "make a lot of noise." But in conservative Jackson-ville, bringing a court case on such grounds could be "a very dangerous thing to do," she said. "You could lose your job at the drop of a hat." She took her kids out of school immediately; some months later, the family moved to Miami.

After listening to these stories, I turned to the one woman in the group who hadn't been married, a twenty-six-year-old Cuban American named Sonia Fandino. Sonia lived at home with her parents and managed a gas sta-tion. I asked her facetiously if she ever planned to get married. "No," she laughed. "But I am planning to have a child soon." How did she plan to become pregnant? I asked. "Artificial insemination," she replied, and every-one in the room broke into laughter.

I thought back to that glimpse of old-style gay parenting when I returned to Newton to visit Mo and Ellen two months after Emma Claire was born. Ellen led me upstairs to the baby's room, where Mo was giving Emma Claire a bath. There, on the changing table that had arrived during my previous visit, was a squawling little baby with big blue eyes. The room was now furnished with two cribs—a large one filled with stuffed animals, and a second, smaller one for Emma Claire. Mo dried the baby, put her in a flannel nightgown, and laid her down in the crib. Ellen and I headed downstairs to the living room, now equipped with a baby's swing chair and decorated with a mobile depict-ing various animals. 40

Once Emma Claire had fallen asleep, Mo joined us. The two filled me in on events since I had last seen them. Childbirth was the toughest thing she had ever done in her life, Mo said. In the middle of the contractions Mo shouted to Ellen, who was holding Mo's legs as she worked to push the baby out, "This is really going to be hard for you when it's your turn!"

In general, the hospital staff had been at ease with them, they said. By coincidence, another lesbian who had become pregnant through AI was in the next room. When Mo mentioned to one nurse that they knew the woman next door, the nurse apparently assumed Mo was a lesbian. She began barraging her with questions: How did she get pregnant? What was AI, anyway? Did she know the baby's father?

According to the hospital rules, only husbands could spend all day in the room with the woman during and after labor, but Ellen remained and no one objected. Another regulation said no visitors except husbands could bring a baby from the nursery to the mother's room. Ellen went in and asked to take Emma Claire. The nurse balked. "I'm a partner," she insisted. The nurse relented, eyeing her suspiciously as she walked out the door with the baby.

Mo's mother came up from Ohio for the birth and stayed for two weeks. Mo had lost a lot of blood during childbirth and was too weak and exhausted to be very enthusiastic about holding Emma Claire. Her mother tried to get her to bond with the baby. But she went to such lengths that Ellen felt she was deliberately trying to freeze her out of any role. Mo's mother was constantly sending Ellen out of the house on errands. She would call Mo "Mommy" in the baby's presence, something Mo and Ellen had agreed not to do. At one point, the grandmother grabbed the baby right out of Ellen's arms and gave her to Mo to hold. Ellen became increasingly convinced that the mother's intention was to make it clear that the baby was Mo's, not Mo *and* Ellen's.

Caught between her mother and her lover, Mo was trying not to take sides. Her mother would come around, she was convinced; she just had to get used to the situation. And she had been helpful during the two weeks after the birth of the baby. The following weekend, Mo and Ellen were planning to bring the baby to visit Mo's parents. But if her mother persisted in trying to demonstrate that Emma Claire was Mo's and Mo's alone, her daughter was ready to insist she "cut the 'Mommy' crap." 45

Our mutual friend Katie, a social worker by profession, suspected that Mo's relations with her parents were about to undergo a major change. Mo, in her view, had always been the family mediator, listening patiently as her mother complained about the travails of having three gay children. Now, with the birth of Mo's baby, Katie thought that Mo would have to become more outspoken in defending the child and affirming her own relationship.

Meanwhile, Ellen reported that people at work were bringing her gifts for her "roommate's" baby. One co-worker gave her a bib; another bought a suit for Emma Claire. Everyone was asking her how the baby was doing. "I've been getting some weird questions," she said. "One of my co-workers asked me, 'Is your roommate being a surrogate mother?' But generally, people seem to go along with it and understand that I come home after work and help take care of the baby." In fact, a male co-worker had called earlier that week to ask Ellen out on a date. "I'm involved," she told him.

A month after the baby was born, a disquieting incident occurred. Ellen's brother-in-law, who held a highly sensitive post in the navy, had been called into his superior's office. "Do you know your sister-in-law is a lesbian?" he was asked. Of course, he knew, he replied. "Just as long as you are aware of it," his superior told him. Apparently, the navy was afraid of a potential blackmail situation.

Ellen's sister had called her up and told her about what had happened. She and Mo were upset and angry. They were puzzled about how the navy could have known about their relationship. Both their names appeared on the home mortgage, they noted. They were also on the mailing lists of the *Gay Community News* and a gay hiking club. Was the military spying on gay organizations? "It could have ruined our lives if we weren't 'out' to our families," said Ellen. Added Mo, her middle-of-the-road approach veering towards militance, "I'd like to know how national security is compromised by my love life!" Ironically, the same week, a federal court of appeals panel in San Francisco had struck down the army's ban on homosexuals.

At the time the United States Navy was questioning Ellen's brother-in- 50 law, rumors were flying in the small Ohio town where Mo's parents live. Mo received a letter of congratulations from a high-school friend; in the letter, the woman noted that her grandmother had heard about the baby at her bridge club. She added that the grandmother had heard that Mo had gotten pregnant through "artificial whatever," a fact that Mo's mother had never revealed. Mo had no idea how the woman could have known. "I was floored," she said. "Information about our personal lives seemed to be sweeping the land. The government was spying on us, and everyone in Ohio was talking about us!"

Despite these minor but dramatic incidents, the new gay parenting as exemplified by Mo and Ellen was still worlds apart from the horrors related by the lesbian mothers in Miami. In Mo and Ellen's case, there would be no ugly custody battles, no ex-husbands exacting revenge, and (one assumed) in liberal Newton, no over-zealous school principals alleging child abuse. But clearly the future would not be easy. The tension between how open or discreet to be about their sexuality and the difficulties of dealing with parents, schools, and society in general were something that Mo and Ellen would have to face squarely.

So far, most of these challenges lay in the future. Parents and baby were doing reasonably well. Ellen's mother and father had been up to visit; some of the neighbors had come by to see Emma Claire. Ellen was still quite determined to have another baby within the next year or two; the sleepless nights since Emma Claire's arrival had not dampened her enthusiasm. On the Friday night after my visit, six lesbian couples, all with babies, were coming by for a potluck.

Still, I couldn't help but speculate on how Emma Claire and all the children of these unusual parenting arrangements would turn out. Would they feel embarrassed about their parents? Protective? Proud? How important would the "absent (and unknown) father" issue be for them as they got older? Would they perceive themselves as different from the other kids? Or would growing up in a community like Newton, where divorced and single-parent families were commonplace, help them feel accepted? Would they be rebellious adolescents trying to prove *they* weren't gay? No one knew. The only studies of children of gay and lesbian parents had been done about traditional gay parenting (after heterosexual marriage), with its complicating factors of divorce and late coming out. Those studies had all been quite positive, but there was no doubt that psychologists and sociologists would have an interesting future studying the children of the lesbian baby boom.

Considerations

1. Miller characterizes parents like Mo and Ellen as pioneers (para. 31). Yet, as Miller describes, the two couples' choices to have children and the changes they foresee in their life-style makes them resemble heterosexual couples who opt for parenthood. How do the particular situations of the gay parents described here redefine the idea of parents and family?

2. In his anecdotes from Florida and Massachusetts, Miller discusses family and community responses to the issue of gay parenting. Look at the range of responses he describes. Which parts of the community seem most able to accept the idea of gay parents? Which parts seem unable to accept it? How are changes in attitudes likely to be put into effect?

3. What do the responses of these two communites to gay parenting indicate about political and public responses to the issue in American culture? What do you think motivates such responses?

Invitation to Write

Homosexuality is rejected in many cultures, including ours, in part because it challenges the established norms of heterosexual society. Write an essay in which you analyze community attitudes toward the gay families Miller describes in light of the challenges homosexuality presents for heterosexual norms. Consider why some people react against homosexuality so strongly and how homosexuals respond to such behavior and attitudes. Is a total acceptance of homosexuality possible in our society? What might the consequences of total acceptance be?

Connections

In the next essay, "Is There a Family?," Jane Collier, Michelle Z. Rosaldo, and Sylvia Yanagisako present various sociological views of the family. They conclude that "The Family is not a concrete 'thing' that fulfills concrete 'needs' but an ideological construct with moral implications" (para. 33). The issue of the homosexual family can be used to expand on this thesis. Examine the various definitions of family given by the three authors and compare them to the definitions Ellen and Mo have to confront. What ideologies and moralities are implied in these definitions? Write an essay in which you use Collier, Rosaldo, and Yanagisako's theories to explore the ideological and political implications of the notion of "family" in Neil Miller's essay.

JANE COLLIER
MICHELLE Z. ROSALDO
SYLVIA YANAGISAKO

Is There a Family?
New Anthropological Views

Collier, Rosaldo, and Yanagisako worked together at Stanford University, where they taught anthropology and performed research in the area of kinship and gender roles. They have also conducted studies individually on related topics. They call themselves "feminist anthropologists" and believe that "a focus on gender can transform our understanding of the world."

Jane Fishborne Collier received her Ph.D. from Tulane University in 1970. Most of her research has been carried out in the Mayan community of Zinacantan in southern Mexico. Her books include *Law and Social Change in Zinacantan* (1973), *Marriage and Inequality in a Classless Society* (1988), and *History and Power in the Study of Law* (1989). Currently, Collier is still teaching at Stanford in the anthropology department.

Michelle Zimbalist Rosaldo had a Ph.D. in social anthropology from Harvard University and did her primary research in the Philippines. Her speciality was anthropological linguistics and oral traditions. She published *Knowledge and Passion* in 1980. She was also among the editors of *Women, Culture, and Society* (1974) and *Feminist Theory: A Critique of Ideology* (1982). She was a professor in the anthropology department at Stanford when she died in 1981.

Sylvia Junko Yanagisako received her Ph.D. from the University of Washington. She is especially interested in the Japanese-American experience and has published a book entitled *Transforming the Past: Tradition and Kinship Among Japanese Americans* (1985). With Jane Collier, she edited *Gender and Kinship: Essays Toward a Unified Analysis* (1988).

The following essay deals with anthropology, the science of human cultures. Early studies focused on isolated tribes and non-European cultures—so-called primitive societies. In recent years, however, anthropologists have looked to their own societies for scientific models. In this spirit, the authors debate ideas about the family that emerged from Western culture and the science of anthropology. The main writer examined in this essay is Bronislaw Malinowski (1884–1942), a Polish-born English anthropologist, who is considered by many to be the founder of modern anthropology. His works include *Argonauts of the Western Pacific* (1922), *Myth in Primitive Societies* (1926), *Crime and Custom in Savage Society* (1926), *Sex and Repression in Savage Society* (1927), and *The Sexual Life of Savages* (1929). Although he proposed that culture should be seen "from the native's point of view," Malinowski had his own cultural bias, as is apparent even in his titles. The authors of this essay reveal that, in defining the family as a functional unit in society, Malinowski voiced the dominant ideology of his time.

THIS ESSAY POSES A RHETORICAL QUESTION in order to argue that most of our talk about families is clouded by unexplored notions of what families "really" are like. It is probably the case, universally, that people expect to have special connections with their genealogically closest relations. But a knowledge of genealogy does not in itself promote understanding of what these special ties are about. The real importance of The Family in contemporary social life and belief has blinded us to its dynamics. Confusing ideal with reality, we fail to appreciate the deep significance of what are, cross-culturally, various ideologies of intimate relationship, and at the same time we fail to reckon with the complex human bonds and experiences all too comfortably sheltered by a faith in the "natural" source of a "nurture" we think is found in the home.

This essay is divided into three parts. The first examines what social scientists mean by The Family. It focuses on the work of Bronislaw Malinowski, the anthropologist who first convinced social scientists that The Family was a universal human institution. The second part also has social scientists as its focus, but it examines works by the nineteenth-century thinkers Malinowski refuted, for if—as we shall argue—Malinowski was wrong in viewing The Family as a universal human institution, it becomes important to explore the work of theorists who did not make Malinowski's mistakes. The final section then draws on the correct insights of nineteenth-century theorists to sketch some implications of viewing The Family, not as a concrete institution designed to fulfill universal human needs, but as an ideological construct associated with the modern state.

Malinowski's Concept of the Family

In 1913 Bronislaw Malinowski published a book called *The Family Among the Australian Aborigines*[1] in which he laid to rest earlier debates about whether all human societies had families. During the nineteenth century, proponents of social evolution argued that primitives were sexually promiscuous and therefore incapable of having families because children would not recognize their fathers.[2] Malinowski refuted this notion by showing that Australian aborigines, who were widely believed to practice "primitive promiscuity," not only had rules regulating who might have intercourse with whom during sexual orgies but also differentiated between legal marriages and casual unions. Malinowski thus "proved" that Australian aborigines had marriage, and so proved that aboriginal children had fathers, because each child's mother had but a single recognized husband.

Malinowski's book did not simply add data to one side of an ongoing debate. It ended the debate altogether, for by distinguishing coitus from conjugal relationships, Malinowski separated questions of sexual behavior from questions of the family's universal existence. Evidence of sexual promiscuity was henceforth irrelevant for deciding whether families existed. Moreover, Malinowski argued that the conjugal relationship, and therefore The Family, had to be universal because it fulfilled a universal human need. As he wrote in a posthumously published book:

> The human infant needs parental protection for a much longer period than does the young of even the highest anthropoid apes. Hence, no culture could endure in which the act of reproduction, that is, mating, pregnancy, and childbirth, was not linked up with the fact of legally-founded parenthood, that is, a relationship in which the father and mother have to look after the children for a long period, and, in turn, derive certain benefits from the care and trouble taken.[3]

In proving the existence of families among Australian aborigines, Malinowski described three features of families that he believed flowed from The Family's universal function of nurturing children. First, he argued that families had to have clear boundaries, for if families were to perform the vital function of nurturing young children, insiders had to be distinguishable from outsiders so that everyone could know which adults were responsible for the care of which children. Malinowski thus argued that families formed bounded social units, and to prove that Australian families formed such units, he demonstrated that aboriginal parents and children recognized one another. Each aboriginal woman had a single husband, even if some husbands had more than one wife and even if husbands occasionally allowed wives to sleep with other men during tribal ceremonies. Malinowski thus proved that each aboriginal child had a recognized mother and father, even if both parents occasionally engaged in sexual relations with outsiders.

Second, Malinowski argued that families had to have a place where family members could be together and where the daily tasks associated with child-rearing could be performed. He demonstrated, for example, that aboriginal parents and their immature children shared a single fire—a home and hearth where children were fed and nurtured—even though, among nomadic aborigines, the fire might be kindled in a different location each night.

Finally, Malinowski argued that family members felt affection for one another—that parents who invested long years in caring for children were rewarded by their own and their children's affections for one another. Malinowski felt that long and intimate association among family members fostered close emotional ties, particularly between parents and children, but also between spouses. Aboriginal parents and their children, for example, could be expected to feel the same emotions for one another as did English parents and children, and as proof of this point, Malinowski recounted touching stories of the efforts made by aboriginal parents to recover children lost during conflicts with other aborigines or with white settlers and efforts made by stolen aboriginal children to find their lost parents.

Malinowski's book on Australian aborigines thus gave social scientists a concept of The Family that consisted of a universal function, the nurturance of young children, mapped onto (1) a bounded set of people who recognized one another and who were distinguishable from other like groups; (2) a definite physical space, a hearth and home; and (3) a particular set of emotions, family love. This concept of The Family as an institution for nurturing young children has been enduring, probably because nurturing children is thought to be the primary function of families in modern industrial societies. The flaw in Malinowski's argument is the flaw common to all functionalist arguments: Because a social institution is observed to perform a necessary function does not mean either that the function would not be performed if the institution did not exist or that the function is responsible for the existence of the institution.

Later anthropologists have challenged Malinowski's idea that families always include fathers, but, ironically, they have kept all the other aspects of his definition. For example, later anthropologists have argued that the basic social unit is not the nuclear family including father but the unit composed of a mother and her children: "Whether or not a mate becomes attached to the mother on some more or less permanent basis is a variable matter."[4] In removing father from the family, however, later anthropologists have nevertheless retained Malinowski's concept of The Family as a functional unit, and so have retained all the features Malinowski took such pains to demonstrate. In the writings of modern anthropologists, the mother-child unit is described as performing the universally necessary function of nurturing young children. A mother and her children form a bounded group, distinguishable from other units of mothers and their children. A mother and her children share a place, a home and hearth. And, finally, a mother and her children share deep emotional bonds based on their prolonged and intimate contact.

Modern anthropologists may have removed father from The Family, but they did not modify the basic social science concept of The Family in which

10

the function of child-rearing is mapped onto a bounded set of people who share a place and who "love" one another. Yet it is exactly this concept of The Family that we, as feminist anthropologists, have found so difficult to apply. Although the biological facts of reproduction, when combined with a sufficiently elastic definition of marriage, make it possible for us, as social scientists, to find both mother-child units and Malinowski's conjugal-pairs-plus-children units in every human society, it is not at all clear that such Families necessarily exhibit the associated features Malinowski "proved" and modern anthropologists echo.

An outside observer, for example, may be able to delimit family boundaries in any and all societies by identifying the children of one woman and that woman's associated mate, but natives may not be interested in making such distinctions. In other words, natives may not be concerned to distinguish family members from outsiders, as Malinowski imagined natives should be when he argued that units of parents and children have to have clear boundaries in order for child-rearing responsibilities to be assigned efficiently. Many languages, for example, have no word to identify the unit of parents and children that English speakers call a "family." Among the Zinacantecos of southern Mexico, the basic social unit is identified as a "house," which may include from one to twenty people.[5] Zinacantecos have no difficulty talking about an individual's parents, children, or spouse; but Zinacantecos do not have a single word that identifies the unit of parents and children in such a way as to cut it off from other like units. In Zinacanteco society, the boundary between "houses" is linguistically marked, while the boundary between "family" units is not.

Just as some languages lack words for identifying units of parents and children, so some "families" lack places. Immature children in every society have to be fed and cared for, but parents and children do not necessarily eat and sleep together as a family in one place. Among the Mundurucu of tropical South America, for example, the men of a village traditionally lived in a men's house together with all the village boys over the age of thirteen; women lived with other women and young children in two or three houses grouped around the men's house.[6] In Mundurucu society, men and women ate and slept apart. Men ate in the men's house, sharing food the women had cooked and delivered to them; women ate with other women and children in their own houses. Married couples also slept apart, meeting only for sexual intercourse.

Finally, people around the world do not necessarily expect family members to "love" one another. People may expect husbands, wives, parents, and children to have strong feelings about one another, but they do not necessarily expect prolonged and intimate contact to breed the loving sentiments Malinowski imagined as universally rewarding parents for the care they invested in children. The mother-daughter relationship, for example, is not always pictured as warm and loving. In modern Zambia, girls are not expected to discuss personal problems with, or seek advice from, their mothers. Rather,

Zambian girls are expected to seek out some older female relative to serve as confidante.[7] Similarly, among the Cheyenne Indians who lived on the American Great Plains during the last century, a mother was expected to have strained relations with her daughters.[8] Mothers are described as continually admonishing their daughters, leading the latter to seek affection from their fathers' sisters.

Of course, anthropologists have recognized that people everywhere do not share our deep faith in the loving, self-sacrificing mother, but in matters of family and motherhood, anthropologists, like all social scientists, have relied more on faith than evidence in constructing theoretical accounts. Because we *believe* mothers to be loving, anthropologists have proposed, for example, that a general explanation of the fact that men marry mother's brothers' daughters more frequently than they marry father's sisters' daughters is that men naturally seek affection (i.e., wives) where they have found affection in the past (i.e., from mothers and their kin).[9]

Looking Backward

The Malinowskian view of The Family as a universal institution—which maps the "function" of "nurturance" onto a collectivity of specific persons (presumably "nuclear" relations) associated with specific spaces ("the home") and specific affective bonds ("love")—corresponds, as we have seen, to that assumed by most contemporary writers on the subject. But a consideration of available ethnographic evidence suggests that the received view is a good deal more problematic than a naive observer might think. If Families in Malinowski's sense are *not* universal, then we must begin to ask about the biases that, in the past, have led us to misconstrue the ethnographic record. The issues here are too complex for thorough explication in this essay, but if we are to better understand the nature of "the family" in the present, it seems worthwhile to explore the question, first, of why so many social thinkers continue to believe in Capital-Letter Families as universal institutions, and second, whether anthropological tradition offers any alternatives to a "necessary and natural" view of what our families are. Only then will we be in a position to suggest "new anthropological perspectives" on the family today.

Our positive critique begins by moving backward. In the next few pages, we suggest that tentative answers to both questions posed above lie in the nineteenth-century intellectual trends that thinkers like Malinowski were at pains to reject. During the second half of the nineteenth century, a number of social and intellectual developments—among them, the evolutionary researches of Charles Darwin; the rise of "urban problems" in fast-growing cities; and the accumulation of data on non-Western peoples by missionaries and agents of the colonial states—contributed to what most of us would now recognize as the beginnings of modern social science. Alternately excited and perplexed by changes in a rapidly industrializing world, thinkers as diverse as socialist Frederick Engels[10] and bourgeois apologist Herbert Spencer[11]—to say nothing of a host of mythographers, historians of religion, and even feminists—attempted to identify the distinctive problems and potentials of their contemporary society by constructing *evolutionary* accounts of "how it all began." At base, a sense of "progress" gave direction to their thought, whether, like Spencer, they believed "man" had advanced from the love of violence to a more civilized love of peace or, like Engels, that humanity had moved from primitive promiscuity and incest toward monogamy and "individual sex love." Proud of their position in the modern world, some of these writers claimed that rules of force had been transcended by new rules of law,[12] while others thought that feminine "mysticism" in the past had been supplanted by a higher male "morality."[13]

At the same time, and whatever else they thought of capitalist social life (some of them criticized, but none wholly abhorred it), these writers also shared a sense of moral emptiness and a fear of instability and loss. Experience argued forcefully to them that moral order in their time did not rest on the unshakable hierarchy—from God to King to Father in the home—enjoyed by Europeans in the past.[14] Thus, whereas Malinowski's functionalism led him to stress the underlying continuities in all human social forms, his nineteenth-century predecessors were concerned to understand the facts and forces that set their experiential world apart. They were interested in comparative and, more narrowly, evolutionary accounts because their lives were torn between celebration and fear of change. For them, the family was important not because it had at all times been the same but because it was at once the moral precondition for, the triumph of, and the victim of developing capitalist society. Without the family and female spheres, thinkers like Ruskin feared we would fall victim to a market that destroys real human bonds.[15] Then again, while men like Engels could decry the impact of the market on familial life and love, he joined with more conservative counterparts to insist that our contemporary familial forms benefited from the individualist morality of modern life and reached to moral and romantic heights unknown before.

Given this purpose and the limited data with which they had to work, it is hardly surprising that the vast majority of what these nineteenth-century writers said is easily dismissed today. They argued that in simpler days such things as incest were the norm; they thought that women ruled in "matriarchal" and peace-loving states or, alternatively, that brute force determined the primitive right and wrong. None of these visions of a more natural, more feminine, more sexy, or more violent primitive world squares with contemporary evidence about what, in technological and organizational terms, might be reckoned relatively "primitive" or "simple" social forms. We would suggest, however, that whatever their mistakes, these nineteenth-century thinkers *can* help us rethink the family today, at least in part because we are (unfortunately) their heirs, in the area of prejudice, and partly because their concern to characterize difference and change gave rise to insights much more promising than their functionalist critics may have thought.

To begin, although nineteenth-century evolutionary theorists did not believe The Family to be universal, the roots of modern assumptions can be seen in their belief that women are, and have at all times been, defined by nurturant, connective, and reproductive roles that *do not change* through time. Most nineteenth-century thinkers imaged social development as a process of differentiation from a relatively confused (and thus incestuous) and indiscriminate female-oriented state to one in which men fight, destroy their "natural" social bonds, and then forge public and political ties to create a human "order." For some, it seemed reasonable to assume that women dominated, as matriarchs, in the undifferentiated early state, but even these theorists believed that women everywhere were "mothers" first, defined by "nurturant" concerns and thus excluded from the business competition, cooperation, social ordering, and social change propelled and dominated by their male counterparts. And so, while nineteenth-century writers differed in their evaluations of such things as "women's status," they all believed that female reproductive roles made women different from and complementary to men and guaranteed both the relative passivity of women in human history and the relative continuity of "feminine" domains and functions in human societies. Social change consisted in the acts of men, who left their mothers behind in shrinking homes. And women's nurturant sphere was recognized as a complementary and necessary corrective to the more competitive pursuits of men, not because these thinkers recognized women as political actors who influence the world, but because they feared the unchecked and morally questionable growth of a male-dominated capitalist market.

For nineteenth-century evolutionists, women were associated, in short, with an unchanging biological role and a romanticized community of the past, while men were imaged as the agents of all social process. And though contemporary thinkers have been ready to dismiss manifold aspects of their now-dated school of thought, on this point we remain, perhaps unwittingly, their heirs. Victorian assumptions about gender and the relationship between competitive male markets and peace-loving female homes were not abandoned in later functionalist schools of thought at least in part because pervasive sexist biases make it easy to forget that women, like men, are important actors in *all* social worlds. Even more, the functionalists, themselves concerned to understand all human social forms in terms of biological "needs," turned out to strengthen earlier beliefs associating action, change, and interest with the deeds of men because they thought of kinship in terms of biologically given ties, of "families" as units geared to reproductive needs, and finally, of women as mere "reproducers" whose contribution to society was essentially defined by the requirements of their homes.

If most modern social scientists have inherited Victorian biases that tend

20

ultimately to support a view uniting women and The Family to an apparently unchanging set of biologically given needs, we have at the same time failed to reckon with the one small area in which Victorian evolutionists were right. They understood, as we do not today, that families—like religions, economies, governments, or courts of law—are *not* unchanging but the product of various social forms, that the relationships of spouses and parents to their young are apt to be different things in different social orders. More particularly, although nineteenth-century writers had primitive society all wrong, they were correct in insisting that *family* in the modern sense—a unit bounded, biologically as well as legally defined, associated with property, self-sufficiency, with affect and a space "inside" the home—is something that emerges not in Stone Age caves but in complex state-governed social forms. Tribal peoples may speak readily of lineages, households, and clans, but—as we have seen—they rarely have a word denoting Family as a particular and limited group of kin; they rarely worry about differences between legitimate and illegitimate heirs or find themselves concerned (as we so often are today) that what children and/or parents do reflects on their family's public image and self-esteem. Political influence in tribal groups in fact consists in adding children to one's home and, far from distinguishing Smith from Jones, encouraging one's neighbors to join one's household as if kin. By contrast, modern bounded Families try to keep their neighbors out. Clearly their character, ideology, and functions are not given for all times. Instead, to borrow the Victorian phrase, The Family is a "moral" unit, a way of organizing and thinking about human relationships in a world in which the domestic is perceived to be in opposition to a politics shaped outside the home, and individuals find themselves dependent on a set of relatively noncontingent ties in order to survive the dictates of an impersonal market and external political order.

In short, what the Victorians recognized and we have tended to forget is, first, that human social life has varied in its "moral"—we might say its "cultural" or "ideological"—forms, and so it takes more than making babies to make Families. And having seen The Family as something more than a response to omnipresent, biologically given needs, they realized too that Families do not everywhere exist; rather, The Family (thought to be universal by most social scientists today) is a moral and ideological unit that appears, not universally, but in particular social orders. The Family as we know it is not a "natural" group created by the claims of "blood" but a sphere of human relationships shaped by a state that recognizes Families as units that hold property, provide for care and welfare, and attend particularly to the young—a sphere conceptualized as a realm of love and intimacy *in opposition* to the more "impersonal" norms that dominate modern economies and politics. One can, in nonstate social forms, find groups of genealogically related people who interact daily and share material resources, but the contents of their daily ties, the ways they think about their bonds and their conception of the relationship between immediate "familial" links and other kinds of sociality, are apt to be different from the ideas and feelings we think rightfully belong to families we know. Stated otherwise, because our notions of The Family are rooted in a contrast between "public" and "private" spheres, we will not find that Families like ours exist in a society where public and political life is radically different from our own.

Victorian thinkers rightly understood the link between the bounded modern Family and the modern state, although they thought the two related by a necessary teleology of moral progress. Our point resembles theirs not in the *explanations* we would seek but in our feeling that if we, today, are interested in change, we must begin to probe and understand change in the families of the past. Here the Victorians, not the functionalists, are our rightful guides because the former recognized that *all* human social ties have "cultural" or "moral" shapes, and more specifically, that the particular "morality" of contemporary familial forms is rooted in a set of processes that link our intimate experiences and bonds to public politics.

Toward a Rethinking

Our perspective on families therefore compels us to listen carefully to what the natives in other societies say about their relationships with genealogically close kin. The same is true of the natives in our own society. Our understanding of families in contemporary American society can be only as rich as our understanding of what The Family represents symbolically to Americans. A complete cultural analysis of The Family as an American ideological construct, of course, is beyond the scope of this essay. But we can indicate some of the directions such an analysis would take and how it would deepen our knowledge of American families.

One of the central notions in the modern American construct of The Family is that of nurturance. When antifeminists attack the Equal Rights Amendment, for example, much of their rhetoric plays on the anticipated loss of the nurturant, intimate bonds we associate with The Family. Likewise, when prolife forces decry abortion, they cast it as the ultimate denial of nurturance. In a sense, these arguments are variations of a functionalist view that weds families to specific functions. The logic of the argument is that because people need nurturance, and people get nurtured in The Family, then people need The Family. Yet if we adopt the perspective that The Family is an ideological unit rather than merely a functional unit, we are encouraged to subject this syllogism to closer scrutiny. We can ask, first, What do people mean by nurturance? Obviously, they mean more than mere nourishment—that is, the provision of food, clothing, and shelter required for biological survival. What is evoked by the word nurturance is a certain kind of relationship: a relationship that entails affection and love, that is based on cooperation as opposed

25

to competition, that is enduring rather than temporary, that is noncontingent rather than contingent upon performance, and that is governed by feeling and morality instead of law and contract.

The reason we have stated these attributes of The Family in terms of oppositions is because in a symbolic system the meanings of concepts are often best illuminated by explicating their opposites. Hence, to understand our American construct of The Family, we first have to map the larger system of constructs of which it is only a part. When we undertake such an analysis of The Family in our society, we discover that what gives shape to much of our conception of The Family is its symbolic opposition to work and business, in other words, to the market relations of capitalism. For it is in the market, where we sell our labor and negotiate contract relations of business, that we associate with competitive, temporary, contingent relations that must be buttressed by law and legal sanctions.

The symbolic opposition between The Family and market relations renders our strong attachment to The Family understandable, but it also discloses the particularity of our construct of The Family. We can hardly be speaking of a universal notion of The Family shared by people everywhere and for all time because people everywhere and for all time have not participated in market relations out of which they have constructed a contrastive notion of the family.

The realization that our idea of The Family is part of a set of symbolic oppositions through which we interpret our experience in a particular society compels us to ask to what extent this set of oppositions reflects real relations between people and to what extent it also shapes them. We do not adhere to a model of culture in which ideology is isolated from people's experience. On the other hand, neither do we construe the connection between people's constructs and people's experience to be a simple one of epiphenomenal reflection. Rather, we are interested in understanding how people come to summarize their experience in folk constructs that gloss over the diversity, complexity, and contradictions in their relationships. If, for example, we consider the second premise of the aforementioned syllogism—the idea that people get "nurtured" in families—we can ask how people reconcile this premise with the fact that relationships in families are not always this simple or altruistic. We need not resort to the evidence offered by social historians (e.g., Philippe Aries[16] and Lawrence Stone[17]) of the harsh treatment and neglect of children and spouses in the history of the Western family, for we need only read our local newspaper to learn of similar abuses among contemporary families. And we can point to other studies, such as Young and Willmott's *Family and Kinship in East London*,[18] that reveal how people often find more intimacy and emotional support in relationships with individuals and groups outside The Family than they do in their relationships with family members.

The point is not that our ancestors or our contemporaries have been uniformly mean and nonnurturant to family members but that we have all been both nice and mean, both generous and ungenerous, to them. In like manner, our actions toward family members are not always motivated by selfless altruism but are also motivated by instrumental self-interest. What is significant is that, despite the fact that our complex relationships are the result of complex motivations, we ideologize relations within The Family as nurturant while casting relationships outside The Family—particularly in the sphere of work and business—as just the opposite.

We must be wary of oversimplifying matters by explaining away those disparities between our notion of the nurturant Family and our real actions toward family members as the predictable failing of imperfect beings. For there is more here than the mere disjunction of the ideal and the real. The American construct of The Family, after all, is complex enough to comprise some key contradictions. The Family is seen as representing not only the antithesis of the market relations of capitalism; it is also sacralized in our minds as the last stronghold against The State, as the symbolic refuge from the intrusions of a public domain that constantly threatens our sense of privacy and self-determination. Consequently, we can hardly be surprised to find that the punishments imposed on people who commit physical violence are lighter when their victims are their own family members.[19] Indeed, the American sense of the privacy of the things that go on inside families is so strong that a smaller percentage of homicides involving family members are prosecuted than those involving strangers.[20] We are faced with the irony that in our society the place where nurturance and noncontingent affection are supposed to be located is simultaneously the place where violence is most tolerated.

There are other dilemmas about The Family that an examination of its ideological nature can help us better understand. For example, the hypothesis that in England and the United States marriages among lower-income ("working-class") groups are characterized by a greater degree of "conjugal role segregation" than are marriages among middle-income groups has generated considerable confusion. Since Bott observed that working-class couples in her study of London families exhibited more "segregated" conjugal roles than "middle-class" couples, who tended toward more "joint" conjugal roles,[21] researchers have come forth with a range of diverse and confusing findings. On the one hand, some researchers have found that working-class couples indeed report more segregated conjugal role-relationships—in other words, clearly differentiated male and female tasks, as well as interests and activities—than do middle-class couples.[22] Other researchers, however, have raised critical methodological questions about how one goes about defining a joint activity and hence measuring the degree of "jointness" in a conjugal relationship.[23] Platt's finding that couples who reported "jointness" in one activity were not particularly likely to report "jointness" in another activity is significant because it demonstrates that "jointness" is not a general

30

characteristic of a relationship that manifests itself uniformly over a range of domains. Couples carry out some activities and tasks together or do them separately but equally; they also have other activities in which they do not both participate. The measurement of the "jointness" of conjugal relationships becomes even more problematic when we recognize that what one individual or couple may label a "joint activity," another individual or couple may consider a "separate activity." In Bott's study, for example, some couples felt that all activities carried out by husband and wife in each other's presence were

> similar in kind regardless of whether the activities were complementary (e.g. sexual intercourse, though no one talked about this directly in the home interview), independent (e.g. husband repairing book while the wife read or knitted), or shared (e.g. washing up together, entertaining friends, going to the pictures together). It was not even necessary that husband and wife should actually be together. As long as they were both at home it was felt that their activities partook of some special, shared, family quality.[24]

In other words, the distinction Bott drew among "joint," differentiated," and "autonomic" (independent) relationships summarized the way people thought and felt about their activities rather than what they were observed to actually do. Again, it is not simply that there is a disjunction between what people say they do and what they in fact do. The more cogent point is that the meaning people attach to action, whether they view it as coordinated and therefore shared or in some other way, is an integral component of that action and cannot be divorced from it in our analysis. When we compare the conjugal relationships of middle-income and low-income people, or any of the family relationships among different class, age, ethnic, and regional sectors of American society, we must recognize that our comparisons rest on differences and similarities in ideological and moral meanings as well as on differences and similarities in action.

Finally, the awareness that The Family is not a concrete "thing" that fulfills concrete "needs" but an ideological construct with moral implications can lead to a more refined analysis of historical change in the American or Western family than has devolved upon us from our functionalist ancestors. The functionalist view of industrialization, urbanization, and family change depicts The Family as responding to alterations in economic and social conditions in rather mechanistic ways. As production gets removed from the family's domain, there is less need for strict rules and clear authority structures in the family to accomplish productive work. At the same time, individuals who now must work for wages in impersonal settings need a haven where they can obtain emotional support and gratification. Hence, The Family becomes more concerned with "expressive" functions, and what emerges is the modern "companionate family." In short, in the functionalist narrative

The Family and its constituent members "adapt" to fulfill functional requirements created for it by the industrialization of production. Once we begin to view The Family as an ideological unit and pay due respect to it as a moral statement, however, we can begin to unravel the more complex, dialectical process through which family relationships and The Family as a construct were mutually transformed. We can examine, for one, the ways in which people and state institutions acted, rather than merely reacted, to assign certain functions to groupings of kin by making them legally responsible for these functions. We can investigate the manner in which the increasing limitations placed on agents of the community and the state with regard to negotiating the relationships between family members enhanced the independence of The Family. We can begin to understand the consequences of social reforms and wage policies for the age and sex inequalities in families. And we can elucidate the interplay between these social changes and the cultural transformations that assigned new meanings and modified old ones to make The Family what we think it to be today.

Ultimately, this sort of rethinking will lead to a questioning of the somewhat contradictory modern views that families are things we need (the more "impersonal" the public world, the more we need them) and at the same time that loving families are disappearing. In a variety of ways, individuals today *do* look to families for a "love" that money cannot buy and find; our contemporary world makes "love" more fragile than most of us hope and "nurturance" more self-interested than we believe.[25] But what we fail to recognize is that familial nurturance and the social forces that turn our ideal families into mere fleeting dreams are *equally* creations of the world we know *today*. Rather than think of the ideal family as a world we lost (or, like the Victorians, as a world just recently achieved), it is important for us to recognize that while families symbolize deep and salient modern themes, contemporary families are unlikely to fulfill our equally modern nurturant needs.

We probably have no cause to fear (or hope) that The Family will dissolve. What we can begin to ask is what we *want* our families to do. Then, distinguishing our hopes from what we have, we can begin to analyze the social forces that enhance or undermine the realization of the kinds of human bonds we need.

35

NOTES

[1]Bronislaw Malinowski, *The Family Among the Australian Aborigines* (London: University of London Press, 1913).

[2]Lewis Henry Morgan, *Ancient Society* (New York: Holt, 1877).

[3]Bronislaw Malinowski, *A Scientific Theory of Culture* (Chapel Hill: University of North Carolina Press, 1944), p. 99.

[4]Robin Fox, *Kinship and Marriage* (London: Penguin, 1967), p. 39.

[5]Evon Z. Vogt, *Zinacantan: A Maya Community in the Highlands of Chiapas* (Cambridge, Mass.: Harvard University Press, 1969).

[6]Yolanda and Robert Murphy, *Women of the Forest* (New York: Columbia University Press, 1974).

[7]Ilsa Schuster, *New Women of Lusaka* (Palo Alto: Mayfield, 1979).

[8]E. Adamson Hoebel, *The Cheyennes: Indians of the Great Plains* (New York: Holt, Rinehart and Winston, 1978).

[9]George C. Homans and David M. Schneider, *Marriage, Authority, and Final Causes* (Glencoe, Ill.: Free Press, 1955).

[10]Frederick Engels, *The Origin of the Family, Private Property and the State,* in *Karl Marx and Frederick Engels: Selected Works,* vol. 2 (Moscow: Foreign Language Publishing House, 1955).

[11]Herbert Spencer, *The Principles of Sociology,* vol. 1, *Domestic Institutions* (New York: Appleton, 1973).

[12]John Stuart Mill, *The Subjection of Women* (London: Longmans, Green, Reader and Dyer, 1869).

[13]J. J. Bachofen, *Das Mutterrecht* (Stuttgart, 1861).

[14]Elizabeth Fee, "The Sexual Politics of Victorian Social Anthropology," in *Clio's Banner Raised,* ed. M. Hartman and L. Banner (New York: Harper & Row, 1974).

[15]John Ruskin, "Of Queen's Gardens," in Sesame and Lilies (London: J. M. Dent, 1907).

[16]Philippe Aries, *Centuries of Childhood,* trans. Robert Baldick (New York: Vintage, 1962).

[17]Lawrence Stone, *The Family, Sex, and Marriage in England 1500–1800* (London: Weidenfeld and Nicholson, 1977).

[18]Michael Young and Peter Willmott, *Family and Kinship in East London* (London: Routledge and Kegan Paul, 1957).

[19]Henry P. Lundsgaarde, *Murder in Space City: A Cultural Analysis of Houston Homicide Patterns* (New York: Oxford University Press, 1977).

[20]Ibid.

[21]Elizabeth Bott, *Family and Social Network: Roles, Norms, and External Relationships in Ordinary Urban Families* (London: Tavistock, 1957).

[22]Herbert J. Gans, *The Urban Villagers* (New York: Free Press, 1962); C. Rosser and C. Harris, *The Family and Social Change* (London: Routledge and Kegan Paul, 1965).

[23]John Platt, "Some Problems in Measuring the Jointness of Conjugal Role-Relationships," *Sociology* 3 (1969): 287–97; Christopher Turner, "Conjugal Roles and Social Networks: A Re-examination of an Hypothesis," *Human Relations* 20(1967): 121–30; and Morris Zelditch, Jr., "Family, Marriage and Kinship," in *A Handbook of Modern Sociology,* ed. R. E. L. Faris (Chicago: Rand McNally, 1964), pp. 680–707.

[24]Bott, *Family and Social Network,* p. 240.

[25]Rayna Rapp, "Family and Class in Contemporary America: Notes Toward an Understanding of Ideology," *Science and Society* 42 (Fall 1978): 278–300.

Considerations

1. In the first part of the essay, the authors argue that although Bronislaw Malinowski's theory of the family contradicted prevailing nineteenth-century theories, which were based on the idea of evolution, he shared with them certain assumptions about women. What are these assumptions? What role do they play in defining the family?

2. In order to support their definition of the family as an ideological construct, the authors examine concepts that reveal the biases of other theorists, such as the belief that most mothers are naturally loving. Look for two or

three other examples of the cultural biases present in the various definitions of the family. What do they reveal about the ideology of the thinkers who propose them?

3. The authors declare themselves "feminist anthropologists" from the beginning of their argument. How is their feminist position reflected in the essay? What assumptions of patriarchal culture do the authors reveal?

Invitation to Write

Toward the end of the essay, the authors propose a sketch of "what The Family represents symbolically to Americans" (para. 24). Television programs and advertising also give us idealized pictures of American families and suggest what family means to American culture. Using concepts developed by the authors, such as assumptions about the roles of women and the opposition between work and family, write an essay in which you define "family" in present-day American culture. To develop your definition, you can apply the authors' concepts to examples from TV shows or advertisements that reflect the symbolic value of the family for Americans.

Connections

"Is There a Family? New Anthropological Views" argues that in American society the family is conceived as being opposed to work and the marketplace. The experience of Scott Myers in "Scott Myers, Entrepreneur" (p. 242), by Bruce Tucker and Paul Leinberger, also suggests that work and family exist as opposites. Does Myers's division of his life between job and family reinforce the definition of the American family that Collier, Rosaldo, and Yanagisako put forth in their essay? Write an essay in which you explain Myers's problems from the anthropologists' theoretical point of view. Consider the way he relates to work as well as the way he sees his role in his family.

ASSIGNMENT SEQUENCE

Functions of the Family

In order to think about why the family remains a viable institution, this sequence begins by asking you to think about the tasks families usually perform and to assess the unique impact of the family in carrying out its traditional responsibilities. Using two specific examples of particular situations—the life of Aunt Fe in "Just Like a Tree" and your own personal experience of family life—you will continue, in a second paper, to think about the way families meet individual needs and the responsibilities family members are willing to assume. In your third paper, you will look at the support networks that are helpful in sustaining family life and how they vary according to different situations. Moving from specific to general cases, you will then look at the way American society constructs the ideal image of the contemporary family and examine that image in light of the predominant anthropological theories that have reigned over the past two hundred years. In your concluding paper, you will think about the connection between the more private world of the family and the public society in which it evolves.

Assignment 1: Exploring Experience

Think about some specific functions and tasks assumed by the family. We may consider routine many of the tasks associated with family life. Child-rearing, educating, taking care of the elderly, developing affectionate relationships, providing economic stability, and ensuring shelter are part of most people's lives; but sometimes the family is unable to assume these responsibilities and must transfer them outside the family. Write a paper in which you consider the consequences to individuals when society at large seeks to provide these services in place of the family. Be sure to discuss the particular impact of the family structure on society and on individuals.

First, pick an example or two of family responsibilities that can also be carried out by social institutions. Look at the ways some of these tasks are performed within a family setting and the way they are carried out within a different social organization. Analyze the differences in each case and consider the possible effects of transferring the task from the family to another group. From your comparison, analyze the influence of the family structure upon individuals' lives.

Assignment 2

Poor old thing; how many times I done come here and washed clothes for her when she couldn't do it herself. How many times I done hoed in that garden, ironed her clothes, wrung a chicken neck for her. You count the days in the year and you'll be pretty close.
—ERNEST J. GAINES, *Just Like a Tree*

Although she is old and apparently unable to care for herself, Aunt Fe can depend on her acquired kin to provide for her. Those who claim her as family gather around her to ease her pain after they are told she is leaving. Their action reflects the way this same network of adults and children has taken an interest in her welfare on a daily basis. Write a paper that discusses Aunt Fe's situation and compares it to the situation of an elderly person in a more urban or suburban community today. Define the resources available to each community and individual, then evaluate the long-term effects on each party.

To understand Aunt Fe's situation in more detail, reread the story and underline different characters' comments that suggest how she manages on a daily basis and how the other characters support her. Then, describe in some detail the situation of an elderly person you know, such as a relative, a neighbor, or a friend's relative. (The person you describe could be more independent than Aunt Fe.) Using these two examples as the basis of your comparison, evaluate the way traditional and contemporary societies provide care for elderly citizens.

Assignment 3

But to reach that point, a specific gay and lesbian community had to achieve a certain degree of cohesion and comfort. As a result, the new parenting was primarily a phenomenon of large cities and the East and West coasts, where gay people had developed the most extensive support systems and felt the most secure.
—NEIL MILLER, *A Time of Change*

Both Neil Miller's essay on gay and lesbian parenting and Ernest J. Gaines's short story "Just Like a Tree" describe families who are not, to use Miller's term, "families of origin" and families who are biologically connected. Using examples from "A Time of Change" and "Just Like a Tree," write a paper that looks at the circumstances and support systems necessary for either kind of family to flourish.

You can begin by looking in detail at the different families in both readings and determine the network of relationships that surround them. For example, in Ernest Gaines's story there are at least three clearly recognizable families: Chuckkie's family, which includes Emile (his father), Leola (his mother), and Lou (his grandmother); Aunt Fe's biological family, represented by Louise and James; and the community members who claim her as family. In Neil Miller's essay there are the gay and lesbian families and the families of Mo and Ellen. In each case, look for the ways families provide and depend upon support. You can also look at the opposite situation, the consequences of a lack of support.

Assignment 4

Our understanding of families in contemporary American society can be only as rich as our understanding of what The Family represents symbolically to Americans.
—JANE COLLIER, MICHELLE Z. ROSALDO, and SYLVIA YANAGISAKO,
Is There a Family? New Anthropological Views

The essay "Is There a Family?" traces the way anthropologists have looked at the family structure and the importance they have attached to it at different points in time. Write a paper in which you examine a popular concept of "The Family" in contemporary American culture. After reading these three contemporary anthropologists' analysis of past views of the family, use a similar method to explain the popularity of the concept you have identified. In your work, justify your conclusions through references to the earlier views discussed by Jane Collier, Michelle Z. Rosaldo, and Sylvia Yanagisako.

To understand "The Family's" symbolic meaning, you will need to move beyond your personal experiences of family life to see how images of the family appear in American culture. To do this, you can look for images of the family in popular culture. Television shows, advertising, movies, and magazines, for example, provide these images. Turn to these sources to find messages about the significance and emotional importance of the family in people's lives. Then return to Collier, Rosaldo, and Yanagisako's essay and decide which of the anthropologist's views on the family are useful to explain the ideas behind the contemporary image of the family.

Assignment 5

The American construct of The Family, after all, is complex enough to comprise some key contradictions. The Family is seen as representing not only the antithesis of the market relations of capitalism; it is also sacralized in our minds as the last stronghold against The State, as the symbolic refuge from the intrusions of a public domain that constantly threatens our sense of privacy and self-determination.
—JANE COLLIER, MICHELLE Z. ROSALDO, and SYLVIA YANAGISAKO,
Is There a Family? New Anthropological Views

In their essay, Collier, Rosaldo, and Yanagisako emphasize that the social construct of the family does not need to reflect the real experiences of individual families. They believe that most people see the family as a private realm, opposed to a public realm. The authors, however, are quick to point out that the reality can be quite different from the image.

Using the experiences of the characters in Ernest Gaines's story and the individuals in Neil Miller's essay, write an essay that examines the relationship between the private realm of the family and the public realm of the surrounding society.

There are key questions you can ask about each reading before you begin to write. One is whether the assumption that families can remain apart and untouched by powerful forces in society is true. Look for mention of political events in Gaines's story and in Miller's essay, and examine the descriptions of people's reactions to them. Another factor to consider is how families stand up against events or circumstances which threaten their members. A third question would be to ask how people succeed in creating a private realm. From your answers, you can begin to consider what people believe about the relationship between their private and public lives, and how accurately they perceive that relationship.

2

Growing Into Adulthood

From early adolescence onwards, I've been ashamed of my "unmanliness." I think I know how that sense of inadequacy was produced in me. I certainly know that my culturally learned view of my own body as "unmanly" comes from the socially constructed contrasts between ideal, heterosexual norms and a withering sense of my own puniness.

—DAVID JACKSON, *One of the Boys*

The weight of these maximum opportunities given to young Americans puts very strong pressure on them, early on, to "prove themselves," to show their parents and the world what they are capable of. But since the expectations have never been clearly defined, and ideally cannot be so, logically there can be no moment when the goal is reached.

—RAYMONDE CARROLL, *Parents and Children*

It is not unusual for an adolescent to feel disconnected from her body—a stranger to herself and to her new developing needs—but I think that to a person living simultaneously in two cultures this phenomenon is intensified.

—JUDITH ORTIZ COFER, *The Looking-Glass Shame*

59

"In all times and in all places" . . . the span between childhood and adulthood, however fleeting or prolonged, has been associated with the acquisition of virtue as it is differently defined in each society. A child may be good and morally obedient, but only in the process of arriving at womanhood or manhood does a human being become capable of virtue—that is, the qualities of mind and body that realize society's ideals.
    —LOUISE J. KAPLAN, *Adolescence: The Farewell to Childhood*

As Louise J. Kaplan points out in her essay "Adolescence: The Farewell to Childhood," the time period contemporary society refers to as adolescence is difficult to define. The saying "some people never grow up" underlines the elusive nature of the phenomenon by suggesting that adults, like children, can be immature, that maturation can occur at any age, and that adolescence may never end. The other readings in this chapter also look at adolescence as a process that happens over time: Adolescence emerges as a period of transition between childhood and adulthood, rather than an identifiable moment of awareness of impending adulthood. In many ways, adolescence is a logical culmination rather than an abrupt shift in perspective and behavior. The essays suggest the writers' awareness that adolescence connects many threads of childhood experience and memory to their adult behavior. These writers return to some of the moments that shaped their adult identities and gain new insight into the role the moments played in their development. While these authors highlight the turbulence of adolescence, they also examine the nature of its power, which leaves a lasting imprint on each individual.

In "One of the Boys," David Jackson recounts the struggles he faced in childhood and adolescence to define himself according to male norms of behavior. Internalizing these norms was a prerequisite to acceptance into an adult world where male bonding created the most powerful social institutions. The camp, the scouts, and the world of the boarding school were previews of the adult world to come. Raymonde Carroll, in her essay "Parents and Children" traces the interactions of parents and children in French and American society. She links child-rearing practices to the cultural assumptions that underlie each society's expectations about what types of adult behavior are valuable. According to Carroll, these expectations define the relationship between individuals and their society, as well as between parents and children. Judith Ortiz Cofer explores the cultural schizophrenia that made her adolescent transition difficult. Her essay "The Looking-Glass Shame" describes how the freedom of her American school conflicted with the strict world of her Puerto Rican home, where her female status reinforced her parents' view of her as a dependent. In "Adolescence: The Farewell to Childhood," Louise Kaplan seeks to define "adolescence" and distinguish it from the biological process of puberty. She analyzes the way this process affects the growth and development of the adult and shapes the adult's possible contributions to his or her society. While reading these essays will not provide a clear-cut definition of the term *adolescence,* the experiences they describe convey the complexity of the process that shapes adolescents as they leave childhood behind and assume the responsibilities of growing up.

David Jackson

One of the Boys

David Jackson was born in 1931 and grew up in Great Britain during the 1950s, a period he describes as dominated by the "He-man" image of male ideology. He became a schoolteacher and dedicated himself to that profession until a debilitating heart disease obliged him to quit at age forty-six. The trauma of heart surgery was accompanied by a mid-life crisis, which made him reflect upon his manhood. The experience of losing what he defines as "masculine control" over his body made him aware of the way gender expectations had shaped his assumptions about his life. He began writing a critical autobiography to "take on a critical reassessment of [his] traditional bodily relations and masculine identity." At present, Jackson edits textbooks, lectures in Great Britain (where he lives), and writes books and articles on teaching English.

The essay "One of the Boys" comes from Jackson's autobiography, *Unmasking Masculinity* (1990). Here, Jackson depicts the humiliating rituals of adolescent boys in their struggle to become "real" men. The cruelty and violence of the jokes, banter, and teasing are all, Jackson argues, the expressions of deep-seated fears.

*B*oys *learn very early that they had better be able to bond. What they learn in order to bond is an elaborate behavioural code of gestures, speech habits, and attitudes, which effectively exclude women from the society of men. Male bonding is how men learn from each other that they are entitled under patriarchy to power in the culture. Male bonding is how men get that power, and male bonding is how it is kept. Therefore, men enforce a taboo against unbonding—a taboo which is fundamental to patriarchal society.*
—JOHN STOLTENBERG, *For Men Against Sexism*[1]

I have to find some male places, groups that won't be so macho, so he [Daniel—her son] can learn from and be with good men and good boys. But look at the male organizations they've built. They're all unacceptable. Curse them. What should a "boys' group" be for? What might they discover, boys together? Hopefully, not "bonding"

63

to exclude females, but just the pleasure of being who they are, to-gether, without woman-hating.

—JUDITH ARCANA, *Every Mother's Son*[2]

From early adolescence onwards, I've been ashamed of my "unmanliness." I think I know how that sense of inadequacy was produced in me. I certainly know that my culturally learned view of my own body as "unmanly" mainly comes from the socially constructed contrasts between ideal, heterosexual norms and a withering sense of my own puniness. But that recently acquired awareness didn't prevent me from feeling inadequate, especially between the ages of about ten and sixteen: ashamed of not having to shave until well after most boys had started; ashamed of my breaking voice, seesawing from husky gruffness to a thin, squeaky piping; ashamed of my ridiculous, unboylike hands—smooth, delicate, and "never seen a hard day's work in their lives"; ashamed of my "half-pint"[3] body, relatively undersized for most of that time; ashamed of being a short-sighted, "specky four-eyes" who couldn't sit in the back row with the troublemakers with my glasses off because I couldn't see the blackboard.

At a more unconscious level that sense of "unmanliness" also came from a deep-seated ambivalence over my gender identification. Problems over separation and individuation[4] from my mother left me confused over the boundary division between my "masculinity" and "femininity." I felt constantly in-between those restrictive categories; partly learning that the privileged activities of boys were rewarded in a male-supremacist culture and that I could benefit in the same kind of way, but also vaguely aware of the dangerous pleasures of a range of feelings, affections, and aesthetic responses that couldn't be choked into the starched-collar category of "masculinity."

For instance, discovering embroidery at primary school. I liked the rhythmic movement of weaving coloured wool threads back and forth through a canvas latticework. I enjoyed slowly building up the cross-stitches into a decorative design. At that time it was a relatively unmoulded me, fluidly moving back and forth across given categories and fixed boundaries, acknowledging a broader spread of myself before the shutters came down.

They came down soon enough in the form of a male teacher who made a special point of reminding me that I couldn't opt for needlework in next term's programme of work. "Boys do handicraft," he pointed out. That's when I realized I had to conform, like other boys, to the social/institutional meanings of what is manly/unmanly. Needlework was sissyish girls' work and any healthy, self-respecting boy should shun it with all his might. I learnt that to be accepted in the male club I had to turn my back on that uncomfortable bundle of feelings, pleasures, and desires and begin to rehearse the defensive practices—Stoltenberg's "code of gestures, speech, habits, and attitudes"—of male bonding. In my case it was certainly my sense of personal precariousness, existing within a social network of male power, that made me so susceptible to the conventional norms of male bonding.

But why did male bonding gain such a grip over me? To explain that I   5
need to explore the origins of male bonding. Heterosexual masculinity, aware of its precarious formation in confusion, ambivalence, and self-doubt, defines itself in opposition to the "other" (women, homosexuals). It strengthens and buttresses its internally cracked condition through jeering at what it most fears, and takes refuge in the solidarity and support of other heterosexual men in groups and organizations.

It's important here to emphasize the power relations between different versions of masculinity as well as between men and women. Hierarchical heterosexual culture achieves its dominating position through its social construction of contrasted, deviant cultures that "normalize" and consolidate its own position.

As Jonathan Dollimore[5] puts it, "the demonised abnormal other" (in other words, the socially powerless, contrasting cultures of women, gays, bisexuals, unbonding men, etc.), "whose alienness reinforces through contrast the rightness of normality." That's why outsiders/"deviants" are treated with such aggressive bullying, mocking, and ridiculing. Through focusing scorn on those who are outside the male bond, the male club overcomes internal tensions and fears (like my fears of "unmanliness") and, in so doing, unites separate individuals into an undifferentiated pack, who can hide within the pack membership while putting pressure on outsiders to join up as well.

So male bonding is not just about group dynamics. It's a political process because it viciously exploits men's internal contradictions and uses these to sustain patriarchal power over other people. I actively sought the reassuring badge of belonging to the male club because of my shaky grip on my masculine identity. I was in a continuous state of fear that my "girlishness" would be discovered and publicly ridiculed, and so, to survive, I learned to consent to the accepted codes and conventions of heterosexual masculinity (that dominating version of masculinity) that made up the rules of the male club.

The tightly organized network of male bonding represents an important institutional force for regulating women and powerless masculinities. It effectively polices the boundaries of what counts as masculinity through "norm-enforcing mechanisms"[6] (like joking, bantering, and swearing), and the dominant cultural features of boys' and men's groups and organizations. Here I want to limit myself to:

(a) looking at joking, bantering, and swearing; and
(b) looking at some examples of boys'/men's groups and their specific cultures and atmospheres.

Joking, Swearing, and Bantering

In primary school and at an all-boys' grammar and boarding school I half   10
belonged and half didn't belong to the dominant peer-group pack. I was
pulled between a class identification with the piss-taking, joking banter of the
"lads" and their rejection of the middle-class, upwardly mobile educational
ideals of the school and an inner unease at the aggressive, brutalizing culture
that the "lads" celebrated and were victims of. To save my own skin, particularly in the boarding school, I had to appear as "one of the lads." To com-
pensate for my vulnerable manner and size, I went out of my way to prove my
masculine virility through successful sporting activities and through my acceptance of the mock bravado and swagger of a joking, peer-group culture.
Hovering on the edge of the group, I wasn't any good at wisecracking one-
liners and smart repartee. But I tried to joke, swore and horseplayed with the
rest of them, and vied for the label of "clown of the class."

This unofficial competition to be the "clown of the class" was always a
strong temptation to play to the gallery, get one over on the teacher, and grab
the limelight through being laughed at. One incident that happened to a
friend of mine was when Chippy Carpenter, a hopelessly inadequate supply
teacher, came to teach us maths.[7]

One of Chippy's unfortunate habits was that flecks of spit used to form in
the corners of his mouth, and these flecks used to spatter my friend and other
pupils sitting in the front desks. Fed up with this and wanting to gain star
attention for himself, my friend appeared in class, sitting in the front row seat
directly in front of the teacher's desk, with a navy-blue mac pulled over his
head. Chippy fell for it and asked him what he thought he was doing in a
maths class. "Keeping myself dry from your spit!" fired back my friend in a
flash.

We made constant jokes about "browners" and "queers," and were always on the lookout for any unguarded hint of effeminacy in each others'
gestures and behaviour to deflect the focus of attention from ourselves. Any
slight diffidences, stuttering oddness, weakness was seized upon by the rest of
the group, held up for public inspection, and devastatingly ridiculed. The
wrong colour or style of vest revealed while undressing in the changing room,
writing a letter to your sister during the weekend compulsory letter-writing
session, or wearing slippers around the dormitory that were suspiciously
furry—all these associations with a culture that wasn't ferociously heterosexual were ruthlessly put down.

As one of the men in David Collinson's investigation of masculinity and
joking in shopfloor culture[8] comments, the pressure to conform through joining in the humour acts as a regulatory mechanism to keep the imbalance of
power between the sexes, and the conflict between different forms of masculinity, intact and unchanging: "You've got to give it or go under. It's a form

of survival, you insult first before they get one back. The more you get embarrassed, the more they do it, so you have to fight back. It can hurt you deep down, although you don't show it."

While you're busy protecting yourself against any sign of vulnerability in   15
yourself, and dishing out the ritual insults, any possibility of challenge to the patriarchal system of male bonding is lost, along with any chance to develop closeness and emotional support with other boys and men. Indeed, the emotional structure of the male bond, as I've mentioned already, is one of defensive confirmation through the use of joking and jeering at the expense of feared others.[9] It not only puts down women through sexist innuendo and at times through brashly overt misogyny but it also reduces men's emotional range to a crippling, self-alienating narrowness.

Stoltenberg's "taboo against unbonding" as an institutional way of sustaining patriarchal power was very real for me in my own life history. I complied with the *status quo* (with unease and discomfort, admittedly) through my fear of being shut out of the male club of "normal men," and made the butt of their insults and teasing. The humour did help me to make a V sign against the middle-class cultural authority of grammar school but it also kept me toeing the line of heterosexual masculinity. The contradictory nature of this joking, brutalized culture always prevented it from gaining the more purposeful cultural resistance attributed to it by Paul Willis.[10] In joining in on the joking and back-slapping, it only made me more firmly entrenched within the assumptions of a male-supremacist culture.

In particular I remember a moment of joking that demonstrates this contradictoriness. Every lunchtime in the grammar-school dinner queue we had to wait out in the cold, patrolled by prefects. We were supposed to be totally regimented and silent in this queue. I was secretly joking with a couple of my dormitory friends, at the end of the queue, about the supposed dangers of too much masturbation. The joke might have gone something like this:

"It's supposed to send you blind, isn't it, if you go at it too hard?" whispered Chris.

"Don't be daft!" I replied, "but it's true that there's a white ring left on your skin between your thumb and your first finger if you wank more than four times a week."

"Oh, go on!" Chris protested, furtively glancing at his own hand.   20

The repeated "Made you look!" joke went up and down the queue of waiting boys, with murmurs, glances, and laughter that was hushed down by the prefects, several times.

The joke was certainly a way of challenging the boredom of queueing and waiting and the authoritarian control of the school regime. But it was also, at the same time, a joke that negotiated[11] inner fears and tensions about developing male sexuality. I was laughing at what I was scared of—dangerous, illegitimate sexuality was being publicly recognized and acknowledged through the "made you look" tactic. The joking form allowed me to negotiate my contradictory feelings of guilt and uncertainty at possibly deviant sexual practices ("wanking more than four times a week"), and my almost fetishistic fascination with my own sexuality. While the joke explores the boundaries of "normal" and "abnormal" male sexuality it does it through shared laughter that reaffirms the safety and solidarity of the male bond. So that the "rightness of normality" within the male club is further cemented because it's been able to strengthen itself in contrast to these dangerously "deviant" sexual habits.

Swearing was another peer-group/male-bonding badge that I frequently displayed to seek acceptance from the group. (Indeed now, in certain contexts where I need to assert my class origins, and possibly release pent-up feelings, I catch myself throwing in a few "fucks.")

Jennifer Coates[12] remarks that there's a "high correlation between peer group status and use of non-standard language" like swearing. So that swearing in my experience was a norm-enforcing mechanism in that to gain approval and status in the male peer group you had to sound tough, aggressive, and cocksure. Intensely aware of my "unmanliness" I unsuccessfully strained to build an impression of virile sophistication and everyday swearing was one of the building blocks I used.

My attempt to gain approval through a deliberately vernacular language form like swearing was done at the expense of women and other, "deviant," masculinities. Sexist slang and swearing is about the linguistic dismemberment of women's bodies through words like "fuck," "tits," "arse" (like "she's got a lovely arse on her!"). And I joined in the swearing with elaborate gusto just to show the other lads that I was one of them.

Masculinity is founded upon its denial and exclusion of the potential for being bisexual. But even in the most swaggering performances these hidden fears and anxieties are always implicitly there. Similarly, banter appears on the surface to be insulting and aggressive but often carries with it a repressed homosexual element. In my personal history mock punching and banter ("You old bastard! What have you been up to then?") gave me an acceptably aggressive form within which I could express some of my frustrated need physically to touch other male friends. I would often put my arm around other boys' necks, thump a friend's shoulder, wrestle, and even have "friendly fights" when, unconsciously perhaps, I wanted to hug and be affectionate. Also with much older boys I used to try and gain a higher peer-group status by exploiting this ambivalence within bantering. I used to humorously insult, tease, and mock them knowing that I wouldn't have to pay the full price for my insults; in fact, knowing that I could get away with it. The older boys put up with my antics, perhaps recognizing that they couldn't be seen to use their full force against an irritating gnat like me.

According to Antony Easthope[13] male bantering is a "way of affirming the bond of love between men while appearing to deny it." Certainly male bonding becomes a more intensely addictive process because of these re-pressed homosexual elements implied within it. But bantering has more forms than Easthope suggests and can be more viciously wounding while still working within the bonding process.

An example from my time as a dormitory prefect in the boarding school shows what I mean. The housemaster had occasional difficulty in finding suitable leaders among the boys, and it was very much as a last resort that he chose me in the fifth form to become a dormitory prefect. I was supposedly in charge of eight other boys in the dormitory. But I was nervously aware that I was smaller than several of the third and fourth formers there.

Every night, lights-out time, with an official ban on talking, was a traumatic moment for me because I was always put into a contradictory position between whether to side with the boys (who wanted to go on talking and giggling all night) or traditional authority (with which I had some class reservations). I usually compromised and we went on talking until I suggested that we'd better go to sleep. Most of the boys accepted that except for one fourth former who merely saw me as a hostile representative of the system of authority at school and in the school house that he was dedicated to undermining.

This fourth former used to spend all his inventiveness in mocking me   30
through banter and other forms. I tried to keep my temper and ignore his needling. I wanted to talk about what was going on. He wanted to keep me at a distance and objectify me as the Enemy.

We used to keep our Sunday suits (worn only for the compulsory church service) in a wardrobe in one of the dormitory corners. And I remember the moment when, with a great deal of pain, I took my suit out one Sunday and found this note in one of my pockets: "*Jackson*—you're a sawn-off runt." As Easthope says, "banter depends on a close, intimate, and personal understanding of the person who is the butt of the attack." I knew, without thinking, that the note was from the fourth former. He was the only person in the dormitory who had the motivation and perverted ingenuity to understand and play on my insecurities as an "unmanly" prefect. His understanding of my castration anxiety ("sawn-off") and my hang-up about being undersized ("runt," the smallest, weakest pig in a litter) was clearly targeted. He sensed minutely and intimately what would eat away at my belief in my masculine identity, and he succeeded. He drew closer to me, through his detailed observation of my weakness and knowing how to really get at me, and in my rising hatred of what he had done I became more closely bonded to him.

Boys'/Men's Groups

An all boys' dormitory in a boarding school. Boys-only boarding schools, like sporting teams, certain pub cultures, working men's clubs, military training establishments, etc., provide the social organizations[14] where patriarchal power can be produced and reproduced through the institutional routines of a vicious form of male bonding.

Except for the time at around five or six when my Dad came home from the AFS[15] there was no more powerfully shaping influence on my masculinity than those years boarding at school. I was never so ruthlessly exposed, night and day, to so many contexts and pressures to mask the full range of my feelings, desires, and interests and to buy into the dormitory framework of a strutting, heterosexual culture. Behind the scenes I had my own one-to-one relationships which kept me relatively sane, but the public arena was taken over by a bullying, misogynistic culture that was defined in brutal opposition to anything vaguely associated with women and homosexuality. Many sensitive and gentle masculinities were trampled in the rush to define themselves in opposition to women that entitled them to entry to the masculine club. Nowhere was this psychological violence more keenly felt than in two dormitory scenes from my childhood.

The cohesion of the male pack in the dormitory was achieved by isolating and victimizing any boys who in their weakness, oddness, or awkwardness they could connect to a despised culture of effeminacy. One of the boys constantly picked on, a boy called Martin, was an outsider like me—sensitive, a mummy's boy, son of a squadron leader down Plymouth way, and self-consciously aware of his own gangling awkwardness. He had a fatal habit of blushing deep red (which in the pack's warped imagination was always linked with the imagined embarrassment of young girls) on hearing anything that was rude and offensive to him. The pack immediately latched on to his blushing and kept on at him, night and day, with endlessly repetitive, mocking comments that were intended to make him blush. Gaining a blush from Mart (like a severed scalp) earned a pack member greater status and made Mart even more hunted.

After one weekend when the rest of the dormitory pack had caught a glimpse of Martin's mother—elegant, smart, well-turned out—while bringing Martin back from Plymouth, we gave him hell. (Notice here how I've become a part of the "we." I couldn't afford to take Martin's side against the pack as I would have been turned on as well. To survive I had to keep silent *within* the pack.) "Does your mother shag then, Martin?" suggested one of the pack. It was painful to watch Mart writhing in embarrassed confusion but we knew if we didn't join in it would be our turn next.

Martin tried to duck the question and offered the pack leaders some cake he had brought back with him from the weekend. They took his cake, recognizing a soft touch when they saw one, but persisted, obsessively, with their taunts. "I bet you watched them shagging together didn't you, Mart?" Martin fumbled with his cake tin and locker door and tried to defend himself in a voice that was trembling on the edge of tears. Underneath what he was saying you could feel him pleading with the pack to let him go. But they didn't. They

35

had him in a corner and the scent of blood was in their nostrils. A voice of victory suddenly rang out: "What are you blushing for, Mart?" and was chorused by the pack together, *"What are you blushing for, Mart?"*

And there it was—a deep, reddening flush burning across his cheeks. Mart just wanted the floor to open up and bury him, to hide his blushes. But the pack had sniffed blood and pursued and harried him until well after lights out. "Are you crying, Mart?" And then, later, on hearing somebody's bed creaking:

"Stop wanking, Cornhill!"

This represented just one night in two years of misery (day and night) for Martin, when he had no place to hide away or be comforted by anybody. After a botched attempt to run away in the third year Martin was taken away and sent to a school much nearer home where he didn't have to board.

The dormitory is painted cream with brown institutional lino on the floor, and nine iron beds are crammed in around the walls. I stand at the centre of a grinning ring of faces. I've a hollow sinking feeling beginning to spread from the pit of my stomach. I look down at the polished brown lino, knowing I mustn't cry but feeling my nose start to twitch with tears. 40

For the second night running they've pinched my pyjamas from under my pillow. My supposed friends, even Martin, have vanished into the anonymity of the grinning ring. They know that if they don't act with the mind of the pack it will be their turn next. Even Chris, who had his pyjamas taken last week, is there now within the ring of faces, mocking and calling me. The pack hunts down any outsiders, and forces them to forget their own contradictory resistances, and teaches them to snarl, like the rest.

The pack leader ambles up to me and pushes the stolen pyjamas right under my nose. Steady now! Keep your cool! I know that I mustn't rise to the temptation of snatching. I know the pack want to goad me into chasing them. I look, mock-casually up at the plaster frieze on the ceiling, pretend to look away, and then I suddenly lunge forward to grab the pyjamas. At that very moment the pack leader whisks them away to another boy within the circle.

I can't help myself now. I know I'm trapped within the rules of the game. I haven't got a choice anymore. I have to become part of the action. I flail this way, that way, arms outspread, trying to intercept the flung pyjamas.

I'm openly sobbing with anger now and with injured pride. They're got me on the run and they know it. I hear myself pleading with them to give my pyjamas back. Mucus and tears are dribbling down my chin. I half-intercept the flying bundle but two pack members land on top of me just as I am about to get my hands on the pyjamas.

The throwing gets more hysterical. I'm shrieking at them now. One of the pack makes a mistake and drops the pyjamas. I get a hand to my pyjama jacket sleeve while the pack seize hold of the other, and I tug with all my 45 might. Two other boys drop on me from behind and try to pull me away. The jacket sleeve is ripped off. The pack stops in alarm.

I hurl abuse at them between my sobs. I grab up the torn remnants and slam off to lock myself in the toilet for half an hour. For the next week I go around in hurt silence hoping the pack will forget my pyjamas and move on to some other victim for next week. But they don't. It's always there in the banter, the incessant jibes, and the repetitively brutalizing actions. I've shown the pack that "I can't take a joke," that I'm easily hurt and offended (like Martin) and I've cried like a girl, and that's the kind of person the pack likes to hunt. The barbaric system of male bonding is achieved at the expense of all those other forms and varieties of masculinity—the misfits and the vulnerable ones like me—that are choked off in their infancy without ever having a proper chance to develop and grow in a more gentle and openly emotional way.

The changing room. The rituals of male solidarity were most clearly seen in that most private and most intimidating place—the sport's changing room as a male preserve.[16] It was one of those male places that held power over regulating "deviant" masculinities through fear of being publicly teased and ridiculed as "girlish," "unmanly," or physically inadequate. I was always half-fearful in those kinds of places, fearful that I would be exposed and jeered at because I was wearing an unconventional vest, socks, or underpants. It was there that I learned to measure negatively my own physical qualities, like the size of my penis and relative absence of body hair, in relation to those ideal, heterosexual, bodily norms. I didn't have much hair where it counted; my pubic hair seemed to be a bit sparse and I had a desperate need of a chest wig! Hairiness, an "insignia of power"[17] and masculine virility, was conspicuously absent on my body. That's one of the reasons why, when I became head of English in a tough comprehensive school in Lancashire, later in life, I grew a straggly beard and then a moustache.

A desire for physical closeness with other boys expressed itself through raucous horseplay in such places. Boys were always chasing each other, trying to flick each other with the edge of their wet towels, catching the other person off guard. Practical jokers thrived in such surroundings. Underpants were always getting nicked, shoelaces tied together, ties losing their expert knots. Sexual innuendoes about the liniment rub, "Fiery Jack!" or "Zambuk," flew around, and jokes about putting bromide[18] in the aftermatch tea when we were playing the Royal Engineers' apprentices just outside Newton Abbot.

The showers were the most terrifying places for "unmanly" boys like me. I used to position myself in the most secret corner of the changing room, protecting myself from being ogled or ridiculed. And frequently I used to skip the shower, hiding my muddy knees and waiting till I got back to the boarding school when I could scrape the mud off my legs in a wash basin without exposing the rest of my body to the public gaze. But the teachers were always on the lookout for boys like me and often forced me to have a shower before I could go.

There was also a forced male camaraderie that made me squirm, such as the communal team baths after rugby matches with the Royal Naval College, Dartmouth. On the field the opposing scrum half had been full of solidarity, with hearty phrases like "Coming in starboard, ship!" just as he was placing the ball at the centre of the scrum. And, inside, in their changing rooms the same kind of pressure towards team spirit had been planned for us by the building of enormous communal baths that a whole team could sit in together. I think I can remember the steamy haze after the match and the echoing shouts and yells as a member of the team was got by the others, debagged, and flung into the bath. 50

I was lucky that day. My team members ignored me, but I had to give in to the pressure to join the rest of the team in the coiling vapours of the bath. And I have to admit that after the bleakness of a raw, November afternoon such warmth was welcome. I just lay back in that steaming, muddy liquid and felt my bones start to melt and dissolve in the heat. And then there was the obligatory round of dirty rugby songs, "Balls to Mr Banglestein, dirty old man," and "Oh, Sir Jasper, do not touch me!"[19]

The wolf cub pack. Male-bonding processes were explicitly encouraged by boys-only organizations like the Boy Scout/Wolf Cub movement in Britain. From 1948 to 1950 I was a member of a wolf cub pack, meeting every week in a church hall, that sexually segregated boys into a group-bonding process and organized them into subgroups of "sixes." The pack was led by an "Akela," a young woman who we were all in love with, and the evenings were very tightly regimented and repetitive.

Obedience to authority was instilled through the wearing of a military-type uniform and weekly routines and rituals. I remember wearing an itchy blue jersey, a green cap, and a neckerchief held together at the front by a leather woggle. And this uniform was inspected every week.

The evening had the opening and ending ritual of the Grand Howl. Even between the ages of eight and ten I smelt something fishy about this strained, worked-up ceremony. While saluting Akela with two fingers held up to the ear, the pack chanted:

> Akela. We will do our best.
> Dib. Dib. Dib. Dib.
> We will do our best.
> Dob. Dob. Dob. Dob.

The ideals of the Scouting movement were the "robust, muscular, Christian ideals"[20] of Charles Kingsley and Thomas Hughes, linked to Baden-Powell's imperialist notions of manliness[21]—physical courage, determination, 55 adventurous action, and resourcefulness—with an emphasis on military drill and discipline. These ideals came through to me, every week, in the form of wildly rowdy, muscular games like "Clear the decks" and "British bulldog" (a Scouting game but played by our wolf pack in 1949).

"Clear the decks" was a deliberately rowdy game to help cubs to let off steam before the more purposeful work of the evening. When Akela shouted "Clear the decks!" you had to make a mad dash to the stage end of the church hall and leap up onto the stage, getting your body off the ground. The last cub was out. Then there were other commands: "Man the boats!" (reach the refuge of chairs arranged in the shape of a boat), "Boom coming over!" (hurl yourself flat on the floor), "Admiral coming aboard!" (stand to stiff attention and salute), and "Freeze!" (become a totally unmoving statue).

As well as careering around like wild things, we were also learning obedience to military authority, respect for hierarchy, and deference to commands. "British bulldog," with its Churchillian emphasis on strength and assertiveness, usually ended up with somebody being hurt, either with a nosebleed or an injured knee or leg.

Victory in this game always went to the most "red-blooded," muscularly built cub. As there was no chance to show skill or intelligence I normally went through the motions in this game, making myself inconspicuous in the main pack and watching out for possible injury.

The game went something like this. Most of the cubs were gathered down one end of the hall and had to charge their way to the other end. The only obstacle to their charge was one cub in the middle of the room who had to try and capture a cub by stopping him in his charge, often holding him down on the floor, and then lifting him off the ground, yelling, "British bulldog!"

At times the cub in the middle was humiliated by not being able to cap- 60 ture one boy and quickly labelled "weakling!" by the others, but usually somebody was caught and hauled off the ground. And then there were two in the middle, then three, four . . . until the tables were turned—the whole wolf pack was trying to stop and capture the last rogue elephant. And that's when boys got hurt. The last cub to get captured was always the largest, toughest, most muscular member of the pack and he always went down with a really ferocious fight, lashing out, kicking and yelling like a cornered beast. Sometimes we all had to sit on him, pinioning him down to the floor and blocking his way, before we were able to get a grip of his legs and arms and lift him off the ground.

The rest of the cub business was always an anticlimax after that. The "difficult arts and practices" of the "backwoodsman, explorers, and frontiersmen" that Baden-Powell explicitly recommended[22]—like learning to tie knots like reef, sheep bend, clovehitch, and bowline and understand compass points—left me a bit cold. The only things I found to be practically useful, and that I could see some point in, were telling the time and tying up my shoelaces properly by myself.

All that talk about badges for collecting, naturalist, gardener, athlete, swimmer, artist, book reader, etc., made me an ardent badge collector. It was very much a contrived set of decontextualized tasks that had to be checked out by an impartial adult in order to be able to persuade your mother or your sister to sew your new badge on your jersey shoulder. Like the "house orderly" badge for example: To be worthy of the badge you had to wash your neckerchief and iron it; sweep and dust a room; cook a meal like sausages and bacon; make your bed; and sew on a button. But it never made me any better at contributing to the daily domestic labour in my own home.[23]

> Linked to these concerns was the value of a simple and spartan
> life away from the debilitating materialism of the city and in response
> to the natural challenges of the rural and colonial frontier.[24]

Baden-Powell was always praising the special importance of the outdoor life (camping, hiking, tracking, etc.) in the training of young boys. Those values certainly filtered down to our wolf cub pack in St Paul's Church, Preston, Paignton. For some time between 1948 and 1950 the pack went for a week's camp back up the Devon coast, close to Combe-in-Teignhead, and I went with them.

It was a very traumatic time for me because it was the first time I had been away from home and I was very homesick. Two episodes stand out for me from that week of dullness and grey drizzle.

The first incident was tent inspection. Every morning we had to prepare for a military-style inspection by folding the groundsheet and blankets very neatly, in straight lines, and displaying them outside the tent, if weather permitted, together with any spare kit we had brought, such as our toilet bags (with my soap in a Bakelite soap dish), shoes, towel, torch, etc.

I remember that I was so anxious with homesickness (another moment of withdrawal from my mother's body?) that I wet the bed (meaning the sleeping bag, blankets, right through to the groundsheet). I guiltily tried to dry them all by hanging them over the tent but they seemed to get wetter because of the rain from the night before.

When Akela came round on her tour of inspection with other adult helpers there was nothing to see from my tent. I just hung my head in shame, tears welled up in my eyes, and I wanted, desperately, to go home.

The other episode was on one of the afternoons, about halfway through the week, when my mother and two sisters came to visit me. I struggled really hard not to show them how homesick I really was. I sensed how much they wanted their son and brother to be bright, cheerful, and energetic, and "having a really good time" like some of the other cubs appeared to be doing. But the desperation was clearly written all over my face, and, on seeing them, I quickly dissolved into tears.

My mother wanted to take me back with her, but I knew I had to stick it out for her sake. The pressure not to be one of those blubbering sissies was already so intense within the pack, and in my wolf cub group (my "six"), that I learnt my first lesson in how to toughen up. During the daytime I tried to busy myself in robust action, sport, joking, and it was only at night that I was haunted by my mother's face.

Drinking and pubs. An early training in conformity to the norms of the dominant, heterosexual peer group prepared me for a later entry into the informal, patriarchal network of men's organizations, like the pub and the football terrace.

In my later teens, drinking talk, like sexual-bravado talk, was an important way of proving that I was "one of the lads." In fact talking about drink, before and after the event, in a supposedly tough, sophisticated manner was often more significant than the actual drinking itself.[25]

Again the irony was that the more the illicit drinking went on as a form of cultural resistance against middle-class school authority, the more we made ourselves susceptible to the routines and practices of patriarchal power. From the moment of dangerous pleasure when we smuggled in bottles of brown ale to drink after lights out when I was about sixteen, the central question about drink was: Could we prove that we were "real men" by taking our drink?

Drinking always presented a test of my virility and masculine identity; could I drink deeply without puking up? Could I prove that I was "one of the lads" by holding my drink? But I soon proved that I couldn't. For a short time at university I got the nickname of "Puker Jackson." It happened like this.

It was student rag week in 1959, and in the all-men's hall where I spent my first year all the talk was of the yearly "giant piss-up" on Saturday night. It was designed to be a pub crawl of as many city-centre pubs as we could take in during the evening. I drifted into this contest, anxious for group approval and acceptance, but not really taking in the implications of this pub crawl.

By then I knew about my tendency to be sick through drinking more than four pints but I didn't want to be left out of that hearty, shoulder-thumping, joking atmosphere of the male peer group. I even took precautions by drinking half a pint of milk before we set off, to line my stomach. But, in the end, it didn't do much good.

We started off quite cautiously by sipping half pints of mild in the first two or three pubs but then I got caught up in the climate of cheery adolescent abandonment. I started to feel queasy after the next two or three pints, and then I lost count of the mixture of shorts (vodka, rum, whisky) and half pints we got down between us. In the end the night became a swirling blur of constant laughter, piss-taking, and violent vomiting.

I puked up first out on the street, and then I spent the whole night crouching over a metal bucket in the student common room, groaning and puking. And there I stayed for the whole of Sunday stretched out on a brown horsehair sofa with a blanket flung over me and promising myself, "Never! I'll never do this again!"

I gained the male club's attention through my feats of puking. There was a tinge of contempt for my not being able to hold my drink in their label "Puker," but, temporarily, I grabbed the limelight through the repeated stories about my night of puking and was granted temporary club membership.

As well as male-bonding processes exploiting men's ambivalent identities, male places like the pub are patriarchal institutions in the way they generate social and cultural relations that "exclude, fragment, and abuse the female sex."[26]

One example from my life history illustrates the point I want to make. Sometimes on Friday evenings between 1968 and 1972, when I was working in a Lancashire comprehensive school in Whitworth, outside Rochdale, I used to stay on at school to play five-a-side football and other sporting activities. Usually, afterwards, a geography teacher called Harry used to suggest a drink and then would drive me to Rochdale station.

I was dimly aware that I ought to have refused and got home to help my ex-wife feed and get to bed our three kids. But the cosy fug of the pub was too much of a lure for me. It was a place where I could escape from my family responsibilities and assert an illusion of independence in a male club atmosphere (all the early evening drinkers were always men). And I knew what I was avoiding by sitting there for another hour—that exhausting, hectic time between six and seven in the evening when the kids had to be sorted out, read to, and put into their pyjamas. It was never as explicitly worked out as this, but a general sense of fatigue, cosiness, and beer kept me rooted to the seat.

The pub's atmosphere, and its joking culture of misogyny, was not only built on the exclusion of women, but on their segregated position in the traditional, sexual division of labour. My leisure time in the pub was bought at the cost of my ex-wife's domestic labour, preparing meals and nurturing my kids back at home. And whereas my official labour as a teacher was paid, my ex-wife's domestic work went unnoticed and unpaid. The pub presented me with a bolt-hole, an exclusively privileged territory, a retreat from the world of domestic responsibilities.

Viewed from the perspective of the late 1980s I regret very much how I benefited from such a taken-for-granted, patriarchal network of men's organizations and male-bonding interactions. But I also regret how that barbaric system was able to regulate men like me into putting fear of our exclusion from the male club before our personal commitments to other people.

NOTES

[1]J. Stoltenberg (1977), "Toward Gender Justice," in J. Snodgrass (ed.), *For Men Against Sexism,* New York, Times Change Press.

[2]J. Arcana (1983), *Every Mother's Son,* London, Women's Press.

[3]A bantering term of abuse that was used by the gang to put me down.

[4]See N. Chodorow (1978), *The Reproduction of Mothering*, Berkeley, Calif., University of California Press.

[5]J. Dollimore (1986), "Homophobia and sexual difference," *Oxford Literary Review*, vol. 8, nos. 1–2. Much of the argument here is indebted to Dollimore's essay.

[6]See J. Coates (1986), *Women, Men, and Language*, London, Longman, and her use-of-social-network theory which is to be found in L. Milroy (1980), *Language and Social Networks*, Oxford, Basil Blackwell.

[7]See P. Willis (1977), *Learning to Labour*, London, Saxon House.

[8]D. Collinson (1988), "Engineering humour! Masculinity, joking, and conflict in shopfloor relations," *Organisation Studies*, vol. 9, no. 2.

[9]See P. Lyman (1987), "The fraternal bond as a joking relationship" in M. Kimmel (ed.), *Changing Men*, London, Sage.

[10]Willis, op. cit.

[11]See Lyman, op. cit.

[12]Coates, op. cit.

[13]A. Easthope (1986), *What a Man's Gotta Do*, London, Paladin.

[14]See B. Rogers (1988), *Men Only*, London, Pandora.

[15]Auxiliary Fire Service set up as Second World War firefighting organisation.

[16]See E. Dunning (1986), "Sports as a male preserve," *Theory, Culture and Society*, vol. 3, no. 1.

[17]See E. Reynaud (1983), *Holy Virility*, London, Pluto: "To be a man you must sport the insignia of power on your arms, legs, armpits, and pubis as early as possible. Beach, swimming pool, and shower can thus become such a nightmare for the adolescent whose virginal skin is still hairless that he often helps nature along in the privacy of the bathroom."

[18]See D. Morgan (1987), *It Will Make a Man of You: Notes on National Service, Masculinity, and Autobiography*, Manchester Sociology Department, University of Manchester, for a similar bromide-in-the-tea folk story.

[19]On the significance of rugby songs see Dunning, op. cit.

[20]Compare Morgan, op. cit.

[21]See V. Hey (1986), *Patriarchy and Pub Culture*, London, Tavistock.

[22]Ibid.

[23]J. Springhall (1987), "Building character in the British boy: the attempt to extend Christian manliness to working-class adolescents, 1880–1914," in J. Mangan and J. Walvin (eds.), *Manliness and Morality*, Manchester, Manchester University Press.

[24]A. Warren (1987), "Popular manliness: Baden-Power, scouting, and the development of manly character," in J. Mangan and J. Walvin (eds.), *Manliness and Morality*, Manchester, Manchester University Press.

[25]In R. S. Baden-Powell (1963), *Scouting for Boys*, London, Pearson.

[26]I'm deeply indebted to Mona McKenzie for detailed information about the Wolf Cub movement.

Considerations

1. Jackson begins his essay with quotations from John Stoltenberg and Judith Arcana. How do these quotations signal the subjects Jackson is going to explore? How are his own discussions related to their comments?

2. Jackson describes the violence of physical and psychological abuse among peers at school. What dilemmas does the situation create for him? What choices does he have? How typical are such dilemmas for any adolescent, irrespective of gender?

3. Jackson often insists that masculine rituals are meant to break the rules

and upset not only the school order but also the higher order of society in general, but he shows that this nonconformism actually leads to a reinforcement of the rules it is meant to defy. How does Jackson suggest that the precepts of masculinity support the established political order?

Invitation to Write

Jackson emphasizes that "there was no more powerfully shaping influence on [his] masculinity than those years boarding at school" (para. 33). His experience is inextricable from his British culture, but all cultures have ways to teach men and women what society expects of them. Write an essay exploring the aspects of British culture that are reinforced in the process of "becoming a man." Think further of the ways in which American culture instructs boys and girls about gender roles and draw some general conclusions regarding the learning of gender roles in today's societies.

Connections

Jackson devotes a major portion of his essay to the examination of male language and the codes and rituals of masculine behavior. Deborah Tannen's "Damned If You Do" (p. 495), which makes a similar connection between gender and social language, may or may not be in agreement with Jackson's observations. Using Tannen's theories, write an essay in which you discuss the examples Jackson presents. For instance, Jackson specifically talks about the role of bragging in creating male bonds. Does Tannen consider the act of bragging in the same light? Explain how their analyses of language patterns reflect their concepts of the male role in each society, and determine whether they share any assumptions about masculine behavior.

RAYMONDE CARROLL

Parents and Children

Raymonde Carroll was born in Tunisia and educated in France and the United States. Her training as an anthropologist and her personal experience of living in different countries have inspired her to reflect upon the process of interpreting cultures, whether they are remote or familiar. In 1980, she published *Nukuoro Stories,* a collection of narratives she gathered while living for three years on Nukuoro, an atoll in the Pacific. Later, using the experience of her life in the United States as well as field research, she wrote *Evidences invisibles* (1988), which was subsequently translated as *Cultural Misunderstandings: The French-American Experience.* Currently, Carroll teaches French at Oberlin College in Ohio.

Carroll's originality as an anthropologist derives from the fact that cultural differences dominated both her childhood and her marriage. She is therefore attentive to the smallest differences in behavior, to the pain that can be caused by misinterpreting an innocuous cultural gesture. Carroll's purpose is to identify the areas in which cultural misunderstandings occur and enable people to recognize them. Her book deals with such intricacies of behavior as the ways French and American people handle money, ask for information, use a telephone, talk about love, apologize for their blunders, and so on.

"Parents and Children" is a chapter from *Cultural Misunderstandings,* in which Carroll explores the differences between French and American child-rearing practices. Besides the anecdotal charm of her examples, the essay is interesting because it reveals the way child-rearing is related to cultural background.

WHILE I WAS LIVING IN FRANCE," an American academic told me, "I often saw the following scene: A child does something which his parents don't like, or one of his parents doesn't like. The parent tells him to stop. The child continues. Nothing happens, the parents don't say anything and don't do anything. The child continues to do what he was doing. The parents repeat, 'Will you stop that?' and it continues. What good does it do to tell children to stop doing something, if nothing happens when they don't?"

An American student who had just spent the year in France after having made several shorter visits told me, still horrified, about her experience in a Parisian student dorm, which she summarized in these indignant terms: "They treated us like children." What had deeply shocked her was that during one residents' meeting, the director of the dormitory announced that she had gone into the students' rooms while they were away, "because you can learn a lot about people by seeing how they keep their rooms." This particular student shared her room with a French woman and unflinchingly accepted the comings and goings of the maid. It was therefore the fact that the director had entered without permission that seemed an intolerable assault on her private life. In addition, she was surprised that the French students, who were in the majority, did not seem to find this intrusion upsetting or even surprising. Similarly, the nightwatchman treated her "like a little girl" the first time she arrived a quarter of an hour after the curfew at 11 P.M. Not knowing where else to go hardly a month after her arrival in Paris, she insistently banged on the door of the dormitory. The night watchman "lectured her" and "yelled at her." She added this remark which I found surprising: "And he didn't even ask me where I had been; he would have found out that I was coming from the other side of Paris where I had seen a play for a class, and that I had a good reason for being late." The last straw (which convinced her to leave the dormitory) was when the director's assistant ("hardly older than I was") reprimanded her for having forgotten to sign the register upon leaving by making a gesture as if to slap her, while she was "in the presence of an American friend who was in France for the first time" (and who therefore could only interpret the scene from an American perspective).

Americans and the French seem to be in complete agreement on only one point: They do not understand (which means they do not approve of) the way in which the children of "the other culture" are raised. Thus, many "American" situations can be displeasing to a French person. Here are a few, such as they were recounted to me:

—I am engaged in an interesting conversation with X, an American. Just as he is about to answer my question, or else at the most important point in my discourse, his child comes in and interrupts our conversation in what I consider to be an intrusive manner. Instead of teaching him manners, X turns and listens to him. He may even get up, apologize for the interruption by saying that he must give or show something to the little one and that he will return "in a few minutes." X comes back, a smile on his lips, asking, "Where were we?" and resumes the conversation. The worst of it is that if the little child comes back because he didn't find what he was looking for or because something is not working or because he is proud of having finished what he was doing and wants to tell X, he won't hesitate to do so. And X will not hesitate to respond. No doubt about it, these Americans have no manners.

—We're at the dinner table. Y, an American, is sitting next to her   5 three-year-old daughter, who has demanded a setting identical to that of the grown-ups (and received it from the hostess, since the mother seemed to think it was only normal) and is "acting cute." She asks for soup, then refuses to eat it. Her mother is trying to persuade her, saying, "You'll see, it's very good." The little girl finally takes a spoonful, then exclaims, "I hate it, it's yucky." The mother says, "You're going to make Z (the hostess) feel bad," or "No, it's very good," or else (are you ready for this?) "Z's cooking doesn't seem to be a hit with the little one." Slaps, that's what they deserve, these kids! And the parents too, while we're at it! You should see them in restaurants. The kids get up, mosey about, sometimes they even come up to your table to make conversation; they eat like pigs, talk loudly, do whatever they please, as if they were at home; they think they can do anything.

—I'm riding in my car, on the main street of a residential neighborhood. It is not a small, out-of-the-way street that is isolated and quiet, and it certainly is not a dead end. It is a major, busy street. I have to slow down. Right in the middle of the street, on the road, children, yes, children are playing baseball, or with frisbees. They stop, "allow me" to go by with big smiles, sometimes even a little tap on my car. Can't they play elsewhere? This isn't a ghetto—there are big parks nearby, huge lawns surrounding their houses. No, they must have the street, and so they take it, that's all there is to it. They are nice enough to let me go by, why should I complain? You should see how they're dressed, barefoot, right in the middle of the street. These Americans are impossible . . .

The preceding examples represent just a partial collage of comments that I have heard repeatedly concerning American children. And I am sure we (French) can all provide examples, which we have either seen or heard about, concerning their "lack of manners." Spoiled, ill-bred, undisciplined; with no manners, no reserve; egotistical, impolite, constantly moving, running all over, touching everything, making noise . . . Everyone has his favorite story, and not only in France. Many French parents who have been living in the United States for a long time, whose children have been raised in the American style "despite" them, complained about American schools during interviews conducted by my students. "No discipline," "they let them do what they want," "not enough homework," "no general education . . . even I, with the little education I have, know the capital of every country in the world. . . . Go find an American who can tell you that." "No respect," "spoiled rotten," are comments I have often heard and recorded myself. "Here, Madame, it is not the parents who raise their children, it is the children who raise their parents. . . . I'm proud to have remained French. . . . But don't get me wrong, I'm also proud of being an American."

Similarly, Americans have much to say about French children, or rather, perhaps, about French parents. Here is an example told to me by an American, who had obviously been mystified by the scene: "We were having a drink at the house of some friends. She's French (like my wife), and he's an American (like me). Our children are having fun together, running in and out of the room, absorbed in chasing each other. The adults' conversation is suddenly interrupted by G., the French lady of the house, who loudly scolds the kids, all the kids, hers and ours, 'because they're making too much noise and preventing us from speaking calmly.' This threatening and screaming happens again—with increasing stridency—each time the children forget G.'s command in the heat of their chasing. When we get home, I mention to my wife that G. was the one who had made any conversation nearly impossible with her loud interruptions." He adds, with a look of amusement, that G. is always complaining about the "rudeness" of Americans, and about the "atrocious" manner in which they bring up their children ("and in addition she annoys me because she always says to her husband and me each time she criticizes Americans, 'not you two, of course, you're the exception, we've found the only two tolerable Americans' . . . but I'm also an American").

Some American students with whom I was studying French magazine advertisements were very impressed by the children's clothing displayed in certain ads; they admired the interesting colors, the quality of the garments, the style. After a few moments' thought, a few of them asked, "But how can they play in these clothes?" I sent them to children's clothing stores, where they could compare the American clothes with those that had been imported from France, feel them, study them. To sum up their reactions: They felt that the French clothes were far prettier but that it was impossible to imagine a child dressed in them doing anything but standing still or sitting down. It would be impossible to imagine a child running or roughhousing, rolling on the ground or even in the grass—in short, playing any game at which one could get dirty. As far as the baby clothes went, they noticed something else they found strange: The snaps or other closings were on the shoulders or at the back of the neck, not between the legs as on the American clothes. This leads one to believe either that one undresses the child completely in order to change diapers or that one doesn't change them very often—which means either that the baby's comfort comes after his or her appearance or that babies are taught to control themselves very early. The French clothes were unanimously condemned, despite their good looks. My students all agreed that a well-dressed child who must constantly be wary of getting dirty, a child who thinks about his clothes, is a victimized child.

The opinion of my students on this subject is the same as that of many Americans. Indeed, more than one American has expressed surprise, in my presence, at how French children can remain quiet (*sage*) for hours. Even the expression *être sage,* or *rester sage,* makes them smile. It is an expression which is (literally) untranslatable into English (in this case, one would use *well-behaved* which is closer to *qui se conduit bien*). For an American, a child

10

who remains quiet for long periods of times is either sick or, in a sense, oppressed by his parents—parents who restrain his movements, his space, his words, and his freedom. An American would say that he is not a child but a small grown-up.

A scene on the platform at the train station in Rambouillet would seem to confirm the American interpretation. A mother says to her daughter (two or three years old) who is squatting, "Come on, get up. . . . I'll help you walk! . . . Just you wait and see." Then, a few seconds later, "I told you not to mess around like that. . . . Now look how dirty you are. . . . Come on, let me wipe off your hand . . . and then you go and put it in your mouth!" And, as if to prevent her daughter from getting her hands dirty again by touching the ground, she picks her up.

A young American who had spent a year in South of France, told me how she had been reprimanded by a little three- or four-year-old French girl in the park. A "teeny-weeny girl" who was passing by, a few steps behind her father, stopped and lectured her on her bare feet, adding that a big girl like her should know better. The father didn't reprimand his daughter. For the American in question, French people "learn to be arrogant" from day one.

And then there are scenes, like the ones described at the beginning of this essay, which evoke the incomprehension or the surprise of the foreigner faced with an unfamiliar situation, a question mark rather than a judgment. Thus the comments of students who have spent some time in French families. One au pair girl said, "When guests were coming for dinner, the parents repeated the rules to the children before the meal." Another one, who took care of a little two-year-old boy in an upper-middle-class family (in a house so large that the children had a separate apartment from their parents, with a remote monitor video camera in their room), said, "I was not supposed to let B. cry, because his father didn't like the noise when they had guests." "When French children are young, the father doesn't pay much attention to them; the children must remain quiet and well-behaved in his presence." "French children do not often sit down just to chat with their parents. One evening, after dinner, I stayed with the parents to talk and watch television. The next morning, their daughter asked me why I had done that." "Madame N. had two sons, a three-year-old and an eight-year-old. The boys always played together, and it was rare to see them with other children. One Sunday, we had a big meal with the entire family. The two boys remained completely still for hours. They didn't say a word at the table. . . . The French demand that a child, even if he is very young, know how to behave himself." "Obedience is very important in French families, the child must respect his parents' wishes and, above all, must not question things. The children are very well-behaved, especially when the father is present. In contrast, when an American child is told to do something by his parents, he often asks "why?" and very often the parents explain why.

In the French family, the father is always right." "In the family I lived with, the mother accompanied her daughter to her piano lessons and stayed there during the lessons. She monitored her daughter's progress, even if she had already heard her play a thousand times at home. American children go by themselves to their music or dance lessons, and even if their mothers go with them, they usually don't stay. In the same way, American parents let their children go to school all alone, or else, very often, with friends. In France, I had to bring the children to school and pick them up every day, even if they lived only two minutes away. There was also a crowd of parents who came to pick up their children. They too lived very close to the school." "Parents protect their children in several ways. Outside, their physical movements are restricted: 'Don't run,' 'calm down,' 'slowly,' 'not so loud,' 'don't yell.' In the bookstore, the mother helps her daughter to choose her books. The mother is really the one who chooses them. American children choose their own books." "French children can play all by themselves. . . . When I brought the little girl to the park, she played with her doll all alone, unless her brother was there, in which case, before going to play with her brother, she liked to say to her doll 'don't get dirty, you hear' in imitation of her mother." "My friend's children were five, ten, and thirteen, but they had no problem in playing together. American children, on the other hand, don't like playing with their little brothers or sisters." "It is not uncommon to see a parent slap his child in public. . . . American parents wait to get home to punish their children, because it is very important that the child not be ridiculed in front of his friends."

This final sentence explains why the American who had told me of her experience in a student dormitory was so annoyed at having been reprimanded, even gently, in front of her American friend who was in France for the first time. She considered herself to be an adult and was treated like a child, and in the cruelest fashion to boot: ridiculed in front of a friend.

I cannot go into all the cases that I collected. But if there were any doubts 15 as to the differences between the French and the Americans in the realm of parent-child relationships, I think that the preceding pages will have sufficed to eliminate them. The analysis of these firsthand reports, of my interviews and observations, helped me become aware of the distance separating the cultural premises informing these relationships.

A French woman told me, to show her joy and approval on the day of her daughter's second marriage, "For me, it's the first time she's marrying," thereby erasing, in one fell swoop, the seven years of her daughter's life which had been dedicated to her first marriage and the first husband, whom—as she was aware—I knew well. Only the second marriage counted for her (as she told all the guests) not only, I think, because she liked and approved of the second husband very much, but also, and especially, I believe, because her daughter, who until then had refused maternity, was expecting a baby and was radiant with joy. In her eyes, her daughter had finally reached maturity. During the intimate reception which followed the ceremony, the mother expressed concern more than once about her daughter's health, insisting that she sit down and rest. The other members of her family, and of her husband's family, were doing the same. My young friend's nice round belly no longer seemed to belong to her. She had suddenly become the repository of a being over whom both families had rights.

Getting married or living together is already a social act, of course, inasmuch as it consists of presenting oneself, if only to one's closest friends and family, as someone's partner in a permanent association (even if it later turns out to be temporary). But neither the family nor society acquires rights over the partner in question. As soon as two people become parents, however, they are expected to become "good parents," under the surveillance of many vigilant eyes. To bring a child into the world is therefore an eminently social act in France. It is easier to understand, in this context, why many French feminists sang the praises of childbirth as self-discovery, as physical joy, as intimately personal, as egotistical. What seems to be a contradiction to American feminists (a feminist expressing joy at being a mother) becomes easily understandable once we see that these women are reclaiming the experience of childbirth for themselves, which goes against the implicit definition of childbirth as a social act.

Indeed, as soon as I become a parent in France, I must answer to society for my behavior toward the child. As a parent, my role is to transform this "malleable, innocent, impressionable, and irresponsible" creature into a social being, a responsible member of the society, which is prepared to integrate him or her in exchange for a pledge of allegiance. This means that on becoming a parent, it is first and foremost to the society that I incur an obligation, a debt, rather than to my child, who comes second. If I give priority to my child, I isolate myself from this society.

A child is therefore a link between his parents and society—others, people in general, whoever is outside of the father-mother-child triangle; and even within this triangle, whoever, at any moment, is outside of the relationship between one parent (mother or father) and the child. In other words, my behavior with respect to my child is constantly subject to the judgment of others, which explains why I am always tempted to justify myself when my child's conduct does not correspond, or might not correspond, to what a third party, even someone totally unknown to me, might expect. If my child "behaves badly," therefore, I am immediately placed in a conflictful situation: I must show others that I know the rules and that I am wearing myself out trying to teach them to my child; at the same time, I must show my child that I love him or her anyway, that the bond between us cannot be destroyed so easily, since it is precisely because of this given of parental love that the child will attempt to change, to improve the conduct that displeases me so because it displeases others. This could even lead me, as a parent, to create a perfect double-bind: "You are not my daughter any more" or "You are not my son any more." As a matter of fact, this threat, which is quite common, can have meaning and thereby bring about results only insofar as it contains its own negation. Indeed, if by saying "You are not my child any more" I were confirming a real rupture, as when I say "You are not my friend any more" or "You are no longer my lover," my child would have no reason to behave differently in order to please me. It is because I, and (French) society, have established my love as noncontingent and the ties that bind us as indestructible, even if we no longer want them, that my threat can have an effect. My child and I know, implicitly, that what I am saying is: "You are behaving yourself in a way that shames me, that makes me feel bad, that hurts me. You are not behaving like the perfect child worthy of my love. Other people's disapproval of your conduct is a reflection on me."

From this perspective, it becomes apparent that the constant commands   20 at the table ("Don't put your elbows on the table," "Sit up straight," "Don't talk with your mouth full," etc.), the scolding in cafés, the "bawling out" in the street, the quick spanking or slap just about anywhere, the lecture, or even, simply, the reproving gesture or look, all fall into a single category. It is less a matter of showing my anger, which would be impolite since I must remain in control of myself in public (hence the "wait till we get home . . . "), than it is of showing others the efforts I am making to bring up my child correctly. In other words, by scolding, slapping, and repeating "Are you going to stop that?" I am justifying myself in the eyes of others. If my child behaves poorly, it is not my fault, I've done everything I could to make things different. I am a "good parent," but I have to fight against the nature of children ("You know how kids are") or, even worse, against "bad influences." The older my child gets, the more the "bad influences" will be responsible for his deviant behavior, and certainly for all criminal conduct. (Question: Are there parents who prevent their children from having a bad influence on their friends?)

The pressure must be very strong for it to maintain such a hold over parents. It is. We are all familiar with the reproving glances that converge upon parents who "don't know how to control their child." If these glances have no effect, bystanders turn to each other with gestures of disapproval for the "guilty parents" and finally resort to making comments indirectly addressed to the parents. In an extreme case, if the parents remain oblivious to even the most clearly expressed reprobation, it is not unusual to see others intervene directly, as often happens at the beach ("It isn't nice to throw sand on people," "If I catch you . . ."). Moreover, in the absence of parents—in the neighborhood, in the street, and so on—neighbors feel invested with parental responsibility with respect to all the children they know and even those they don't ("If your mother (father) could see you . . . "). A little scene, which I very recently witnessed in Paris, illustrates this perfectly. A waiting room, filled with various families. It is a long wait, people are getting impatient, children are running around, but in what is still a "tolerable" fashion. One little boy has obviously gone too far, as a grandmother, who is part of our group, tells me: "There was a little boy who was kicking his grandmother, so I caught him and told him, 'You're tired, aren't you, I'm sure you didn't mean to kick your grandmother, but you're very tired. Now be a good little boy and go ask your grandmother to forgive you.' Really, I wouldn't want to be his grandmother." The woman who told me this seemed satisfied and rather proud of her action (she told me about it several times), of having put the little boy on the right track. I think she would have been scandalized if I had told her even in a polite manner that "she should mind her own business" or that she had assumed rights that in no way were hers, which would probably have been the American interpretation of the scene.

This assumption of responsibility works both ways. A child by himself (or with other children) who is crying will be consoled, protected, helped, and reassured by a passing adult. Thus, on the whole, all adults are responsible for all children, and, within this group, certain adults have the exclusive care of certain children, their own, but on condition that they "pass the test" to which they are constantly subjected by any member of the group.

To understand the American situation, one need only in a sense reverse all the signs. Of course, in this case too, the parents take responsibility for the education of their children. But the essential difference is that this responsibility is theirs alone. When I (an American) become a parent, I incur an obligation to my children rather than to society, which comes second. My obligation is not to teach my children the rules and practices of society, but above all to give them every possible chance to discover and develop their "natural qualities," to exploit their gifts, and to blossom.

Thus, when I raise my child in the French style, in a sense what I am doing is clearing a patch of ground, pulling out the weeds, cutting, planting, and so on, in order to make a beautiful garden which will be in perfect harmony with the other gardens. This means that I have in mind a clear idea of the results I want to obtain and of what I must do to obtain them. My only difficulty will lie in the nature of the soil, given that I apply myself regularly to the task, that is. But when I raise my child American-style, it is almost as if I were planting a seed in the ground without knowing for sure what type of seed it was. I must devote myself to giving it food, air, space, light, a supporting stake if necessary, care, water—in short, all that the seed needs to develop as best it can. And then I wait, I follow the developments closely, I attend to any needs what may arise, and I try to guess what type of plant it will be. I can hope for the best, of course. But if I try to give shape to my dreams, to transform my tomato seed into a potato, for example, I am not a "good parent." To be a good parent, I must therefore give my children every chance, every "opportunity" possible, and then "let nature take its course." If I teach them good manners and social practices, it is to give them an additional chance, knowing that they will need these things to "succeed" in life, to fulfill themselves—that music, dance, and sports lessons, books, toys and all types of gadgets, will favor their development. Once I have assured them a "higher education," that is to say, four years of study at the universities of their choice, I will have done everything possible to give them the best means to realize all their dreams, to choose who and what they want to be.

In other words, it is the French parents who are put to the test; their role as spokespersons for society and their performance as teachers are evaluated. But it is the American children who are put to the test; it is up to them to show their parents what they can do with the chances that have been given them; up to them to prove that they haven't wasted these chances but made maximum use of them; up to them to satisfy the hopes their parents have blindly placed in them. 25

From this perspective, it becomes clear that French childhood is an apprenticeship, during which one learns the rules and acquires "good habits"; it is a time of discipline, of imitation of models, of preparation for the role of adult. As one French informant told me, "we had a lot of homework to do and little time to play." American childhood is, on the contrary, a period of great freedom, of games, of experimentation and exploration, during which restrictions are only imposed when there is a serious threat of danger.

In the same vein, American parents avoid as much as possible criticizing their children, making fun of their tastes, or telling them constantly "how to do things." French parents, on the other hand, train their children to "defend themselves well," verbally that is. Thus, by ordering the child "not to speak if he has nothing to say," "not to act cute," or "not to say silly things," I force her or him to discover the best ways of retaining my attention. According to an American informant, "In France, if the child has something to say, others listen to him. But the child can't take too much time and still retain his audience; if he delays, the family finishes his sentences for him. This gets him in the habit of formulating his ideas better before he speaks. Children learn to speak quickly and to be interesting." To be amusing as well. That is to say, the child is encouraged to imitate adults but not to copy them "like a parrot." The implicit message is "do like me, but differently." While teaching my child the rules by criticizing or making fun of him or her ("you're really going out like that?"; "you look ridiculous in those clothes"; "Come on, you're joking; you couldn't be going out dressed like that"; "A green shirt and red shorts? Sure . . . going to the circus?"), I force him or her at the same time to break free of me by affirming very definite tastes and well-formed opinions.

GROWING INTO ADULTHOOD

An American parent will try to do exactly the opposite. As an "ideal" parent, I will patiently listen to all that my child wants to tell me without interrupting, I will compliment him or her for having dressed without assistance (in the beginning), with no comment on the strange assortment he or she has chosen. Later, I will allow my child to buy the clothes he or she chooses, even if they make my hair stand on end, if my suggestions ("don't you think that . . .") have been rejected. The most important thing here, as in all the games we play together, is to give children plenty of room to make their own mistakes and to find their own solutions.

When a child reaches adolescence (the exact age is unimportant, let's just say that it represents the period between childhood and adulthood), the situation seems to reverse itself. For French children, the prize for this long apprenticeship, for these years of obedience and good conduct, is the freedom to do what they want, that is, to stay out late, to "have a good time," maybe to get drunk, to have sexual experiences, to travel, and so on. Even if their parents continue their roles as educators and critics, deep down they recognize the adolescents' right to "do exactly as they please," or at least they resign themselves to this ("youth must have its fling"). The fact that the adolescent continues to be fed, housed, and clothed by his or her parents in no way affects his or her "independence": I am independent if I know what I want and do what I want no matter how things look from the outside. It is therefore possible for my parents to continue to remonstrate with me, to "give me orders," or to advise me; I may grow impatient with this, but it is essentially unimportant, since I can always let them "say what they want," let them play their roles, without it producing any greater change in my behavior than a nominal acquiescence. Thus, in the student dormitory described by the American earlier, it is likely that the French students weren't bothered by the director's inspection of their rooms, the assistant's remonstrances, or the night watchmen's yelling and lecturing because all that corresponded to the quasi-parental roles that these people in charge were supposed to assume, and all one had to do was let them play their roles in order to be "left in peace." On the other hand, it seems to me that a French student would have found any questions from the night watchman concerning her arrival at the dormitory after the curfew out of place (and would have refused to answer them), whereas the American student regretted the fact that he had accused her without giving her the opportunity to explain her lateness and justify it.

American adolescents insist more on the exterior signs of independence. 30
The first sign will be economic: Very early on, they will show that they can earn money and "take care of themselves," that is, pay for everything they would consider it "childish" to expect parents to pay for (records, a stereo, sporting equipment, a motor bike, etc.). This is often interpreted by French

people as indisputable proof of the "well-known American materialism." In fact, what young Americans are doing, is, on the contrary, proving that they are capable of taking care of themselves, showing that they are capable of putting to good use the chances their parents made every effort (to the point of sacrifice) to give them. The second exterior sign of independence is affective: It is important to "leave home," even if one gets along marvelously with one's parents, if only to reassure them. American parents worry if their children hesitate to "stand on their own two feet," if they give what parents interpret as signs of "dependency," of "insecurity," of an "unhealthy" need for protection, or if they "act like children." This means that even if, deep down, I (an American) think that my child is still immature, it is important that the outward signs I give to the child show the opposite, not because I am a hypocrite but because I am convinced that it will help him or her to reach maturity. And it is even more important that I do this in the presence of others—in the presence of my child's friends as well as in the presence of mine.

In exchange, all my children's "successes" belong to them alone. I can go to all their tennis matches, or anxiously attend their concerts, but I would indignantly reject the slightest suggestion that they owe their success to me in any way. I only gave them the chance.

Since Americans "do what they want," in a sense, from childhood, it is much less important for them to "know" what they want very early on. Parents accept, if they do not encourage, having their children "experience different life-styles," hesitate between careers—in short, not "settle down too soon," which could reduce their chances and restrict their potential (which explains why most programs of university study, including law and medicine, include four preliminary years of college). The weight of these maximum opportunities given to young Americans puts very strong pressure on them, early on, to "prove themselves," to show their parents (and the world) what they are capable of. But since the expectations have never been clearly defined, and ideally cannot be so, logically there can be no moment when the goal is reached. The implicit parental injunction is to always seize every opportunity, to climb farther and higher, without rest, to always be "on the go." Not to do so is to condemn oneself to mediocrity, to wasted chances, to the ultimate failure which consists of not exploiting one's human potential to the fullest.

One of the consequences of all of the above is that the majority of French people interviewed have better memories of their adolescence ("it was sheer madness") than of their childhood, happy as it may have been. Childhood is full of restrictions; adolescence is, or is reconstructed in retrospect to be, a burst of freedom, memorable experiences with friends, a kind of happy interlude. One can let loose and kid around, have an attack of the giggles, or play "practical jokes," which Americans of the same age have trouble understanding, because for them these are the hallmarks of childish behavior.

In contrast, when Americans reach adolescence, they are suddenly confronted with all sorts of expectations, real or imagined; they are expected to take on responsibilities and to perform. It is time for them to take their places on a stage from which they will no longer step down without a profound sense of failure. Hence the nervousness, the panic which often seizes American adolescents when they must say goodbye to the total freedom, the games and carefree attitude of their childhood world. For the majority of Americans, childhood becomes a paradise lost. Whether or not I had a happy childhood is irrelevant; if I hadn't, it means that I was cheated twice: cheated of my right to "opportunities" and cheated of my right to a few years of paradise, to that blessed time when I neither had to be an adult nor pretend to be one.

Thus, whereas young Americans do not understand why young French people often "act like children," young French people in the United States often remark that young Americans are "too serious," that they "don't know how to have fun," that they "give boring parties," in short, that they "act like adults."

These differences between young American and French people, this systematic inversion of the signs, so to speak, between the two systems, are also found in the relationships between children and adults in the two cultures.

While French parents educate their children, they cannot, at the same time, be their playmates, save in exceptional circumstances when the rules are, so to speak, suspended. And in this case, the parent plays at being a child, thus putting him- or herself on the same level as the child. Whenever he or she wants to play, the French child turns to the other children in the family, no matter what their ages, and is heartily encouraged by his or her parents to do so. He or she is also encouraged to serve as a replacement for the parents when with the younger children, at school and in the street. Parents reinforce this solidarity between the children by refusing to intervene in case of a dispute. In the words of one informant, "When I went to my mother, I got an extra smack . . . so it didn't take me long to learn." It is therefore up to the children to "work things out among themselves." And never, never should they come and "tell"; this is definitely not a way of getting on the parents' good side, but quite the contrary. Little by little, this system teaches children to stick together against parental authority. And this relationship is reproduced at school. At the same time, within the family structure, each parent establishes an independent relationship with each child, and each child does the same with his or her brothers and sisters. Each family member is therefore engaged in a network of independent relationships and is witness to (or judge of) the relationships between each family member and the others. In the case of an argument between two family members, this allows a third, who is un-involved in the dispute, to play the role of the go-between, to interpret one's behavior for the other ("You know, you have to understand your father"; "You know, your mother is very tired these days"; "Don't get angry, he's studying for finals and is very nervous"). The child therefore gets used to a multitude of simultaneous relationships and to the presence of intermediaries, of go-betweens.

The role played by the intermediary in "arranging the situation" explains why a parent's intervention at school and, as we shall see, at the university is accepted or at least tolerated by French children, whereas it would be unac-ceptable if not unbearable to American children. Thus, a French couple, in France, asked me to explain the higher education system in the United States because their son wanted to go there. Both of them were educated and "mod-ern." I explained. Armed with my experience of frequent cultural misunder-standings, I was preparing to discuss what I consider to be most important, that is to say, the expectations to which French people would not be accus-tomed. To illustrate this, I began to tell a story that some (French) friends had just told me, about how they had furiously intervened at the *grande école* (a unique French institution) because their son, it seems, had been slighted by the "incompetence" of some of its staff. I was about to say that this type of thing could not happen in the United States or would be considered very in-appropriate (by the son himself, who would feel he was being taken charge of "like a child") when, fortunately for the relationship between the couple and myself, I was interrupted by the mother who said, "Oh, yes, it's like Alain," and told me, indignantly, about all of her protests at the medical school in which her son was enrolled concerning the "stupid" aggravation they had given him. I immediately stopped talking, experiencing the dizzy sensation one feels at the edge of a cliff.

American children are encouraged very early on to play with other children their own age (and therefore outside of the family), to "make friends," to learn to establish relationships with strangers, to "become popular" among their peers. At home, they seek the approval or encouragement (and, hope-fully, some day, admiration) of their parents; it is therefore only logical that they feel in competition with their brothers and sisters. The same thing hap-pens at school: They must both make friends among their classmates and compete with them for the attention and approval of teachers, and later on of professors, for whom they will "do the best they can." This competition is not meant to be destructive; rather it aims to stimulate children, to extract or elicit the best possible performance from each one, and "may the best one win." And like the parent, the teacher will not allow him- or herself to criticize a student's work in public, but will give the student the means to find and de-velop the area he or she can excel in. A teacher who makes curt, scornful, or even joking comments about each paper he or she returns, as would be possible in the French system, might be considered sick or deranged—in any case, inept at teaching. The class would simply be deserted, as I've seen happen in an American university to a young instructor right off the boat from France. The American student, accustomed since childhood to explanations rather than to pronouncements or encouragements to emulate, does not hesitate to ask questions, to discuss, to disagree, to question—behavior which always surprises French students visiting the United States. What surprises them even more is that the professor does not take the question as a sign of hostility, a challenge to his or her authority, but treats it as a sign of intellectual independence, or a sincere desire to better understand the question or to participate in the discussion of a subject that interests her or him—an attitude which a "good" professor will seek to encourage. We should note here that American students spontaneously turn to the professor rather than to their classmates, thereby recreating the relationship they have established with their parents. The relationship is of concern only to two people. No one has the right to intervene, to "interfere" in this relationship, not even, in the family, the other parent.

For the young French person, then, reaching maturity consists of assuming the role for which my parents and other educators have prepared me, that of being an "educator" (in the broadest sense) in turn, of taking my place and taking on my responsibilities in society, and beginning the cycle all over again. Whatever my age, though, my conduct will always be a reflection on my parents, who share my successes as well as my disappointments. At this time, I will also begin to attend to my parents' well-being and will tacitly commit myself to taking care of them in their old age, to reversing the roles. I will, in turn, be judged, by whoever feels it is his right, on the way in which I treat my parents.

For an American, maturity is a much more fluid concept which varies from person to person. I can, therefore, be a responsible adult (I have a permanent job, a house, a family, I pay my bills and taxes) and still be considered immature by certain people, whereas others will envy the fact that I have retained a certain "childlike" side (a taste for taking risks, a capacity for wonderment and amazement, a refusal to accept the impossible, etc.). In the end, I alone decide if I have reached maturity or not. And just as my parents always went out of their way to allow me to be responsible for myself, often at the price of a strict control on their desires to do otherwise, so I will not treat my old parents as children by inflicting on them the "indignity" of taking care of them (at my home) but will make certain of the security and comfort of their environment and of the possibility of their having a "social life" with people whose company they appreciate, that is to say, people their own age. My family and I will visit them, but they have earned the right to have a quiet or fast-paced life, as they choose, in any case a life free of the demands and tears of small children. For a French person, however, this means that Americans "abandon" their aged parents.

Faced with such profound cultural differences at practically each stage in the life cycle, we can only marvel, not at the number of sources for misunderstandings, but rather at the possibilities for—and the existence of—any understandings at all.

Considerations

1. From the beginning of her essay, Carroll presents French and American views on how children should behave. The French see American children as "spoiled, ill-bred, undisciplined; with no manners, no reserve; egotistical, impolite, constantly moving, running all over, touching everything, making noise" (para. 7). Although Americans seem to be as shocked by the behavior of French children, we never hear their judgments in Carroll's essay. Why do you think such judgments are absent on the American side? What kind of judgments would an American make?

2. Carroll opens her essay with an example presented by an American academic living in France. She never analyzes this particular example; she uses it only to demonstrate the American's incomprehension of French behavior. Consider her example more closely. Imagine that you have witnessed the scene. What would your first impression about the French parents be? How would you respond to such a situation? Having read Carroll's analysis of French and American behavior, can you explain your response?

3. What differences between French and American culture become apparent in Carroll's discussion of child-rearing?

Invitation to Write

Carroll believes that Americans raise their children in the spirit of independence and competition, which are basic cultural values in the United States. To the French, American children look ill-bred, or to put it differently, "bad." Carroll implies that American parents also have a notion of "good" and "bad" when it comes to their children. Write an essay in which you explore the notions of good and bad in relation to children as they are understood in the United States. (For examples, you may refer to personal experience, children you know, or juvenile characters in movies or television shows.) Use Carroll's characterizations of American culture to explain why certain qualities are admired and encouraged in children, whereas others are not.

Connections

Carroll's statements about child-rearing may be accurate as far as middle-class, mainstream Americans are concerned, but she tends to ignore the differentiations which occur in a culture due to social class, ethnic background, race, religion, and geographical location. In the next selection, "The Looking-Glass Shame," Judith Ortiz Cofer draws a portrait of a young girl's experience growing up between two cultures. Write an essay in which you analyze and interpret the attitudes of this Puerto Rican family toward raising children according to the approach taken by Carroll. Try to figure out what cultural values are involved in the rules the Puerto Rican parents impose on their children. You may draw comparisons between Ortiz Cofer's upbringing and the examples of French and American child-rearing described by Carroll in order to support your argument.

JUDITH ORTIZ COFER

The Looking-Glass Shame

Judith Ortiz Cofer was born in 1952 in Puerto Rico. Although her family moved to Paterson, New Jersey, to accompany her father, who was in the U.S. Navy, they spent long periods of time with her maternal grandmother in Puerto Rico. She describes the cultural duality of her childhood in her narrative *Silent Dancing* (1990), which was awarded the 1991 PEN/Marth Albrand Special Citation for Nonfiction. Ortiz Cofer has also published two books of poetry, *Terms of Survival* (1987) and *Reaching for the Mainland* (1987), as well as a novel, *The Line of the Sun* (1989). Ortiz Cofer received a grant from the Witter Bynner Foundation in 1988 and a Fellowship in Poetry from the National Endowment for the Arts in 1989. She now lives in Athens, Georgia.

No matter what form her writing takes, Ortiz Cofer's main interest is in the way art transforms experience. On page 12 of *Silent Dancing*, she explains the role of personal experience in her writing:

> Much of my writing begins as a meditation on past events. But memory for me is the "jumping off" point; I am not, in my poetry and my fiction writing, a slave to memory. I like to believe that the poem or story contains the "truth" of art, rather than the factual, historical truth.

The following narrative is one of the final chapters in *Silent Dancing*. Ortiz Cofer describes here the first signs of her adolescence and her first love. The typical adolescent problems are intensified by her situation as a young immigrant. On the one hand, she is isolated from her schoolmates who, although they seem to go through the same experience, do not want to share it with her; on the other, she feels estranged from her family and divided between her mother's romantic desire to go back to Puerto Rico and her father's more lucid and bitter realization that there is no future for him in either his native or his adopted home.

At any rate, the looking-glass shame has lasted all my life.
　　　　　　　　　—VIRGINIA WOOLF, *Moments of Being*

In her memoir *Moments of Being*, Virginia Woolf tells of a frightening dream she had as a young girl in which, as she looked at herself in the mirror, she saw something moving in the background: ". . . a horrible face—the face of an animal . . ." over her shoulder. She never forgot that "other face in the glass" perhaps because it was both alien and familiar. It is not unusual for an adolescent to feel disconnected from her body—a stranger to herself and to her new developing needs—but I think that to a person living simultaneously in two cultures this phenomenon is intensified.

Even as I dealt with the trauma of leaving childhood, I saw that "cultural schizophrenia" was undoing many others around me at different stages of their lives. Society gives clues and provides rituals for the adolescent but withholds support. As I entered my freshman year of high school in a parochial school, I was given a new uniform to wear: a skirt and blouse as opposed to the severe blue jumper with straps, to accommodate for developing breasts, I suppose, although I would have little to accommodate for an excruciatingly long time—being a "skinny bones," as my classmates often called me, with no hips or breasts to speak of. But the warnings began, nevertheless. At home my mother constantly reminded me that I was now a "señorita" and needed to behave accordingly; but she never explained exactly what that entailed. She had said the same thing when I had started menstruating a couple of years before. At school the classrooms and the cafeteria were segregated into "boyside" and "girlside." The nuns kept a hawkeye on the length of the girls' skirts, which had to come to below the knee at a time when the mini-skirt was becoming the micro-skirt out in the streets.

After school, I would see several of the "popular" girls walk down to the corner out of sight from the school, and get into cars with public school boys. Many of the others went down to the drugstore to have a soda and talk loudly and irreverently about the school and the nuns. Most of them were middle-class Italian and Irish kids. I was the only Puerto Rican student, having gotten in after taking a rigorous academic test and after the priest visited our apartment to ascertain that we were a good Catholic family. I felt lost in the sea of bright white faces and teased blond hair of the girls who were not unkind to me but did not, at least that crucial first year, include me in their groups that traveled together to skating rinks, basketball games, pizza parlors—those activities that they would talk about on Monday in their rapid-fire English as we all waited to be let into the building.

Not that I would have been allowed to go to these places. I lived in the carefully constructed facsimile of a Puerto Rican home my mother had created. Every day I crossed the border of two countries: I would spend the day in the pine-scented parochial school building where exquisitely proper behavior was the rule strictly enforced by the soft-spoken nuns, who could, upon observing an infraction of their many rules, turn into despots—and never raise their voices—as they destroyed your peace of mind with threats of shameful exposure and/or expulsion. But there was order, quiet, respect for logic, and there, also, I received the information I was always hungry for. I liked reading books, and I took immense pleasure in the praise of the teachers for my attentiveness and my good grades. So what, I thought to myself, if I was not invited to the homes of my classmates, who did not live in my neighborhood, anyway. I lived in the city core, in an apartment that may have housed an Italian or Irish family a generation before. Now they were prosperous and had moved to the suburbs and the Puerto Ricans had moved into the "immigrant" apartment buildings. That year I actually felt a sense of burning shame at the fact that I did not have to take a bus or be picked up in a car to go home. I lived only a few blocks away from the church and the school which had been built in the heart of the city by the original wave of Irish Catholics—for *their* convenience. The Puerto Ricans had built no churches.

I would walk home every day from school. I had fifteen minutes to get home before my mother panicked and came after me. I did not want that to happen. She was so different from my classmates' mothers that I was embarrassed to be seen with her. While most of the other mothers were stoutly built women with dignified grey hair who exuded motherliness, my mother was an exotic young beauty, black hair down to her waist and a propensity for wearing bright colors and spike heels. I would have died of shame if one of my classmates had seen her sensuous walk and the looks she elicited from the men on our block. And she would have embraced me in public, too, for she never learned moderation in her emotions, or restraint for her gesturing hands and loud laughter. She kept herself a "native" in that apartment she rarely left, except on my father's arm, or to get one of us from school. I had had to have a shouting match with her to convince her that I no longer needed to be escorted back and forth from school in the ninth grade.

My mother carried the island of Puerto Rico over her head like the mantilla she wore to church on Sunday. She was "doing time" in the U.S. She did not know how long her sentence would last, or why she was being punished with exile, but she was only doing it for her children. She kept herself "pure" for her eventual return to the island by denying herself a social life (which would have connected her too much with the place); by never learning but the most basic survival English; and by her ability to create an environment in our home that was a comfort to her, but a shock to my senses, and I suppose, to my younger brother's, both of us having to enter and exit this twilight zone of sights and smells that meant *casa* to her.

In our apartment we spoke Spanish, we ate rice and beans with meats prepared in *adobo*, that mouth-watering mixture of spices, and we listened to

5

romantic ballads sung by Daniel Santos which my mother played on the record-player. She read letters from her family in Puerto Rico and from our father. Although she loved getting his letters, his descriptions of the Roman Coliseum or the Acropolis did not interest her as much as news from *casa*—her mother and her many brothers and sisters.

Most of my mother's sentences began with *En casa* . . . : At her Mama's house things were done like this and like that. At any place in the world other than her beloved *Isla* my mother would have been homesick: Perpetual nostalgia, constant talk of return, that was my mother's chosen method of survival. When she looked into her looking-glass, what did she see? Another face, an old woman nagging, nagging, at her—*Don't bury me in foreign soil* . . .

> A sailor went to sea, sea, sea,
> To see what he could see, see, see,
> And all that he could see, see, see,
> Was the bottom of the deep, blue
> Sea, sea, sea.

The black girls sang this jump-rope song faster and faster in the concrete play yard of the public school, perhaps not thinking of the words, landlocked in the city, never having seen the deep, blue sea. I thought of my father when I heard it.

The deep blue sea for my father was loneliness. He had joined the U.S. military service at eighteen, the very same year he had married, because for the young men of Puerto Rico who did not have money in 1951, it was the only promise of a future away from the cane fields of the island or the factories of New York City. He had been brought up to expect better things. My father had excelled in school and was president of his senior class. In my mother, whom he met when she was just fourteen, he must have seen the opposite of himself. He had forsaken his early dreams for her love, and later for the future of his children.

His absences from home seemed to be harder on him than on us. Whatever happened to him during those years, most of it, I will never know. Each time he came home he was a quieter man. It was as if he were drowning in silence and no one could save him. His main concern was our education, and I remember showing him my school papers, which he would pore over as if he were reading a fascinating book.

He would listen attentively while Mother recounted the ordinary routine of our days to him, taking it all in like nourishment. He asked endless questions. Nothing was too trivial for his ears. It was as if he were attempting to live vicariously each day he had missed with us. And he never talked about the past; unlike our mother, he had no yearning to return to the Island that held no promise for him. But he did not deprive her of her dream of home either. And her need to be with her family may have been what prompted him to devise the complex system of back-and-forth travel that I experienced most of my childhood. Every time he went to Europe for six months, we went back with Mother to her mother's *casa*; upon his return to Brooklyn Yard, he would wire us, and we would come back. Cold/hot, English/Spanish; that was our life.

I remember my father as a man who rarely looked into mirrors. He would even comb his hair looking down. What was he afraid of seeing? Perhaps the monster over his shoulder was his lost potential. He was a sensitive, intellectual man whose energies had to be entirely devoted to survival. And that is how many minds are wasted in the travails of immigrant life.

And so, life was difficult for my parents, and that means that it was no more and no less painful than for others like them: for the struggle, *la lucha*, goes on all around for people who want to be a piece that fits in the American puzzle, to get a share in the big picture; but, of course, I see that in retrospect. At fourteen and for a few years after, my concerns were mainly focused on the alarms going off in my body warning me of pain or pleasure ahead.

I fell in love, or my hormones awakened from their long slumber in my body, and suddenly the goal of my days was focused on one thing: to catch a glimpse of my secret love. And it had to remain secret, because I had, of course, in the great tradition of tragic romance, chosen to love a boy who was totally out of my reach. He was not Puerto Rican; he was Italian and rich. He was also an older man. He was a senior at the high school when I came in as a freshman. I first saw him in the hall, leaning casually on a wall that was the border line between girlside and boyside for underclassmen. He looked extraordinarily like a young Marlon Brando—down to the ironic little smile. The total of what I knew about the boy who starred in every one of my awkward fantasies was this: that he was the nephew of the man who owned the supermarket on my block; that he often had parties at his parents' beautiful home in the suburbs which I would hear about; that this family had money (which came to our school in many ways)—and this fact made my knees weak: and that he worked at the store near my apartment building on weekends and in the summer.

My mother could not understand why I became so eager to be the one sent out on her endless errands. I pounced on every opportunity from Friday to late Saturday afternoon to go after eggs, cigarettes, milk (I tried to drink as much of it as possible, although I hated the stuff)—the staple items that she would order from the "American" store.

Week after week I wandered up and down the aisles, taking furtive glances at the stock room in the back, breathlessly hoping to see my prince. Not that I had a plan. I felt like a pilgrim waiting for a glimpse of Mecca. I did not expect him to notice me. It was sweet agony.

One day I did see him. Dressed in a white outfit like a surgeon: white pants and shirt, white cap, and (gross sight, but not to my love-glazed eyes) blood-smeared butcher's apron. He was helping to drag a side of beef into the freezer storage area of the store. I must have stood there like an idiot, because

15

I remember that he did see me, he even spoke to me! I could have died. I think he said, "Excuse me," and smiled vaguely in my direction.

After that, I *willed* occasions to go to the supermarket. I watched my mother's pack of cigarettes empty ever so slowly. I wanted her to smoke them fast. I drank milk and forced it on my brother (although a second glass for him had to be bought with my share of Fig Newton cookies which we both liked, but we were restricted to one row each). I gave my cookies up for love, and watched my mother smoke her L&M's with so little enthusiasm that I thought (God, no!) that she might be cutting down on her smoking or maybe even giving up the habit. At this crucial time!

I thought I had kept my lonely romance a secret. Often I cried hot tears 20 on my pillow for the things that kept us apart. In my mind there was no doubt that he would never notice me (and that is why I felt free to stare at him—I was invisible). He could not see me because I was a skinny Puerto Rican girl, a freshman who did not belong to any group he associated with.

At the end of the year I found out that I had not been invisible. I learned one little lesson about human nature—adulation leaves a scent, one that we are all equipped to recognize, and no matter how insignificant the source, we seek it.

In June the nuns at our school would always arrange for some cultural extravaganza. In my freshman year it was a Roman banquet. We had been studying Greek drama (as a prelude to church history—it was at a fast clip that we galloped through Sophocles and Euripedes toward the early Christian martyrs), and our young, energetic Sister Agnes was in the mood for spectacle. She ordered the entire student body (it was a small group of under 300 students) to have our mothers make us togas out of sheets. She handed out a pattern on mimeo pages fresh out of the machine. I remember the intense smell of the alcohol on the sheets of paper, and how almost everyone in the auditorium brought theirs to their noses and inhaled deeply—mimeographed handouts were the school-day buzz that the new Xerox generation of kids is missing out on. Then, as the last couple of weeks of school dragged on, the city of Paterson becoming a concrete oven, and us wilting in our uncomfortable uniforms, we labored like frantic Roman slaves to build a splendid banquet hall in our small auditorium. Sister Agnes wanted a raised dais where the host and hostess would be regally enthroned.

She had already chosen our Senator and Lady from among our ranks. The Lady was to be a beautiful new student named Sophia, a recent Polish immigrant, whose English was still practically unintelligible, but whose features, classically perfect without a trace of makeup, enthralled us. Everyone talked about her gold hair cascading past her waist, and her voice which could carry a note right up to heaven in choir. The nuns wanted her for God. They kept saying that she had vocation. We just looked at her in awe, and the boys seemed afraid of her. She just smiled and did as she was told. I don't know what she thought of it all. The main privilege of beauty is that others will do almost everything for you, including thinking.

Her partner was to be our best basketball player, a tall, red-haired senior whose family sent its many offspring to our school. Together, Sophia and her senator looked like the best combination of immigrant genes our community could produce. It did not occur to me to ask then whether anything but their physical beauty qualified them for the starring roles in our production. I had the highest average in the church history class, but I was given the part of one of many "Roman Citizens." I was to sit in front of the plastic fruit and recite a greeting in Latin along with the rest of the school when our hosts came into the hall and took their places on their throne.

On the night of our banquet, my father escorted me in my toga to the   25
door of our school. I felt foolish in my awkwardly draped sheet (blouse and skirt required underneath). My mother had no great skill as a seamstress. The best she could do was hem a skirt or a pair of pants. That night I would have traded her for a peasant woman with a golden needle. I saw other Roman ladies emerging from their parents' cars looking authentic in sheets of material that folded over their bodies like the garments on a statue by Michelangelo. How did they do it? How was it that I always got it just slightly wrong, and worse, I believed that other people were just too polite to mention it. "The poor little Puerto Rican girl," I could hear them thinking. But in reality, I must have been my worst critic, self-conscious as I was.

Soon, we were all sitting at our circle of tables joined together around the dais. Sophia glittered like a golden statue. Her smile was beatific: a perfect, silent Roman lady. Her "senator" looked uncomfortable, glancing around at his buddies, perhaps waiting for the ridicule that he would surely get in the locker room later. The nuns in their black habits stood in the background watching us. What were they supposed to be, the Fates? Nubian slaves? The dancing girls did their modest little dance to tinny music from their finger cymbals, then the speeches were made. Then the grape juice "wine" was raised in a toast to the Roman Empire we all knew would fall within the week—before finals anyway.

All during the program I had been in a state of controlled hysteria. My secret love sat across the room from me looking supremely bored. I watched his every move, taking him in gluttonously. I relished the shadow of his eyelashes on his ruddy cheeks, his pouty lips smirking sarcastically at the ridiculous sight of our little play. Once he slumped down on his chair, and our sergeant-at-arms nun came over and tapped him sharply on his shoulder. He drew himself up slowly, with disdain. I loved his rebellious spirit. I believed myself still invisible to him in my "nothing" status as I looked upon my beloved. But toward the end of the evening, as we stood chanting our farewells in Latin, he looked straight across the room and into my eyes! How did I survive the killing power of those dark pupils? I trembled in a new way. I was not cold—I was burning! Yet I shook from the inside out, feeling light-headed, dizzy.

The room began to empty and I headed for the girls' lavatory. I wanted to relish the miracle in silence. I did not think for a minute that anything more would follow. I was satisfied with the enormous favor of a look from my beloved. I took my time, knowing that my father would be waiting outside for me, impatient, perhaps glowing in the dark in his phosphorescent white Navy uniform. The others would ride home. I would walk home with my father, both of us in costume. I wanted as few witnesses as possible. When I could no longer hear the crowds in the hallway, I emerged from the bathroom, still under the spell of those mesmerizing eyes.

The lights had been turned off in the hallway and all I could see was the lighted stairwell, at the bottom of which a nun would be stationed. My father would be waiting just outside. I nearly screamed when I felt someone grab me by the waist. But my mouth was quickly covered by someone else's mouth. I was being kissed. My first kiss and I could not even tell who it was. I pulled away to see that face not two inches away from mine. It was he. He smiled down at me. Did I have a silly expression on my face? My glasses felt crooked on my nose. I was unable to move or to speak. More gently, he lifted my chin and touched his lips to mine. This time I did not forget to enjoy it. Then, like the phantom lover that he was, he walked away into the darkened corridor and disappeared.

I don't know how long I stood there. My body was changing right there   30
in the hallway of a Catholic school. My cells were tuning up like musicians in an orchestra, and my heart was a chorus. It was an opera I was composing, and I wanted to stand very still and just listen. But, of course, I heard my father's voice talking to the nun. I was in trouble if he had had to ask about me. I hurried down the stairs making up a story on the way about feeling sick. That would explain my flushed face and it would buy me a little privacy when I got home.

The next day Father announced at the breakfast table that he was leaving on a six-month tour of Europe with the Navy in a few weeks and, that at the end of the school year my mother, my brother, and I would be sent to Puerto Rico to stay for half a year at Mamá's (my mother's mother) house. I was devastated. This was the usual routine for us. We had always gone to Mamá's to stay when Father was away for long periods. But this year it was different for me. I was in love, and . . . my heart knocked against my bony chest at this thought . . . he loved me too? I broke into sobs and left the table.

In the next week I discovered the inexorable truth about parents. They can actually carry on with their plans right through tears, threats, and the awful spectacle of a teenager's broken heart. My father left me to my mother who impassively packed while I explained over and over that I was at a crucial time in my studies and that if I left my entire life would be ruined. All she would say was, "You are an intelligent girl, you'll catch up." Her head was filled with visions of *casa* and family reunions, long gossip sessions with her mamá and sisters. What did she care that I was losing my one chance at true love?

In the meantime I tried desperately to see him. I thought he would look for me too. But the few times I saw him in the hallway, he was always rushing away. It would be long weeks of confusion and pain before I realized that the kiss was nothing but a little trophy for his ego. He had no interest in me other than as his adorer. He was flattered by my silent worship of him, and he had *bestowed* a kiss on me to please himself, and to fan the flames. I learned a lesson about the battle of the sexes then that I have never forgotten: The object is not always to win, but most times simply to keep your opponent (synonymous at times with "the loved one") guessing.

But this is too cynical a view to sustain in the face of that overwhelming rush of emotion that is first love. And in thinking back about my own experience with it, I can be objective only to the point where I recall how sweet the anguish was, how caught up in the moment I felt, and how every nerve in my body was involved in this salute to life. Later, much later, after what seemed like an eternity of dragging the weight of unrequited love around with me, I learned to make myself visible and to relish the little battles required to win the greatest prize of all. And much later, I read and understood Camus's statement about the subject that concerns both adolescent and philosopher alike: If love were easy, life would be too simple.

Considerations

1. Ortiz Cofer begins her narrative by connecting her title to a quotation drawn from Virginia Woolf—a writer Ortiz Cofer considers her literary mentor. In what context does the looking glass suggested in the title reappear later in the narrative? What images does Ortiz Cofer suggest could be found there? What is Ortiz Cofer's equivalent of Woolf's monster in the mirror? How does this image reinforce Ortiz Cofer's thesis?

2. In the conclusion of the narrative, Ortiz Cofer declares, "I learned to make myself visible" (para. 34). What experiences does she describe that contribute to her sense of not being visible? What is the source of her sense of invisibility in each instance?

Invitation to Write

Most people, at some point in their lives, have experienced the feeling of being out of place or different. Since Ortiz Cofer is struggling to negotiate two cultures, she is more acutely aware of the conditions of her exclusion. Yet her feeling that she "always got it just slightly wrong" is also symbolic of her lack of belonging. Write an essay in which you discover and analyze the causes of her isolation. Think about other circumstances in which a person can feel excluded or out of place, such as a teenager among adults, a city dweller among farmers, a farmer in the city, a person of one race in another racial group, or an immigrant among natives. Try to reach a more general conclusion about the feeling of not being accepted as one of the group.

Connections

In "American Horse" (p. 330), Louise Erdrich's story of American Indian experience, the characters are also caught between two cultures. Although American Indians are the only people in America who aren't immigrants, Ortiz Cofer's statement that "many minds are wasted in the travails of immigrant life" (para. 13) can be extrapolated to describe the condition of the characters portrayed by Erdrich. Using examples from both readings, write an essay that shows how contradictory standards can affect people who are forced to live in two cultures at the same time. Observe the different ways the older and younger generations respond to a different culture. Is the happiness of the children conditional upon the "wasting" of the parents? Why or why not?

LOUISE J. KAPLAN

Adolescence: The Farewell to Childhood

Louise J. Kaplan was born in New York City and graduated from Brooklyn College. She has been an associate professor in the graduate clinical psychology programs at both New York University and the City College of New York. A former director of the Mother-Infant Research Nursery at NYU and the Child and Adolescent Clinic of the Psychological Center at City University of New York, she has also been a member of the faculty of the Seminar of the New School for Social Research. Kaplan is currently a member of the Professional Advisory Committee of the Margaret S. Mahler Research Foundation.

Kaplan's books include *Oneness and Separateness: From Infant to Individual* (1978), *Adolescence: The Farewell to Childhood* (1984), *Female Perversions: The Temptation of Emma Bovary* (1991) and, with Donald M. Kaplan and Armand Schwerner, *The Domes Day Dictionary.* As both a post-Freudian psychoanalyst and a psychologist, Kaplan is interested in applying the concepts of psychoanalysis to literary studies and to investigation of the relationships between different age groups within a culture. The following essay on adolescence comes from the introductory and concluding chapters of her book *Adolescence: The Farewell to Childhood.* Besides probing into adolescent psychology, Kaplan investigates the social ways in which adolescents are guided into adulthood in both tribal and modern cultures.

BETWEEN THE CLOSING MOMENTS of childhood and the yet-to-be of womanhood and manhood is that ambiguous time of life we have come to refer to as adolescence. In contrast to the factual clarity of a word such as "puberty"—the biological condition of having acquired mature genitals and the functional capacity to reproduce—"adolescence" embodies all the connotative uncertainties of emotional and social growth. There is little controversy about the existence of puberty. Even the experts who question the existence of adolescence agree that the average girl arrives at puberty between ages fourteen and

107

sixteen and the average boy between fifteen and seventeen, give or take a year or two. Adolescence, on the other hand, is a widely debated concept. It—if indeed "it" exists at all—may last anywhere from a week to the decade or so typical in contemporary Western societies.

On the subject of adolescence about the only affirmative declaration specialists will agree to is that it is a psychological process somehow associated with puberty, a process that will vary from person to person, family to family, society to society, and from one epoch, era, century, decade to the next. When consensus is desired they omit the word "psychological." Anyone who has ever embarked on a search for some unified theory of adolescence knows that the safest strategy is to take refuge among the folds of this agreeable social relativism. The manifest behaviors of adolescents are contradictory and overwhelming in their diversity. But when one decides not to go along with the fashionable doubt about the feasibility of a meaningful concept of adolescence, then soon enough the seemingly contradictory data are no longer unfriendly antagonists. Diversity becomes simply an expectable characteristic of the issues of adolescence, an invitation for exploration.

The facts of puberty provide a reliable anchor. Girls and boys do become women and men. Girls begin menstruating and soon after produce fertile ova. Boys begin ejaculating and in a few years the ejaculate will contain mature sperm. That girls and boys themselves attach psychological significance to these dramatic events, and that the adults around them respond to such changing physical status we can be certain.

As it turns out, human beings respond to the approach or advent of puberty in a characteristically human way. All the more remarkable for its sturdy resistance to changing circumstances, one response repeatedly asserts itself. In every period of human history some recognition is accorded to the potential threat to society of this transition period. Both changing child and adult world make an effort to harness an emerging genitality to the prevailing social norms and to the moral order—whatever these may be. Sexuality and morality always mature in tandem, and everything else grows up around them.

As remotely different from our modern ways of dealing with adolescence ⁵ as they appear to be, the puberty rites of hunter-gatherer peoples reveal the same themes, dilemmas, plights, and resolutions.

In hunter-gatherer societies the rites of initiation into adulthood involve mutilation of the body, among them, depending on the society: pulling out a tooth, cutting off the little finger above the last joint, cutting off the earlobe or perforating the earlobe or nasal septum, tattooing, scarifying the face, chest, back, legs, and arms, excising the clitoris, perforating the hymen, subincising the penis, cutting off the foreskin. The human body is treated like a piece of wood whose surfaces can be trimmed, broken through, written on, whose irregular projections can be carved away or shaped into whatever a society designates as womanly or manly.

The scarifications etch the body with a permanent record of the dilemmas of existence. They posit such contrasts as male/female, line/circle, lineage/age group, ancestors/descendants, and, most important, past/future. The oppositions are resolved in the scars. In the last opposition, that of past and future, the scar represents the emergence of a present moment that is capable of drawing on the past as it creates the future. The present is not thought of as a hairline between "was" and "yet-to-be" but as a space filled with history and potentiality.

The scarifications, amputations, excisions, and perforations are permanent body transformations. They are marks of membership in a community of peers, signs of incorporation into adulthood. Most directly they signify the irreversible differences between woman and man. The ritual initiations into manhood and womanhood also typically include a few temporary body transformations, such as paring the nails, pulling out the scalp hair or cutting off a few locks, painting the body with clay, menstrual blood, semen, or saliva, or wearing special garments, masks, jewelry. Whether permanent or temporary, the body transformations are meant to divest youthful sexual vitalities of their social threat and transform them into a source of social rejuvenation.

Usually a girl's puberty rite is closely linked to her actual physiological pubescence, which in one respect at least is inescapably noticeable. In many societies it is thought that a girl becomes a woman when she menstruates. There are no comparably definitive changes to suggest the attainment of manhood. With boys it is not uncommon for the rites to take place several years before or after the onset of the physical changes leading to manhood. In some instances the official puberty rite occurs every four or five years, so that boys of different ages and degrees of sexual development undergo initiation together.

Regardless of the age assigned for becoming adult, the overall significance remains the same. An individual is separated from the asexual world of childhood and initiated into adult sexuality and adult moral responsibility. Permission to be a sexually functioning adult is granted under conditions of initiation into the moral order. In all rites of passage, but particularly in those associated with puberty, the sexual and moral realms intertwine. 10

The ceremonies for boys are frequently derived from some idea of separation from the world of women and children. At one or another moment over a period of time the boy is required to give up his emotional attachment to his mother—who weeps for him. He becomes attached to all men. He abandons his boyhood sports and games along with his domestic ties to his mother. After the ceremony of severing the bonds of childhood the boy is instructed by a designated sponsor or group of teachers in the duties and moral responsibilities of his community.

In some tribes the boy will be considered dead for the period of his novitiate. He is separated from his usual environment and secluded, either alone or with a group of same-sexed peers. He undergoes a physical or mental weakening, which is meant to eradicate all recollection of childhood. He is subjected to flagellation and other physical ordeals. Intoxication with palm wine, tobacco, or peyote induces anesthesia and amnesia. His former personality is erased. Toward the end of this trial period come the transition rites, which may include body mutilations and painting of the body. During the transitional period, sometimes referred to as the "sacred time," the child-adult speaks a special language and eats special foods. After weeks or months or years he is deemed ready for instruction in the tribal law, totem ceremonies, recitations of songs and myths.

In many societies women are likened to children. They are regarded as closer to nature, more controlled by nature and on more intimate terms with it than men. As she approaches puberty a girl's rupture with childhood need not be as definitive as a boy's. However, a woman's intimacy with the mysterious forces of nature requires that her pubescent physiology be brought under control as soon as possible. The female rites of passage tend to have the effect of binding a girl to a home place, which more often than not is the home of her childhood. Whereas boys are initiated into the public sphere, girls are initiated into the domestic sphere.

At menarche, nettles and grass may be inserted into the vagina to "cause" the bleeding and impel the girl into womanhood. The young girl will be instructed by older women in the patterns of behavior her society assigns to menstruating women. The feminine tribal lore takes the form of rules for the prevention of defilement—the cooking and sexual taboos associated with menstruation.

The onset of menstruation is the commonest occasion of a girl's initiation, but it is not the only one.[1] A girl may be considered ripe for initiation when her breasts begin to form, a development that precedes menstruation by a few years. The girl's breasts are rubbed with fat. A circle of red ocher is painted around each nipple. In some societies a girl whose breasts are beginning to develop is instructed to enlarge her labia by pulling and stroking or placing vegetable irritants, herbs, or leaves into her vagina. The lips of her vulva may be enlarged by an older woman who stretches them and lightly punctures the vaginal tissue in several places. A woman with thick vaginal lips is considered beautiful.

The molding of the girl into womanhood is meant to control her physicality but also to change her inner qualities. She is a beautiful and good woman if she is kind, cheerful, friendly, unselfish, strong, capable of enduring much.

The growing of the girl, though it does not involve a violent severing of her ties with childhood, impresses on her the necessity for subduing her phys-

---

[1] . . . The puberty rites I am describing are sometimes composites derived from several societies and sometimes concern only one or two specific societies. [Author's note]

ical self in order to attain feminine virtue. Her body is scarified and molded. She is enclosed in a designated space within her own household or village, in a hogan or seclusion chamber, surrounded by a mound of earth, buried from her waist down in a pit of sand. Her separation from childhood does not require a removal in actual space. Like a caterpillar that must be enclosed in a cocoon and undergo a quiet, unseen metamorphosis to then emerge from the chrysalis as a butterfly, the girl undergoes transformation to maturity, but by way of imaginary adventures. These acts may take the form of an identification with a mythic heroine or the undertaking of a cosmic journey. Often the metamorphosis entails both mythic patterns. However far-reaching the imaginary journey, it takes place in a cocoon—the family nest or nearby hut.

Through her identification with a mythic heroine, the initiand abandons the historical moment in which she lives. She enters the primordial, atemporal zone. Her acts are eternal in duration, ever renewed, ever repeated. Like the heroines she impersonates, the girl is infinitely creative and virtuous. The gifts she acquires are never solely for herself. She appropriates for herself the personal qualities of the mythic heroine: fruitfulness and courage. She reappropriates for her society the gifts of civilization: grain, agriculture, medicine. Her personal initiation benefits society as a whole and, beyond this, the entire cosmos. Though at the close of the ritual she must reenter historical time, the girl retains her creative powers. Thereafter her existence partakes of divine virtue.

When the girl undertakes a cosmic journey she is *symbolically* liberated from the limitations of her household or village. She is freed from the restrictions of the safe world of childhood. Her journey is an ordeal, a descent into the underworld or beneath the sea or above through the dark cosmos, a confrontation with all manner of demonic powers. The girl returns from her journey utterly transformed. She is no longer an immature child whose field of activity is restricted to domestic matters. She is a mature woman who is expected to transcend the boundaries of the mundane existence to which she is henceforth consigned, a cosmic being who contains within herself the universe at large. Though she reenters the household and village of her childhood, she retains forever the virtues and cosmic powers of all those who have undertaken the sacred journey. The women and men who have accompanied her on her journey or have listened to her tale or sung the songs or danced the dances with her will see once again through her eyes all they once knew so well and then forgot.

Whether they undertake their passage into adulthood in actual time and space or enclosed in a domestic cocoon, pubescent boys and girls are considered neophytes. The neophyte is a blank slate on which is inscribed the wisdom of society. A neophyte is without gender, anonymous as a piece of wood or bit of clay or mote of dust, mere matter whose form will be impressed on

20

it by society. In some instances the neophytes act as though they are newborns who have forgotten how to walk or eat. They pretend that they must be re-taught all the gestures of ordinary life. As they relearn the ways of the world, they are becoming adult. Just before becoming adult the boy or girl partici-pates in a dramatization of the encounter between the generations. The mas-culine scenario is a fight or competition that stresses the discontinuity between childhood and adulthood. The feminine scenario entails a confrontation with cosmic forces. The novitiate takes on a new identity and frequently a new name. The dead child has been resurrected into adulthood.

All rites of passage embrace a double series of separations with a tran-sition between. Puberty rites begin with a separation from childhood, a separation that is at the same time an incorporation into a sacred environ-ment. The sacred world is a transitional realm, a margin, both exit and entrance, a cocoon, a mound of earth, a gateway, a passage, a journey between childhood and adulthood. In the sacred realm the individual is suspended, perhaps above the earth or below the sea or in the underworld, temporarily isolated from the anchorage of everyday life. Here the past is put away in preparation for the future. Here the child learns that access to adult sexuality requires a revision of the moral life of childhood—a moral life that has been based solely on family attachments and peer camarade-rie. The passage through the sacred realm endows an individual with qual-ities she did not possess as a child.

Although she may not remember what occurred, she will retain forever an aura of the experience of the hunger, fear, grief, loneliness associated with her separation from the world of childhood. The youngster learns that her family is no longer her sole refuge, protection, security. The ceremonies of the sacred realm are a cultural means for deflecting emotional energies away from the childhood past in order that they may be invested in emotional identifications and anchorage within the larger social group.

Later there must be a second separation, this time from the "unreal" sa-cred realm, which is then followed by a ritual of reincorporation in which the emotions associated with the physiology of sexuality and reproduction are divested of their antisocial qualities.

There is a pretense that society has controlled the natural processes, that the rites have prevented the natural world from usurping the social order. An appearance of orderliness is imposed on disorderly events—on unruly nature and socially incompatible desires. The ceremonies of reentry assert the au-thority of tradition. The rite of reentry stresses obedience to prescribed ways of performing sex, giving birth, teaching children. There is an assignment to the individual of circumscribed domestic, social, and religious roles. Permis-sion is granted to be an active participant in the rites of birth, marriage, pu-berty, burial. Thus at the conclusion of the ceremonies of puberty, order is restored; a child has become caregiver and lawgiver. The message is that although there has occurred a drama of threatening emotional intensity, nothing new will happen.

But the rites also proclaim that there is something larger than the personal 25 or the social. By participating in the passage from one realm of existence into another, even the most wretched human is witness to the dilemmas of the omnipotent gods, who though they rule the cosmos must also reckon with their powers to create and destroy. The mortal being encounters the eternal dilemmas of virtue, sin, and ethical responsibility. The self has been enlarged to accommodate the divine. The individual has become a participant in the system that rules the cosmos.

"In all times and in all places"—in Constantinople, northwestern Zambia, Victorian England, Sparta, Arabia, the Machado tributary of the Amazon, Hispaniola, medieval France, Babylonia, the Kidepo Valley, Carthage, Mohenjo-Daro, Patagonia, Kyūshū, Nouakchott, Dresden—the time span between childhood and adulthood, however fleeting or prolonged, has been associated with the acquisition of virtue as it is differently defined in each society. A child may be good and morally obedient, but only in the process of arriving at womanhood or manhood does a human being become capable of virtue—that is, the qualities of mind and body that realize the society's ideals.

In classical thought the virtues of prudence, courage, justice, temperance were thought to be forms of conduct that could be imposed on human nature through training and discipline. In Christian theology, faith, hope, and charity were virtues assumed to be innate dispositions residing in all humans, potential in the infant and child but actualizable only in women and men. By the fourteenth century the classical and early Christian virtues were combined as the seven cardinal virtues, which were meant to stand in opposition to the seven deadly sins: Prudence could tame covetousness, courage conquer lust, justice regulate anger, temperance overcome gluttony, faith defeat sloth, hope diminish pride, charity assuage envy.

The Latin word *virtus*, which means "manliness" or "valor," makes explicit the association between moral excellence and male sexual power. *Virtus* is a reminder also that virtue, like the process of adolescence, is often a privilege granted only to special persons. In its original renderings *virtus* was restricted to supernatural or divine beings. Through identification with some divine figure a human might acquire the power of virtue. Virtue is a constant, but interpretations of it fluctuate. Chastity is frequently considered a virtue in young women but a failure of valor in young men. An unchaste woman is said to be "of easy virtue."

While virtue and ethics are not synonymous, implicit in the concept of virtue is that when these ideal qualities reside within the person, that person is capable of reflecting on human behaviors and evaluating the consequences of those behaviors for other persons, whether they are family members, neighbors, colleagues, or society at large, and then acting according to that evaluation. Nevertheless we cannot presume that the ethical sense automatically follows from virtue as night follows day. As we know, ideals of virtue have been promoted in one class or sector of a society as a way of excluding or dominating others.

Clearly the social order does not bestow all the advantages or impose the identical moral trials on all those growing up into womanhood and manhood. Some children are encouraged to pass through to adulthood tranquilly and unobtrusively. Or, if they must be raucous and sow a few wild oats, they are expected to do so as quickly as possible and then simmer down to a conventional adult life—with or without virtue or the ethical sensibilities.

The growth changes of pubescence can and often do take place without any recognizable rite of passage. Not all hunter-gatherer societies have puberty rites. In some, only the boys are initiated into adulthood; in others, only the girls. In Western societies, as in some hunter-gatherer societies and in all the ancient civilizations, the time to *adolescere*, or "grow up into adulthood," was originally granted exclusively to young men of the upper classes and to a few intellectual, religious, artistic, or otherwise gifted girls and boys. Until the emancipation of the working class and the advent of the youth movements in the early twentieth century the term "youth" was generally understood to imply a young man of mental or financial advantage, one who could be counted on to benefit from the conveniences and inconveniences of virtue. The underclasses, like the majority of women, were treated as obedient children who reflexively proceeded without benefit of transition into an obedient and dutiful adulthood. Whatever moral strengths they had acquired during childhood would suffice for the uneventful, uncomplicated adult lives they were about to lead. A husband's virtue could protect the wife, the lord's his serfs, a knight's his pages and his damsels.

Now the benefits and trials of adolescence are technically available to every person between the ages of thirteen and twenty-three. It is a characteristic of modernization that the privileges of adolescence became rights granted to all youth. Adolescence was enmeshed with Romantic ideology: revolution, naturalness, spontaneity, idealism, emancipation, liberty, sexual freedom. It is not surprising that such apparently easy availability of liberty and sexual freedom should be regarded doubtfully by parents, educators, theologians, philosophers. One response to such doubt has been to regard adolescents with tolerant condescension. We can think of them provisionally as innocent victims who are powerless and naïve. Sooner or later, however, they begin to be perceived as victimizers—sinister, amoral, hostile invaders of adult territory.

Now that adolescence is accessible to the multitude and not restricted to gentlemen and lords, many adults are taking alarm at what seems to be a barbaric horde of scruffy girls and boys out to dismantle the structures of society. It is hard to see any virtue in it all. When the grown-ups see in its stead is considerable evidence of pride, covetousness, anger, gluttony, envy, sloth, and a great deal of lust. On occasion, not long ago, the enmity between adults and adolescents erupted into real warfare, with guns, knives, rocks, and tear gas. More usually, however, the generational antagonisms are masked and more insidious.

A characteristic unique to the human species is immense mental agility, especially when it comes to coping with fear. One technique is straightforward denial. Our minds look away and pretend that nothing is happening. A trickier version of denial is trivialization of what we fear. And so we invent "teenagers," the Val girls, the Nintendo addicts, the army of soporific sloths whose classroom thoughts are intent on one matter—getting home to watch the soaps. Another favored trivialization of youth is the image of the illiterate, greasy-haired, leather-jacketed "hood" with the heart of gold. He may not know much about grammar or history, but put him on the dance floor and he is transformed into a divine being. He's got rhythm. And what's more, he goes to church.

By far the most popular image is the teenager ensconced in his or her armchair, feet up on a desk, jabbering for hours on the phone, surrounded by a cozy mess of unopened textbooks, gym clothes, hair dryer, teddy bear, and tennis racket, half-eaten pizza and hot dog, Coke bottle, posters of Springsteen and Madonna and other superstars plastered across every inch of wall space, including the doors and closets. Annoying and frustrating, these silly kids. But they'll soon grow out of it.

Another technique for reducing anxiety is to become as much like the object of fear as possible. The method, identification with the aggressor, comes naturally to little children, who fear and envy the extraordinary power they attribute to parents, dentists, policemen. So they roar like ferocious lions; they dress up like monsters, as they soberly administer injections to dolls, toy soldiers, stuffed animals, and trucks.

Grown-ups, when they feel intimidated by adolescent barbarisms, can get fairly rambunctious themselves. Besides, sometimes those enviable teenagers seem to be having a lot of fun. After a generational truce during World War II, when young men between the ages of seventeen and twenty-six were too busy soldiering to be a challenge to their elders, the generational antagonisms took a surprising turn. The grown-ups began to emulate youth. Middle-aged parents revived their sexual appetites. They donned gaudy T-shirts, jeans, jumpsuits, psychedelic jewels. They pranced at the discos. They vied with their teenagers for youthful sexual partners.

Not to be outdone by youth, the adults simulated Woodstock. A common sight at professional meetings was groups of psychologists, philosophers, ministers, college professors, doctors, social workers, and lawyers, sandaled or barefoot, decked out in feathers, ethnic skirts and shirts, jeans, Indian beads, headbands, plunking guitars, chanting mantras, grunting like the Dead, sprawled in the lobbies, on the lawns, or along the poolsides of the various

Hiltons and Sheratons. But soon the Age of Aquarius was over. In hindsight many of these sobered, gray-haired, burned-out elders have begun to lament the caricatures of youth they had allowed themselves to become. . . .

Every human society endeavors to preserve itself by inventing the adolescence it requires. Yet, to put it another way, we could say that every society invents the adolescence it deserves and then regards that invention as monstrous, saintly, or heroic. Adults are prone to create myths about the meaning of adolescence. Whatever their political or personal inclinations, whether they glorify nature or revere society, whether they are identified with youth or they are detractors of youth, most adults find it imperative to defuse the awesome vitalities of these monsters, saints, and heroes. . . .

During adolescence, what has belonged to the lowest part of the mental   40
life is changed into what is highest in the human mind by our scale of values. The method—omnipotence of gesture, love of self, primary narcissism—is there from birth. But not until adolescence are our personal aspirations, our dreams of glory transposed into those aspirations that might serve all of humanity. When our personalized dreams of glory are impersonalized, they kindle in us a wish to preserve the species as we once preserved our own love of self. Adolescents are the bearers of cultural renewal, those cycles of generation and regeneration that link our limited individual destinies with the destiny of the species.

More than birth, marriage, or death, adolescence entails the most highly elaborated drama of the passage from one realm of existence into another. It is then that the individual passes from family life into cultural existence. The puberty rites of the hunter-gatherer peoples were a dramatization of this passage. A young person became a responsible member of the social and moral order by *actively* participating in the drama of her own passage into adulthood. Even more, the drama imparted to her existence from then on—however mundane and limited it was destined to be—was an aura of something larger than life. And those who listened to the tales or sang the songs with her remembered all they once knew and then forgot. In a performance that may have extended for a week, a month, a season, several years, the metaphors of existence were brought into play—music, dance, song, the recitation of the sacred texts and tribal lore, masks, jewelry, body decorations, symbolic enactments, scarifications and mutilations that mature a child into an adult, the legends of losing old dialogues, finding new ones, refinding the old ones.

Modern adolescence, when it is not trivialized or aborted by some deformity of family life or social convention, is an inner drama no less encompassing in its metaphorical reach. By temporarily abandoning the modes of ordinary existence the young person enters a sacred zone in which time is eternal and limitless, in which experience is reversible and recoverable. Time is regenerated; the past is reactualized and transformed into a future mode; the forging of a personal life becomes connected with the possibilities of a new society, a new

humanity. In modern societies the drama does not end with everything returning to the beginning. We can no longer expect that young people will undergo
their personal ordeals and then return to us with an unqualified acceptance of
things as they are. When things are rotten in Denmark the young will be quick
to sniff out the decay and corruption. Modern youth resist the idea that they,
or the social order, are hopelessly determined by the past. They counter our
conservative, reductionist tendencies with their inspirations—exploration, innovation, aspiration. In finding out who they are and who they are not, adolescents mobilize the energies of the archaic past and use them to extend the
cultural dimensions of the future.

The sacred world they pass through, which is outside time, outside the
order and protection of civilized life, can be a lonely and frightening place.
The demons they encounter there are not masked representations of evil and
violence and crude sexuality but their own internal demons—their unruly desires, their untamed consciences that afflict them with threats of defilement,
castration, mutilation, starvation, exile. Adolescents encounter within themselves elemental passions in their raw, simplified forms. These encounters,
frightening and emotionally painful as they are at the time, will later allow for
a more generous and humane appreciation of the human plight.

In the interval between giving up the old dialogues and finding new ones,
there are long periods of time when there is an absence of love dialogue. The
dread of loss of dialogue, a loss that is like a falling-away into an eternal
nothingness where one will never be held again, can make submissive cowards of us all. But adolescents risk it. They risk also the loneliness and fear of
departing from one realm of existence and entering a new but as yet unknown
realm. They come to know within themselves the hopelessness when there is
no place for desire to go, no person to love, no ability to divert sexual hunger
into friendship or activity. They learn what it means to lose the past and to
recognize that it will never come again.

Most adults do not care to be reminded of these anguished emotional 45
states. In late adolescence and young adulthood some youths have not forgotten; they are still close enough to such experiences to feel compassion for
those who suffer as they once did. They see their beloved, once vigorous, productive grandparents now aging, decaying, moving closer to that finite moment of death. "Is this what life is all about?" they ask. "A frantic race with
time and then a long eventless ending?" Young people, those who allow
themselves to remember the loneliness and grief of their recent years, have
more compassion and tenderness toward the elderly than most middle-aged
adults. Nothing—not avarice, not pride, not scrupulousness, not impulsive-
ness—so disillusions a youth about her parents as the seemingly inhumane
way they treat her grandparents.

It has been said that one of the most touching expressions of our
specifically human morality is the care of elderly, lonely, or infirm parents by

their children. But in the modern world we grown-ups run from the elderly as we might run from a plague. Their very presence is a nagging reminder of the despair and stagnation that might await us. Our own dread of the finitude of time overwhelms our compassion. We leave the entire matter to "the assistant postmaster," who will efficiently dispense the welfare checks and arrange for tidy housing. The elderly, except perhaps for those with wealth or power, are treated as castoffs, leftovers that in the most charitable of circumstances we confine to their retirement communities.

Youth, because they are facing forward toward a new life, can endure what it means to grow old. They can still recall the violence and disorder of spirit, the grief, the loneliness, the loss of dialogue when a person must depart from one realm of existence and enter another. They have an emotional grasp that enables them to engage in a meaningful dialogue with the aged. The young, for example, are certainly more appreciative than we are of the nostalgic "ramblings" of their grandparents. And they often find in these retrospective accounts a certain wisdom that we too often ignore. A young person's willingness to listen keeps alive the memories of the golden days. Her compassionate gestures counter the dread of loss of dialogue. The descent into nothingness is halted. Even though they are soon to be forever separated from the universe, the elderly are reminded of regeneration and renewal. In the presence of a youth they feel held. For the moment, at least, they sense that life is not a meaningless passage of time, that their own individual destinies are linked to some larger, eternal human destiny.

In this we see another legacy of adolescence: the sense that departure from one realm to another need not entail a severing of bonds but rather may offer an expansion and renewal of our common humanity.

Soon after a newborn has been severed from the womb he enters into his first human dialogue, a dialogue that reminds him of that fetus-placenta-amniotic fluid-mother he once knew. In order for him to become a person with his own unique selfhood, he must depart from that realm of human oneness and enter a new realm of humanness. He undergoes the separation-individuation of his first three years of life. In the process he will expand the range of his emotional capacities, release himself from the humiliating dependencies of nursery morality, and extend himself into the law and order of family life. His separation-individuation does not sever his attachment to his mother; it enlarges the meaning of that attachment. In a similar way, the adolescent's second psychological birth leads to expansion of a child's emotional and intellectual reach, a quickening of the tender and affectionate bonds to the parents, a humanizing enlargement of the sexual and moral passions.

Yet we have come to view the adolescent opportunity to grow up and 50 achieve a new level of identity as a time for rupturing the bonds of family attachment. Even the experts have become prey to this version of things. In fact, the intensity of an adolescent's resistance to growing up may be gauged by how desperately and how far he must flee, actually or emotionally, from the intimacies of family life in order to preserve his sense of self.

A young child releases himself from the bondage of nursery passions by taking in, internalizing, what he then imagines to be parental inhibitions, authority, ideals. These early internalizations of the parents allow the child to become a relatively civilized human being who can regulate and manage his desires. He has achieved at least a certain degree of independence from external authority. But his new internal masters are exceedingly harsh and demanding. For a child to become a responsible adult these exaggeratedly idealized versions of the parents must undergo some revision. And the infantile desires that are attached to the parental idealizations must also undergo revision so that they can be transferred outside the family.

As we know, whenever passions are about to be deployed to another person, another realm, another order of existence, the event always begins as a variation of violence. An adolescent, however, is not trying to get rid of the parents or to demolish the existing order of things. She may look like a wild, untamed creature, but her adolescent madness is a sign of her warfare on desire and her attempts to transform the infantile idealizations into something more humane and less exalted than they once were. In this way she enlarges her passions and is able to extend them into new relationships with peers, lovers, children, grandparents, *and* her parents, who can now be forgiven for being less perfect than they were once imagined to be.

If into the bargain the adolescent extracts permission to aspire toward values and ideals that go beyond the realities of everyday life, it will be the result of a personal inner struggle, a struggle that cannot be ordained by any social order. But the formation of that inner structure of the mind we call the adult ego-ideal can be fostered only in a social order that confirms the intimate cogwheeling of generations—a society that sponsors the connections between sexual dialogue and moral dialogue at every phase of the life cycle.

The way it now stands, the interests of civilization are served if a person simply leaves the childhood family unit to procreate a new family, works at an assigned job, obeys a few uncomplicated moral commandments. When infant-parent love attachments are thought to be necessary to the preservation of society, some societies do what they can to protect the family unit. But even in our contemporary Western societies, with their narrowness of historical perspectives and trivialized moral values, some adolescents, employing all the means that nature has given them, do become adults who are more concerned with expanding the boundaries of human existence than with preserving the social order exactly as it is. They may move us all a little further into the light.

The articulation of an individual life with its environmental niche is like a kaleidoscope with infinite flecks of colored glass which might be turned a million times and still not produce all its potential designs. The moral potential of the retarded primate is not infinite, but it is much vaster than we have 55

yet dared to imagine. This eminent anthropoid who need not give up searching, who need not return to the beginning and always repeat the past, who has
within her flexible responses, inventive solutions, limitless curiosity, will always have to reckon with the forms of civilization that are the safety net of
her existence. She may have it within her to control nature, to uproot the
earth she inhabits, to dominate and even extinguish all the animals below her
on the *scala naturae*, to achieve power over the helplessness and the powerless, to fly off to the distant galaxies, but she must still preserve civilization or
her species will die out. At the same time, in order to make life on this harsh
and confusing planet more bearable, she must find a way to preserve the resting places, beyond society, pleasure, or reality. Organized human societies
could last a while without cultural aspirations, but no society has survived for
long without them.

Civilization itself can be preserved and be passed on from one generation
to another without change. Even so, there are always metaphors, rituals, temples, and tribal lore that will express the idea of "no change." Adolescence
can be a great drama of passion and upheaval in which at the end everything
returns to the beginning. Even so, the green light beckons. We are born with
an irresistible urge to push on, to strike out for the territory. When obedience
to the authority of the social order leaves no room for the expression of personal power or a sense of moral dignity, we feel less than we might be—we
feel false to ourselves.

An actual human history is bound and finite. We will have made only one
life, leaving our other possible lives by the wayside, dimly remembered,
haunting the life we actually lead. Sometimes we will imagine that our real life
is the life we didn't lead, or we will sense nameless feelings coursing through
our breast. There is a realm of existence in which the history of infinite possibilities continues. We call it the resting place, the transitional zone, the inter-
mediate realm, culture, metaphor, illusion. Here we temper the sense of the
finite, unbolt the breast, and become aware of life's flow and hear its winding
murmur. And though the adolescent becomes an adult who will live but one
finite life, for a time she has lived in the realm of infinite possibility. Another
legacy the adult inherits from her adolescent years is the inner experience that
once she might have played all parts in the human comedy, that once she was
true to herself and to her powers.

When adolescence is over, the young adult's character is etched with the
inner struggles she has undergone. The changing woman has not been a passive recapitulator of infancy; she has been an active reviser. Her strategies, her
losses, her defeats, her triumphs, her new solutions leave their imprint on the
adult form. Later in life she may further humanize her conscience, she may
find some more extended ways of loving and caring, she may even rediscover
the powers she merely imagined during adolescence. It is part of her species-
specific inheritance that no matter how set or rigid her character, there is

always some flexibility, always some curiosity to be reawakened. But for an adult to change her ways requires immense effort and risk and a great expense of spirit. In adolescence the forces of growth are a spur to innovation and moral renewal. Adolescence is the conjugator of a human life. When it is over, who we are and what we might become are not as open to change. We are never as flexible again.

Some youths conclude their journey by settling back into the familiar civilized routines. They reinstate, albeit with a few new flourishes and minor alterations, the frozen plots of childhood. They are ruled again by the inflexible dictates of should and ought, dominated by seeking and finding sexual gratification—but only this way and not that way. They try to assuage dread by returning to the safety of the schoolyard. They never quite yield up the wish to be totally cared for and protected by some all-powerful idol, even if that idol should turn out to be a tyrant. They are forever young. But they have lost their youthfulness.

It could be said that the number of adults who have faltered in this 60 journey out of childhood is exceedingly large. But this is the case only when we measure what we became against the possibilities that were there. This is a harsh and primitive way to evaluate a human life. Every now and then, when a woman is pregnant, when a newborn leaves the womb to enter the world, when a child reaches puberty, when someone is married or someone dies, there is a resting place. We go to weddings. We go to funerals. We begin something. We remark that it is finished. We look back on our youthful years as the hopeful time when it did seem possible to radically change the course of our personal fate. We forget the loneliness, the pain of loss, the narcissistic anguish, the wrestlings with desire, the torments of our unruly, unlovely, disobedient bodies. We dimly remember the return of exquisite passion, the longings that loosened us from the confining safety of childhood.

Considerations

1. At the start of her essay, Kaplan remarks that "sexuality and morality always mature in tandem, and everything else grows up around them" (para. 4). Why is it important to develop a moral sense and a sense of responsibility once one becomes sexually mature?

2. Kaplan describes the way in which adolescents are introduced to adulthood at the onset of puberty. Gender differences guide this process: Girls are socialized in different ways than boys. What do you think are the reasons for and purposes of these differences?

3. Kaplan compares views of youth that are suggested by earlier puberty rites to current attitudes toward adolescence. What does this comparison

suggest about adolescence? What kinds of conclusions does she draw on the basis of the comparison?

Invitation to Write

Kaplan begins her book with a description of the puberty rites that mark the passage from childhood to adulthood. She writes that "the puberty rites of the hunter-gatherer peoples were a dramatization of this passage" (para. 41), and she concludes that modern adolescence also "is an inner drama no less encompassing in its metaphorical reach" (para. 42). What kinds of outer signs dramatize the passage from youth to adulthood in our society? Write an essay in which you analyze Kaplan's examples of various rites of passage, explaining their symbolic meaning. Discuss also some particular events in a modern adolescent's life which might be said to represent "rites of passage." Decide whether Kaplan is right to associate tribal rites of passage with the modern manifestations of adolescence.

Connections

In the essay on page 80, "Parents and Children," Raymonde Carroll makes clear distinctions between American and French children and adolescents. Kaplan's analogies between tribal "rites of passage" and their modern counterparts in America suggest that she might consider the problems of adolescence to be the same all over the world. Write an essay in which you explore the questions about adolescence that Kaplan raises. Pay attention to cultural specificity. Use Carroll's argument and examples to confront Kaplan's theory and determine whether there are any universal features of adolescence.

ASSIGNMENT SEQUENCE

Growing Into Adulthood

The first question in this sequence asks you to reflect upon how the process of becoming an adult can vary, even among individuals in the same culture. Drawing on your own observations of the ways males and females in American culture follow different paths toward adulthood, you will consider the implications of the gender-based rituals that govern adolescence. Next, following in David Jackson's footsteps, you will examine the interactions of individuals with their peers and what they learn from this experience. In your third paper, you will consider Jackson's essay again, this time in light of Raymonde Carroll's comment about the ways children are raised in French and American society. You will extend Carroll's analysis to Jackson's British society in order to see what values emerge as important. Turning again to Jackson's essay, and to Judith Ortiz Cofer's narrative and Louise Kaplan's theory, you will next write on the relationship between an adolescent's sense of psychological belonging and his or her own body. For your final paper, you will look at all the readings in terms of Louise Kaplan's idea that during the period between childhood and adulthood, individuals learn to become "capable of virtue." To do so, you will need to decide how each society discussed in this sequence would define that term and how much virtue Kaplan would see in each society's accepted model of behavior.

Assignment 1: Exploring Experience

As Louise Kaplan writes in "Adolescence: The Farewell to Childhood," and as the other readings in this chapter make us aware, people do not arrive at adulthood by a uniform route. For the authors of these essays, establishing an adult identity is inextricably linked to establishing a gender identity. Therefore their essays discuss how the two processes intertwine. Write a paper that discusses to what degree American rituals of adolescence reflect different expectations about the adult roles of men and women. From your experience or observation, consider what role gender plays in the lives of American teenagers as they grow up.

Rather than beginning with generalizations, start your paper with a description and analysis of two or three social rituals that mark milestone moments in the lives of American adolescents. Think about and discuss how they differ for males and females. Topics to consider could include the high school senior prom, graduation honors, family celebrations, college acceptance, or roles in personal relationships. From your observations, draw conclusions about the importance of gender in the lives of individuals as they move toward adult roles in contemporary American society.

Assignment 2

Again the irony was that the more the illicit drinking went on as a form of cultural resistance against middle-class school authority, the more we made ourselves susceptible to the routines and practices of patriarchal power. From the moment of dangerous pleasure when we smuggled in bottles of brown ale to drink after lights out when I was about sixteen, the central question about drink was: Could we prove that we were "real men" by taking our drink?
    —DAVID JACKSON, *One of the Boys*

In "One of the Boys," David Jackson uses several examples that show that membership in a group of his peers was crucial to his childhood development. For instance, resistance to adult authority depended on forming relationships with his peers. His use of the term "irony" suggests that this particular experience had a double and unexpected effect. Write a paper in which you examine how peer relationships and the need for group approval both encourage and get in the way of growing up.

In your paper, be sure to examine in depth at least one example described by Jackson. Identify the way this situation helped him modify childish behavior to absorb values of the adult society. Also consider the long-range ramifications and Jackson's evaluation of its lasting effect on him after he became an adult. Then consider examples from your own knowledge about the effects of belonging to a group of peers in American society. One example that you could examine is the role social groups like fraternities and sororities play in providing opportunities for friendships and independence, as well as exerting a strong influence on the lives of their members. Consider whether Jackson would be likely to see them as the American equivalent of the more casual British social drinking groups he writes about.

Assignment 3

From this perspective, it becomes clear that French childhood is an apprenticeship, during which one learns the rules and acquires "good habits"; it is a time of discipline, of imitation of models, of preparation for the role of adult. . . . American childhood is, on the contrary, a period of great freedom, of games, of experimentation and

exploration, during which restrictions are only imposed when there is a serious threat of danger.
—RAYMONDE CARROLL, *Parents and Children*

In her essay, "Parents and Children," Raymonde Carroll closely links a society's pattern of child-rearing with its deepest values. According to her analysis, French parents see their obligation to society as the most important one, while American parents believe that their greatest obligation is to their children. After reading David Jackson's description, in "One of the Boys," of the way some British children grow up, think about how Carroll would define a British parent's sense of obligation. Decide what Carroll would say about how British adults shape children's behavior to instill particular values, and write a paper that examines David Jackson's narrative using her ideas.

Base your observations on topics that Carroll examines in her essay on French and American behaviors, such as the relationships of children with their parents, siblings, and peers. You could also consider the attitudes British, French, and American parents have toward letting others have authority over their children. Decide if Carroll would see British attitudes as closer to French or to American attitudes, or if she would need to establish a different category for them.

Assignment 4

It is not unusual for an adolescent to feel disconnected from her body—a stranger to herself and to her new developing needs—but I think that to a person living simultaneously in two cultures this phenomenon is intensified.
—JUDITH ORTIZ COFER, *The Looking-Glass Shame*

In "The Looking-Glass Shame," Judith Ortiz Cofer describes her experience of moving each day from an American world of school to a Puerto Rican world *"en casa."* In a sense, David Jackson, in "One of the Boys," also moves between two cultures, which are represented in the world ruled by the masculine code and the gender-neutral world of his childhood. Ortiz Cofer's suggestion that her psychological sense of being out of place reflects a sense of disassociation from the physical body is also true of Jackson's experience. In a different context, Louise Kaplan's essay "Adolescence: The Farewell to Childhood" discusses the physical and psychological correlations in coming-of-age rituals. Using these three readings, write a paper that examines how adolescents experience a link between a sense of their physical presence and a psychological sense of belonging.

Find and analyze at least one description of an adolescent's body in each of these three readings. Determine whether the example suggests a sense of connection or of disconnection between the adolescent and his or her body. Then discuss how the adolescents' feelings about their physical presence suggest an attitude about the choices facing them as adults. From your analyses, decide how their immediate environments contribute to the feelings adolescents experience about growing up.

Assignment 5

A child may be good and morally obedient, but only in the process of arriving at womanhood or manhood does a human being become capable of virtue—that is, the qualities of mind and body that realize the society's ideals.
    —LOUISE J. KAPLAN, *Adolescence: The Farewell to Childhood*

Louise Kaplan's description of the passage to adulthood both in contemporary and earlier societies defines adolescence as a period of growth. According to Kaplan, this period of growth allows each individual to learn to represent the most characteristic and the best qualities of each society. After reading Louise Kaplan's "Adolescence: The Farewell to Childhood," Raymonde Carroll's "Parents and Children," David Jackson's "One of the Boys," and Judith Ortiz Cofer's "The Looking-Glass Shame," think about what types of adults British, French, and Puerto Rican societies appear to value. Then write a paper that suggests how Kaplan would respond to the processes shaping adults in each society, justifying your analysis in terms of the theory she presents.

To write this paper, you will need to look closely at each reading to identify the adult behavior that each society wants to encourage. These writers indicate a sense of understanding this model when they describe behavior that wins adult approval. You can also find a sense of what constitutes "virtuous," or valued, behavior in the conflicts the adolescents experience as they try to adapt to their society's norms. After you have established the values apparent in each society's definition, explain how Kaplan would evaluate them.

Defining Women's Lives

*D*on't snort," said Mehri. "It wasn't your fate yet to get married, and it wasn't mine yet either, and we'll see what Turan's fate will be."

"Ah, fate . . ." said Tala, with a sigh like a sob.

"Fate, ha!" cried Mahin, "You know what I'll do with my fate? I'll pee on it." They all laughed.

—ERIKA FRIEDL, *A Betrothal, a Rape, and a Guess About Turan's Fate*

Although my scores are superb, the guidance counselor has recommended the secretarial track; when I protested, the conference with my parents was arranged. My mother's preference is clear: the secretarial track—college is for boys; I will need to make a "good living" until I marry and have children.

—MARIANNA DE MARCO TORGOVNICK,
On Being White, Female, and Born in Bensonhurst

She is defined and differentiated with reference to man and not he with reference to her; she is the incidental, the inessential as opposed to the essential. He is the Subject, he is the Absolute—she is the Other.

—SIMONE DE BEAUVOIR, *Introduction to* The Second Sex

127

In recent history, the roles of women in Western societies have been radically transformed, at least on the surface. The resurgence of feminism in the second half of the twentieth century contributed to women's awareness that traditional roles could be reshaped. Many women have entered traditionally male professions such as law and medicine. As if in response to Beauvoir's observation that men have controlled the present through their ability to write the past, feminist historians have redefined history in terms of women's often unrecognized contributions to sustaining daily life. Still, change has come more slowly in non-Western countries, and even in America, deeper inequalities persist. While some changes can be implemented through legislation, attitudes cannot be legislated. Change can, however, occur through other processes.

This chapter explores the social processes that define women in traditional ways, as well as women's ability to interact with those processes. It raises questions about the nature of gender roles by asking you to consider how traditional fixed roles are maintained and altered, and it looks at the ability of societies to "impose" behavior and the power women have to shape the conditions of their lives.

In "A Betrothal, a Rape, and a Guess About Turan's Fate," Erika Friedl transcribes the conversation of Iranian women in a village courtyard as they discuss the recent attack on their friend Turan. Their speculations about her "fate" establish that the guidelines for women's behavior vary in response to particular situations. Furthermore, their gathering shows how Iranian women participate in defining norms of acceptable behavior. In her essay "On Being White, Female, and Born in Bensonhurst," Marianna De Marco Torgovnick, whose own life did not follow the preordained pattern of a rigid social order, writes about the conditions of life in Bensonhurst when she was growing up. Finally, Simone de Beauvoir's introduction to a classic feminist text, *The Second Sex,* surveys the position of women after World War II and seeks to explain how women's role in society has evolved.

ERIKA FRIEDL

A Betrothal,
a Rape, and a Guess About
Turan's Fate

Erika Friedl is an anthropologist who spent over five years living in a rural Iranian village in order to study the lives of the women who live there. She published a number of scholarly articles based on the research she undertook during this time. Her research, which was supported by grants from the National Endowment for the Humanities, the Social Science Research Council, the Wenner-Gren Foundation for Anthropological Research, and Western Michigan University, provided the material for *Women of Deh Koh: Lives in an Iranian Village (1989)*.

Women of Deh Koh approaches its subject in a style totally different from that of traditional anthropological studies. In it, Friedl explains that although the available scientific and social analyses of Middle Eastern women are correct, they present a fragmented view of women because they "do not lend themselves easily to conveying the feeling of interconnectedness the people themselves feel as members of their culture." The narrative and dialogue format Friedl uses gives a fuller view of Iranian culture and results in a kind of experimental social science reporting, the effectiveness of which she firmly believes in.

The following selection is chapter six of *Women of Deh Koh*. The lively dialogue of several women focuses on a rape that took place in the village. It reveals their conceptions about the roles of men and women in their society, about proper behavior, and about the religious principles on which these are founded. "Deh Koh" is not an actual name; it merely means "mountain village," and it is used to guarantee anonymity to the women Friedl studied, as well as to indicate that this village is representative of many others in Iran.

ANIMATED DISCUSSIONS IN DEH KOH are polyphonic and contrapuntal. Everybody talks more or less simultaneously, indeed often seemingly to themselves in monologues interlaced with comments, responses, and questions flying in all directions. Rendering such conversation two-dimensionally in writing gives it a structure and logical sequence it does not really possess. It also levels the tonal quality and the volume—Mehri's screechy soprano and Tala's booming alto are assigned the same value on paper. This is a pity, but what is being said stands out a lot of clearer in print than in the chorus, and, besides, what is written cannot be argued away.

This was also Banu's opinion that warm afternoon in May on her shady, narrow verandah.

"A description of Abbas is being sent around in the whole area, a big poster, I know. My mother has seen it because brother Rahmat has one; she told me so herself this morning—all the revolutionary guards have it . . ."

"His photograph too?" Leila was leaning against a wooden pillar, fanning her broad, freckled face with her veil. "I would like to see one; I don't think I have ever seen Abbas."

"So what?" said Mahin, "a scoundrel." She snorted loudly.   5

There were five of them squatting on an old rug on the verandah of the small house behind Tamas's big courtyard. Notwithstanding appearances of extreme modesty and stone-walled seclusion, the dusty place had been the social center for the younger women of the neighborhood ever since Banu had moved there from her father's house as her cousin's wife. There was not really enough room for them in her uncle's (and father-in-law's) place, next to her own father's house—separated from it by a wall since her grandfather had died—especially after another son got married only a few months later. When their first son was born, her husband had invested his small savings in two adobe rooms surrounded by a wall outside the old house, in a corner left open by the odd angles of the old compound's yard walls. Living in the shadows of both parents had made that move acceptable for Banu although her husband was at home only rarely. At night, a cousin or sister or her grandmother often would keep her company, or else she went home to sleep. During the days neighbors dropped in regularly for no apparent reason. No one could say why it felt so good to sit with Banu on her small verandah, looking at the single scraggly walnut tree next to the barely tray-sized pool, the dusty yard, and the oppressively close walls all around it, but it did. True, hers was a safe place for unmarried girls like Mahin, because Banu's husband was working in town and no other man was living there or was likely to show up unexpectedly. Secluded behind the massive wall, even the most careful woman could let her veil-wrap slide down safely without having to fear embarrassment or rebuke. True also that Banu was easy to look at: small limbed, light skinned, with a broad mouth that smiled easily in a delicate face dominated by large eyes of light brown color under straight black brows. She was well liked by all, respected, lively, full of stories and good sense, a woman who had gone to school for eight years and knew things without being uppity about it. But whatever the reason, there were never any lonely afternoons for her.

That day, Mehri—prim, slow, and tightlipped—had brought her spindle and fleece over from her own house to escape one of Begom's bouts of quarrelsomeness. Leila had dropped in on her way home from school. Mahin, the oldest unmarried girl in the neighborhood—straight backed and with eyebrows perpetually arched, giving her small face an expression of mocking disapproval—was cleaning rice on a tray for the dinner she would cook later. She lived only a small apricot orchard and a bramble hedge away and was a frequent visitor on Banu's porch. Tala, on one of her extended visits at her father's place two courtyards up the hill, was working with fast, big hands embroidering a huge red vase on a pillowcase, and Banu herself was stitching a boldly colored zig-zag pattern on a bag made of a piece of sacking. Presently, work stopped. The topic of conversation was absorbing.

"Turan will have to do something, for sure," Mahin was saying, letting rice idly flow through her fingers.

"Yes, but what? What?" said Tala fiercely. When she spoke, everything on her moved—eyes, head, arms; her whole body was in it, and whiffs of very sweet perfume rose around her.

"Well, she was his fiancée, after all, ever since she was *this* small," said   10
Banu, indicating a midgety size. "She told me herself, in school. We were together in school until I got married."

"She is no longer his fiancée," said Leila. "Her people broke it off when Abbas lost his head over Setara and married her instead of Turan. A lovesick man . . ."

"Scoundrel," Mahin hissed, tossing her head.

". . . a lovesick man is worse than a drunkard, I say," Leila finished her sentence, throwing up both her arms. Her black veil-wrap slid down into the dirt below the verandah.

"It was Setara's fault," said Mehri. "I know because Huri told us, and Huri knows because she is a neighbor of Setara. Setara made eyes at him. Shameless widows! He never said he did not want to marry Turan. He wanted them both."

"The dirty-eyed bandit! Well, her people said no, and Turan said no, and   15
good for her." Mahin was emphatic. She tossed her head again and plunked the rice tray behind her on the floor. "Even Setara divorced him when he was thrown in jail a year ago because he was in a car-theft gang."

"That's when he went after Turan again, so she told me, although her people returned all the gifts—imagine, everything: clothes, jewelry, rice, butterfat, everything." Banu was shaking her head in wonderment. "They really did it correctly. Our religious law says . . ."

"Even Setara said Turan was lucky not to have married him," said Mahin. "She went to Turan's people and told them herself, and wept."

"They even made a pilgrimage to the shrine in Shiraz. I know, because my mother was on the same bus with them," said Tala.

"He wanted her anyway. Bandar's wife Aftab told me—you know, she is a cousin of Abbas, so she knows—'Mehri,' she said to me, 'they still owe him a refrigerator and a sack of rice.' That's what they are fighting about. But Abbas wanted her anyway, and after Setara divorced him they should have gone through with it." Mehri, screwing up her lips in disapproval, gave her spindle a decisive twirl, threw it down on the ground below the low verandah with an expert flick, and twisted some feet of yarn out of the fleece wrapped around her right arm.

Mahin produced a grand gesture of contempt which scared a loudly protest- 20
ing chicken right across the abandoned tray with rice. "A thief, a jailbird . . ." she cried.

"People say her brothers said she shouldn't go to school any longer," said Mehri. "It is a long way to school here, all the way from Mahmudabad. Dangerous. An hour at least."

"He should have been kept in jail," said Mahin.

"And they were right, I say, about her walking to school, with him just out of jail. She should have stayed home. Nothing would have happened," said Mehri with conviction. "Now, my own brothers never would have let me . . ."

"She was not alone, though, ever. It was *his* fault," cried Tala. "He is rotten . . ."

"Usually there are four or five girls from Mahmudabad coming to school 25
here. They always walk together. But it was final exam and Turan and this other girl were out later than the others. Just their bad luck," Banu said. She was fanning her baby, who was sleeping next to her on the ample folds of her skirts with her rice-sack bag. The sacking was stamped *Louisiana*. "And our religious law says . . ."

"A girl shouldn't go to school if it is so far away. It just shows," said Mehri. "My brothers . . ."

Mahin snorted twice.

"It is his fault, though," Tala said again. "He followed them."

"They were walking fast too, through the lonely wilderness there," said Leila, with a faraway look on her face.

"He was waiting for them down by the bridge," said Mehri "Maybe he 30
just wanted to talk to her. She was his fiancée. Maybe . . ."

"But if he wanted no harm, why did he have to crack her head with a rock?" cried Tala.

"I am sure he wanted to kill her," said Mahin darkly, wagging a finger at Mehri.

"He must be a strong fellow," said Leila, dreamy eyed. "I have never seen him, though."

"He didn't crack her head either. He only tied her hands and feet with a rope—and why would he do this if it was not that he wanted her?" Mehri, challenge in her eye, was stabbing the rug with her spindle. "He could have killed her, but he didn't."

"Really strong, a devil . . ."

"Nothing but rocks and trees around there, not a soul, and the brook is so noisy, one can't hear one's own voice . . ." said Banu sadly.

"He jumped out from behind a rock . . . oh, dear me, poor Turan!" Tala shook herself violently, and another cloud of perfume spread around her.

"The people say the girl who was with her—I mean, I would be scared to walk there practically alone, really I would—people say she passed out from shock," said Leila.

"No, no, she ran away . . ."

"It was *her* head he cracked with a rock . . ."

"She hid behind a tree . . ."

"Coward," cried Mahin.

"Anyway," said Leila, "she wasn't there when he bound Turan or whatever, you know. I mean, they say he did it with a finger . . . imagine!" Mahin raised her eyebrows higher yet and turned her face to look up into the walnut tree. Mehri hid a red face behind her veil and giggled. Tala shot Leila a nervous glance.

"The police doctor says she is all right, she is still a virgin," said Banu.

Mahin snorted loudly. "And how does *he* know?"

"It was a woman doctor who examined her," said Banu. She shooed another chicken away from Mahin's rice and spread the end of Mahin's dropped veil over the tray.

"With a finger . . . I mean, the things that happen in this world . . . and she was maybe screaming and yelling all the time," Leila said, her faced flushed.

"She was gagged," said Mehri

"How do you know? Maybe she passed out too. I am sure she did. I would," said Tala.

"The two men who found her had heard her yell. Two men from Mahmudabad. I don't know who. Abbas would have finished his job otherwise, but he had no time," said Leila.

"Maybe he would have killed her," said Tala.

Banu clucked "tsk, tsk, tsk," and shook her head.

"The son of a bitch," Mahin said, with feeling.

"Well, the other girl had left, and he was alone with her . . ." Leila filled a pause with heavy meaning.

"Men are dirty," said Tala.

"When Abbas saw the two other men coming, he took off into the mountains," said Banu, "but they recognized him. He had a gun, too."

"I have never seen him," Leila said again. "He must be awful to look at."

"The whole family is bad," said Mehri, "just like this beggar Aftab and her people. Really lightweight, no honor, no substance." Her long face was pinched with offended righteousness.

"If he is anything like his brother, he has a dark face, huh," said Leila.

"They are all sort of bad in Mahmudabad. Two of his brothers are in jail still because of the stolen cars," Mehri went on.   60

"No, Yusuf says they broke into a bank or a store or something like this," said Tala. "It was not only cars."

"Cursed semen. All his children will be bad . . . seven generations," said Mahin.

"In the Koran . . ." Banu tried.

"Well, sometimes the children of bad fathers turn out well. So maybe, if Turan would marry him after all, and had children . . ." Tala's loud voice was trailing off. She swatted at some flies with her red vase.

"Setara says he has money stashed away someplace, from his thievery,"   65
said Mehri. "It was never found."

"Unlawful money, cursed money," Mahin said.

At this point Leila's little girl appeared in the narrow court gate in dirty cotton pants and a pink shirt too big for her. She ran up to her mother, just about disappeared in the many folds of her wide skirts, and whispered, "Grandmother says—she says come home right away, she has something to tell you."

Leila murmured something like, "The black death on the old woman." Aloud, readjusting her daughter's scarf over her matted hair, she said, "Instantly, my sweetheart, right away—go tell your grandmother I am on my way. Now go, hurry, run, my dear, my life, run run!" The little girl left reluctantly and slowly. "Old woman!" Leila murmured again, defiantly. Fingers spread, she moved her hand in the direction of her house in a quick gesture of contempt. "Humph," she said.

But the others had gone on. "Abbas isn't poor," Mehri was saying, "and if it is her fate, she'll marry him."

"She'll have to do something," said Mahin. There was a moment of si-   70
lence. Somebody sighed. Banu unhappily was looking at her sleeping baby under her veil. The sun had gone low enough to illuminate the cooking pots stacked on the rim of the pool. Two shovels appeared above the wall, moving along at a good speed on the shoulders of invisible men in the alley. Leila followed them with her eyes and started to fish for her veil.

"I guess," Banu said at length, "she'll probably have to kill herself . . . although the religion . . . it is a sin . . . but then again . . ."

"Poor thing," Mahin said.

There was more silence. Sparrows were twittering around the glistening water. Tala started to shake her head. "No, no," she said, finally, "no, she is innocent. They'll execute him, for sure. They have to—the revolutionary guards will shoot him. He is guilty . . ."

"They don't even have him," said Banu. "It has been, what? Four days or five now. Who knows where he is? He fled; he has taken to the mountains, maybe he is in Iraq by now or with the rebels in Kurdistan."

"Imagine if he were still around and you would be sitting at home, alone- 75 like, and he would come through the door . . . huh, I would faint right away," said Leila, wide eyed.

"You don't even know what he looks like, you would be very polite to him," said Tala.

"Huh, huh!" cried Leila, shuddering.

"Aftab says Turan's brothers are after him with guns," said Mehri.

"So, big deal. She has only two, and one is not older than twelve or so. A lot of help, this!" said Banu. "Besides, it is a matter for the judge, for the Islamic Court . . ."

"And she says his people and her people have a bitter fight because they 80 blame each other for this mess," said Mehri.

A little boy of about three, dressed in nothing more elaborate than a short, dirty T-shirt and big plastic sandals, was strolling in through the gate. Tala was the first to spot him. "Hamid, Hamid," she shouted at him, "run home quickly or else the rooster will get your little you-know-what!" Banu turned and smiled. It was her nephew. "Look, look, watch out for the rooster, here he comes!" Hamid looked at the rooster and the women, picked up a pebble as a weapon, but then decided it wasn't a good time to visit Aunt Banu after all and ran out. Tala and Leila giggled, Mahin grunted.

"Imagine," said Leila, "imagine if Hamid would have been Abbas . . . terrible!"

"People say somebody saw him in Shiraz . . ."

"I have heard they caught him on the other side of the mountain . . ."

"No, I told you, all the revolutionary guard posts in the area got pictures 85 of him and a description, so they all can look out for him," said Banu. "He has disappeared."

"But if they catch him they'll execute him," said Tala, "for sure!"

"If. . . ." Mahin said, darkly.

Banu's baby stretched. Flies were buzzing. Leila's little daughter reappeared in the doorway. Leaning against the gate, she watched both the women and the lane, blowing huge gum bubbles.

"If she is pregnant she'll kill herself, she'll have to," said Banu. "Although strictly by the rules of our Prophet . . ." Mahin was nodding emphatically.

"But it was only a finger—she is still a virgin, she'll get a husband, for 90 sure," said Leila. "One can't get pregnant with only a . . . well, I mean!"

"No way, never," cried Tala, "She won't get a husband after this. For sure they'll execute him, or at least they'll beat him up awfully. Remember what they did with Heidar Afghani?"

"They'll flog him publicly and then they'll let him go. And then what?" asked Leila.

"Turan should flee, go someplace," Mahin said, but this suggestion was met with noises of doubt.

"You are crazy," said Mehri. "Where can a girl like her go?"

"But what can she do here?" Mahin was passionate. "Just pretend there   95
was nothing? People won't let her. Her people won't even let her finish school after this, I am sure."

"Suicide," Banu murmured, "poison, like my stepmother . . . and last year the miller's wife . . ."

"What does she herself say?" asked Tala.

"She says she won't marry him, no matter what," Mehri said.

"Yes, I know," added Banu. "My brother Rahmat says the judge told her she has to marry Abbas as soon as they catch him. They'll force him, too. She really has no choice but to . . ."

"Force! Brutality! Injustice!" cried Mahin. Banu's baby stirred again and   100
started to whine. Banu patted his back.

"Aftab says his people say they no longer want Turan," said Mehri, "but . . ."

"Rahmat says the judge . . ."

". . . but anyway, if it is her fate to marry, she'll marry," Mehri continued.

"Besides, they'll make it worth her while, for sure," said Tala. "They'll give her a handsome gift, and a big golden pendant with 'Allah' engraved on it, and a nice wristwatch, and in the end she'll agree; what else can she do?"

"If he is so crazy about her anyway . . ." said Leila.   105

"They'll beat her up at home until she says yes, just like my folks tried it with me. For a golden 'Allah' and a thousand Toman they are ready to sell a girl!" Mahin's voice was gloomy. She snorted again and picked up her tray.

"Don't snort," said Mehri. "It wasn't your fate yet to get married, and it wasn't mine yet either, and we'll see what Turan's fate will be."

"Ah, fate . . ." said Tala, with a sigh like a sob.

"Fate, ha!" cried Mahin. "You know what I'll do with my fate? I'll pee on it." They all laughed.

Banu's baby started to bawl and Leila's daughter in the doorway got impa-   110
tient. "Mother," she shouted, "Hey, listen, Mother, Grandmother says . . ."

For the moment, concern for Turan's fate gave way to the demands of a waning afternoon.

Considerations

1. Friedl considers her choice of using conversational narrative an important feature of her book. Do you think your perception of either Turan's story or the village women's reaction to it would be different if she had presented the situation in an expository form, without dialogue and dramatization? How?

2. One of the women, Mehri, agrees with Turan's brothers that Turan should not have walked to school knowing that Abbas was out of jail. She stresses that Turan "should have stayed home" (para. 23). What does her statement and other information in the essay tell you about the sharing of space in this community? Which spaces might be considered "male" spaces? Which spaces might be called "female" spaces? What are the reasons behind such divisions?

Invitation to Write

Friedl's narrative provides a glimpse into the lives of Iranian women living in rural areas. The women react differently to Turan's situation and propose different solutions; it seems that a consensus is hard to reach because they have difficulty in referring to what has happened to Turan as rape. While they find Abbas's behavior despicable, they also seem to find him fascinating and attractive. Write an essay in which you explore the reasons for the women's difficulties in assessing the nature of Abbas's violence against Turan. Compare the women's indecision with the difficulties our own society has in defining rape and show the relationship between the concept of rape and what society deems to be proper behavior for women.

Connections

By presenting male-female relationships in an Iranian village from the women's point of view, Friedl manages to show what that society expects from both females and males. David Gilmore's essay "Performative Excellence: Circum-Mediterranean" (p. 190) examines the expectations placed on men, primarily in Spain. How do Gilmore's examples compare to those we can find in Turan's story? Using the concept of "masculinity" developed by Gilmore, write an essay in which you define the male role in the Iranian village portrayed by Friedl. Abbas is certainly the basic example of masculine behavior, but the idea of "masculinity" can also be deduced from other comments the women make about men in general and about themselves.

MARIANNA DE MARCO TORGOVNICK

On Being White,
Female, and Born in Bensonhurst

Marianna De Marco Torgovnick was born in 1949 and grew up in
the predominantly Italian-American neighborhood of Bensonhurst,
New York. She has published books on literature, society, and the
arts, including *Closure in the Novel* (1981) and *The Visual Arts, Pic-*
torialism, and the Novel: James, Lawrence, and Woolf (1985). Her
most recent work, *Gone Primitive: Savage Intellects, Modern Lives*
(1990), reveals the relation between the concept of primitivism, colonialism, and sexuality by analyzing works of fiction as well as biographical and anthropological texts. At present, she is writing a
sequel to this book, as well as a collection of essays that combine
autobiographical material with cultural criticism. Her essays have
appeared in *South Atlantic Quarterly, Partisan Review,* and *Art*
Forum. Torgovnick plans to continue writing for both a general public and a scholarly audience. Currently, she teaches nineteenth- and
twentieth-century literature at Duke University.

The following essay first appeared in *Partisan Review* and was
reprinted in *The Best American Essays 1991.* "On Being White, Female, and Born in Bensonhurst" provides a good example of the way
personal history can be used to formulate cultural criticism. She
chooses to discuss those aspects of her experience that make her representative of an entire category of Americans caught between a distaste for their parent's prejudices and an undeniable gratitude to
these parents. By revealing their complexity, Torgovnick upsets our
normal perception of racial relations. Literally, she urges us not to see
the world in black and white.

T HE MAFIA PROTECTS THE NEIGHBORHOOD, our fathers say, with that peculiar satisfied pride with which law-abiding Italian Americans refer to the
Mafia: The Mafia protects the neighborhood from "the coloreds." In the
fifties and sixties, I heard that information repeated, in whispers, in neighborhood parks and in the yard at school in Bensonhurst. The same information
probably passes today in the parks (the word now "blacks," not "coloreds")

but perhaps no longer in the schoolyards. From buses each morning, from neighborhoods outside Bensonhurst, spill children of all colors and backgrounds—American black, West Indian black, Hispanic, and Asian. But the blacks are the only ones especially marked for notice. Bensonhurst is no longer entirely protected from "the coloreds." But in a deeper sense, at least for Italian Americans, Bensonhurst never changes.

Italian-American life continues pretty much as I remember it. Families with young children live side by side with older couples whose children are long gone to the suburbs. Many of those families live "down the block" from the last generation or, sometimes still, live together with parents or grandparents. When a young family leaves, as sometimes happens, for Long Island or New Jersey or (very common now) for Staten Island, another arrives, without any special effort being required, from Italy or a poorer neighborhood in New York. They fill the neat but anonymous houses that make up the mostly tree-lined streets: two-, three-, or four-family houses for the most part (this is a working, lower– to middle–middle-class area, and people need rents to pay mortgages), with a few single-family or small apartment houses tossed in at random. Tomato plants, fig trees, and plaster madonnas often decorate small but well-tended yards which face out onto the street; the grassy front lawn, like the grassy back yard, is relatively uncommon.

Crisscrossing the neighborhood and marking out ethnic zones—Italian, Irish, and Jewish, for the most part, though there are some Asian Americans and some people (usually Protestants) called simply Americans—are the great shopping streets: Eighty-sixth Street, Kings Highway, Bay Parkway, Eighteenth Avenue, each with its own distinctive character. On Eighty-sixth Street, crowds bustle along sidewalks lined with ample, packed fruit stands. Women wheeling shopping carts or baby strollers check the fruit carefully, piece by piece, and often bargain with the dealer, cajoling for a better price or letting him know that the vegetables, this time, aren't up to snuff. A few blocks down, the fruit stands are gone and the streets are lined with clothing and record shops, mobbed by teenagers. Occasionally, the el rumbles overhead, a few stops out of Coney Island on its way to the city, a trip of around one hour.

On summer nights, neighbors congregate on stoops which during the day serve as play yards for children. Air-conditioning exists everywhere in Bensonhurst, but people still sit outside in the summer—to supervise children, to gossip, to stare at strangers. "*Buona sera,*" I say, or "*Buona notte,*" as I am ritually presented to Sal and Lily and Louie, the neighbors sitting on the stoop. "*Grazie,*" I say when they praise my children or my appearance. It's the only time I use Italian, which I learned at high school, although my parents (both second-generation Italian Americans, my father Sicilian, my mother Calabrian) speak it at home to each other but never to me or my brother. My accent is the Tuscan accent taught at school, not the southern Italian accents of my parents and the neighbors.

It's important to greet and please the neighbors; any break in this deco-   5
rum would seriously offend and aggrieve my parents. For the neighbors are
the stern arbiters of conduct in Bensonhurst. Does Mary keep a clean house?
Did Gina wear black long enough after her mother's death? Was the food
good at Tony's wedding? The neighbors know and pass judgment. Any news
of family scandal (my brother's divorce, for example) provokes from my
mother the agonized words: "But what will I *tell* people?" I sometimes collaborate in devising a plausible script.

A large sign on the church I attended as a child sums up for me the ethos
of Bensonhurst. The sign urges contributions to the church building fund with
the message, in huge letters: "EACH YEAR ST. SIMON AND JUDE SAVES THIS
NEIGHBORHOOD ONE MILLION DOLLARS IN TAXES." Passing the church on the
way from largely Jewish and middle-class Sheepshead Bay (where my in-laws
live) to Bensonhurst, year after year, my husband and I look for the sign and
laugh at the crass level of its pitch, its utter lack of attention to things spiritual. But we also understand exactly the values it represents.

In the summer of 1989, my parents were visiting me at my house in Durham, North Carolina, from the apartment in Bensonhurst where they have
lived since 1942; three small rooms, rent-controlled, floor clean enough to eat
off, every corner and crevice known and organized. My parents' longevity in
a single apartment is unusual even for Bensonhurst, but not that unusual;
many people live for decades in the same place or more within a ten-block
radius. When I lived in this apartment, there were four rooms; one has since
been ceded to a demanding landlord, one of the various landlords who have
haunted my parents' life and must always be appeased lest the ultimate
threat—removal from the rent-controlled apartment—be brought into play.
That summer, during their visit, on August 23 (my younger daughter's birthday) a shocking, disturbing, news report issued from the neighborhood: It had
become another Howard Beach.

Three black men, walking casually through the streets at night, were attacked by a group of whites. One was shot dead, mistaken, as it turned out,
for another black youth who was dating a white, although part-Hispanic, girl
in the neighborhood. It all made sense: the crudely protective men, expecting
to see a black arriving at the girl's house and overreacting; the rebellious girl
dating the outsider boy; the black dead as a sacrifice to the feelings of the
neighborhood.

I might have felt outrage, I might have felt guilt or shame, I might have
despised the people among whom I grew up. In a way I felt all four emotions
when I heard the news. I expect that there were many people in Bensonhurst
who felt the same rush of emotions. But mostly I felt that, given the set-up,
this was the only way things could have happened. I detested the racial killing,
but I also understood it. Those streets, which should be public property available to all, belong to the neighborhood. All the people sitting on the stoops on

August 23 knew that as well as they knew their own names. The black men walking through probably knew it too—though their casual walk sought to deny the fact that, for the neighbors, even the simple act of blacks walking through the neighborhood would be seen as invasion.

Italian Americans in Bensonhurst are notable for their cohesiveness and provinciality; the slightest pressure turns those qualities into prejudice and racism. Their cohesiveness is based on the stable economic and ethical level that links generation to generation, keeping Italian Americans in Bensonhurst and the Italian-American community alive as the Jewish-American community of my youth is no longer alive. (Its young people routinely moved to the suburbs or beyond and were never replaced, so that Jews in Bensonhurst today are almost all very old people.) Their provinciality results from the Italian Americans' devotion to jealous distinctions and discriminations. Jews are suspect, but (the old Italian women admit) "they make good husbands." The Irish are okay, fellow Catholics, but not really "like us"; they make bad husbands because they drink and gamble. Even Italians come in varieties, by region (Sicilian, Calabrian, Neapolitan, very rarely any region further north) and by history in this country (the newly arrived and ridiculed "gaffoon" versus the second or third generation).

Bensonhurst is a neighborhood dedicated to believing that its values are the only values; it tends toward certain forms of inertia. When my parents visit me in Durham, they routinely take chairs from the kitchen and sit out on the lawn in front of the house, not on the chairs on the back deck; then they complain that the streets are too quiet. When they walk around my neighborhood (these De Marcos who have friends named Travaglianti and Occhipinti), they look at the mailboxes and report that my neighbors have strange names. Prices at my local supermarket are compared, in unbelievable detail, with prices on Eighty-sixth Street. Any rearrangement of my kitchen since their last visit is registered and criticized. Difference is not only unwelcome, it is unacceptable. One of the most characteristic things my mother ever said was in response to my plans for renovating my house in Durham. When she heard my plans, she looked around, crossed her arms, and said, "If it was me, I wouldn't change nothing." My father once asked me to level with him about a Jewish boyfriend who lived in a different part of the neighborhood, reacting to his Jewishness, but even more to the fact that he often wore Bermuda shorts: "Tell me something, Marianna. Is he a Communist?" Such are the standards of normality and political thinking in Bensonhurst.

I often think that one important difference between Italian Americans in New York neighborhoods like Bensonhurst and Italian Americans elsewhere is that the others moved on—to upstate New York, to Pennsylvania, to the Midwest. Though they frequently settled in communities of fellow Italians, they did move on. Bensonhurst Italian Americans seem to have felt that one large move, over the ocean, was enough. Future moves could be only local:

from the Lower East Side, for example, to Brooklyn, or from one part of Brooklyn to another. Bensonhurst was for many of these people the summa of expectations. If their America were to be drawn as a *New Yorker* cover, Manhattan itself would be tiny in proportion to Bensonhurst and to its satellites, Staten Island, New Jersey, and Long Island.

"Oh, no," my father says when he hears the news about the shooting. Though he still refers to blacks as "coloreds," he's not really a racist and is upset that this innocent youth was shot in his neighborhood. He has no trouble acknowledging the wrongness of the death. But then, like all the news accounts, he turns to the fact, repeated over and over, that the blacks had been on their way to look at a used car when they encountered the hostile mob of whites. The explanation is right before him but, "Yeah," he says, still shaking his head. "yeah, but what were they *doing* there? They didn't belong."

Over the next few days, the television news is even more disturbing. Rows of screaming Italians lining the streets, most of them looking like my relatives. I focus especially on one woman who resembles almost completely my mother: stocky but not fat, mid-seventies but well preserved, full face showing only minimal wrinkles, ample steel-gray hair neatly if rigidly coifed in a modified beehive hairdo left over from the sixties. She shakes her fist at the camera, protesting the arrest of the Italian-American youths in the neighborhood and the incursion of more blacks into the neighborhood, protesting the shooting. I look a little nervously at my mother (the parent I resemble), but she has not even noticed the woman and stares impassively at the television.

What has Bensonhurst to do with what I teach today and write? Why did   15
I need to write about this killing in Bensonhurst, but not in the manner of a news account or a statistical sociological analysis? Within days of hearing the news, I began to plan this essay, to tell the world what I knew, even though I was aware that I could publish the piece only someplace my parents or their neighbors would never see or hear about it. I sometimes think that I looked around from my baby carriage and decided that someday, the sooner the better, I would get out of Bensonhurst. Now, much to my surprise, Bensonhurst—the antipodes of the intellectual life I sought, the least interesting of places—had become a respectable intellectual topic. People would be willing to hear about Bensonhurst—and all by the dubious virtue of a racial killing in the streets.

The story as I would have to tell it would be to some extent a class narrative: about the difference between working class and upper middle class, dependence and a profession, Bensonhurst and a posh suburb. But I need to make it clear that I do not imagine myself as writing from a position of enormous self-satisfaction, or even enormous distance. You can take the girl out of Bensonhurst (that much is clear), but you may not be able to take Bensonhurst out of the girl. And upward mobility is not the essence of the story, though it is an important marker and symbol.

In Durham today, I live in a twelve-room house surrounded by an acre of trees. When I sit on my back deck on summer evenings, no houses are visible through the trees. I have a guaranteed income, teaching English at an excellent university, removed by my years of education from the fundamental economic and social conditions of Bensonhurst. The one time my mother ever expressed pleasure at my work was when I got tenure, what my father still calls, with no irony intended, "ten years." "What does that mean?" my mother asked when she heard the news. Then she reached back into her experience as a garment worker, subject to periodic layoffs. "Does it mean they can't fire you just for nothing and can't lay you off?" When I said that was exactly what it means, she said, "Very good. Congratulations. That's *wonderful.*" I was free from the *padrones,* from the network of petty anxieties that had formed, in large part, her very existence. Of course, I wasn't really free of petty anxieties: Would my salary increase keep pace with my colleagues', how would my office compare, would this essay be accepted for publication, am I happy? The line between these worries and my mother's is the line between the working class and the upper middle class.

But getting out of Bensonhurst never meant to me a big house, or nice clothes, or a large income. And it never meant feeling good about looking down on what I left behind or hiding my background. Getting out of Bensonhurst meant freedom—to experiment, to grow, to change. It also meant knowledge in some grand, abstract way. All the material possessions I have acquired, I acquired simply along the way—and for the first twelve years after I left Bensonhurst, I chose to acquire almost nothing at all. Now, as I write about the neighborhood, I recognize that although I've come far in physical and material distance, the emotional distance is harder to gauge. Bensonhurst has everything to do with who I am and even with what I write. Occasionally I get reminded of my roots, of their simultaneously choking and nutritive power.

Scene one: It's after a lecture at Duke, given by a visiting professor from Princeton. The lecture was long and a little dull and—bad luck—I had agreed to be one of the people having dinner with the lecturer afterward. We settle into our table at the restaurant: this man, me, the head of the comparative literature program (also a professor of German), and a couple I like who teach French, the husband at my university, the wife at one nearby. The conversation is sluggish, as it often is when a stranger, like the visiting professor, has to be assimilated into a group, so I ask the visitor from Princeton a question to personalize things a bit. "How did you get interested in what you do? What made you become a professor of German?" The man gets going and begins talking about how it was really unlikely that he, a nice Jewish boy from Bensonhurst, would have chosen, in the mid-fifties, to study German. Unlikely indeed.

I remember seeing *Judgment at Nuremberg* in a local movie theater and 20 having a woman in the row in back of me get hysterical when some clips of a concentration camp were shown. "My God," she screamed in a European accent, "look at what they did. Murderers, MURDERERS!"—and she had to be supported out by her family. I couldn't see, in the dark, whether her arm bore the neatly tattooed numbers that the arms of some of my classmates' parents did—and that always affected me with a thrill of horror. Ten years older than me, this man had lived more directly through those feelings, lived with and *among* those feelings. The first chance he got, he raced to study in Germany. I myself have twice chosen not to visit Germany, but I understand his impulse to identify with the Other as a way of getting out of the neighborhood.

At the dinner, the memory about the movie pops into my mind but I pick up instead on the Bensonhurst—I'm also from there, but Italian American. Like a flash, he asks something I haven't been asked in years: Where did I go to high school and (a more common question) what was my maiden name? I went to Lafayette High School, I say, and my name was De Marco. Everything changes: his facial expression, his posture, his accent, his voice. "Soo, Dee Maw-ko," he says, "dun anything wrong at school today—got enny pink slips? Wanna meet me later at the parrk or maybe bye the Baye?" When I laugh, recognizing the stereotype that Italians get pink slips for misconduct at school and the notorious chemistry between Italian women and Jewish men, he says, back in this Princetonian voice: "My God, for a minute I felt like I was turning into a werewolf."

It's odd that although I can remember almost nothing else about this man—his face, his body type, even his name—I remember this lapse into his "real self" with enormous vividness. I am especially struck by how easily he was able to slip into the old, generic Brooklyn accent. I myself have no memory of ever speaking in that accent, though I also have no memory of trying not to speak it, except for teaching myself, carefully, to say "oil" rather than "earl."

But the surprises aren't over. The female French professor, whom I have known for at least five years, reveals for the first time that she is also from the neighborhood, though she lived across the other side of Kings Highway, went to a different, more elite high school, and was Irish American. Three of six professors, sitting at an eclectic vegetarian restaurant in Durham, all from Bensonhurst—a neighborhood where (I swear) you couldn't get the *New York Times* at any of the local stores.

Scene two: I still live in Bensonhurst. I'm waiting for my parents to return from a conference at my school, where they've been summoned to discuss my transition from elementary to junior high school. I am already a full year younger than any of my classmates, having skipped a grade, a not uncommon occurrence for "gifted" youngsters. Now the school is worried about putting me in an accelerated track through junior high, since that would make me two years younger. A compromise was reached: I would be put in a special program for gifted children, but one that took three, not two, years. It sounds okay.

Three years later, another wait. My parents have gone to school this time   25
to make another decision. Lafayette High School has three tracks: academic, for potentially college-bound kids; secretarial, mostly for Italian-American girls or girls with low aptitude-test scores (the high school is de facto segregated, so none of the tracks is as yet racially coded, though they are coded by ethnic group and gender); and vocational, mostly for boys with the same attributes, ethnic or intellectual. Although my scores are superb, the guidance counselor has recommended the secretarial track; when I protested, the conference with my parents was arranged. My mother's preference is clear: the secretarial track—college is for boys; I will need to make a "good living" until I marry and have children. My father also prefers the secretarial track, but he wavers, half proud of my aberrantly high scores, half worried. I press the attack, saying that if I were Jewish I would have been placed, without question, in the academic track. I tell him I have sneaked a peek at my files and know that my IQ is at genius level. I am allowed to insist on the change into the academic track.

What I did, and I was ashamed of it even then, was to play upon my father's competitive feelings with Jews: His daughter could and should be as good as theirs. In the bank where he was a messenger, and at the insurance company where he worked in the mailroom, my father worked with Jews, who were almost always his immediate supervisors. Several times, my father was offered the supervisory job but turned it down after long conversations with my mother about the dangers of making a change, the difficulty of giving orders to friends. After her work in a local garment shop, after cooking dinner and washing the floor each night, my mother often did piecework making bows; sometimes I would help her for fun, but it *wasn't* fun, and I was free to stop while she continued for long, tedious hours to increase the family income. Once a week, her part-time boss, Dave, would come by to pick up the boxes of bows. Short, round, with his shirttails sloppily tucked into his pants and a cigar almost always dangling from his lips, Dave was stereotyped Jew but also, my parents always said, a nice guy, a decent man.

Years later, similar choices come up, and I show the same assertiveness I showed with my father, the same ability to deal for survival, but tinged with Bensonhurst caution. Where will I go to college? Not to Brooklyn College, the flagship of the city system—I know that, but don't press the invitations I have received to apply to prestigious schools outside of New York. The choice comes down to two: Barnard, which gives me a full scholarship, minus five hundred dollars a year that all scholarship students are expected to contribute from summer earnings, or New York University, which offers me one thousand dollars above tuition as a bribe. I waver. My parents stand firm: They are already losing money by letting me go to college; I owe it to the family to contribute the extra thousand dollars plus my summer earnings. Besides, my mother adds, harping on a favorite theme, there are no boys at Barnard; at NYU I'm more likely to meet someone to marry. I go to NYU and do marry in my senior year, but he is someone I didn't meet at college. I was secretly relieved, I now think (though at the time I thought I was just placating my parents' conventionality), to be out of the marriage sweepstakes.

The first boy who ever asked me for a date was Robert Lubitz, in eighth grade: tall and skinny to my average height and teenage chubbiness. I turned him down, thinking we would make a ridiculous couple. Day after day, I cast my eyes at stylish Juliano, the class cutup; day after day, I captivated Robert Lubitz. Occasionally, one of my brother's Italian-American friends would ask me out, and I would go, often to ROTC dances. My specialty was making political remarks so shocking that the guys rarely asked me again. After a while I recognized destiny: The Jewish man was a passport out of Bensonhurst. I, of course, did marry a Jewish man, who gave me my freedom and, very important, helped remove me from the expectations of Bensonhurst. Though raised in a largely Jewish section of Brooklyn, he had gone to college in Ohio and knew how important it was, as he put it, "to get past the Brooklyn Bridge." We met on neutral ground, in Central Park, at a performance of Shakespeare. The Jewish-Italian marriage is a common enough catastrophe in Bensonhurst for my parents to have accepted, even welcomed, mine—though my parents continued to treat my husband like an outsider for the first twenty years ("Now Marianna. Here's what's going on with you brother. But don't tell-a you husband").

Along the way I make other choices, more fully marked by Bensonhurst cautiousness. I am attracted to journalism or the arts as careers, but the prospects for income seem iffy. I choose instead to imagine myself as a teacher. Only the availability of NDEA fellowships when I graduate, with their generous terms, propels me from high school teaching (a thought I never much relished) to college teaching (which seems like a brave new world). Within the college teaching profession, I choose offbeat specializations: the novel, interdisciplinary approaches (not something clear and clubby like Milton or the eighteenth century). Eventually I write the book I like best about primitive others as they figure within Western obsessions: My identification with "the Other," my sense of being "Other," surfaces at last. I avoid all mentoring structures for a long time but accept aid when it comes to me on the basis of what I perceive to be merit. I'm still, deep down, Italian-American Bensonhurst, though by this time I'm a lot of other things as well.

Scene three: In the summer of 1988, a little more than a year before the shooting in Bensonhurst, my father woke up trembling and in what appeared to be a fit. Hospitalization revealed that he had a pocket of blood on his brain, a frequent consequence of falls for older people. About a year earlier, I had stayed home, using my children as an excuse, when my aunt, my father's 30 much-loved sister, died, missing her funeral; only now does my mother tell me how much my father resented my taking his suggestion that I stay home. Now, confronted with what is described as brain surgery but turns out to be less dramatic than it sounds, I fly home immediately.

My brother drives three hours back and forth from New Jersey every day to chauffeur me and my mother to the hospital: he is being a fine Italian-American son. For the first time in years, we have long conversations alone. He is two years older than I am, a chemical engineer who has also left the neighborhood but has remained closer to its values, with a suburban, Republican inflection. He talks a lot about New York, saying that (except for neighborhoods like Bensonhurst) it's a "third-world city now." It's the summer of the Tawana Brawley incident, when Brawley accused white men of abducting her and smearing racial slurs on her body with her own excrement. My brother is filled with dislike for Al Sharpton and Brawley's other vocal supporters in the black community—not because they're black, he says, but because they're troublemakers, stirring things up. The city is drenched in racial hatred that makes itself felt in the halls of the hospital: Italians and Jews in the beds and as doctors; blacks as nurses and orderlies.

This is first time since I left New York in 1975 that I have visited Brooklyn without once getting into Manhattan. It's the first time I have spent several days alone with my mother, living in her apartment in Bensonhurst. My every move is scrutinized and commented on. I feel like I am going to go crazy.

Finally, it's clear that my father is going to be fine, and I can go home. She insists on accompanying me to the travel agent to get my ticket for home, even though I really want to be alone. The agency (a Mafia front?) has no one who knows how to ticket me for the exotic destination of North Carolina and no computer for doing so. The one person who can perform this feat by hand is out. I have to kill time for an hour and suggest to my mother that she go home, to be there for my brother when he arrives from Jersey. We stop in a Pork Store, where I buy a stash of cheeses, sausages, and other delicacies unavailable in Durham. My mother walks home with the shopping bags, and I'm on my own.

More than anything I want a kind of *sorbetto* or ice I remember from my childhood, a *cremolata*, almond-vanilla-flavored with large chunks of nuts. I pop into the local bakery (at the unlikely hour of 11 A.M.) and ask for a *cremolata*, usually eaten after dinner. The woman—a younger version of my mother—refuses: They haven't made a fresh ice yet, and what's left from the day before is too icy, no good. I explain that I'm about to get on a plane for North Carolina and want that ice, good or not. But she has her standards and holds her ground, even though North Carolina has about the same status in her mind as Timbuktoo and she knows I will be banished, perhaps forever, from the land of *cremolata*.

Then, while I'm taking a walk, enjoying my solitude, I have another idea. 35 On the block behind my parents' house, there's a club for men, for men from a particular town or region in Italy: six or seven tables, some on the sidewalk beneath a garish red, green, and white sign; no women allowed or welcome unless they're with men, and no women at all during the day when the real business of the club—a game of cards for old men—is in progress. Still, I know that inside the club would be coffee and a *cremolata* ice. I'm thirty-eight, well dressed, very respectable looking; I know what I want. I also know I'm not supposed to enter that club. I enter anyway, asking the teenage boy behind the counter firmly, in my most professional tones, for a *cremolata* ice. Dazzled, he complies immediately. The old men at the card table have been staring at this scene, unable to place me exactly, though my facial type is familiar. Finally, a few old men's hisses pierce the air. "*Strega,*" I hear as I leave, "*mala strega*"—"witch," or "brazen whore." I have been in Bensonhurst less than a week, but I have managed to reproduce, on my final day there for this visit, the conditions of my youth. Knowing the rules, I have broken them. I shake hands with my discreetly rebellious past, still an outsider walking through the neighborhood, marked and insulted—though unlikely to be shot.

Considerations

1. Torgovnick paraphrases an old saying when she declares, "You can take the girl out of Bensonhurst ... , but you may not be able to take Bensonhurst out of the girl" (para. 16). How successful has Torgovnick been in taking Bensonhurst out of herself, that is, in breaking away from the values and attitudes of her native community? Can you find any residue of those attitudes in the text?

2. "Crisscrossing the neighborhood and marking out ethnic zones . . . are the great shopping streets" (para. 3). The topography of the neighborhood suggests to Torgovnick the racial and ethnic divisions. What other cultural or social divisions are marked by divisions of space?

3. At the conclusion of her essay, Torgovnick tells of her decision to enter a club for Italian-American men in order to order a special kind of ice cream: "I also know I'm not supposed to enter that club. I enter anyway . . ." (para. 35). How are the other choices she discusses throughout the essay mirrored in this final scene?

Invitation to Write

"Occasionally I get reminded of my roots, of their simultaneously choking and nutritive power" (para. 18). When Torgovnick speaks about her choices, she shows how they were determined by her upbringing. When presented with a choice she was inclined to take the alternative that was least acceptable to Bensonhurst people; yet, at crucial moments in her life, she cautiously chose what her parents would have recommended. How do her choices illustrate the "roots" metaphor in the preceding quotation? Write an essay in which you explore the influence of family and cultural environment on individual choices by considering Torgovnick's case. Based on her sense of cultural heritage, as well as your own sense of what family can give an individual, show how important it is for anyone to come to terms with one's family tradition. Explain what elements of family life inspire both rebellion and nostalgia about it.

Connections

In "On Being White, Female, and Born in Bensonhurst," Marianna Torgovnick sketches the portrait of a close-knit community made up mainly of Italian immigrants. She stresses the fact that "Italian Americans . . . are notable for their cohesiveness and provinciality; the slightest pressure turns those qualities into prejudice and racism" (para. 10). In spite of the obvious difference, the racially and ethnically homogeneous community of Gaines's story "Just Like a Tree" (p. 5) is also quite tightly knit and, perhaps, predisposed to prejudice. Write an essay in which you explore the relation between a sense of community and the development of prejudice on the basis of a comparison between the Bensonhurst of Torgovnick's essay and the Southern community described by Gaines. Do not shy away from pointing out the differences, but try to get deeper than the surface. A superficial difference may turn out to be a profound similarity.

SIMONE DE BEAUVOIR

Introduction to The Second Sex

Simone de Beauvoir was born in 1908, in France, into a traditional Catholic family. Her early years were very restricted by parental control, but dwindling family fortunes led her parents to decide to educate her, which eventually provided Beauvoir with opportunities for independence and intellectual accomplishment. After graduating from the Sorbonne, she became first a teacher, then a writer, and later a respected spokesperson for the French Existentialist movement and other political causes. As a student, she considered herself exceptional, and this led her to identify more with men than with women. However, she later became aware that her life was limited by her society's attitudes toward gender. With the publication of her most famous work, *The Second Sex* (1949), Beauvoir, who had already earned recognition as a leading and innovative feminist thinker, was recognized as a founder of modern feminism. Beauvoir also wrote novels, including *The Mandarins* (1954), works of criticism, and a four-volume autobiography. Beauvoir spent the last years of her life editing the papers of Jean-Paul Sartre, with whom she had had a long history of both romance and intellectual friendship. She died in Paris in 1986.

In the introduction to *The Second Sex* (translated in 1952 by H. M. Parshley), Beauvoir focuses on the cultural conditions that determine a woman's role. She argues, in fact, that women are treated as alien and inferior beings.

FOR A LONG TIME I HAVE HESITATED to write a book on woman. The subject is irritating, especially to women; and it is not new. Enough ink has been spilled in the quarreling over feminism, now practically over, and perhaps we should say no more about it. It is still talked about, however, for the voluminous nonsense uttered during the last century seems to have done little to illuminate the problem. After all, is there a problem? And if so, what is it? Are there women, really? Most assuredly the theory of the eternal feminine still has its adherents who will whisper in your ear: "Even in Russia women still are *women*"; and other erudite persons—sometimes the very same—say with a sigh: "Woman is losing her way, woman is lost." One wonders if women still exist, if they will always exist, whether or not it is desirable that they should, what place they occupy in this world, what their place should be. "What has become of women?" was asked recently in an ephemeral magazine.[1]

But first we must ask: What is a woman? *"Tota mulier in utero,"* says one, "woman is a womb." But in speaking of certain women, connoisseurs declare that they are not women, although they are equipped with a uterus like the rest. All agree in recognizing the fact that females exist in the human species; today as always they make up about one half of humanity. And yet we are told that femininity is in danger; we are exhorted to be women, remain women, become women. It would appear, then, that every female human being is not necessarily a woman; to be so considered she must share in that mysterious and threatened reality known as femininity. Is this attribute something secreted by the ovaries? Or is it a Platonic essence, a product of the philosophic imagination? Is a rustling petticoat enough to bring it down to earth? Although some women try zealously to incarnate this essence, it is hardly patentable. It is frequently described in vague and dazzling terms that seem to have been borrowed from the vocabulary of the seers, and indeed, in the times of St. Thomas, it was considered an essence as certainly defined as the somniferous virtue of the poppy.

But conceptualism has lost ground. The biological and social sciences no longer admit the existence of unchangeably fixed entities that determine given characteristics, such as those ascribed to woman, the Jew, or the Negro. Science regards any characteristic as a reaction dependent in part upon a *situation*. If today femininity no longer exists, then it never existed. But does the word *woman*, then, have no specific content? This is stoutly affirmed by those who hold to the philosophy of the enlightenment, of rationalism, of nominalism; women, to them, are merely the human beings arbitrarily designated by the word *woman*. Many American women particularly are prepared to think that there is no longer any place for woman as such; if a backward individual still takes herself for a woman, her friends advise her to be psychoanalyzed and thus get rid of this obsession. In regard to a work, *Modern Woman: The Lost Sex*, which in other respects has its irritating features, Dorothy Parker has written: "I cannot be just to books which treat of woman as woman. . . . My idea is that all of us, men as well as women, should be regarded as human beings." But nominalism is a rather inadequate doctrine, and the antifeminists have had no trouble in showing that women simply *are not* men. Surely woman is, like man, a human being; but such a declaration is abstract. The fact is that every concrete human being is always a singular, separate individual. To decline to accept such notions as the eternal feminine, the black soul, the Jewish character, is not to deny that Jews, Negroes, women exist today—

---

[1] *Franchise*, dead today. [Author's note]

this denial does not represent a liberation for those concerned, but rather a flight from reality. Some years ago a well-known woman writer refused to permit her portrait to appear in a series of photographs especially devoted to women writers; she wished to be counted among the men. But in order to gain this privilege she made use of her husband's influence! Women who assert that they are men lay claim none the less to masculine consideration and respect. I recall also a young Trotskyite standing on a platform at a boisterous meeting and getting ready to use her fists, in spite of her evident fragility. She was denying her feminine weakness; but it was for love of a militant male whose equal she wished to be. The attitude of defiance of many American women proves that they are haunted by a sense of their femininity. In truth, to go for a walk with one's eyes open is enough to demonstrate that humanity is divided into two classes of individuals whose clothes, faces, bodies, smiles, gaits, interests, and occupations are manifestly different. Perhaps these differences are superficial, perhaps they are destined to disappear. What is certain is that right now they do most obviously exist.

If her functioning as a female is not enough to define woman, if we decline also to explain her through "the eternal feminine," and if nevertheless we admit, provisionally, that women do exist, then we must face the question: What is a woman?

To state the question is, to me, to suggest, at once, a preliminary answer. 5
The fact that I ask it is in itself significant. A man would never get the notion of writing a book on the peculiar situation of the human male.[2] But if I wish to define myself, I must first of all say: "I am a woman"; on this truth must be based all further discussion. A man never begins by presenting himself as an individual of a certain sex; it goes without saying that he is a man. The terms *masculine* and *feminine* are used symmetrically only as a matter of form, as on legal papers. In actuality the relation of the two sexes is not quite like that of two electrical poles, for man represents both the positive and the neutral, as is indicated by the common use of *man* to designate human beings in general; whereas woman represents only the negative, defined by limiting criteria, without reciprocity. In the midst of an abstract discussion it is vexing to hear a man say: "You think thus and so because you are a woman"; but I know that my only defense is to reply: "I think thus and so because it is true," thereby removing my subjective self from the argument. It would be out of the question to reply: "And you think the contrary because you are a man," for it is understood that the fact of being a man is no peculiarity. A man is in the right in being a man; it is the woman who is in the wrong. It amounts to this: "Just as for the ancients there was an absolute vertical with reference to which

[2]The Kinsey Report (Alfred C. Kinsey and others, *Sexual Behavior in the Human Male* [W. B. Saunders Co., 1948]) is no exception, for it is limited to describing the sexual characteristics of American men, which is quite a different matter. [Author's note]

the oblique was defined, so there is an absolute human type, the masculine. Woman has ovaries, a uterus; these peculiarities imprison her in her subjectivity, circumscribe her within the limits of her own nature. It is often said that she thinks with her glands. Man superbly ignores the fact that his anatomy also includes glands, such as the testicles, and that they secrete hormones. He thinks of his body as a direct and normal connection with the world, which he believes he apprehends objectively, whereas he regards the body of woman as a hindrance, a prison, weighed down by everything peculiar to it. "The female is a female by virtue of a certain *lack* of qualities," said Aristotle; "we should regard the female nature as afflicted with a natural defectiveness." And St. Thomas for his part pronounced woman to be an "imperfect man," an "incidental" being. This is symbolized in Genesis where Eve is depicted as made from what Bossuet called "a supernumerary bone" of Adam.

Thus humanity is male and man defines woman not in herself but as relative to him; she is not regarded as an autonomous being. Michelet writes: "Woman, the relative being. . . ." And Benda is most positive in his *Rapport d'Uriel:* "The body of man makes sense in itself quite apart from that of woman, whereas the latter seems wanting in significance by itself. . . . Man can think of himself without woman. She cannot think of herself without man." And she is simply what man decrees; thus she is called "the sex," by which is meant that she appears essentially to the male as a sexual being. For him she is sex—absolute sex, no less. She is defined and differentiated with reference to man and not he with reference to her; she is the incidental, the inessential as opposed to the essential. He is the Subject, he is the Absolute— she is the Other.[3]

The category of the *Other* is as primordial as consciousness itself. In the most primitive societies, in the most ancient mythologies, one finds the expression of a duality—that of the Self and the Other. This duality was not originally attached to the division of the sexes; it was not dependent upon any

---

[3]E. Lévinas expresses this idea most explicitly in his essay *Temps et l'Autre.* "Is there not a case in which otherness, alterity *[altérité],* unquestionably marks the nature of a being, as its essence, an instance of otherness not consisting purely and simply in the opposition of two species of the same genus? I think that the feminine represents the contrary in its absolute sense, this contrariness being in no wise affected by any relation between it and its correlative and thus remaining absolutely other. Sex is not a certain specific difference . . . no more is the sexual difference a mere contradiction. . . . Nor does this difference lie in the duality of two complementary terms, for two complementary terms imply a pre-existing whole. . . . Otherness reaches its full flowering in the feminine, a term of the same rank as consciousness but of opposite meaning."

I suppose that Lévinas does not forget that woman, too, is aware of her own consciousness, or ego. But it is striking that he deliberately takes a man's point of view, disregarding the reciprocity of subject and object. When he writes that woman is mystery, he implies that she is mystery for man. Thus his description, which is intended to be objective, is in fact an assertion of masculine privilege. [Author's note]

empirical facts. It is revealed in such works as that of Granet on Chinese thought and those of Dumézil on the East Indies and Rome. The feminine element was at first no more involved in such pairs as Varuna-Mitra, Uranus-Zeus, Sun-Moon, and Day-Night than it was in the contrasts between Good and Evil, lucky and unlucky auspices, right and left, God and Lucifer. Otherness is a fundamental category of human thought.

Thus it is that no group ever sets itself up as the One without at once setting up the Other over against itself. If three travelers chance to occupy the same compartment, that is enough to make vaguely hostile "others" out of all the rest of the passengers on the train. In small-town eyes all persons not belonging to the village are "strangers" and suspect; to the native of a country all who inhabit other countries are "foreigners"; Jews are "different" for the anti-Semite, Negroes are "inferior" for American racists, aborigines are "natives" for colonists, proletarians are the "lower class" for the privileged.

Lévi-Strauss, at the end of a profound work on the various forms of primitive societies, reaches the following conclusion: "Passage from the state of Nature to the state of Culture is marked by man's ability to view biological relations as a series of contrasts; duality, alternation, opposition, and symmetry, whether under definite or vague forms, constitute not so much phenomena to be explained as fundamental and immediately given data of social reality."[4] These phenomena would be incomprehensible if in fact human society were simply a *Mitsein* or fellowship based on solidarity and friendliness. Things become clear, on the contrary, if, following Hegel, we find in consciousness itself a fundamental hostility toward every other consciousness; the subject can be posed only in being opposed—he sets himself up as the essential, as opposed to the other, the inessential, the object.

But the other consciousness, the other ego, sets up a reciprocal claim. The native traveling abroad is shocked to find himself in turn regarded as a "stranger" by the natives of neighboring countries. As a matter of fact, wars, festivals, trading, treaties, and contests among tribes, nations, and classes tend to deprive the concept *Other* of its absolute sense and to make manifest its relativity; willy-nilly, individuals and groups are forced to realize the reciprocity of their relations. How is it, then, that this reciprocity has not been recognized between the sexes, that one of the contrasting terms is set up as the sole essential, denying any relativity in regard to its correlative and defining the latter as pure otherness? Why is it that women do not dispute male sovereignty? No subject will readily volunteer to become the object, the inessential; it is not the Other who, in defining himself as the Other, establishes the One. The Other is posed as such by the One in defining himself as the One. But if

10

[4]See C. Lévi-Strauss, *Les Structures élémentaires de la parenté.* My thanks are due to C. Lévi-Strauss for his kindness in furnishing me with the proofs of his work, which, among others, I have used liberally in Part II [of *The Second Sex*]. [Author's note]

the Other is not to regain the status of being the One, he must be submissive enough to accept this alien point of view. Whence comes this submission in the case of woman?

There are, to be sure, other cases in which a certain category has been able to dominate another completely for a time. Very often this privilege depends upon inequality of numbers—the majority imposes its rule upon the minority or persecutes it. But women are not a minority, like the American Negroes or the Jews; there are as many women as men on earth. Again, the two groups concerned have often been originally independent; they may have been formerly unaware of each other's existence, or perhaps they recognized each other's autonomy. But a historical event has resulted in the subjugation of the weaker by the stronger. The scattering of the Jews, the introduction of slavery into America, the conquests of imperialism are examples in point. In these cases the oppressed retained at least the memory of former days; they possessed in common a past, a tradition, sometimes a religion or a culture.

The parallel drawn by Bebel between women and the proletariat is valid in that neither ever formed a minority or a separate collective unit of mankind. And instead of a single historical event it is in both cases a historical development that explains their status as a class and accounts for the membership of *particular individuals* in that class. But proletarians have not always existed, whereas there have always been women. They are women in virtue of their anatomy and physiology. Throughout history they have always been subordinated to men,[5] and hence their dependency is not the result of a historical event or a social change—it was not something that *occurred*. The reason why otherness in this case seems to be an absolute is in part that it lacks the contingent or incidental nature of historical facts. A condition brought about at a certain time can be abolished at some other time, as the Negroes of Haiti and others have proved; but it might seem that a natural condition is beyond the possibility of change. In truth, however, the nature of things is no more immutably given, once for all, than is historical reality. If woman seems to be the inessential which never becomes the essential, it is because she herself fails to bring about this change. Proletarians say "We"; Negroes also. Regarding themselves as subjects, they transform the bourgeois, the whites, into "others." But women do not say "We," except at some congress of feminists or similar formal demonstration; men say "women," and women use the same word in referring to themselves. They do not authentically assume a subjective attitude. The proletarians have accomplished the revolution in Russia, the Negroes in Haiti, the Indochinese are battling for it in Indochina; but the women's effort has never been anything more than a symbolic agitation. They

---

[5]With rare exceptions, perhaps, like certain matriarchal rulers, queens, and the like. [Translator's note]

have gained only what men have been willing to grant; they have taken nothing, they have only received.

The reason for this is that women lack concrete means for organizing themselves into a unit which can stand face to face with the correlative unit. They have no past, no history, no religion of their own; and they have no such solidarity of work and interest as that of the proletariat. They are not even promiscuously herded together in the way that creates community feeling among the American Negroes, the ghetto Jews, the workers of Saint-Denis, or the factory hands of Renault. They live dispersed among the males, attached through residence, housework, economic condition, and social standing to certain men—fathers or husbands—more firmly than they are to other women. If they belong to the bourgeoisie, they feel solidarity with men of that class, not with proletarian women; if they are white, their allegiance is to white men, not to Negro women. The proletariat can propose to massacre the ruling class, and a sufficiently fanatical Jew or Negro might dream of getting sole possession of the atomic bomb and making humanity wholly Jewish or black; but woman cannot even dream of exterminating the males. The bond that unites her to her oppressors is not comparable to any other. The division of the sexes is a biological fact, not an event in human history. Male and female stand opposed within a primordial *Mitsein,* and woman has not broken it. The couple is a fundamental unity with its two halves riveted together, and the cleavage of society along the line of sex is impossible. Here is to be found the basic trait of woman: She is the Other in a totality of which the two components are necessary to one another.

One could suppose that this reciprocity might have facilitated the liberation of woman. When Hercules sat at the feet of Omphale and helped with her spinning, his desire for her held him captive; but why did she fail to gain a lasting power? To revenge herself on Jason, Medea killed their children; and this grim legend would seem to suggest that she might have obtained a formidable influence over him through his love for his offspring. In *Lysistrata* Aristophanes gaily depicts a band of women who joined forces to gain social ends through the sexual needs of their men; but this is only a play. In the legend of the Sabine women, the latter soon abandoned their plan of remaining sterile to punish their ravishers. In truth woman has not been socially emancipated through man's need—sexual desire and the desire for offspring—which makes the male dependent for satisfaction upon the female.

Master and slave, also, are united by a reciprocal need, in this case economic, which does not liberate the slave. In the relation of master to slave the master does not make a point of the need that he has for the other; he has in his grasp the power of satisfying this need through his own action; whereas the slave, in his dependent condition, his hope and fear, is quite conscious of the need he has for his master. Even if the need is at bottom equally urgent for both, it always works in favor of the oppressor and against the oppressed. That is why the liberation of the working class, for example, has been slow.

Now, woman has always been man's dependent, if not his slave; the two sexes have never shared the world in equality. And even today woman is heavily handicapped, though her situation is beginning to change. Almost nowhere is her legal status the same as man's,[6] and frequently it is much to her disadvantage. Even when her rights are legally recognized in the abstract, long-standing custom prevents their full expression in the mores. In the economic sphere men and women can almost be said to make up two castes; other things being equal, the former hold the better jobs, get higher wages, and have more opportunity for success than their new competitors. In industry and politics men have a great many more positions and they monopolize the most important posts. In addition to all this, they enjoy a traditional prestige that the education of children tends in every way to support, for the present enshrines the past—and in the past all history has been made by men. At the present time, when women are beginning to take part in the affairs of the world, it is still a world that belongs to men—they have no doubt of it at all and women have scarcely any. To decline to be the Other, to refuse to be a party to the deal—this would be for women to renounce all the advantages conferred upon them by their alliance with the superior caste. Man-the-sovereign will provide woman-the-liege with material protection and will undertake the moral justification of her existence; thus she can evade at once both economic risk and the metaphysical risk of a liberty in which ends and aims must be contrived without assistance. Indeed, along with the ethical urge of each individual to affirm his subjective existence, there is also the temptation to forgo liberty and become a thing. This is an inauspicious road, for he who takes it—passive, lost, ruined—becomes henceforth the creature of another's will, frustrated in his transcendence and deprived of every value. But it is an easy road; on it one avoids the strain involved in undertaking an authentic existence. When man makes of woman the *Other,* he may, then, expect her to manifest deep-seated tendencies toward complicity. Thus, woman may fail to lay claim to the status of subject because she lacks definite resources, because she feels the necessary bond that ties her to man regardless of reciprocity, and because she is often very well pleased with her role as the *Other.*

But it will be asked at once: How did all this begin? It is easy to see that the duality of the sexes, like any duality, gives rise to conflict. And doubtless the winner will assume the status of absolute. But why should man have won from the start? It seems possible that women could have won the victory; or that the outcome of the conflict might never have been decided. How is it that

---

[6]At the moment an "equal rights" amendment to the Constitution of the United States is before Congress. [Translator's note]

this world has always belonged to the men and that things have begun to change only recently? Is this change a good thing? Will it bring about an equal sharing of the world between men and women?

These questions are not new, and they have often been answered. But the very fact that woman *is the Other* tends to cast suspicion upon all the justifications that men have ever been able to provide for it. These have all too evidently been dictated by men's interest. A little-known feminist of the seventeenth century, Poulain de la Barre, put it this way: "All that has been written about women by men should be suspect, for the men are at once judge and party to the lawsuit." Everywhere, at all times, the males have displayed their satisfaction in feeling that they are the lords of creation. "Blessed be God . . . that He did not make me a woman," say the Jews in their morning prayers, while their wives pray on a note of resignation: "Blessed be the Lord, who created me according to His will." The first among the blessings for which Plato thanked the gods was that he had been created free, not enslaved; the second, a man, not a woman. But the males could not enjoy this privilege fully unless they believed it to be founded on the absolute and the eternal; they sought to make the fact of their supremacy into a right. "Being men, those who have made and compiled the laws have favored their own sex, and jurists have elevated these laws into principles," to quote Poulain de la Barre once more.

Legislators, priests, philosophers, writers, and scientists have striven to show that the subordinate position of woman is willed in heaven and advantageous on earth. The religions invented by men reflect this wish for domination. In the legends of Eve and Pandora men have taken up arms against women. They have made use of philosophy and theology, as the quotations from Aristotle and St. Thomas have shown. Since ancient times satirists and moralists have delighted in showing up the weaknesses of women. We are familiar with the savage indictments hurled against women throughout French literature. Montherlant, for example, follows the tradition of Jean de Meung, though with less gusto. This hostility may at times be well founded, often it is gratuitous; but in truth it more or less successfully conceals a desire for self-justification. As Montaigne says, "It is easier to accuse one sex than to excuse the other." Sometimes what is going on is clear enough. For instance, the Roman law limiting the rights of woman cited "the imbecility, the instability of the sex" just when the weakening of family ties seemed to threaten the interests of male heirs. And in the effort to keep the married woman under guardianship, appeal was made in the sixteenth century to the authority of St. Augustine, who declared that "woman is a creature neither decisive nor constant," at a time when the single woman was thought capable of managing her property. Montaigne understood clearly how arbitrary and unjust was woman's appointed lot: "Women are not in the wrong when they decline to accept the rules laid down for them, since the men make these rules without consulting them. No wonder intrigue and strife abound." But he did not go so far as to champion their cause.

It was only later, in the eighteenth century, that genuinely democratic 20 men began to view the matter objectively. Diderot, among others, strove to show that woman is, like man, a human being. Later John Stuart Mill came fervently to her defense. But these philosophers displayed unusual impartiality. In the nineteenth century the feminist quarrel became again a quarrel of partisans. One of the consequences of the industrial revolution was the entrance of women into productive labor, and it was just here that the claims of the feminists emerged from the realm of theory and acquired an economic basis, while their opponents became the more aggressive. Although landed property lost power to some extent, the bourgeoisie clung to the old morality that found the guarantee of private property in the solidity of the family. Woman was ordered back into the home the more harshly as her emancipation became a real menace. Even within the working class the men endeavored to restrain woman's liberation, because they began to see the women as dangerous competitors—the more so because they were accustomed to work for lower wages.

In proving woman's inferiority, the antifeminists then began to draw not only upon religion, philosophy, and theology, as before, but also upon science—biology, experimental psychology, etc. At most they were willing to grant "equality in difference" to the *other* sex. That profitable formula is most significant; it is precisely like the "equal but separate" formula of the Jim Crow laws aimed at the North American Negroes. As is well known, this so-called equalitarian segregation has resulted only in the most extreme discrimination. The similarity just noted is in no way due to chance, for whether it is a race, a caste, a class, or a sex that is reduced to a position of inferiority, the methods of justification are the same. "The eternal feminine" corresponds to "the black soul" and to "the Jewish character." True, the Jewish problem is on the whole very different from the other two—to the anti-Semite the Jew is not so much an inferior as he is an enemy for whom there is to be granted no place on earth, for whom annihilation is the fate desired. But there are deep similarities between the situation of woman and that of the Negro. Both are being emancipated today from a like paternalism, and the former master class wishes to "keep them in their place"—that is, the place chosen for them. In both cases the former masters lavish more or less sincere eulogies, either on the virtues of "the good Negro" with his dormant, childish, merry soul—the submissive Negro—or on the merits of the woman who is "truly feminine"— that is, frivolous, infantile, irresponsible—the submissive woman. In both cases the dominant class bases its argument on a state of affairs that it has itself created. As George Bernard Shaw puts it, in substance, "The American white relegates the black to the rank of shoeshine boy; and he concludes from this that the black is good for nothing but shining shoes." This vicious circle is met with in all analogous circumstances; when an individual (or a group of individuals) is kept in a situation of inferiority, the fact is that he *is* inferior. But the significance of the verb *to be* must be rightly understood here; it is in bad faith to give it a static value when it really has the dynamic Hegelian sense of "to have become." Yes, women on the whole *are* today inferior to men; that is, their situation affords them fewer possibilities. The question is: Should that state of affairs continue?

Many men hope that it will continue; not all have given up the battle. The conservative bourgeoisie still see in the emancipation of women a menace to their morality and their interests. Some men dread feminine competition. Recently a male student wrote in the *Hebdo-Latin:* "Every woman student who goes into medicine or law robs us of a job." He never questioned his rights in this world. And economic interests are not the only ones concerned. One of the benefits that oppression confers upon the oppressors is that the most humble among them is made to *feel* superior; thus, a "poor white" in the South can console himself with the thought that he is not a "dirty nigger"—and the more prosperous whites cleverly exploit this pride.

Similarly, the most mediocre of males feels himself a demigod as compared with women. It was much easier for M. de Montherlant to think himself a hero when he faced women (and women chosen for his purpose) than when he was obliged to act the man among men—something many women have done better than he, for that matter. And in September 1948, in one of his articles in the *Figaro littéraire*, Claude Mauriac—whose great originality is admired by all—could[7] write regarding woman: "*We* listen on a tone [*sic!*] of polite indifference . . . to the most brilliant among them, well knowing that her wit reflects more or less luminously ideas that come from *us.*" Evidently the speaker referred to is not reflecting the ideas of Mauriac himself, for no one knows of his having any. It may be that she reflects ideas originating with men, but then, even among men there are those who have been known to appropriate ideas not their own; and one can well ask whether Claude Mauriac might not find more interesting a conversation reflecting Descartes, Marx, or Gide rather than himself. What is really remarkable is that by using the questionable *we* he identifies himself with St. Paul, Hegel, Lenin, and Nietzsche, and from the lofty eminence of their grandeur looks down disdainfully upon the bevy of women who make bold to converse with him on a footing of equality. In truth, I know of more than one woman who would refuse to suffer with patience Mauriac's "tone of polite indifference."

I have lingered on this example because the masculine attitude is here displayed with disarming ingenuousness. But men profit in many more subtle ways from the otherness, the alterity of woman. Here is miraculous balm for

---

[7]Or at least he thought he could. [Author's note]

those afflicted with an inferiority complex, and indeed no one is more arrogant toward women, more aggressive or scornful, then the man who is anxious about his virility. Those who are not fear-ridden in the presence of their fellow men are much more disposed to recognize a fellow creature in woman; but even to these the myth of woman, the Other, is precious for many reasons.[8] They cannot be blamed for not cheerfully relinquishing all the benefits they derive from the myth, for they realize what they would lose in relinquishing woman as they fancy her to be, while they fail to realize what they have to gain from the woman of tomorrow. Refusal to pose oneself as the Subject, unique and absolute, requires great self-denial. Furthermore, the vast majority of men make no such claim explicitly. They do not *postulate* woman as inferior, for today they are too thoroughly imbued with the ideal of democracy not to recognize all human beings as equals.

In the bosom of the family, woman seems in the eyes of childhood and youth to be clothed in the same social dignity as the adult males. Later on, the young man, desiring and loving, experiences the resistance, the independence of the woman desired and loved; in marriage, he respects woman as wife and mother, and in the concrete events of conjugal life she stands there before him as a free being. He can therefore feel that social subordination as between the sexes no longer exists and that on the whole, in spite of differences, woman is an equal. As, however, he observes some points of inferiority—the most important being unfitness for the professions—he attributes these to natural causes. When he is in a cooperative and benevolent relation with woman, his theme is the principle of abstract equality, and he does not base his attitude upon such inequality as may exist. But when he is in conflict with her, the situation is reversed: His theme will be the existing inequality, and he will even take it as justification for denying abstract equality.[9]

So it is that many men will affirm as if in good faith that women *are* the equals of man and that they have nothing to clamor for, while *at the same time* they will say that women can never be the equals of man and that their demands are in vain. It is, in point of fact, a difficult matter for man to realize the extreme importance of social discriminations which seem outwardly

[8]A significant article on this theme by Michel Carrouges appeared in No. 292 of the *Cahiers du Sud.* He writes indignantly: "Would that there were no woman-myth at all but only a cohort of cooks, matrons, prostitutes, and bluestockings serving functions of pleasure or usefulness!" That is to say, in his view woman has no existence in and for herself; he thinks only of her *function* in the male world. Her reason for existence lies in man. But then, in fact, her poetic "function" as a myth might be more valued than any other. The real problem is precisely to find out why woman should be defined with relation to man. [Author's note]

[9]For example, a man will say that he considers his wife in no wise degraded because she has no gainful occupation. The profession of housewife is just as lofty, and so on. But when the first quarrel comes he will exclaim: "Why, you couldn't make your living without me!" [Author's note]

insignificant but which produce in woman moral and intellectual effects so profound that they appear to spring from her original nature. The most sympathetic of men never fully comprehend woman's concrete situation. And there is no reason to put much trust in the men when they rush to the defense of privileges whose full extent they can hardly measure. We shall not, then, permit ourselves to be intimidated by the number and violence of the attacks launched against women, nor to be entrapped by the self-seeking eulogies bestowed on the "true woman," nor to profit by the enthusiasm for woman's destiny manifested by men who would not for the world have any part of it.

We should consider the arguments of the feminists with no less suspicion, however, for very often their controversial aim deprives them of all real value. If the "woman question" seems trivial, it is because masculine arrogance has made of it a "quarrel"; and when quarreling, one no longer reasons well. People have tirelessly sought to prove that woman is superior, inferior, or equal to man. Some say that, having been created after Adam, she is evidently a secondary being; others say on the contrary that Adam was only a rough draft and that God succeeded in producing the human being in perfection when He created Eve. Woman's brain is smaller; yes, but it is relatively larger. Christ was made a man; yes, but perhaps for his greater humility. Each argument at once suggests its opposite, and both are often fallacious. If we are to gain understanding, we must get out of these ruts; we must discard the vague notions of superiority, inferiority, equality which have hitherto corrupted every discussion of the subject and start afresh.

Very well, but just how shall we pose the question? And, to begin with, who are we to propound it at all? Man is at once judge and party to the case; but so is woman. What we need is an angel—neither man nor woman—but where shall we find one? Still, the angel would be poorly qualified to speak, for an angel is ignorant of all the basic facts involved in the problem. With a hermaphrodite we should be no better off, for here the situation is most peculiar; the hermaphrodite is not really the combination of a whole man and a whole woman, but consists of parts of each and thus is neither. It looks to me as if there are, after all, certain women who are best qualified to elucidate the situation of woman. Let us not be misled by the sophism that because Epimendies was a Cretan he was necessarily a liar; it is not a mysterious essence that compels men and women to act in good or in bad faith, it is their situation that inclines them more or less toward the search for truth. Many of today's women, fortunate in the restoration of all the privileges pertaining to the estate of the human being, can afford the luxury of impartiality—we even recognize its necessity. We are no longer like our partisan elders; by and large we have won the game. In recent debates on the status of women the United Nations has persistently maintained that the equality of the sexes is now becoming a reality, and already some of us have never had to sense in our femininity an inconvenience or an obstacle. Many problems appear to us to be more pressing than those which concern us in particular, and this detachment even allows us to hope that our attitude will be objective. Still, we know the feminine world more intimately than do the men because we have our roots in it, we grasp more immediately than do men what it means to a human being to be feminine; and we are more concerned with such knowledge. I have said that there are more pressing problems, but this does not prevent us from seeing some importance in asking how the fact of being women will affect our lives. What opportunities precisely have been given us and what withheld? What fate awaits our younger sisters, and what directions should they take? It is significant that books by women on women are in general animated in our day less by a wish to demand our rights than by an effort toward clarity and understanding. As we emerge from an era of excessive controversy, this book is offered as one attempt among others to confirm that statement.

But it is doubtless impossible to approach any human problem with a mind free from bias. The way in which questions are put, the points of view assumed, presuppose a relativity of interest; all characteristics imply values, and every objective description, so called, implies an ethical background. Rather than attempt to conceal principles more or less definitely implied, it is better to state them openly at the beginning. This will make it unnecessary to specify on every page in just what sense one uses such words as *superior, inferior, better, worse, progress, reaction,* and the like. If we survey some of the works on woman, we note that one of the points of view most frequently adopted is that of the public good, the general interest; and one always means by this the benefit of society as one wishes it to be maintained or established. For our part, we hold that the only public good is that which assures the private good of the citizens; we shall pass judgment on institutions according to their effectiveness in giving concrete opportunities to individuals. But we do not confuse the idea of private interest with that of happiness, although that is another common point of view. Are not women of the harem more happy than women voters? Is not the housekeeper happier than the working-woman? It is not too clear just what the word *happy* really means and still less what true values it may mask. There is no possibility of measuring the happiness of others, and it is always easy to describe as happy the situation in which one wishes to place them.

In particular those who are condemned to stagnation are often pro- 30
nounced happy on the pretext that happiness consists in being at rest. This notion we reject, for our perspective is that of existentialist ethics. Every subject plays his part as such specifically through exploits or projects that serve as a mode of transcendence; he achieves liberty only through a continual reaching out toward other liberties. There is no justification for present existence other than its expansion into an indefinitely open future. Every time

transcendence falls back into immanence, stagnation, there is a degradation of existence into the *"en-soi"*—the brutish life of subjection to given conditions—and of liberty into constraint and contingence. This downfall represents a moral fault if the subject consents to it; if it is inflicted upon him, it spells frustration and oppression. In both cases it is an absolute evil. Every individual concerned to justify his existence feels that his existence involves an undefined need to transcend himself, to engage in freely chosen projects.

Now, what peculiarly signalizes the situation of woman is that she—a free and autonomous being like all human creatures—nevertheless finds herself living in a world where men compel her to assume the status of the Other. They propose to stabilize her as object and to doom her to immanence since her transcendence is to be overshadowed and forever transcended by another ego *(conscience)* which is essential and sovereign. The drama of woman lies in this conflict between the fundamental aspirations of every subject (ego)—who always regards the self as the essential—and the compulsions of a situation in which she is the inessential. How can a human being in woman's situation attain fulfillment? What roads are open to her? Which are blocked? How can independence be recovered in a state of dependency? What circumstances limit woman's liberty and how can they be overcome? These are the fundamental questions on which I would fain throw some light. This means that I am interested in the fortunes of the individual as defined not in terms of happiness but in terms of liberty.

Considerations

1. Beauvoir is writing about women's position in society. How would you characterize her point of view? Do you feel that she identifies more closely with the situations of the women or of the men she discusses? How can you tell? Give two or three examples from the text to support your point of view.

2. Although Beauvoir's essay presents a feminist position, she occasionally writes seemingly contradictory statements like "A man is in the right in being a man" (para. 5). Find other similar examples of statements that seem puzzling and contradictory. What is Beauvoir's purpose in using such statements? How are they used in the context of the essay?

3. In the course of her essay, Beauvoir takes a simple word like *other*, which we all know and are familiar with, and transforms it into a concept, which she uses to describe the situation of women. What does Beauvoir mean by "Other"? Have a close look at the stages of the concept's development. How does the concept apply to other groups besides women?

Invitation to Write

Beauvoir wrote her essay in the first half of the twentieth century. The situation she describes is basically that of the French and western European women of her time. Write an essay in which you establish how much (if any) of Beauvoir's argument still holds true in American society today. Is her argument valid today in other societies with which you are familiar? (In your essay, you can answer these questions from the male or female point of view.)

Connections

In her essay "Damned If You Do" (p. 495) Deborah Tannen describes how people's gender expectations cause them to evaluate differently the language and behavior of men and women. Considering Tannen's observations, would Beauvoir be able to say that women speak an "other" language? Write an essay using Beauvoir's concept of "other" applied to the language of women. Consider the differences between masculine and feminine language and explain them from Beauvoir's point of view. Given these differences, evaluate also the possibility of finding a common means of communication between men and women.

Defining Women's Lives

This sequence begins by asking you to consider how American society defines women's roles and how American women respond to that definition. Your conclusions, combined with your observations about the women described in Friedl's essay, will form the basis of your second paper, in which you consider the processes at work in shaping the definition of women's roles and how women themselves—whether in America or in another culture—participate in shaping that definition. The third assignment asks you to compare the boundaries of the lives of women in traditional communities, whether in Iran or closer to home. Moving from specific experiences to a more theoretical perspective, assignment 4 directs you to examine closely the text by Beauvoir. Here you will apply to her own work Beauvoir's observations about the attitudes behind gender classification. Finally, the last assignment gives you the opportunity to apply Beauvoir's ideas to the particular experiences of the women in the readings, as well as to your own experience. In a sense, you will test her theory by applying it to specific situations. If you think her theory helps provide a good basis for finding a common thread of meaning in the experiences of the women presented in the readings, you can use her ideas to make meaningful connections between theory and experience as well as among the lives of different women. If you reject or modify Beauvoir's ideas, you can define your own position as the first step toward constructing a theory of your own.

Assignment 1: Exploring Experience

Over the past two decades, many of the legal barriers that have oppressed women have been abolished. While this change has provided American women with more opportunities to redefine their roles and to take on new challenges, they often find that society's expectations about their behavior have not kept pace with the law. Write a paper in which you explore the way American society now defines women's roles and the impact of these expectations on women's lives.

Begin your paper by drawing on examples based on your own experience, the experience of family and friends, situations you have read about in newspapers or magazines, movie plots, or television programs. Use examples that focus on women's roles as students, professionals, politicians, homemakers, and parents. As a student, you could consider whether female students are treated differently than male students by teachers and the administration in the classroom, in the career counseling office, or on the playing fields. As you study your examples, ask what each example reveals about society's expectations for women. Decide if these expectations reflect a belief in equal opportunities for men and women. Also, ask how these expectations are communicated.

Assignment 2

*"People say her brothers said she shouldn't go to school any longer,"
said Mehri. "It is a long way to school here, all the way from
Mahmudabad. Dangerous. An hour at least."*
                                     —ERIKA FRIEDL, *A Betrothal, a Rape,*
                                     and a Guess About Turan's Fate

The women's discussion of Turan's situation and the brief glimpse of their own lives offered by Erika Friedl suggest the paths Iranian women must follow to avoid danger and criticism. Yet, the discussion in the courtyard suggests that the women's reactions are shaped as much by their membership in a female community as by their position in the larger society. Using examples from Friedl's text and your own knowledge of American society, write a paper that examines the way women's roles are defined by their cultures, and by the way women participate in this process.

To write this paper, consider specific examples from Friedl's description of the Iranian women's experience as well as the examples involving American women you developed in the first assignment. Go back to Friedl's text and underline two or three examples that suggest what the women see as "good" and "bad" fates. Explain how their definitions reflect their culture's views of women, and then look at their responses to these views. Consider their discussion with other women as part of their response. Then consider your previous discussion of the roles open to American women and their responses to these definitions of their roles. After you describe their responses, draw a conclusion about the long-term consequences of those responses.

Assignment 3

*I know what I want. I also know I'm not supposed to enter the club.
I enter anyway.*
                                     —MARIANNA DE MARCO TORGOVNICK,
                                     On Being White, Female, and Born in Bensonhurst

Boundaries that clearly establish geographic territories on maps are actually invisible on the land they divide. Unless a marker or fence has been placed on the land, a person walking across a border or boundary might not know it is actually there. Marianna De Marco Torgovnick begins and ends her essay by looking at different types of boundaries, visible and invisible, that were reinforced in Bensonhurst. Write a paper in which you investigate the presence and effect of these boundaries, and compare them to the boundaries that the Iranian women in Erika Friedl's selection must not or will not cross.

As you reread Torgovnick's essay to begin your assignment, underline as many passages referring to boundaries, stated or implicit, as possible. Include boundaries formed by class, gender, education, and religion and boundaries that create physical spaces, psychological spaces, or both. Turning to Friedl's description of the Iranian women, proceed in a similar fashion. After you look at both essays, analyze the relationship between physical and psychological boundaries and how such boundaries affect women. Use your analyses as the basis for an essay in which you explore the effect of visible and invisible boundaries on women's lives and the consequences of both respecting and crossing these boundaries.

Assignment 4

In actuality the relation of the two sexes is not quite like that of two electrical poles, for man represents both the positive and the neutral, as is indicated by the common use of man *to designate human beings in general; whereas woman represents only the negative, defined by limiting criteria, without reciprocity. In the midst of an abstract discussion it is vexing to hear a man say: "You think thus and so because you are a woman.". . .*
—SIMONE DE BEAUVOIR, *Introduction to* The Second Sex

Simone de Beauvoir poses the question "What is a woman?" and then presents us with a long list of answers drawn from literature, philosophy, and conversation. She gives us a range of viewpoints, using different voices. Write a paper in which you identify and examine the use of different voices in Beauvoir's essay. From your observations, determine whether Beauvoir participates in the process of casting people into the role of an "Other."

First, go back through Beauvoir's "Introduction to *The Second Sex*" and listen closely to the voices she hears in several of the examples she considers. As you look at three or four of them, ask yourself what Beauvoir is telling you about male or female behavior. For instance, when she writes "woman represents only the negative," Beauvoir is not giving her view of women but presenting what she suggests is a male point of view, the point of view that she believes shapes the opinion of society. As you look for examples, consider those statements Beauvoir attributes to men, her own statements about women, and the statements in which the speaker's gender remains unidentified. When the statements' speakers are unidentified, decide whether Beauvoir implies their gender, according to her analysis of male and female attitudes. Read her examples, keeping in mind her reaction to the "male" comments which "vex" her, and considering her own assumptions about male and female behavior.

Assignment 5

Reconsider the experiences of the women you have discussed in previous papers in light of Simone de Beauvoir's viewpoint. Specifically, explore Beauvoir's contribution to the discussion of social roles based on gender by testing it against your own analyses.

Begin by going back to the examples you discussed in previous papers. What might Beauvoir say about your descriptions of women's experience in contemporary American culture, about the lives of Turan and the women in Erika Friedl's essay, or about Marianna Torgovnick's use of the word *difference?* Does her response challenge or confirm your own? Discussing her response and your own will help you construct your own theory about the role of women in society.

Next, bring your ideas together in a paper that presents your theory about the role of women in modern society. Explain how reading and thinking about Beauvoir's ideas has shaped or reshaped your ideas. Or if reading Beauvoir has not changed your ideas, explain why you feel Beauvoir might need to look at the examples from another point of view, and then propose a revision of her theory.

4

Defining Men's Lives

Only the adults knew how bad things were. Sandy and I were allowed to go on believing that a father was indestructible—and ours turned out to be just that. Despite a raw emotional nature that makes him prey to intractable worry, his life has been distinguished by the power of resurgence.

—PHILIP ROTH, *His Roth*

Had his heart not throbbed with thousands of others that day as each time he closed his eyes he saw a vision of something exciting, a legacy of responsibilities that demanded a warrior's spirit? . . . But it seemed to him now that a common goal had been lost sight of and he lamented it. He could not help but feel that the warriors had laid down their arrows and had parted different ways to fend for themselves.

—LEONARD KIBERA, *The Spider's Web*

The real man gains renown by standing between his family and destruction, absorbing the blows of fate with equanimity. Mediterranean manhood is the reward given to the man who is an efficient protector of the web of primordial ties, the guardian of his society's moral and material integuments.

—DAVID GILMORE,
Performative Excellence: Circum-Mediterranean

171

Traditionally, men have been considered society's warriors. This aggressive image of male behavior may still be deeply entrenched in American and other cultures. But men have begun redefining their roles, just as women began challenging their traditional roles in the 1960s and 1970s. As they struggle with questions about their own identities, many men feel that the social roles open to them have been as rigidly defined as the roles open to women. Some theorists of male gender studies have examined the cost and responsibilities of being male, and other theorists have studied the reasons for the emergence of the traditional roles for males. This attention to traditional definitions of the male role has allowed for its redefinition. Today, varied images of men coexist alongside the traditional models of male behavior; for example, some men cook, clean, and care for their children while their wives go to work. As they explore new roles, men are finding it acceptable to express their feelings and respond with behaviors previously reserved for women. Even if the structure of society has not changed radically, men have more varied images of manhood open to them: John Wayne or Kevin Costner, GI Joe or Aladdin, the Frugal Gourmet or Norman Schwarzkopf, Robert Bly or Clint Eastwood.

The readings by Philip Roth, Leonard Kibera, and David Gilmore pose some interesting questions about expectations of male behavior. As you read, you will find that some ideas about manhood cross cultures while others do not. You will also examine the relationship between the private and public definitions of acceptable male behavior, observing the way modifications in one realm affect roles developed in the other. Philip Roth's brief memoir about his father, "His Roth," demonstrates the way children grow up associating particular attitudes and behaviors with either male or female parents. His father's behavior could be considered conventional and atypical at the same time. In his short story "The Spider's Web," Leonard Kibera describes how social upheaval that disrupts traditional gender roles disorients individuals who have no new models to substitute for them. David Gilmore's more theoretical essay, "Performative Excellence: Circum-Mediterranean," looks at images of manhood in one particular region of the world. He explores the persistence of these images by suggesting their functional role in Mediterranean society. Gilmore demonstrates that despite changes in traditional societies, traditional ideas of male behavior remain powerful.

PHILIP ROTH

His Roth

Philip Roth was born in 1933 in Newark, New Jersey, where he grew up and attended high school and his first year of college. He graduated from Bucknell University in 1954 and later received an M.A. in English from the University of Chicago. After a brief stint in the army, Roth returned to the University of Chicago to study for his doctorate. There, he worked on the literary magazine and began to write the short stories collected in his first published work, *Good-Bye, Columbus* (1959). He left graduate school to become a full-time writer, soon winning several grants, fellowships, and an appointment to teach at the Writer's Workshop at the University of Iowa. Roth has published numerous novels, including *When She Was Good* (1967), *Portnoy's Complaint* (1969), *The Great American Novel* (1973), and the trilogy of Zuckerman novels, *Zuckerman Bound* (1985). He has also taught at Princeton University and the University of Pennsylvania.

Roth's novels often draw on his personal knowledge of Jewish-American life. He has written frequently about his family background and his relationship with his father. The following article, which appeared in the Summer 1988 issue of *Granta,* is the prologue to *The Facts* (1988) and is closely related to *Patrimony* (1991), Roth's book exploring his relationship with his father in great depth. Both of these books and the following excerpt blend nostalgia and pain with humor and optimism. In them, much of Roth's best writing consists of his portrayal of his father, Herman Roth—who was eighty-six years old, a widower, and a retired insurance manager—during the moments when he was debilitated by illness.

ONE DAY IN LATE OCTOBER 1944, I was astonished to find my father, whose workday ordinarily began at seven and many nights didn't end until ten, sitting alone at the kitchen table in the middle of the afternoon. He was going into the hospital unexpectedly to have his appendix removed. Though he had already packed a bag to take with him, he had waited for my brother, Sandy, and me to get home from school to tell us not to be alarmed. "Nothing to it," he assured us, though we all knew that two of his brothers had died back in the 1920s from complications following difficult appendectomies. My mother, the president that year of our school's parent-teacher association, happened, quite unusually, to be away overnight in Atlantic City at a state-wide PTA convention. My father had phoned her hotel, however, to tell her the news, and she had immediately begun preparations to return home. That would do it, I was sure: My mother's domestic ingenuity was on a par with Robinson Crusoe's, and as for nursing us all through our illnesses, we couldn't have received much better care from Florence Nightingale. As was usual in our household, everything was now under control.

By the time her train pulled into Newark that evening, the surgeon had opened him up, seen the mess, and despaired for my father's chances. At the age of forty-three, he was put on the critical list and given less than a fifty-fifty chance to survive.

Only the adults knew how bad things were. Sandy and I were allowed to go on believing that a father was indestructible—and ours turned out to be just that. Despite a raw emotional nature that makes him prey to intractable worry, his life has been distinguished by the power of resurgence. I've never intimately known anyone else—aside from my brother and me—to swing as swiftly through so wide a range of moods, anyone else to take things so hard, to be so openly racked by a serious setback, and yet, after the blow has rever-berated down to the quick, to clamber back so aggressively, to recover lost ground and get going again.

He was saved by the new sulfa powder, developed during the early years of the war to treat battlefront wounds. Surviving was an awful ordeal none the less, his weakness from the near-fatal peritonitis exacerbated by a ten-day siege of hiccups during which he was unable to sleep or to keep down food. After he'd lost nearly thirty pounds, his shrunken face disclosed itself to us as a replica of my elderly grandmother's, the face of the mother whom he and all his brothers adored (towards the father—laconic, authoritarian, remote, an immigrant who'd trained in Galicia to be a rabbi but worked in America in a hat factory—their feelings were more confused). Bertha Zahnstecker Roth was a simple old-country woman, good-hearted, given to neither melancholy nor complaint, yet her everyday facial expression made it plain that she nursed no illusions about life's being easy. My father's resemblance to his mother would not appear so eerily again until he himself reached his eighties, and then only when he was in the grip of a struggle that stripped an otherwise physically youthful old man of his seeming impregnability, leaving him bewil-dered not so much because of the eye problem or the difficulty with his gait that had made serious inroads on his self-sufficiency but because he felt all at once abandoned by the masterful accomplice and overturner of obstacles, his determination.

When he was driven home from Newark's Beth Israel Hospital after   5 six weeks in bed there, he barely had the strength, even with our assistance, to make it up the short back staircase to our second-storey apartment. It was December 1944 by then, a cold winter day, but through the windows the sunlight illuminated my parents' bedroom. Sandy and I came in to talk to him, both of us shy and grateful and, of course, stunned by how helpless he appeared seated weakly in a lone chair in the corner of the room. Seeing his sons together like that, my father could no longer control himself and began to sob. He was alive, the sun was shining, his wife was not widowed nor his boys fatherless—family life would now resume. It was not so complicated that an eleven-year-old couldn't understand his father's tears. I just didn't see, as he so clearly could, why or how it should have turned out differently.

I knew only two boys in our neighborhood whose families were fatherless, and thought of them as no less blighted than the blind girl who attended our school for a while and had to be read to and shepherded everywhere. The fatherless boys seemed almost equally marked and set apart; in the aftermath of their fathers' deaths, they too struck me as scary and a little taboo. Though one was a model of obedience and the other a trouble-maker, everything either of them did or said seemed determined by his being a boy with a dead father and, however innocently I arrived at this notion, I was probably right.

I knew no child whose family was divided by divorce. Outside of the movie magazines and the tabloid headlines, it didn't exist, certainly not among Jews like us. Jews didn't get divorced—not because divorce was forbidden by Jewish law but because that was the way they were. If Jewish fathers didn't come home drunk and beat their wives—and in our neighbourhood, which was Jewry to me, I'd never heard of any who did—that too was because of the way they were. In our lore, the Jewish family was an inviolate haven against every form of menace, from personal isolation to gentile hostility. Regardless of internal friction and strife, it was assumed to be an indissoluble consolidation. *Hear, O Israel, the family is God, the family is One.*

Family indivisibility, the first commandment.

In the late 1940s, when my father's younger brother, Bernie, proclaimed his intention of divorcing the wife of nearly twenty years who was the mother of his two daughters, my mother and father were as stunned as if they'd heard that he'd killed somebody. Had Bernie committed murder and gone to jail for life, they would probably have rallied behind him despite the abominable, inexplicable deed. But when he made up his mind not merely to divorce but to do so to marry a younger woman, their support went instantly to the "victims," the sister-in-law and the nieces. For his transgression, a breach of faith with his wife, his children, his entire clan—a dereliction of his duty as a Jew *and* as a Roth—Bernie encountered virtually universal condemnation.

That family rupture only began to mend when time revealed that no one 10 had been destroyed by the divorce; in fact, anguished as they were by the break-up of their household, Bernie's ex-wife and his two girls were never remotely as indignant as the rest of the relatives. The healing owed a lot to Bernie himself, a more diplomatic man than most of his judges, but also to the fact that for my father the demand of family solidarity and the bond of family history exceeded even *his* admonishing instincts. It was to be another forty-odd years, however, before the two brothers threw their arms around each other and hungrily embraced in an unmistakable act of unqualified reconciliation. This occurred a few weeks before Bernie's death, in his late seventies, when his heart was failing rapidly and nobody, beginning with himself, expected him to last much longer.

I had driven my father over to see Bernie and his wife, Ruth, in their condominium in a retirement village in north-western Connecticut, twenty miles from my own home. It was Bernie's turn now to wear the little face of his unillusioned, stoical old mother; when he came to the door to let us in, there in his features was that stark resemblance that seemed to emerge in all the Roth brothers when they were up against it.

Ordinarily the two men would have met with a handshake, but when my father stepped into the hallway, so much was clear both about the time that was left to Bernie and about all those decades, seemingly stretching back to the beginning of time, during which they had been alive as their parents' offspring, that the handshake was swallowed up in a forceful hug that lasted minutes and left them in tears. They seemed to be saying goodbye to everyone already gone as well as to each other, the last two surviving children of the dour hat-blocker Sender and the imperturbable *balabusta* Bertha. Safely in his brother's arms, Bernie seemed also to be saying goodbye to himself. There was nothing to guard against or defend against or resent anymore, nothing even to remember. In these brothers, men so deeply swayed, despite their dissimilarity, by identical strains of family emotion, everything remembered had been distilled into pure, barely bearable feeling.

In the car afterwards my father said, "We haven't held each other like that since we were small boys. My brother's dying, Philip. I used to push him around in his carriage. There were nine of us, with my mother and father. I'll be the last one left."

While we drove back to my house (where he was staying in the upstairs back bedroom, a room in which he says he never fails to sleep like a baby) he recounted the struggles of each of his five brothers—with bankruptcies, illnesses, and in-laws, with marital dissension and bad loans, and with children, with their Gonerils, their Regans, and their Cordelias. He recalled for me the martyrdom of his only sister, what she and all the family had gone through when her husband the book-keeper who liked the horses had served a little time for embezzlement.

It wasn't exactly the first time I was hearing these stories. Narrative is the form that his knowledge takes, and his repertoire has never been large: family, family, family, Newark, Newark, Newark, Jew, Jew, Jew. Somewhat like mine.

I naively believed as a child that I would always have a father present, and the truth seems to be that I always will. However awkward the union may sometimes have been, vulnerable to differences of opinion, to false expectations, to radically divergent experiences of America, strained by the colliding of two impatient, equally willful temperaments and marred by masculine clumsiness, the link to him has been omnipresent. What's more, now, when he no longer commands my attention by his bulging biceps and his moral strictures, now, when he is no longer the biggest man I have to contend with—and when I am not all that far from being an old man myself—I am able to laugh at his jokes and hold his hand and concern myself with his well-being, I'm able to love him the way I wanted to when I was sixteen, seventeen, and eighteen but when, what with dealing with him and feeling at odds with him, it was simply an impossibility. *The* impossibility, for all that I always respected him for his particular burden and his struggle within a system that he didn't choose. The mythological role of a Jewish boy growing up in a family like mine—to become the hero one's father failed to be—I may even have achieved by now, but not at all in the way that was pre-ordained. After nearly forty years of living far from home, I'm equipped at last to be the most loving of sons—just, however, when he has another agenda. He is trying to die. He doesn't say that, nor, probably, does he think of it in those words, but that's his job now and, fight as he will to survive, he understands, as he always has, what the real work is.

Trying to die isn't like trying to commit suicide—it may actually be harder, because what you are trying to do is what you least want to have happen; you dread it but there it is and it must be done, and by no one but you. Twice in the last few years he has taken a shot at it, on two different occasions suddenly became so ill that I, who was then living abroad half the year, flew back to America to find him with barely enough strength to walk from the sofa to the TV set without clutching at every chair in between. And though each time the doctor, after a painstaking examination, was unable to find anything wrong with him, he none the less went to bed every night expecting not to awaken in the morning and, when he did awaken in the morning, he was fifteen minutes just getting himself into a sitting position on the edge of the bed and another hour shaving and dressing. Then, for God knows how long, he slouched unmoving over a bowl of cereal for which he had absolutely no appetite.

I was as certain as he was that this was it, yet neither time could he pull it

15

off and, over a period of weeks, he recovered his strength and became himself again, loathing Reagan, defending Israel, phoning relatives, attending funerals, writing to newspapers, castigating William Buckley, watching MacNeil-Lehrer, exhorting his grown grandchildren, remembering in detail our own dead, and relentlessly, exactingly—and without having been asked—monitoring the caloric intake of the nice woman he lives with. It would seem that to prevail here, to try dying and to *do* it, he will have to work even harder than he did in the insurance business, where he achieved a remarkable success for a man with his social and educational handicaps. Of course, here too he'll eventually succeed—though clearly, despite his record of assiduous application to every job he has ever been assigned, things won't be easy. But then they never have been.

Needless to say, the link to my father was never so voluptuously tangible as the colossal bond to my mother's flesh, whose metamorphosed incarnation was a sleek black seal-skin coat into which I, the younger, the privileged, the pampered papoose, blissfully wormed myself whenever my father chauffeured us home to New Jersey on a winter Sunday from our semi-annual excursion to Radio City Music Hall and Manhattan's Chinatown: The unnameable animal-me bearing her dead father's name, the protoplasm-me, boy-baby, and body-burrower-in-training, joined by every nerve-ending to her smile and her seal-skin coat, while his resolute dutifulness, his relentless industriousness, his unreasoning obstinacy and harsh resentments, his illusions, his innocence, his allegiances, his fears were to constitute the original mould for the American, Jew, citizen, man, even for the writer, I would become. To be at all is to be her Philip, but in the embroilment with the buffeting world, my history still takes its spin from beginning as his Roth.

Considerations

1. From Roth's descriptions of his father, how do you think the latter defines his role as the head of the family? How does young Philip view his father in that role? How does becoming an adult change Roth's view of his father?

2. Roth starts talking about his father by narrating the appendectomy incident. Why do you think he starts with a crisis situation? What is the significance of his father's operation? What is the significance of the details concerning the degradation of his body?

3. At the end of his narrative, Roth describes himself as his mother's "Philip" but his father's "Roth." How is this remark connected to the title? What kinds of family relationships are indicated by the use of the names?

Invitation to Write

Roth's narrative is mainly concerned with his father, but it also discloses powerful beliefs about the Jewish family and the role of each of its members in maintaining its unity. To what extent is his family particularly Jewish? Write an essay in which you explore the relationship between Judaism and the notion of family as it emerges in Roth's narrative. Think about his relationship with his parents and their family values, and try to determine whether they are specifically Jewish or, more generally, American. Compare Roth's notion of the family when he was a child to your own contemporary notion of family in order to draw your conclusions.

Connections

Both Roth, in the above essay, and Richard Rodriguez, in "Complexion" (p. 465), reach back to their childhoods to produce powerful descriptions of their fathers. Although both essays seem to focus more on the role of the fathers, they also tell us a great deal about the importance the two writers attach to being their fathers' sons. In spite of certain moments of rebellion against their fathers, they are both haunted by nostalgia. Write an essay in which you explore the influence the fathers have on their sons in the essays by Roth and Rodriguez. Examine the importance of the values that the authors inherited from their families, and determine the degree to which each of them identifies with his father. This latter issue should consider their ethnic backgrounds, which make their relationships even more complicated than many American father-son relationships.

LEONARD KIBERA

The Spider's Web

Leonard Kibera was born in Kenya around 1940—the exact date of his birth is uncertain. In 1968, together with his brother Samuel Kahiga, he published *Potent Ash,* a volume of short stories that deals with events during the days of Kenya's "Emergency" in the middle 1950s, when the so-called Mau-mau revolt sought to overthrow the British rule. In 1967, the short play entitled *Potent Ash,* based on the short story which gave the volume its title, was published by *New African Literature and the Arts.* The play won third prize in the BBC African drama contest and was produced in London on the BBC's *African Services.* In 1971, Kibera published his first novel, *Voices in the Dark.* The novel expressed his vision of postindependence, which in Kenya was a time of national questioning and tensions. Kibera's stylistic and structural devices—a disjointed approach to reality, swinging back and forth in time—make his topic even more compelling.

"The Spider's Web" was published in 1972 in *Présence Africaine* and later reprinted in *African Short Stories* (1985), edited by Chinua Achebe and C. L. Innes. Like Kibera's others works, this story probes into the meaning of the Kenyan experience after independence. The spirit of British rule lingered in the former colony, perverting relationships and defying long-standing traditions. Kibera's story is difficult to read because he often resorts to metaphors and symbolic representations that are tangential to the main action. The story's ambiguous ending is also a challenge to simplified notions about the problems faced by the citizens of the liberated African countries.

INSIDE THE COFFIN, HIS BODY had become rigid. He tried to turn and only felt the prick of the nail. It had been hammered carelessly through the lid, just falling short of his shoulder. There was no pain but he felt irretrievable and alone, hemmed within the mean, stuffy box, knowing that outside was air. *As dust to dust* . . . the pious preacher intoned out there, not without an edge of triumph. *This suicide, brethren* . . . ! They had no right, these people had no right at all. They sang so mournfully over him, almost as if it would disappoint them to see him come back. But he would jump out yet, he would send the rusty nails flying back at them and teach that cheap-jack of an undertaker

180

how to convert old trunks. He was not a third-class citizen. *Let me out!* But he could not find the energy to cry out or even turn a little from the nail on his shoulder, as the people out there hastened to cash in another tune, for the padre might at any moment cry *Amen!* and commit the flesh deep into the belly of the earth whence it came. Somebody was weeping righteously in between the pauses. He thought it was Mrs Njogu. Then in the dead silence that followed he was being posted into the hole and felt himself burning up already as his mean little trunk creaked at the joints and nudged its darkness in on him like a load of sins. *Careful, careful, he is not a heap of rubbish . . .* That was Mr Njogu. Down, slowly down, the careless rope issued in snappy mean measures like a spider's web and knocked his little trunk against the sides to warn the loud gates that he was coming to whoever would receive him. It caved in slowly, the earth, he could feel, and for the first time he felt important. He seemed to matter now, as all eyes no doubt narrowed into the dark hole at this moment, with everybody hissing *poor soul; gently, gently.* Then *snap!* The rope gave way—one portion of the dangling thing preferring to recoil into the tight-fisted hands out there—and he felt shot towards the bottom head-downwards, exploding into the gates of hell with a loud, unceremonious *Bang!*

Ngotho woke up with a jump. He mopped the sweat on the tail of his sheet. This kind of thing would bring him no good. Before, he had been dreaming of beer parties or women or fights with bees as he tried to smoke them out for honey. Now, lately, it seemed that when he wasn't being smoked out of this city where he so very much belonged and yet never belonged, he was either pleading his case at the White Gates or being condemned to hell in cheap coffins. *This kind of thing just isn't healthy . . .*

But he was in top form. He flung the blanket away. He bent his arms at the elbow for exercise. He shot them up and held them there like a surrender. *No that will not do.* He bent them again and pressed his fingers on his shoulders. They gathered strength, knitting into a ball so that his knuckles sharpened. Then he shot a dangerous fist to the left and held it there, tightly, not yielding a step, until he felt all stiff and blood pumped at his forehead. Dizziness overpowered him and his hand fell dead on the bed. Then a spasm uncoiled his right which came heavily on the wall and, pained, cowered. Was he still a stranger to the small dimensions of his only room even after eight years?

But it wasn't the first time anyhow. So, undaunted, he sprang twice on the bed for more exercise. Avoiding the spring that had fetched his thigh yesterday morning between the bulges in the old mattress, he hummed *Africa nchi yetu* and shot his leg down the bed. Swa—ah! That would be three shillings for another sheet through the back doors of the Koya Mosque. Ngotho dragged himself out of bed.

It was a beautiful Sunday morning. He had nothing to worry about so long as he did not make the mistake of going to church. Churches depressed

5

him. But that dream still bothered him. *(At least they could have used a less precipitate rope.)* And those nails, didn't he have enough things pricking him since Mrs Knight gave him a five-pound handshake saying Meet you in England and Mrs Njogu came buzzing in as his new memsahib borrowing two shillings from him?

Ngotho folded his arms at his chest and yawned. He took his moustache thoughtfully between his fingers and curled it sharp like horns. At least she could have returned it. It was not as if the cost of living had risen the way employers took things for granted these days. He stood at the door of the two-room house which he shared with the other servant who, unlike him, didn't cook for memsahib. Instead, Kago went on errands, trimmed the grass, and swept the compound, taking care to trace well the dog's mess for the night. Already Ngotho could see the early riser as good as sniffing and scanning the compound after the erratic manner of Wambui last night. (Wambui was the brown Alsatian dragged from the village and surprised into civilisation, a dog-collar, and tinned bones by Mrs Njogu. A friend of hers, Elsie Bloom, kept one and they took their bitches for a walk together.) Ngotho cleared his throat.

"Hei, Kago!"

Kago, who was getting frostbite, rubbed his thumb between the toes and turned round.

"How is the dog's breakfast?"

"Nyukwa!"   10

Ngotho laughed.

"You don't have to insult my mother," he said. "Tinned bones for Wambui and corn flakes for memsahib are the same thing. We both hang if we don't get them."

Kago leant on his broom, scratched the top of his head dull-wittedly, and at last saw that Ngotho had a point there.

He was a good soul, Kago was, and subservient as a child. There was no doubt about his ready aggressiveness where men of his class were concerned it was true, but when it came to Mrs Njogu he wound tail between his legs and stammered. This morning he was feeling at peace with the world.

"Perhaps you are right," he said, to Ngotho. Then diving his thumb be-   15
tween the toes he asked if there was a small thing going on that afternoon—
like a beer party.

"The Queen!"

At the mention of the name, Kago forgot everything about drinking, swerved round, and felt a thousand confused things beat into his head simultaneously. Should he go on sweeping and sniffing or should he get the Bob's Tinned? Should he untin the Bob's Tinned or should he run for the Sunday paper? Mrs Njogu, alias queen, wasn't she more likely to want Wambui brushed behind the ear? Or was she now coming to ask him why the rope lay at the door while Wambui ran about untied?

With his bottom towards memsahib's door, Kago assumed a busy pose and peeped through his legs. But memsahib wasn't bothered about him. At least not yet. She stood at the door legs askew and admonished Ngotho about the corn flakes.

Kago breathed a sigh of relief and took a wild sweep at the broom. He saw Ngotho back against the wall of their servant's-quarters and suppressed a laugh. After taking a torrent of English words, Ngotho seemed to tread carefully the fifty violent paces between the two doors, the irreconcilable gap between the classes. As he approached Mrs Njogu, he seemed to sweep a tactful curve off the path, as if to move up the wall first and then try to back in slowly towards the master's door and hope memsahib would make way. For her part, the queen flapped her wings and spread herself luxuriously, as good as saying, You will have to kneel and dive in through my legs. Then she stuck out her tongue twice, heaved her breasts, spat milk and honey onto the path, and disappeared into the hive. Ngotho followed her.

Kago scratched his big toe and sat down to laugh.

Breakfast for memsahib was over. Ngotho came out of the house to cut out the painful corn in his toe with the kitchen knife. He could take the risk and it pleased him. But he had to move to the other end of the wall. Mr Njogu was flushing the toilet and he might chance to open the small blurred window and see the otherwise clean kitchen knife glittering in the sun on dirty toe nails.

Breakfast. Couldn't memsahib trust him with the sugar or milk even after four years? Must she buzz around him as he measured breakfast-for-two? He had nothing against corn flakes. In fact ever since she became suspicious, he had found himself eating more of her meals whenever she was not in sight, also taking some sugar in his breast pocket. But he had come to hate himself for it and felt it was a coward's way out. Still, what was he to do? Mrs Njogu had become more and more of a stranger and he had even caught himself looking at her from an angle where formerly he had stared her straight in the face. He had wanted to talk to her, to assure her that he was still her trusted servant, but everything had become more entangled and sensitive. She would only say he was criticising, and if he wasn't happy what was he waiting for? But if he left, where was he to go? Unemployment had turned loose upon the country as it had never done before. Housewives around would receive the news of his impertinence blown high and wide over Mrs Njogu's telephone before he approached them for a job, and set their dogs on him.

Ngotho scratched at his grey hair and knew that respect for age had completely bereft his people. Was this the girl he once knew as Lois back in his home village? She had even been friends with his own daughter. A shy, young thing with pimples and thin legs. Lois had taught at the village school and was everybody's good example. She preferred to wear cheap skirts than see her aging parents starve for lack of money.

20

"Be like Lois," mothers warned their daughters and even spanked them to press the point. What they meant in fact was that their daughters should, like Lois, stay unmarried longer and not simply run off with some young man in a neat tie who refused to pay the dowry. Matters soon became worse for such girls when suddenly Lois became heroine of the village. She went to jail.

It was a General Knowledge class. Lois put the problem word squarely on the blackboard. The lady supervisor who went round the schools stood squarely at the other end, looking down the class. Lois swung her stick up and down the class and said,

"What is the Commonwealth, children? Don't be shy, what does this word mean?"

The girls chewed their thumbs.

"Come on! All right. We shall start from the *beginning*. Who rules England?"

Slowly, the girls turned their heads round and faced the white supervisor. Elizabeth, they knew they should say. But how could Lois bring them to this? England sounded venerable enough. Must they go further now and let the white lady there at the back hear the Queen of England mispronounced, or even uttered by these tender things with the stain of last night's onions in their breath? Who would be the first? They knit their knuckles under the desks, looked into their exercise books, and one by one said they didn't know. One or two brave ones threw their heads back again, met with a strange look in the white queen's eye which spelt disaster, immediately swung their eyes onto the blackboard, and catching sight of Lois's stick, began to cry.

"It is as if you have never heard of it." Lois was losing patience. "All right, I'll give you another start. Last start. What is our country?"

Simultaneously, a flash of hands shot up from under the desks and thirty-four breaths of maize and onions clamoured.

"A colony."

Slowly, the lady supervisor measured out light taps down the class and having eliminated the gap that came between master and servant, stood face to face with Lois.

The children chewed at their rubbers.

Then the white queen slapped Lois across the mouth and started for the door. But Lois caught her by the hair, slapped her back once, twice, and spat into her face. Then she gave her a football kick and swept her out with a right.

When at last Lois looked back into the class, she only saw torn exercise books flung on the floor. Thirty-four pairs of legs had fled home through the window, partly to be comforted from the queen's government which was certain to come, and partly to spread the formidable news of their new queen and heroine.

Queen, she certainly was, Ngotho thought as he say by the wall and backed against it. Corn flakes in bed; expensive skirts; cigarettes. Was this

her? Mr Njogu had come straight from the University College in time to secure a shining job occupied for years by a mzungu. Then a neat car was seen
to park by Lois's house. In due course these visits became more frequent and
alarming, but no villager was surprised when eventually Njogu succeeded in
dragging Lois away from decent society. He said paying the dowry was for
people in the mountains.

As luck would have it for Ngotho, Mr and Mrs Knight left and Mr and
Mrs Njogu came to occupy the house. He was glad to cook and wash a black
man's towels for a change. And, for a short time at any rate, he was indeed
happy. Everybody had sworn that they were going to build something together, something challenging and responsible, something that would make a
black man respectable in his own country. He had been willing to serve, to
keep up the fire that had eventually smoked out the white man. From now on
there would be no more revenge, and no more exploitation. Beyond this, he
didn't expect much for himself; he knew that there would always be masters
and servants.

Ngotho scratched himself between the legs and sunk against the wall. He
stared at the spider that slowly built its web meticulously under the verandah
roof. He threw a light stone at it and only alerted the spider.

Had his heart not throbbed with thousands of others that day as each   40
time he closed his eyes he saw a vision of something exciting, a legacy of
responsibilities that demanded a warrior's spirit? Had he not prayed for oneness deep from the heart? But it seemed to him now that a common goal had
been lost sight of and he lamented it. He could not help but feel that the
warriors had laid down their arrows and had parted different ways to fend for
themselves. And as he thought of their households, he saw only the image of
Lois who he dared call nothing but memsahib now. She swam big and muscular in his mind.

Ngotho wondered whether this was the compound he used to know. Was
this part connecting master and servant the one that had been so straight during Mrs Knight?

Certainly he would never want her back. He had been kicked several
times by Mr Knight and had felt what it was like to be hit with a frying pan
by Mrs Knight as she reminded him to be grateful. But it had all been so
direct, no ceremonies: They didn't like his broad nose. They said so. They
thought there were rats under his bed. There were. They teased that he hated
everything white and yet his hair was going white on his head like snow, a
cool white protector while below the black animal simmered and plotted:
Wouldn't he want it cut? No, he wouldn't. Occasionally, they would be impressed by a well-turned turkey or chicken and say so over talk of the white
man's responsibility in Africa. If they were not in the mood they just dismissed
him and told him not to forget the coffee. Ngotho knew that all this was
because they were becoming uneasy and frightened, and that perhaps they

had to point the gun at all black men now at a time when even the church had taken sides. But whatever the situation in the house, there was nevertheless a frankness about the black-and-white relationship were no ceremonies or apologies were necessary in a world of mutual distrust and hate. And if Mrs Knight scolded him all over the house, it was Mr Knight who seemed to eventually lock the bedroom door and come heavily on top of her and everybody else although, Ngotho thought, they were all ruled by a woman in England.

Ngotho walked heavily to the young tree planted three years ago by Mrs Njogu and wondered why he should have swept a curve off the path that morning, as memsahib filled the door. He knew it wasn't the first time he had done that. Everything had become crooked, subtle, and he had to watch his step. His monthly vernacular paper said so. He felt cornered. He gripped the young tree by the scruff of the neck and shook it furiously. What the hell was wrong with some men anyway? Had Mr Njogu become a male weakling in a fat queen bee's hive, slowly being milked dry and sapless, dying? Where was the old warrior who at the end of the battle would go home to his wife and make her moan under his heavy sweat? All he could see now as he shook the tree was a line of neat houses. There, the warriors had come to their battle's end and parted, to forget other warriors and to be mothered to sleep without even knowing it, meeting only occasionally to drink beer and sing traditional songs. And where previously the bow and arrow lay by the bed-post, Ngotho now only saw a conspiracy of round tablets while a *Handbook of Novel Techniques* lay by the pillow.

He had tried to understand. But as he looked at their pregnant wives he could foresee nothing but a new generation of innocent snobs, who would be chauffeured off to school in neat caps hooded over their eyes so as to obstruct vision. There they would learn that the other side of the city was dirty. Ngotho spat right under the tree. Once or twice he would have liked to kick Mr Njogu. He looked all so sensibly handsome and clean as he buzzed after his wife on a broken wing and—a spot of jam on his tie—said he wanted the key to the car.

He had also become very sensitive and self-conscious. Ngotho couldn't complain a little or even make a joke about the taxes without somebody detecting a subtler intention behind the smile, where the servant was supposed to be on a full-scale plotting. And there was behind the master and the queen now a bigger design, a kind of pattern meticulously fenced above the hive; a subtle web, at the centre of which lurked the spider which protected, watched, and jailed. Ngotho knew only too well that the web had been slowly, quietly in the making and a pebble thrown at it would at best alert and fall back impotent on the ground.

He took a look at the other end of the compound. Kago had fallen asleep, while Wambui ran about untied, the rope still lying at the door. Kago wore an indifferent grin. Ngotho felt overpowered, trapped, alone. He spat in Kago's direction and plucked a twig off one of the branches on the tree. The tree began to bleed. He tightened his grip and shed the reluctant leaves down. Just what had gone wrong with God?

The old one had faithfully done his job when that fig tree near Ngotho's village withered away as predicted by the tribal seer. It had been the local news and lately, it was rumoured, some businessman would honour the old god by erecting a hotel on the spot. Ngotho hardly believed in any god at all. The one lived in corrupted blood, the other in pulpits of hypocrisy. But at least while they kept neat themselves they could have honoured the old in a cleaner way. How could this new saviour part the warriors different ways into isolated compartments, to flush their uneasy hotel toilets all over the old one?

Ngotho passed a reverent hand over his wrinkled forehead and up his white hair. He plucked another twig off the dangerous tree. Something was droning above his ear.

"What are you doing to my tree?"

The buzzing had turned into a scream. 50

"I—I want to pick my teeth," Ngotho unwrapped a row of defiant molars.

The queen flapped her wings and landed squarely on the ground. Then she was heaving heavily, staring at him out of small eyes. He tried to back away from her eyes. Beyond her, in the background, he caught sight of Mr Njogu through the bedroom window polishing his spectacles on his pyjama sleeve, trying desperately to focus—clearly—on the situation outside. A flap of the wing and Ngotho felt hit right across the mouth, by the hand that had once hit the white lady. Then the queen wobbled in midflight, settled at the door, and screamed at Mr Njogu to come out and prove he was a man.

Mr Njogu didn't like what he saw. He threw his glasses away and preferred to see things blurred.

"These women," he muttered, and waved them away with a neat pyjama sleeve. Then he buried his head under the blanket and snored. It was ten o'clock.

Ngotho stood paralysed. He had never been hit by a woman before, out- 55 side of his mother's hut. Involuntarily, he felt his eyes snap shut and his eyelids burn red, violently, in the sun. Then out of the spider's web in his mind, policemen, magistrates, and third-class undertakers flew in profusion. He opened up, sweating, and the kitchen knife in his hand fell down, stabbing the base of the tree where it vibrated once, twice, and fell flat on its side, dead.

Then with a cry, he grabbed it and rushed into the house. But Mr Njogu saw him coming as the knife glittered nearer and clearer in his direction, and leapt out of bed.

Suddenly the horror of what he had done caught Ngotho. He could hear the queen at least crying hysterically into the telephone, while Mr Njogu locked himself in the toilet and began weeping. Ngotho looked at the kitchen knife in his hand. He had only succeeded in stabbing Mr Njogu in the thigh, and the knife had now turned red on him. Soon the sticky web would stretch a thread. And he would be caught as he never thought he would when first he felt glad to work for Lois.

He saw Wambui's rope still lying in a noose. Then he went into his room and locked the door.

Considerations

1. Early in the story, after Ngotho wakes from his nightmare, he reflects that his dreams have recently changed radically from pleasant images to alarming ones. How would you explain this change in his dreams and the nightmare that awakens him?

2. During the course of the story, Ngotho reflects upon the way Mrs. Njogu's name has evolved from "Lois" to "the queen." As her name indicates, she grows more powerful in the eyes of Ngotho. From Ngotho's point of view, where does her power come from? How does he react to it?

3. The story is rich with symbols and metaphorical representations. The image of Lois as a queen bee is only one of them. Locate two or three other symbols in the story and determine what they might represent. How do they function separately, and what kind of pattern do they form in the story as a whole?

Invitation to Write

This story expresses Ngotho's confusion and feelings of helplessness. Because it is told from his point of view, we tend to sympathize with him and to see him as a victim of the lingering colonial spirit embodied by Lois, the "queen." However, his hate and frustration are not determined only by his position as a servant, but also by the fact that his exploiter is a woman. Think of situations you have witnessed where a relationship defined essentially from the point of view of class or race is complicated by gender roles. Then take a closer look at his remarks about Lois and about her husband. Write an essay in which you explore the complexity of the relationship between Ngotho and Lois. Determine how much of Ngotho's frustration derives from the fact that he is socially inferior and how much he is hurt in his masculine pride. Consider the indigenous conceptions about the roles of men and women in his society as they become evident in his complaints. Draw a more general conclusion about the overlapping of gender and class or race divisions.

Connections

In his essay "The Westernization of the World" (p. 553), Paul Harrison comments upon the situation that results when colonial masters leave, only to be replaced by an indigenous class of Western-educated upstarts. Given his analysis, how would Harrison look at the relationship between Ngotho and the Njogus? Write an essay that examines the events in Kibera's story in light of Harrison's analysis of the economic and cultural effects of westernization. Which aspects of the story's postcolonial situation become clearer when Harrison's comments are considered? How do Harrison's ideas offer ways to help imagine more about the conditions of the characters' lives? Point out the circumstances in the story that would seem to elude Harrison's analysis.

DAVID GILMORE

Performative Excellence: Circum-Mediterranean

David D. Gilmore was born in 1943 and is now a professor of anthropology at the State University of New York at Stony Brook. He is the author of several books, including *People of the Plain: Class and Community in Lower Andalusia* (1980), *Aggression and Community: Paradoxes and Andalusian Culture* (1987), and *Manhood in the Making: Cultural Concepts of Masculinity* (1990). As an anthropologist, Gilmore is concerned with observing and analyzing patterns of behavior, especially in Andalusia, Spain.

Manhood in the Making, from which this selection is taken, addresses the question of masculinity in many cultures ranging from Europe to East and South Asia, East Africa, South America, the Caribbean, and Micronesia. Using his own and other anthropologists' research, Gilmore aims to establish whether there is a universal concept of manhood. He concludes that, while such a concept would be hard to sustain, the roles of men are universally determined by their society's conditions of production. He rejects the idea that masculinity is self-serving, egotistical, and uncaring and finds that, in most cultures, aggressive behavior itself is motivated by the necessity of protecting the family. The following essay, "Performative Excellence: Circum-Mediterranean," is representative of Gilmore's research in Spain and gives the general lines upon which most notions of masculinity are constructed.

In Glendiot idiom, there is less focus on "being a good man" than on "being good at being a man"—a stance that stresses performative excellence, *the ability to foreground manhood by means of deeds that strikingly "speak for themselves."*
—MICHAEL HERZFELD, *The Poetics of Manhood*

The lands of the Mediterranean Basin have for centuries been in close contact through trade, intermarriage, intellectual and cultural exchange, mutual colonization, and the pursuit of common regional interests (Braudel 1972; Peristiany 1965; Davis 1977). The use of terms such as *Mediterranean* or *Circum-*

Mediterranean (Pitt-Rivers 1963; Giovannini 1987) to categorize these lands is not meant to imply a "culture area" as that term has been used in American ecological anthropology—for Mediterranean societies are as diverse and varied as anywhere else in the world—but rather to serve as a concept of heuristic convenience in ethnographic analysis and comparison (Pitt-Rivers 1977:viii). Although not representing a unity in the sense of cultural homogeneity (Herzfeld 1980), many Mediterranean societies place importance on "certain institutions" (Pitt-Rivers 1977:ix) that invite comparison. Aside from obvious resemblances in ecology, settlement patterns, and economic adaptations, what seems to provide a basis of comparison more than anything else is, in fact, a shared image of manhood. In his magisterial survey, *People of the Mediterranean,* John Davis (1977:22) writes,

> Many observers assert the unity of the Mediterranean on various grounds, some of them more plausible than others. At a straightforward, noncausal level, anthropologists, tourists, even Mediterranean people themselves notice some common cultural features: attitudes, elements of culture that are recognizably similar in a large proportion of Mediterranean societies and that are readily intelligible to other Mediterranean people. "I also have a moustache," is the phrase happily recorded by J. G. Peristiany. . . . In an emblematic way, it serves to denote not only manliness, which is so common a concern around the Mediterranean, but also a style of anthropological argument.

This invocation of the mustache, of course, is shorthand for saying I am a man, too, the equal of any, so afford me the respect of the hirsute sex. By appealing to this common denominator, the statement is both a warning and an evocation of the fiercely egalitarian (and competitive) values shared by many otherwise diverse peoples of the region.

In the Mediterranean area, most men are deeply committed to an image of manliness because it is part of their personal honor or reputation. But this image not only brings respect to the bearer; it also brings security to his family, lineage, or village, as these groups, sharing a collective identity, reflect the man's reputation and are protected by it. Because of its competitive, sexually aggressive aspects, Mediterranean male imagery has been perceived, at least in some of the Latin countries, as self-serving, disruptive, and isolating, a matter of "personal vice" and a "social evil" (Pitt-Rivers 1961:118). This is part of a distancing stereotype shared by many northern visitors who for their own reasons assume the south to be "different" (Herzfeld 1987). But this overlooks the very important and often constructive group implications of the male image as it exists in many Mediterranean societies and which, as we shall see later, is not so different in effect from masculine imagery elsewhere. I want to explore the implications of these male ideals . . . as the first step in our quest for the meaning of manhood.

We begin our discussion of masculine imagery in the Mediterranean societies by taking a negative example. This is the man who is not "good at being a man," in Michael Herzfeld's felicitous phrase above. What does he lack? Let me start by describing such a case from my own fieldwork in the Andalusian pueblo of Fuenmayor (a pseudonym). Although the following discussion is geared to southern Spain and to other areas in the northern littoral of the Mediterranean, much of what I say here relates to parts of the Islamic Middle East as well.

Lorenzo

Like many other men in the Mediterranean area with whom they share the common sensibilities alluded to by Davis, the Andalusians of Spain's deep south are dedicated to proving their manliness publicly. Even more than other Iberians, they are fervent followers of what the Spanish critic Enrique Tierno Galván (1961:74–76) has called a quasi-religious Hispanic "faith in manhood." If you measure up in this regard, you are "very much a man" (*muy hombre*), "very virile" (*muy macho*), or "lots of man" (*mucho hombre*). If not, you are *flojo*, a weak and pathetic impostor. The polysemous term *flojo* literally means empty, lazy, or flaccid; it is used also to describe a dead battery, a flat tire, or some other hopeless tool that does not work. It connotes flabby inadequacy, uselessness, or inefficiency.

Our example, Lorenzo, was a callow fellow in his late twenties, a perennial student and bachelor. A gentle character of outstanding native intelligence, Lorenzo was the only person from Fuenmayor ever to have attended graduate school to pursue a doctorate, in this case in classic Castilian literature. But he was unable for various reasons ever to complete his dissertation, so he remained in a kind of occupational limbo, unable to find suitable work, indecisive, and feckless. Because of his erudition, unusual in such backwater towns, Lorenzo was generally acknowledged as a sort of locally grown genius. Many people had high hopes for him. But the more traditionally minded people in town were not among his admirers. They found him reprehensible for their own curmudgeonly reasons, for in the important matter of gender appropriateness, Lorenzo was considered highly eccentric, even deviant. "A grave case," one townsman put it.

People pointed first to his living arrangements. Oddly, even perversely, Lorenzo stayed indoors with his widowed mother, studying, reading books, contemplating things, rarely leaving his cramped scholar's cloister. He had no discernible job, and as he earned no money, he contributed nothing concrete to his family's impoverished larder, a fact that made him appear parasitic to many. He lived off his uncomplaining old mother, herself hardworking but poor. Withdrawn and secretive, Lorenzo made no visible efforts to change this state of affairs; nor did he often, as other men are wont to do, enter the masculine world of the bars to drink with cronies, palaver, debate, or engage in the usual convivial banter. When he did, he drank little. Rarely did he enter into the aggressively competitive card games or the drunken bluster that men enjoy and expect from their fellows.

Perhaps most bizarre, Lorenzo avoided young women, claiming not to have time for romance. Along with his other faults, Lorenzo was actually intensely shy with girls. This is a very unusual dereliction indeed, one that is always greeted with real dismay by both men and women in Spain. Sexual shyness is more than a casual flaw in an Andalusian youth; it is a serious, even tragic inadequacy. The entire village bemoans shyness as a personal calamity and collective disgrace. People said that Lorenzo was afraid of girls, afraid to try his luck, afraid to gamble in the game of love. They believe that a real man must break down the wall of female resistance that separates the sexes; otherwise, God forbid, he will never marry and will sire no heirs. If that happens, everyone suffers, for children are God's gift to family, village, and nation.

Being a sensitive soul, Lorenzo was quite aware of the demands made upon him by importuning kith and kin. He felt the pressure to go out and run after women. He knew he was supposed to target a likely wife, get a paying job, and start a family. A cultural rebel by default or disinclination, he felt himself to be a man of modern, "European" sensibilities. Above all, he wanted to remain beyond that "stupid rigmarole" of traditional southern expectations, as he called it. He was clearly an agnostic in regards to Tierno Galván's Spanish faith in manhood.

One evening, after we had spent a pleasant hour talking about such things as the place of Cervantes in world literature, he looked up at me with his great, sad brown eyes and confessed his cultural transgressions. He began by confiding his anxieties about the aggressive courting that is a man's presumed function. "I know you have to throw yourself violently at women," he said glumly, "but I prefer not to," adding, "It's just not me." Taking up his book, he shook his head and cast his mournful eyes to the ground with a shrug, awaiting a comforting word from a sympathetic and, he believed, enlightened foreigner. It was obvious he was pathologically afraid of rejection.

Because he was a decent and honest man, Lorenzo had his small circle of friends in the town. Like Lorenzo, they were all educated people. Given to introspective brooding, he was the subject of much concern among them. They feared he would never marry, bachelorhood being accounted the most lamentable fate outside of blatant homosexuality, which is truly disgusting to them. With the best intentions in mind, these people often took me aside to ask me if I did not think it was sad that Lorenzo was so withdrawn, and what should be done about him? Finally, one perceptive friend, discussing Lorenzo's case at length as we often did, summed up the problem in an unforgettable phrase that caused me to ponder. He expressed admiration for Lorenzo's brains, but he noted his friend's debilitating unhappiness, his social estrangement; he told me in all seriousness and as a matter obviously much considered that Lorenzo's problem was his failure "as a man." I asked him what he meant by this, and he explained that, although Lorenzo had pursued knowledge with a modicum of success, he had "forgotten" how to be a man, and this forgetting was the cause of his troubles. This friend laid the blame for Lorenzo's alienation squarely on a characterological defect of role-playing, a kind of stage fright. Shaking his head sadly, he uttered an aphoristic diagnosis: "Como hombre, no sirve" (literally, as a man he just doesn't serve, or work). He added, "Pobrecito, no sirve pa' na'" (poor guy, he's totally useless).

Spoken by a concerned friend in a tone of commiseration rather than reproach, this phrase, "no sirve," has much meaning. Loosely translated, it means that as man Lorenzo fails muster in some practical way, the Spanish verb *servir* meaning to get things done, to work in the sense of proficiency or serviceability. There is a sense of the measurable quantity here—visible results. But what are these practical accomplishments of Andalusian manliness? Let me digress briefly in order to place Lorenzo and his apostasy from Tierno's "faith" in the broader context of the Circum-Mediterranean area by offering some comparisons from across the sea.

Manly Services

Lorenzo's friends made a connection between manhood and some code of effective or "serviceable" behavior. This echoes Chandos's (1984:246) description of the British public-school elite, the English locution connoting utility being both etymologically and conceptually cognate to the Spanish *sirve*. But more than simply serving, this behavior in Lorenzo's community had to be public, on the community stage, as it were. A man's effectiveness is measured as others see him in action, where they can evaluate his performance. This conflation of masculinity and efficaciousness into a theatrical image of performing finds powerful echoes in other Mediterranean lands. Let us take, for example, Greece. Luckily we have excellent data for that country, thanks to the untiring efforts of Michael Herzfeld. There, too, the manly man is one who performs, as Herzfeld has it, center stage. His role-playing is manifested in "foregrounded" deeds, in actions that are seen by everyone and therefore have the potential to be judged collectively. As Herzfeld says of the Greeks he studied, the excellent man, the admired man, is not necessarily a "good" man in some abstract moral sense. Rather he is *good at being a man*. This means not only adequate performance within set patterns (the male script); it also means publicity, being on view and having the courage to expose oneself to risk. In addition, it means decisive action that works or serves a purpose, action that meets tests and solves real problems consensually perceived as important.

A subtle and perceptive fieldworker, Herzfeld (1985a) describes for the village of Glendi in Crete—an island of Mediterranean cultural synthesis—the archetype of social acceptance that is most relevant to the present case. To be a man in Crete and Andalusia means a pragmatic, agential modality, an involvement in the public arena of acts and deeds and visible, concrete accomplishments. This showy modality has nothing to do with the security or domestic pleasures of the home or with introspection. These things are associated with self-doubts, hesitancy, withdrawal into the wings, that is, with passivity. It is here that Lorenzo, back in Spain, has been deficient. He is, above all else, a recessive man, staying demurely at home, avoiding life's challenges and opportunities. Manhood at both ends of the sea seems to imply a nexus of gregarious engagement, a male praxis endlessly conjoined on the stage of community life.

If we go back in time we find some intriguing echoes. The ancient Greeks also admired an outgoing, risk-taking manliness of effective action. They also judged a man not for being good but for whether or not he was useful in the role he played on the communal stage—an "efficient or defective working part of the communal mechanism" (Dover 1978:108). Their agonistic view of life is the ethos that informs the restless heroism of the Homeric sagas with a call to dramatic, even grandiose, gestures (Gouldner 1965). But this image is also associated with ideals of manly virtue that the ancient Greeks, like some of their modern descendants, held and still hold dear in its vulgar manifestation as *filotimo*, masculine pride or self-esteem (Herzfeld 1980:342–45). The Spaniards or Italians might call this right to pride by some cognate of "honor," *honra* or *onore,* or perhaps respect. It conveys a self-image deeply involved with the endless search for worldly success and fame, for approbation and admiration in the judgmental eyes of others. This emphasis on the dramatic gesture appears early in Greek culture. It shows up in Homer, in the *Iliad* most visibly: in Achilles' willingness to trade a long, uneventful life for a brief one filled with honor and glory, and in Agamemnon's willingness to trade several months of his life for an honorable death on the battlefield at Troy (Slater 1968:35).

This quest for fame and for the glorious deed as a measure of masculine virtue took on a life of its own in the ancient eastern Mediterranean world. Indeed, in the flourishing Athens of the fifth century B.C. male life seems to have been an unremitting struggle for personal aggrandizement—for "fame and honor, or for such goals as could lead to these (wealth, power, and so forth)" (ibid.:38). Despite the Greek emphasis on moderation that we cherish today, this obsessive glory-seeking grew more and more a part of Greek masculine ideals, to the point where the chronicler Thucydides was motivated to chastise his countrymen: "Reckless audacity came to be considered the courage of a loyal ally; prudent hesitation specious cowardice; moderation was held to be a cloak for unmanliness" (1951, iii:82). One mythological model of this manly man covered in glory, the embodiment of this Greek ideal, is the intrepid and wily traveler Odysseus.

The *Odyssey* is a parable of this kind of dramatized manliness uniting practical effect and moral vision. Its hero sets forth, engaging in countless struggles, surviving through physical strength and clever stratagems fair and foul. After innumerable encounters with the dangers and monsters of the world, he returns triumphantly in the final act to succor wife and kin, the ultimate heroic Greek male. Odysseus is no saint; he is portrayed as a trickster and manipulator. But his tricks "work." They have the desired end: the rescue of the endangered wife left at home, Penelope, and the restoration of the family's honor, threatened by the opportunistic suitors. The Homeric epic captures in legend the thrust of this peripatetic, pragmatic, and serviceable Mediterranean manhood.

From a psychological point of view, it is clear that this ancient morality of man-acting has something to do with the cultural encoding of impulse sublimation. An inspirational model of right action, it directs energies away from self-absorption and introspection toward a strategy of practical problem-solving and worldly concerns. The manly image in ancient Greece as well as in modern Andalusia is an inducement toward ceaseless enterprise judged by measurable ends. In an important sense, it is more than simply the sublimation of libido and aggression into culturally approved channels of practical achievement; it is also the encouragement to resist their opposites: indolence, self-doubt, squeamishness, hesitancy, the impulse to withdraw or surrender, the "sleepiness" of quietude (symbolized in Greek legend by death by drowning—a universal metaphor for returning to the womb). As well as a commitment to commanding action in an agonistic context, an aggressive stance in service to proximate goals—what Gouldner has called the Greek contest system—manliness in much of the Mediterranean world can be called a social agoraphilia, a love for the sunlit public places, for crowds, for the proscenium of life. Such open contexts are associated not only with exposure and sociability but also with risk and opportunity, with the possibility of the grand exploit and the conspicuous deed. We can thus describe Lorenzo's first failure as a man as a refusal to sally forth into the fray.

A Northern Parallel

This phototropic manly adventurism is not confined to the Mediterranean cultures by any means. In the north of Europe, too, didactic tales pitting risk-taking against withdrawal abound, attesting to a widespread European archetype. There is a very telling parallel, for example, in the story of the knight Tannhäuser as borrowed by Wagner from the sixteenth-century *Volkslied von Tannhäuser* by Jobst Gutknecht. In the old German legend, the hero, in a moment of moral weakness, has been granted his heart's desire to live with

Venus in her fabulous mountain, the Venusberg. His every desire is immediately fulfilled by the voluptuous goddess and her attendants, the Naiads and Sirens. But he is alone and estranged and has grown weary of this barren subterranean paradise. Wagner's version begins in a gloomy cave, where Tannhäuser is engaged in a violent internal struggle. Should he remain a happy but passive captive, his needs instantly gratified by the goddess and her minions, or should he renounce all this and return to the sunlit world of conflict and danger? After much hesitation, the hero renounces the decadent pleasures of the engulfing Venus, who would deprive him of his chance at battling the world. "I must return to the world of men. I stand prepared for battle," he sings, "even for death and nothingness" (I, i). Tannhäuser's achievement in abandoning the goddess, like Odysseus's triumph over the Sirens, is a means of moral regeneration through the acceptance of existential struggle. The knight has mastered the most primitive of the demands of the pleasure principle—the temptation to drown in the arms of an omnipotent woman, to withdraw into a puerile cocoon of pleasure and safety. As in the *Odyssey,* the scene of the great decision is one in which water imagery abounds: murky grottos, dim pools, misty waterfalls.

German culture, too, at least in its prewar manifestations, had its "real man" traditions, ideals of manly courage deriving from martial Prussian prototypes. In fact, "masculinism" is deeply ingrained in the Teutonic ideal, and not only its militaristic or Wagnerian manifestations, as Klaus Theweleit has shown in his book on Weimar culture, *Male Fantasies* (1987:55).

Sex and Marriage

It is, of course, a commonplace version of this kind of mighty inner struggle against self-withdrawal that Lorenzo had become embroiled in and that he seemed to be losing in Spain. But there is more at stake here than a show of self-mastery and competitive fitness. There is also sex; or rather, an aggressive role in courtship. Lorenzo's friends bemoaned his failure to go out and capture a wife. "As a man he does not serve" refers explicitly to wife-capture and phallic predation. [20]

In some Muslin areas, for example, rural Turkey (Bates 1974) and the southern Balkans (Lockwood 1974), this predation often takes the form of actual bride theft or prenuptial rape, often involving kidnapping or violence. Such things used to occur also in parts of southern Italy, where some men first raped and then married reluctant brides. Wife-by-capture is still common in parts of rural Greece (Herzfeld 1985b). This assertive courting, minus the violence, is an important, even essential requirement of manhood in Spain as well. It is a recurrent aspect of the male image in many parts of southern Europe, whereas it seems less critical in the northern countries.

Most of what we know about Mediterranean ideas of manhood, in fact, concerns their more expressive components—more precisely, their sexual assertiveness (Pitt-Rivers 1977): The *maschismo* of Spain and the *maschio* of Sicily (Giovannini 1987) are examples. There is also the *rajula* (virility) complex of Morocco (Geertz 1979:364), which has been likened specifically to Hispanic *machismo* by a female anthropologist (Mernissi 1975:4–5). There are parallels in the Balkans, which anthropological observers Simic (1969, 1983) and Denich (1974), male and female scholars respectively, independently identify with the *machismo* of Hispanic culture. A real man in these countries is forceful in courtship as well as a fearless man of action. Both sex and economic enterprise are competitive and risky, because they place a man against his fellows in the quest for the most prized resource of all—women. Defeat and humiliation are always possible.

In Sicily, for instance, masculine honor is always bound up with aggression and potency. A real man in Sicily is "a man with big testicles" (Blok 1981:432–33); his potency is firmly established. Among the Sarakatsani of Greece, also, an adult male must be "well endowed with testicles" (Campbell 1964:269), quick to arousal, insatiable in the act. Such beliefs also hold true for much of Spain, especially the south (Pitt-Rivers 1965, 1977; Brandes 1980, 1981; Mitchell 1988), where a real man is said to have much *cojones,* or balls. Such big-balled men, naturally, tower over and dominate their less well-endowed and more phlegmatic fellows.

Yet there is more to this than competitive lechery (which, incidentally, is not as highly regarded in the Muslim countries, for in Islam unbridled lust is held to be socially disruptive and immoral for both sexes [Bates and Rassam 1983:215]). This extra dimension is important for a deeper understanding of the social matrix of Circum-Mediterranean ideas of manhood that I mentioned above. Even in those parts of southern Europe where the Don Juan model of sexual assertiveness is highly valued, a man's assigned task is not just to make endless conquests but to spread his seed. Beyond mere promiscuity, the ultimate test is that of competence in reproduction, that is, impregnating one's wife. For example, in Italy, "only a wife's pregnancy could sustain her husband's masculinity" (Bell 1979:105). Most importantly, therefore, the Mediterranean emphasis on manliness means results; it means procreating offspring (preferably boys). At the level of community endorsement, it is legitimate reproductive success, more than simply erotic acrobatics—a critical fact often overlooked by experts on Mediterranean honor who stress its disruptive or competitive elements (Pitt-Rivers 1977:11). Simply stated, it means creating a large and vigorous family. Promiscuous adventurism represents a prior (youthful) testing ground to a more serious (adult) purpose. Sexuality and economic self-sufficiency work in parallel ways.

In southern Spain, for example, people will heap scorn upon a married man without children, no matter how sexually active he may have been prior to marriage. What counts is results, not the preliminaries. Although both husband and wife suffer in prestige, the blame of barrenness is placed squarely on him, not his wife, for it is always the man who is expected to initiate (and accomplish) things. "Is he a man?" the people sneer. Scurrilous gossip circulates about his physiological defects. He is said to be incompetent, a sexual bungler, a clown. His mother-in-law becomes outraged. His loins are useless, she says, "no sirven," they don't work. Solutions are sought in both medical and magical means. People say that he has failed in his husbandly duty. In being sexually ineffectual, he has failed at being a man.

Beyond Sex: Provisioning

Aside from potency, men must seek to provision dependents by contributing mightily to the family patrimony. This, too, is measured by the efficiency quotient, by results (Davis 1977:77). What counts, again, is performance in the work role, measured in sacrifice or service to family needs. What has to be emphasized here is the sense of social sacrifice that this masculine work-duty entails. The worker in the fields often despises manual labor of any sort, because it rarely benefits him personally. For example, the rural Andalusians say that work is a "curse" (Gilmore 1980:55), because it can never make a man rich. For the poor man, working means contracting under humiliating conditions for a day-wage, battling with his fellows for fleeting opportunities in the workplace, and laboring in the fields picking cotton and weeding sunflowers from dawn to dusk. Synonymous with suffering, work is something that most men will freely admit they hate and would avoid if they could.

Yet for the worker, the peasant, or any man who must earn his bread, work is also a responsibility—never questioned—of feeding dependents. And here, as in matters of sex and fatherly duty, the worker's reputation as a citizen and a man is closely bound up with clearly defined service to family. A man who shirks these obligations renounces his claim to both respectability and manhood; he becomes a despised less-than-man, a wastrel, a *gamberro*. The latter term means an irresponsible reprobate who acts like a carefree child or who lives parasitically off women. Although it is true that women in Andalusia are often wage-earners too, the husband, to be a real man, must contribute the lion's share of income to support wife and family like a pillar and to keep the feminine machine of domestic production running smoothly. A man works hard, sometimes desperately, because, as they say, *se obliga*, you are bound to your family, not because you like it. In this sense, Spanish men are, as Brandes notes (1980:210), like men everywhere, actively pursuing the breadwinning role as a measure of their manhood. The only difference is that they rarely get pleasure or personal satisfaction from the miserable work available to them.

In southern Italy, much the same attitude is found. John Davis (1973: 94–95) writes of the town of Pisticci: "Work is also justified in terms of the family of the man who works: 'If it were not for my family, I'd not be wearing myself out' (*non mi sacrifico*). The ability of a husband to support his wife and children is as important a component of his honour as his control of his wife's sexuality. Independence of others, in this context, thus implies both his economic and sexual honour. . . . Work, then, is not regarded as having any intrinsic rewards. Men work to produce food and some cash for their families."

This sacrifice in the service of family, this contribution to household and kin, is, in fact, what Mediterranean notions of honor are all about. Honor is about being good *at being a man,* which means building up and buttressing the family or kindred—the basic building blocks of society—no matter what the personal cost: "[Mediterranean] honor as ideology helps shore up the identify of a group (a family or a lineage) and commit to it the loyalties of otherwise doubtful members. Honor defines the group's social boundaries, contributing to its defense against the claims of equivalent competing groups" (Schneider 1971:17).

The emphasis on male honor as a domestic duty is widespread in the 30 Mediterranean. In his seminal survey of the literature, John Davis, like Jane Schneider in the quote above, finds confirmation for his view of masculine honor as deriving from work and economic industry as much as from sexual success: "It should be said at the outset that honour is not primarily to do with sexual intercourse. . . . but with performance of roles and is related to economic resources because feeding family, looking after women, maintaining a following, can be done more easily when the family is not poor" (1977:77).

Sometimes this kind of economic service can be quantified in terms of money or other objects of value, or it can be expressed in material accumulations that are passed on to women and children, such as dowries. For example, Ernestine Friedl (1962), writing about a Greek peasant village in contemporary Boeotia, describes the honor of fathers as grounded in their ability to provide large dowries in cash and valuables to their daughters. This success assures them of the best in-laws, contributes to family prestige, and consequently enhances their image as provider. Manhood is measured at least partly in money, a man's only direct way of nourishing children. Manhood, then, as call to action, can be interpreted as a kind of moral compunction to provision kith and kin.

Man-the-Protector

After impregnating and provisioning comes bravery. Being a man in Andalusia, for example, is also based on what the people call *hombría.* Technically this simply means manliness, but it differs from the expressly virile or economic performances described above. Rather, hombría is physical and moral courage. Having no specific behavioral correlatives, it forms an intransitive component: It means standing up for yourself as an independent and proud actor, holding your own when challenged. Spaniards also call this *dignidad* (dignity). It is not based on threatening people or on violence, for Andalusians despise bullies and deplore physical roughness, which to them is mere buffoonery. Generalized as to context, hombría means a courageous and stoic demeanor in the face of any threat; most important, it means defending one's honor and that of one's family. It shows not aggressiveness in a physical sense but an unshakable loyalty to social group that signals the ultimate deterrent to challenge. The restraint on violence is always based on the capacity for violence, so that reputation is vital here.

As a form of masculine self-control and courage, hombría is shown multitudinously. For example, in Fuenmayor, a group of young men may wander down to the municipal cemetery late at night after a few drinks to display their disdain for ghosts. They take with them a hammer and a nail or spike. Posturing drunkenly together, they pound the nail into the cemetery's stucco wall. Challenging all manner of goblins and ghouls, they recite in unison the following formula to the rhythm of the hammer blows:

Aquí hinco clavo	I here drive a spike
del tio monero	before goblin or sprite
venga quién venga,	and whatever appear,
aquí lo espero!	I remain without fear!

The last man to run away wins the laurels as the bravest, the most manly. Sometimes adolescents will challenge each other to spend a night in the cemetery in a manner of competitive testing, but otherwise hombría is nonconfrontational, as the defiance is displaced onto a supernatural (nonsocial) adversary. Nevertheless, as the above example shows, it is competitive and, like virility and economic performance, needs proof in visible symbols and accomplishments. Hombría judges a man's fitness to defend his family. Pitt-Rivers (1961:89) has depicted it best: "The quintessence of manliness is fearlessness, readiness to defend one's own pride and that of one's family." Beyond this, hombría also has a specifically political connotation that enlarges its role in Spain.

For the past century, Spain, and Andalusia in particular, has been a land of political struggle. Class consciousness is strong as a result of deep antagonism between landowners and laborers (Martinez-Alier 1971). Hombría among the embattled workers and peasants has taken on a strongly political coloration from this class opposition: loyalty to social class. Among peasants and workers, manliness is expressed not only by loyalty to kindred but also by loyalty to the laboring class and by an active participation in the struggle for workers' rights. For example, workers are very manly who uphold laborers' rights by refusing to back down in labor disputes. This was an especially courageous act under the Franco dictatorship but is still admired today among the committed. Charismatic labor leaders—especially those jailed and beaten by the Franco police, as was Marcelino Camacho, the head of the underground Workers' Commissions—are highly admired as being very virile. In their group they are men with "lots of balls," envied by men, attractive to women. In the eyes of their political enemies they may be hated, but they are also respected and feared.

A concrete example: There was in Fuenmayor the famous case of the militant agitator nicknamed "Robustiano" (the Robust One), so called for his athletic build and his formidable courage. After the Civil War, when his left-leaning family was decimated by the Nationalists in the postwar persecutions, he had openly defied the Franco police by continuing his revolutionary activities. Beatings, threats, and blackballing had no effect. After each return from jail he took up the struggle anew, winning admiration from all sides, including his jailers. Despite torture, he never betrayed his comrades, always taking police abuse stoically as a matter of course. Robustiano developed a huge and loyal following; today he is remembered as one of the martyrs who kept up the workers' spirits during the dark days of the dictatorship. Beyond this, people remember Robustiano as a real man, an apotheosis of the Andalusian ideal of manhood.

Apart from politics, this call to dramatic action in defense of one's comrades finds echoes throughout the Mediterranean region where social class is less important than other primordial ties, as among patrilineal peoples of the African littoral. For example, among the Kabyles of Algeria, according to Bourdieu (1965, 1979a), the main attribute of the real man is that he stands up to other men and fiercely defends his agnates. "All informants give as the essential characteristic of the man of honour the fact that he *faces* others," Bourdieu remarks (1979a:128). A real man suffers no slights to self or, more importantly, to family or lineage. Nearby, in eastern Morocco, true men are those who stand ever ready to defend their families against outside threats; they "unite in defense of their livelihoods and collective identity" (Marcus 1987:50).

Likewise, among the Sarakatsani shepherds of modern-day Greece (Campbell 1964:269–70), the true man is described as *varvatos,* clearly cognate to the Italian *barbato,* bearded or hairy. Aside from indicating strength and virility (the facial hair again), this also "describes a certain ruthless ability in any form of endeavour" in defense of his kindred. Virile Sarakatsani shepherds are those who meet the demands of pastoral life in which " 'reputation' is impossible without strength" (ibid.:317). In this way the Sarakatsani man gains the respect of competitors and fends off threats to his domain. Thus he maintains his kindred's delicate position in a tough environment. "The reputation for manliness of the men of the family is a deterrent against external outrage" (ibid.:271). Campbell sees this stress on manliness in essentially

35

functional terms. "Here again," he writes (ibid.:270), "we see the *'efficient'* aspect of manliness" (emphasis added).

Man-the-protector is everywhere encountered in the Mediterranean area. Throughout, bureaucratic protections are weakly developed, states are unstable, feuding is endemic, and political alignments, like patronage, are shifting and unreliable. Because of the capriciousness of fortunes and the scarcity of resources, a man ekes out a living and sustains his family through toughness and maneuvering. For example, in Sicily, *"un vero uomo"* (a real man) is defined by "strength, power, and cunning necessary to protect his women" (Giovannini 1987:68). At the same time, of course, the successfully protective man in Sicily or Andalusia garners praise through courageous feats and gains renown for himself as an individual. This inseparable functional linkage of personal and group benefit is one of the most ancient moral notions found in the Mediterranean civilizations. One finds it already in ancient seafaring Greece in the voyager Odysseus. His very name, from *Odyne* (the ability to cause pain and the readiness to do so), implies a willingness to expose oneself to conflict, risk, and trouble and to strive against overwhelming odds in order to achieve great exploits. "To be Odysseus, then, is to adopt the attitude of the hunter of dangerous game: to deliberately expose one's self, but thereafter to take every advantage that the exposed position admits; the immediate purpose is injury, but the ultimate purpose is recognition and the sense of great exploit" (Dimrock 1967:57).

But Odysseus's ultimate goal is not simply one vainglorious exploit after another. All his wayfaring heroism is directed at a higher purpose: to rescue wife and child and to disperse the sinister suitors who threaten them both. The real man gains renown by standing between his family and destruction, absorbing the blows of fate with equanimity. Mediterranean manhood is the reward given to the man who is an efficient protector of the web of primordial ties, the guardian of his society's moral and material integuments.

Autonomous Wayfarers

The ideals of manliness found in these places in the Mediterranean seem to have three moral imperatives: first, impregnating one's wife; second, provisioning dependents; third, protecting the family. These criteria demand assertiveness and resolve. All must be performed relentlessly in the loyal service of the "collective identities" of the self.   40

One other element needs mention. The above depend upon something deeper: a mobility of action, a personal autonomy. A man can do nothing if his hands are tied. If he is going to hunt dangerous game and, like Odysseus, save his family, he needs absolute freedom of movement. Equally important as sex and economic resourcefulness is the underlying appeal to independent action as the starting point of manly self-identity. To enter upon the road to manhood, a man must travel light and be free to improvise and to respond, unencumbered, to challenge. He must have a moral captaincy. In southern Spain, as reported by Brandes (1980:210), dependency for an Andalusian peasant is not just shameful; it is also a negation of his manly image. Personal autonomy is the goal for each and every man; without it, his defensive posture collapses. His strategic mobility is lost, exposing his family to ruin. This theme, too, has political implications in Spain.

An example comes from George Collier's account of the Spanish Civil War in an Andalusian village. Collier (1987:90) points out the role played by masculine pride in the labor movements of workers and peasants in western Andalusia. He describes the critical political connotations of what he calls the "cultural terms in which Andalusians relate autonomy to masculine honor" and the virtues attached to asserting this masculinity (ibid.:96). Collier's discussion of the violent conflicts between landowners and laborers during the Second Republic (1931–36) in the pueblo of Los Olivos (Huelva Province) shows that a driving force behind their confrontations was this issue of personal autonomy. The peasants and workers were defending not only their political rights but also their self-image as men from the domineering tactics of the rich and powerful. Autonomy permitted them to defend their family's honor. Encumbered or dependent, they could not perform their manly heroics. Their revolutionism, as Collier brilliantly shows, was as much a product of a manhood image as their political and economic demands. This was particularly true of southern Spain, but Collier sees this mixture of political ideology and masculine self-image as something more widely Mediterranean:

> Villagers in Los Olivos held to the ideal of masculine autonomy characteristic of property relations and the system of honor in the agrarian societies of the Mediterranean. . . . The prepotent male discouraged challenges by continually reasserting this masculinity and potential for physical aggression while he guarded against assaults on the virtue of his women and stood up to others to protect his family's honor. . . . The ideal of masculine autonomy thus charged employer-employee relations with special tension. In having to accept someone else's orders, the employee implicitly acknowledged his lack of full autonomy and his vulnerability to potential dishonor. (Ibid.:96–97).

To be dependent upon another man is bad enough, but to acknowledge dependence upon a woman is worse. The reason, of course, is that this inverts the normal order of family ties, which in turn destroys the formal basis for manhood. For instance, in Morocco, as reported by Hildred Geertz (1979: 369), the major values of *rajula,* or manly pride, are "personal autonomy and force," which imply dominating and provisioning rather than being dominated and provisioned by women. There is indeed no greater fear among men than the loss of this personal autonomy to a dominant woman.

In Morocco there is in fact a recurrent anxiety that a man will fall under the magical spell of a powerful woman, a demonic seductress who will entrap him forever, as Venus entrapped Tannhaüser, or as Circe attempted to enslave Odysseus, causing him to forget his masculine role (Dwyer 1978). The psychological anthropologist Vincent Crapanzano has written an entire book about a Moroccan who lived in terror of such a demonic female *jinn*. He tells us that this anxiety is widespread: "This theme of enslavement by a women—the inverse of the articulated standards of male-female relations, of sex and marriage—pervades Moroccan folklore" (1980:102). There, as in Spain, a man must gain full and total independence from women as a necessary criterion of manhood. How can he provide for dependents and protect them when he himself is dependent like a child? This inversion of sex roles, because it turns wife into mother, subverts both the man and the family unit, sending both down to corruption and defeat.

Sexual Segregation

Many of these themes—activity versus passivity, extroversion versus introversion, autonomy versus dependence—are expressed in the physical context of Mediterranean rural community life. The requirement that the male separate conclusively from women could be no more clearly expressed than in the prohibitions against domesticity that pervade the ethnographic literature. In many Mediterranean societies (Gilmore 1982:194–96), the worlds of men and women are strictly demarcated. Male and female realms are, as Duvignaud says of Tunisia, "two separate worlds that pass without touching" (1977:16). Men are forced by this moral convention of spatial segregation to leave home during the day and to venture forth into the risky world outside. Like Lorenzo, a man hiding in the shadows of home during the daytime is immediately suspect. His masculinity is out of place and thus questionable. A real man must be out-of-doors among men, facing others, staring them down. In Cyprus, for example, a man who lingers at home with wife and children will have his manhood questioned: "What sort of man is he? He prefers hanging about the house with women" (Loizos 1975:92). And among the Algerian Kabyle described by Bourdieu (1979b:141), his fellows will malign a homebody for much the same reason: "A man who spends too much time at home in the daytime is suspect or ridiculous: He is 'a house man,' who 'broods at home like a hen at roost.' A self-respecting man must offer himself to be seen, constantly put himself in the gaze of others, confront them, face up to them (*qabel*). He is a man among men." So we can see the manly image working to catapult men out of the refuge of the house into the cockpit of enterprise.

Another Eccentric

To conclude, I will describe another negative case from Andalusia that illustrates these last points. There was a man in Fuenmayor who was a notorious homebody and whose family suffered the consequences. Alfredo was a rubicund little merchant with the non-Castilian surname Tissot (his ancestors had emigrated from Catalonia generations earlier). A sedentary man of middle age, he operated a small grocery establishment from out of his home—nothing unusual for men with small retail businesses. But Alfredo was unusual that in that he rarely ventured out from his home, where he lived with his wife and two pretty grown daughters.

In Andalusia, as in Cyprus or Algeria, a man is expected to spend his free time outdoors, backslapping and glad-handing. This world is the street, the bar, the fields—public places where a man is seen. He must not give the impression of being under the spell of the home, a clinger to wife or mother. While out, men are also expected to become involved in standard masculine rivalries: games of cards and dominoes, competitive drinking and spending, and contests of braggadocio and song. Although aware of such expectations, Alfredo resisted them, because, as he confided to me one day, such socializing was a waste of time and money—you have to spend money in the bars; you have to buy rounds of drinks for the company of fellows, and you have to tipple and make merry. You have to boast and puff yourself up before your cronies. All this conviviality was expensive and boring, so the chubby grocer stayed at home with his family. He read books and watched television at night or went over his accounts.

Like all other townsmen, Alfredo was under the scrutiny of public opinion and was accountable as a man. Although grudgingly admitting his modest business acumen (said however to be based on his wife's capital), the townspeople did not accept his lame excuses for inappropriate comportment. As a descendant of distrusted ethnic outsiders (Catalans are known as a race of workaholics and misers), he was expected to display strange attitudes, but his refusal to enter the public world of men in favor of home was greeted with outrage and indignation. Especially vilified was his stinginess with both time and money, which was felt as an insult to the other men of the pueblo, a calculated withdrawal from the male role, which demands not just familiar provisioning but a certain degree of generosity in the wider society. A man of means is expected to spend freely and thus to support his community. People say such a man owes something to the town. Alfredo's withdrawal damaged both his own prestige and that of his family, which suffered equally in the public spotlight.

One hot afternoon, as I was walking past the Tissot house with a group of friends, my companions made passing comments on Alfredo's strangeness. "What kind of man is he," they muttered, pointing at his sealed and cloistered house, "spending his time at home?" Glowering ominously, they likened him to a mother hen. They offered colorful explanations for his contemptible secretiveness, alluding to certain despicable character traits such as cheapness and egoism. But beyond these picayune moral defects, my informants found something truly repulsive in the merchant's domesticity, furtiveness, and sedentariness. They suggested a basic failure at a deeper level in the most important thing of all: man-acting. Carrying this character assassination further, my informants left the realm of observable fact and ventured into gossipy speculation, which is common in such matters of serious deviance. Unequivocal explanations are deemed necessary when deeply felt customs are violated.

The men then told me their suspicions about Alfredo. In the telling I could   50
feel a palpable relaxation of their anxiety about him, for they had reduced the deviance to root causes that they could scapegoat and consensually reject in a way that corroborated their own self-image. It all boiled down to Alfredo's failure as a man. This was shown incontrovertibly, as in the case of Lorenzo, by his shadowy introversion. As a consequence of his withdrawn uxoriousness, in the minds of his fellows, the Tissot household, bereft of sexual respectability, was held necessarily to be abnormal in terms of sexual functioning. Its very existence was, therefore, by local standards, attributable to aberrant practices. Since Alfredo was not a real man, as his community had decided, then his daughters, by logical extension, could not be the product of his own seed. The explanation that tied all together (since the eccentric Catalan was also known as a moderately wealthy man) was that he was a panderer and a pimp for his wife, and his daughters and his wealth were the result of her secret whoring. The villagers had thus conceptually, if inaccurately, reversed provider and dependent roles in this ugly and ridiculous slander. The associated success of insemination was stolen by a hostile act of imagination. Poor Alfredo was utterly incapable of combatting this malicious attack because he had cut himself off from male communication, so he and his family suffered from the slights and contempt reserved for deviants.

Hypothetically classified as unnatural, then, Alfredo's inexplicable character traits fell into a kind of preordained order of the man-who-is-no-man. For example, there was the matter of his cooking. He was known to help wife and daughters in the kitchen, cutting, chopping, and so on, performing tasks absolutely unnatural to the male physiology and musculature. Andalusians recognize that there are professional chefs, but they are men who have learned a trade to earn a living, and so they retain their claim to manhood. At home, even chefs do not cook; their wives do. But Alfredo was said to help eagerly out of his own perverted volition. "Is he a man?" people scoffed, "cooking, hanging about in the kitchen like that?" The Andalusians believe fervidly that male and female anatomy provide for different, complementary skills. It was true that Alfredo helped in the kitchen. Since he invited me into his home (in itself an act of unusual, even deviant hospitality), I saw him. He never hid this indictable bit of information from me. I came to know him fairly well on these occasions. Being a didactic and helpful sort of man in a fussy way, he instructed my wife and myself in the proper preparation of certain specialities of Spanish cuisine, providing precise, often compulsive directions for grinding ingredients to make a tasty gazpacho. I learned how to whip up a savory, if smelly, garlic soup in the gleaming Tissot kitchen. He always watched that everything was done in the proper order. For example, the bread always went in the pot after you added the vinegar: no improvising here. Beaming maternally, the homebody took pride in his knowledge of local recipes and in my vocal appreciation of his culinary skills.

But his fellows in the streets laughed at him, scorning his hurried excuses, grimacing disgustedly when I spoke of him, holding both him and his superfluous wife in contempt. The placid pleasure Alfredo took in his own odd domesticity hastened his withdrawal from manly assemblages and activities. The introverted grocer failed to make it as a man by local standards. This failure in turn robbed his family of respectability, plunging them all into disrepute, so that, for example, his two daughters had to find fiancés in other towns. Alfredo's fatal flaw was that he failed even to present himself for the test of manhood. He failed, most decisively, to separate: His public identity was blurred by the proximity of women. He had withdrawn into a sheltered cocoon of domesticity, self-indulgently satisfied with good food and easeful luxury, unwilling or afraid to enter the risky ring of manhood. This withdrawal made the other men uncomfortable, so they conceptually emasculated him and stole his family's honor, placing them all beyond the pale and obviating the threat they represented.

And yet, Alfredo was for other men a subject of endless discussion and debate. Perhaps, despite their protestations, there was something about him that, though also repellent, attracted these tough, virile men? Or possibly he presented to them some contumacious principle—living well without visibly working, perhaps—that caused ambivalent feelings that had to be expunged through projection and denial?

WORKS CITED

Bates, Daniel G. 1974. Normative and alternative systems of marriage among the Yörük of southeastern Turkey. *Anthropological Quarterly* 47:270–87.

Bates, Daniel G., and Amal Rassam. 1983. *Peoples and Cultures of the Middle East.* Englewood Cliffs, N.J.: Prentice-Hall.

Bell, Rudolf M. 1979. *Fate and Honor, Family and Village: Demographic and Cultural Change in Rural Italy since 1800.* Chicago: University of Chicago Press.

Blok, Anton. 1981. Rams and billy-goats: a key to the Mediterranean code of honour. *Man* 16:427–40.

Bourdieu, Pierre. 1965. The sentiment of honour in Kabyle society. In *Honour and Shame: The Values of Mediterranean Society,* ed. J.-G. Peristiany, pp. 191–241. Chicago: University of Chicago Press.

———.1979a. The sense of honour. In *Algeria 1960: Essays by Pierre Bourdieu*. Cambridge: Cambridge University Press.

———.1979b. The Kabyle house, or the world reversed. In *Algeria 1960: Essays by Pierre Bourdieu*. Cambridge: Cambridge University Press.

Brandes, Stanley H. 1980. *Metaphors of Masculinity: Sex and Status in Andalusian Folklore*. Philadelphia: University of Pennsylvania Press.

———. 1981. Like wounded stags: male sexual ideology in an Andalusian town. In *Sexual Meanings*, ed. Sherry B. Ortner and Harriet Whitehead, pp. 216–39. Cambridge: Cambridge University Press.

Braudel, Fernand, 1972. *The Mediterranean and the Mediterranean World in the Age of Philip II*, 2 vols, trans. Siân Reynolds. New York: Harper and Row.

Campbell, J. K. 1964. *Honour, Family, and Patronage*. Oxford: Clarendon Press.

Chandos, John. 1984. *Boys Together: English Public Schools, 1800–1864*. New Haven: Yale University Press.

Collier, George A. 1987. *The Socialists of Rural Andalusia: Unacknowledged Revolutionaries*. Stanford: Stanford University Press.

Crapanzano, Vincent. 1980. *Tuhami: Portrait of a Moroccan*. Chicago: University of Chicago Press.

Davis, John. 1973. *Land and Family in Pisticci*. London: Athalone Press.

———. 1977. *People of the Mediterranean*. London: Routledge and Kegan Paul.

Denich, Bette. 1974. Sex and power in the Balkans. In *Women, Culture, and Society*, ed. Michelle Rosaldo and Louise Lamphere, pp. 243–62. Stanford: Stanford University Press.

Dimrock, George E., Jr. 1967. The name of Odysseus. In *Essays on the Odyssey: Selected Modern Criticism*, ed. Charles H. Taylor, Jr., pp. 54–72. Bloomington: Indiana University Press.

Dover, Kenneth J. 1978. *Greek Homosexuality*. Cambridge, Mass.: Harvard University Press.

Duvignaud, Jean. 1977. *Change at Shebika: Report from a North African Village*, trans. F. Frenaye. New York: Pantheon.

Dwyer, Daisy. 1978. *Images and Self-Images: Male and Female in Morocco*. New York: Columbia University Press.

Friedl, Ernestine. 1962. *Vasilika: Village in Modern Greece*. New York: Holt, Rinehart and Winston.

Geertz, Hildred. 1979. The meanings of family ties. In *Meaning and Order in Moroccan Society*, ed. Clifford Geertz, H. Geertz, and L. Rosen, pp. 315–86. New York: Cambridge University Press.

Gilmore, David D. 1980. *The People of the Plain*. New York: Columbia University Press.

———. 1982. Anthropology of the Mediterranean area. *Annual Review of Anthropology* 11:175–205.

Giovannini, Maureen. 1987. Female chastity codes in the Circum-Mediterranean: comparative perspectives. In *Honor and Shame and the Unity of the Mediterranean*, ed. David D. Gilmore, pp. 61–74. Washington, D.C.: American Anthropological Association, Special Pub. no. 22.

Gouldner, Alvin W. 1965. *Enter Plato: Classical Greece and the Origins of Social Theory*. New York: Basic Books.

Herzfeld, Michael. 1980. Honour and shame: some problems in the comparative analysis of moral systems. *Man* 15:339–51.

———. 1985a. *The Poetics of Manhood: Contest and Identity in a Cretan Mountain village*. Princeton: Princeton University Press.

———. 1985b. Gender pragmatics: agency, speech, and bride-theft in a Cretan mountain village. *Anthropology* 9:25–44.

———. 1987. *Anthropology Through the Looking-Glass: Critical Ethnography in the Margins of Europe*. Cambridge: Cambridge University Press.

Lockwood, William G. 1974. Bride theft and social maneuverability in western Bosnia. *Anthropological Quarterly* 47:253–69.

Loizos, Peter. 1975. *The Greek Gift.* New York: St. Martin's Press.

Martinez-Alier, Juan. 1971. *Labourers and Landowners in Southern Spain.* London: St. Martin's Press.

Mernissi, Fatima. 1975. *Beyond the Veil.* New York: Schenckman.

Mitchell, Timothy J. 1988. *Violence and Piety in Spanish Folklore.* Philadelphia: University of Pennsylvania Press.

Peristiany, J.-G., ed. 1965. *Honour and Shame: The Values of Mediterranean Society.* London: Weidenfeld and Nicolson.

Pitt-Rivers, Julian. 1961. *The People of the Sierra.* Chicago: University of Chicago Press.

———. 1965. Honour and social status. In *Honour and Shame,* ed. J.-G. Peristiany, pp. 19–77. London: Weidenfeld and Nicolson.

———. 1977. *The Fate of Shechem.* Cambridge: Cambridge University Press.

———, ed. 1963. *Mediterranean Countrymen.* Paris: Mouton.

Schneider, Jane. 1971. Of vigilance and virgins. *Ethnology* 9:1–24.

Simic, Andrei. 1969. Management of the male image in Yugoslavia. *Anthropological Quarterly* 42:89–101.

———. 1983. Machismo and cryptomatriarchy: power, affect, and authority in the contemporary Yugoslav family. *Ethos* 11:66–86.

Slater, Philip F. 1968. *The Glory of Hera.* Boston: Beacon Press.

Theweleit, Klaus. 1987. *Male Fantasies,* trans. S. Conway, Erica Carter, and Chris Turner. Minneapolis: University of Minnesota Press.

Thucydides. 1951. *The Complete Writings: The Peloponnesian Wars,* ed. J. H. Finley, Jr., trans. Richard Crawley. New York: Modern Library.

Tierno Galván, Enrique. 1961. Los toros, acontecimiento nacional. In *Desde el Espectáculo a la Trivilización,* pp. 53–77. Madrid: Taurus.

Considerations

1. Gilmore begins his essay with the story of Lorenzo, who is perceived by his fellow townsmen as a failure. Why is he a failure in the eyes of the community? How would you describe Gilmore's own attitude toward Lorenzo and his situation? To what extent does Gilmore identify with Lorenzo?

2. Gilmore concludes his essay with a second negative example, the story of Alfredo. Why does he need a second example of a failure? How does the failure illustrate the norm? How useful is this second example to Gilmore in expanding and restating his earlier points?

Invitation to Write

At the beginning of his essay, Gilmore states that, although he is looking at the male image in Mediterranean societies, he will eventually show that it is not so different from the male imagery found elsewhere (para. 2). Write an essay that analyzes his definition of masculinity and tests its validity with examples from American culture. Think about the values Americans consider masculine, about the role models American males have to live up to, about how popular culture (movies, TV, etc.) portrays the American male. In

Gilmore's style, you may think of both positive and negative examples of masculinity in order to reveal the ideal American male.

Connections

In his essay "One of the Boys (p. 63), David Jackson also discusses expectations of male behavior. Although their subject is the same, Jackson and Gilmore look at it from different perspectives and apparently reach different conclusions. Write an essay in which you determine how their different frames of reference shape the author's divergent interpretations. You will have to take into account the fact that Jackson is personally involved in the action he describes, whereas Gilmore is talking about a culture that is not his own. If you find both arguments valid, explain how you have been persuaded by each of them.

ASSIGNMENT SEQUENCE
Defining Men's Lives

The first assignment in this sequence asks you to take a close look at the models of male behavior that are popular today. Looking at some specific examples, you will decide what messages they send about masculine roles. Next, you will use your experience and Philip Roth's story to investigate the way messages about gender are conveyed to children. Then, in your third paper, you will consider David Gilmore's description of the social implications of traditional male gender roles. You will decide if American men's roles resemble the roles of Mediterranean men in both the private and the public spheres. You turn next to see how well Gilmore's analysis can be applied to men in African society: You will decide how looking at Ngotho's behavior through Gilmore's framework of analysis provides insight into that character and his situation. Returning again to Ngotho's experience and the descriptions of Roth's father, you will explore the effects of powerlessness on the image of men. Finally, you test Gilmore's idea that even if no universal male exists, the traditional view of men as protector and provider can be found everywhere in some degree.

Assignment 1: Exploring Experience

Images of American manhood bombard us from many different directions. They come from the lives of men we know and men we read about: fathers, brothers, friends, popular heroes, movie stars, sports stars, and traditional heroes. Descriptions of male behavior appear on television, in movies, in books, in newspapers, in song lyrics, and in advertising. Write a paper in which you use some of these sources to explore commonly shared ideas about American men and to develop a model of American manhood.

Begin your paper by focusing on two or three specific examples of acceptable or unacceptable behavior for men. Use examples that draw on the behavior of public figures or private individuals you know, or analyze the model of behavior presented in a particular movie or television show. Explore the images connected with these models and decide what kinds of ideas about masculinity the imagery and/or behavior project.

Assignment 2

To be at all is to be her Philip, but in the embroilment with the buffeting world, my history still takes its spin from beginning as his Roth.
—PHILIP ROTH, *His Roth*

Philip Roth ends his memoir "His Roth" with the conclusion that his public identity "in the world" is linked to his relationship with his father. He implies that his relationship with his mother is more private, intimate, and elemental. He also indicates that each parent represented for him a set of attitudes, behaviors, and responsibilities. Write a paper in which you use your own childhood experience and Roth's experience to reflect upon the way children grow up seeing the world categorized according to gender. Also, consider how messages about gender roles are communicated to children.

To write this paper you will need to observe how Roth categorizes his world by gender. Look for examples in his memoir where he attributes particular behaviors to each parent. Analyze his attitude toward what he observes and the values he attaches to each parent. Then, turning to your own childhood, think about roles and behaviors that you learned were appropriate for men or appropriate for women, or for male and female children. Analyze the messages communicated by this division of the world along gender lines. Looking at your data, explain the process at work in the creation of expectations about gender behavior.

Assignment 3

The ideals of manliness found in these places in the Mediterranean seem to have three moral imperatives: first, impregnating one's wife; second, provisioning dependents; third, protecting the family. These criteria demand assertiveness and resolve. All must be performed relentlessly in the loyal service of the "collective identities" of the self.

—DAVID GILMORE,
Performative Excellence: Circum-Mediterranean

Here, David Gilmore summarizes the cultural assumptions about male behavior that are held by people in the Mediterranean area. Although the geographical region he covers is large and he sees varied patterns of behavior, he arrives at a "basic" model of male behavior. Write a paper in which you decide how well Gilmore's description of male behavior reflects the image of manhood present in American society. Explain how the presence or absence of the Mediterranean model can be explained in terms of general social values as well as more personal ones.

Begin your paper by introducing two distinct ideas: First, identify and explain Gilmore's definition of manhood in the Mediterranean; second, present your own definition of American manhood. You can refer back to your first paper and the definition you developed there. Discuss how your definition reflects both private and public values. Explore how the expectations about individual behavior reflect the values and priorities held by the society as a whole.

Assignment 4

What the hell was wrong with some men anyway? Had Mr Njogu become a male weakling in a fat queen bee's hive, slowly being milked dry and sapless, dying? Where was the old warrior who at the end of the battle would go home to his wife and make her moan under his heavy sweat?

—LEONARD KIBERA, *The Spider's Web*

In Leonard Kibera's story "The Spider's Web," Ngotho is perplexed by the radical changes in his world. One of those changes is the distribution of power between Mr. and Mrs. Njogu, and Mr. Njogu's inability to act like a traditional man. Using David Gilmore's framework of analysis, explain how the behavior of men like Mr. Njogu and Ngotho reflects other changes in this postcolonial African country.

In your paper, focus on the link between the men's private and public behavior. Consider how shifts in political structure and social values have affected Njogu's and Ngotho's ability to uphold the traditional ideal described by Ngotho. Discuss how Gilmore would interpret the connections between private and public, looking at some of the same topics he considers in relation to Mediterranean men, such as their roles as protectors and providers.

Assignment 5

He was a good soul, Kago was, and subservient as a child. There was no doubt about his ready aggressiveness where men of his class were concerned it was true, but when it came to Mrs Njogu he wound tail between his legs and stammered.

—LEONARD KIBERA, *The Spider's Web*

Philip Roth's memoir and Leonard Kibera's short story suggest models of male behavior that influence the ideas of their characters. While the characters are men who value traditional standards of behavior, the circumstances of their lives place them in situations where they, unlike traditional men, sometimes exhibit powerlessness. Write a paper in which you examine the causes of powerlessness in the cases of Roth's father and of the African men, their responses to it, and the ways in which it is described.

As you reread these texts, locate the passages that show that the characters have clearly defined ideas about the way men should behave. Then locate those situations that show the powerlessness of the characters. Examine these two different sets of circumstances to determine how the men's lives have changed and how these changes influence their relationships to others.

Assignment 6

Although there may be no "Universal Male," we may perhaps speak of a "Ubiquitous Male" based on these criteria of performance. We might call this quasi-global personage something like "Man-the-Impregnator-Protector-Provider."
                    —DAVID GILMORE, *Manhood in the Making*

In this conclusion to his book *Manhood in the Making: Cultural Concepts of Masculinity,* David Gilmore notes that societies that emphasize assertive manhood focus on three main aspects of male behavior.

In your papers, you have discussed the images of manhood in several texts as well as the culture in which you live. For your final paper, decide if you agree with Gilmore's statement suggesting there is a "ubiquitous" or omnipresent idea of manhood. Apply Gilmore's definition of man as a performer to the men in Philip Roth's memoir, Leonard Kibera's story, and your definition of American manhood to see if it explains the representations of manhood in each case.

Think about the way these men in different geographical locations fit Gilmore's generalized theory. Their behavior may not prove his theory, but be sure to look beyond specific, superficial behavior; look also at the perceived obligations that were placed on them by their gender. That is, decide if these men share the values attached to manhood described by Gilmore, even if they can't act on them. Use your conclusions to demonstrate whether or not you would agree with Gilmore's statement.

5

Working in the World

He tells me they pay him three dollars and thirty-five cents an hour—the minimum. He gets up at four to come to work; his bus fare is three dollars, and lunch from the catering truck almost always costs six dollars a day. He is so tired at the end of the day, he cannot stay awake.
—WAKAKO YAMAUCHI, *Maybe*

In a very real way, we in industry spoiled the old community life of Japan, and something had to replace it. So in today's Japan, companies like ours are the new communities, and their managers have a responsibility to create conditions in which people can enjoy a community life.
—ISAMU YAMASHITA, as quoted by ROBERT C. CHRISTOPHER,
The Fruits of Industry

The experience convinced Scott that he would never get where he wanted to go as long as he stayed inside a large corporation. He resolved to commit himself only to tasks that would enhance his own career—eventually outside Memorex.
"Had the company been different," he says, "I might have stayed. But there was no reason to. No one really cared what you did. You were penalized for being entrepreneurial. I knew I would get a check whether I sold or not. And no one seemed to share the same goal."
—BRUCE TUCKER and PAUL LEINBERGER,
Scott Myers, Entrepreneur

217

What constitutes the alienation of labor? First, that the work is external *to the worker, that it is not part of his nature; and that, consequently, he does not fulfill himself in his work but denies himself, has a feeling of misery rather than well-being, does not develop freely his mental and physical energies but is physically exhausted and mentally debased.*
—KARL MARX, *Alienated Labor*

Even though we live in an age when the nature of work and our economy are undergoing radical shifts, for most people the need to work remains an inescapable "given" of life. Yet while most people must work, they are motivated to work for different reasons and have different responses to the same work situation. For many, work is routine, even degrading. Illegal aliens, unskilled laborers, and the unemployed willing to take any job are virtually powerless to change the types of work available to them and the conditions of the workplace. Some work, like volunteer work or a homemaker's work, is satisfying but unpaid. For some individuals, work is a tolerable means to an end—a paycheck. Their real interests lie outside their work, in their hobbies and activities that engage them in the deepest expression of themselves and involve them in a community of like-minded people. For a happy few, work represents love and a challenge, allowing them to get paid for doing what they want to be doing anyway. For artists, writers, scientists, and many professionals, interest and work usually become inseparable. Under ideal conditions, work is a source of tremendous personal growth; the worker meets challenges, has opportunities to explore and develop interests, shares her interests with others, and obtains status and the chance to belong to a community of co-workers. No wonder, then, that studies show that, along with their paychecks, many unemployed individuals lose self-esteem and often suffer from depression.

Analysis of the nature of work and its role in individual lives requires consideration of the economic, social, and psychological impact work has on individuals and groups of people, as well as the conditions that make work a debilitating or satisfying experience. The readings in this chapter explore many of these aspects of work. Wakako Yamauchi's story "Maybe" examines the powerlessness of immigrant workers and the way work can provide a sense of community for even the most disenfranchised workers. In his essay "The Fruits of Industry," Robert C. Christopher evaluates the Japanese economic success in terms of the employee-employer relationship that develops a model corporate community. In "Scott Myers, Entrepreneur," Bruce Tucker and Paul Leinberger narrate the experiences of a talented man who works first for a large American corporation and then for himself. Finally, "Alienated Labor," drawn from the classic writings of Karl Marx, provides a theoretical base from which to examine the relationship of workers to work and to each other.

WAKAKO YAMAUCHI

Maybe

Wakako Yamauchi was born in 1924 in Westmoreland, California. Her parents were Japanese immigrants who farmed in Imperial Valley. But the Great Depression made her family abandon farming and move to Oceanside, California, in an unsuccessful effort to escape their poverty. After the United States entered World War II, in 1941, Yamauchi and her family, like many other Japanese Americans, were forced to live in an internment camp. Yamauchi's internment at Postern in Arizona interrupted her high school education, which wasn't completed until after the war. During the war, Yamauchi joined the *Postern Chronicle* as a staff artist, which gave her the opportunity to work with the writer Hisaye Yamamoto, whom she had always admired. Later in her life, when Yamauchi turned from painting to writing, she claimed Yamamoto as her mentor and friend. Although Yamauchi did some writing as a columnist while at Postern, her real development as a writer occurred years after her release from the camp. She had continued to study art but turned to writing in order to express her haunting memories of the Japanese-American experience. At present, Yamauchi lives in Gardena, California.

   Yamauchi's work has appeared in journals, newspapers, and numerous anthologies. Among her best-known stories are "And the Soul Shall Dance" (1976?), "Songs My Mother Taught Me" (1977), "Boatman on Toneh River" (1983), "Surviving the Wasteland Years" (1988), and "Makapoo Bay" (1989). She has also written several plays that explore the lives of Japanese Americans, including *And the Soul Shall Dance* (based on the story), *The Music Lessons*, *12-I-A*, and *Memento*.

   In "Maybe," Yamauchi's narrator, a Japanese American, describes the exploitation of Mexican migrant workers by their American employer and his Latin American wife. Beyond the inhumane work conditions, Florence observes and deplores the workers' isolation and alienation in the midst of prosperous Americans.

WHEN I AM OUT OF SORTS, I often drive to the outer edge of the city to calm myself. I love the outskirts. It reminds me of the land as it must have looked before we covered the earth with cement. I find there a feeling of the prairie where I was born. Sometimes when I see an old house with peeling paint squatting on a mound of dry weeds, the setting sun bleaching its west wall, I think I hear the children that have played there, perhaps now as old as myself—if they have survived the depression, three wars, sickness, and heartbreak. At this point I remember where I am in the scheme of things, smaller than a grain of sand and as dispensable. It comforts me.

One day on such a drive, I found the factory just outside of town. Here narrow roads through low hills, and frame houses, shutters askew like unfocused eyes, along with rusting cars and oil drums, cling to the chain link fence that banks a structured city drain. The lots here are oddly shaped; city planners had exercised eminent domain and sliced the properties at their convenience, creating instant prosperity to the owners (providing rabbit skin coats and hand-tooled boots), maiming the lots for that brief prosperity (a tuft of fur caught in the chain links, a weathered boot lying with the flotsam in the weeds). A sign on the outer wall of the factory, HELP, succinct, desperate, still with a touch of humor, gave me courage to walk in. After all, I was no less in need, my alimony had dwindled to a trickle; after eight years, that's about par for course, my attorney said. Even after twenty-five years of marriage, he said. That's life. The owner himself, Chuck White, took me in like a lost member of a tribe. We're of the same generation.

I am embarrassed to tell you the name of the company; it's too presumptuous for the two stories of rotting wood and broken windows and air conditioners hanging off the walls. Those that still function, spin out tails of spidery dust in the tepid air. But that's only in the offices and not for the majority of us.

I will call it Zodiac Prints. When I joined them, they were printing signs of the zodiac on T-shirts and cloth posters. I was hired as a quality-control person. They put me at the end of a long conveyor belt that slowly passes through several silk screens, each a different color, and a drying process. I check the colors, the print, and the material for flaws, and I stack and bundle the finished product. They don't say Zodiac 'til *I* say they say Zodiac.

Although I was the last hired, I was sent to the end of the belt largely because of Chuck White. White people (no pun intended) do not observe the difference between native Japanese and Japanese Americans. As I said, I was born in the southern California desert, but people are often amazed that I can speak English and I guess Chuck White associates me with Japanese industry (Sony, Toyota, etc.), and just for walking in and asking for a job, I went to the back of the line which in this case is the top of the bottom. This inability of white America to differentiate had worked against thousands of us Japanese Americans in 1942 when we were all put in concentration camps, blamed for Japan's attack on Pearl Harbor. Since then there have been other harrowing moments: the save-the-whale issue, the slaughter of dolphins, and always during trade treaties over Japanese exports—each movement sending waves of guilt by association. On the extreme, some of us have been clubbed to death by our super patriots and we have always been admonished to go back where we came from.

Anyway, back at the Zodiac, the story I hear is that Chuck White was having financial trouble and had taken steps toward declaring bankruptcy. He planned to drop out, wipe off the slate of debts, and start clean at another place under his wife's name—Zenobia. They say it isn't the first time Chuck did this, but the first with the new wife.

Preparations for the change had been made; a new site was selected, new business cards with Zenobia's name were printed and Zenobia was coming in daily to get a working knowledge of the business. Then suddenly the orders came pouring in and with it thousands of dollars. New people had to be hired. The factory started to hum again and the move was postponed. This is where I came in.

They say Zenobia, Colombian by birth, a ravishing overweight beauty at least twenty years Chuck White's junior (like my husband's new wife), changed from a quiet housewife to a formidable boss as easily as she would put on a coat, wearing all the executive qualities, the harassed eyes, the no-nonsense walk, the imperial forefinger, and also a touch of paternal benevolence—the sodas and tacos on the days that we worked overtime. Most of the workers are from Mexico, Nicaragua, and Costa Rica. The sales staff is white but they are not often at the factory.

Zenobia watches me when she thinks I'm not looking. I catch her reflection on the dirty glass panes and when I turn to face her, she flashes her perfect teeth. She doesn't like me. Maybe I remind her of someone. Maybe she's amazed that I can speak English. China, she call me. Maybe she thinks I'm a communist.

Most of the time she's busy on the phone or is rushing off somewhere in her silver Mercedes. Probably to the bank. She wears Gloria Vanderbilt jeans and carries a Gucci bag and smells of expensive perfume. When Chuck White is out of town, she moves me from one floor to the other for unimportant reasons. Just to let me know how superfluous I am.

So it goes. I've had worse things happen to me and nothing about this job causes me to lose sleep. Almost nothing. There's a certain confidence in knowing you're over-qualified and Zenobia does not diminish me. Besides, I like the second floor; the project is more interesting. They tie-dye there. Twenty people bend over paint troughs, dipping and squeezing shirts, skirts, and other things and the items hang to dry on rows and rows of lines, dripping and making puddles of color on the worn floor.

There are three big German Shepherd dogs in the factory. During the worst of his days (I'm told), Chuck White had to sell his Bel Air house but Zenobia would not let him sell the dogs. So the dogs live in the ramshackle factory and they follow Umberto, who feeds and cleans up after them, everywhere he goes—roaming the floors (they're not permitted outside), up and down the stairs, stumbled on and cursed by the workers, in and out of rooms. When Umberto is not here, these monstrous animals lie disconsolately on the floor wherever their depression happens to drop them. Umberto calls them by name and rubs their monster heads and they thump their powerful tails and slosh him with saliva. He's patient and gentle. He's twenty-four and quite handsome.

Everyone here who is from the other Americas is between seventeen and twenty-five. They all speak Spanish, some a little English, and they generally work quietly, obeying Zenobia or Rachel (the floorlady) without question or comment. In the late afternoons and on pay days, Jesus (El Savior) begins to sing and an excitement prevails even though we groan and laugh at his comic straining for high notes. I am reminded of my own youth, after being released from camp, the period that I spent working in factories, looking over the boys, waiting for the end of the day, looking forward to my pay check, mentally parceling out the money—to the lay-away at Lerner's, for rent, for food, for bus tokens. Fridays were just like these with another Jesus singing and cutting up, with everyone waiting for the factory whistle so we could go on with our real lives. I've come a full circle, back to a place that has remained unchanged in the changing times, in the age of the Pac Man and the computer. Maybe all displaced people go through a period of innocence before the desire to own, the ambition to be, propel us away from simple pleasures. The return is sweet with remembrance, along with a little sorrow—for the loss of innocence. But I'm older now and none of the senses are so acute and no pain so unbearable. And yet . . .

On a coffee break, I walk to the low hills for a breath of fresh air. Reynaldo and Anabella sit on top of the knoll on a scrap of plastic. Reynaldo is in charge of the keys to the factory and is married to Anabella. She doesn't speak much English so she always stays close to him, letting him transact the business of their lives. Faded pop cans lie in the dry grass.

"How romantic," I say to them.   15

"It is hot in the factory," Reynaldo says. Anabella whispers something.

"We are thinking about our son," Reynaldo says.

Why, Anabella looks no more than seventeen. I tell him this.

"She is twenty-one, same as me," Reynaldo says. "We are married already five years. Our son is in Mexico still. Today is his birthday."

Walking down the hill, I am filled with their longing. I stop to look back   20
at them. Anabella waves.

Umberto is not conscientious about cleaning the factory. The women's bathroom is dotted with dog droppings. I complain and Umberto tells me not to use it.

"I cannot clean everything all the time and do the work also," he says. "The dogs, you know, they do it all the time. I cannot keep up. Go to the office toilet."

He tells me they pay him three dollars and thirty-five cents an hour—the minimum. He gets up at four to come to work; his bus fare is three dollars, and lunch from the catering truck almost always costs six dollars a day. He is so tired at the end of the day, he cannot stay awake. He shakes his head. "I am still a young man," he says.

The reedy whistle of the catering truck rises above the factory noises and a surge of people run to meet it. The chatter grows bright with food words: tortillas, polla, naranja. My high school Spanish is inadequate; I wish I knew what else is said. Umberto sits on the ground to eat, carefully placing the paper plate in the circle of his legs. I feel the sublime intimacy of the man and his food.

To get to the office bathroom, I must pass through Chuck White's office. 25
He sits at a big desk looking over invoices in a pool of sunlight. The floor is carpeted, the walls are papered; the room is an oasis in the factory. He looks up briefly and smiles—almost an apology. "The other bathroom is filthy," I say. He nods and returns to his papers. No doubt he's heard of the fastidious Japanese.

Someone tried to bring some class to the bathroom and had painted the walls a dark green and installed a pair of fancy faucets in the sink. An electric hotplate on a crate destroys the ambience and there is a bottle of shampoo on the floor. The toilet here doesn't flush right either.

Umberto tells me that Reynaldo and Anabella live in the factory at night. I see no bed, no blankets, no clothes—only the hotplate and shampoo in the office bathroom. I think about the eerie loneliness of this huge factory at night, the three dogs groaning and snuffling and shuffling, the doors that hardly close, and Reynaldo and Anabella copulating on the production table with the smell of dogs and the spoiling vegetable dyes and the summer moon shining on their skin. And in the morning I see them putting away the evidence of their living: the underwear, the socks, the toothbrushes, combs, and towels.

But Umberto says Zenobia knows about this. She lets them stay because they have nowhere else to go. Umberto himself shares rent with six other people. "I have no room for them," he says.

In winter icy winds will blow through those broken windows and ill-fitting doors and the production table will be cold and hard, I tell Umberto.

"That's winter," he shrugs. 30

Reynaldo makes a sandwich from a loaf of Weber's bread and pressed meat. He spreads the bread with a thin swipe of mayonnaise and eats this with a gusto that can come only from hunger or habit. Anabella buys fried chicken, frijoles, and tortillas from the truck and shares these with Reynaldo. She eats slowly and sensually, careful not to lose a morsel from the chicken bones. She eats a sandwich too. I make fun; I point to her stomach and ask, "How many months?" She holds up four fingers.

I have a feeling Zenobia likes the sales staff as little as she does me. They bring her extravagant gifts and she puts on a dazzling smile and turns away, quickly dropping the smile as though she hopes her hypocrisy would be discovered. But on her birthday she invites them all to a party—everyone except me. I'd already contributed five dollars toward her gift and I had signed the birthday card.

She's happy all day, smiling and humming, but I pretend not to know what's up and try to look happy too. What do I care? If she has a conscience at all, she'll feel rotten when she sees my name on the card. I wish Rachel had let me do the shopping; I'd have fixed her good (I thought I'd given up feelings like that).

At the party they say Zenobia drinks too much and kisses all the young men. That's because she married an old man, Umberto says. Late in the evening she sniffs cocaine and turns up the music and wants to dance with all the guys. Chuck White serves the cake and goes to bed. Neighbors call to complain about the noise and everyone gets nervous thinking about police and raids and such things. These are always on the top of an undocumented alien's mind, Umberto says. Zenobia doesn't care; she married a white man and holds a green card. Umberto says everyone in the factory except the sales staff is undocumented. Reynaldo comes to sit with us.

"Are you illegal too?" I ask.   35

Reynaldo nods. "Everybody is. In this factory, in all the restaurants around here, all these places," he waves his hands. "These places, they would not stand without us." He pokes my arm and laughs. "Hey, you want to marry me? I'll give you one thousand dollars," he says.

"What will we do with Anabella?" I say.

"After the divorce, I will marry her," he says.

"But I have children older than you," I say.

He moves away and calls back, "One thousand dollars, Florence." An-   40
abella smiles at me.

Andrea smiles at the bus stop with a plastic purse clasped to her breast. She is seventeen and the prettiest girl in the factory, but today she looks awful. It's before the lunch hour. "Is she sick?" I ask Umberto.

"Well, Chuck told her to go home," he says.

The story is, Zenobia was so anxious to get an order off, she told Andrea to remove the bands before time and dry the shirts. Andrea did this, but she put the shirts in the tumble dryer and the wet dyes ran together and the whole order was ruined. Chuck White found the mess and fired Andrea. Even after he was told about Zenobia's instructions, he would not relent. "She should know better," he said and went to his office and closed the door.

Umberto taps his head. "She should know better," he says.

"Look how she holds her purse," I say.   45

"Well, she's sad," he says.

"Her mother will ask what happened and she'll have to say she lost her job."

"Rachel will find another for her," Umberto says.

"What will happen if she doesn't?" I ask.

"Then I will find for her," he says.   50

Reynaldo punches my arm every time he passes by, mocking me softly, "One thousand dollars, Florence." Sometimes he catches my eye from across the room and mouths, "One thousand dollars."

I call a young single friend to ask if she would marry Reynaldo. She is divorced and always in need of money but she tells me that immigration laws require a full three years of marriage before they will issue green cards. "That's longer than some real marriages last," my friend says. "One thousand dollars for three years is three hundred and thirty-three dollars a year," she says.

"And thirty-three cents," I add.

"I turned down ten thousand for the same service," she says. "And I could very well meet someone myself in three years. A real marriage, you know what I mean?

I give Reynaldo the bad news. He looks hurt even though we only joke about   55
it. I tell him my friend says three years is too long to be tied to a stranger.

"I just want my green card so I can bring my son here," he says. "My son was two years when we left him. He already forgot me, I think." Anabella turns her face away.

"I can't marry you, Reynaldo," I say.

"I know," he says. After a while he walks away.

I'm afraid I shall leave Zodiac soon. In the deceptive simplicity of the lives here, there is a quality I am unable to face. It's the underbelly of a smile. I know it well.

I remember our life in the Arizona camp—the first day our family entered   60
that empty barrack room (our home for the next four years), my father squatted on the dusty floor, his head deep in his shoulders, and my mother unwrapped a roll of salami and sliced it for us. I wanted so much to cry, but my

mother gripped my arm and gave me the meat. I turned to my father; he looked up and smiled. Two years later, the day I was to leave them and relocate to Chicago, my mother stood by the army truck that was to take us to the train in Parker. She had not wanted me to leave because my father was in the hospital with stomach ulcers. She did not touch me. The corners of her mouth wavered once, then turned up in a smile. And in the same tradition I smiled when he told me he was marrying a young woman from Japan. "That's good," I said.

It did not seem so brave or so sad then. Maybe living it is easier than remembering or watching someone else living it. My son is in Mexico still, ha-ha; he will soon forget me.

Late in the afternoon Reynaldo comes back to me and pokes my arm. "Thank you for telling your friend to marry me," he says.

"I'm sorry it didn't work out," I say. I ask him if he crossed the border at Tijuana. My sister lives in National City, just north of the border. I remember those immigration round-ups that show periodically on television nightly news: soft gray blurs running in the California twilight, crouching, routed out of bushes, herded into covered pick-up trucks, their faces impassive.

"We crossed the river in Texas," he says.

"You swam the Rio Grande at night?" I ask.

Reynaldo nods. "Anabella, you know, she does not swim so I . . ." he crooks his left arm to make a circle for Anabella's head and with his right arm he makes swimming strokes and looks at me and smiles.

65

Maybe it does not seem so brave or so sad to him. Maybe I should spare myself the pain.

Considerations

1. At several places in the story, the narrator, Florence, is reminded of her experiences growing up as a Japanese American. Find two such reminiscences and explain how they connect with the subject matter and main narrative line of the story.

2. Florence seems to be a competent worker, and she establishes friendly relationships with most of the people at Zodiac Prints, including the owner, Chuck White, and other workers like Reynaldo and Umberto. Her relation with Zenobia is different, however. How do you explain the way Zenobia behaves to Florence? What reasons can you suggest for Zenobia's singling her out from among the other workers?

Invitation to Write

Yamauchi's story focuses more on the human relationships at Zodiac Prints than on the work actually done or the product produced. In this sense, her story could be read as a social commentary on working conditions at a particular moment in late twentieth-century America. What exactly are these conditions? Referring back to any jobs (paid or volunteer) that you have held, write an essay in which you examine the relations between working and social conditions as they are presented by Yamauchi's story. Consider the role played by the phenomenon of immigration and the way it influences or radically changes the relationship between employers and employees. Think of other factors that can determine this kind of relationship, such as age, degree of education, or family connections, and find some examples from your own experience that will make your conclusions more general.

Connections

In "Alienated Labor" (p. 254), Karl Marx suggests that people's relationships to their jobs are gauged on an entirely different scale from that which gauges their relationships to each other. His essay moves towards the conclusion that

> human alienation, and above all the relation of man to himself, is first realized and expressed in the relationship between each man and other men. Thus in the relationship of alienated labor every man regards other men according to the standards and relationships in which he finds himself placed as a worker. (para. 36)

Write an essay in which you use Yamauchi's story "Maybe" to construct a response to Marx's point of view. Explore the concept of alienation and the supplementary meaning it acquires in Yamauchi's story, where the workers are literally aliens. Look at the ways workers relate to their work and to each other and determine whether the situation of these workers supports Marx's assertions.

ROBERT C. CHRISTOPHER

The Fruits of Industry

Robert C. Christopher was born in 1924, educated at Yale, and now works for *Newsweek* magazine. There he writes on foreign affairs and business, analyzing corporate America from both an economic and a social point of view. Christopher is especially interested in American-Japanese relations; his interest in Japanese culture was first aroused over fifty years ago when he began learning Japanese in a U.S. Army school. Christopher has written articles for *Time* Magazine, *The New York Times Magazine,* the *London Sunday Times,* and numerous other periodicals. He has also written a book about American-Japanese relations called *Second to None: American Companies in Japan* (1986). His most recent work is *Crashing the Gates: The DeWASPing of America's Power Elite* (1989). His book *The Japanese Mind: The Goliath Explained* (1982) presents a culmination of his study of Japanese society and is based on his personal contacts with Japanese individuals and organizations. The essay that follows is a chapter from this book, which Christopher characterizes as a "psychic and institutional guidebook to today's Japan."

In "The Fruits of Industry," Christopher examines the Japanese cultural ideals reflected in their business practices. His insights into Japanese culture are useful in understanding the Japanese point of view and improving communication with that culture.

IT WAS TEN THIRTY AT NIGHT, and on the stool next to mine in the Orchid Bar of Tokyo's Hotel Okura a British businessman was sipping moodily at a snifter of brandy. He was, he explained, about to head home to London empty-handed, having failed to land a big contract because the product his company made did not meet the standards of reliability insisted upon by a potential Japanese client. In due course, the Englishman ordered a second brandy and savored it in silence, all the while staring intently at a pair of Japanese bartenders who were deftly mixing and dispensing a bewildering variety of drinks to forty or fifty customers. Finally, his snifter empty, the Englishman abruptly jumped up off his bar stool and, just before disappearing into the night, said loudly to no one in particular: "They are so damned efficient, these people, that it's bloody frightening."

In so saying, the frustrated Briton was of course voicing a sentiment now shared by most of the world's non-Japanese population. Only fifteen years ago, eminent Europeans like France's Jean-Jacques Servan-Schreiber were pointing with alarm to "the American challenge" and glumly predicting the imminent economic takeover of the world by U.S.-controlled multinational corporations. Today all that is forgotten and it is the Japanese challenge that obsesses businessmen, labor leaders, and politicians all the way from Detroit to Düsseldorf. How do they do it? Westerners ask in anguished wonderment. How have the inhabitants of a relatively small country with virtually no natural resources managed to build in so short a time the world's second-largest industrial economy? What are the secrets that have enabled Japan to surpass the once-impregnable United States in automobile production, rival it in steel production, and unleash upon the world at large a torrent of consumer goods so high in quality and reasonable in price that in one field after another, the developed nations of the West have fallen back upon protectionism, overt or disguised, as the only way to prevent destruction of their domestic industries?

Back in the '60s and early '70s, when they had not yet perceived the full dimensions of the Japanese challenge, most Western businessmen and politicians were inclined to attribute the superior competitiveness of so many Japanese products to some kind of Oriental trickery. Cheap labor was the explanation, they said. Or more darkly yet, they accused the Japanese of widespread dumping—selling goods abroad at prices below their cost of production.

But as the years went by and Japan's great modern corporations steadily expanded their foreign beachheads in one industry after another, the charge of unfair competition became harder and harder to sustain as the primary explanation for Japan's export successes. Clearly, no manufacturer, not even an inscrutable Oriental one, can go on, decade in and decade out, continually selling his products at a loss. And the cheap-labor argument, though still frequently heard, does not stand up to close examination either. For one thing, Japan's most successful manufacturers have for some time been steadily reducing their dependence on human labor: Japan's newer steel mills, auto plants, and TV assembly lines are considerably more automated and "robotized" than most comparable Western facilities. In any case, overall labor costs in Japan now equal or surpass those prevailing in most of Western Europe and in some instances actually surpass those in the United States itself. Yet Japanese automakers now sell more cars in the United States than all their European competitors combined.

Faced with these awkward facts, realists in the West began to search for more sophisticated explanations for the superior competitiveness of the Japanese. One reason for it, some people suggested, was that Japanese industry 5 had been fortunate enough to have most of its plants bombed off the face of the earth during World War II and thus, unlike American industry, had been left with no choice but to replace obsolescent factories and mills with more modern and efficient ones. An even more intriguing suggestion was the concept of "Japan, Inc." developed by American business consultant James Abegglen. This was a vision of the Japanese economy as a kind of seamless web in which politicians, bureaucrats, and businessmen all worked industriously toward mutually agreed-upon ends. As oversimplified by some of its popularizers, however, it was often reduced to the proposition that unlike the U.S. government, the government of Japan invariably seeks, by fair means or foul, to strengthen private industry and advance its interests.

There was some truth to both these suggestions, but again, as time wore on, it became clear that neither of them by itself could fully account for the Japanese miracle. World War II bomb damage, extensive as it was, has very little relevance to the current efficiency of the Japanese auto industry, which existed only in rudimentary form in the 1940s, and it has none whatsoever to Japanese dominance of consumer electronics, an industry which did not exist at all then. And while the Japanese government has indeed played a vital role in the nurturing of Japanese industry, that role does not, as many Americans appear to believe, involve extraordinarily heavy financial aid to industry. In one important respect, in fact, Tokyo is actually less openhanded than Washington: Where the U.S. government underwrites close to 50 percent of all the research and development efforts of American corporations—including more than 35 percent of all nonmilitary research—only about 25 percent of the R&D money spent in Japan comes from government agencies.

In short, if one is intellectually honest, it is very difficult to find an ego-salving set of excuses for the fact that American industry in recent years has so frequently been outperformed by Japanese industry. In recognition of this, an increasing number of Americans—perhaps the most influential being Harvard professor Ezra Vogel, the author of *Japan as Number One: Lessons for America*—have come up with a revisionist interpretation of the Japanese challenge. The real explanation of the Japanese success story, the revisionists say, is that in a number of respects—social, economic, and administrative—Japan operates more intelligently and efficiently than Western societies do. The basic message preached by the revisionists, at least as it gets through to most American businessmen, bureaucrats, and politicians, is a simple one: Observe what the Japanese do and then try your damnedest to do likewise.

If only because it reflects a sensible degree of modesty—a virtue that has never loomed large in the American national character—the revisionists' approach surely represents a step in the right direction. But as a prescription for concrete action it also carries some inherent risks. To determine what if any economic devices the United States can reasonably hope to borrow from Japan, it is first necessary to arrive at a clear understanding of how big

Japanese corporations actually operate—and why they can and do operate that way.

A half century ago, my great-uncle Will Lee lived in a small Connecticut town owned by the Talcotts, an old Yankee family whose ancestors had reputedly acquired the place from a sachem called Uncas the Mohegan.

When I say that the Talcotts owned Talcottville, I mean exactly that. They were more than just the owners of the woolen mill that was the heart of the community and gave employment to most of Talcottville's men. They also owned every house in town, had built the local school, and in the manner of eighteenth-century English squires, had appointed the rector of the local church. Talcottville, in short, was at once a business enterprise and a community.

Today, like most of the scores of other such communities that once dotted the United States, Talcottville is no longer a company town—and most Americans would not regret the change. On the contrary, nearly all of us in this country regard the increasing rarity of communities owned or dominated by a single company as a sign of progress. To be dependent on your employer not only for your income but also for your housing, your recreation, and even, in a sense, your social life is, by contemporary American standards, an unacceptable infringement on personal freedom. It is therefore somewhat disconcerting to discover that in up-and-coming Japan the state of affairs is almost exactly the reverse. Since World War II, in fact, Japan's major business enterprises have increasingly developed into something approaching self-contained communities. This is not to say that Japan has become simply one vast collection of company towns. What has been happening there is something considerably more complex—something first drawn to my attention by Isamu Yamashita, the chairman of Mitsui Zosen (or, as it is known in English, the Mitsui Engineering and Shipbuilding Company).

Yamashita, a stocky, unassuming engineer who has worked for Mitsui Zosen for nearly fifty years, is one of Japan's most capable and hardheaded executives. Most of our conversation dealt with very pragmatic matters, such as the techniques by which he had achieved a dramatically successful diversification of his company's activities.

But when I asked him a cliché Harvard Business School question—what basic line of business did Mitsui Zosen consider itself to be in—Yamashita suddenly waxed philosophical. Mitsui Zosen, he allowed, was essentially in the business of surviving.

"You have to remember," he went on, "that only fifty years ago we Japanese were still living in an essentially feudal system. As a general thing, people in those days stuck to the communities where they were born. But after World War II, when Japan began reindustrializing, people started to flock to the big industrial complexes, and the old sense of geographic community largely broke down. In a very real way, we in industry spoiled the old community life of Japan, and something had to replace it. So in today's Japan, companies like ours are the new communities, and their managers have a responsibility to create conditions in which people can enjoy a community life. Above all, of course, we managers have the overriding responsibility of keeping the community alive."

At first blush this seemed an interesting but slightly artificial construct— 15
the sort of thing thrown out by a young sociologist desperately seeking a topic for a Ph.D thesis. But just how true it really is was driven home to me a couple of weeks later when I spent an afternoon with Toru Iijima, a foreman in the Nissan Motor Company's Oppama assembly plant, which sits on the western shore of Tokyo Bay near the great naval base of Yokosuka.

At thirty-seven, Toru Iijima is a lean, handsome man of uncommon dignity and self-possession. I have, in fact, rarely met anyone who struck me as being more in command of his own soul than Iijima. Yet for him the sun rises and sets on Nissan.

A car nut since childhood, Iijima passed up public high school to attend the Nissan Vocational School. From there he went directly to the stamping shop of the Oppama plant. Today, twenty years later, he is still in the stamping shop, but now he has fifteen people working under him.

When he first went to work at Oppama, Iijima lived in a bachelor dormitory that Nissan maintains at Oppama. In due course he married a girl who also worked at Nissan, and for a while they lived in a company-owned apartment. Then a baby came along—today the Iijimas have two sons, thirteen and ten—and Iijima decided to buy his own home. With the help of Nissan's real estate subsidiary, he was able to do so at considerably less than the exorbitant price that housing in the Tokyo megalopolis normally commands. And his payments are relatively easy to handle because of the installment savings program Nissan makes available to its employees—a kind of credit union that pays higher interest than ordinary banks and lends money more cheaply.

A devoted father, Iijima spends much of his free time on barbecues and hikes with his family. But he is also a keen athlete who makes frequent use of the plant gymnasium at Oppama, competing with other Nissan workers in a variety of sports. On vacations he usually drives his wife and children to the mountains in his Nissan Sunny (Datsun 210)—which he bought at an employee discount.

If all this makes Toru Iijima sound like a mindless creation of Nissan, it 20
does him a great injustice. When I asked him if he wanted his sons to go to university so they could become Nissan engineers, he threw me a cool, level look. "I hope they will do whatever they want," he said. "They have to have their own way of life."

Nonetheless, Nissan provides Iijima with the same sense of belonging that Talcottville gave to my great-uncle Will. The thought of looking for a better job elsewhere or, more to the point, of being cast adrift by Nissan literally never crosses Iijima's mind. He knows that unless he commits some heinous offense, he will never be fired. And he knows, too, that if the Oppama plant were ever obliged to reduce production drastically, Nissan would make every effort to find useful employment for any redundant personnel. (Not too far from Oppama, in fact, there is dramatic evidence of the lengths to which a Japanese company will go to take care of its employees: When Nippon Steel was forced to close down one of its furnaces at Kimitsu, on the other side of Tokyo Bay, it promptly set up an agricultural subsidiary in the area and put the displaced furnacemen to work raising cattle.)

For Toru Iijima, Nissan is more than the source of his income. It is a living organism with which he identifies to a degree surpassed only by his identification with his family and his country. "Nissan," he told me, sounding remarkably like Isamu Yamashita, "must survive for long, long years, and the quality of its work must be maintained through all those years." For that reason, he feels great responsibility for the training of younger workers and for ensuring that the members of his shift remain "very active" in suggesting improvements in working methods. He also expects the more experienced members of his shift to spot anything wrong with a car that passes through their hands even if the error was made in another part of the plant. "The whole responsibility for every car we touch is on our shoulders," he says. "If I hear that a car produced by Nissan has any problems, I feel personally guilty."

From casual conversations with people like Toru Iijima, it is tempting to conclude—as many Americans have—that Japanese workers have somehow been brainwashed into utter docility by their bosses. But there is one great flaw in that theory: Japanese executives manifest precisely the same attitudes as their assembly-line workers.

Of the scores of Japanese senior executives I have interviewed over the years, I can recall only two who did not sooner or later make a point of informing me that they had spent their entire working lives with one company. And nearly all Japan's current crop of top executives are quick to tell you that they started out on the assembly line or in some equally humble job. (This is a fact that sometimes has rather anomalous results: It is doubtful, for example, that the chief executive of any American corporation can boast, as Mitsui Zosen's Yamashita does, that he was once the leader of his company's labor union.)

The reason for the extraordinary corporate fidelity of Japanese executives 25 is not simply, as foreigners often assume, that they fear change or regard job-hopping as a manifestation of frivolity. Rather, like their workers, they conceive of corporations as communities that, in a certain sense, are collectively managed and hence cannot be successfully led by anyone not intimately familiar with the collective psyche. "In this country you just don't get a company like Chrysler calling in a top Ford executive to run its affairs," one of Japan's most respected businessmen told me. "That would be almost as unthinkable as it would be for New Yorkers to elect a mayor who had lived all his life in Chicago."

Moreover, this sense of the corporation as a unique, continuing entity provides Japanese executives, like their workers, with a high degree of financial and emotional security. Indeed, in a Japanese company, as in the political life of a small American city, dedication and hard work are often more prized than brilliance.

Just how true this is was spelled out for me by Yoshiya Ariyoshi, for many years the elder statesman of the giant shipping line named Nippon Yusen Kaisha (NYK). Heavily influenced by his youthful experiences in Europe—as an NYK representative in Hitler's Germany, he took the risky step of issuing steamship tickets on credit to Jewish families frantic to escape the Thousand Year Reich—Mr. Ariyoshi was unusual among Japanese of his generation in that when he was dealing with Westerners he made his points directly and forcefully. "I know it is hard for Americans to understand," Ariyoshi told me, "but in Japan it's quite customary for a twenty-year-old to receive only a third of the salary of a forty-year-old who is doing exactly the same work. In most companies here all employees except for the top executives are paid according to seniority. To you Americans that would seem to destroy incentive. But in Japan if the other members of your group work hard and you don't, you will eventually be ostracized. And being excluded from the group is the most appalling thing any Japanese can imagine."

As Ariyoshi himself confessed, this reliance on peer pressure can on occasion backfire. "At Japan National Railways, it is the people who work hard that are ostracized," he said ruefully. And an increasing number of Japanese executives feel that as a spur to efficiency and creativity the wage system should be modified so as to put more weight on individual performance. Already some big corporations have begun to edge cautiously away from seniority as the sole criterion of salary, and Taiji Ubukata, president of Ishikawajima-Harima Heavy Industries, foresees the day when "perhaps 60 to 70 percent of wages will be based on seniority and the rest on such things as merit and productivity." But even so limited a resort to the merit system is not a universally popular idea. "It seems to me," one promising young *sarariman* told me, "that our traditional system suits the Japanese character better."

Important as they may be, in other words, financial rewards do not loom as large in corporate life in Japan as they do in the United States—and that is even truer for executives than for workers. It is doubtful that in all of Japan's booming auto industry there is a single person who makes as much as a quarter of the income enjoyed by the top half-dozen men in Detroit. The typical big Japanese corporation, in fact, pays its president less than $150,000 a year—partly because he would have to pay out 80 percent of anything over that amount in income tax. And unless he founded his company himself, a Japanese executive cannot hope for stock options, deferred-compensation plans, or any of the other gimmicks through which top American managers contrive to become personally wealthy.

In Japanese eyes, this relative deprivation is more than compensated for by the psychic and social security that comes with success. If a Japanese executive reaches the top rungs of his company, the mandatory retirement age—usually somewhere in the sixties for management personnel—will be raised for him or even, as it was in Mr. Ariyoshi's case, effectively suspended entirely. It is by no means uncommon in Japanese business for a men to serve successively as his company's president, then chairman, and finally, in extreme old age, honorary chairman.

But even if an executive is only moderately successful and never rises above the bottom rungs of senior management, he does not have to resign himself, as most American executives must, to being put out to pasture in his late fifties or early sixties. Though he will be required to observe his company's mandatory retirement age, more likely than not his colleagues will find him a "postretirement job" in the management of one of the company's subsidiaries or subcontractors. And thus a centrally important element in his life—his membership in the corporate community—remains intact.

To the hardheaded European or American businessman, it may seem a long leap from the institution of "lifetime employment" to the concept of the Japanese corporation as at least a partial surrogate for the traditional geographic community. But only if you make that leap does it become possible to explain, rather than merely describe, some of the aspects of Japanese economic life that foreigners find most mystifying.

Consider, for example, the fact that the typical Japanese labor union represents the workers of only one company and, as a routine matter, adjusts its wage, bonus and overtime demands to the prosperity of that particular company at contract time. Most Westerners who are aware of this phenomenon tend to attribute it either to the passivity of Japanese labor or to the Machiavellian practices of Japanese management. But while both these factors may apply in some slight degree, the fundamental explanation for the close cooperation between unions and management lies in a strongly perceived identity of interest between the two. In many Japanese companies, the union's leadership is treated almost as an arm of management. At Mitsui Shipbuilding, for example, the chief executive officer meets every quarter with the leaders of the company's union (the union president at the time of my visit was a young university graduate who presumably would eventually move into executive ranks himself) and fills them in on all major corporate developments. "So when it comes time for a new wage settlement," Mr. Yamashita told me, "the union already knows the situation of the company and doesn't make exorbitant demands."

Essentially, the reason a big Japanese corporation can operate in this fashion is that its employees accept that their prosperity as individuals is directly dependent upon the prosperity of the economic community to which they belong. Far more than American or European workers, Japanese workers take it for granted that just as an individual must sometimes sacrifice to ensure national survival, so he must sometimes sacrifice to ensure corporate survival.

As Yutaka Takeda, a senior executive of Shin Nippon Steel, once pointed out to me, however, there is an important corollary to this assumption: In the majority of Japanese corporations, the class struggle does not enter strongly into labor-management relations. To be sure, Japanese companies are extremely hierarchical organizations in which everyone is keenly aware of his or her place. But everyone is also made to feel an indispensable part of the community—a fact that many Japanese argue constitutes a crucial difference between American and Japanese industry.

"American executives are too aristocratic," charges a Japanese businessman who knows the United States very well. "Very few of them have ever worked on a production line themselves, and they have little or no contact with their workers, whom they treat as interchangeable parts. Here in Japan it's routine for the president of a big department store, if he has no other engagement, to have lunch in the company cafeteria, mingling with the salesclerks and other employees. And that's not just a gimmick. All of us—everyone of us in Japan—believe that the rise or fall of our organization rests on the individual shoulders of each one of us."

It is at least in part this sense of being a valued member of a social unit that explains the extraordinary degree of loyalty Japanese workers feel toward their companies—an attitude closely akin to the civic boosterism of many Americans. For a Westerner it is a sobering experience to hear, as I have, a twenty-three-year-old clerk discourse on the history, products, and procedures of her corporation with all the uncritical earnestness of an American high school teacher expounding on the ineffable wisdom of the Founding Fathers.

Still another desirable consequence of the concept of the corporation as a community is the relative immunity of Japanese industry to the plague of mergers and takeovers that has afflicted American industry in recent years. Big Japanese corporations do occasionally merge or absorb one another, but such occurrences are rare—and traumatic. "For one major company here to take over another," a Japanese government official explained, "is nearly as unsettling as it would be if Connecticut took over Rhode Island. It causes all kinds of psychological and social upheaval."

This is not to say that Japanese industry does not have its own version of the American conglomerate. But Japanese-style conglomerates—the potent collections of twenty to thirty companies such as the "Mitsui group" and the "Mitsubishi group"—are more like loosely linked political confederations than artificial, balance-sheet empires such as Litton Industries.

Typically, at least 50 percent of the stock of, say, a Mitsui company is 40 owned by other Mitsui companies. The performance of the managers of one Mitsui company is, therefore, judged by their peers in other Mitsui companies—and the crucial element in that evaluation is how effectively this particular set of managers has acted to ensure the survival of its company and of the Mitsui group as a whole.

It is precisely here, in my view, that the more-than-commercial role of the major Japanese companies has made its biggest contribution to Japan's economic success. "American managers," Yoshiya Ariyoshi once told me disapprovingly, "are judged by their stockholders on the basis of how big a profit they turned in last quarter and what they can be expected to turn in next quarter. That forces them to focus on the short term, like a baseball player worrying about his batting average. Our system, with its heavy emphasis on the survival of the institution, forces managers to think constantly about the long term."

From time to time, representatives of U.S. cities or states that are trying to attract Japanese investment seek out Richard Rabinowitz to get the benefit of the expertise on Japan he has acquired in the course of twenty years of highly successful law practice there. "I always give them pretty much the same advice," says Rabinowitz. "I tell them to give the Japanese they are wooing reassurances about the existence of a literate work force in their particular region, the degree of physical security the area offers, and what it has in the way of cultural facilities and amenities—in short, the kind of reassurances the citizens of any advanced nation want when they are considering a business venture in a less-developed society."

Courtesy, of course, does not permit most Japanese to refer openly to the United States as a less advanced nation than Japan. On the contrary, almost every Japanese businessman with whom I have discussed the relative performances of the Japanese and American economies has been quick to tell me of the enormous debt his particular industry owes to "our elder brothers in America." Given the role of the elder brother in the traditional Japanese family, this is an expression of extreme deference; and in thus emphasizing their sense of indebtedness to their American counterparts Japanese businessmen are in no way insincere. An extremely high proportion of the technology currently employed by the most advanced sectors of Japanese industry was originally developed in the United States, and it is no accident that the coveted quality-control award for which Japanese firms bitterly compete each year is named after an American statistician, W. Edwards Deming. "Productivity and quality control are both games we learned from the Americans," admits

Ichiro Shioji, the president of the Confederation of Japanese Automobile Workers' Unions.

Such deference is always flattering—until you stop to reflect that very often the Japanese apply what they have borrowed from the United States in the way of technology, managerial devices, and manufacturing techniques more effectively than Americans now do. It is this embarrassing fact above all that in recent years has led a certain number of Americans to suggest that it would be wise for U.S. industry to determine what it is that the Japanese do differently and then emulate them.

To support this argument, its most simplistic proponents sometimes point 45 to Japanese companies that have purchased or launched U.S. subsidiaries, have operated them Japanese style (in some cases right down to mass morning calisthenics for employees) and, in the process, have prospered mightily. But while some of these case histories are accurate enough, they tend, in my view, to be deceptive. When you press hard enough, a surprising number of Japanese industrialists privately express reservations about the performance of their American subsidiaries. One deeply pro-American Tokyo executive proudly described to me how his company had acquired a money-losing U.S. concern and rendered it profitable in the space of a single year. In the next breath, however, he confessed that because of sloppy work practices among the employees in his U.S. plant, the number of defective units it produced ran nearly 50 percent higher than in his Japanese plants. Another top Japanese manager confessed with an embarrassed laugh that when his company acquired a well-established U.S. manufacturing company, "we found that the way they were doing things over there was twenty years behind us." Glumly, he added that in his opinion, it would be a very long time before the U.S. operation achieved Japanese levels of productivity—if indeed it ever did.

In the view of many of the Japanese industrialists I have talked with, nearly all Japanese firms that have successfully employed their own style of management in the United States fall into a special category. "They're in fields where they don't have to deal with tough, industry-wide unions," the chief executive of a major Japanese manufacturing company bluntly declared. Somewhat more cautiously, Jiro Tokuyama of the Nomura School of Advanced Management told me: "It's significant, I think, that the Japanese companies that have done best in the United States mostly have American subsidiaries with only a thousand employees or less. In such cases, it's relatively easy to apply what I call Japan's 'lubricant system'—which is to say greater humanism in industrial relations and a greater sense of participation on the part of ordinary workers. But whether this would work in a U.S. company with five or six thousand employees I'm not so sure."

Obviously, it would be foolish to suggest that there is no possibility whatever of successfully transferring Japanese managerial and manufacturing techniques to the United States. Some transfer of this kind is already occurring. A number of U.S. firms have taken a careful look at Japanese business strategies and, as a result, are themselves experimenting with such things as heavier reliance upon subcontractors and "guaranteed" employment. Perhaps the most widespread reimportation from Japan has been the "quality-control circle"—a group of eight to a dozen workers from the same division of a company who are encouraged to engage in regular brainstorming sessions in order to find ways of increasing their own productivity and the reliability of the goods they produce.

But while these and other specific Japanese practices can no doubt be usefully adapted to the American environment, there would seem to be clear limits to the degree to which U.S. industry can hope to remodel itself in the Japanese image. On the strength of his intimate knowledge of both countries, Jiro Tokuyama, for one, has concluded that most of the differences between Japanese and American managerial techniques are merely symptoms of a far deeper and probably ineradicable difference. "The contradiction between the two countries is not basically economic but rather is one of social systems," he asserts. Sounding the same theme, Yoshiya Ariyoshi rhetorically demanded of me: "How can anyone reasonably expect Americans—individualistic and independent-minded Americans—to behave like group-oriented Japanese?"

Because "individualistic" and "independent-minded" are positive words in our lexicon, most Americans instinctively preen themselves when they hear a question like Mr. Ariyoshi's. That, unfortunately, tends to obscure an important fact: It is group orientation that in large part explains the heavy emphasis on long-term planning which many Japanese businessmen regard as the key factor in Japanese managerial strategy.

Nearly all Americans who possess any familiarity with Japanese business freely concede—or angrily charge—that Japanese corporations are far readier than American ones to mortgage the present in order to secure the future. To win a foothold in a promising new industry or market, Japan's major companies routinely make heavy investments that cannot be expected to produce profits for a long time to come. But the fact that Japanese managers take such action far more freely and more frequently than their American counterparts does not stem from greater cunning or superior intelligence. Rather, it is a function of the climate in which they operate.

Unlike his American counterparts, in fact, a Japanese executive would endanger his own career prospects if he sought to maximize short-term profits at the risk of his company's long-term health. There are at least two reasons for this. Where U.S. stockholders for the most part are primarily interested in a company's current earnings and their impact on the price of its shares, the interlocking directorates that exercise effective control of so many Japanese corporations tend, as Mr. Ariyoshi pointed out, to focus on a company's prospects for long-term survival. And this emphasis upon the company as an enduring institution is reinforced by the fact that although they now do far more equity financing than they used to, Japanese corporations still typically rely upon bank loans to meet a much higher percentage of their capital requirements than American corporations do. Inevitably, companies with massive bank loans are inclined to pay close attention to the views of their bankers. But unlike stockholders, bankers do not stand to gain directly from a quick boost in corporate earnings or share prices; their main concern is that a company which has borrowed from them stay in business and go on paying off the interest on its debts.

Besides all these institutional forces, there is another consideration which, I believe, helps significantly to deter Japanese executives from settling for quick and impermanent fixes. Because they identify so completely with one company and rarely indulge in job-hopping, they have a greater stake in the long-range implications of their decisions than America's far more mobile managers necessarily do. Instead of consoling himself with the thought that he can always skip off to greener pastures, a Japanese executive knows that unless in the meantime he has died or retired, he will still be around to face any untoward consequences that his current decisions may ultimately have upon his company's fortunes.

Considerations

1. What major differences does Christopher see between Japanese and American attitudes toward work? How would you compare the attitudes of Japanese and American workers? of Japanese and American managers?

2. Christopher writes very positively about the Japanese corporate system. What does he see as positive in the system? What are some possible concerns or disadvantages that he does not consider? Why does he not present them?

Invitation to Write

Christopher suggests that the Japanese model of industry reflects the value the Japanese place on community, while the American model emphasizes the value Americans place on personal freedom. Using the information Christopher presents, it is easy to imagine that, in accepting a job with a Japanese corporation, an American worker would have to get used to a lot of new rules. Write an essay in which you determine the adjustments an American worker would have to make in order to conform to Japanese norms regarding work. Consider the difficulties she or he might have and the reasons for such difficulties. After evaluating this hypothetical experience, answer the question implied by Christopher: Can we accept the revisionist's point of view that copying Japanese methods will lead to a similar economic success in America?

Connections

Imagine that several Japanese corporate executives interviewed by Christopher are invited to the United States to review the situation of American corporations and to offer advice to American business leaders. Using Christopher's essay as the basis of your understanding of the Japanese attitudes toward work, show how these executives might evaluate the situation they encounter at Zodiac Prints, the company described in the story "Maybe" (p. 219) by Wakako Yamauchi. Write an essay in which you describe their probable reaction to some of the specific practices and attitudes present in the factory, and speculate about the suggestions for improvement they would make to the management. You might begin by focusing on any one example of Florence's experience that Yamauchi describes in detail.

BRUCE TUCKER
PAUL LEINBERGER

Scott Myers, Entrepreneur

Bruce Tucker, born in 1948, is a freelance writer from Highland Park, New Jersey. His interests include art, critical theory, and American culture. In addition to *The New Individualists*, which he wrote with Paul Leinberger, he collaborated with James Brown on *James Brown: The Godfather of Soul* (1990). His current projects include an anthology of contemporary critical theory essays, which he is editing, and a larger study of the relationship between American art and culture.

Paul Leinberger, born in 1947, has held a number of jobs similar to the ones he and Bruce Tucker analyze in *The New Individualists*. He has been an executive for a large clothing company, an urban planner in Chicago, and a private consultant. Currently, he divides his time between management consulting, market research, and urban planning. He lives in Palo Alto, California.

"Scott Myers, Entrepreneur" is taken from the first chapter of *The New Individualists: The Generations After The Organization Man* (1991). *The Organization Man*, written in 1956 by William H. Whyte, Jr., described the "men in the grey suits" whose loyalty to their corporations played a central role in their lives and in the lives of their spouses. Leinberger and Tucker discovered that the sons and daughters of these loyal corporate employees did not choose to work for corporations and could not even imagine the same kind of loyalty to a large corporation. Many had seen the devotion of their fathers to the corporation replaced by a sense of failure and disillusionment. Scott Myers is typical in his response to the former generation's experience and his desire to find a different situation for himself. The essay also suggests the different roles of work in the lives of individuals and raises the issue of divided loyalties between work and family.

SCOTT MYERS, MANEUVERING HIS MAZDA through traffic and onto the San Tomas Expressway, is smiling. On this damp and cold spring morning, he is not wearing a coat and tie, the mandatory uniform of the organization man he had worn for almost a decade. A polo shirt, a pair of cotton wash pants, and loafers suffice. For the past eight years he has dreamed of this day, and now, March 1987, he is about to fulfill his wish to be in business for himself. During the short trip up the valley from his home in Cupertino, where he lives with his wife Charity and their two children, he talks about how he arrived at this day.

"I quit college after one year," he says. "I was not into studying at the time. I flunked out of most of my classes. It was a waste of my time and my dad's money. I went to Colorado and messed around the mountains for about nine months. I had a camping trailer and I lived out in the hills and basically did whatever it took to get food. Construction, mostly.

"I was a real dropout. I just hadn't gotten plugged into a useful life. I had given no thought to what I wanted to do. The building of houses was just something I landed in—learned from scratch, no thought to it, making just enough to live on. I went from paycheck to paycheck. But I got tired of getting up at five in the morning and going out in the cold to build houses. So I went back to school."

Born in 1953, Scott is the youngest of Ray and Bee Myers's three sons. Scott understands very well what his father's thirty-three-year commitment to Continental meant, and he intends to make good use of the lessons he learned growing up as the son of an organization man.

He is his father's son through and through. But when he was wandering   5
the Colorado mountains in the early 1970s, the gap between them could not have been wider. Along with many members of his generation at the time, including older brother Randy, he hardly seemed the son of a senior corporate executive. And his parents, like many at the time, must have asked themselves if this could really be the son they had brought up in suburban Park Forest, Illinois, and neighboring Flossmoor.

Scott stopped wandering in the spring of 1972. Not only did he hate working in the predawn cold of the Rockies, he also wanted a student deferment from the draft, so he returned to school at his father's alma mater, DePauw University in Greencastle, Indiana. But a small, liberal arts school in the rolling hills of southern Indiana was not Scott's idea of what education should be.

"I did not like DePauw at all," Scott says. "It was useless. I told my dad that many times. I felt it was too sheltered. It was a place where parents sent their kids so they wouldn't have to deal with reality. You had to live in the dorm, so you couldn't have any of the responsibilities that I wanted at that age. The college cooked your meals and your parents paid your bills. That wasn't the kind of place I was looking for."

He transferred to Indiana University in Bloomington and eventually persuaded his then-girlfriend Charity to join him. Charity provided a stabilizing influence. By the time they were graduated in 1976, he in biology, she in microbiology, they'd decided that graduate school offered the best route to good jobs. His aimless days now far behind him, Scott headed for business school at Northwestern University. Charity enrolled in the Ph.D. program in medical research.

Scott had watched his two older brothers take dramatically different courses in their lives and he thought he could learn from both. Scott loved Randy and remembered fondly the time they had spent together after Scott had first dropped out of DePauw. But Scott also knew that Randy's life was not for him. He wondered what kind of future there was for a construction contractor in the mountains above Boulder, Colorado. Scott's older brother, by contrast, had taken the opposite course from Randy, becoming the model son of the family—graduating from college on time, earning an advanced degree, and going to work for a major corporation.

Scott wanted the freedom and expansiveness he saw in Randy's life, but   10
he wanted more opportunities than he saw coming Randy's way. He also liked the respectability and predictability that characterized his other brother's career, but he was wary of the corporate straitjacket. Scott thought he could have the best of both brothers' lives—and on his own terms.

Scott loops his Mazda onto Great America Parkway and heads west into the heart of Silicon Valley, past such industry giants as Sun and Tandem. The commute has not gone badly as it might have, and the rain is stopping. He turns south onto El Camino Real and into a district more reminiscent of Guadalajara than of the manicured, muted center of high technology in America. His new company occupies part of the second floor of a plain, brown stucco, commercial building that also houses a florist, a hairdresser, a certified public accountant, and a bureau of the *Korean Times* newspaper. This part of Santa Clara is the kind of multicultural mecca California is becoming famous for— home to many of the immigrant groups who have come to the valley in recent years from the Pacific Rim, Mexico, and Central America. The street signs along El Camino attest to the area's diverse population and diverse appeals: L'Amour Shoppe Contemporary Books, Ultimate Interiors, Korean Books, and Wet Pleasures (a store that sells skin-diving equipment). A Mexican restaurant sits on one corner, a Japanese fast-food place on the other, and a Chinese carryout across the street.

"It's not the high-rent district," says Scott, "but then we could do what we're doing just about anywhere. All we need is space for our computers and a bunch of telephones. We wanted cheap and close to home."

It has been only a few weeks since Scott left Memorex Corporation, where he spent the previous ten years of his professional life. In 1978, while vacationing in California, Scott told his wife Charity that they should move there and never look back. Never having lived outside Indiana, she agreed to take their next summer vacation there, and if they could both find jobs, try it for two years only. On the last day of the vacation, in 1978, they both received job offers—he from Memorex, a high technology company, and she from Syntex, one of the nation's largest drug manufacturers.

Scott joined the finance department in a development position that moved him within the company every six months. The idea was to give him a feel for many parts of the business, move him into the corporate mainstream, and make him into a "Memorex kind of guy." All it did was bore Scott.

"The first job I had was writing debits and credits at the end of each 15 month. I could not believe anyone did that for a living. I remember the shock. I had been there three weeks and been through the desk procedures and I had no idea what it all meant, like: 'You mean I have to write debits and credits— MBAs don't do that!'"

It was perhaps youthful naivete to think he would not have to perform mundane duties, but his response typifies the high expectations many members of his generation have about work, unlike the more modest expectations their fathers had. As Ray Myers, whose first job for Continental Illinois bank had been as a glorified salesman, says, "I would have been quite content to do that for the rest of my life." Not so Scott, or other organization offspring, who, as a matter of course, expect their jobs not only to be stimulating, but to allow them to be recognized for their personal achievements. Nor for Scott is the organization man's credo of seeing to it that others get the credit. He searched frantically for another job in the company.

"I took a job in systems development," he says, "doing financial planning programs for various departments. I would install financial planning systems and then go in and teach people how to use them. I'd do the programming and then do the teaching."

At first he liked it, but not for long.

"Memorex is a funny place. I'd been there only six months when I decided I was going someplace else. I was in the process of leaving ever since then. The reason I stayed had nothing to do with loyalty. It's just that whenever I got to the point where I actually went looking for another job, an opportunity would come along inside and I would take it. I reasoned that I would never get such an opportunity elsewhere because of lack of experience.

"A while back I switched from finance into sales. I had become bored 20 with finance and I knew that if I was going to move up or ever be successful on my own I needed sales experience. I got involved helping a group that was setting up a software company to package and sell to the marketplace. It was a typical Memorex sort of deal—a skunkworks without support. No one on top said: 'No, you can't do it.' But, on the other hand, they gave us little money to do it. Their attitude was if it doesn't work, they don't want their name on it; if it does work, they want it. But they were unwilling to back the effort."

Failure might jeopardize the careers of all the participants in the project. Nevertheless, Scott saw it as an opportunity to learn and to run a small operation. He took the assignment.

Shortly thereafter, Memorex was sold to Burroughs (which, subsequently, was merged with Sperry to become Unisys) and Scott's little in-house software business found itself on the wrong side of a major corporate policy struggle. Burroughs was not interested in Memorex's small businesses; it had bought the company to gain control of Memorex's main product lines—disk drives and tape drives. Out went Scott's fledgling division and project.

The experience convinced Scott that he would never get where he wanted to go as long as he stayed inside a large corporation. He resolved to commit himself only to tasks that would enhance his own career—eventually outside Memorex.

"Had the company been different," he says, "I might have stayed. But there was no reason to. No one really cared what you did. You were penalized for being entrepreneurial. I knew I would get a check whether I sold or not. And no one seemed to share the same goal."

Scott's criticisms resemble those that were being heard in many of the nation's largest corporations at mid-decade. America, according to Peter F. Drucker, was entering an era of innovation. Yet most corporations remained content to manage the past. Try as they might, many venerable American companies had virtually no idea how to solve the multiple problems that were developing. Many no longer understood their marketplace; many seemed incapable of handling the transition to a global, knowledge-based economy; and few understood their own young managers—most of whom were the sons and daughters of organization men.

"That little software division was a different story," says Scott. "We were like a little family. We shared the same goals, shared the same risks, and felt like we were all in this venture together."

Members of the group began to talk about starting their own business.

"One of the technical guys on the Memorex team had left the company and gone out on his own. He was a brilliant technician and the kind of guy who could have done everything, except for the fact that there are only so many hours in a day. I hired him back as a consultant to me, and it was then we started talking. When things stated to fall apart at Memorex, I decided to join this group of guys on the weekends. We defined a new product, did market research, figured out what the product should be, specced it out, and started rolling.

"For over a year and a half we worked that way," he says. "I spent most of my weekends and some evenings working with them while continuing my job at Memorex."

He admits his frequent absences from home were hard on Charity, who, after the birth of their second child, had decided to stay at home. Much to her surprise—and some dismay—she was left the job of child-rearing, mostly alone. She understood, at least intellectually, the pressures Scott was under. Nevertheless, it was not easy, for either of them. Scott, unlike the organization man before him, does not view this as a natural or desirable state of affairs.

"I want to be more involved with my kids," he insists. "What that means is that I don't expect and don't want Charity's role and my role to be as clearly defined as they were when I was growing up. For example, my father never cooked. His job was to bring in the groceries and that was it. All very well defined. I want it to be different. I don't cook, but I do the dishes sometimes and on Sundays I do 50 percent of the housecleaning. I never saw my dad do any of that stuff."

But Scott's good intentions and the reality of holding down a job while trying to build a new company made for a wide gap between vision and reality—and revealed that the gap between him and his father was perhaps narrower than it seemed.

"Having children really tore up our life-style," he says. "I had a real problem with that. I had a hard time with the lack of control over my time. I could no longer do what I wanted to do when I wanted to do it. You do what is necessary for the child at that point. And though I understood that was the right thing to do, I resented it. I was dedicated to my work and having a child made it difficult for me."

The conflict Scott feels between his role as a father and the importance of his work is hardly unique, for his experience bears the marks of powerful social and economic changes transforming the "Leave It to Beaver" family of the organization man and creating the new American family.

In 1987, with Scott working and Charity at home with the children, the 35 Myerses were among an ever-dwindling group of American families with men as the sole wage earners. By 1988 only 15 percent of American families fit the male-as-sole-wage-earner profile, falling from as high as 42 percent in 1960. Ironically, "traditional" households are far more common in the high-stress, entrepreneurial world of Silicon Valley than most people would think. Some see it as a coping mechanism—the only way family life can be sustained in such a high-anxiety setting, while others attribute it to the blatant sexism rampant in many fields of engineering.

Though Scott and Charity were among the small group in their generation managing to have a family on one (male) income, their struggle to define appropriate roles and to find time and energy for work, children, and marriage were not so different from those facing their peers in two-earner households. Finding that balance has not been easy.

Perhaps Scott could have easily resolved his dilemma by adopting his father as a role model, in the unlikely event that Charity would have gone along. But Scott wanted to be a different kind of father, with a "less clearly defined role" than his father had. He wanted to share fully the emotional responsibility and the physical care of his children and said, at least, that he wanted to do half the housework.

But such liberation from traditional roles is not easily accomplished—it requires far more than good intentions. He could have chosen to arrange his life so he could spend more time with his family, but instead he chose the demands of starting a company. Feeling driven by his role as provider, he felt his primary responsibility was "put to bread on the table." Yet he wanted to be more involved with his children. Unlike men and women of their parents' generation, who had sharply defined role models to follow, Scott and Charity had no models to guide them through this contemporary dilemma. So, in the final analysis, Scott fell back on, however reluctantly, the organization-man model. Like many middle-class men, then and now, his identity comes from his work—he is what he does. He feels *more* responsible for his work even while wishing to be more involved with home and family.

As sociologist Arlie Hochschild details (with Anne Machung) in *The Second Shift: Working Parents and the Revolution at Home*, many wives find themselves similarly conflicted, but in the opposite direction. "One reason women take a deeper interest than men in the problems of juggling work with family life," she writes, "is that even when husbands happily shared the hours of work, their wives felt more *responsible* for home and children." If the husband puts his work first and his wife puts home and children first, her behavior tends to reinforce his. Under such circumstances, a substantial change in roles does not come easily.

Though the old way of being parents—in the style of the organization man and his wife—grew increasingly difficult to justify, new relationships between husbands and wives evolved little beyond the rhetorical stage. For the organization offspring, reared in the middle-class paradigm of "breadwinners" and "homemakers," the transition to whatever new form the American family will take will undoubtedly be one of the most difficult struggles they will face. For most, like Scott and Charity, it will occupy center stage, its ramifications played out in their lives every day. But for them, at least, the odds of their winning the struggle increased substantially when Scott's high expectations clashed dramatically with corporate reality. 40

On the evening of Sunday, December 7, 1986, in the first-class cabin of a Detroit-bound jet high above the clouds over the Midwest, W. Michael Blumenthal, then chairman and chief executive officer (CEO) of Unisys and former treasury secretary in the Carter administration, eased back in his seat and settled into a copy of the Sunday *New York Times*. Thumbing through *Business World*, a new magazinelike section of the paper, he landed on a story that caught his eye. He took a sip of his drink and began to read.

On the third page of the article, he came upon a reference to Memorex, a company Unisys had recently acquired. His attention quickened. But what he read he did not like. By the time he finished the story, he was seething with anger, eager to take action. But trapped at thirty-five thousand feet, in the days before air phones, he was forced to wait until the plant touched down at Chicago's O'Hare airport. When it did, he stormed off the plane and headed for a bank of phones. He called his second-in-command, Paul Stern, at home.

"Did you see the Sunday *Times?*" Blumenthal barked. He didn't wait for a response. "There's this guy from Memorex who's quoted in an article. I want you to find out who he is and get rid of him. I want this guy out. *Now.*"

Stern, who had not seen the article, asked why.

"He's quoted as saying, 'I don't have any loyalty to the company; I'm in it for me.' Get rid of him." 45

Stern immediately called the president of Memorex, who had not seen the article either but knew what had to be done. On Monday morning he called the head of Marketing and Sales, who assured the president he would take immediate action.

Or so the story goes. Whether it is correct in every detail is a matter of speculation, but that is how it moved through the halls of Memorex in late 1986 and early 1987.

That fateful Monday the employee quoted in the article went to work as usual. He vaguely sensed that he might be in a little trouble if upper management had seen the story. Senior managers at Unisys were not known for allowing deviations from the corporate line. Unisys was a long way from the kind of free-form, slightly irreverent high-tech upstarts that had become common in Silicon Valley.

Unisys was, in fact, a classic organization-man company, a merger of two of the most successful technology companies of the fifties and sixties, Burroughs and Sperry. The resulting company was, as John Sculley of Apple Computer might phrase it, a "second-wave" company all the way, a place where "people are fearful of saying what they really think because they don't trust each other ... [where] people believe their opinions can get them in trouble." At Unisys, managers pledged their loyalty to the company whether or not they genuinely felt such a bond. You knew your place and played by the rules.

Monday came and went with business as usual. Tuesday came and went without mention of the article. But on Wednesday afternoon, just as the offending employee was beginning to conclude that he had nothing to worry about, he was summoned without explanation to an urgent meeting with his boss. 50

The Memorex manager heading into the vortex that fading December afternoon was Scott Myers, Ray Myers's youngest son. The quote that enraged CEO Blumenthal had appeared as a caption under a picture of Myers sitting in his Memorex office in Santa Clara. Entitled " 'Organization Man' Revisited," the article was the first published account of what would become [the book *The New Individualists*].

Scott's offhand comment about loyalty, he realized, had been careless and perhaps unwise—not good corporate politics. Yet, on the other hand, it had been the truth. It was the way he felt.

He walked into his boss's office expecting the worst. But the boss began merely by detailing the bizarre chain of events that had brought them to this meeting. Then he asked for an explanation. Scott attempted to put his remark in context, to explain the circumstances. What he had meant by saying that he was "in it for me" was that he expected his job to offer him real challenges, give him opportunities to learn and apply new skills, and make substantial contributions to getting the job done and, not incidentally, give him some sense of satisfaction and self-esteem. What kind of employees did the corporation want, after all? Timeservers? Toadies whose chief talent is paying lip service to loyalty until the time comes for them to start collecting their pensions?

But neither Scott's explanation nor the real attitude of his immediate supervisor mattered. The fact remained that the highest-ranking officer of the corporation wanted the young manager out. Out he would go.

Though Scott did not know it at the time, those traumatic days in December 1986 were fortuitous. It was in the months preceding that fateful December day that he and his friends had been working on the venture that Unisys had abandoned. Meeting on evenings and weekends, they had been painstakingly developing a business plan of their own and moving closer to the time when they could all walk away from one of the world's largest corporations. Their intention was not to beat the company at its own game but, rather, to show what they could accomplish, to be recognized for their talent and ability, and to control their own destinies. Thus, while Scott Myers's boss moved ever closer to carrying out CEO Blumenthal's orders, Scott's course of action was already laid out for him. Scott quit before the final showdown could occur.

Who was right? From an organization man's perspective, Scott's breezy dismissal of corporate loyalty betrayed, at best, a scepticism detrimental to the best interests of the corporation or, at worst, a cynicism born of serious maladjustment (the inability to adapt to corporate life) or a wanton disrespect for the legitimate authority of the organization. To the organization man, a young manager like Scott Myers should have learned—and come to believe—the "organization man's litany," which Whyte suggested went like this: "Be loyal to the company and the company will be loyal to you. After all, if you do a good job for the organization, it is only good sense for the organization to be good to you, because that will be best for everyone."

Scott Myers revealed that he believed otherwise. His remark violated the essential, if unwritten, contract that had bound the individual to the organization since World War II. Myers had declared that the individual, rather than the organization, should be paramount. In challenging pieties about corporate loyalty, he was questioning the legitimacy of the organization's authority and, perhaps most cogently, the organization man's premise that "the goals of the individual and the goals of the organization will work out to be one and the same."

In Scott Myers's attitude, one begins to glimpse the organization offspring's complex and often contradictory relationship to organizations and organizational life. One begins also to comprehend the dramatic form that individualism has taken for this generation of middle-class Americans and how individualism has changed in the past three decades.

In the reaction of CEO Blumenthal, one sees vividly the striking and emotionally charged differences that have come to separate the views of the generation now running America's largest organizations from those of the vast majority of managers under their command. From the perspective of the organization man, Scott's honesty about his work represented a threat to legitimate authority—a breakdown of the values that have governed organizational life during the postwar period. The organization man asks: What must be done when legitimacy is challenged? How can a CEO ensure that his commands will be followed? What good is a hierarchy, in which one's right to govern and lead is vested in one's position, if young managers do not take it seriously? How can you mandate loyalty? Blumenthal's answer was simple: Instill fear. Thus, when he demanded Scott Myers's head, he was sending a message to the entire corporation.

But to a new generation of managers—managers whose loyalty is not to 60 the organization but to doing the job right in the interests of their own self-development—the meaning of the Myers incident was far different from its significance for Blumenthal. And bark and bluster as he might, Blumenthal sent a different message through Unisys than the one he intended.

On the Monday following publication of the *Times* article, Scott began to receive congratulatory calls from co-workers. They said, in effect: "Nice going, Scott. You said what I believe. Like you, I want to work for a company that recognizes my contributions, allows me to determine how my work should be accomplished, and creates an atmosphere in which the emphasis is on knowledge and skill, not on issues of authority and rank." By telling an interviewer how he really felt, Scott Myers articulated what so many in his generation believe almost as a matter of course. And Blumenthal's autocratic and unreasoning action merely confirmed for them the truth of their perspective.

Scott Myers never set out to make waves. He had always been a hardworking and enthusiastic employee. But he could not pretend to be something other than what he was—someone, like so many in his generation, whose relationship to power and authority is governed by a new and much-changed view of organizations and organizational life. At Unisys, the new generation collided with the old, though neither had intended it. And it is far from clear that Unisys won.

Since Scott left Memorex, his life has changed dramatically. He and his partners went on to develop and market a successful software product for mainframe computers. The product was so successful that they were able to negotiate the sale of the product to a major software company in summer 1989.

With the money earned from the sale, Scott's chief partner was able to realize a dream—to live in the high Sierras on the shore of one of the world's most beautiful bodies of water, Lake Tahoe. There he spends much of his time doing what he loves best—writing computer software—and the remainder of his time hiking, skiing, and taking in the grandeur of the lake. The partner continues to work just as hard as he did when he lived in the Bay Area, but now he works on his own terms, not someone else's.

Scott also achieved a long-held goal—to arrange his life so he could spend more time with his wife and now three children. First, he and his chief partner created a new organization consisting of two separate companies. Once again, they identified another area of the computer mainframe market where advanced software can help companies achieve greater efficiency. But this time, in keeping with his often-stated desire to work toward greater integration of his work life and family life, Scott set up shop at home. The new organization is located in the corner of the Myers's master bedroom. From there, with his computers, telephones, a fax machine, and modems, Scott and his new company are prepared to take on a new challenge. 65

To an organization man, Scott's new life looks like an employment nightmare. He has no job security, no clearly defined career path, no company health insurance or retirement benefits. He must continually juggle temporary employees, consultants, and suppliers. He has none of the prestige that goes with a corporate title, no staff, no company parking space, and no membership in a corporate health club. All he has to look forward to are wild swings in income and the constant anxiety of never knowing where the next client is going to come from.

But Scott has found what he had always been looking for. He has a job he can control; a career path that will change as he changes; an opportunity to be recognized for what he accomplishes, rather than for where he sits in a hierarchy; and a work life that is in balance with the rest of his existence. Michael Blumenthal got his wish: Scott Myers is out. And Scott could not be happier.

Considerations

1. After reading this piece, how would you describe Scott Myers's personality and temperament? What biographical information and descriptions of his personality might help you predict his eventual departure from Memorex?

2. After reviewing the description of the values and attitudes prevalent

among the Memorex management, describe the attitudes you would expect to find among workers toward each other and their work.

3. When he describes his first attempt to become an entrepreneur, Myers says, "We were like a little family" (para. 26). What ideas about the family does this association suggest?

Invitation to Write

Scott Myers's main problem with Memorex is that he is not allowed to be creative and get satisfaction from his work. However, there are also family issues involved: "The conflict Scott feels between his role as a father and the importance of his work is hardly unique, for his experience bears the marks of powerful social and economic changes transforming the 'Leave it to Beaver' family of the organization man and creating the new American family" (para. 34). His experience suggests a deep connection between family life and the way production is organized. Write an essay in which you explore this connection by analyzing the various episodes that lead to his break with the company. Add your own examples to show the extent to which work patterns influence family life.

Connections

In many ways the organizations referred to in Tucker and Leinberger's essay resemble the Japanese corporations described by Robert C. Christopher in the preceding essay, "The Fruits of Industry." Compare the basic principles that underlie the activities of both American and Japanese corporations. Have a close look at the way they treat the individual worker and determine whether economic success is directly related to the suppression of individual needs and satisfactions. Write an essay in which you explore the relation between the purposes of the organization and the individual's aims. Use Scott Myers's objections against the corporation he worked for in order to enhance your argument.

KARL MARX

Alienated Labor

Karl Marx, the German philosopher and economist, was born in 1818. He studied at the University of Berlin in the late 1830s. In 1848, Marx published *The Communist Manifesto,* which he wrote in collaboration with Friedrich Engels. Soon after, he settled in London, where he spent the rest of his life. He defined his political doctrine in *Das Kapital,* written in 1867, and founded the International Workingmen's Association, known as the First International, in 1864. Many commentators have believed that Marx's philosophy, later called Marxism, interpreted all economic and historic events in terms of a human desire for comfort and monetary gain. Other commentators think this is a misreading of his philosophy that ignores Marx's emphasis on the need for spiritual development, which is made possible by liberation from economic enslavement. Marx argued that the concentration of wealth in the hands of a few rich capitalists would lead to a revolt on the part of the workers, who would eventually organize society on a collective basis. Because of this, Marx, who died in 1883, is considered by many to be the father of the World Communism that dominated the governments of Eastern Europe and the former Soviet Union until 1990.

"Alienated Labor," here translated by T. B. Bottomore, is one of four *Economic and Philosophical Manuscripts* written in 1844. This early work presents Marx's analysis of the effect of the working conditions of his day upon individuals.

WE HAVE BEGUN FROM the presuppositions of political economy. We have accepted its terminology and its laws. We presupposed private property, the separation of labor, capital and land, as also of wages, profit and rent, the division of labor, competition, the concept of exchange value, etc. From political economy itself, in its own words, we have shown that the worker sinks to the level of a commodity, and to a most miserable commodity; that the misery of the worker increases with the power and volume of his production; that the necessary result of competition is the accumulation of capital in a few hands, and thus a restoration of monopoly in a more terrible form; and finally that the distinction between capitalist and landlord, and between agricultural laborer and industrial worker, must disappear and the whole of society divide into the two classes of property *owners* and propertyless *workers*.

Political economy begins with the fact of private property; it does not explain it. It conceives the *material process* of private property, as this occurs in reality, in general and abstract formulas which then serve it as laws. It does not *comprehend* these laws; that is, it does not show how they arise out of the nature of private property. Political economy provides no explanation of the basis of the distinction of labor from capital, of capital from land. When, for example, the relation of wages to profits is defined, this is explained in terms of the interests of capitalists; in other words, what should be explained is assumed. Similarly, competition is referred to at every point and is explained in terms of external conditions. Political economy tells us nothing about the extent to which these external and apparently accidental conditions are simply the expression of a necessary development. We have seen how exchange itself seems an accidental fact. The only moving forces which political economy recognizes are *avarice* and the *war between the avaricious, competition.*

Just because political economy fails to understand the interconnections within this movement it was possible to oppose the doctrine of competition to that of monopoly, the doctrine of freedom of the crafts to that of the guilds, the doctrine of the division of landed property to that of the great estates; for competition, freedom of crafts, and the division of landed property were conceived only as accidental consequences brought about by will and force, rather than as necessary, inevitable, and natural consequences of monopoly, the guild system, and feudal property.

Thus we have now to grasp the real connection between this whole system of alienation—private property, acquisitiveness, the separation of labor, capital and land, exchange and competition, value and the devaluation of man, monopoly and competition—and the system of *money.*

Let us not begin our explanation, as does the economist, from a legendary   5
primordial condition. Such a primordial condition does not explain anything; it merely removes the question into a gray and nebulous distance. It asserts as a fact or event what it should deduce, namely, the necessary relation between two things; for example, between the division of labor and exchange. In the same way theology explains the origin of evil by the fall of man; that is, it asserts as a historical fact what it should explain.

We shall begin from a *contemporary* economic fact. The worker becomes poorer the more wealth he produces and the more his production increases in power and extent. The worker becomes an ever cheaper commodity the more goods he creates. The *devaluation* of the human world increases in direct relation with the *increase in value* of the world of things. Labor does not only create goods; it also produces itself and the worker as a *commodity,* and indeed in the same proportion as it produces goods.

This fact simply implies that the object produced by labor, its product, now stands opposed to it as an *alien being,* as a *power independent* of the producer. The product of labor is labor which has been embodied in an object and turned into a physical thing; this product is an *objectification* of labor. The performance of work is at the same time its objectification. The performance of work appears in the sphere of political economy as a *vitiation* of the worker, objectification as a *loss* and as *servitude to the object,* and appropriation as *alienation.*

So much does the performance of work appear as vitiation that the worker is vitiated to the point of starvation. So much does objectification appear as loss of the object that the worker is deprived of the most essential things not only of life but also of work. Labor itself becomes an object which he can acquire only by the greatest effort and with unpredictable interruptions. So much does the appropriation of the object appear as alienation that the more objects the worker produces the fewer he can possess and the more he falls under the domination of his product, of capital.

All these consequences follow from the fact that the worker is related to the *product of his labor* as to an *alien* object. For it is clear on this presupposition that the more the worker expends himself in work the more powerful becomes the world of objects which he creates in fact of himself, the poorer he becomes in his inner life, and the less he belongs to himself. It is just the same as in religion. The more of himself man attributes to God the less he has left in himself. The worker puts his life into the object, and his life then belongs no longer to himself but to the object. The greater his activity, therefore, the less he possesses. What is embodied in the product of his labor is no longer his own. The greater this product is, therefore, the more he is diminished. The *alienation* of the worker in his product means not only that his labor becomes an object, assumes an *external* existence, but that it exists independently, *outside himself,* and alien to him, and that it stands opposed to him as an autonomous power. The life which he has given to the object sets itself against him as an alien and hostile force.

Let us now examine more closely the phenomenon of *objectification,* the worker's production and the *alienation* and *loss* of the object it produces, which is involved in it. The worker can create nothing without *nature,* without the *sensuous external world.* The latter is the material in which his labor is realized, in which it is active, out of which and through which it produces things.

But just as nature affords the *means of existence* of labor in the sense that labor cannot *live* without objects upon which it can be exercised, so also it provides the *means of existence* in a narrower sense; namely the means of physical existence for the *worker* himself. Thus, the more the worker *appropriates* the external world of sensuous nature by his labor the more he deprives himself of *means of existence,* in two respects: first, that the sensuous external world becomes progressively less an object belonging to his labor or a means of existence of his labor, and secondly, that it becomes progressively less a means of existence in the direct sense, a means for the physical subsistence of the worker.

In both respects, therefore, the worker becomes a slave of the object; first, in that he receives an *object of work,* i.e., receives *work,* and secondly that he receives *means of subsistence.* Thus the object enables him to exist, first as a *worker* and secondly, as a *physical subject.* The culmination of this enslavement is that he can only maintain himself as a *physical subject* so far as he is a *worker,* and that it is only as a *physical subject* that he is a worker.

(The alienation of the worker in his object is expressed as follows in the laws of political economy: The more the worker produces the less he has to consume; the more value he creates the more worthless he becomes; the more refined his product the more crude and misshapen the worker; the more civilized the product the more barbarous the worker; the more powerful the work the more feeble the worker; the more the work manifests intelligence the more the worker declines in intelligence and becomes a slave of nature.)

Political economy conceals the alienation in the nature of labor insofar as it does not examine the direct relationship between the worker (work) and production. Labor certainly produces marvels for the rich but it produces privation for the worker. It produces palaces, but hovels for the worker. It produces beauty, but deformity for the worker. It replaces labor by machinery, but it casts some of the workers back into a barbarous kind of work and turns the others into machines. It produces intelligence, but also stupidity and cretinism for the workers.

The direct relationship of labor to its products is the relationship of the 15 *worker to the objects of his production.* The relationship of property owners to the objects of production and to production itself is merely a *consequence* of this first relationship and confirms it. We shall consider this second aspect later.

Thus, when we ask what is the important relationship of labor, we are concerned with the relationship of the *worker* to production.

So far we have considered the alienation of the worker only from one aspect; namely, *his relationship with the products of his labor.* However, alienation appears not only in the result, but also in the *process,* of *production,* within *productive activity* itself. How could the worker stand in an alien relationship to the product of his activity if he did not alienate himself in the act of production itself? The product is indeed only the *résumé* of activity, of production. Consequently, if the product of labor is alienation, production itself must be active alienation—the alienation of activity and the activity of alienation. The alienation of the object of labor merely summarizes the alienation in the work activity itself.

What constitutes the alienation of labor? First, that the work is *external* to the worker, that it is not part of his nature; and that, consequently, he does not fulfill himself in his work but denies himself, has a feeling of misery rather than well-being, does not develop freely his mental and physical energies but is physically exhausted and mentally debased. The worker therefore feels himself at home only during his leisure time, whereas at work he feels homeless. His work is not voluntary but imposed, *forced labor*. It is not the satisfaction of a need, but only a *means* for satisfying other needs. Its alien character is clearly shown by the fact that as soon as there is no physical or other compulsion it is avoided like the plague. External labor, labor in which man alienates himself, is a labor of self-sacrifice, of mortification. Finally, the external character of work for the worker is shown by the fact that it is not his own work but work for someone else, that in work he does not belong to himself but to another person.

Just as in religion the spontaneous activity of human fantasy, of the human brain and heart, reacts independently as an alien activity of gods or devils upon the individual, so the activity of the worker is not his own spontaneous activity. It is another's activity and a loss of his own spontaneity.

We arrive at the result that man (the worker) feels himself to be freely active only in his animal functions—eating, drinking, and procreating, or at most also in his dwelling and in personal adornment—while in his human functions he is reduced to an animal. The animal becomes human and the human becomes animal.

Eating, drinking, and procreating are of course also genuine human functions. But abstractly considered, apart from the environment of other human activities, and turned into final and sole ends, they are animal functions.

We have now considered the act of alienation of practical human activity, labor, from two aspects: (1) the relationship of the worker to the *product of labor* as an alien object which dominates him. This relationship is at the same time the relationship to the sensuous external world, to natural objects, as an alien and hostile world; (2) the relationship of labor to the *act of production* within *labor*. This is the relationship of the worker to his own activity as something alien and not belonging to him, activity as suffering (passivity), strength as powerlessness, creation as emasculation, the *personal* physical and mental energy of the worker, his personal life (for what is life but activity?) as an activity which is directed against himself, independent of him and not belonging to him. This is *self-alienation* as against the above-mentioned alienation of the *thing*.

We have now to infer a third characteristic of *alienated labor* from the two we have considered.

Man is a species-being[1] not only in the sense that he makes the commu-

---

[1]The term "species-being" is taken from Feuerbach's *Das Wesen des Christentums* (The Essence of Christianity). Feuerbach used the notion in making a distinction between consciousness in man and in animals. Man is conscious not merely of himself as an individual but of the human species or "human essence." [Translator's note]

nity (his own as well as those of other things) his object both practically and theoretically, but also (and this is simply another expression for the same thing) in the sense that he treats himself as the present, living species, as a *universal* and consequently free being.

Species-life, for man as for animals, has its physical basis in the fact that man (like animals) lives from inorganic nature, and since man is more universal than an animal so the range of inorganic nature from which he lives is more universal. Plants, animals, minerals, air, light, etc. constitute, from the theoretical aspect, a part of human consciousness as objects of natural science and art; they are man's spiritual inorganic nature, his intellectual means of life, which he must first prepare for enjoyment and perpetuation. So also, from the practical aspect they form a part of human life and activity. In practice man lives only from these natural products, whether in the form of food, heating, clothing, housing, etc. The universality of man appears in practice in the universality which makes the whole of nature into his inorganic body: (1) as a direct means of life; and equally (2) as the material object and instrument of his life activity. Nature is the *inorganic body* of man; that is to say, nature excluding the human body itself. To say that man *lives* from nature means that nature is his *body* with which he must remain in a continuous interchange in order not to die. The statement that the physical and mental life of man, and nature, are interdependent means simply that nature is interdependent with itself, for man is a part of nature.

Since alienated labor: (1) alienates nature from man; and (2) alienates man from himself, from his own active function, his life activity; so it alienates him from the species. It makes *species-life* into a means of individual life. In the first place it alienates species-life and individual life, and secondly, it turns the latter, as an abstraction, into the purpose of the former, also in its abstract and alienated form.

For labor, *life activity, productive life,* now appear to man only as *means* for the satisfaction of a need, the need to maintain his physical existence. Productive life is, however, species-life. It is life creating life. In the type of life activity resides the whole character of a species, its species-character; and free, conscious activity is the species-character of human beings. Life itself appears only as a *means of life.*

The animal is one with its life activity. It does not distinguish the activity from itself. It is *its activity.* But man makes his life activity itself an object of his will and consciousness. He has a conscious life activity. It is not a determination with which he is completely identified. Conscious life activity distinguishes man from the life activity of animals. Only for this reason is he a species-being. Or rather, he is only a self-conscious being, i.e. his own life is an object for him, because he is a species-being. Only for this reason is his activity free activity. Alienated labor reverses the relationship, in that man because he is a self-conscious being makes his life activity, his *being,* only a means for his *existence.*

The practical construction of an *objective world,* the *manipulation* of inorganic nature, is the confirmation of man as a conscious species-being, i.e. a being who treats the species as his own being or himself as a species-being. Of course, animals also produce. They construct nests, dwellings, as in the case of bees, beavers, ants, etc. But they only produce what is strictly necessary for themselves or their young. They produce only in a single direction, while man produces universally. They produce only under the compulsion of direct physical need, while man produces when he is free from physical need and only truly produces in freedom from such need. Animals produce only themselves, while man reproduces the whole of nature. The products of animal production belong directly to their physical bodies, while man is free in face of his product. Animals construct only in accordance with the standards and needs of the species to which they belong, while man knows how to produce in accordance with the standards of every species and knows how to apply the appropriate standard to the object. Thus man constructs also in accordance with the laws of beauty.

It is just in his work upon the objective world that man really proves   30
himself as a *species-being.* This production is his active species life. By means of it nature appears as *his* work and his reality. The object of labor is, therefore, the *objectification of man's species life;* for he no longer reproduces himself merely intellectually, as in consciousness, but actively and in a real sense, and he sees his own reflection in a world which he has constructed. While, therefore, alienated labor takes away the object of production from man, it also takes away his *species life,* his real objectivity as a species-being, and changes his advantage over animals into a disadvantage insofar as his inorganic body, nature, is taken from him.

Just as alienated labor transforms free and self-directed activity into a means, so it transforms the species life of man into a means of physical existence.

Consciousness, which man has from his species, is transformed through alienation so that species life becomes only a means for him.

(3) Thus alienated labor turns the *species life of man,* and also nature as his mental species-property, into an *alien* being and into a *means* for his *individual existence.* It alienates from man his own body, external nature, his mental life and his *human* life.

(4) A direct consequence of the alienation of man from the product of his labor, from his life activity, and from his species life is that *man is alienated* from other *men.* When man confronts himself he also confronts *other* men. What is true of man's relationship to his work, to the product of his work, and to himself, is also true of his relationship to other men, to their labor, and to the objects of their labor.

In general, the statement that man is alienated from his species life means   35 that each man is alienated from others, and that each of the others is likewise alienated from human life.

Human alienation, and above all the relation of man to himself, is first realized and expressed in the relationship between each man and other men. Thus in the relationship of alienated labor every man regards other men according to the standards and relationships in which he finds himself placed as a worker.

We began with an economic fact, the alienation of the worker and his production. We have expressed this fact in conceptual terms as *alienated labor,* and in analyzing the concept we have merely analyzed an economic fact.

Let us now examine further how this concept of alienated labor must express and reveal itself in reality. If the product of labor is alien to me and confronts me as an alien power, to whom does it belong? If my own activity does not belong to me but is an alien, forced activity, to whom does it belong? To a being *other* than myself. And who is this being? The *gods*? It is apparent in the earliest stages of advanced production, e.g., temple building, etc. in Egypt, India, Mexico, and in the service rendered to gods, that the product belonged to the gods. But the gods alone were never the lords of labor. And no more was *nature*. What a contradiction it would be if the more man subjugates nature by his labor, and the more the marvels of the gods are rendered superfluous by the marvels of industry, he should abstain from his joy in producing and his enjoyment of the product for love of these powers.

The *alien* being to whom labor and the product of labor belong, to whose service labor is devoted, and to whose enjoyment the product of labor goes, can only be *man* himself. If the product of labor does not belong to the worker, but confronts him as an alien power, this can only be because it belongs to *a man other than the worker*. If his activity is a torment to him it must be a source of enjoyment and pleasure to another. Not the gods, nor nature, but only man himself can be this alien power over men.

Consider the earlier statement that the relation of man to himself is first realized, objectified, through his relation to other men. If therefore he is related to the product of his labor, his objectified labor, as to an *alien,* hostile, powerful, and independent object, he is related in such a way that another alien, hostile, powerful, and independent man is the lord of this object. If he is related to his own activity as to unfree activity, then he is related to it as activity in the service, and under the domination, coercion, and yoke of another man.

Every self-alienation of man, from himself and from nature, appears in the relation which he postulates between other men and himself and nature. Thus religious self-alienation is necessarily exemplified in the relation between laity and priest, or, since it is here a question of the spiritual world, between the laity and a mediator. In the real world of practice this self-alienation can only be expressed in the real, practical relation of man to his fellow-men. The medium through which alienation occurs is itself a *practical* one. Through alienated labor, therefore, man not only produces his relation to the object and to the process of production as to alien and hostile men; he also produces the relation of other men to his production and his product, and the relation between himself and other men. Just as he creates his own production as a vitiation, a punishment, and his own product as a loss, as a product which does not belong to him, so he creates the domination of the nonproducer over production and its product. As he alienates his own activity, so he bestows upon the stranger an activity which is not his own.

Considerations

1. In this essay, Marx makes numerous observations about the dehumanizing effects of work upon the worker. What kinds of changes do you think are suggested by his criticisms?

2. Marx suggests that alienation results from capitalist development. What does he mean by alienation? What kind of damage can alienation produce? What forms of alienation are more damaging than others?

3. Along his argument, Marx resorts, more than once, to religious analogies. What do you think is the significance of these analogies? Locate two or three of them and explain them in their context.

Invitation to Write

Today's work situations are clearly not the same ones Marx observed, since his analysis reflects the situation of workers in western Europe in the nineteenth century. While some aspects of working remain familiar, changes in technology, the establishment of unions, the passing of labor legislation, and many other developments have had an impact on the relationship between the worker and his or her work. Using your observations and personal experience of work, write a paper that examines whether or not modern working conditions result in the same types of alienation Marx describes in his essay.

Connections

When Marx discusses the alienation of labor, he comes close to describing Scott Myers's experience with the corporation, as reported by Bruce Tucker and Paul Leinberger in their essay "Scott Myers, Entrepreneur" (p. 242). Consider Marx's analysis:

The work is *external* to the worker . . . he does not fulfill himself in his work but denies himself, has a feeling of misery rather than well-being, does not develop freely his mental and physical energies but is physically exhausted and mentally debased. The worker therefore feels at home only during his leisure time, whereas at work he feels homeless. (para. 18)

Write an essay in which you compare the more or less abstract "worker," which Marx uses in his argument, to Scott Myers, who is a real person confronted with similar problems. Consider not only the similarities, which could make him a typical case of alienation, but also the differences, which may indicate that Marx's theory is not beyond criticism. You may also suggest alterations of his theory based on your conclusions about Myers.

Assignment Sequence
Working in the World

The first assignment in the sequence will allow you to use your own work experience to determine what conditions make working a meaningful experience. In your next paper you will examine the working conditions at a small manufacturing company, Zodiac Prints, described in Wakako Yamauchi's short story, in light of your previous analysis. You will also determine how your view of the situation compares to that of the worker who narrates the story. In the third assignment, you will consider the factors that reduce the power of workers to shape their own jobs, using Wakako Yamauchi's story and Bruce Tucker and Paul Leinberger's text as the basis of your discussion. In the next assignment, you will again consider the situation of the workers, along with other conditions of working that reveal the relationship between cultural values and attitudes toward work. In your next paper, you will apply Robert C. Christopher's analysis of the connection between culture and work to Yamauchi and Tucker and Leinberger's texts, which describe the American work situation. The fifth assignment will ask you to become more theoretical; it will require that you closely read Karl Marx's essay "Alienated Labor" to determine his view of the kinds of working conditions men and women need. Then you will continue working with Marx's theory and write a paper that uses it to view the experiences described by Christopher, Yamauchi, and Tucker and Leinberger. After reading all the texts, you will use them, along with your own experience, in a final paper to offer a view of the conditions that make work a satisfying experience for human beings.

Assignment 1: Exploring Experience

By the time you've arrived at college, you've probably had several jobs and enough experience to start analyzing the conditions that make working a satisfying or unsatisfying experience. For the first assignment, write a paper that recalls an earlier job you held and how it has shaped your attitudes and understanding about work.

Describing your job is a good way to begin your paper. Focus your paper by looking at two or three specific situations that show how your particular experiences on this job shaped your conclusions about work. Look at several specific aspects of the work that made it unsatisfying or rewarding, such as its economic rewards, your feelings about your boss, your relationships with your co-workers, the status associated with the position, contributions of the job to your professional development, or any way you feel this job prepared you for life in general. After you discuss your experiences, use them to reach a conclusion about the conditions that make work satisfying.

Assignment 2

I'm afraid I shall leave Zodiac soon. In the deceptive simplicity of the lives here, there is a quality I am unable to face. It's the underbelly of a smile. I know it well.

—WAKAKO YAMAUCHI, *Maybe*

In this statement, Florence, the main character of Wakako Yamauchi's "Maybe," makes a direct connection between a situation in her working life and her past experience of personal unhappiness. She looks at work in human terms and at workers as individuals, identifying with her co-workers on the basis of her own experience. Write a paper in which you use the conclusions from your first paper to evaluate the nature of the working conditions at Zodiac Prints. Decide how closely your own evaluation of the situation reflects the implied analysis offered by Florence.

Begin by analyzing one or two specific examples of the conditions at Zodiac using the conclusions you established in your first paper. Then examine Florence's reactions to her own situation and the experiences of others. As part of your discussion, include an examination of Florence's personal experiences and the way she is treated at Zodiac. Discuss whether your conclusions and Florence's reactions reinforce each other or whether they provide different ways of looking at these workers' lives.

Assignment 3

That fateful Monday the employee quoted in the article went to work as usual. He vaguely sensed that he might be in a little trouble if upper management had seen the story. Senior managers at Unisys were not known for allowing deviations from the corporate line.

—BRUCE TUCKER and PAUL LEINBERGER,
Scott Myers, Entrepreneur

In Wakako Yamauchi's story, Florence is a divorced, unemployed housewife from a minority ethnic group. Scott Myers, as described by Bruce Tucker and Paul Leinberger, is a gainfully employed, professional Caucasian male. Despite these differences, both Florence and Scott Myers have little control over the conditions of their work. Write a paper that explores their powerlessness, using both cases to develop a discussion about the conditions that alienate workers from their work.

To gather material for your paper, choose several examples from both texts that reveal the conditions they face at work. Look for examples that establish the amount of control they have over their work, their participation in decision making, and management's attitude toward them. Even more importantly, analyze the reasons they are placed in these situations and how these reasons affect their ability to control their work lives.

Assignment 4

Nearly all of us in this country regard the increasing rarity of communities owned or dominated by a single company as a sign of progress. To be dependent on your employer not only for your income but also for your housing, your recreation, and even, in a sense, your social life is, by contemporary American standards, an unacceptable infringement on personal freedom. It is therefore somewhat disconcerting to discover that in up-and-coming Japan the state of affairs is almost exactly the reverse.
—ROBERT C. CHRISTOPHER, *The Fruits of Industry*

Robert C. Christopher's observation from "The Fruits of Industry" points to the way American and Japanese attitudes toward work rest upon very different cultural assumptions. Write a paper in which you expand on Christopher's evaluation by considering the cultural values that shape the American work experiences described by Wakako Yamauchi and by Bruce Tucker and Paul Leinberger.

In order to focus your paper, look at two or three issues from the Japanese work experience that Christopher raised. You may consider employer-employee relationships, feelings toward co-workers, loyalty, product quality, working conditions, or training of the work force. Then consider the Japanese cultural assumptions that underlie their work experiences. Do the same for the American experience. For example, if in your paper you look at the issue of employers' treatment of employees, consider the treatment of employees of Zodiac and at Unisys. Then extract the values underlying the employers' attitudes and the assumptions they reflect about relationships between individuals and organizations.

Assignment 5

What constitutes the alienation of labor? First, that the work is external to the worker, that it is not part of his nature; and that, consequently, he does not fulfill himself in his work but denies himself, has a feeling of misery rather than well-being, does not develop freely his mental and physical energies but is physically exhausted and mentally debased.

—KARL MARX, *Alienated Labor*

In his tract "Alienated Labor," Marx seeks to demonstrate many of the ways in which workers (most people) are negatively affected by working in an age where "the whole of society divide[s] into the two classes of property *owners* and propertyless *workers*" (para. 1). Write a paper in which you review his criticisms in order to explain what working conditions Marx believes human beings should experience.

To write this paper, read beyond Marx's descriptions of actual conditions and try to infer his view of the optimal work conditions. To begin this assignment you can make a list of some of the negative conditions Marx cites. For example, think of the several forms of alienation that he describes as the negative consequences of the current system and put them on your list. As you follow Marx's discussion of them, jot down conditions that Marx would identify as able to eliminate this kind of alienation. As you write this paper, feel free to relate Marx's theoretical ideas to examples of work and working conditions you currently observe, if they offer examples that help define Marx's position.

Assignment 6

A direct consequence of the alienation of man from the product of his labor, from his life activity, and from his species life is that man *is* alienated *from other* men. *When man confronts himself he also confronts* other *men. What is true of man's relationship to his work, to the product of his work, and to himself, is also true of his relationship to other men, to their labor, and to the objects of their labor.*

—KARL MARX, *Alienated Labor*

While Karl Marx developed his theories as a response to working conditions in nineteenth-century Europe, many of the issues he discussed are still unresolved. Topics such as the effect of work on the worker, worker-employer relationships, and relations of the worker to the workplace and to other employees, are still the focus of contemporary discussions about work. Write a paper in which you use Marx's ideas to argue how he would most likely evaluate the situations of workers in the Japan described by Robert C. Christopher in "The Fruits of Industry," at the fictional Zodiac Prints in Wakako Yamauchi's "Maybe," and in an American corporation like Unisys, described by Bruce Tucker and Paul Leinberger in "Scott Myers, Entrepreneur."

In this paper you will need to think about how Marx might have looked at twentieth-century work experiences in other cultures and how these examples would lead him to modify or uphold his original statements about work in capitalist societies. To help you assess his reaction to the four different situations, consider each situation in light of one or two aspects of work Marx mentions in the preceding quotation. Choose from the workers' relationships to their own work, to the product of their work, to themselves, to their co-workers, and to other workers' labor and achievements.

Assignment 7

The readings in this chapter reveal workers' attitudes toward their work and imply the presence or absence of conditions that make work satisfying. From your reading of these texts and your own exploration of the subject in your earlier paper, write a paper in which you define and analyze the conditions that must be present for people to find work a meaningful and satisfying experience. In your paper, you will also need to examine the conditions that do not lead to this result.

To write your paper, pick three or four conditions that you think must be present. Discuss these conditions in light of particular examples from the texts and your own experience. Explain how the examples show the positive effects of these conditions or the negative consequences of their absence. Then build these conditions into your own theory of how to make work a satisfying experience.

Individuals in Communities

No one had been invited to her new pebble-dash house, and the two sisters who called unannounced were left standing on the doorstep, with some flimsy excuse about her distempering the kitchen ceiling. She was determined to remain aloof, and as if to emphasize the point she had venetian blinds fitted.

—EDNA O'BRIEN, *The Widow*

We can't afford not to care about other people in a place this small. Our survival, in a way, depends on minimizing privacy because the lack of it draws us into each other's lives, and that's a major resource in a little town where there aren't a thousand entertainments.

—LINDA THURSTON, as quoted by
WILLIAM LEAST HEAT-MOON, *The Emma Chase*

Through such reasoning, it has become possible to maintain a self-image of generosity toward, and solidarity with, one's "community" without bearing any responsibility to "them"—the other "community."

—ROBERT REICH, *The Global Elite*

Human beings are often thought of as "social animals." Among the complex relationships we establish are those we share with others in a community. The word "community" reflects its original meaning of having goals, interests, needs, or concerns "in common." By joining others we can create strong relationships to support our individual lives. In its most common appearance, this term refers to a collection of people sharing a small territory marked by geographical boundaries. However, communities needn't be bound geographically. People have many different kinds of associations that identify them as members of a group with interests and concerns in common. People usually turn to their community for support in their endeavors or for assistance in time of need.

Our traditional American images of community reflect the idealized role it has played in the eyes of many, whether we think of individuals coming together for barn raisings or banding together for survival in a hostile and threatening wilderness. These kinds of ideas color images of community with a nostalgic tint that obscures the other, less appealing, consequences of membership in a community. When people are closely connected to others, those others take a very strong interest in their lives. Since groups cohere and operate by consensus, groups of any kind expect their members to share the group's values. Members who hold divergent positions often find themselves confronting the group's definition of acceptable behavior. Membership in communities, then, will have both positive and negative consequences, raising questions as to how much leeway exists in individual development and to what point the interests of individuals become subordinated to the greater good of the community. Life in a community can be nourishing, a source of conflict, or a negotiation between those extremes.

The readings in this chapter help you explore some of these issues. "The Widow," Edna O'Brien's short story about a woman's life in an Irish village, reveals a less-than-nostalgic view of rural life. In "The Emma Chase," William Least Heat-Moon interviews a woman who holds traditional ideas of community, but infuses them with her more contemporary political principles. Finally, Robert Reich looks at the differences between contemporary American communities in his essay "The Global Elite." He sees a great difference between traditional American communities and contemporary towns where socially and economically elite groups live.

EDNA O'BRIEN

The Widow

Edna O'Brien was born in county Clare, Ireland. She grew up on a farm. Her family had once been prosperous but was reduced to poverty after the loss of their fortune. There were few books in her house, but she remembers a world rich in stories told by various family members. After attending a convent school, she left for Dublin, where she made a living writing brief sketches for a newspaper until she married. In 1960 she moved with her family to London, where she published her first novel, *The Country Girls*, which explored the erotic lives of young Catholic girls. This novel and her seven subsequent books were banned in Ireland because of their nonconformity to Catholic norms. Although she has lived in London since the banning of her first book, Ireland is often the setting of her more than twenty books. These include several collections of short stories, among them *The Love Object* (1968), *A Scandalous Woman* (1974), *A Rose in the Heart* (1978), *Returning* (1981), and *A Fanatic Heart: Selected Stories* (1984). Her seven novels include *August Is a Wicked Month* (1964), *Night* (1972), and *The High Road* (1989). She was awarded the *Yorkshire Post* Novel Award in 1971. Her work appears frequently in *New Yorker* magazine, where the story "The Widow" was published in 1989.

"The Widow" is reminiscent of romantic stories in which an unconventional pair of lovers confront the opposition of their elders. But, this story also reworks O'Brien's major theme of woman's alienation from a society that suppresses her inclinations and desires. The community's point of view adopted in the narrative makes it hard to understand Bridget's behavior, but it exposes the community's suffocating control over the individual.

BRIDGET WAS HER NAME. She played cards like a trooper, and her tipple was gin-and-lime. She kept lodgers, but only select lodgers: people who came for the dapping, or maybe a barrister who would come overnight to discuss a case with a client or with a solicitor.

The creamery manager was the first guest to be more or less permanent. After a few months it was clear he wasn't going to build the bungalow that he had said he would, and after a few more months he was inviting girls to the house as if it were his own. Oh the stories, the stories! Card parties, drink, and God knows what else. No one dared ask expressly. Brazen women in finery, with nail varnish and lizard handbags and so forth, often came, sometimes staying for the weekend. Bridget had devoted the sitting room to him and his guests, choosing to say that whatever they wanted to do was their business.

She worked in the daytime, in a local shop, where she was a bookkeeper. She kept herself very much to herself—sat in her little office with its opaque beaded-glass panelling, and wrote out the bills and paid for commodities, and rarely, if ever, came out to the shop to serve customers. The owner and she got on well. He called her Biddy, short for Bridget, which meant, of course, that they were good friends. Occasionally she would emerge from her glass booth to congratulate a young mother on having a baby or to sympathize with someone over a death, but this, as people said, was a formality, a mere gesture. No one had been invited to her new pebble-dash house, and the two sisters who called unannounced were left standing on the doorstep, with some flimsy excuse about her distempering the kitchen ceiling. She was determined to remain aloof, and as if to emphasize the point she had venetian blinds fitted.

You may ask, as the postmistress had asked—the postmistress her sworn enemy—"Why have venetian blinds drawn at all times, winter and summer, daylight and dark? What is Bridget trying to hide?" What went on there at night, after she strolled home, carrying a few tasties that the owner of the shop had given her, such as slices of bacon or tins of salmon? It was rumored that she changed from her dark shop overall into brighter clothes. A child had seen her carrying in a scuttle of coal. So there was a fire in the parlor, people were heard to say.

Parties began to take place, and many a night a strange car or two, or even three, would park outside her driveway and remain there till well near dawn. Often people were heard emerging, singing "She'll be comin' 'round the mountain when she comes, when she comes." Such frivolities inevitably lead to scandals, and there came one that stunned the parish. A priest died in the house. He was not a local priest but had arrived in one of those strange cars with strange registration numbers. The story was that he went up to the bathroom, missed a step as he came out, and then, of course—it could happen to anyone—tripped and fell. He fell all the way down the fifteen steps of stairs, smashed his head on the grandfather clock that was at the bottom, and lay unconscious on the floor. The commotion was something terrible, as Rita, a neighbor, reported. There were screams from inside the house. The creamery manager, it seems, staggered to his car, but was too inebriated to even start the engine; then a young lady followed, drove off, and shortly after the local curate arrived at the house with the viaticum. An hour later, the ambulance took the priest to the hospital, but he was already dead.

Bridget put a brave face on it. Instead of hiding her understandable guilt, she acknowledged it. She spoke over and over again of the fatal night, the fun that had preceded the tragedy, the priest, not touching a drop, regaling them with the most wonderful account of being admitted to the Vatican—not for an audience, as he had thought, but to see the treasures. "Thousands of pounds' worth of treasures . . . thousands of pounds' worth of treasures!" he had apparently said as he described a picture or a sculpture or a chalice or vestments. Then Bridget would go on to describe how they had all played a game of forty-five and before they knew where they were it was three in the morning and Father So-and-So rose to return home, going upstairs first. He had had, as she said, glass after glass of lemonade. Then the terrible thud, and their not believing what it was, and the creamery manager getting up from the table and going out to the hall, and then a girl going out, and then the screams. Bridget made it known that she would never forgive herself for not having had a stronger bulb on the landing. At the High Mass for the priest's remains, she wore a long black lace thing, which she had not taken out since her beloved husband had died.

Her husband had been drowned years before, which is why she was generally known as the Widow. They had been married only a few months and were lovebirds. They had lived in another house then—a little house with a porch that caught the sun, where they grew geraniums and begonias and even a few tomatoes. Her despair at his death was so terrible it was legendary. Her roar, when the news was broken to her, rent the parish, and was said to have been heard in distant parishes. Babies in the cots heard it, as did old people who were deaf and sitting beside the fire, as did the men working out in the fields. When she was told that her husband had drowned, she would not believe it, her husband was not dead; he was a strong swimmer; he swam down at the docks every evening of his life before his tea. She rebelled by roaring. She roared all that evening and all that night. Nobody in the village could sleep. When they found his body in the morning with reeds matted around it, her cries reached a gargantuan pitch. She could not be let to go to the chapel. Women held her down to keep her from going berserk.

Then, two days after he was buried, when the cattle began to trample over the grave and treat it as any old grave, she stopped her keening. Soon after, she put on a perfectly calm, cheerful, resigned countenance. She told everyone that she was a busy woman now and had much to do. She had to write to thank all the mourners, and thank the priests who officiated at the High Mass, and then decide what to do about her husband's clothes. Above all, she was determined to sell her house. She was advised against it, but nothing would deter her. That house was for Bill and herself—"Darling Bill," as she called him—and only by leaving it would the memory, the inviolate memory, of their mornings and their evenings and their nights and their tête-à-têtes remain intact.

She sold the house easily, though far too cheaply, and went back up the country to live with her own folks—a brother and a deaf-mute sister. No one in the village heard of her until a few years later, when her brother died and her sister went to an institution. Unable to manage the tillage and foddering, Bridget sold the farm and moved back to the town. She was a changed woman when she came back—very much more in charge of herself. Very much more the toff, as people said. She got her job as a bookkeeper in the shop and started to build a house, and while it was being built many conjectured that she had a second husband in mind. There were rumors about bachelors seen talking to her, and especially one who came from America and took her to the dog track in Limerick a few Saturday nights in a row and bought her gins. The news of her drinking soon spread, and the verdict was that she could bend the elbow with any man. Hence, being installed in her new house was not the neighborly affair it might have been. There was no housewarming, for instance; no little gifts of cream or homemade black puddings or porter cake; no good-luck horseshoe on her door. In short, the people ostracized her. She seemed not to mind, having always kept to herself anyway. She had a good wardrobe, she had a good job, and as soon as she started to keep select boarders—only two, or at the most three—everybody remarked that she was getting above herself. Her house was sarcastically called the Pleasure Dome, and sometimes, more maliciously, she was coupled with the song "Biddy the Whore, who lived in a hotel without any door."

Her first two guests were strangers—men who were doing some survey   10
for the land commission, and whom all the farmers suspected of being meddlesome. They and Bridget became the best of friends—sat outside on deck chairs and were heard laughing; went to Mass together, the last Mass on Sundays; and in the evening imbibed, either at home or in the hotel. When they left, the creamery manager arrived—a big man with wide shoulders and a large, reddish face. He was voluble, affectionate. He touched people's lapels, particularly women's, and he was not shy about asking for a kiss. A few of the girls professed to have spurned him. The old maids, who mistrusted him, watched him when he left the creamery at half past five in the evening to see if he would go straight to his lodgings or across to the town to have a pint or two. They would lie in wait behind walls, or behind the windows of their sitting rooms. He rarely mentioned Bridget by name but referred to her as the Landlady, often adding how saucy she was, and what a terrific cook. He was especially fond of her lamb stew, which, as people said, was really mutton stew.

Soon the creamery manager, whose name was Michael, acquired a steady girlfriend called Mea. Mea was a bank clerk from the city, and she came in her car at weekends and stayed two nights. He would splash himself with eau de cologne on the evenings she was expected, and was to be seen traipsing in front of the house, so eager was he to see her. They never kissed on the steps but always inside and left some of the local snoopers, especially the women, demented with curiosity as to what happened next. She could, as Bridget told the shopkeeper, who then told it to everyone else, twist Michael around her little finger. She was subject, it seemed, to the most fitful moods—sometimes bright as a hummingbird, other times professing to have a headache or a sinus or a stomach ache, and refusing even to speak to him. Once, she locked herself in her bedroom and did not come out for the whole evening. She ate like a bird, bleached her hair with egg yolk and lemon, and cut a great dash at Mass or devotions, always managing to have a different hat or a different head scarf each Sunday. It was noticed that she hardly prayed at all—that she looked around, summing up the people, sneering at them—and that she was not certain when were the times to stand and when were the times to kneel, but would look around to gauge what others were doing.

"Ah, it's her sweet mystery . . . her sweet mystery," Michael had told Bridget, who had told the shopkeeper, who had, of course, told others. Before long, Mea and Michael were engaged, and Mea was coming not only two nights a week but three nights a week, and driving all around with him to see if there were any uninhabited houses or bungalows, because of course they would want their own place. Each week, as well, she brought some item of furniture, usually something bulky—a mirror or a wardrobe or a whatnot or a bureau—and he was heard to say that she was furniture mad. In jest he would ask the men why he was putting a rope around his neck.

They were to be married in June, but one evening early in May there was a rift. Michael broke it off. It happened at the hotel, just as the crowd was wishing them well and making innuendos about the patter of little feet. Michael was very drunk—his drinking had got heavy over the past few weeks— and suddenly he turned to Mea and said, very candidly and almost tearfully, that he could not go through with it. She was to keep the ring; he wanted everything to end in good faith. She slapped him, there and then, three times on the cheek in front of everyone. "How dare you," she said with the acerbity of a governess, and then she ran out and he followed, and soon they drove off down the Shannon Road—no doubt to patch things up, as people said. But Michael was adamant. The engagement was broken off.

She left that night, and Michael hid for three days. He went back to the creamery, drawn and unshaven, and on that Friday he learned of her suit for breach of promise by reading of it in the weekly newspaper. There were photos of him and Mea, mention of some little lovey-dovey exchanges, and even a photo of Bridget, who Mea said had had too much influence over him and was probably responsible for the rift. Mea also talked about her broken heart, the several plans she had made, the house that she envisaged, the little rose garden, then discussed her bottom drawer, which was full of linen and lavender sachets and so on. Above all, she bemoaned the fact that her romantic future with any other man was out of the question; in short, that her life was destroyed. Michael received a solicitor's letter, consulted his local solicitor, and was said to have paid her a hefty compensation. Then he went on the batter for a few weeks and was carted to the Cistercian monastery, and finally came home looking thinner and much more subdued. "A gold-digger, a gold-digger, that's what she was," Bridget would say whenever Mea's name was mentioned, and in time the matter was forgotten.

It was perceived—first by the postmistress, then by another woman, who spoke about it to several others—that Bridget and the creamery manager were flirting openly. Soon after, they were seen holding hands as they took a walk down the Chapel Road after the Benediction. They had lingered in the chapel, allowing the others to leave. It was the sacristan who saw them, and ran and told it in the town, once she had recovered from her fright. People asked if she was certain, or if she had not imagined it. "That I may drop dead if it's not true," she said, putting her hand to the gray wool cardigan that covered her sunken bosom.

The inappropriateness of this was more than they could stomach. After all, she was a widow, and she was a woman in her forties, who ought to know better. Neighbors began to watch more carefully, especially at night, to see how many lights went on in the upstairs rooms—to see if they had separate bedrooms or were living in mortal sin. The less censorious said it was a flash in the pan and soon he would have another beauty in tow, so that all, all were flabbergasted the morning Bridget stood in the doorway of the shop and announced her engagement. To prove it, a lozenge of blue shimmered on her finger, and her eyes were dancing as the people gaped at her.

Before long, Bridget bought a car and Michael gave her driving lessons on the Dock Road, the very road where her husband had walked to his death. Michael stopped soliciting young girls, even the young buttermaker in the creamery, and told strangers how happy he was, and that up to now all the women he had known were mere bonbons, and that this was *It*.

Her happiness was too much for people to take; they called her a hussy, they predicted another breach of promise, they waited for the downfall. Some of the older women went to the parish priest about it, but when they arrived the parish priest was in such a grump about the contributions toward a new altar that he told them to pull their socks up and try to raise money by selling cakes and jellies and things at a bazaar. He suspected why they had come, because the creamery manager had gone to him alone, and stayed an hour, and no doubt gave him a substantial offering for Masses.

To put a good complexion on the engagement period, a youngster was brought to Bridget's house from the country, a boy so daft that he dug up the tubers of the irises in mistake for onions—in short, no chaperon. They were to be married in December, which left Bridget two months to pack up her job and prepare her trousseau. She was always to be seen flying in her red car now, a menace to pedestrians and cattle that strayed on the roadside. To ingratiate herself, as they said, she offered people lifts to the city, or offered to do errands for them. Some, being weak, accepted these favors, but not the diehards. A few of the men, it is true, praised her, said what spunk she had. She was much older than Michael, and, moreover, she had got him off the booze; he only drank wine now—table wine.

A week before the wedding, the pair went to the local pub, which they 20 had got out of the habit of doing, and stood drinks to everyone. The shopkeeper, proposing the toast, said he knew that Biddy and Michael had everyone's blessing. People clapped, then someone sang. Then Biddy, being a little tipsy, tapped her glass with her engagement stone and said she was going to give a little recitation. Without further ado, she stood up, smiled that sort of urchin smile of hers, ran her tongue over her lips, another habit, and recited a poem entitled "People Will Talk." It was a lunge at all those mischievous, prurient people who begrudged her her little flourish. It may have been—indeed, many people said that it was—this audacious provocation that wreaked the havoc of the next weeks. Had she confided in a few local women, she might have been saved, but she did not confide; she stood aloof with her man, her eyes gleaming, her happiness assured.

It never came to light who exactly had begun it, but suddenly the word went round, the skeleton that had been lurking for years—that her husband had not drowned by accident, he had taken his own life. His predicament, it was said, was so grinding that he saw no way out of it. He went down to the docks that evening, after yet another hideous row with her, pen and paper in his pocket, and wrote his farewell note. It was in his trousers pocket before they handed it to her. Why else had she roared for three days, they asked, and why was she unfit to attend her own husband's funeral or the High Mass? Why else did she recover so soon but that she was a wicked, heartless harlot? The creamery manager, they predicted would be a scapegoat once the marriage vows were exchanged. First one person whispered it, then another, and then another; the story slipped from house to house, from mouth to mouth, and before long it reached Bridget's appalled ears. As if that were not shock enough, she received one morning an anonymous letter saying that her husband-to-be would know of her skeleton shortly. She flung the letter into the stove, then tried in vain to retrieve it. Luckily, Michael was still upstairs, asleep in his own room. It was then that she made her first mistake—she ran around trying to bribe people, asking them not to mention this terrible rumor, not to tell the creamery manager, for God's sake not to tell. The more she tried to quash the talk, the more people concluded her guilt. She lost all composure. She could be seen in her bare feet or in her nightgown running up the road to meet the postman, to ward off any other dreadful bulletins.

After that morning, she dared not let Michael go anywhere alone, in case someone told him. She knew, or at least clung to the belief, that no one at work would risk telling him, for fear of being fired on the spot. But in the street or on the way to Mass or at the pub—these were the danger zones, and for weeks she followed him everywhere, so that he began to show signs of impatience and said that she was a hairy Molly, clinging to him. Her looks, which had improved since the engagement, took a turn for the worse, and she was what she once had been—a scraggy older woman, with thin hair and skin that was much too yellow.

Michael saw that she was distraught, but did not understand it. It seems he told the young buttermaker that his missus had got the jitters and the sooner they got married the better. Even while he was saying this, his missus-to-be was grasping at any straw. She confided in the shopkeeper, who advised her to tell Michael, but she broke down and even flared up, mistrusting her one friend. "Why not take the bull by the horns and tell him straight out?" he had said. She couldn't. He would jilt her. Had he not already jilted a younger and comelier girl, and was she, Bridget, not haunted by the same prospect? It was then that she remembered the old woman who had lived across the road from her husband and herself and had later moved back to the country. She would go to find this woman, who would swear that she had never heard a voice raised, and that in fact Bridget and her first husband used to sit in the sun porch in the evening, among the geraniums and the begonias, whispering, holding hands, and canoodling.

Then a little respite came. Michael decided to go home to his own folks for a week, and that was a godsend. They would then meet in Limerick, with a small sprinkling of relatives, and there they would be married in the Augustinian church. One of the friars was a friend of Michael's, and he had already made the arrangements. Because of the breach-of-promise episode, it was going to be a very hushed-up affair.

Before leaving, Michael tackled her. He sat her in the little armchair by the kitchen stove, where they had often, so often, joked and cuddled. He asked her if perhaps she was having second thoughts about things, if perhaps she did not love him. Her eyes filled up with tears. She said, "No, no, Michael . . . no." She was so in love, she confessed, that she was afraid that it would go wrong. Then he kissed her and reproved her for being a daft little hen of a woman, and they waltzed around the kitchen, promising things that they would do when they were married, like putting a skylight in the kitchen, and getting a new range so that she did not have to dirty her fingers with the ashes and clinkers. He loved her little hands, he said, and he kissed them. "Num, num," he said, as if he were eating them, as if they were jam tarts.

As she told the shopkeeper later, they had a blissful farewell. He tried to coax out of her what she was planning to wear at the wedding, but she sang dumb. "I sang dumb," she said, and described how she ran upstairs to get the

25

old fox collar, with its little foxy snout and beady eyes, and threatened him with it, went "Yap, yap, yap." They played hide-and-seek, they laughed, they teased one another, but on no account would she allow him into the room where her trousseau was stored—her voile gown and her satin shoes, and her piles of new undies, and the fleecy bed jacket. Their farewell was so tender that Michael even debated if he should cancel his journey. "God blast it, I'm over twenty-one," he said. But she persuaded him to go, insisted. She knew it was essential that he be away from this place, where any mischief-maker could say, "I believe your intended wife drove her first husband to his death." She could not risk it. There was something about Michael, although she never told him this, that reminded her of her first husband: They were both childlike and affectionate, and they both had gruff tempers but were quick to apologize—to lay a bar of chocolate or a gift on the pillow as an appeasement. She loved them in much the same way—the same gushing, bubbly, childish way that she had loved at twenty—and, miraculously, her love was reciprocated.

The day after he left, Bridget set out to see the old woman. She was cheerful in the town when she stopped to buy petrol. She even told the young attendant that she was thinking of throwing a party, and asked if he would like to come. "Deffo" was what he claimed to have said.

No one of us ever knew what ensued with the old woman, because it was on the way back that it happened. It was a treacherous bit of road, always known to be; it twisted, then straightened, then forked suddenly and ridged under a thick canopy of beech trees. Lorries and cars had crashed there so often that people said there was a curse on that stretch. A witch had once lived nearby—a witch who defied the hierarchy and plied strange pagan cures. Peopled wondered if the aftermath of this witch was not the cause of all these disasters, and holy water had been sprinkled there many a time by the priests.

It was after dark when the accident happened. Bridget had gone to the old woman, and afterward had gone to a hotel in the nearest town and treated herself to a drink. It may have been that she went to the hotel to celebrate, to taste for the first time the joy, as well as the certainty of her future. Maybe the old woman had said, "I'll tell them how happy you and Bill were," or had cried, remembering that other time, when she was not old, when she did not have cataracts in her eyes, when the nice young couple invited her across the road for a glass of stout or a cup of tea. Or maybe the old woman had forgotten almost everything and just held her hand and stared. Whatever took place was never known, but in the hotel where Bridget drank the gin-and-lime and bought the crisps she chattered with the owner and asked him for his card, saying that she would be coming back there with her husband for a dinner. The locality, she said, was lucky for her, and she felt she owed it a little recompense. Half an hour later, she was around a tree, the car up on its hind legs, like an animal, her face on the dashboard, askew, her eyes wide open.

Some workmen who had been tarring the road heard the screech of the   30
crash, and ran from a little caravan where they were cooking supper. None of
them knew her. Two stayed while the third went to the lodge of a big house
to ask to use the telephone. The woman in the gate lodge was a bit strange
and did not want to let them in, so they had to go up to the big house, and
quite a long time passed before the ambulance and the guards came. But the
consensus was that she had died on the spot. She was brought back to the
local hospital, where a young nurse laid her out in white. The mourners who
came the next day were surprised, even aghast, that her face was so beauti-
fully smooth, without cuts or gashes. It was makeup, they claimed, perfect
makeup, and what a scandalous thing to adorn a corpse.

Michael knelt beside her and roared intemperately, as she had once
roared, leaving no one in doubt that he loved her passionately. At the grave
he tried to talk to her, tried to stop them from lowering the coffin. He knew
everything now; he knew her plight and was helpless to do anything about it.
She had quite a large funeral, but beneath the prayers and the murmurs were
the whispers of how drunk she had been when she got into that car. They said
her face had been disfigured, but that some silly nurse had made her look
presentable, had doctored the truth, sent her to her Maker with this monstrous camouflage—some chit of a nurse, as wayward as Bridget herself had
been.

Considerations

1. When Biddy returned to the village and built a new house, there was no
housewarming because "the people ostracized her" (para. 9). They quickly
excluded her from belonging to their community. What do you think they
found most offensive about Biddy? What could she have done to make people
accept her?

2. Judging from the town's reaction to Biddy, what kinds of values do the
people in this town live by? How are people expected to behave?

3. It is clear that Edna O'Brien's story is set in Ireland, but the time when
the action takes place is never specified. Judging by the way people behave, by
the standards they consider necessary, and by the details concerning the state
of technology, can you determine when this story could have taken place?

Invitation to Write

Although O'Brien's story is set in Ireland, and the setting is an inextricable
part of the story, the type of community she describes can be found elsewhere.
Establish the main characteristics of this community, the rules it lives by, and

the ways in which it enforces its rules. Formulate a definition of what you think the people living there mean by "community" and determine what role community is supposed to play in an individual's life. Then write an essay in which you explore the effects of community life on the individual, as illustrated by O'Brien's story. Think also of examples of communities that might resemble this one and incorporate them in your argument.

Connections

In his essay "Performative Excellence: Circum-Mediterranean" (p. 190), David Gilmore discusses the role of the community in establishing and perpetuating the ideals of manhood. In O'Brien's story, the community also plays a crucial role in setting limits for Bridget's behavior. Write an essay in which you explore the role of community in determining individual behavior and defining masculinity and femininity. Use examples from O'Brien's story and Gilmore's essay to show the consequences of the community's intervention in individual lives. Consider how the communities react to the choices made by individuals, and how they express appreciation or disapproval of individual behavior.

WILLIAM LEAST HEAT-MOON

The Emma Chase

William Least Heat-Moon is the pen name of William Trogdon.
Least Heat-Moon's ancestors were Irish, English, and Osage. He received a bachelor's degree in photojournalism and a doctorate in English from the University of Missouri. Least Heat-Moon has written
two books, both of which chronicle his traveling experiences in the
United States. His first book, *Blue Highways,* describes his 1978
journey across the United States. His recent book, *PrairyErth* (1991),
is a detailed account of Chase County in Kansas. In it he investigates
the geological, historical, and social life in "the most easterly part of
the Far West" to present a picture of the current state of human beings on the planet.

   "The Emma Chase" comes from this recent book. It was part of
an excerpt first published in *The Atlantic Monthly* in September
1991. The introduction to the *Atlantic's* excerpt clearly establishes
Least Heat-Moon's view that Kansas represents a distillation of
American experience, spirit, and values—a view also held by many
other writers. "The Emma Chase" is descriptive and contemplative,
meditating on the history of the community as well as on the way its
members interpret and plan their own lives in a time of change.

BROADWAY, WEST SIDE, A STOREFRONT WINDOW, and painted on the plate
glass a cup of steaming coffee, morning, Cottonwood Falls, the Emma Chase
Café, November 1984: I'm inside and finishing a fine western omelet and in a
moment will take on the planks of homemade wheat-bread—just as soon as
the shadow from the window coffee cup passes across my little notebook. The
men's table (a bold woman sometimes sits at it, but rare is the man who sits
at the women's table) has already emptied, and now the other one too. On the
west wall hangs a portrait of a woman from the time of Rutherford B. Hayes,
and she, her hair parted centrally, turns a bit to the left as if to answer someone in the street, her high collar crisp, her eyebrow ever so slightly raised, her
lips pursed as if she's about to speak. (Someone calls out from the kitchen to
the new waitress, *On your ticket, what's this U.P.?* and the girl says, *Up,* and
from the kitchen, *You can't have scrambled eggs up.*) The portrait is of *the
woman history forgot,* Emma Chase, who said, *You can't start a revolution*

on an empty stomach. She was not wife, daughter, sister, or mother of Salmon P. Chase, the great enemy of slavery and Lincoln's chief justice, whose name the county carries. Emma stands in no man's shadow but in the dark recess that the past mostly is. In this county, she's famous for having been forgotten; after all, who remembers it was on the back of one of Emma's envelopes that Lincoln outlined his Emancipation Proclamation? That's been the story in the Falls, anyway.

Most countians now understand that Emma "A-Cookie-in-Every-Jar" Chase has the reality of an idea and an ideal. When Linda Pretzer Thurston decided to open the café a couple of years ago, she cast about for a name, something local, something feminine, and she searched the volumes of the *Chase County Historical Sketches* for an embodiment of certain values but came away unsatisfied by or unaware of the facts, such as those of 1889 about Minnie Morgan of Cottonwood, one of the first women in the county elected mayor and *the* first—and probably the only one—to serve with an all-female city council. Minnie has stood in a few dark historical corridors herself: Her daughter's biography of the family in the *Historical Sketches* speaks of wild plums and a neighbor who threw her family's clothes down the cistern to save them from a prairie fire, and it mentions her father's founding of the county newspaper the *Leader,* but it says not one word about Minnie's mayoralty or her advocacy of woman suffrage. There has not been a female mayor since.

So, the café had no name until one night at the family supper table Linda and her identical twin said simultaneously in response to something she's now forgotten, *The Emma Chase!* Soon, newspaper ads for the café printed Emma's chocolate chip cookie recipe, and they asked townspeople to search their attic trunks for information about her. One day Whitt Laughridge came in with a large, framed portrait of an unidentified woman he'd found in the historical society vault. Thurston said, *Yes! At last we've got Emma!* Unsatisfied with history, she had invented a persona and then had to invent ways to get people to accept the name. Her ads and fabricated history worked so well that she, who grew up five miles west in Elmdale, *she* became to the citizens *Emma down at the café,* and she doesn't mind.

There are other things she does object to, such as the racist joke a fellow told a while ago at the men's table and to which she said loudly from across the room, *Did you hear that one at church, Ray?* and sometimes to sexist comments she'll recite from the café refrigerator, covered with stick-on slogans like a large, upright bumper: THE ROOSTER CROWS BUT THE HEN DELIVERS or WOMEN'S RIGHTS—REAGAN'S WRONGS.

Linda Thurston is trim and pretty, a dark strawberry blonde given to   5
large, swinging earrings; today she wears a pair of silvery stars almost of a size to be hoisted atop the courthouse cupola for Christmas. She sits down across from me to see what I'm scratching in my notebook. Now I'm copying what is on her coffee mug:

I HAVE A B.A., M.A., PH.D.
ALL I NEED NOW IS A GOOD J.O.B.

Her doctorate is in child psychology, she is thirty-nine, divorced, and has a son, John. She calls across the little café to the new waitress, *We can't do scrambled eggs over easy.*

We talk, and then she brings the guest book to me. In it are names from many states and also from Russia, Italy, Israel, and she says, *My friends say I'm the white Aunt Jemima of the women's movement, a radicalized, store-front feminist whose job is to get cowboys to eat quiche Lorraine even if they call it quick lorn. I'm an aproned militant known for scratch pies, soups, and breads, the one who's taught a waitress Lamaze-breathing on a café floor.*

A man, his spine crumbling with age, his eyesight almost gone, comes up and holds out a palm of change for his coffee, and Linda takes out thirty-five cents, forget the tax.

Three years ago she and her young son lived near Kansas City, Kansas, where she worked with battered women and handicapped children, some of whose fathers couldn't remember their child's name; they all were poor city people who lived anonymously. She was also president of a large chapter of the National Organization for Women, and she campaigned and typed and marched. When Ronald Reagan became president and inner-city social programs started disappearing, she found herself depressed and beginning to wonder who the enemy was, where the battlefield was, and she didn't understand why ideas so apparently democratic and humane were so despised and thwarted, and she was no longer sure what it meant to help the disadvantaged or to be a feminist. Women seemed in retreat from action to the easier, safer battles of awareness. Things were retrogressing.

On a trip home to Elmdale she learned that the old and closed Village Inn Café was for sale, and she looked it over, found a broken-down and fouled building, and, suddenly, a fight against dirt and dilapidation, enemies you could lay your rubber-gloved hands on, looked good, especially when she heard the county-seat citizens wanted a pleasant place once again to sit down with a coffee and find out whose cattle it was that went through the ice, whose horse had sent him over the fence. A group of Broadway businesspeople met in Bell's western clothing store and offered to buy the café building and lease it to her until she could pay for it—after all, she was a native—and so Linda Thurston decided to live out her fantasy of running a little homey restaurant, and she moved back to Chase County, where, she hoped, *the Hills could heal.* Her friend Linda Woody, a state lobbyist for NOW, had also wearied of the struggle against Reaganism, and joined her, and the once dingy, moribund café became unofficially the Retreat for Burned-Out Social Activists, a place where the women could serve homilies, history, and cold pasta salad.

Linda Thurston says: *I saw it as a haven of rest from political struggles, a* 10
place I'd have time to write up my research. If we could undermine a few
stereotypes along the way and wake up a few people, that was fine too. I've
never seen my return as going home so much as going forward to my roots,
but I don't think I'll stay long enough to grow old here—unless I already
have. I believe when the time comes to go back to whatever, I'll know where
that is. I've learned you can go home again, but I don't know whether you can
stay home again.

Refurbishing the café became a community task: The seventy-eight-year-
old furniture dealer power-sanded the chipped floor, the clothier painted, a
drywaller showed the women how to mud plasterboard. They came to love
the exhaustion of such work. Then they got to the Wolf stove, which yielded
its encrusted grease to no woman, man, or method from scrapers to torches.
One day two fellows came in with an idea: They dismantled the range, put it
in the back of a pickup, hauled it to the county highway yard, turned a steam
hose on it, and reassembled it into the beauty of new sculpture, and someone
happily wrote on the blackboard Thurston had set up to list possible names
for the place: the Clean Stove Café. Also on the board were the Double L, the
Quarthouse, and Soup and Psychological Services, this last already beginning
to have some meaning.

The women did not flaunt their politics, and the town was enough impressed with their hard work to ignore their ERA NOW! bumper stickers, and
strollers stopped in to watch the work or help out or just pour themselves a
cup of free coffee. After six weeks of reconstruction, the women papered over
the street windows to create suspense for the opening a couple of days later
while they completed last details. In a county where beef stands second only
to Christianity, where gravy and chicken-fried steak are the bases from which
all culinary judgments proceed, the women offered eggplant parmigiana, lin-
guine with clams, gazpacho, fettuccine Alfredo—and chicken-fried steak.
Business was excellent, and the first day they sold out of pasta primavera, and
the women were certain they could keep their pledge never to serve french
fries or factory white bread. All their eggs came from Chase farms; on weekends, in season, they prepared calf fries fresh from county pastures (and tolerated jokes attendant to feminists grilling ballocks), and they catered meals to
businessmen in lodge meetings and ranch hands at corrals.

Linda says to me: *Scratch cooking all the way. The highest compliment is*
a woman saying, "This is as good as I make at home." But the men bitched
all the time about no french fries or white bread so we gave in and cut our
own fry potatoes and baked our own white bread, but, still today, if you want
a grilled cheese between a couple of slices of Rainbo, you'll just have to go
someplace else. That's the only little thing we haven't compromised on.

We've never changed our deeper values because we refuse to divorce
being café owners from our feminism. We're tolerated for it and sometimes

we're defined by it: I heard a man ask his friend what a crêpe was and why something like that would even be on the menu, and the waitress told him, "They're for the ERA." And that's right. We employ only women, and we try to bring to them what we've learned. In the first days of the café, a wealthy lady told me there were no battered women in the county, and she believed that, but she's been misled—the problem is just buried. Not long ago at the health fair in the school gym we sponsored a display about services for abused women and children, and we found out later that some people were afraid to stand in front of it because a neighbor might think they were abused. And one day a woman said to me, she was holding back tears, "You ought to get out of here—the longer you stay, the worse you'll feel about yourself as a woman." Maybe that's a minority view, but it's valid. The other side is that people here are still close to their pioneer ancestors, and they all can tell stories about strong and capable grandmothers. For a long time women have owned businesses in the county, so we're accepted, but then the café isn't a hardware store or a transmission shop.

The young waitress has just given a single check to a man sitting with two women, and Linda explains to her to give each person one, and she says, *Don't assume the male always pays,* and to me, *Separate checks also protect privacy—people watch and read something into who picks up the tab.* I ask whether lack of privacy isn't the worst thing about a small town, and she says, *And also the best. I love going to the post office in the morning and knowing everybody. The only time we honk a car horn is with a wave. It's touching when somebody asks about my son or my dad's health. We can't afford not to care about other people in a place this small. Our survival, in a way, depends on minimizing privacy because the lack of it draws us into each other's lives, and that's a major resource in a little town where there aren't a thousand entertainments. There's an elderly man who lost his little granddaughter to a drunk, a hit-and-run driver, a few months ago. Every time the old gentleman comes into the Emma Chase, he retells the story, and every time people listen. What's that worth to a person? Or to a community? A café like this serves to bond us.*

I'm scribbling things down, and she watches and says, *Growing up in this county I learned not to ask questions. If people want you to know something, they'll tell you.* I say that I must be a popular fellow, what with a question mark in every sentence, and she says, *You don't count. You don't live here. Besides, the word is out that you're in the county. You'll be tolerated even if they do think you're about a half bubble off plumb.* She watches me write that down, and she says, *We can't afford to ostracize each other just because we don't like this one's politics or the way that one raises her kids. You can get away with it in a city—picking and choosing—but here we're already picked. Participation by everybody discourages change, and the radical gets cut off. But if we give aberrant behavior a wide berth we don't usually reject it com-*

15

pletely. Every merchant on Broadway can tell a story about some petty shop-lifter whose pilfering has been ignored to avoid a bigger problem. For an out-sider it's different: If you—yourself—would espouse something terribly un-popular like government ownership of land they'll just question your sanity, but pocket a candy bar and they'll have you arrested. If I do either one, it would be just the reverse. We have limits, of course. The first and most pow-erful enforcement is gossip and scorn. They're the sap and sinew of a small town.

When she gets up to ready the kitchen for lunch, I ask whether she or the Emma Chase has ever been scorned, and she says, *You'd be more likely to hear that than I would.*

Now, late afternoon, October 1988: The painted coffee cup still steams on the window, and stalwart Emma Chase looks over the stacked chairs and onto Broadway, and the dank odor of an old and unused building slips between the locked twin doors. The café has been closed for nearly a year, and there's nothing more than a hope of somebody reopening it, although everyone is tired of coffee in Styrofoam cups and factory cookies in the Senior Citizens' Center a few doors down. Linda Woody has gone to Washington as a NOW lobbyist, and Linda Thurston is sixty miles up the road at Kansas State University, an assistant professor in rural special education. The café is for sale, and she's asking eight thousand dollars less than she paid for it, in spite of its becoming known as one of the best small-town eateries in the state, in spite of a Kansas Citian's offer to underwrite the franchising of Emma Chase cafés.

I've just returned from lunch with her in the student union, where she said, *Standing in front of that big Wolf stove I kept remembering my degree and how useless it was becoming with every fried egg. I'm forty-three, and I'm ten years behind my colleagues. I worked long hours at the café, and my feet hurt all the time, and I got arthritis in my hands, and finally I realized I didn't want to work that hard day after day and still not earn enough money to send my son to college. Every other businessperson on Broadway has at least one additional source of income—the furniture dealer runs a funeral par-lor, the owners of the two dress shops have their husbands' incomes, the filling station man has another in Strong City. The Emma Chase would sup-port one frugal person, but it wouldn't even do that without weekend city people. Tourists coming to see the Hills, bicycle clubs—they kept us alive after we earned a name around the state by being special. But there were local folks who never came in, and I'd ask them what it would take to get them inside, and they'd say, "We let the kids decide where we're going to eat out, and they choose McDonald's." How does a box of toys in the Emma Chase compete against television commercials? And there's something else: Good home-cooking is common in the county. Franchise food is the novelty, espe-*

cially when it's twenty miles away. What our café offered, city people wanted, but they also wanted clean floors, and the cowboys were afraid to come in and get the floor dirty.

I asked, was it a loss, and she said, *I lost some money and something* 20 *professionally because I never found time to write, but I realized my fantasy, and I was at home for the last two years of my father's life. And I got to live again according to the dictates of rainfall and the price of cattle and grain and the outbreaks of chicken pox. I was part of a community rebuilding its café, and working with those helpers let me see men again as people instead of the enemy. It meant something for my son to go to school with children of neighbors I went to school with. And—I think I can say this—because of the café, I see my femaleness differently: Now I think feminism means being connected with other people, not just with other feminists.*

She was quiet for some time, and then she said, *There were losses, no question, but there was only one real failure: We never did get the farmers to eat alfalfa sprouts. They know silage when they see it. Maybe we should have tried it with gravy.*

Considerations

1. Linda Thurston describes her return to Elmdale as "going forward to my roots" (para. 10). She seems to understand her community and its values, but she clearly does not share all of its beliefs. Which of her community's values does she accept? Which of her community's values does she seek to change?

2. Least Heat-Moon writes that Linda Thurston "decided to live out her fantasy of running a homey little restaurant" (para. 9). What does his use of the word "fantasy" suggest about her project? Do you think it is her word, or his? Why?

Invitation to Write

When Linda Thurston decided to open a café in Cottonwood Falls, "she cast about for a name . . . for an embodiment of certain values" (para. 2). What are the values that Linda wants to be embodied in the name? Write an essay in which you clarify Linda's ideas about what a community is or should be. Determine whether the other members of the community agree with her definition and whether her community is indeed what she thinks it is. Respond to her definition of community in light of your own ideas on the subject.

Connections

Robert Reich gives us an idea of what the term "community" has come to mean in late-twentieth-century America. In "The Global Elite" (p. 290), he writes about the disappearance of traditional communities and their replacement by a new set of allegiances. Write an essay in which you measure Reich's evaluations against Thurston's experience. In the process you will have to question his ideas regarding the speed at which these changes take place, and also determine whether Linda Thurston's attitude is nostalgic or simply anachronistic.

ROBERT REICH

The Global Elite

Robert B. Reich is an instructor in political economy at Harvard University's John F. Kennedy School of Government. He is the author of numerous books on government, business, and the international economy, including *The Next American Frontier* (1983), *Tales of a New America* (1987), *The Power of Public Ideas* (1988), and *The Resurgent Liberal and Other Unfashionable Prophesies* (1989). He holds a degree from Yale Law School.

The article "The Global Elite," adapted from *The Work of Nations: Preparing Ourselves for 21st-Century Capitalism* (1991), was first published in the *New York Times Magazine* in January 1991. "The Global Elite" focuses on the changes technology has produced in social life, and traces the new formations of community, which both displace and replace the older forms.

THE IDEA OF "COMMUNITY" has always held a special attraction for Americans. In a 1984 speech, President Ronald Reagan celebrated America's "bedrock"—"its communities where neighbors help one another, where families bring up kids together, where American values are born." Governor Mario M. Cuomo of New York, with a very different political leaning, has been almost as lyrical. "Community . . . is the reality on which our national life has been founded," he said in 1987.

There is only one problem with this picture. Most Americans no longer live in traditional communities. They live in suburban subdivisions bordered by highways and sprinkled with shopping malls, or in tony condominiums and residential clusters, or in ramshackle apartment buildings and housing projects. Most of them commute to work and socialize on some basis other than geographic proximity. And most people pick up and move to a different neighborhood every five years or so.

But Americans generally have one thing in common with their neighbors: They have similar incomes. And that simple fact lies at the heart of the new community. This means that their educational backgrounds are likely to be similar, that they pay roughly the same in taxes, and that they indulge in the same consumer impulses. "Tell me someone's ZIP code," the founder of a direct-mail company once bragged, "and I can predict what they eat, drink, drive—even think."

Americans who own their homes usually share one political cause with their neighbors: a near obsessive concern with maintaining or upgrading property values. And this common interest is responsible for much of what has brought neighbors together in recent years. Complete strangers, although they may live on the same street or in the same condominium complex, suddenly feel intense solidarity when it is rumored that low-income housing will be constructed in their midst or that a poorer school district will be consolidated with their own.

The renewed emphasis on "community" in American life has justified and   5
legitimized these economic enclaves. If generosity and solidarity end at the border of similarly valued properties, then the most fortunate can be virtuous citizens at little cost. Since most people in one neighborhood or town are equally well off, there is no cause for a guilty conscience. If inhabitants of another area are poorer, let them look to one another. Why should *we* pay for *their* schools?

So the argument goes, without acknowledging that the critical assumption has already been made: "We" and "they" belong to fundamentally different communities. Through such reasoning, it has become possible to maintain a self-image of generosity toward, and solidarity with, one's "community" without bearing any responsibility to "them"—the other "community."

America's high earners—the fortunate top fifth—thus feel increasingly justified in paying only what is necessary to insure that everyone in their community is sufficiently well educated and has access to the public services they need to succeed.

Last year, the top fifth of working Americans took home more money than the other four-fifths put together—the highest portion in postwar history. These high earners will relinquish somewhat more of their income to the Federal Government this year than in 1990 as a result of last fall's tax changes, although considerably less than in the late 1970s, when the tax code was more progressive. But the continuing debate over whether the wealthy are paying their fair share of taxes obscures a larger issue, with more profound implications for America: The fortunate fifth is quietly seceding from the rest of the nation.

This is occurring gradually, without much awareness by members of the top group—or, for that matter, by anyone else. And the Government is speeding this process as Washington shifts responsibility for many public services to state and local governments.

The secession is taking several forms. In many cities and towns, the   10
wealthy have in effect withdrawn their dollars from the support of public spaces and institutions shared by all and dedicated the savings to their own

private services. As public parks and playgrounds deteriorate, there is a pro-
liferation of private health clubs, golf clubs, tennis clubs, skating clubs, and
every other type of recreational association in which costs are shared among
members. Condominiums and the omnipresent residential communities dun
their members to undertake work that financially strapped local governments
can no longer afford to do well—maintaining roads, mending sidewalks,
pruning trees, repairing street lights, cleaning swimming pools, paying for life-
guards, and, notably, hiring security guards to protect life and property. (The
number of private security guards in the United States now exceeds the number of public police officers.)

Of course, wealthier Americans have been withdrawing into their own
neighborhoods and clubs for generations. But the new secession is more dramatic because the highest earners now inhabit a different economy from other
Americans. The new elite is linked by jet, modem, fax, satellite, and fiber-
optic cable to the great commercial and recreational centers of the world, but
it is not particularly connected to the rest of the nation.

That is because the work this group does is becoming less tied to the
activities of other Americans. Most of their jobs consist of analyzing and ma-
nipulating symbols—words, numbers, or visual images. Among the most
prominent of these "symbolic analysts" are management consultants, lawyers, software and design engineers, research scientists, corporate executives,
financial advisers, strategic planners, advertising executives, television and
movie producers, and other workers whose job titles include terms like "strategy," "planning," "consultant," "policy," "resources," or "engineer."

These workers typically spend long hours in meetings or on the telephone
and even longer hours in planes or hotels—advising, making presentations,
giving briefings, and making deals. Periodically, they issue reports, plans, designs, drafts, briefs, blueprints, analyses, memorandums, layouts, renderings,
scripts, or projections. In contrast with people whose jobs tend to be tedious
and repetitive, symbolic analysts find their work varied and intellectually
challenging. In fact, the work is often enjoyable.

These symbolic analysts are in ever greater demand in a world market
that places an increasing value on identifying and solving problems. Requests
for their software designs, financial advice, or engineering blueprints come
from all parts of the globe. This largely explains why most (but by no means
all) symbolic analysts have become wealthier, even as the ever-growing
worldwide supply of unskilled labor continues to depress the wages of other
Americans.

Successful Americans have not completely disengaged themselves from the   15
lives of their less fortunate compatriots. Some devote substantial resources
and energies to helping the rest of society, not through their tax payments, but
through voluntary efforts. "Generosity is a reflection of what one does with

his or her resources—and not what he or she advocates the government do with everyone's money," Ronald Reagan said in 1984.

The argument is fair enough. Government is not the only device for redistributing wealth. In his speech accepting the Presidential nomination at the Republican National Convention in 1988, George Bush said that the real magnanimity of America was to be found in a "brilliant diversity" of private charities, "spread like stars, like a thousand points of light in a broad and peaceful sky."

No nation congratulates itself more enthusiastically on its charitable acts than America; none engages in a greater number of charity balls, bake sales, benefit auctions, and border-to-border hand holdings for good causes. Much of this is sincerely motivated and admirable.

But close examination reveals that many of these acts of benevolence do not help the needy. Particularly suspect is the private giving of those in the top income-tax bracket. Studies have revealed that their largess does not flow mainly to social services for the poor—to better schools, health clinics, or recreational centers. Instead, most voluntary contributions of wealthy Americans go to the places and institutions that entertain, inspire, cure, or educate wealthy Americans—art museums, opera houses, theaters, orchestras, ballet companies, private hospitals, and elite universities.

And even these charitable contributions are relatively skimpy. Last year, American households with incomes of less than $10,000 gave an average of 5.5 percent of their earnings to charity or to a religious organization; those making more than $100,000 a year gave only 2.9 percent. After the 1986 tax-code overhaul reduced the benefits of charitable giving, the very rich became even stingier. According to Internal Revenue Service data, taxpayers earning $500,000 or more slashed their average donations to $16,062 in 1988 from $47,432 in 1980.

Corporate philanthropy is following the same general pattern. In recent years, the largest American corporations have been sounding the alarm about the nation's fast deteriorating primary and secondary schools. Few are more eloquent and impassioned about the need for better schools than American executives. "How well we educate all of our children will determine our competitiveness globally, and our economic health domestically, and our communities' character and vitality," said a report of The Business Roundtable, a New York–based association of top executives.

Accordingly, there are numerous "partnerships" between corporations and public schools: scholarships for poor children qualified to attend college, and programs in which businesses adopt individual schools by making conspicuous donations of computers, books, and, on occasion, even money. That such activities are loudly touted by corporate public relations staffs should not detract from the good they do.

Despite the hoopla, business donations to education and charitable causes actually tapered off markedly in the 1980s, even as the economy boomed. In the 1970s, corporate giving to education jumped an average of 15 percent a year. In 1990, however, giving was only 5 percent over that in 1989; in 1989 it was 3 percent over 1988. Moreover, most of this money goes to colleges and universities—in particular, to the alma maters of symbolic analysts, who expect their children and grandchildren to follow in their footsteps. Only 1.5 percent of corporate giving in the late 1980s was to public primary and secondary schools.

Notably, these contributions have been smaller than the amounts corporations are receiving from states and communities in the form of subsidies or tax breaks. Companies are quietly procuring such deals by threatening to move their operations—and jobs—to places around the world with a more congenial tax climate. The paradoxical result has been even less corporate revenue to spend on schools and other community services than before. The executives of General Motors, for example, who have been among the loudest to proclaim the need for better schools, have also been among the most relentless in pursuing local tax abatements and in challenging their tax assessments. G.M.'s successful efforts to reduce its taxes in North Tarrytown, N.Y., where the company has had a factory since 1914, cut local revenues by $1 million in 1990, part of a larger shortfall that forced the town to lay off scores of teachers.

The secession of the fortunate fifth has been most apparent in how and where they have chosen to work and live. In effect, most of America's large urban centers have splintered into two separate cities. One is composed of those whose symbolic and analytic services are linked to the world economy. The other consists of local service workers—custodians, security guards, taxi drivers, clerical aides, parking attendants, salespeople, restaurant employees—whose jobs are dependent on the symbolic analysts. Few blue-collar manufacturing workers remain in American cities. Between 1953 and 1984, for example, New York City lost about 600,000 factory jobs; in the same interval, it added about 700,000 jobs for symbolic analysts and service workers.

The separation of symbolic analysts from local service workers within cities has been reinforced in several ways. Most large cities now possess two school systems—a private one for the children of the top-earning group and a public one for the children of service workers, the remaining blue-collar workers, and the unemployed. Symbolic analysts spend considerable time and energy insuring that their children gain entrance to good private schools, and then small fortunes keeping them there—dollars that under a more progressive tax code might finance better public education.

People with high incomes live, shop, and work within areas of cities that, if not beautiful, are at least esthetically tolerable and reasonably safe; precincts not meeting these minimum standards of charm and security have been left to the less fortunate.

Here again, symbolic analysts have pooled their resources to the exclusive benefit of themselves. Public funds have been spent in earnest on downtown "revitalization" projects, entailing the construction of clusters of post-modern office buildings (complete with fiber-optic cables, private branch exchanges, satellite dishes, and other communications equipment linking them to the rest of the world), multilevel parking garages, hotels with glass-enclosed atriums, upscale shopping plazas and galleries, theaters, convention centers, and luxury condominiums.

Ideally, these complexes are entirely self-contained, with air-conditioned walkways linking residences, businesses, and recreational space. The lucky resident is able to shop, work, and attend the theater without risking direct contact with the outside world—that is, the other city.

When not living in urban enclaves, symbolic analysts are increasingly congregating in suburbs and exurbs where corporate headquarters have been relocated, research parks have been created, and where bucolic universities have spawned entrepreneurial ventures. Among the most desirable of such locations are Princeton, N.J.; northern Westchester and Putnam Counties in New York; Palo Alto, Calif.; Austin, Tex.; Bethesda, Md.; and Raleigh-Durham, N.C.

Engineers and strategists of American auto companies, for example, do 30 not live in Flint or Saginaw, Mich., where the blue-collar workers reside; they cluster in their own towns of Troy, Warren, and Auburn Hills. Likewise, the vast majority of the financial specialists, lawyers, and executives working for the insurance companies of Hartford would never consider living there; after all, Hartford is the nation's fourth-poorest city. Instead, they flock to Windsor, Middlebury, West Hartford, and other towns that are among the wealthiest in the country.

This trend, too, has been growing for decades. But technology has accelerated it. Today's symbolic analysts linked directly to the rest of the globe can choose to live and work in the most pastoral of settings.

The secession has been encouraged by the Federal Government. For the last decade, Washington has in effect shifted responsibility for many public services to local governments. At their peak, Federal grants made up 25 percent of state and local spending in the late 1970s. Today, the Federal share has dwindled to 17 percent. Direct aid to local governments, in the form of programs introduced in the Johnson and Nixon Administrations, has been the hardest hit by budget cuts. In the 1980s, Federal dollars for clean water, job training and transfers, low-income housing, sewage treatment, and garbage disposal shrank by some $50 billion a year, and Washington's share of spending on local transit declined by 50 percent. (The Bush Administration has proposed that states and localities take on even more of the costs of building and maintaining roads, and wants to cut Federal aid for mass transit.) In 1990, New York City received only 9.6 percent of all its revenue from the Federal Government, compared with 16 percent in 1981.

States have quickly transferred many of these new expenses to fiscally strapped cities and towns, with a result that by the start of the 1990s, localities were bearing more than half of the costs of water and sewage, roads, parks, welfare, and public schools. In New York State, the local communities' share has risen to about 75 percent of these costs.

Cities and towns with affluent inhabitants can bear these burdens relatively easily. Poorer ones, faced with the twin problems of lower incomes and greater demand for social services, have had far more difficulty. And as the gap between the richest and poorest communities has widened, the shift in responsibility for public services to cities and towns has functioned as another means of relieving wealthier Americans of the cost of aiding less fortunate citizens.

The result has been a growing inequality in basic social and community services. While the city tax rate in Philadelphia, for example, is about triple that of communities around it, the suburbs enjoy far better schools, hospitals, recreation, and police protection. Eighty-five percent of the richest families in the greater Philadelphia area live outside the city limits, and 80 percent of the region's poorest live inside. The quality of a city's infrastructure—roads, bridges, sewage, water treatment—is likewise related to the average income of its inhabitants.

The growing inequality in government services has been most apparent in the public schools. The Federal Government's share of the costs of primary and secondary education has dwindled to about 6 percent. The bulk of the cost is divided about equally between the states and local school districts. States with a higher concentration of wealthy residents can afford to spend more on their schools than other states. In 1989, the average public-school teacher in Arkansas, for example, received $21,700; in Connecticut, $37,300.

Even among adjoining suburban towns in the same state the differences can be quite large. Consider three Boston-area communities located within minutes of one another. All are predominantly white, and most residents within each town earn about the same as their neighbors. But the disparity of incomes between towns is substantial.

Belmont, northwest of Boston, is inhabited mainly by symbolic analysts and their families. In 1988, the average teacher in its public schools earned $36,100. Only 3 percent of Belmont's eighteen-year-olds dropped out of high school, and more than 80 percent of graduating seniors chose to go on to a four-year college.

Just east of Belmont is Somerville, most of whose residents are low-wage service workers. In 1988, the average Somerville teacher earned $29,400. A third of the town's eighteen-year-olds did not finish high school, and fewer than a third planned to attend college.

Chelsea, across the Mystic River from Somerville, is the poorest of the three towns. Most of its inhabitants are unskilled, and many are unemployed or only employed part time. The average teacher in Chelsea, facing tougher educational challenges than his or her counterparts in Belmont, earned $26,200 in 1988, almost a third less than the average teacher in the more affluent town just a few miles away. More than half of Chelsea's eighteen-year-olds did not graduate from high school, and only 10 percent planned to attend college.

Similar disparities can be found all over the nation. Students at Highland Park High School in a wealthy suburb of Dallas, for example, enjoy a campus with a planetarium, indoor swimming pool, closed-circuit television studio and state-of-the-art science laboratory. Highland Park spends about $6,000 a year to educate each student. This is almost twice that spent per pupil by the towns of Wilmer and Hutchins in southern Dallas County. According to Texas education officials, the richest school district in the state spends $19,300 a year per pupil; its poorest, $2,100 a year.

The courts have become involved in trying to repair such imbalances, but the issues are not open to easy judicial remedy.

The four-fifths of Americans left in the wake of the secession of the fortunate fifth include many poor blacks, but racial exclusion is neither the primary motive for the separation nor a necessary consequence. Lower-income whites are similarly excluded, and high-income black symbolic analysts are often welcomed. The segregation is economic rather than racial, although economically motivated separation often results in *de facto* racial segregation. Where courts have found a pattern of racially motivated segregation, it usually has involved lower-income white communities bordering on lower-income black neighborhoods.

In states where courts have ordered equalized state spending in school districts, the vast differences in a town's property values—and thus local tax revenues—continue to result in substantial inequities. Where courts or state governments have tried to impose limits on what affluent communities can pay their teachers, not a few parents in upscale towns have simply removed their children from the public schools and applied the money they might otherwise have willingly paid in higher taxes to private school tuitions instead. And, of course, even if statewide expenditures were better equalized, poorer states would continue to be at a substantial disadvantage.

In all these ways, the gap between America's symbolic analysts and everyone else is widening into a chasm. Their secession from the rest of the population raises fundamental questions about the future of American society. In the new global economy—in which money, technologies, and corporations cross borders effortlessly—a citizen's standard of living depends more and more on skills and insights, and on the infrastructure needed to link these abilities to the rest of the world. But the most skilled and insightful Americans, who are already positioned to thrive in the world market, are now able to slip the bonds of national allegiance, and by so doing disengage themselves from their less-favored fellows. The stark political challenge in the decades ahead will be to reaffirm that, even though America is no longer a separate and distinct economy, it is still a society whose members have abiding obligations to one another.

Considerations

1. Reich spends most of his essay analyzing the ways in which American communities are changing. Judging from his criticisms and observations, how do you think Reich would define the word "community"? Try to infer what he thinks is the basis of community.

2. Reich keeps using the word "secession" to describe the separation of wealthy Americans from their less fortunate neighbors. He also notes that symbolic analysts are separated from their business partners, with whom they communicate by telephone, fax, and modem. What attitudes on the part of the elite, as described by Reich, distinguish between "secession" and "separation"?

Invitation to Write

Over the past several decades, many downtown shopping areas have suffered from economic decay and stagnation as shoppers spend more time and money in modern suburban and urban shopping malls. Visiting malls has become a source of recreation for many people, especially adolescents. In his essay, Reich looks at the appearance of private clubs, schools, and other exclusive areas of the city where "symbolic analysts" work and shop. Write an essay in which you analyze the phenomenon of shopping malls, taking into account Reich's comments on the privatization of services in America. In light of Reich's discussion, decide whether malls recreate the downtown shopping areas they replace or whether they are another reflection of economic segregation. What is the impact of their separation from a residential community?

Connections

In "If You Can Talk to a Guy" (p. 483), Jane Staw and Mary Swander present a picture of a more traditional community where people do remain in contact with each other through both conversation and memory. How would this community compare to those described by Reich? Write an essay in which you analyze the relationships in the communities described by Staw and Swander, and discuss their possible futures on the basis of the trends in community life proposed by Reich. Look at Reich's essay to determine whether any of the dangers he points out seem to be present in the Minnesota communities visited by Staw and Swander.

ASSIGNMENT SEQUENCE

Individuals in Communities

This sequence begins by asking you to explore your own experience as a member of a community in order to think about the relationships between individuals and their communities. Applying your knowledge of the dynamics of coexistence and conflict in your own community, you will proceed in the next assignment to take a close look at the tensions mirrored in the social order of a small Irish village. You will consider how some of the forces at work in your own community may or may not be at work there. The next assignment asks you to look at the same Irish community, as well as at a small Midwestern town in order to see how individuals within these environments succeed in establishing places for themselves within their communities. Next you will consider an analysis of the way American communities have changed. Finally, in the fifth assignment, you will reconsider some of the earlier examples of community that you discussed in order to test Robert Reich's theories and ideas about the forces that create and destroy communities.

Assignment 1: Exploring Experience

Since you have lived in at least one geographic community and may belong to other types of communities as well, you have firsthand knowledge of the subject. Write a paper that describes your relationship to a community and how this relationship has affected your own life.

An obvious way to approach this assignment would be to describe the community you have in mind and your own relationship to it. While your community might be a town or geographic unit, it might be a group that unites people with some common interest or goal. It would therefore be helpful for your readers to know what kinds of people belong to this community and what interests unite them. Outline the goals and accomplishments of the group or the values and objectives of the community. Focus on individuals who represent it and the issues that mobilize or divide its members. You might remember and tell a story about your community that exemplifies its values or demonstrates cooperation or conflict. Then explain how your connection to this particular community has influenced your own life.

Assignment 2

Without further ado, she stood up, smiled that sort of urchin smile of hers, ran her tongue over her lips, another habit, and recited a poem entitled "People Will Talk." It was a lunge at all those mischievous, prurient people who begrudged her her little flourish. It may have been—indeed, many people said that it was—this audacious provocation that wreaked the havoc of the next weeks.

—EDNA O'BRIEN, *The Widow*

Edna O'Brien's short story "The Widow" shows the experience of a woman who lives in a community but is never accepted by it. When Biddy recites her poem she openly recognizes the community's criticism of her behavior. Write a paper in which you analyze the relationship between Biddy and her community, suggesting the causes and consequences of incompatibility, and comparing the relationship between Biddy and her community to the relationship between your community and yourself, which you described in assignment 1. Use these two descriptions to consider the way communities influence individuals to share a community's values.

Begin your paper by examining the episode where Biddy openly confronts the town by reciting the poem, or other moments in the story where she flouts the town's values with her speech and behavior. Underline examples of actions that place Biddy in danger of scrutiny by her neighbors. Sometimes the best indication of these moments lies in the comments that the story's narrative repeats as the villagers circulate conversation, gossip, and observations about Biddy. These are the comments of the "people who will talk," and you will need to look closely at several of these moments, as well as your examples from your first paper, to reach a conclusion about the causes of the tension between Biddy and her neighbors. Then add them to your own knowledge of community life and dynamics.

Assignment 3

I was part of a community rebuilding its café, and working with those helpers let me see men again as people instead of the enemy. It meant something for my son to go to school with children of neighbors I went to school with. And   I think I can say this—because of the café, I see my femaleness differently: Now I think feminism means being connected with other people, not just with other feminists.

—LINDA THURSTON as quoted by
WILLIAM LEAST HEAT-MOON, *The Emma Chase*

William Least Heat-Moon, in "The Emma Chase," shows that Linda Thurston's ability to rediscover the importance of community and to reconnect with the community she grew up in does not mean that she accepts all of its attitudes and values. Yet unlike Biddy in Edna O'Brien's "The Widow," Thurston is able to earn the community's respect and acceptance. Write a paper in which you examine the situations of the two women and explore the reasons behind their two very different relationships with their communities.

In order to understand the differences in their situations, pick one or two examples from each reading that describe a situation of potential or actual conflict between the women and their communities. Articulate the community values that appear threatened, the way the women respond to their communities' concerns, and the factors that enable the women to succeed or fail in gaining their communities' respect for their different values.

Assignment 4

Most Americans no longer live in traditional communities. They live in suburban subdivisions bordered by highways and sprinkled with shopping malls, or in tony condominiums and residential clusters, or in ramshackle apartment buildings and housing projects.
—ROBERT REICH, *The Global Elite*

Robert Reich begins his essay "The Global Elite" by giving examples that stress the importance of community life to Americans, and then presents details of American life to show that most Americans no longer know what it would be like to live in a traditional community. He suggests a great deal about what is wrong with the "new" community in which most Americans now live, but he never directly tells his readers what image of community he would use to replace it. Write a paper in which you use the criticisms in Reich's text to construct the model of community he envisions but never explicitly describes. Decide whether or not Reich is returning to a traditional view of community or is developing a new model.

To focus your paper, evaluate the actual communities Reich describes by comparing them to the traditional model that Reich suggests used to exist. Explain why these newer communities cause Reich great concern. Note the weaknesses or advantages present in each case, and any possible solutions he might suggest, using comments in the text to support your ideas. Decide if you think these solutions offer a traditional or alternative view of communities.

Assignment 5

So the argument goes, without acknowledging that the critical assumption has already been made: "We" and "they" belong to fundamentally different communities.

—ROBERT REICH, *The Global Elite*

Robert Reich believes that the breakdown of the traditional form of community and its reconstitution along economic lines separates the "haves" from the "have-nots," dividing people along the lines of "us" and "them." Looking at the two more traditional communities presented in the texts by Edna O'Brien and William Least Heat-Moon, write a paper that uses Reich's framework of economic analysis to explain the presence or absence of these types of divisions within each community. Decide to what extent Reich's analysis could be used to explain the presence or absence of conflict in each community.

Begin with Reich's description of these "new" American communities and see if they in any way resemble the Irish community or the town of Cottonwood Falls. In both Least Heat-Moon's and O'Brien's texts, consider whether people in the communities see differences in economic status to be of primary or secondary importance in their relationships with other people. Although you don't have a detailed economic profile of each community, you do have enough information about Thurston and Biddy to decide how their economic status affects their relation to the community and if other factors are more or less important in defining their position in the community.

7

Environments of Prejudice

And there seemed to be no way whatever to remove this cloud that stood between them and the sun, between them and love and life and power, between them and whatever it was that they wanted. One did not have to be very bright to realize how little one could do to change one's situation; one did not have to be abnormally sensitive to be worn down to a cutting edge by the incessant and gratuitous humiliation and danger one encountered every working day, all day long.
—JAMES BALDWIN, *Whose Child Are You?*

"I want you to remember this if you wanna stay friends with Carl."
He looked at me as we drove alongside the river. "You gotta decide where you stand. You either decide never to hang around blacks for the rest of your life, or you decide you're going to stand by us and get ignored by whites. That's the choice."
—HARUHIKO YOSHIMEKI, *Learning the Language*

Not one thing escaped Vicki Koob's trained and cataloguing gaze. She made note of the cupboard that held only commodity flour and coffee. The unsanitary tin oil drum beneath the kitchen window, full of empty surplus pork cans and beer bottles, caught her eye as did Uncle Lawrence's physical and mental deteriorations. She quickly described these "benchmarks of alcoholic dependency within the extended family of Woodrow (Buddy) American Horse" as she walked around the room with the little notebook open, pushed against her belly to steady it.

—LOUISE ERDRICH, *American Horse*

I cannot tell you how angry it makes me to hear people from North America tell me how much they love England, how beautiful England is, with its traditions. All they see is some frumpy, wrinkled-up person passing by in a carriage waving at a crowd. But what I see is the millions of people, of whom I am just one, made orphans: no motherland, no fatherland, no gods, no mounds of earth for holy ground, no excess of love which might lead to the things that an excess of love sometimes brings, and worst and most painful of all, no tongue.

—JAMAICA KINCAID, *A Small Place*

Prejudgment, a term linked linguistically and etymologically to "prejudice," denotes an initial movement toward setting up categories based on race, gender, sex, age, ethnicity, or other characteristics. Prejudgment becomes prejudice when people are unable to adjust their ideas to recognize the individuality of people, seeing them in negative and derogatory ways. Prejudice can have devastating consequences. Unfortunately, it's easy to name many of its victims: the Jew in Nazi Germany, the Japanese American in the United States during World War II, the African American in Bensonhurst, the Caucasian American in riot-torn Los Angeles, or the foreign student in the Deep South.

The readings in this chapter examine the psychological, political, and economic grounds of prejudice and racism. They explore the way individual behavior can reflect the prejudice of society and politics, as well as the way individuals sometimes resist the prejudicial views imposed upon them.

Aware of the boundaries that bordered his neighborhood and the danger that threatened any African-American male who crossed them, James Baldwin, in "Whose Child Are You?," describes the fortunate choices that helped him survive in an environment from which few African-American males escaped unscarred.

Haruhiko Yoshimeki's experience in Louisiana makes it clear that all groups tend to look upon outsiders with prejudgment and prejudice. In an environment of prejudice, the mere appearance of an unfamiliar person can be interpreted as a hostile act, especially if that person has an unfamiliar appearance. The adults in Yoshimeki's narrative sense the danger of crossing clearly drawn boundaries. On the playground, between neighborhoods, or on the bus, the children learn to internalize their parents' fear.

The prejudice described in Louise Erdrich's story, "American Horse," is subtle and disguised. A social worker decides that Buddy's American Indian family is unable to care for him. But Erdrich knows that the social worker's judgment echoes the decisions of earlier European Americans to place American Indian children in boarding schools where knowledge of their own culture, considered inferior, was obliterated.

Growing up in Antigua, Jamaica Kincaid did not see, until much later, the conditions of prejudice that shaped her life. Her essay "A Small Place" conveys her childhood innocence, as well as her later realization that the "bad manners" of the English on Antigua were really an expression of their racism and prejudice. These authors reflect upon the ways in which encounters with prejudice affect individual lives. Considered together, the readings begin to develop a definition of the dynamics of prejudice.

JAMES BALDWIN

Whose Child Are You?

James Baldwin was born in Harlem, New York, in 1924. Along with his eight brothers and sisters, he grew up in great poverty in the Harlem ghetto, an experience that gave him the early desire to break out of his environment. Although he hated his stepfather, he was deeply impressed by his preaching, and he himself became a preacher at the Fireside Pentecostal Assembly after his conversion in 1938. In 1942, he completed high school and left the ministry, because he decided that religion did not provide any solutions to the problems of poor blacks. He dedicated himself to writing and received encouragement and support from Richard Wright—an already famous African-American writer. Baldwin's first book, *Go Tell It on the Mountain,* was published in 1953 and was based on his own early experiences. Subsequently, not only did he become an important spokesperson for African Americans and a civil rights activist, but he earned a place among the most important writers of the twentieth century as well. Baldwin spent many years in France, as an expatriate, and died there in 1987.

Baldwin's subjects, which derive from his own life and preoccupations, often focus on issues of race, politics, love, and homosexuality. His style reflects his earlier career as a preacher. Baldwin's works include novels, essays, plays, and a collection of short stories. This selection is from *The Fire Next Time* (1963), in which he uses his own childhood memories to describe the African-American experience. Baldwin looks back on his troubled adolescence with deeper understanding. His description of the neighborhood produces a vivid picture of what it meant to be an African-American teenager in the 1930s.

I UNDERWENT, DURING THE SUMMER that I became fourteen, a prolonged religious crisis. I use the word "religious" in the common, and arbitrary, sense, meaning that I then discovered God, His saints and angels, and His blazing Hell. And since I had been born in a Christian nation, I accepted this Deity as the only one. I supposed Him to exist only within the walls of a church—in fact, of *our* church—and I also supposed that God and safety were synonymous. The word "safety" brings us to the real meaning of the word "religious" as we use it. Therefore, to state it in another, more accurate way, I became, during my fourteenth year, for the first time in my life, afraid—afraid of the evil within me and afraid of the evil without. What I saw around me that summer in Harlem was what I had always seen; nothing had changed. But now, without any warning, the whores and pimps and racketeers on the Avenue had become a personal menace. It had not before occurred to me that I could become one of them, but now I realized that we had been produced by the same circumstances. Many of my comrades were clearly headed for the Avenue, and my father said that I was headed that way, too. My friends began to drink and smoke, and embarked—at first avid, then groaning—on their sexual careers. Girls, only slightly older than I was, who sang in the choir or taught Sunday school, the children of holy parents, underwent, before my eyes, their incredible metamorphosis, of which the most bewildering aspect was not their budding breasts or their rounding behinds but something deeper and more subtle, in their eyes, their heat, their odor, and the inflection of their voices. Like the strangers on the Avenue, they became, in the twinkling of an eye, unutterably different and fantastically *present*. Owing to the way I had been raised, the abrupt discomfort that all this aroused in me and the fact that I had no idea what my voice or my mind or my body was likely to do next caused me to consider myself one of the most depraved people on earth. Matters were not helped by the fact that these holy girls seemed rather to enjoy my terrified lapses, our grim, guilty, tormented experiments, which were at once as chill and joyless as the Russian steppes and hotter, by far, than all the fires of Hell.

Yet there was something deeper than these changes, and less definable, that frightened me. It was real in both the boys and the girls, but it was, somehow, more vivid in the boys. In the case of the girls, one watched them turning into matrons before they had become women. They began to manifest a curious and really rather terrifying single-mindedness. It is hard to say exactly how this was conveyed: something implacable in the set of the lips, something farseeing (seeing what?) in the eyes, some new and crushing determination in the walk, something peremptory in the voice. They did not tease us, the boys, any more; they reprimanded us sharply, saying, "You better be thinking about your soul!" For the girls also saw the evidence on the Avenue, knew what the price would be, for them, of one misstep, knew that they had to be protected and that we were the only protection there was. They understood that they must act as God's decoys, saving the souls of the boys for Jesus and binding the bodies of the boys in marriage. For this was the beginning of our burning time, and "It is better," said St. Paul—who elsewhere, with a most unusual and stunning exactness, described himself as a "wretched man"—"to marry than to burn." And I began to feel in the boys a curious, wary, bewildered despair, as though they were now settling in for the long, hard winter of life. I did not know then what it was that I was reacting to; I put it to myself that they were letting themselves go. In the same way that the girls were destined to gain as much weight as their mothers, the boys, it was clear, would rise no higher than their fathers. School began to reveal itself, therefore, as a child's game that one could not win, and boys dropped out of school and went to work. My father wanted me to do the same. I refused, even though I no longer had any illusions about what an education could do for me; I had already encountered too many college-graduate handymen. My friends were now "downtown," busy, as they put it, "fighting the man." They began to care less about the way they looked, the way they dressed, the things they did; presently, one found them in twos and threes and fours, in a hallway, sharing a jug of wine or a bottle of whiskey, talking, cursing, fighting, sometimes weeping: lost, and unable to say what it was that oppressed them, except that they knew it was "the man"—the white man. And there seemed to be no way whatever to remove this cloud that stood between them and the sun, between them and love and life and power, between them and whatever it was that they wanted. One did not have to be very bright to realize how little one could do to change one's situation; one did not have to be abnormally sensitive to be worn down to a cutting edge by the incessant and gratuitous humiliation and danger one encountered every working day, all day long. The humiliation did not apply merely to working days, or workers; I was thirteen and was crossing Fifth Avenue on my way to the Forty-second Street library, and the cop in the middle of the street muttered as I passed him, "Why don't you niggers stay uptown where you belong?" When I was ten, and didn't look, certainly, any older, two policemen amused themselves with me by frisking me, making comic (and terrifying) speculations concerning my ancestry and probable sexual prowess, and for good measure, leaving me flat on my back in one of Harlem's empty lots. Just before and then during the Second World War, many of my friends fled into the service, all to be changed there, and rarely for the better, many to be ruined, and many to die. Others fled to other states and cities—that is, to other ghettos. Some went on wine or whiskey or the needle, and are still on it. And others, like me, fled into the church.

For the wages of sin were visible everywhere, in every wine-stained and urine-splashed hallway, in every clanging ambulance bell, in every scar on the faces of the pimps and their whores, in every helpless, newborn baby being brought into this danger, in every knife and pistol fight on the Avenue, and in every disastrous bulletin: a cousin, mother of six, suddenly gone mad, the children parceled out here and there; an indestructible aunt rewarded for years of hard labor by a slow, agonizing death in a terrible small room; someone's bright son blown into eternity by his own hand; another turned robber and carried off to jail. It was a summer of dreadful speculations and discoveries, of which these were not the worst. Crime became real, for example—for the first time—not as *a* possibility but as *the* possibility. One would never defeat one's circumstances by working and saving one's pennies; one would never, by working, acquire that many pennies, and, besides, the social treatment accorded even the most successful Negroes proved that one needed, in order to be free, something more than a bank account. One needed a handle, a lever, a means of inspiring fear. It was absolutely clear that the police would whip you and take you in as long as they could get away with it, and that everyone else—housewives, taxi drivers, elevator boys, dishwashers, bartenders, lawyers, judges, doctors, and grocers—would never, by the operation of any generous human feeling, cease to use you as an outlet for his frustrations and hostilities. Neither civilized reason nor Christian love would cause any of those people to treat you as they presumably wanted to be treated; only the fear of your power to retaliate would cause them to do that, or to seem to do it, which was (and is) good enough. There appears to be a vast amount of confusion on this point, but I do not know many Negroes who are eager to be "accepted" by white people, still less to be loved by them; they, the blacks, simply don't wish to be beaten over the head by the whites every instant of our brief passage on this planet. White people in this country will have quite enough to do in learning how to accept and love themselves and each other, and when they have achieved this—which will not be tomorrow and may very well be never—the Negro problem will no longer exist, for it will no longer be needed.

People more advantageously placed than we in Harlem were, and are, will no doubt find the psychology and the view of human nature sketched above dismal and shocking in the extreme. But the Negro's experience of the white world cannot possibly create in him any respect for the standards by which the white world claims to live. His own condition is overwhelming proof that white people do not live by these standards. Negro servants have been smuggling odds and ends out of white homes for generations, and white people have been delighted to have them do it, because it has assuaged a dim guilt and testified to the intrinsic superiority of white people. Even the most doltish and servile Negro could scarcely fail to be impressed by the disparity between his situation and that of the people for whom he worked; Negroes who were neither doltish nor servile did not feel that they were doing anything wrong when they robbed white people. In spite of the Puritan-Yankee equation of virtue with well-being, Negroes had excellent reasons for doubting that money was made or kept by any very striking adherence to the Christian virtues; it certainly did not work that way for black Christians. In any case, white people, who had robbed black people of their liberty and who profited by this theft every hour that they lived, had no moral ground on which to stand. They had the judges, the juries, the shotguns, the law—in a word, power. But it was a criminal power, to be feared but not respected, and to be outwitted in any way whatever. And those virtues preached but not practiced by the white world were merely another means of holding Negroes in subjection.

It turned out, then, that summer, that the moral barriers that I had sup- 5
posed to exist between me and the dangers of a criminal career were so tenu-
ous as to be nearly nonexistent. I certainly could not discover any principled
reason for not becoming a criminal, and it is not my poor, God-fearing parents who are to be indicted for the lack but this society. I was icily determined—more determined, really, than I then knew—never to make my peace
with the ghetto but to die and go to Hell before I would let any white man spit
on me, before I would accept my "place" in this republic. I did not intend to
allow the white people of this country to tell me who I was, and limit me that
way, and polish me off that way. And yet, of course, at the same time, I *was*
being spat on and defined and described and limited, and could have been
polished off with no effort whatever. Every Negro boy—in my situation during those years, at least—who reaches this point realizes, at once, profoundly,
because he wants to live, that he stands in great peril and must find, with
speed, a "thing," a gimmick, to lift him out, to start him on his way. *And it
does not matter what the gimmick is.* It was this last realization that terrified
me and—since it revealed that the door opened on so many dangers—helped
to hurl me into the church. And, by an unforeseeable paradox, it was my
career in the church that turned out, precisely, to be my gimmick.

For when I tried to assess my capabilities, I realized that I had almost
none. In order to achieve the life I wanted, I had been dealt, it seemed to me,
the worst possible hand. I could not become a prizefighter—many of us tried
but very few succeeded. I could not sing. I could not dance. I had been well
conditioned by the world in which I grew up, so I did not yet dare take the
idea of becoming a writer seriously. The only other possibility seemed to involve my becoming one of the sordid people on the Avenue, who were not
really as sordid as I then imagined but who frightened me terribly, both because I did not want to live that life and because of what they made me feel.
Everything inflamed me, and that was bad enough, but I myself had also become a source of fire and temptation. I had been far too well raised, alas, to
suppose that any of the extremely explicit overtures made to me that summer,
sometimes by boys and girls but also, more alarmingly, by older men and
women, had anything to do with my attractiveness. On the contrary, since the
Harlem idea of seduction is, to put it mildly, blunt, whatever these people saw
in me merely confirmed my sense of my depravity.

It is certainly sad that the awakening of one's senses should lead to such
a merciless judgment of oneself—to say nothing of the time and anguish one
spends in the effort to arrive at any other—but it is also inevitable that a literal
attempt to mortify the flesh should be made among black people like those
with whom I grew up. Negroes in this country—and Negroes do not, strictly
or legally speaking, exist in any other—are taught really to despise themselves
from the moment their eyes open on the world. This world is white and they
are black. White people hold the power, which means that they are superior

to blacks (intrinsically, that is: God decreed it so), and the world has innumerable ways of making this difference known and felt and feared. Long before the Negro child perceives this difference, and even longer before he understands it, he has begun to react to it, he has begun to be controlled by it. Every effort made by the child's elders to prepare him for a fate from which they cannot protect him causes him secretly, in terror, to begin to await, without knowing that he is doing so, his mysterious and inexorable punishment. He must be "good" not only in order to please his parents and not only to avoid being punished by them; behind their authority stands another, nameless and impersonal, infinitely harder to please, and bottomlessly cruel. And this filters into the child's consciousness through his parents' tone of voice as he is being exhorted, punished, or loved; in the sudden, uncontrollable note of fear heard in his mother's or his father's voice when he has strayed beyond some particular boundary. He does not know what the boundary is, and he can get no explanation of it, which is frightening enough, but the fear he hears in the voices of his elders is more frightening still. The fear that I heard in my father's voice, for example, when he realized that I really *believed* I could do anything a white boy could do, and had every intention of proving it, was not at all like the fear I heard when one of us was ill or had fallen down the stairs or strayed too far from the house. It was another fear, a fear that the child, in challenging the white world's assumptions, was putting himself in the path of destruction. A child cannot, thank Heaven, know how vast and how merciless is the nature of power, with what unbelievable cruelty people treat each other. He reacts to the fear in his parents' voices because his parents hold up the world for him and he has no protection without them. I defended myself, as I imagined, against the fear my father made me feel by remembering that he was very old-fashioned. Also, I prided myself on the fact that I already knew how to outwit him. To defend oneself against a fear is simply to insure that one will, one day, be conquered by it; fears must be faced. As for one's wits, it is just not true that one can live by them—not, that is, if one wishes really to live. That summer, in any case, all the fears with which I had grown up, and which were now a part of me and controlled my vision of the world, rose up like a wall between the world and me, and drove me into the church.

As I look back, everything I did seems curiously deliberate, though it certainly did not seem deliberate then. For example, I did not join the church of which my father was a member and in which he preached. My best friend in school, who attended a different church, had already "surrendered his life to the Lord," and he was very anxious about my soul's salvation. (I wasn't, but any human attention was better than none.) One Saturday afternoon, he took me to his church. There were no services that day, the church was empty, except for some women cleaning and some other women praying. My friend took me into the back room to meet his pastor—a woman. There she sat, in her robes, smiling, an extremely proud and handsome woman, with Africa,

Europe, and the America of the American Indian blended in her face. She was perhaps forty-five or fifty at this time, and in our world she was a very celebrated woman. My friend was about to introduce me when she looked at me and smiled and said, "Whose little boy are you?" Now this, unbelievably, was precisely the phrase used by pimps and racketeers on the Avenue when they suggested, both humorously and intensely, that I "hang out" with them. Perhaps part of the terror they had caused me to feel came from the fact that I unquestionably wanted to be *somebody's* little boy. I was so frightened, and at the mercy of so many conundrums, that inevitably, that summer, *someone* would have taken me over; one doesn't, in Harlem, long remain standing on any auction block. It was my good luck—perhaps—that I found myself in the church racket instead of some other, and surrendered to a spiritual seduction long before I came to any carnal knowledge. For when the pastor asked me, with that marvelous smile, "Whose little boy are you?" my heart replied at once, "Why, yours."

Considerations

1. In this selection Baldwin discusses those experiences of his youth which led him to surrender himself to religion. Adolescence itself confronted him with many questions, but his problems are not generated only by age. What other factors contribute to his confusion? How do all these factors relate to each other?

2. Did Baldwin's religious devotion survive his adolescence? Look for passages in the text which indicate whether, at the time when he writes, he is still a believer. Is his adult attitude to religion what you would have expected? What in the text encourages you to form such an expectation?

Invitation to Write

Baldwin describes the summer when he was fourteen as "a summer of dreadful speculations and discoveries" (para. 3). Comparing his experience with what you would consider a typical adolescent experience today, write an essay about his discoveries and the way they determine his choices. How much influence does the social environment have on the choices an adolescent makes?

Connections

One of the purposes of Baldwin's essay is to explain the difficult choices he was forced to make in order to survive adolescence. Louise J. Kaplan's essay, "Adolescence: The Farewell to Childhood (p. 107)," also discusses the types of choices adolescents make and the consequences such choices have on a person's development. She comes close to describing Baldwin's experience in her statement: "When obedience to the authority of the social order leaves no room for the expression of personal power or a sense of moral dignity, we feel less than we might be—we feel false to ourselves" (para. 56). How does Baldwin's decision to rebel against paternal authority illustrate Kaplan's argument that adolescent rebellion can be a positive reaction? Write an essay in which you discuss Baldwin's experiences in Kaplan's conceptual frame. You can expand the discussion to define the role of adolescent rebellion in social change.

HARUHIKO YOSHIMEKI

Learning the Language

Haruhiko Yoshimeki was born in Odawara, Japan, in 1957. He came to the United States in 1965, when his father was offered a visiting professorship at Louisiana State University. Going to school in Baton Rouge, Yoshimeki got acquainted with the racial prejudices of the region. Later he returned with his family to Japan. Yoshimeki has written two novels. The first, *Zipangu,* published in 1986, won *Gunzo* magazine's New Novelist Award. Yoshimeki's second novel, *Louisiana Pile Driving,* based on his life, was published in Japan by *Gunzo* magazine in March 1989. Later both novels were published together in one volume.

"Learning the Language," the first translation of Yoshimeki's work in the United States, originally appeared in *Ploughshares* magazine in 1990 under the title "From *Louisiana Pile Driving.*" Translated by Etsuko Takahashi and Don Lee, this excerpt recalls Yoshimeki's experiences at an elementary school in Louisiana from 1965 to 1967, years when desegregation laws went into effect in the United States. The Japanese youngster has to contend not only with the bigotry of the locals but also with the difficulty of deciding what side to be on in the ongoing racial conflict of the town.

IN 1965, WHEN I WAS NINE, my father moved us from Japan to Baton Rouge, Louisiana. He had been an exchange student at Louisiana State University years ago, and now LSU had invited him to be a visiting professor in the agriculture department.

We rented an apartment near campus, across the street from a grove of wild berries. Long ago someone had tried to plant a garden of crape myrtles there, but the garden had been overwhelmed by the berries, thousands of dense, entangled runners. Every weekday morning, I would crawl through a narrow tunnel in the grove—a shortcut to the other side—looking at the stitch pattern of shadows. I would emerge in the backyard of the Protestant church and wait for the school bus with the other children.

I attended Louisiana State University Terrace Elementary School, which had some rather strict rules of behavior. On the school bus, boys were to sit on the left side, girls on the right. Recess on the spacious school grounds was

317

segregated as well, with the basketball court as the demarcation area. Once, I got into trouble because I had inadvertently wandered into forbidden territory, and my father was summoned by the principal.

"Doctor," the lady principal said, "I'm certainly not discouraging him from being friends with the other children, *all* of them. Just the opposite. But in order for him to do that, he must adhere to the rules, and, of course, he really must learn the language. Don't you think he should learn the language? I imagine it must be so inconvenient for him, not knowing the language."

My father promised her he would see to it that I learned the language. He had his own opinions about the rules of behavior, the unique and strict morality of the people, in Baton Rouge. "Americans call it the Bible Belt," he tried to explain. One time my mother had helped his colleague's wife put on a kimono for a party. "They're from Michigan," he said. "Had she been born and raised by a good family in Louisiana, she wouldn't let even a woman touch her body." 5

My homeroom teacher gave me an American name, Harry, and told me not to use my real name from that point on because it was a Japanese word. My first lesson in English was to memorize the Pledge of Allegiance to the American flag. Every morning, all the students had to stand up and make an oath to the Star-Spangled Banner, which hung at the upper left side of the chalkboard. "I pledge allegiance to the flag of the United States of America, and the Republic for which it stands, one nation under God, indivisible, with liberty and justice for all." It seemed like an extremely odd ritual. When I told my parents about it, my mother laughed and said that she had had to do the same sort of thing for the Japanese flag when she and her family had lived in Taiwan during the war.

Terrace Elementary School, supposedly a more liberal institution because it was part of the university, was nearly all white for my first two years there. Twenty-some students were in my class, and of those, only two were black. In the entire school, from the first to ninth grades, there were a total of only five or six black children.

One of the black students in my class was the son of a minister, and the other one's father managed a used car dealership. Both boys wore stiffly starched white shirts, ties, and well-polished leather shoes to school every day. They looked wonderful, better than any of the white kids, when they arrived at school in the morning, but they looked pretty miserable when they left in the afternoon, dirty and disheveled from having to wear the clothes while playing basketball in gym class or softball during lunch break.

Theodore Henderson, the car dealer's son, told us once that some men from the Chamber of Commerce were harassing his father. "They say they'll destroy the company so I can't come to school anymore. 'Mr. Martel, we're not doing anything wrong,' my dad says, and they go, 'Look, slave, don't you dare even think about wanting an ordinary life.' You believe it? They called him *slave!*"

Ted was a cocky kid, maybe given to a bit of exaggeration. He knew how   10
we'd react to the story, and he was enjoying the attention, smirking a little.

I believed him, though. "What are you going to do?" I asked, horrified.

One of the girls nudged me. She told me to drop the subject, not to get
involved. As a Southern Protestant, she felt she had an obligation to tutor me
on the correct standards of Louisiana life.

The teachers—especially the white female ones—were extremely tough
on Ted and the other boy. The women were older and quite experienced as
educators, but they were, people said, strictly opposed to the civil rights
movement. Whenever one of the boys couldn't answer a question or made a
minor error, the teachers would chastise him harshly. They called the boys
lazy, said they lacked concentration. They often told them they were a negative influence on the other students.

I didn't feel particularly self-conscious about being an Asian until a young
Army officer came to visit our school one day. It was in the middle of the
Vietnam War; it must have been about a year after we had moved to Baton
Rouge, since by then I had learned the language and could understand him.

People often ask me what kinds of things I saw or heard in Louisiana   15
during that time. They want to know about protests, sit-ins, draft cards being
burned. The truth is, I hardly remember a thing. It was, I guess, pretty quiet
at LSU, since the lecture by the young officer is practically my sole memory of
anything related to the Vietnam War.

All the students were assembled in the high-ceilinged cafeteria, and we
were treated to orange sherbet, compliments of the military. Then the officer
began his lecture. "Hello, boys and girls of Louisiana State University Terrace
Elementary School," he boomed. "I just came back from a place called Saigon
last month. Before that, I was in Chu Lai. I assume you have never heard
those names before. Those cities are in a country called Vietnam, and I was
fighting a war in Vietnam. I'm here today to explain why we are fighting that
war.

"First of all, war isn't as horrible as you might think. Even in the jungle,
I had McDonald's hamburgers for lunch. Of course, personally, I prefer
Burger King, but you can't have everything."

All the students in the cafeteria laughed, so I did, too.

"When we're in the jungle, U.S. Army helicopters bring us everything we
need, including all our meals, which are delicious. They are called C rations.
Of course, we don't have TVs, so we can't watch *The Green Hornet* or *Mission: Impossible,* but otherwise we live a pretty ordinary life, just like you're
living with your mommy and daddy. The only difference I can think of is that
we have a task to fight to enemy.

"The Vietnamese are good people, but they're very stupid. These Asians   20
are about to be deprived of their homes, their money, even their lives by the
Communists, but they can't defend themselves. They're cowards. They're

weaklings, loose and slack. These Asians are so slack, they don't take baths at all, and they're always stinky. Can you imagine that? They can't even take care of their own bodies! Asian people are just not capable of improving themselves unless we Americans look after them. It's an obligation and responsibility that we Americans have, and we should feel proud of ourselves for bearing this task."

Each time the officer mentioned the word *Asian,* several kids turned around and looked at me. There was one other Asian in the school, an Indian boy, but no one looked at him.

"Don't worry," Joan Elkins said, patting my hand. "None of us think you're an Asian."

I asked Mr. Rody, one of my father's assistants in the laboratory, if eventually I would have to go to Vietnam if we stayed in America. Mr. Rody was a big, cheerful man, the son of a Texas rancher; he was always kind to me, took me to places with his wife Jane on holidays.

"Who suggested such a thing?" Mr. Rody asked.

I told him and Jane about the young officer's lecture.   25

Jane sighed. "Do you have any reason to fight the Vietnamese?" she asked me.

I said I really didn't understand what the Vietnamese were.

"Me neither," Jane said.

Then Mr. Rody started talking about the Mexicans who crossed the border into Texas. "I'm always telling your father to visit my parents' ranch. Then you could see for yourself. They wander around with their entire family and set up tents in the rocks. They're always making all kinds of trouble, stealing cows even. You know what happens then?" He lifted his hands, squinted one eye, and imitated the sound of a rifle report.

I asked him if the Mexicans were similar to the Vietnamese.   30

"I'm not exactly sure," he said.

Machiko-San

She couldn't speak any English at all, although she had been living in Baton Rouge for almost five years. She rented a house along a bank of the Mississippi River, an isolated residential area for whites who had come to the state to start fresh. Once these people obtained jobs, they moved to better neighborhoods as soon as they could, but Machiko remained.

She said she was from Niigata, an industrial seaport in Central Honshu, but my mother suspected she was actually from a very rural area, somewhere outside of the city, because Machiko used an expression which was indigenous to farmers. My mother's own family had been poor. She had grown up on a farm near Namie, Fukushima, and as a little girl she had heard people call cooked rice either *hito-take* or *futa-take* (first-cooked, second-cooked).

Even today, whenever Machiko's name comes up, Mother still makes a point of saying that Machiko must have been from a very rural area, citing those phrases, *hito-take, futa-take,* a distinction between fresh rice and recooked rice which only peasants need to make.

Machiko had met her husband, a pilot in the U.S. Air Force who was stationed in Japan, during the Korean War. They had four children, a boy and three girls, and then her husband died in a training accident. Machiko came to Baton Rouge to seek the support of her in-laws, but they refused her. They wouldn't admit a Japanese as a member of their family. Eventually they moved to Arkansas to evade her. Nonetheless, Machiko decided to stay in America, living off the benefits provided by the Air Force.

"It's too difficult for a woman with four children of mixed race to live in   35
Japan," she said.

I thought it strange that she couldn't speak English.

"I used to understand it, more or less, but I've forgotten it all now," she told me.

I think she had simply decided to refuse the United States of America and everything about it, including its language, just as she had been refused. She would take the Air Force benefits, which were her due, but nothing else.

As soon as Machiko sent her children off to school in the morning, she would lock all the doors in the house and shut herself inside all day, waiting for them to return. Occasionally, in the evenings, she ventured out to do some shopping, but she needed an interpreter even for that simple task, and she didn't have a car, so she would have to enlist someone's help. She spent most of her time on the telephone.

She would call my mother or Yoko and Yukie, the two other war brides   40
in Baton Rouge, and she would talk and talk. Once she started, she didn't quit for three or four hours.

"She's such a drag," Yoko would say.

In the beginning of the summer in 1967, a group from the prefectural assembly visited my father. The group, whose members belonged to the Opposition Party, had been invited to come to LSU by the Ministry of Agriculture and Forestry in Japan. On the last day of their visit, war brides became the topic of conversation at dinner. The assembly members said American soldiers who married yellow only chose yellow because they couldn't get anyone to marry them in America. It was a national shame that Japanese women succumbed to them, they said. Children of mixed race were a "symbol of the disgrace of the war," they said. The assembly members were relatively intelligent people, but they were in a cavalier mood—it was their last day, and they had completed all their work.

My father kicked them out of the house.

The Ministry of Agriculture and Forestry subsequently received some complaints. My father was an entomologist, specializing in insects which harmed rice plants, and he had hoped to be a leader in this field of research. Eventually, he was forced to find another vocation.

I don't remember much about Machiko's three daughters—one was named Cindy, another Lucy, the third's I've forgotten—but Lenny, the son, the first-born, I remember very well. Whenever we went to New Orleans, my father invited Machiko's family to accompany us, which made for a tight squeeze in the car, and my father liked having Lenny beside him as he drove, liked talking to him. Everyone—my parents, Yoko, Yukie—said Lenny was a loving, devoted son. He was always there for Machiko when something happened, when something important had to be decided.

I didn't like him. Around his neighborhood, little kids collected scrap for pocket change, and I heard Lenny extorted money from them to give to his sisters. "He's just like a little *yakuza*, a gangster," I told my father.

My father told me that there were many things I could learn from Lenny, that maybe I should hang around him more. I knew there was a deeper meaning to this suggestion, but I still didn't like Lenny.

The last time I talked to him was in 1971. We were living in Bangkok then, and one night he called my father. Lucy had been hit by a car. It hadn't looked like she was seriously injured, so Machiko signed an affidavit to receive $2,000, admitting that Lucy had ignored the red light as she was crossing the street. The truth was, the driver had ignored the light. Lenny had tried to keep Machiko from signing the affidavit, but Machiko had insisted they needed the money for Lucy's medical bills. Now, six months later, the vision in Lucy's left eye was failing. Because of the affidavit, no lawyer would take the case. As a last resort, Lenny had called my father, who would go out of his way to help, contacting his old colleagues at LSU.

I got on the phone with Lenny that night. "What's going on? What happened?" I asked him.

"Nothing," he said coldly.

I remember him telling me something once. "I know what you Japanese think of my mom," he had said to me.

We haven't heard from Machiko or her family since then. I don't know how they're doing at all.

Black School

University Lake extended from the campus to the Protestant church near our apartment. On the campus shore was an arbor and a small, vaguely Oriental-looking garden. I had no idea what country in the Orient had such gardens.

"It's Japanese, of course," Mr. Rody, my father's assistant in the laboratory, said. "You've seen them in Japan, haven't you?"

Professor Newsome, who was the chairman of the agriculture department, thought it was a Chinese garden.

"It looks like Thai to me," my father said. "It's not Japanese, that's for sure."

Beside the arbor was a swamp, and from the yard of the Protestant church I could see a house trailer on a little patch of solid ground there—an island of sorts. An old white couple lived in the trailer. Mr. Rody told me they were Communists, antiwar activists. "They're afraid the military'll get them. They's why they're living there. If they need to escape, they can just jump in the lake," he laughed.

I asked Mr. Rody what the people did for work.

"Collect empty bottles to sell. Fish in the lake."

"That's all?"   60

"Yup. That's all."

My mother said she'd never seen any real Communists before. When they showed the hippies on the West Coast on TV, I thought they were Communists.

On the north side of the lake, on a little hill, was a city park. We were about half an hour from the closest black quarter, and most of the time, we hardly saw any blacks around the area at all. But once a month or so, groups of them (they never came alone) would show up at the park for barbecues. The congregation would swell, eventually number in the thousands, or so it seemed. Every time it happened, all the whites disappeared. The parties were lively, lasting until midnight on the hill surrounded by trees. The following morning, a garbage truck would be specially dispatched to pick up the refuse.

"If there weren't that many of them, they might get hurt," my father told me.

I was confused. What did he mean?   65

"This is that kind of place," he said.

My mother repeatedly warned me not to go to the park when the blacks were having their barbecues. "When there's only one person of a different race," she said, "there's no telling what might happen."

People often inquire about the racism in Louisiana. I usually say that it's true, it was severe. We saw and heard of many incidents, some of which had an indirect influence on us, but we were never badly harmed. I probably faced more discrimination when I returned to Japan—a foreigner in my own country. Except for on TV, I never saw the KKK. Even in Louisiana, I have to tell people, they don't put on white hoods and costumes and just walk around. Some are disappointed to hear this. There's always that tendency, I suppose, to think of the United States, especially the Deep South, as a place of significant and profound meaning.

After two years, the white school I attended turned into a black school. I didn't know about the change until I started the new semester. Over the summer, the school policies had been amended, relaxing the admission standards, and the residents of the black quarter rushed to enroll their children: Lunch cost only a dollar-fifty, and their kids could study where the white kids studied. What happened at the city park happened at Terrace Elementary School. Nearly all the white kids transferred out to private schools.

My father had heard about the policy change, but he hadn't expected   70
things to become so extreme. Professor Everett and his other colleagues tried to find a white school for me, but they were all full by that time. I stayed at Terrace.

I looked at my new classmates with curiosity. Compared to white girls, black girls seemed much more precocious, appeared to know much about life. They teased me shamelessly, putting their hands on their waists and wiggling their hips at me. The male students quickly established a hierarchical order of bosses, who never seemed to change expressions, a *Noh*-mask for a face, and who spoke in low, barely understandable voices.

Once, our homeroom teacher had her car keys stolen during lunch. Mrs. Bush was a beautiful blond-haired lady from Alabama, a graduate student at the university, a recent bride. Carrying art supplies from her car to the building, she had left her keys in the car door, and when she came back, they were gone. She thought someone in our geology class, where she was having discipline problems, had taken them to spite her.

That afternoon, as she stretched to hang a map over the chalkboard, a student snapped a rubber band at her, hitting her slip, which peeked out from her skirt. She whipped around, her face reddening. "What'd you do that for?" she screamed. "Why, you junkyard dogs!"

She glared at the black kids. "Give me my keys. They're mine. I said give them to me!"

No one said a word. Mrs. Bush started pacing between the students'   75
desks. Directly outside the window, a squirrel on an oak tree shook the Spanish moss, which resembled gray rags, and the classroom resounded with the dry little noise.

Suddenly Darcy May, who was sitting in the back said, "Cedric, what were you doing by Mrs. Bush's car, anyway?"

Mrs. Bush pleaded, "Darcy May, please tell me what you know."

"I'd forgotten about it," the girl said, "but I just remembered—"

Cedric Smith ran from his front seat and slapped Darcy May in the face.

"Stop that right now!" Mrs. Bush said, grabbing Cedric's arm. "You're   80
coming with me to the principal's office."

After they left, a boy, one of the bosses, said to Darcy May, "You know what's going to happen, don't you? We can't do nothing at school, but we'll get you, you can be sure of that. We'll strip you of all your clothes and make you walk down the street, all naked."

"You might as well take off her panties, too," a girl said. "Show her cunt so no man will ever care for her."

Darcy May began crying.

I don't know if they really did such a horrible thing to her, but something like that happened nearly every day. It wasn't rare to see torn clothes, noses or mouths bleeding. I couldn't believe these were the fights of elementary school students. There were both male and female gangs, and they were very exclusive. The school had not been an exclusive place when it had been a white school.

I became friendly with a black boy named Richard. I've forgotten his last name, but I remember that everyone called him by his middle name, Carl. He said he had a second middle name as well. He seemed so proud of all his names, I imagined he recited the entire list whenever he was introduced to anyone.

Carl was considered harmless. He didn't belong to any of the gangs, and no one took him seriously. He carried around a box with his collection of miniature cars inside, and during recess he would open the box and line the cars up in a row, beaming. He was always congenial to me, except for the one time I asked him what his father did: He said he owned a shoe store and then told me not to ask anything more.

After school one day, I rode with him in his mother's car to visit their house in the black quarter. They lived on a gentle slope behind a tall building which was under construction. All the houses were flat and wooden, in disarray, spread out to hug the shore of the river, painted either white or turquoise.

There was a skinny lady with white hair sitting on Carl's porch. She stared at me. "Who is that?" she asked sharply.

"A friend of mine," Carl said.

"From school?"

"Yeah. He's Japanese."

"Who cares," she said.

Carl told me the woman was his grandmother and that she had been a dancer as a young woman.

"Tell Becky to get rid of that honeycomb," she yelled as we opened the screen door to the house. "You got to get on her or she'll never do it."

"I've got three sisters. Becky's the oldest. She's a big pain in the butt," Carl said.

He showed me his collection of cars. I had a keen interest in automobiles when I lived in America. Both Carl and I liked the old-fashioned models, big, showy ones with fins, and he had quite a few miniatures of them. Some of the small towns outside of Baton Rouge held demolition derbies, cars with all kinds of stickers and decorations performing battle royal, and it seemed a shame to me a crash those great, old-fashioned finned models.

As Carl and I were looking at his collection, people gathered at the door. Some even entered his room, which smelled like paint thinner, to scrutinize me.

"He's Japanese," his grandmother said. "Could you tell? Looks like a Chinese, but I knew he was Japanese from the first moment I saw him."

Carl smirked. His grandmother had rounded up the neighbors for a look-see at the Asian boy.

In the meantime, my mother and father had found out I'd gone to the black quarter. All the elementary school students were supposed to take the bus unless their parents were picking them up, and the school bus driver had noticed I was missing. The principal asked if anyone knew where I was.

"Harry? He went off with Carl," someone said. Several students had seen me getting into Carl's mother's car. The principal called my mother, who couldn't really understand what was being said. Her English was never that good. She knew enough, though, to be alarmed, and she tried to reach my father at the laboratory. He wasn't available; he was in the middle of a lecture. She contacted Professor Kim, a Korean who knew Japanese. He learned what was going on and alerted my father.

Professor Newsome was furious. He had Mr. Rody and Jane recruit some black students, thinking they'd be helpful when they came to fetch me in the black quarter. He also called the police. Later, he severely scolded me, saying the police officer had yelled to him, "What kind of child is this?"

But by that time, I was on my way home. Carl's grandmother had summoned the rest of the family to take a look at me, and Carl's brother-in-law, who'd just finished working at the ice cream factory, immediately voiced concern.

"This is not good," he said. "The police'll bug us about this."

"But he's Carl's classmate," Carl's grandmother said. "And besides, he's not even white."

"Yeah, I'm not white," I said.

"It don't matter, it's not gonna do us any good," he said, looking at me.

He drove me home, or close to my home (he told me it was a little difficult for him to go into my neighborhood and dropped me off nearby). He gave me a note for my parents, which explained that my going there had been an unfortunate, careless mistake, and all parties concerned should be careful not to let it happen again.

Everyone was grateful that I was safe. Professor Kim even admired the responsibility shown by Carl's brother-in-law, but Professor Newsome was exasperated, angrier than I'd ever seen him. He had urged my father to transfer me to a white school from the start. "I never thought you could be such a fool," he said.

My father told him he had taught me to treat blacks no differently than anyone else, like he did.

"You should've taught him not to associate with them at all, not to talk to them even if they talk to him," Professor Newsome said. "That's what you have to do if he's going to go to a school with black kids."

"My son isn't going to spend the rest of his life in Louisiana. Isn't that a little too much to ask of him?"

"Listen, don't disparage our customs. I've never disparaged yours, have I?" Professor Newsome told him. "What you just said isn't relevant, anyway. Can't you understand what kind of danger your son was in?"

My mother put the ice cream which Carl's brother-in-law had given to me into the trash can.

I thought about the conversation I had had with the brother-in-law on the drive home. He had asked me why I hadn't switched schools like everyone else. "All the other white kids switched schools, didn't they?"

"There's still some white kids there. Not that many, though." The few children remaining hadn't been able to afford a transfer.

"What about you? Why didn't your parents get you out?"

"I'm not really sure. I guess they didn't think there'd be so many black kids all of a sudden. I guess they didn't think they really had to move me to another school."

He turned on the radio. Nat King Cole sang "Time and the River." The brother-in-law was silent for a while, then asked, "How long is your family gonna stay here? You gonna live here forever?"

"We're going back to Japan sometime. I don't know when exactly."

"Well, this isn't my job, it's your parents', but I want to tell you something. I want you to remember this if you wanna stay friends with Carl." He looked at me as we drove alongside the river. "You gotta decide where you stand. You either decide never to hang around blacks for the rest of your life, or you decide you're going to stand by us and get ignored by whites. That's the choice. You have to choose one or the other. You have to make up your mind. You can't take both. You make a decision by tomorrow. Let's say if you decide never to talk to Carl—that's okay, that can't be helped. I'll talk to Carl about it."

"Why do I have to decide?"

"Because being neutral's the worst thing you can do. You're unfair to everybody, being neutral."

"I wanna stay friends with Carl."

"All right, but if I hear you're still hanging around with the white kids, too, I'll tell Carl never to talk to you again."

The ice cream on my lap was melting, the condensation dripping onto my pants. "I still don't understand why I have to decide," I said.

He thought for a moment. "Have you ever been to New Orleans?" he asked.

"We go there once or twice a month."

"There's a city bus there. You ever take it?"

"No."

"I figured. You see, only blacks and poor whites use them, and on the bus, blacks have to give up their seats for the whites when the bus gets full. That's the rule. When it's full, blacks have to stand up. It's determined by law. What would you do?"

"What do you mean?"

"You're on the bus, and you've got a seat. It starts to get crowded, and it's full now. Would you stand up?"

"No, I wouldn't."

"Then you're on the whites' side. We consider you white, understand? This is the funny thing, though," he told me. "If you stood up, the whites would treat you like a black. I guess you just can't win, but it don't matter. If you live in America, you got no choice. You gotta decide. You gotta choose one way or the other." 135

Considerations

1. At different points in Yoshimeki's account, people of one race make comments about people of other races. Find two or three examples of such comments and decide whether you would consider them to be racist. How do you define the term *racist* and how do you explain your decision to use or not use this term when discussing your examples?

2. In the beginning of his essay, Yoshimeki remembers the school principal who tells his father that Harry "must adhere to the rules, and, of course, he really must learn the language" (para. 4). Although he eventually learns English, Yoshimeki has more difficulty learning the language of cultural codes—the "rules." How would you account for Yoshimeki's difficulty in learning to adjust to the cultural conventions of life in Louisiana?

Invitation to Write

In "Learning the Language," Yoshimeki describes his experience of coming to terms with life in a culture different from his own, one that appears to be complicated by its division along racial lines. Yoshimeki's narrative records his first encounters with situations in which the differences among people are pointed out to him. These teachings seem absurd by comparison with young Yoshimeki's own perceptions, which are not determined by prejudice. Write an essay in which you analyze the ways his experiences taught Yoshimeki about prejudice. Then think of the ways we all encounter cultural differences and are taught about them, comparing your examples to Yoshimeki's experience. From your comparison, reach a general conclusion about how racial attitudes are culturally determined.

Connections

As a newcomer to Louisiana, Yoshimeki doesn't understand the behavior and attitudes he observes among the adults and children of both races. For example, he does not believe the behavior of the African-American children in his class was appropriate to their ages, and he does not understand why some territories, such as the park or Carl's house, are forbidden to whites and himself. Although he suffers discrimination from the whites, he has difficulty identifying with, or even making sense of, the African Americans' behavior. In the preceding essay, "Whose Child Are You?," Baldwin writes about experiencing racism as a child from an African-American point of view. Write an essay in which you use Baldwin's insights into African-American experience to explain the attitudes and values that Yoshimeki, as a child, cannot understand.

LOUISE ERDRICH

American Horse

Louise Erdrich was born in Little Falls, North Dakota, in 1954. Her father's family is German American, and her mother's is Turtle Mountain Chippewa. Erdrich graduated from Dartmouth College in 1976 and has a master's degree in creative writing from Johns Hopkins University.

Erdrich had already published two stories when "The World's Greatest Fisherman," a story she submitted to a national competition, won the Nelson Algren Award in 1982. Later this story became the first chapter in *Love Medicine*, which was named the best work of fiction by the National Book Critics Circle in 1984. Erdrich often works in collaboration with her husband, Michael Dorris, but they usually publish their books under one author's name. Their recent work, *The Crown of Columbus* (1991), is an exception in that it is signed by both. Erdrich's books include two volumes of poetry and the novels *Love Medicine* (1984), *The Beet Queen* (1986), and *Tracks* (1988), which are the first three parts of a family saga.

The following short story will be part of the saga's final volume called *American Horse*. "American Horse" was first published in 1983 and was reprinted in Paula Gunn Allen's anthology *Spider Woman's Granddaughter* (1989). Allen reads this story as a reworking of traditional narratives involving the theft of a miraculous child, a wicked witch, and trickery. She also sees a parallel between the story's last scene and legends in which the evil Raven enthralls his victims by making them eat. Allen notes that in the legends, such victims can escape if they reverse the trick played on them.

THE WOMAN SLEEPING ON THE COT in the woodshed was Albertine American Horse. The name was left over from her mother's short marriage. The boy was the son of the man she had loved and let go. Buddy was on the cot too, sitting on the edge because he's been awake three hours watching out for his mother and besides, she took up the whole cot. Her feet hung over the edge, limp and brown as two trout. Her long arms reached out and slapped at things she saw in her dreams.

Buddy had been knocked awake out of hiding in a washing machine while herds of policemen with dogs searched through a large building with many tiny rooms. When the arm came down, Buddy screamed because it had a blue cuff and sharp silver buttons. "Tss," his mother mumbled, half awake, "wasn't nothing." But Buddy sat up after her breathing went deep again, and he watched.

There was something coming and he knew it.

It was coming from very far off but he had a picture of it in his mind. It was a large thing made of metal with many barbed hooks, points, and drag chains on it, something like a giant potato peeler that rolled out of the sky, scraping clouds down with it and jabbing or crushing everything that lay in its path on the ground.

Buddy watched his mother. If he woke her up, she would know what to do about the thing, but he thought he'd wait until he saw it for sure before he shook her. She was pretty, sleeping, and he liked knowing he could look at her as long and close up as he wanted. He took a strand of her hair and held it in his hands as if it was the rein to a delicate beast. She was strong enough and could pull him along like the horse their name was.

Buddy had his mother's and his grandmother's name because his father had been a big mistake.

"They're all mistakes, even your father. But *you* are the best thing that ever happened to me."

That was what she said when he asked.

Even Kadie, the boyfriend crippled from being in a car wreck, was not as good a thing that had happened to his mother as Buddy was. "He was a medium-sized mistake," she said. "He's hurt and I shouldn't even say that, but it's the truth." At the moment, Buddy knew that being the best thing in his mother's life, he was also the reason they were hiding from the cops.

He wanted to touch the satin roses sewed on her pink tee shirt, but he knew he shouldn't do that even in her sleep. If she woke up and found him touching the roses, she would say, "Quit that, Buddy." Sometimes she told him to stop hugging her like a gorilla. She never said that in the mean voice she used when he oppressed her, but when she said that he loosened up anyway.

There were times he felt like hugging her so hard and in such a special way that she would say to him, "Let's get married." There were also times he closed his eyes and wished that she would die, only a few times, but still it haunted him that his wish might come true. He and Uncle Lawrence would be left alone. Buddy wasn't worried, though, about his mother getting married to somebody else. She had said to her friend, Madonna, "All men suck," when she thought Buddy wasn't listening. He had made an uncertain sound, and when they heard him they took him in their arms.

"Except for you, Buddy," his mother said. "All except for you and maybe Uncle Lawrence, although he's pushing it."

"The cops suck the worst, though," Buddy whispered to his mother's sleeping face, "because they're after us." He felt tired again, slumped down, and put his legs beneath the blanket. He closed his eyes and got the feeling that the cot was lifting up beneath him, that it was arching its canvas back and then traveling, traveling very fast and in the wrong direction for when he looked up he saw the three of them were advancing to meet the great metal thing with hooks and barbs and all sorts of sharp equipment to catch their bodies and draw their blood. He heard its insides as it rushed toward them, purring softly like a powerful motor and then they were right in its shadow. He pulled the reins as hard as he could and the beast reared, lifting him. His mother clapped her her hand across his mouth.

"Okay," she said. "Lay low. They're outside and they're gonna hunt."

She touched his shoulder and Buddy leaned over with her to look through   15
a crack in the boards.

They were out there all right, Albertine saw them. Two officers and that social worker woman. Vicki Koob. There had been no whistle, no dream, no voice to warn her that they were coming. There was only the crunching sound of cinders in the yard, the engine purring, the dust sifting off their car in a fine light brownish cloud and settling around them.

The three people came to a halt in their husk of metal—the car emblazoned with the North Dakota State Highway Patrol emblem which is the glowing profile of the Sioux policeman, Red Tomahawk, the one who killed Sitting Bull. Albertine gave Buddy the blanket and told him that he might have to wrap it around him and hide underneath the cot.

"We're gonna wait and see what they do." She took him in her lap and hunched her arms around him. "Don't worry," she whispered against his ear. "Lawrence knows how to fool them."

Buddy didn't want to look at the car and the people. He felt his mother's heart beating beneath his ear so fast it seemed to push the satin roses in and out. He put his face to them carefully and breathed the deep, soft powdery woman smell of her. That smell was also in her little face cream bottles, in her brushes, and around the washbowl after she used it. The satin felt so unbearably smooth against his cheek that he had to press closer. She didn't push him away, like he expected, but hugged him still tighter until he felt as close as he had ever been to back inside her again where she said he came from. Within the smells of her things, her soft skin, and the satin of her roses, he closed his eyes then, and took his breaths softly and quickly with her heart.

They were out there, but they didn't dare get out of the car yet because of   20
Lawrence's big, ragged dogs. Three of these dogs had loped up the dirt driveway with the car. They were rangy, alert, and bounced up and down on their cushioned paws like wolves. They didn't waste their energy barking, but po-

sitioned themselves quietly, one at either car door and the third in front of the bellied-out screen door to Uncle Lawrence's house. It was six in the morning but the wind was up already, blowing dust, ruffling their short moth-eaten coats. The big brown one on Vicki Koob's side had unusual black and white markings, stripes almost, like a hyena and he grinned at her, tongue out and teeth showing.

"Shoo!" Miss Koob opened her door with a quick jerk.

The brown dog sidestepped the door and jumped before her, tiptoeing. Its dirty white muzzle curled and its eyes crossed suddenly as if it was zeroing its cross-hair sights in on the exact place it would bite her. She ducked back and slammed the door.

"It's mean," she told Officer Brackett. He was printing out some type of form. The other officer, Harmony, a slow man, had not yet reacted to the car's halt. He had been sitting quietly in the back seat, but now he rolled down his window and with no change in expression unsnapped his holster and drew his pistol out and pointed it at the dog on his side. The dog smacked down on its belly, wiggled under the car, and was out and around the back of the house before Harmony drew his gun back. The other dogs vanished with him. From wherever they had disappeared to they began to yap and howl, and the door to the low shoebox-style house fell open.

"Heya, what's going on?"

Uncle Lawrence put his head out the door and opened wide the one eye   25
he had in working order. The eye bulged impossibly wider in outrage when he saw the police car. But the eyes of the two officers and Miss Vicki Koob were wide open too because they had never seen Uncle Lawrence in his sleeping getup or, indeed, witnessed anything like it. For his ribs, which were cracked from a bad fall and still mending, Uncle Lawrence wore a thick white corset laced up the front with a striped sneaker's lace. His glass eye and his set of dentures were still out for the night so his face puckered here and there, around its absences and scars, like a damaged but fierce little cake. Although he had a few gray streaks now, Uncle Lawrence's hair was still thick, and because he wore a special contraption of elastic straps around his head every night, two oiled waves always crested on either side of his middle part. All of this would have been sufficient to astonish, even without the most striking part of his outfit—the smoking jacket. It was made of black satin and hung open around his corset, dragging a tasseled belt. Gold thread dragons struggled up the lapels and blasted their furry red breath around his neck. As Lawrence walked down the steps, he put his arms up in surrender and the gold tassels in the inner seams of his sleeves dropped into view.

"My heavens, what a sight." Vicki Koob was impressed.

"A character," apologized Officer Harmony.

As a tribal police officer who could be counted on to help out the State Patrol, Harmony thought he always had to explain about Indians or get twice as tough to show he did not favor them. He was slow-moving and shy but two jumps ahead of other people all the same, and now, as he watched Uncle Lawrence's splendid approach, he gazed speculatively at the torn and bulging pocket of the smoking jacket. Harmony had been inside Uncle Lawrence's house before and knew that above his draped orange-crate shelf of war medals a blue-black German luger was hung carefully in a net of flat-headed nails and fishing line. Thinking of this deadly exhibition, he got out of the car and shambled toward Lawrence with a dreamy little smile of welcome on his face. But when he searched Lawrence, he found that the bulging pocket held only the lonesome-looking dentures from Lawrence's empty jaw. They were still dripping denture polish.

"I had been cleaning them when you arrived," Uncle Lawrence explained with acid dignity.

He took the toothbrush from his other pocket and aimed it like a rifle.   30

"Quit that, you old idiot." Harmony tossed the toothbrush away. "For once you ain't done nothing. We came for your nephew."

Lawrence looked at Harmony with a faint air of puzzlement.

"Ma Frere, listen," threatened Harmony amiably, "those two white people in the car came to get him for the welfare. They got papers on your nephew that give them the right to take him."

"Papers?" Uncle Lawrence puffed out his deeply pitted cheeks. "Let me see them papers."

The two of them walked over to Vicki's side of the car and she pulled a   35 copy of the court order from her purse. Lawrence put his teeth back in and adjusted them with busy workings of his jaw.

"Just a minute," he reached into his breast pocket as he bent close to Miss Vicki Koob. "I can't read these without I have in my eye."

He took the eye from his breast pocket delicately, and as he popped it into his face, the social worker's mouth fell open in a consternated O.

"What is this," she cried in a little voice.

Uncle Lawrence looked at her mildly. The white glass of the eye was cold as lard. The black iris was strangely charged and menacing.

"He's nuts," Brackett huffed along the side of Vicki's neck. "Never mind   40 him."

Vicki's hair had sweated down her nape in tiny corkscrews and some of the hairs were so long and dangly now that they disappeared into the zippered back of her dress. Brackett noticed this as he spoke into her ear. His face grew red and the backs of his hands prickled. He slid under the steering wheel and got out of the car. He walked around the hood to stand with Leo Harmony.

"We could take you in too," said Brackett roughly. Lawrence eyed the officers in what was taken as defiance. "If you don't cooperate, we'll get out the handcuffs," they warned.

One of Lawrence's arms was stiff and would not move until he'd rubbed it with witch hazel in the morning. His other arm worked fine though, and he stuck it out in front of Brackett.

"Get them handcuffs," he urged them. "Put me in a welfare home."

Brackett snapped one side of the handcuffs on Lawrence's good arm and   45
the other to the handle of the police car.

"That's to hold you," he said. "We're wasting our time. Harmony, you search that little shed over by the tall grass and Miss Koob and myself will search the house."

"My rights is violated!" Lawrence shrieked suddenly. They ignored him. He tugged at the handcuff and thought of the good heavy file he kept in his tool box and the German luger oiled and ready but never loaded, because of Buddy, over his shelf. He should have used it on these bad ones, even Harmony in his big-time white man job. He wouldn't last long in that job anyway before somebody gave him what for.

"It's a damn scheme," said Uncle Lawrence, rattling his chains against the car. He looked over at the shed and thought maybe Albertine and Buddy had sneaked away before the car pulled into the yard. But he sagged, seeing Albertine move like a shadow within the boards. "Oh, it's all a damn scheme," he muttered again.

"I want to find that boy and salvage him," Vicki Koob explained to Officer Brackett as they walked into the house. "Look at his family life—the old man crazy as a bedbug, the mother intoxicated somewhere."

Brackett nodded, energetic, eager. He was a short hopeful redhead who   50
failed consistently to win the hearts of women. Vicki Koob intrigued him. Now, as he watched, she pulled a tiny pen out of an ornamental clip on her blouse. It was attached to a retractable line that would suck the pen back, like a child eating one strand of spaghetti. Something about the pen on its line excited Brackett to the point of discomfort. His hand shook as he opened the screendoor and stepped in, beckoning Miss Koob to follow.

They could see the house was empty at first glance. It was only one rectangular room with whitewashed walls and a little gas stove in the middle. They had already come through the cooking lean-to with the other stove and washstand and rusty old refrigerator. That refrigerator had nothing in it but some wrinkled potatoes and a package of turkey necks. Vicki Koob noted in her perfect-bound notebook. The beds along the walls of the big room were covered with quilts that Albertine's mother, Sophie, had made from bits of old wool coats and pants that the Sisters sold in bundles at the mission. There was no one hiding beneath the beds. No one was under the little aluminum dinette table covered with a green oilcloth, or the soft brown wood chairs tucked up to it. One wall of the big room was filled with neatly stacked crates of things—old tools and springs and small half-dismantled appliances. Five or six television sets were stacked against the wall. Their control panels spewed colored wires and at least one was cracked all the way across. Only the top-most set, with coathanger antenna angled sensitively to catch the bounding signals around Little Shell, looked like it could possibly work.

Not one thing escaped Vicki Koob's trained and cataloguing gaze. She made note of the cupboard that held only commodity flour and coffee. The unsanitary tin oil drum beneath the kitchen window, full of empty surplus pork cans and beer bottles, caught her eye as did Uncle Lawrence's physical and mental deteriorations. She quickly described these "benchmarks of alcoholic dependency within the extended family of Woodrow (Buddy) American Horse" as she walked around the room with the little notebook open, pushed against her belly to steady it. Although Vicki had been there before, Albertine's presence had always made it difficult for her to take notes.

"Twice the maximum allowable space between door and threshold," she wrote now. "Probably no insulation. Two three-inch cracks in walls inadequately sealed with white-washed mud." She made a mental note but could see no point in describing Lawrence's stuffed reclining chair that only reclined, the shadeless lamp with its plastic orchid in the bubble glass base, or the three-dimensional picture of Jesus that Lawrence had once demonstrated to her. When plugged in, lights rolled behind the water the Lord stood on so that he seemed to be strolling although he never actually went forward, of course, but only pushed the glowing waves behind him forever like a poor tame rat in a treadmill.

Brackett cleared his throat with a nervous rasp and touched Vicki's shoulder. "What are you writing?"

She moved away and continued to scribble as if thoroughly absorbed in her work. "Officer Brackett displays an undue amount of interest in my person," she wrote. "Perhaps?"

He snatched playfully at the book, but she hugged it to her chest and moved off smiling. More curls had fallen, wetted to the base of her neck. Looking out the window, she sighed long and loud.

"All night on brush rollers for this. What a joke."

Brackett shoved his hands in his pockets. His mouth opened slightly, then shut with a small throttled cluck.

When Albertine saw Harmony ambling across the yard with his big brown thumbs in his belt, his placid smile, and his tiny black eyes moving back and forth, she put Buddy under the cot. Harmony stopped at the shed and stood quietly. He spread his arms to show her he hadn't drawn his big police gun.

"Ma Cousin," he said in the Michif dialect that people used if they were relatives or sometimes if they needed gas or a couple of dollars, "why don't you come out here and stop this foolishness?"

"I ain't your cousin," Albertine said. Anger boiled up in her suddenly. "I ain't related to no pigs."

She bit her lip and watched him through the cracks, circling, a big tan punching dummy with his boots full of sand so he never stayed down once he fell. He was empty inside, all stale air. But he knew how to get to her so much better than a white cop could. And now he was circling because he wasn't sure she didn't have a weapon, maybe a knife or the German luger that was the only thing that her father, Albert American Horse, had left his wife and daughter besides his name. Harmony knew that Albertine was a tall strong woman who took two big men to subdue when she didn't want to go in the drunk tank. She had hard hips, broad shoulders, and stood tall like her Sioux father, the American Horse who was killed threshing in Belle Prairie.

"I feel bad to have to do this," Harmony said to Albertine. "But for godsakes, let's nobody get hurt. Come on out with the boy, why don't you? I know you got him in there."

Albertine did not give herself away this time. She let him wonder. Slowly   65
and quietly she pulled her belt through its loops and wrapped it around and around her hand until only the big oval buckle with turquoise chunks shaped into a butterfly stuck out over her knuckles. Harmony was talking but she wasn't listening to what he said. She was listening to the pitch of his voice, the tone of it that would tighten or tremble at a certain moment when he decided to rush the shed. He kept talking slowly and reasonably, flexing the dialect from time to time, even mentioning her father.

"He was a damn good man. I don't care what they say, Albertine, I knew him."

Albertine looked at the stone butterfly that spread its wings across her fist. The wings looked light and cool, not heavy. It almost looked like it was ready to fly. Harmony wanted to get to Albertine through her father but she would not think about American Horse. She concentrated on the sky blue stone.

Yet the shape of the stone, the color, betrayed her.

She saw her father suddenly, bending at the grille of their old gray car. She was small then. The memory came from so long ago it seemed like a dream—narrowly focused, snapshot-clear. He was bending by the grille in the sun. It was hot summer. Wings of sweat, dark blue, spread across the back of his work shirt. He always wore soft blue shirts, the color a shade cloudier than this stone. His stiff hair had grown out of its short haircut and flopped over his forehead. When he stood up and turned away from the car, Albertine saw that he had a butterfly.

"It's dead," he told her. "Broke its wings and died on the grille."   70

She must have been five, maybe six, wearing one of the boy's tee shirts Mama bleached in Hilex-water. American Horse took the butterfly, a black and yellow one, and rubbed it on Albertine's collarbone and chest and arms until the color and the powder of it were blended into her skin.

"For grace," he said.

And Albertine had felt a strange lightening in her arms, in her chest, when he did this and said, "For grace." The way he said it, grace meant everything the butterfly was. The sharp delicate wings. The way it floated over grass. The way its wings seemed to breathe fanning in the sun. The wisdom of the way it blended into flowers or changed into a leaf. In herself she felt the same kind of possibilities and closed her eyes almost in shock or pain, she felt so light and powerful at that moment.

Then her father had caught her and thrown her high into the air. She could not remember landing in his arms or landing at all. She only remembered the sun filling her eyes and the world tipping crazily behind her, out of sight.

"He was a damn good man," Harmony said again.   75

Albertine heard his starched uniform gathering before his boots hit the ground. Once, twice, three times. It took four solid jumps to get right where she wanted him. She kicked the plank door open when he reached for the handle and the corner caught him on the jaw. He faltered, and Albertine hit him flat on the chin with the butterfly. She hit him so hard the shock of it went up her arm like a string pulled taut. Her fist opened, numb, and she let the belt unloop before she closed her hand on the tip end of it and sent the stone butterfly swooping out in a wide circle around her as if it was on the end of a leash. Harmony reeled backward as she walked toward him swinging the belt. She expected him to fall but he just stumbled. And then he took the gun from his hip.

Albertine let the belt go limp. She and Harmony stood within feet of each other, breathing. Each heard the human sound of air going in and out of the other person's lungs. Each read the face of the other as if deciphering letters carved into softly eroding veins of stone. Albertine saw the pattern of tiny arteries that age, drink, and hard living had blown to the surface of the man's face. She saw the spoked wheels of his iris and the arteries like tangled threads that sewed him up. She saw the living net of springs and tissue that held him together, and trapped him. She saw the random, intimate plan of his person.

She took a quick shallow breath and her face went strange and tight. She saw the black veins in the wings of the butterfly, roads burnt into a map, and then she was located somewhere in the net of veins and sinew that was the tragic complexity of the world so she did not see Officer Brackett and Vicki Koob rushing toward her, but felt them instead like flies caught in the same web, rocking it.

"Albertine!" Vicki Koob had stopped in the grass. Her voice was shrill and tight. "It's better this way, Albertine. We're going to help you."

Albertine straightened, threw her shoulders back. Her father's hand was   80
on her chest and shoulders lightening her wonderfully. Then on wings of her father's hands, on dead butterfly wings, Albertine lifted into the air and flew toward the others. The light powerful feeling swept her up the way she had

floated higher, seeing the grass below. It was her father throwing her up into the air and out of danger. Her arms opened for bullets but no bullets came. Harmony did not shoot. Instead, he raised his fist and brought it down hard on her head.

Albertine did not fall immediately, but stood in his arms a moment. Perhaps she gazed still farther back behind the covering of his face. Perhaps she was completely stunned and did not think as she sagged and fell. She face rolled forward and hair covered her features, so it was impossible for Harmony to see with just what particular expression she gazed into the head-splitting wheel of light, or blackness, that overcame her.

Harmony turned the vehicle onto the gravel road that led back to town. He had convinced the other two that Albertine was more trouble than she was worth, and so they left her behind, and Lawrence too. He stood swearing in his cinder driveway as the car rolled out of sight. Buddy sat between the social worker and Officer Brackett. Vicki tried to hold Buddy fast and keep her arm down at the same time, for the words she'd screamed at Albertine had broken the seal of antiperspirant beneath her arms. She was sweating now as though she's stored an ocean up inside of her. Sweat rolled down her back in a shallow river and pooled at her waist and between her breasts. A thin sheen of water came out on her forearms, her face. Vicki gave an irritated moan but Brackett seemed not to take notice, or take offense at least. Air-conditioned breezes were sweeping over the seat anyway, and very soon they would be comfortable. She smiled at Brackett over Buddy's head. The man grinned back. Buddy stirred. Vicki remembered the emergency chocolate bar she kept in her purse, fished it out, and offered it to Buddy. He did not react, so she closed his fingers over the package and peeled the paper off one end.

The car accelerated. Buddy felt the road and wheels pummeling each other and the rush of the heavy motor purring in high gear. Buddy knew that what he'd seen in his mind that morning, the thing coming out of the sky with barbs and chains, had hooked him. Somehow he was caught and held in the sour tin smell of the pale woman's armpit. Somehow he was pinned between their pounds of breathless flesh. He looked at the chocolate in his hand. He was squeezing the bar so hard that a thin brown trickle had melted down his arm. Automatically he put the bar in his mouth.

As he bit down he saw his mother very clearly, just as she had been when she carried him from the shed. She was stretched flat on the ground, on her stomach, and her arms were curled around her head as if in sleep. One leg was drawn up and it looked for all the world like she was running full tilt into the ground, as though she had been trying to pass into the earth, to bury herself, but at the last moment something had stopped her.

There was no blood on Albertine, but Buddy tasted blood now at the sight of her, for he bit down hard and cut his own lip. He ate the chocolate, 85 every bit of it, tasting his mother's blood. And when he had the chocolate down inside him and all licked off his hands, he opened his mouth to say thank you to the woman, as his mother had taught him. But instead of a thank you coming out he was astonished to hear a great rattling scream, and then another, rip out of him like pieces of his own body and whirl onto the sharp things all around him.

Considerations

1. When Albertine looks out the window, she sees a social worker and two police officers, one of whom is Officer Harmony of the tribal police. Albertine knows that "he knew how to get to her so much better than a white cop could" (para. 63). How would you explain her statement? What is Harmony's role in this story?

2. Both Buddy and his mother, Albertine, experience visions in this story. Buddy imagines a "large thing made of metal" (para. 4), while Albertine remembers the crushed butterfly in her father's hand. Why does Erdrich introduce these images? What is their significance in the context of the story?

Invitation to Write

We continually hear that the nature of the American family is changing. Still, most of us, like Vicki Koob, seem to have certain expectations about what a typical family is like. In fact, it is on the basis of such expectations that Vicki Koob decides that it is in Buddy's best interest to be taken away from his mother and uncle. Write an essay in which you explore the reasons why the American Horse family does not meet our society's definition of what constitutes a "typical" family. Consider the roles that men and women are supposed to play in the family, how children are nurtured and educated, as well as the ties that unite family members. Consider also the cultural and social factors that might affect family relations among American Indians.

Connections

The story "American Horse" opens with Buddy's nightmare vision of the evil forces that will take him away. It soon becomes clear that Buddy's nightmare is a symbol for Vicki Koob and the police. However, Koob and the policemen see themselves in the roles of "rescuers," and the notes Koob takes after entering Uncle Lawrence's house indicate that she is highly critical of the conditions she finds. Paula Gunn Allen's essay "Where I Come from Is Like This" (p. 390) provides a way to understand these two very different points of view.

341

Write an essay in which you use Allen's analysis of the mainstream American view of American Indian culture to explain the attitudes of the social worker and the policemen, as well as Albertine's response, in this story. Use Allen's essay to locate the underlying assumptions that explain both Koob's statement "It's better this way, Albertine. We're going to help you" (para. 79) and Albertine's response to it.

JAMAICA KINCAID

A Small Place

Jamaica Kincaid was born in St. Johns, Antigua, in 1945. She was educated in England and now lives in the United States. Kincaid is the author of three books of fiction. *At the Bottom of the River* (1984) won the Morton Dauwen Zabel Award of the American Academy and Institute of Arts and Letters. *Annie John* (1985) is a semi-autobiographical novel, and her most recent work, *Lucy* (1990), follows the experiences of a young woman recently arrived in the United States. Her nonfiction work, *A Small Place* (1988), is a passionate essay about growing up in Antigua under English colonial rule and learning firsthand about the unequal relationship between colonizer and colonized. Kincaid now lives in Vermont and is a contributing writer to *The New Yorker* magazine.

The essay that follows is the second chapter of *A Small Place*. Kincaid's powerful voice unmasks the colonial exploitation and unfolds the drama of a people who have been robbed of their history and culture. She credits the English not only with the destruction of her culture but also with creating the problematic identity she and people like her have acquired as a result of colonization. It is an identity that revolves around an unappeased anger from which she feels there is no escape.

THE ANTIGUA THAT I KNEW, the Antigua in which I grew up, is not the Antigua you, a tourist, would see now. That Antigua no longer exists. That Antigua no longer exists partly for the usual reason, the passing of time, and partly because the bad-minded people who used to rule over it, the English, no longer do so. (But the English have become such a pitiful lot these days, with hardly any idea what to do with themselves now that they no longer have one quarter of the earth's human population bowing and scraping before them. They don't seem to know that this empire business was all wrong and they should, at least, be wearing sackcloth and ashes in token penance of the wrongs committed, the irrevocableness of their bad deeds, for no natural disaster imaginable could equal the harm they did. Actual death might have been better. And so all this fuss over empire—what went wrong here, what went wrong there—always makes me quite crazy, for I can say to them what went wrong: They should never have left their home, their precious England, a place they loved so much, a place they had to leave but could never forget. And so everywhere they went they turned it into England; and everybody they met they turned English. But no place could ever really be England, and nobody who did not look exactly like them would ever be English, so you can imagine the destruction of people and land that came from that. The English hate each other and they hate England, and the reason they are so miserable now is that they have no place else to go and nobody else to feel better than.) But let me show you the Antigua that I used to know.

In the Antigua that I knew, we lived on a street named after an English maritime criminal, Horatio Nelson, and all the other streets around us were named after some other English maritime criminals. There was Rodney Street, there was Hood Street, there was Hawkins Street, and there was Drake Street. There were flamboyant trees and mahogany trees lining East Street. Government House, the place where the Governor, the person standing in for the Queen, lived, was on East Street. Government House was surrounded by a high white wall—and to show how cowed we must have been, no one ever wrote bad things on it; it remained clean and white and high. (I once stood in hot sun for hours so that I could see a putty-faced Princess from England disappear behind these walls. I was seven years old at the time, and I thought, She has a putty face.) There was the library on lower High Street, above the Department of the Treasury, and it was in that part of High Street that all colonial government business took place. In that part of High Street, you could cash a cheque at the Treasury, read a book in the library, post a letter at the post office, appear before a magistrate in court. (Since we were ruled by the English, we also had their laws. There was a law against using abusive language. Can you imagine such a law among people for whom making a spectacle of yourself through speech is everything? When West Indians went to England, the police there had to get a glossary of bad West Indian words so they could understand whether they were hearing abusive language or not.) It was in that same part of High Street that you could get a passport in another government office. In the middle of High Street was the Barclays Bank. The Barclay brothers, who started Barclays Bank, were slave-traders. That is how they made their money. When the English outlawed the slave trade, the Barclay brothers went into banking. It made them even richer. It's possible that when they saw how rich banking made them, they gave themselves a good beating for opposing an end to slave trading (for surely they would have opposed that), but then again, they may have been visionaries and agitated for an end to slavery, for look at how rich they became with their banks borrowing from (through their savings) the descendants of the slaves and then lending back to them. But people just a little older than I am can recite the name of and the day the first black person was hired as a cashier at this very same

Barclays Bank in Antigua. Do you ever wonder why some people blow things up? I can imagine that if my life had taken a certain turn, there would be the Barclays Bank, and there I would be, both of us in ashes. Do you ever try to understand why people like me cannot get over the past, cannot forgive and cannot forget? There is the Barclays Bank. The Barclay brothers are dead. The human beings they traded, the human beings who to them were only commodities, are dead. It should not have been that they came to the same end, and heaven is not enough of a reward for one or hell enough of a punishment for the other. People who think about these things believe that every bad deed, even every bad thought, carries with it its own retribution. So do you see the queer thing about people like me? Sometimes we hold your retribution.

And then there was another place, called the Mill Reef Club. It was built by some people from North America who wanted to live in Antigua and spend their holidays in Antigua but who seemed not to like Antiguans (black people) at all, for the Mill Reef Club declared itself completely private, and the only Antiguans (black people) allowed to go there were servants. People can recite the name of the first Antiguan (black person) to eat a sandwich at the clubhouse and the day on which it happened; people can recite the name of the first Antiguan (black person) to play golf on the golf course and the day on which the event took place. In those days, we Antiguans thought that the people at the Mill Reef Club had such bad manners, like pigs; they were behaving in a bad way, like pigs. There they were, strangers in someone else's home, and then they refused to talk to their hosts or have anything human, anything intimate, to do with them. I believe they gave scholarships to one or two bright people each year so they could go overseas and study; I believe they gave money to children's charities; these things must have made them seem to themselves very big and good, but to us there they were, pigs living in that sty (the Mill Reef Club). And what were these people from North America, these people from England, these people from Europe, with their bad behaviour, doing on this little island? For they so enjoyed behaving badly, as if there was pleasure immeasurable to be had from not acting like a human being. Let me tell you about a man; trained as a dentist, he took it on himself to say he was a doctor, specialising in treating children's illnesses. No one objected—certainly not us. He came to Antigua as a refugee (running away from Hitler) from Czechoslovakia. This man hated us so much that he would send his wife to inspect us before we were admitted into his presence, and she would make sure that we didn't smell, that we didn't have dirt under our fingernails, and that nothing else about us—apart from the colour of our skin—should offend the doctor. (I can remember once, when I had whooping cough and I took a turn for the worse, that my mother, before bundling me up and taking me off to see this man, examined me carefully to see that I had no bad smells or dirt in the crease of my neck, behind my ears, or anywhere else. Every horrible thing that a housefly could do was known by heart to my mother, and in her innocence she thought that she and the doctor shared the same crazy obsession—germs.) Then there was a headmistress of a girls' school, hired through the colonial office in England and sent to Antigua to run this school which only in my lifetime began to accept girls who were born outside a marriage; in Antigua it had never dawned on anyone that this was a way of keeping black children out of this school. This woman was twenty-six years old, not too long out of university, from Northern Ireland, and she told these girls over and over again to stop behaving as if they were monkeys just out of trees. No one ever dreamed that the word for any of this was racism. We thought these people were so ill-mannered and we were so surprised by this, for they were far away from their home, and we believed that the farther away you were from your home the better you should behave. (This is because if your bad behaviour gets you in trouble you have your family not too far off to help defend you.) We thought they were un-Christian-like; we thought they were small-minded; we thought they were like animals, a bit below human standards as we understood those standards to be. We felt superior to all these people; we thought that perhaps the English among them who behaved this way weren't English at all, for the English were supposed to be civilised, and this behaviour was so much like that of an animal, the thing we were before the English rescued us, that maybe they weren't from the real England at all but from another England, one we were not familiar with, not at all from the England we were told about, not at all from the England we could never be from, the England that was so far away, the England that not even a boat could take us to, the England that, no matter what we did, we could never be of. We felt superior, for we were so much better behaved and we were full of grace, and these people were so badly behaved and they were so completely empty of grace. (Of course, I now see that good behaviour is the proper posture of the weak, of children.) We were taught the names of the Kings of England. In Antigua, the twenty-fourth of May was a holiday— Queen Victoria's official birthday. We didn't say to ourselves, Hasn't this extremely unappealing person been dead for years and years? Instead, we were glad for a holiday. Once, at dinner (this happened in my present life), I was sitting across from an Englishman, one of those smart people who know how to run things that England still turns out but who now, since the demise of the empire, have nothing to do; they look so sad, sitting on the rubbish heap of history. I was reciting my usual litany of things I hold against England and the English, and to round things off I said, "And do you know that we had to celebrate Queen Victoria's birthday?" So he said that every year, at the school he attended in England, they marked the day she died. I said, "Well, apart from the fact that she belonged to you and so anything you did about her was proper, at least you knew she died." So that was England to us—Queen Victoria and the glorious day of her coming into the world, a beautiful place, a blessed place, a living and blessed thing, not the ugly, piggish individuals we met. I cannot tell you how angry it makes me to hear people from North America tell me how much they love England, how beautiful England is, with its traditions. All they see is some frumpy, wrinkled-up person passing by in a carriage waving at a crowd. But what I see is the millions of people, of whom I am just one, made orphans: no motherland, no fatherland, no gods, no mounds of earth for holy ground, no excess of love which might lead to the things that an excess of love sometimes brings, and worst and most painful of all, no tongue. (For isn't it odd that the only language I have in which to speak of this crime is the language of the criminal who committed the crime? And what can that really mean? For the language of the criminal can contain only the goodness of the criminal's deed. The language of the criminal can explain and express the deed only from the criminal's point of view. It cannot contain the horror of the deed, the injustice of the deed, the agony, the humiliation inflicted on me. When I say to the criminal, "This is wrong, this is wrong, this is wrong," or, "This deed is bad, and this other deed is bad, and this one is also very, very bad," the criminal understands the word "wrong" in this way: It is wrong when "he" doesn't get his fair share of profits from the crime just committed; he understands the word "bad" in this way: A fellow criminal betrayed a trust. That must be why, when I say, "I am filled with rage," the criminal says, "But why?" And when I blow things up and make life generally unlivable for the criminal (is my life not unlivable, too?) the criminal is shocked, surprised. But nothing can erase my rage—not an apology, not a large sum of money, not the death of the criminal—for this wrong can never be made right, and only the impossible can make me still: Can a way be found to make what happened not have happened? And so look at this prolonged visit to the bile duct that I am making, look at how bitter, how dyspeptic just to sit and think about these things makes me. I attended a school named after a Princess of England. Years and years later, I read somewhere that this Princess made her tour of the West Indies (which included Antigua, and on that tour she dedicated my school) because she had fallen in love with a married man, and since she was not allowed to marry a divorced man she was sent to visit us to get over her affair with him. How well I remember that all of Antigua turned out to see this Princess person, how every building that she would enter was repaired and painted so that it looked brand-new, how every beach she would sun herself on had to look as if no one had ever sunned there before (I wonder now what they did about the poor sea? I mean, can a sea be made to look brand-new?), and how everybody she met was the best Antiguan body to meet, and no one told us that this person we were putting ourselves out for on such a big scale, this person we were getting worked up about as if she were God Himself, was in our midst because of something so common, so everyday: Her life was not working out the way she had hoped, her life was one big mess. Have I given you the impression that the Antigua I grew up in revolved almost completely around England? Well, that was so. I met the world through England, and if the world wanted to meet me it would have to do so through England.

Are you saying to yourself, "Can't she get beyond all that, everything happened so long ago, and how does she know that if things had been the other way around her ancestors wouldn't have behaved just as badly, because, after all, doesn't everybody behave badly given the opportunity?"

Our perception of this Antigua—the perception we had of this place ruled   5
by these bad-minded people—was not a political perception. The English were ill-mannered, not racists; the school headmistress was especially ill-mannered, not a racist; the doctor was crazy—he didn't even speak English properly, and he came from a strangely named place, he also was not a racist; the people at the Mill Reef Club were puzzling (why go and live in a place populated mostly by people you cannot stand), not racists.

Have you ever wondered to yourself why it is that all people like me seem to have learned from you is how to imprison and murder each other, how to govern badly, and how to take the wealth of our country and place it in Swiss bank accounts? Have you ever wondered why it is that all we seem to have learned from you is how to corrupt our societies and how to be tyrants? You will have to accept that this is mostly your fault. Let me just show you how you looked to us. You came. You took things that were not yours, and you did not even, for appearances' sake, ask first. You could have said, "May I have this, please?" and even though it would have been clear to everybody that a yes or no from us would have been of no consequence you might have looked so much better. Believe me, it would have gone a long way. I would have had to admit that at least you were polite. You murdered people. You imprisoned people. You robbed people. You opened your own banks and you put our money in them. The accounts were in your name. The banks were in your name. There must have been some good people among you, but they stayed home. And that is the point. That is why they are good. They stayed home. But still, when you think about it, you must be a little sad. The people like me, finally, after years and years of agitation, made deeply moving and eloquent speeches against the wrongness of your domination over us, and then finally, after the mutilated bodies of you, your wife, and your children were found in your beautiful and spacious bungalow at the edge of your rubber plantation—found by one of your many house servants (none of it was ever yours; it was never, ever yours)—you say to me, "Well, I wash my hands of all of you, I am leaving now," and you leave, and from afar you watch as we do to ourselves the very things you used to do to us. And you might feel that there was more to you than that, you might feel that you had understood the meaning of the Age of Enlightenment (though, as far as I can see, it had done you very little good); you loved knowledge, and wherever you went you made sure to build a school, a library (yes, and in both of these places you distorted or erased my history and glorified your own). But then again, perhaps as you observe the debacle in which I now exist, the utter ruin that I say is my life, perhaps you are remembering that you had always felt people like me cannot run things, people like me will never grasp the idea of Gross National Product, people like me will never be able to take command of the thing the most simpleminded among you can master, people like me will never understand the notion of rule by law, people like me cannot really think in abstractions, people like me cannot be objective, we make everything so personal. You will forget your part in the whole setup, that bureaucracy is one of your inventions, that Gross National Product is one of your inventions, and all the laws that you know mysteriously favour you. Do you know why people like me are shy about being capitalists? Well, it's because we, for as long as we have known you, *were* capital, like bales of cotton and sacks of sugar, and you were the commanding, cruel capitalists, and the memory of this is so strong, the experience so recent, that we can't quite bring ourselves to embrace this idea that you think so much of. As for what we were like before we met you, I no longer care. No periods of time over which my ancestors held sway, no documentation of complex civilisations, is any comfort to me. Even if I really came from people who were living like monkeys in trees, it was better to be that than what happened to me, what I became after I met you.

Considerations

1. Kincaid begins her essay by explaining that she will describe an Antigua that no longer exists. What do her descriptions suggest about the way she viewed life in Antigua when she was a child? What changes do you see between her childhood view of Antigua and her adult view of those same years?

2. In several places in her essay, Kincaid refers to the English as criminals. For example, she says that streets were named after English criminals (para. 2). Consider examples where she makes such references. What definition of "criminal" is suggested by these examples? To what extent does such a definition reflect English/Western morality?

Invitation to Write

Kincaid remembers that when she was a child, the Antiguans felt superior to the English "for we were so much better behaved and we were full of grace" (para. 3). But as an adult, she sees that same good behavior as a sign of weakness. Hindsight has complicated her interpretation of what she felt and allowed her to reframe her experience in different terms. Write an essay in which you examine the process involved in reframing earlier perceptions of the world. As you write, think about the new knowledge and understanding that contributes to the change in perspective.

Connections

Kincaid addresses her essay to "you, a tourist" (para. 1). In "The Westernization of the World (p. 553), Paul Harrison also has a lot to say about tourism. Can Kincaid's views of tourists, both past and present, be explained in Harrison's terms? Write an essay in which you present her view of tourism and compare it with Paul Harrison's in "The Westernization of the World." Consider the effects of tourism on both the environment and the lives of the native inhabitants of the tourist destinations. Finally, determine whether tourism helps or hurts relations between cultures.

ASSIGNMENT SEQUENCE
Environments of Prejudice

In this sequence, you will first look at the way prejudgment can impose a framework that distorts an individual's reality. In order to understand the process by which this distortion takes place, you will be asked to describe and analyze a moment in your own experience when you were misperceived by someone. In the second assignment, you will examine the line between prejudgment and prejudice. Here you will look at James Baldwin's discovery in "Whose Child Are You?" of the definitions offered to him as he grew up, as well as the experience you described previously, to assess the links between those definitions and prejudice. Next you will turn to Yoshimeki's narrative "Learning the Language" and again to Baldwin's essay to examine the role that parents play in teaching children about prejudice. The questions raised in the fourth assignment send you back once more to Baldwin's essay to examine the perpetuation of prejudice from still a different perspective. As you move from a familial to a larger social context, you will analyze the experience of Jamaica Kincaid in "A Small Place" and of the characters in Louise Erdrich's story "American Horse," according to Baldwin's view of how social and political institutions maintain racism. Finally, the last assignment in the sequence asks you to reflect upon the ways prejudice is perpetuated in today's society, and the way people can resist and move beyond it.

Assignment 1: Exploring Experience

Think of an occasion when people's reactions to you puzzled or disturbed you because you felt you were being misjudged or treated as "different." Using your experience, write a paper that describes this situation and your reaction to it.

Begin with a description of the situation you encountered, your behavior, and people's reactions to you. Explain why you felt people were prejudging you, and how you reacted. In your paper, identify the basis on which you were judged: race, age, gender, religion, occupation, or other category. Evaluate the way you handled the situation and decide whether you were encountering prejudice.

Assignment 2

*I was icily determined—more determined, really, than I then knew—
never to make my peace with the ghetto but to die and go to Hell
before I would let any white man spit on me, before I would accept
my "place" in this republic.*
—JAMES BALDWIN, *Whose Child Are You?*

Baldwin calls the summer of his fourteenth year a summer of crises. In addition to the usual adolescent experiences of growing up, Baldwin began to understand that his particular situation was much more complex. Behind the known circumstances of his life lurked threats previously hidden and repressed by his parents and himself. Use Baldwin's experience and your first assignment to write a paper in which you look at the relationship between imposing preconceived definitions upon people and prejudice. How powerful are these definitions in shaping people's ideas about themselves and how much power do individuals have to reshape these definitions?

Before writing, reread Baldwin's essay and underline several instances in which Baldwin suggests that he was reacting to someone else's attempt to define him, whether he was resisting an unspoken threat or consciously choosing an alternative definition of himself. Consider how his responses at these particular moments shaped and defined his own idea of himself. Going back to your earlier paper, reexamine your reaction in a similar situation and evaluate the way you responded to people's expectations. Use these specific instances to focus your paper and lead you to your conclusions.

Assignment 3

Both Yoshimeki and Baldwin relate their experiences of encountering prejudice as a child. Often they present them from a child's point of view. In both stories, parents react to the perceived threats to children's safety that arise when racial boundaries are ignored. Write an essay examining the reactions of both writers' parents, and the way these reactions shaped the children's perception of the world.

To begin your essay, look back through both texts and underline those passages in which parents demonstrate a reaction to a prejudice they know exists. What is the reaction of the child at this point in each essay? What is the reaction of the adult writer to the same situation? From these three sets of reactions, decide how each author suggests parents (and adults in general) convey messages about how to behave in the face of prejudiced attitudes.

Assignment 4

It was a criminal power, to be feared but not respected, and to be outwitted in any way whatever.
　　　　　　　　　　　　—JAMES BALWDIN, *Whose Child Are You?*

In Louise Erdrich's story "American Horse," the narrator never directly judges the behavior of any of the individuals involved. Still, the story presents descriptions of behavior and attitudes that reveal assumptions and expectations. Like the policemen in James Baldwin's story, the social worker and her companions have "the judges, the juries, the shotguns, the law—in a word, power" (Baldwin, para. 4). Jamaica Kincaid writes about other institutions of power—the school, the library, and the country club—that hold up England as the civilized ideal.

Use Baldwin's analysis of the power structure to examine the relationship between political power and prejudice in Jamaica Kincaid's Antigua and Louise Erdrich's reservation in North Dakota. Write an essay in which you decide how Baldwin would apply his analysis of power and resistance to Kincaid's experience and the lives of the characters in "American Horse."

As you reread the essays, note the various institutions that appear in each and think about the way they affect the lives of people who come in contact with them. Focus your paper on at least one example from each reading to discuss the relationship between individuals who represent authority and individuals who respond to them. Bring Baldwin's analysis of the dynamics of power to these examples and use it to expand Kincaid's, Albertine's, or Buddy's understanding of their situation.

Assignment 5

Using the four texts by Erdrich, Yoshimeki, Baldwin, and Kincaid, along with the personal experience you described earlier, write a paper that explores the way individuals in societies, acting on their own or as representatives of social institutions, perpetuate prejudice and racism. Also suggest the way people could begin to change the process and environments that make racism and prejudice possible.

Begin your essay by noting some of the conditions, suggested by these writers, which reinforce the prejudice communicated to the children involved. After examining the process by which children learn about prejudice, look at other conditions that contribute to racist or prejudiced attitudes. You can also use your own experience of being misperceived to support your analysis. In your paper, when you write about the way prejudice can be challenged, and change effected, be sure to consider the ideas suggested by these authors.

8

Stories That Shape
Our Lives

Dorothy Parker, she read. What a wonderful name. Maybe I'll change my name to Dorothy, Dorothy Louise Manning. Dot Manning. Dottie, Dottie Leigh, Dot.

—ELLEN GILCHRIST, *Music*

I used to believe everything my mother said, even when I didn't know what she meant. Once when I was little, she told me she knew it would rain because lost ghosts were circling near our windows, calling "Woo-woo" to be let in. She said doors would unlock themselves in the middle of the night unless we checked twice. She said a mirror could see only my face, but she could see me inside out even when I was not in the room.

—AMY TAN, *Without Wood*

Through all the centuries of war and death and cultural and psychic destruction have endured the women who raise the children and tend the fires, who pass along the tales and the traditions, who weep and bury the dead, who are the dead, and who never forget.

—PAULA GUNN ALLEN, *Where I Come from Is Like This*

353

I thought he was lying. I thought he was making up a kind of horror story to shock me and give his moral that much more starch. But it was true. I asked around. I brought it up during History class in junior high school, and my teacher, after silencing me and stepping me off to the back of the room, told me it was indeed so.

—GARRETT HONGO, *Kubota*

We are often unaware of the narratives that shape our lives, that teach us who we are and who we can become. The effects of some narratives, such as historical, political, and cultural myths, are fairly apparent; others are hidden. School experiences teach us the dominant cultural narratives, giving us ideas held in common, but in our daily and personal lives we listen to stories that give us more specific ideas about our identities and distinctiveness, and that serve as models for our behavior. Stories passed down by family members often provide the key to a family's sense of identity: For example, if you know that your great-grandfather sailed around the world before he was twelve, you can explain your own desire to travel; you may know stories about how your grandparents lived during the Great Depression, where your parents met, or why your parents decided to immigrate; and your parents' stories of your childhood experiences might help you define who you are.

Stories that guide you can come to you not only from your family but also from the culture you live in: Myths, movies, television shows, and books are all powerful forms of story-telling. The chapter that follows asks you to examine the importance a particular story had in shaping your own life, and to think about the role of stories—both formal and informal—in helping people define the possibilities open to them in their lives.

The individuals in this chapter hear many different kinds of stories, including stories of family and cultural identity. They are able to weave these stories into their lives as they discover the narrative shape guiding their own experiences. In Ellen Gilchrist's story "Music," the undaunted heroine, Rhoda, fashions romantic scenarios for herself and other figures in her life, revealing her penchant for adapting literary narratives in order to empower herself. Amy Tan's story "Without Wood" describes the power of childhood belief in a mother's strange and wondrous stories and the need of the heroine to recapture that belief, as well as a belief in herself. Paula Gunn Allen, who has Laguna Indian ancestors, discusses the importance of all the stories she heard daily, which kept alive the oral tradition that sustains American Indian identity; in her essay "Where I Come from Is Like This," she demonstrates how this tradition adapts and counters stories from outside the culture. Finally, Garrett Hongo's essay "Kubota" also interprets family stories as a living inheritance. When

Hongo becomes the heir of his grandfather Kubota's story about Japanese-American experience during World War II, the private story he inherits restores public history to him as well. All the texts demonstrate the power of narratives, as well as the powerlessness that accompanies the silence when no stories are told.

ELLEN GILCHRIST

Music

Ellen Gilchrist was born in 1935 in Vicksburg, Mississippi, and was educated at Millsaps College, where she received her bachelor's degree in 1967. She also attended the University of Arkansas in 1976. Gilchrist's first collection of short stories, *In the Land of Dreamy Dreams* (1981), brought her public recognition and success; her second collection, *Victory over Japan* (1984), won the 1984 American Book Award for Fiction. Gilchrist has also written a volume of poetry, *The Land Surveyor's Daughter* (1979); several volumes of short stories, including *Drunk with Love* (1987), *Light Can Be Both Wave and Particle* (1989), and *I Cannot Get You Close Enough* (1990); and the novels *The Annunciation* (1983), *The Anna Papers* (1988), and *Net of Jewels* (1992).

The originality of Gilchrist's stories derives from their vivid depiction of rebellious women, especially Southern women, challenging the codes of genteel behavior. Gilchrist has won critical praise for her ability to concentrate on details that recreate the texture of Southern life. Like many of Gilchrist's early stories, which focus on the problems of young women, "Music," a story found in *Victory over Japan,* presents Rhoda (a recurring character in Gilchrist's work) during her troubled and rebellious adolescence. Rhoda's character illustrates the difficulties of growing up in the South in the fifties.

RHODA WAS FOURTEEN YEARS OLD the summer her father dragged her off to Clay County, Kentucky, to make her stop smoking and acting like a movie star. She was fourteen years old, a holy and terrible age, and her desire for beauty and romance drove her all day long and pursued her if she slept.

"Te amo," she whispered to herself in Latin class. "Te amo, Bob Rosen," sending the heat of her passions across the classroom and out through the window and across two states to a hospital room in Saint Louis, where a college boy lay recovering from a series of operations Rhoda had decided would be fatal.

"And you as well must die, beloved dust," she quoted to herself. "Oh, sleep forever in your Latmian cave, Mortal Endymion, darling of the moon," she whispered, and sometimes it was Bob Rosen's lanky body stretched out in

357

the cave beside his saxophone that she envisioned and sometimes it was her own lush, apricot-colored skin growing cold against the rocks in the moonlight.

Rhoda was fourteen years old that spring and her true love had been cruelly taken from her and she had started smoking because there was nothing left to do now but be a writer.

She was fourteen years old and she would sit on the porch at night looking down the hill that led through the small town of Franklin, Kentucky, and think about the stars, wondering where heaven could be in all that vastness, feeling betrayed by her mother's pale Episcopalianism and the fate that had brought her to this small town right in the middle of her sophomore year in high school. She would sit on the porch stuffing chocolate chip cookies into her mouth, drinking endless homemade chocolate milkshakes, smoking endless Lucky Strike cigarettes, watching her mother's transplanted roses move steadily across the trellis, taking Bob Rosen's thin letters in and out of their envelopes, holding them against her face, then going up to the new bedroom, to the soft, blue sheets, stuffed with cookies and ice cream and cigarettes and rage.

"Is that you, Rhoda?" her father would call out as she passed his bedroom. "Is that you, sweetie? Come tell us goodnight." And she would go into their bedroom and lean over and kiss him.

"You just ought to smell yourself," he would say, sitting up, pushing her away. "You just ought to smell those nasty cigarettes." And as soon as she went into her room he would go downstairs and empty all the ashtrays to make sure the house wouldn't burn down while he was sleeping.

"I've got to make her stop that goddamn smoking," he would say, climbing back into the bed. "I'm goddamned if I'm going to put up with that."

"I'd like to know how you're going to stop it," Rhoda's mother said. "I'd like to see anyone make Rhoda do anything she doesn't want to do. Not to mention that you're hardly ever here."

"Goddammit, Ariane, don't start that this time of night." And he rolled over on his side of the bed and began to plot his campaign against Rhoda's cigarettes.

Dudley Manning wasn't afraid of Rhoda, even if she was as stubborn as a goat. Dudley Manning wasn't afraid of anything. He had gotten up at dawn every day for years and believed in himself and followed his luck wherever it led him, dragging his sweet Southern wife and his children behind him, and now, in his fortieth year, he was about to become a millionaire.

He was about to become a millionaire and he was in love with a beautiful woman who was not his wife and it was the strangest spring he had ever known. When he added up the figures in his account books he was filled with awe at his own achievements, amazed at what he had made of himself, and to make up for it he talked a lot about luck and pretended to be humble but deep down inside he believed there was nothing he couldn't do, even love two women at once, even make Rhoda stop smoking.

Both Dudley and Rhoda were early risers. If he was in town he would be waiting in the kitchen when she came down to breakfast, dressed in his khakis, his pens in his pocket, his glasses on his nose, sitting at the table going over his papers, his head full of the clean new ideas of morning.

"How many more days of school do you have?" he said to her one morning, watching her light the first of her cigarettes without saying anything about it.

"Just this week," she said. "Just until Friday. I'm making A's, Daddy. 15 This is the easiest school I've ever been to."

"Well, don't be smart-alecky about it, Rhoda," he said. "If you've got a good mind it's only because God gave it to you."

"God didn't give me anything," she said. "Because there isn't any God."

"Well, let's don't get into an argument about that this morning," Dudley said. "As soon as you finish school I want you to drive up to the mines with me for a few days."

"For how long?" she said.

"We won't be gone long," he said. "I just want to take you to the mines 20 to look things over."

Rhoda french-inhaled, blowing the smoke out into the sunlight coming through the kitchen windows, imagining herself on a tour of her father's mines, the workers with their caps in their hands smiling at her as she walked politely among them. Rhoda liked that idea. She dropped two saccharin tablets into her coffee and sat down at the table, enjoying her fantasy.

"Is that what you're having for breakfast?" he said.

"I'm on a diet," Rhoda said. "I'm on a black coffee diet."

He looked down at his poached eggs, cutting into the yellow with his knife. I can wait, he said to himself. As God is my witness I can wait until Sunday.

Rhoda poured herself another cup of coffee and went upstairs to write 25 Bob Rosen before she left for school.

Dear Bob [the letter began],

School is almost over. I made straight A's, of course, as per your instructions. This school is so easy it's crazy.

They read one of my newspaper columns on the radio in Nashville. Everyone in Franklin goes around saying my mother writes my columns. Can you believe that? Allison Hotchkiss, that's my editor, say she's going to write an editorial about it saying I really write them.

I turned my bedroom into an office and took out the tacky dressing table mother made me and got a desk and put my typewriter on

*it and made striped drapes, green and black and white. I think you
would approve.*

*Sunday Daddy is taking me to Manchester, Kentucky, to look
over the coal mines. He's going to let me drive. He lets me drive* all
the time. *I live for your letters.*

> *Te amo,*
> *Rhoda*

She put the letter in a pale blue envelope, sealed it, dripped some Toujours
Moi lavishly onto it in several places, and threw herself down on her bed.

She pressed her face deep down into her comforter pretending it was Bob
Rosen's smooth cool skin. "Oh, Bob, Bob," she whispered to the comforter.
"Oh, honey, don't die, don't die, please don't die." She could feel the tears
coming. She reached out and caressed the seam of the comforter, pretending
it was the scar on Bob Rosen's neck.

The last night she had been with him he had just come home from an
operation for a mysterious tumor that he didn't want to talk about. It would
be better soon, was all he would say about it. Before long he would be as good
as new.

They had driven out of town and parked the old Pontiac underneath a
tree beside a pasture. It was September and Rhoda had lain in his arms smelling the clean smell of his new sweater, touching the fresh red scars on his
neck, looking out the window to memorize every detail of the scene, the black
tree, the September pasture, the white horse leaning against the fence, the
palms of his hands, the taste of their cigarettes, the night breeze, the exact
temperature of the air, saying to herself over and over, I must remember everything. This will have to last me forever and ever and ever.

"I want you to do it to me," she said. "Whatever it is they do."

"I can't," he said. "I couldn't do that now. It's too much trouble to make   30
love to a virgin." He was laughing. "Besides, it's hard to do it in a car."

"But I'm leaving," she said. "I might not ever see you again."

"Not tonight," he said. "I still don't feel very good, Rhoda."

"What if I come back and visit," she said. "Will you do it then? When
you feel better."

"If you still want me to I will," he said. "If you come back to visit and we
both want to, I will."

"Do you promise?" she said, hugging him fiercely.   35

"I promise," he said. "On my honor I promise to do it when you come to
visit."

But Rhoda was not allowed to go to Saint Louis to visit. Either her
mother guessed her intentions or else she seized the opportunity to do what
she had been wanting to do all along and stop her daughter from seeing a boy
with a Jewish last name.

There were weeks of pleadings and threats. It all ended one Sunday night when Mrs. Manning lost her temper and made the statement that Jews were little peddlers who went through the Delta selling needles and pins.

"You don't know what you're talking about," Rhoda screamed. "He's not a peddler, and I love him and I'm going to love him until I die." Rhoda pulled her arms away from her mother's hands.

"I'm going up there this weekend to see him," she screamed. "Daddy   40 promised me I could and you're not going to stop me and if you try to stop me I'll kill you and I'll run away and I'll never come back."

"You are not going to Saint Louis and that's the end of this conversation and if you don't calm down I'll call a doctor and have you locked up. I think you're crazy, Rhoda. I really do."

"I'm not crazy," Rhoda screamed. "You're the one that's crazy."

"You and your father think you're so smart," her mother said. She was shaking but she held her ground, moving around behind a Queen Anne chair. "Well, I don't care how smart you are, you're not going to get on a train and go off to Saint Louis, Missouri, to see a man when you're only fourteen years old, and that, Miss Rhoda K. Manning, is that."

"I'm going to kill you," Rhoda said. "I really am. I'm going to kill you," and she thought for a moment that she would kill her, but then she noticed her grandmother's Limoges hot chocolate pot sitting on top of the piano holding a spray of yellow jasmine, and she walked over to the piano and picked it up and threw it all the way across the room and smashed it into a wall beside a framed print of "The Blue Boy."

"I hate you," Rhoda said. "I wish you were dead." And while her mother   45 stared in disbelief at the wreck of the sainted hot chocolate pot, Rhoda walked out of the house and got in the car and drove off down the steep driveway. I hate her guts, she said to herself. I hope she cries herself to death.

She shifted into second gear and drove off toward her father's office, quoting to herself from Edna Millay. "Now by this moon, before this moon shall wane, I shall be dead or I shall be with you."

But in the end Rhoda didn't die. Neither did she kill her mother. Neither did she go to Saint Louis to give her virginity to her reluctant lover.

The Sunday of the trip Rhoda woke at dawn feeling very excited and changed clothes four or five times trying to decide how she wanted to look for her inspection of the mines.

Rhoda had never even seen a picture of a strip mine. In her imagination she and her father would be riding an elevator down into the heart of a mountain where obsequious masked miners were lined up to shake her hand. Later that evening the captain of the football team would be coming over to the hotel to meet her and take her somewhere for a drive.

She pulled on a pair of pink pedal pushers and a long navy blue sweat   50 shirt, threw every single thing she could possibly imagine wearing into a large suitcase, and started down the stairs to where her father was calling for her to hurry up.

Her mother followed her out of the house holding a buttered biscuit on a linen napkin. "Please eat something before you leave," she said. "There isn't a decent restaurant after you leave Bowling Green."

"I told you I don't want anything to eat," Rhoda said. "I'm on a diet." She stared at the biscuit as though it were a coral snake.

"One biscuit isn't going to hurt you," her mother said. "I made you a lunch, chicken and carrot sticks and apples."

"I don't want it," Rhoda said. "Don't put any food in this car, Mother."

"Just because you never eat doesn't mean your father won't get hungry.   55
You don't have to eat any of it unless you want to." Their eyes met. Then they sighed and looked away.

Her father appeared at the door and climbed in behind the wheel of the secondhand Cadillac.

"Let's go, Sweet Sister," he said, cruising down the driveway, turning onto the road leading to Bowling Green and due east into the hill country. Usually this was his favorite moment of the week, starting the long drive into the rich Kentucky hills where his energy and intelligence had created the long black rows of figures in the account books, figures that meant Rhoda would never know what it was to be really afraid or uncertain or powerless.

"How long will it take?" Rhoda asked.

"Don't worry about that," he said. "Just look out the window and enjoy the ride. This is beautiful country we're driving through."

"I can't right now," Rhoda said. "I want to read the new book Allison   60
gave me. It's a book of poems."

She settled down into the seat and opened the book.

> *Oh, gallant was the first love, and glittering and fine;*
> *The second love was water, in a clear blue cup;*
> *The third love was his, and the fourth was mine.*
> *And after that, I always get them all mixed up.*

Oh, God, this is good, she thought. She sat up straighter, wanting to kiss the book. Oh, God, this is really good. She turned the book over to look at the picture of the author. It was a photograph of a small bright face in full profile staring off into the mysterious brightly lit world of a poet's life.

Dorothy Parker, she read. What a wonderful name. Maybe I'll change my name to Dorothy, Dorothy Louise Manning. Dot Manning. Dottie, Dottie Leigh, Dot.

Rhoda pulled a pack of Lucky Strikes out of her purse, tamped it on the dashboard, opened it, extracted a cigarette, and lit it with a gold Ronson lighter. She inhaled deeply and went back to the book.

Her father gripped the wheel, trying to concentrate on the beauty of the   65
morning, the green fields, the small, neat farmhouses, the red barns, the cattle
and horses. He moved his eyes from all that order to his fourteen-year-old
daughter slumped beside him with her nose buried in a book, her plump
fingers languishing in the air, holding a cigarette. He slowed down, pulled the
car onto the side of the road, and killed the motor.

"What's wrong?" Rhoda said. "Why are you stopping?"

"Because you are going to put out that goddamn cigarette this very minute and you're going to give me the package and you're not going to smoke
another cigarette around me as long as you live," he said.

"I will not do any such thing," Rhoda said. "It's a free country."

"Give me the cigarette, Rhoda," he said. "Hand it here."

"Give me one good reason why I should," she said. But her voice let   70
her down. She knew there wasn't any use in arguing. This was not her soft
little mother she was dealing with. This was Dudley Manning, who had
been a famous baseball player until he quit when she was born. Who before that had gone to the Olympics on a relay team. There were scrapbooks full of his clippings in Rhoda's house. No matter where the Man-
nings went those scrapbooks sat on a table in the den. *Manning Hits One
Over The Fence*, the headlines read. *Manning Saves The Day. Manning
Does It Again.* And he was not the only one. His cousin, Philip Manning,
down in Jackson, Mississippi, was famous too. Who was the father of the
famous Crystal Manning, Rhoda's cousin who had a fur coat when she
was ten. And Leland Manning, who was her cousin Lele's daddy. Leland
had been the captain of the Tulane football team before he drank himself
to death in the Delta.

Rhoda sighed, thinking of all that, and gave in for the moment. "Give me
one good reason and I might," she repeated.

"I don't have to give you a reason for a goddamn thing," he said. "Give
the cigarette here, Rhoda. Right this minute." He reached out and took it and
she didn't resist. "Goddamn, these things smell awful," he said, crushing it in
the ashtray. He reached in her pocketbook and got the package and threw it
out the window.

"Only white trash throw things out on the road," Rhoda said. "You'd
kill me if I did that."

"Well, let's just be quiet and get to where we're going." He started the
motor and drove back out onto the highway. Rhoda crunched down lower in
the seat, pretending to read her book. Who cares, she thought. I'll get some as
soon as we stop for gas.

Getting cigarettes at filling stations was not as easy as Rhoda thought it   75
was going to be. This was God's country they were driving into now, the hills
rising up higher and higher, strange, silent little houses back off the road.
Rhoda could feel the eyes looking out at her from behind the silent windows.

Poor white trash, Rhoda's mother would have called them. The salt of the earth, her father would have said.

This was God's country and these people took things like children smoking cigarettes seriously. At both places where they stopped there was a sign by the cash register, *No Cigarettes Sold To Minors.*

Rhoda had moved to the back seat of the Cadillac and was stretched out on the seat reading her book. She found another poem she liked and she was memorizing it.

> *Four be the things I'd be better without,*
> *Love, curiosity, freckles and doubt.*
> *Three be the things I shall never attain,*
> *Envy, content and sufficient champagne.*

Oh, God, I love this book, she thought. *This Dorothy Parker is just like me.* Rhoda was remembering a night when she got drunk in Clarkesville, Mississippi, with her cousin, Baby Gwen Barksdale. They got drunk on tequila LaGrande Conroy brought back from Mexico, and Rhoda had slept all night in the bathtub so she would be near the toilet when she vomited.

She put her head down on her arm and giggled, thinking about waking up in the bathtub. Then a plan occurred to her.

"Stop and let me go to the bathroom," she said to her father. "I think I'm going to throw up." 80

"Oh, Lord," he said. "I knew you shouldn't have gotten in the back seat. Well, hold on. I'll stop the first place I see." He pushed his hat back off his forehead and began looking for a place to stop, glancing back over his shoulder every now and then to see if she was all right. Rhoda had a long history of throwing up on car trips so he was taking this seriously. Finally he saw a combination store and filling station at a bend in the road and pulled up beside the front door.

"I'll be all right," Rhoda said, jumping out of the car. "You stay here. I'll be right back."

She walked dramatically up the wooden steps and pushed open the screen door. It was so quiet and dark inside she thought for a moment the store was closed. She looked around. She was in a rough, high-ceilinged room with saddles and pieces of farm equipment hanging from the rafters and a sparse array of canned goods on wooden shelves behind a counter. On the counter were five or six large glass jars filled with different kinds of Nabisco cookies. Rhoda stared at the cookie jars, wanting to stick her hand down inside and take out great fistfuls of Lorna Doones and Oreos. She fought off her hunger and raised her eyes to the display of chewing tobacco and cigarettes.

The smells of the store rose up to meet her, fecund and rich, moist and cool, as if the store was an extension of the earth outside. Rhoda looked down at the board floor. She felt she could have dropped a sunflower seed on the floor and it would instantly sprout and take bloom, growing quick, moving down into the earth and upwards toward the rafters.

"Is anybody here?" she said softly, then louder. "Is anybody here?"   85

A woman in a cotton dress appeared in a door, staring at Rhoda out of very intense, very blue eyes.

"Can I buy a pack of cigarettes from you?" Rhoda said. "My dad's in the car. He sent me to get them."

"What kind of cigarettes you looking for?" the woman said, moving to the space between the cash register and the cookie jars.

"Some Luckies if you have them," Rhoda said. "He said to just get anything you had if you didn't have that."

"They're a quarter," the woman said, reaching behind herself to take the   90 package down and lay it on the counter, not smiling, but not being unkind either.

"Thank you," Rhoda said, laying the quarter down on the counter. "Do you have any matches?"

"Sure," the woman said, holding out a box of kitchen matches. Rhoda took a few, letting her eyes leave the woman's face and come to rest on the jars of Oreos. They looked wonderful and light, as though they had been there a long time and grown soft around the edges.

The woman was smiling now. "You want one of those cookies?" she said. "You want one, you go on and have one. It's free."

"Oh, no thank you," Rhoda said. "I'm on a diet. Look, do you have a ladies' room I can use?"

"It's out back," the woman said. "You can have one of them cookies if   95 you want it. Like I said, it won't cost you nothing."

"I guess I'd better get going," Rhoda said. "My dad's in a hurry. But thank you anyway. And thanks for the matches." Rhoda hurried down the aisle, slipped out the back door and leaned up against the back of the store, tearing the paper off the cigarettes. She pulled one out, lit it, and inhaled deeply, blowing the smoke out in front of her, watching it rise up into the air, casting a veil over the hills that rose up behind and to the left of her. She had never been in such a strange country. It looked as though no one ever did anything to their yards or roads or fences. It looked as though there might not be a clock for miles.

She inhaled again, feeling dizzy and full. She had just taken the cigarette out of her mouth when her father came bursting out of the door and grabbed both of her wrists in his hands.

"Let go of me," she said. "Let go of me this minute." She struggled to free herself, ready to kick or claw or bite, ready for a real fight, but he held her off. "Drop the cigarette, Rhoda," he said. "Drop it on the ground."

"I'll kill you," she said. "As soon as I get away I'm running away to Florida. Let go of me, Daddy. Do you hear me?"

"I hear you," he said. The veins were standing out on his forehead. His 100
face was so close Rhoda could see his freckles and the line where his false
front tooth was joined to what was left of the real one. He had lost the tooth
in a baseball game the day Rhoda was born. That was how he told the story.
"I lost that tooth the day Rhoda was born," he would say. "I was playing left
field against Memphis in the old Crump Stadium. I slid into second and the
second baseman got me with his shoe."

"You can smoke all you want to when you get down to Florida," he was
saying now. "But you're not smoking on this trip. So you might as well calm
down before I drive off and leave you here."

"I don't care," she said. "Go on and leave. I'll just call up Mother and
she'll come and get me." She was struggling to free her wrists but she could
not move them inside his hands. "Let go of me, you big bully," she added.

"Will you calm down and give me the cigarettes?"

"All right," she said, but the minute he let go of her hands she turned and
began to hit him on the shoulders, pounding her fists up and down on his
back, not daring to put any real force behind the blows. He pretended to
cower under the assault. She caught his eye and saw that he was laughing at
her and she had to fight the desire to laugh with him.

"I'm getting in the car," she said. "I'm sick of this place." She walked 105
grandly around to the front of the store, got into the car, tore open the lunch
and began to devour it, tearing the chicken off the bones with her teeth, swal-
lowing great hunks without even bothering to chew them. "I'm never speaking to you again as long as I live," she said, her mouth full of chicken breast.
"You are not my father."

"Suits me, Miss Smart-alecky Movie Star," he said, putting his hat back
on his head. "Soon as we get home you can head on out for Florida. You just
let me know when you're leaving so I can give you some money for the bus."

"I hate you," Rhoda mumbled to herself, starting in on the homemade
raisin cookies. I hate your guts. I hope you go to hell forever, she thought,
breaking a cookie into pieces so she could pick out the raisins.

It was late afternoon when the Cadillac picked its way up a rocky red clay
driveway to a housetrailer nestled in the curve of a hill beside a stand of pine
trees.

"Where are we going?" Rhoda said. "Would you just tell me that?"

"We're going to see Maud and Joe Samples," he said. "Joe's an old hand 110
around here. He's my right-hand man in Clay County. Now you just be polite
and try to learn something, Sister. These are real folks you're about to meet."

"Why are we going here first?" Rhoda said. "Aren't we going to a hotel?"

"There isn't any hotel," her father said. "Does this look like someplace they'd have hotels? Maud and Joe are going to put you up for me while I'm off working."

"I'm going to stay here?" Rhoda said. "In this trailer?"

"Just wait until you see the inside," her father said. "It's like the inside of a boat, everything all planned out and just the right amount of space for things. I wish your mother'd let me live in a trailer."

They were almost to the door now. A plump smiling woman came out onto the wooden platform and waited for them with her hands on her hips, smiling wider and wider as they got nearer.

"There's Maud," Dudley said. "She's the sweetest woman in the world and the best cook in Kentucky. Hey there, Miss Maud," he called out.

"Mr. D," she said, opening the car door for them. "Joe Samples' been waiting on you all day and here you show up bringing this beautiful girl just like you promised. I've made you some blackberry pies. Come on inside this trailer." Maud smiled deep into Rhoda's face. Her eyes were as blue as the ones on the woman in the store. Rhoda's mother had blue eyes, but not this brilliant and not this blue. These eyes were from another world, another century.

"Come on in and see Joe," Maud said. "He's been having a fit for you to get here."

They went inside and Dudley showed Rhoda all around the trailer, praising the design of trailers. Maud turned on the tiny oven and they had blackberry pie and bread and butter sandwiches and Rhoda abandoned her diet and ate two pieces of the pie, covering it with thick whipped cream.

The men went off to talk business and Maud took Rhoda to a small room at the back of the trailer decorated to match a handmade quilt of the sunrise.

There were yellow ruffled curtains at the windows and a tiny dressing table with a yellow ruffle skirt around the edges. Rhoda was enchanted by the smallness of everything and the way the windows looked out onto layers of green trees and bushes.

Lying on the dresser was a white leather Bible and a display of small white pamphlets, *Alcohol And You, When Jesus Reaches For A Drink, You Are Not Alone, Sorry Isn't Enough, Taking No For An Answer.*

It embarrassed Rhoda even to read the titles of anything as tacky as the pamphlets, but she didn't let on she thought it was tacky, not with Maud sitting on the bed telling her how pretty she was every other second and asking her questions about herself and saying how wonderful her father was.

"We love Mr. D to death," she said. "It's like he was one of our own."

He appeared in the door. "Rhoda, if you're settled in I'll be leaving now," he said. "I've got to drive to Knoxville to do some business but I'll be back here Tuesday morning to take you to the mines." He handed her three twenty-dollar bills. "Here," he said. "In case you need anything."

He left then and hurried out to the car, trying to figure out how long it would take him to get to Knoxville, to where Valerie sat alone in a hotel room waiting for this night they had planned for so long. He felt the sweet hot guilt rise up in his face and the sweet hot longing in his legs and hands.

I'm sorry, Jesus, he thought, pulling out onto the highway. I know it's wrong and I know we're doing wrong. So go on and punish me if you have to but just let me make it there and back before you start in on me.

He set the cruising speed at exactly fifty-five miles an hour and began to sing to himself as he drove.

> *"Oh, sure as the vine grows around the stump*
> *You're my darling sugar lump,"* he sang, and;

> *"Froggy went a-courting and he did ride,*
> *Huhhrummp, Huhhrummp,*
> *Froggy went a-courting and he did ride, Huhhrummp,*

> *What you gonna have for the wedding supper?*
> *Black-eyed peas and bread and butter, Huhhrummp,*
> *huhhrummp . . ."*

Rhoda was up and dressed when her father came to get her on Tuesday morning. It was still dark outside but a rooster had begun to crow in the distance. Maud bustled all about the little kitchen making much of them, filling their plates with biscuits and fried eggs and ham and gravy.

Then they got into the Cadillac and began to drive toward the mine. Dud- 130 ley was driving slowly, pointing out everything to her as they rode along.

"Up on that knoll," he said, "that's where the Traylors live. Rooster Traylor's a man about my age. Last year his mother shot one of the Galtney women for breaking up Rooster's marriage and now the Galtneys have got to shoot someone in the Traylor family."

"That's terrible," Rhoda said.

"No it isn't, Sister," he said, warming into the argument. "These people take care of their own problems."

"They actually shoot each other?" she said. "And you think that's okay? You think that's funny?"

"I think it's just as good as waiting around for some judge and jury to do 135 it for you."

"Then you're just crazy," Rhoda said. "You're as crazy as you can be."

"Well, let's don't argue about it this morning. Come on. I've got some-thing to show you." He pulled the car off the road and they walked into the woods, following a set of bulldozer tracks that made a crude path into the trees. It was quiet in the woods and smelled of pine and sassafras. Rhoda watched her father's strong body moving in front of her, striking along, in-specting everything, noticing everything, commenting on everything.

"Look at this," he said. "Look at all this beauty, honey. Look at how beautiful all this is. This is the real world. Not those goddamn movies and beauty parlors and magazines. This is the world that God made. This is where people are really happy."

"There isn't any God," she said. "Nobody that knows anything believes in God, Daddy. That's just a lot of old stuff . . ."

"I'm telling you, Rhoda," he said. "It breaks my heart to see the way   140 you're growing up." He stopped underneath a tree, took a seat on a log, and turned his face to hers. Tears were forming in his eyes. He was famous in the family for being able to cry on cue. "You've just got to learn to listen to someone. You've got to get some common sense in your head. I swear to God, I worry about you all the time." The tears were falling now. "I just can't stand to see the way you're growing up. I don't know where you get all those crazy ideas you come up with."

Rhoda looked down, caught off guard by the tears. No matter how many times he pulled that with the tears she fell for it for a moment. The summer forest was all around them, soft deep earth beneath their feet, morning light falling through the leaves, and the things that passed between them were too hard to understand. Their brown eyes met and locked and after that they were bound to start an argument for no one can bear to be that happy or that close to another human being.

"Well, I'll tell you one thing," Rhoda said. "It's a free country and I can smoke if I want to and you can't keep me from doing it by locking me up in a trailer with some poor white trash."

"What did you say?" he said, getting a look on his face that would have scared a grown man to death. "What did you just say, Rhoda?"

"I said I'm sick and tired of being locked up in that damned old trailer with those corny people and nothing to read but religious magazines. I want to get some cigarettes and I want you to take me home so I can see my friends and get my column written for next week."

"Oh, God, Sister," he said. "Haven't I taught you anything? Maud Sam-   145 ples is the salt of the earth. That woman raised seven children. She knows things you and I will never know as long as we live."

"Well, no she doesn't," Rhoda said. "She's just an old white trash country woman and if Momma knew where I was she'd have a fit."

"Your momma is a very stupid person," he said. "And I'm sorry I ever let her raise you." He turned his back to her then and stalked on out of the woods to a road that ran like a red scar up the side of the mountain. "Come on," he said. "I'm going to take you up there and show you where coal comes from. Maybe you can learn one thing this week."

"I learn things all the time," she said. "I already know more than half the people I know . . . I know . . ."

"Please don't talk anymore this morning," he said. "I'm burned out talking to you."

He put her into a jeep and began driving up the steep unpaved road. In a minute he was feeling better, cheered up by the sight of the big Caterpillar tractors moving dirt. If there was one thing that always cheered him up it was the sight of a big shovel moving dirt. "This is Blue Gem coal," he said. "The hardest in the area. See the layers. Topsoil, then gravel and dirt or clay, then slate, then thirteen feet of pure coal. Some people think it was made by dinosaurs. Other people think God put it there."

"This is it?" she said. "This is the mine?" It looked like one of his road construction projects. Same yellow tractors, same disorderly activity. The only difference seemed to be the huge piles of coal and a conveyor belt going down the mountain to a train.

"This is it," he said. "This is where they stored the old dinosaurs."

"Well, it is made out of dinosaurs," she said. "There were a lot of leaves and trees and dinosaurs and then they died and the coal and oil is made out of them."

"All right," he said. "Let's say I'll go along with the coal. But tell me this, who made the slate then? Who put the slate right on top of the coal everywhere it's found in this world? Who laid the slate down on top of the dinosaurs?"

"I don't know who put the slate there," she said. "We haven't got that far yet."

"You haven't got that far?" he said. "You mean the scientists haven't got as far as the slate yet? Well, Sister, that's the problem with you folks that evolved out of monkeys. You're still half-baked. You aren't finished like us old dumb ones that God made."

"I didn't say the scientists hadn't got that far," she said. "I just said I hadn't got that far."

"It's a funny thing to me how all those dinosaurs came up here to die in the mountains and none of them died in the farmland," he said. "It sure would have made it a lot easier on us miners if they'd died down there on the flat."

While she was groping around for an answer he went right on. "Tell me this, Sister," he said. "Are any of your monkey ancestors in there with the dinosaurs, or is it just plain dinosaurs? I'd like to know who all I'm digging up . . . I'd like to give credit . . ."

The jeep had come to a stop and Joe was coming towards them, hurrying out of the small tin-roofed office with a worried look on his face. "Mr. D, you better call up to Jellico. Beb's been looking everywhere for you. They had a run-in with a teamster organizer. You got to call him right away."

"What's wrong?" Rhoda said. "What happened?"

"Nothing you need to worry about, Sister," her father said. He turned to Joe. "Go find Preacher and tell him to drive Rhoda back to your house. You go on now, honey. I've got work to do." He gave her a kiss on the cheek and disappeared into the office. A small shriveled-looking man came limping out of a building and climbed into the driver's seat. "I'm Preacher," he said. "Mr. Joe tole me to drive you up to his place."

"All right," Rhoda said. "I guess that's okay with me." Preacher put the jeep in gear and drove it slowly down the winding rutted road. By the time they got to the bottom Rhoda had thought of a better plan. "I'll drive now," she said. "I'll drive myself to Maud's. It's all right with my father. He lets me drive all the time. You can walk back, can't you?" Preacher didn't know what to say to that. He was an old drunk that Dudley and Joe kept around to run errands. He was so used to taking orders that finally he climbed down out of the jeep and did as he was told. "Show me the way to town," Rhoda said. "Draw me a map. I have to go by town on my way to Maud's." Preacher scratched his head, then bent over and drew her a little map in the dust on the hood. Rhoda studied the map, put the jeep into the first forward gear she could find, and drove off down the road to the little town of Manchester, Kentucky, studying the diagram on the gearshift as she drove.

She parked beside a boardwalk that led through the main street of town and started off looking for a store that sold cigarettes. One of the stores had dresses in the window. In the center was a red strapless sundress with a white jacket. $6.95, the price tag said. I hate the way I look, she decided. I hate these tacky pants. I've got sixty dollars. I don't have to look like this if I don't want to. I can buy anything I want.

She went inside, asked the clerk to take the dress out of the window and 165 in a few minutes she emerged from the store wearing the dress and a pair of leather sandals with two-inch heels. The jacket was thrown carelessly over her shoulder like Gene Tierney in *Leave Her to Heaven*. I look great in red, she was thinking, catching a glimpse of herself in a store window. It isn't true that redheaded people can't wear red. She walked on down the boardwalk, admiring herself in every window.

She walked for two blocks looking for a place to try her luck getting cigarettes. She was almost to the end of the boardwalk when she came to a pool hall. She stood in the door looking in, smelling the dark smell of tobacco and beer. The room was deserted except for a man leaning on a cue stick beside a table and a boy with black hair seated behind a cash register reading a book. The boy's name was Johnny Hazard and he was sixteen years old. The book he was reading was *U.S.A.* by John Dos Passos. A woman who came to Manchester to teach poetry writing had given him the book. She had made a dust jacket for it out of brown paper so he could read it in public. On the spine of the jacket she had written *American History*.

"I'd like a package of Lucky Strikes," Rhoda said, holding out a twenty-dollar bill in his direction.

"We don't sell cigarettes to minors," he said. "It's against the law."

"I'm not a minor," Rhoda said. "I'm eighteen. I'm Rhoda Manning. My daddy owns the mine."

"Which mine?" he said. He was watching her breasts as she talked, get- 170 ting caught up in the apricot skin against the soft red dress.

"The mine," she said. "The Manning mine. I just got here the other day. I haven't been downtown before."

"So, how do you like our town?"

"Please sell me some cigarettes," she said. "I'm about to have a fit for a Lucky."

"I can't sell you cigarettes," he said. "You're not any more eighteen years old than my dog."

"Yes, I am," she said. "I drove here in a jeep, doesn't that prove any- 175 thing?" She was looking at his wide shoulders and the tough flat chest beneath his plaid shirt.

"Are you a football player?" she said.

"When I have time," he said. "When I don't have to work on the nights they have games."

"I'm a cheerleader where I live," Rhoda said. "I just got elected again for next year."

"What kind of a jeep?" he said.

"An old one," she said. "It's filthy dirty. They use it at the mine." She had 180 just noticed the package of Camels in his breast pocket.

"If you won't sell me a whole package, how about selling me one," she said. "I'll give you a dollar for a cigarette." She raised the twenty-dollar bill and laid it down on the glass counter.

He ignored the twenty-dollar bill, opened the cash register, removed a quarter, and walked over to the jukebox. He walked with a precise, balanced sort of cockiness, as if he knew he could walk any way he wanted but had carefully chosen this particular walk as his own. He walked across the room through the rectangle of light coming in the door, walking as though he were the first boy ever to be in the world, the first boy ever to walk across a room and put a quarter into a jukebox. He pushed a button and music filled the room.

> *Kaw-Liga was a wooden Indian a-standing by the door,*
> *He fell in love with an Indian maid*
> *Over in the antique store.*

"My uncle wrote that song," he said, coming back to her. "But it got ripped off by some promoters in Nashville. I'll make you a deal," he said. "I'll give you a cigarette if you'll give me a ride somewhere I have to go." "All right," Rhoda said. "Where do you want to go?"

"Out to my cousin's," he said. "It isn't far."

"Fine," Rhoda said. Johnny told the lone pool player to keep an eye on 185 things and the two of them walked out into the sunlight, walking together very formally down the street to where the jeep was parked.

"Why don't you let me drive," he said. "It might be easier." She agreed and he drove on up the mountain to a house that looked deserted. He went in and returned carrying a guitar in a case, a blanket, and a quart bottle with a piece of wax paper tied around the top with a rubber band.

"What's in the bottle?" Rhoda said.

"Lemonade, with a little sweetening in it."

"Like whiskey?"

"Yeah. Like whiskey. Do you ever drink it?"   190

"Sure," she said. "I drink a lot. In Saint Louis we had this club called The Four Roses that met every Monday at Donna Duston's house to get drunk. I thought it up, the club I mean."

"Well, here's your cigarette," he said. He took the package from his pocket and offered her one, holding it near his chest so she had to get in close to take it.

"Oh, God," she said. "Oh, thank you so much. I'm about to die for a ciggie. I haven't had one in days. Because my father dragged me up here to make me stop smoking. He's always trying to make me do something I don't want to do. But it never works. I'm very hardheaded, like him." She took the light Johnny offered her and blew out the smoke in a small controlled stream. "God, I love to smoke," she said.

"I'm glad I could help you out," he said. "Anytime you want one when you're here you just come on over. Look," he said. "I'm going somewhere you might want to see, if you're not in a hurry to get back. You got time to go and see something with me?"

"What is it?" she asked.   195

"Something worth seeing," he said. "The best thing in Clay County there is to see."

"Sure," she said. "I'll go. I never turn down an adventure. Why not, that's what my cousins in the Delta always say. Whyyyyyyy not." They drove up the mountain and parked and began to walk into the woods along a path. The woods were deeper here than where Rhoda had been that morning, dense and green and cool. She felt silly walking in the woods in the little high-heeled sandals, but she held on to Johnny's hand and followed him deeper and deeper into the trees, feeling grown up and brave and romantic. I'll bet he thinks I'm the bravest girl he ever met, she thought. I'll bet he thinks at last he's met a girl who's not afraid of anything. Rhoda was walking along imagining tearing off a piece of her dress for a tourniquet in case Johnny was bit by a poisonous snake. She was pulling the tourniquet tighter and tighter when the trees opened onto a small brilliant blue pond. The water was so blue Rhoda thought for a moment it must be some sort of trick. He stood there watching her while she took it in.

"What do you think?" he said at last.

"My God," she said. "What is it?"

"It's Blue Pond," he said. "People come from all over the world to see it." 200

"Who made it?" Rhoda said. "Where did it come from?"

"Springs. Rock springs. No one knows how deep down it goes, but more than a hundred feet because divers have been that far."

"I wish I could swim in it," Rhoda said. "I'd like to jump in there and swim all day."

"Come over here, cheerleader," he said. "Come sit over here by me and we'll watch the light on it. I brought this teacher from New York here last year. She said it was the best thing she'd ever seen in her life. She's a writer. Anyway, the thing she likes about Blue Pond is watching the light change on the water. She taught me a lot when she was here. About things like that."

Rhoda moved nearer to him, trying to hold in her stomach. 205

"My father really likes this part of the country," she said. "He says people up here are the salt of the earth. He says all the people up here are direct descendants from England and Scotland and Wales. I think he wants us to move up here and stay, but my mother won't let us. It's all because the unions keep messing with his mine that he has to be up here all the time. If it wasn't for the unions everything would be going fine. You aren't for the unions, are you?"

"I'm for myself," Johnny said. "And for my kinfolks." He was tired of her talking then and reached for her and pulled her into his arms, paying no attention to her small resistances, until finally she was stretched out under him on the earth and he moved the dress from her breasts and held them in his hands. He could smell the wild smell of her craziness and after a while he took the dress off and the soft white cotton underpants and touched her over and over again. Then he entered her with the way he had of doing things, gently and with a good sense of the natural rhythms of the earth.

I'm doing it, Rhoda thought. I'm doing it. This is doing it. This is what it feels like to be doing it.

"This doesn't hurt a bit," she said out loud. "I think I love you, Johnny. I love, love, love you. I've been waiting all my life for you."

"Don't talk so much," he said. "It's better if you stop talking." 210

And Rhoda was quiet and he made love to her as the sun was leaving the earth and the afternoon breeze moved in the trees. Here was every possible tree, hickory and white oak and redwood and sumac and maple, all in thick foliage now, and he made love to her with great tenderness, forgetting he had set out to fuck the boss's daughter, and he kept on making love to her until she began to tighten around him, not knowing what she was doing, or where she was going, or even that there was anyplace to be going to.

Dudley was waiting outside the trailer when she drove up. There was a sky full of cold stars behind him, and he was pacing up and down and talking to himself like a crazy man. Maud was inside the trailer crying her heart out and only Joe had kept his head and was going back and forth from one to the other telling them everything would be all right.

Dudley was pacing up and down talking to Jesus. I know I had it coming, he was saying. I know goddamn well I had it coming. But not her. Where in the hell is she? You get her back in one piece and I'll call Valerie and break it off. I won't see Valerie ever again as long as I live. *But you've got to get me back my little girl. Goddammit, you get me back my girl.*

Then he was crying, his head thrown back and raised up to the stars as the jeep came banging up the hill in third gear. Rhoda parked it and got out and started walking toward him, all bravado and disdain.

Dudley smelled it on her before he even touched her. Smelled it all over her and began to shake her, screaming at her to tell him who it had been. Then Joe came running out from the trailer and threw his hundred and fifty pounds between them, and Maud was right behind him. She led Rhoda into the trailer and put her into bed and sat beside her, bathing her head with a damp towel until she fell asleep.

"I'll find out who it was," Dudley said, shaking his fist. "I'll find out who it was."

"You don't know it was anybody," Joe said. "You don't even know what happened, Mr. D. Now you got to calm down and in the morning we'll find out what happened. More than likely she's just been holed up somewhere trying to scare you."

"I know what happened," Dudley said. "I already know what happened."

"Well, you can find out who it was and you can kill him if you have to," Joe said. "If it's true and you still want to in the morning, you can kill him."

But there would be no killing. By the time the moon was high, Johnny Hazard was halfway between Lexington, Kentucky, and Cincinnati, Ohio, with a bus ticket he bought with the fifty dollars he'd taken from Rhoda's pocket. He had called the poetry teacher and told her he was coming. Johnny had decided it was time to see the world. After all, that very afternoon a rich cheerleader had cried in his arms and given him her cherry. There was no telling what might happen next.

Much later that night Rhoda woke up in the small room, hearing the wind come up in the trees. The window was open and the moon, now low in the sky and covered with mist, poured a diffused light upon the bed. Rhoda sat up in the bed and shivered. Why did I do that with him? she thought. Why in the world did I do that? But I couldn't help it, she decided. He's so sophisticated and he's so good-looking and he's a wonderful driver and he plays a guitar. She moved her hands along her thighs, trying to remember exactly what it was they had done, trying to remember the details, wondering where she could find him in the morning.

But Dudley had other plans for Rhoda in the morning. By noon she was on her way home in a chartered plane. Rhoda had never been on an airplane of any kind before, but she didn't let on.

"I'm thinking of starting a diary," she was saying to the pilot, arranging her skirt so her knees would show. "A lot of unusual things have been happening to me lately. The boy I love is dying of cancer in Saint Louis. It's very sad, but I have to put up with it. He wants me to write a lot of books and dedicate them to his memory."

The pilot didn't seem to be paying much attention, so Rhoda gave up on him and went back into her own head.

In her head Bob Rosen was alive after all. He was walking along a street in Greenwich Village and passed a bookstore with a window full of her books, many copies stacked in a pyramid with her picture on every cover. He recognized the photograph, ran into the bookstore, grabbed a book, opened it, and saw the dedication. *To Bob Rosen, Te Amo Forever, Rhoda.*

Then Bob Rosen, or maybe it was Johnny Hazard, or maybe this unfriendly pilot, stood there on that city street, looking up at the sky, holding the book against his chest, crying and broken-hearted because Rhoda was lost to him forever, this famous author, who could have been his, lost to him forever.

Thirty years later Rhoda woke up in a hotel room in New York City. There was a letter lying on the floor where she had thrown it when she went to bed. She picked it up and read it again. *Take my name off that book,* the letter said. *Imagine a girl with your advantages writing a book like that. Your mother is so ashamed of you.*

Goddamn you, Rhoda thought. Goddamn you to hell. She climbed back into the bed and pulled the pillows over her head. She lay there for a while feeling sorry for herself. Then she got up and walked across the room and pulled a legal pad out of a briefcase and started writing.

Dear Father,

You take my name off those checks you send those television preachers and those goddamn right-wing politicians. That name has come to me from a hundred generations of men and women . . . also, in the future let my mother speak for herself about my work.

Love,
Rhoda

P.S. The slate was put there by the second law of thermodynamics. Some folks call it gravity. Other folks call it God.

I guess it was the second law, she thought. It was the second law or the third law or something like that. She leaned back in the chair, looking at the ceiling. Maybe I'd better find out before I mail it.

Considerations

1. "You and your father think you're so smart," says Rhoda's mother during a fight with her daughter (para. 43). Although her father sees Rhoda as an opponent, her mother views them as a pair. Which of Rhoda's personality traits do you think her mother has in mind when she makes this comparison? How would you define Rhoda's relationship with her father?

2. Rhoda's behavior scandalizes her parents. What is she actually searching for with all the experimentation she does? What are her own motivations for smoking, going on a diet, falling in love with Rosen, and having sex with a stranger? Who are her models for this kind of behavior?

Invitation to Write

Rhoda seems to be a rather rebellious teenager whose behavior makes it difficult for us to sympathize with her feelings. On the other hand, her objections to her parents' attitudes are sometimes valid. Write an essay in which you explore the generational gap between Rhoda and her parents. Determine how much of her rebellion is directed toward her parents' protectiveness and how much of it signals the ideals of a new generation. Also determine which of the conflicts between Rhoda and her parents would take place in our society today, and explain why some of her problems no longer occur among young people.

Connections

In Garrett Hongo's "Kubota" (p. 398), the grandfather's memories build a story in which young Hongo's identity begins. Rhoda's identity, on the other hand, is constructed of stories that project her image into the future. By comparison to Hongo's, Rhoda's identity seems fabricated by her imagination; however, if we look at them closely, her stories follow established cultural representations of success. Write an essay in which you explore the importance of role models for the younger generation based on examples from the two texts.

Look at both texts, locating the images that the two characters hold as role models, and establish the relations between such images and cultural values. Think of the contexts in which the images young people follow are generated and explain why Hongo remains attached to his family's past while Rhoda tries to escape it. You may also debate whether she succeeds in escaping it.

AMY TAN

Without Wood

Born in 1952 in Oakland, California, Amy Tan claims—tongue in cheek—that she disappointed her Chinese immigrant parents by becoming neither a neurosurgeon nor an accomplished pianist. Instead, she earned a master's degree in linguistics from San Jose State University and worked as a consultant to programs for disabled children. With the encouragement of a weekly writers' group, where she presented her work, Tan became a freelance writer. Her first book, *The Joy Luck Club* (1989), won the 1990 Bay Area Reviewers Award, was a finalist for the National Book Award and the National Book Critics Circle Award, and was recently made into a film. She has also published essays in *Life, The State of the Language,* and *The Threepenny Review.* Her shorter fiction has been published in *The Atlantic Monthly, Grand Street, McCall's,* and other literary magazines. Her most recent novel, *The Kitchen God's Wife* (1991), was selected by the *New York Times* as a notable book of the year. Tan made her first trip to China, a place central to her fiction, in 1987. She currently lives in San Francisco where she is working on another novel.

Although it may be read as an independent story, "Without Wood" is actually an excerpt from *The Joy Luck Club.* The novel is made up of the individual stories narrated by Chinese women immigrants and their American daughters. Taken together, these stories give the effect of a jigsaw puzzle. The lives of the mothers and daughters complete and illuminate each other, all the while resisting classifications and easy explanations. These women's search for identity is complicated beyond the normal complexity of gender by the cultures to which they are simultaneously exposed. "Without Wood" reveals some of these complexities. It continues the story of Rose Hsu Jordan, who defied her parents by marrying a Caucasian. Now she is about to divorce him. Rose's problem is that, having learned the lessons of American culture, she finds herself confused by too many choices.

I USED TO BELIEVE EVERYTHING my mother said, even when I didn't know what she meant. Once when I was little, she told me she knew it would rain because lost ghosts were circling near our windows, calling "Woo-woo" to be

379

let in. She said doors would unlock themselves in the middle of the night unless we checked twice. She said a mirror could see only my face, but she could see me inside out even when I was not in the room.

And all these things seemed true to me. The power of her words was that strong.

She said that if I listened to her, later I would know what she knew: where true words came from, always from up high, above everything else. And if I didn't listen to her, she said my ear would bend too easily to other people, all saying words that had no lasting meaning, because they came from the bottom of their hearts, where their own desires lived, a place where I could not belong.

The words my mother spoke did come from up high. As I recall, I was always looking up at her face as I lay on my pillow. In those days my sisters and I all slept in the same double bed. Janice, my oldest sister, had an allergy that made one nostril sing like a bird at night, so we called her Whistling Nose. Ruth was Ugly Foot because she could spread her toes out in the shape of a witch's claw. I was Scaredy Eyes because I would squeeze shut my eyes so I wouldn't have to see the dark, which Janice and Ruth said was a dumb thing to do. During those early years, I was the last to fall asleep. I clung to the bed, refusing to leave this world for dreams.

"Your sisters have already gone to see Old Mr. Chou," my mother would   5
whisper in Chinese. According to my mother, Old Mr. Chou was the guardian of a door that opened into dreams. "Are you ready to go see Old Mr. Chou, too?" And every night I would shake my head.

"Old Mr. Chou takes me to bad places," I cried.

Old Mr. Chou took my sisters to sleep. They never remembered anything from the night before. But Old Mr. Chou would swing the door wide open for me, and as I tried to walk in, he would slam it fast, hoping to squash me like a fly. That's why I would always dart back into wakefulness.

But eventually Old Mr. Chou would get tired and leave the door unwatched. The bed would grow heavy at the top and slowly tilt. And I would slide headfirst, in through Old Mr. Chou's door, and land in a house without doors or windows.

I remember one time I dreamt of falling through a hole in Old Mr. Chou's floor. I found myself in a nighttime garden and Old Mr. Chou was shouting, "Who's in my backyard?" I ran away. Soon I found myself stomping on plants with veins of blood, running through fields of snapdragons that changed colors like stoplights, until I came to a giant playground filled with row after row of square sandboxes. In each sandbox was a new doll. And my mother, who was not there but could see me inside out, told Old Mr. Chou she knew which doll I would pick. So I decided to pick one that was entirely different.

"Stop her! Stop her!" cried my mother. As I tried to run away, Old Mr.   10
Chou chased me, shouting, "See what happens when you don't listen to your mother!" And I became paralyzed, too scared to move in any direction.

The next morning, I told my mother what happened, and she laughed and said, "Don't pay attention to Old Mr. Chou. He is only a dream. You only have to listen to me."

And I cried, "But Old Mr. Chou listens to you too."

More than thirty years later, my mother was still trying to make me listen. A month after I told her that Ted and I were getting a divorce, I met her at church, at the funeral of China Mary, a wonderful ninety-two-year-old woman who had played godmother to every child who passed through the doors of the First Chinese Baptist Church.

"You are getting too thin," my mother said in her pained voice when I sat down next to her. "You must eat more."

"I'm fine," I said, and I smiled for proof. "And besides, wasn't it you who   15
said my clothes were always too tight?"

"Eat more," she insisted and then she nudged me with a little spiral-bound book hand-titled "Cooking the Chinese Way by China Mary Chan." They were selling them at the door, only five dollars each, to raise money for the Refugee Scholarship Fund.

The organ music stopped and the minister cleared his throat. He was not the regular pastor; I recognized him as Wing, a boy who used to steal baseball cards with my brother Luke. Only later Wing went to divinity school, thanks to China Mary, and Luke went to the county jail for selling stolen car stereos.

"I can still hear her voice," Wing said to the mourners. "She said God made me with all the right ingredients, so it'd be a shame if I burned in hell."

"Already cre-*mated*," my mother whispered matter-of-factly, nodding toward the altar, where a framed color photo of China Mary stood. I held my finger to my lips the way librarians do, but she didn't get it.

"That one, we bought it." She was pointing to a large spray of yellow   20
chrysanthemums and red roses. "Thirty-four dollars. All artificial, so it will last forever. You can pay me later. Janice and Matthew also chip in some. You have money?"

"Yes, Ted sent me a check."

Then the minister asked everyone to bow in prayer. My mother was quiet at last, dabbing her nose with Kleenex while the minister talked: "I can just see her now, wowing the angels with her Chinese cooking and gung-ho attitude."

And when heads lifted, everyone rose to sing hymn number 335, China Mary's favorite: "You can be an-gel, ev-ery day on earth . . ."

But my mother was not singing. She was staring at me. "Why does he send you a check?" I kept looking at the hymnal, singing: "Send-ing rays of sun-shine, full of joy from birth."

And so she grimly answered her own question: "He is doing monkey   25
business with someone else."

Monkey business? Ted? I wanted to laugh—her choice of words, but also the idea! Cool, silent, hairless Ted, whose breathing pattern didn't alter one bit in the height of passion? I could just see him, grunting "Ooh-ooh-ooh" while scratching his armpits, then bouncing and shrieking across the mattress trying to grab a breast.

"No, I don't think so," I said.

"Why not?"

"I don't think we should talk about Ted now, not here."

"Why can you talk about this with a psyche-atric and not with mother?" 30

"Psychiatrist."

"Psyche-atricks," she corrected herself.

"A mother is best. A mother knows what is inside you," she said above the singing voices. "A psyche-atricks will only make you *hulihudu*, make you see *heimongmong.*"

Back home, I thought about what she said. And it was true. Lately I had been feeling *hulihudu*. And everything around me seemed to be *heimongmong.* These were words I had never thought about in English terms. I suppose the closest in meaning would be "confused" and "dark fog."

But really, the words mean much more than that. Maybe they can't be 35
easily translated because they refer to a sensation that only Chinese people have, as if you were falling headfirst through Old Mr. Chou's door, then trying to find your way back. But you're so scared you can't open your eyes, so you get on your hands and knees and grope in the dark, listening for voices to tell you which way to go.

I had been talking to too many people, my friends, everybody it seems, except Ted. To each person I told a different story. Yet each version was true, I was certain of it, at least at the moment that I told it.

To my friend Waverly, I said I never knew how much I loved Ted until I saw how much he could hurt me. I felt such pain, literally a *physical* pain, as if someone had torn off both my arms without anesthesia, without sewing me back up.

"Have you ever had them torn off *with* anesthesia? God! I've never seen you so hysterical," said Waverly. "You want my opinion, you're better off without him. It hurts only because it's taken you fifteen years to see what an emotional wimp he is. Listen, I know what it feels like."

To my friend Lena, I said I was better off without Ted. After the initial shock, I realized I didn't miss him at all. I just missed the way I felt when I was with him.

"Which was what?" Lena gasped. "You were depressed. You were ma- 40
nipulated into thinking you were nothing next to him. And now you think you're nothing without him. If I were you, I'd get the name of a good lawyer and go for everything you can. Get even."

I told my psychiatrist I was obsessed with revenge. I dreamt of calling Ted up and inviting him to dinner, to one of those trendy who's-who places, like

Café Majestic or Rosalie's. And after he started the first course and was nice and relaxed, I would say, "It's not that easy, Ted." From my purse I would take out a voodoo doll which Lena had already lent me from her props department. I would aim my escargot fork at a strategic spot on the voodoo doll and I would say, out loud, in front of all the fashionable restaurant patrons, "Ted, you're such an impotent bastard and I'm going to make sure you stay that way." *Wham!*

Saying this, I felt I had raced to the top of a big turning point in my life, a new me after just weeks of psychotherapy. But my psychiatrist just looked bored, his hand still propped under his chin. "It seems you've been experiencing some very powerful feelings," he said, sleepy-eyed. "I think we should think about them more next week."

And so I didn't know what to think anymore. For the next few weeks, I inventoried my life, going from room to room trying to remember the history of everything in the house: things I had collected before I met Ted (the hand-blown glasses, the macrame wall hangings, and the rocker I had recaned); things we bought together right after we were married (most of the big furniture); things people gave us (the glass-domed clock that no longer worked, three sake sets, four teapots); things he picked out (the signed lithographs, none of them beyond number twenty-five in a series of two hundred fifty, the Steuben crystal strawberries); and things I picked out because I couldn't bear to see them left behind (the mismatched candlestick holders from garage sales, an antique quilt with a hole in it, odd-shaped vials that once contained ointments, spices, and perfumes).

I had started to inventory the bookshelves when I got a letter from Ted, a note actually, written hurriedly in ballpoint on his prescription notepad. "Sign 4x where indicated," it read. And then in fountain-pen blue ink, "enc: check, to tide you over until settlement."

The note was clipped to our divorce papers, along with a check for ten thousand dollars, signed in the same fountain-pen blue ink on the note. And instead of being grateful, I was hurt.

Why had he sent the check with the papers? Why the two different pens? Was the check an afterthought? How long had he sat in his office determining how much money was enough? And why had he chosen to sign it with *that* pen?

I still remember the look on his face last year when he carefully undid the gold foil wrap, the surprise in his eyes as he slowly examined every angle of the pen by the light of the Christmas tree. He kissed me forehead. "I'll use it only to sign important things," he had promised me.

Remembering that, holding the check, all I could do was sit on the edge of the couch feeling my head getting heavy at the top. I stared at the x's on the divorce papers, the wording on the prescription notepad, the two colors of ink, the date of the check, the careful way in which he wrote, "Ten thousand only and no cents."

I sat there quietly, trying to listen to my heart, to make the right decision. But then I realized I didn't know what the choices were. And so I put the papers and the check away, in a drawer where I kept store coupons which I never threw away and which I never used either.

My mother once told me why I was so confused all the time. She said I was without wood. Born without wood so that I listened to too many people. She knew this, because once she had almost become this way. 50

"A girl is like a young tree," she said. "You must stand tall and listen to your mother standing next to you. That is the only way to grow strong and straight. But if you bend to listen to other people, you will grow crooked and weak. You will fall to the ground with the first strong wind. And then you will be like a weed, growing wild in any direction, running along the ground until someone pulls you out and throws you away."

But by the time she told me this, it was too late. I had already begun to bend. I had started going to school, where a teacher named Mrs. Berry lined us up and marched us in and out of rooms, up and down hallways while she called out, "Boys and girls, follow me." And if you didn't listen to her, she would make you bend over and whack you with a yardstick ten times.

I still listened to my mother, but I also learned how to let her words blow through me. And sometimes I filled my mind with other people's thoughts—all in English—so that when she looked at me inside out, she would be confused by what she saw.

Over the years, I learned to choose from the best opinions. Chinese people had Chinese opinions. American people had American opinions. And in almost every case, the American version was much better.

It was only later that I discovered there was a serious flaw with the American version. There were too many choices, so it was easy to get confused and pick the wrong thing. That's how I felt about my situation with Ted. There was so much to think about, so much to decide. Each decision meant a turn in another direction. 55

The check, for example. I wondered if Ted was really trying to trick me, to get me to admit that I was giving up, that I wouldn't fight the divorce. And if I cashed it, he might later say the amount was the whole settlement. Then I got a little sentimental and imagined, only for a moment, that he had sent me ten thousand dollars because he truly loved me; he was telling me in his own way how much I meant to him. Until I realized that ten thousand dollars was nothing to him, that I was nothing to him.

I thought about putting an end to this torture and signing the divorce papers. And I was just about to take the papers out of the coupon drawer when I remembered the house.

I thought to myself, I love this house. The big oak door that opens into a foyer filled with stained-glass windows. The sunlight in the breakfast room, the south view of the city from the front parlor. The herb and flower garden

Ted had planted. He used to work in the garden every weekend, kneeling on a green rubber pad, obsessively inspecting every leaf as if he were manicuring fingernails. He assigned plants to certain planter boxes. Tulips could not be mixed with perennials. A cutting of aloe vera that Lena gave me did not belong anywhere because we had no other succulents.

I looked out the window and saw the calla lilies had fallen and turned brown, the daisies had been crushed down by their own weight, the lettuce gone to seed. Runner weeds were growing between the flagstone walkways that would between the planter boxes. The whole thing had grown wild from months of neglect.

And seeing the garden in this forgotten condition reminded me of some- 60 thing I once read in a fortune cookie: When a husband stops paying attention to the garden, he's thinking of pulling up roots. When was the last time Ted pruned the rosemary back? When was the last time he squirted Snail B-Gone around the flower beds?

I quickly walked down the garden shed, looking for pesticides and weed killer, as if the amount left in the bottle, the expiration date, anything would give me some idea of what was happening in my life. And then I put the bottle down. I had the sense someone was watching me and laughing.

I went back in the house, this time to call a lawyer. But as I started to dial, I became confused. I put the receiver down. What could I say? What did I want from divorce—when I never knew what I had wanted with marriage?

The next morning, I was still thinking about my marriage: fifteen years of living in Ted's shadow. I lay in bed, my eyes squeezed shut, unable to make the simplest decisions.

I stayed in bed for three days, getting up only to go to the bathroom or to heat up another can of chicken noodle soup. But mostly I slept. I took the sleeping pills Ted had left behind in the medicine cabinet. And for the first time I can recall, I had no dreams. All I could remember was falling smoothly into a dark space with no feeling of dimension or direction. I was the only person in this blackness. And every time I woke up, I took another pill and went back to this place.

But on the fourth day, I had a nightmare. In the dark, I couldn't see Old 65 Mr. Chou, but he said he would find me, and when he did, he would squish me into the ground. He was sounding a bell, and the louder the bell rang the closer he was to finding me. I held my breath to keep from screaming, but the bell got louder and louder until I burst awake.

It was the phone. It must have rung for an hour nonstop. I picked it up.

"Now that you are up, I am bringing you leftover dishes," said my mother. She sounded as if she could see me now. But the room was dark, the curtains closed tight.

"Ma, I can't . . ." I said. "I can't see you now. I'm busy."

"Too busy for mother?"

"I have an appointment . . . with my psychiatrist."   70

She was quiet for a while. "Why do you not speak up for yourself?" she finally said in her pained voice. "Why can you not talk to your husband?"

"Ma," I said, feeling drained. "Please. Don't tell me to save my marriage anymore. It's hard enough as it is."

"I am not telling you to save your marriage," she protested. "I only say you should speak up."

When I hung up, the phone rang again. It was my psychiatrist's receptionist. I had missed my appointment that morning, as well as two days ago. Did I want to reschedule? I said I would look at my schedule and call back.

And five minutes later the phone rang again.   75

"Where've you been?" It was Ted.

I began to shake. "Out," I said.

"I've been trying to reach you for the last three days. I even called the phone company to check the line."

And I knew he had done that, not out of any concern for me, but because when he wants something, he gets impatient and irrational about people who make him wait.

"You know it's been two weeks," he said with obvious irritation.   80

"Two weeks?"

"You haven't cashed the check or returned the papers. I wanted to be nice about this, Rose. I can get someone to officially serve the papers, you know."

"You can?"

And then without missing a beat, he proceeded to say what he really wanted, which was more despicable than all the terrible things I had imagined.

He wanted the papers returned, signed. He wanted the house. He wanted   85
the whole thing to be over as soon as possible. Because he wanted to get married again, to someone else.

Before I could stop myself, I gasped. "You mean you *were* doing monkey business with someone else?" I was so humiliated I almost started to cry.

And then for the first time in months, after being in limbo all that time, everything stopped. All the questions: gone. There were no choices. I had an empty feeling—and I felt free, wild. From high inside my head I could hear someone laughing.

"What's so funny?" said Ted angrily.

"Sorry," I said. "It's just that . . ." and I was trying hard to stifle my giggles, but one of them escaped through my nose with a snort, which made me laugh more. And then Ted's silence made me laugh even harder.

I was still gasping when I tried to begin again in a more even voice. "Lis-   90
ten, Ted, sorry. . . I think the best thing is for you to come over after work." I didn't know why I said that, but I felt right saying it.

"There's nothing to talk about, Rose."

"I know," I said in a voice so calm it surprised even me. "I just want to show you something. And don't worry, you'll get your papers. Believe me."

I had no plan. I didn't know what I would say to him later. I knew only that I wanted Ted to see me one more time before the divorce.

What I ended up showing him was the garden. By the time he arrived, the late-afternoon fog had already blown in. I had the divorce papers in the pocket of my windbreaker. Ted was shivering in his sports jacket as he surveyed the damage to the garden.

"What a mess," I heard him mutter to himself, trying to shake his pant   95
leg loose of a blackberry vine that had meandered onto the walkway. And I knew he was calculating how long it would take to get the place back into order.

"I like it this way," I said, patting the tops of overgrown carrots, their orange heads pushing through the earth as if about to be born. And then I saw the weeds: Some had sprouted in and out of the cracks in the patio. Others had anchored on the side of the house. And even more had found refuge under loose shingles and were on their way to climbing up to the roof. No way to pull them out once they've buried themselves in the masonry; you'd end up pulling the whole building down.

Ted was picking up plums from the ground and tossing them over the fence into the neighbor's yard. "Where are the papers?" he finally said.

I handed them to him and he stuffed them in the inside pocket of his jacket. He faced me and I saw his eyes, the look I had once mistaken for kindness and protection. "You don't have to move out right away," he said. "I know you'll want at least a month to find a place."

"I've already found a place," I said quickly, because right then I knew where I was going to live. His eyebrows raised in surprise and he smiled—for the briefest moment—until I said, "Here."

"What's that?" he said sharply. His eyebrows were still up, but now there   100
was no smile.

"I said I'm staying here," I announced again.

"Who says?" He folded his arms across his chest, squinted his eyes, examining my face as if he knew it would crack at any moment. That expression of his used to terrify me into stammers.

Now I felt nothing, no fear, no anger. "I say I'm staying, and my lawyer will too, once we serve you the papers," I said.

Ted pulled out the divorce papers and stared at them. His x's were still there, the blanks were still blank. "What do you think you're doing? Exactly what?" he said.

And the answer, the one that was important above everything else, ran   105
through my body and fell from my lips: "You can't just pull me out of your life and throw me away."

I saw what I wanted: his eyes, confused, then scared. He was *hulihudu.* The power of my words was that strong.

That night I dreamt I was wandering through the garden. The trees and bushes were covered with mist. And then I spotted Old Mr. Chou and my mother off in the distance, their busy movements swirling the fog around them. They were bending over one of the planter boxes.

"There she is!" cried my mother. Old Mr. Chou smiled at me and waved. I walked up to my mother and saw that she was hovering over something, as if she were tending a baby.

"See," she said, beaming, "I have just planted them this morning, some for you, some for me."

And below the *heimongmong,* all along the ground, were weeds already 110 spilling out over the edges, running wild in every direction.

Considerations

1. Rose begins the account of her painful divorce by recounting her childhood memories of Old Mr. Chou. She refers to him throughout the story, and he reappears in a dream at the end. How do you interpret Mr. Chou's presence? How do Rose's references to him help clarify her character or her situation?

2. Although Rose grows up believing that American opinions are better, she later realizes that American opinions present so many choices that "it was easy to get confused and pick the wrong thing" (para. 55). How do you explain her change from a woman immobilized by indecision to one who clearly sees her choices?

3. After her marriage fails, Rose tells each of her friends a different story. Why? If she is not a liar, how do you explain her need to vary the account of her problems?

Invitation to Write

Even when Rose thinks and narrates in English, Chinese metaphors pervade her language. They are all translated into English, but sometimes they produce confusion because they overlap with English metaphors. "The bottom of their hearts," for instance, is a dark place, where Rose cannot belong (para. 3), whereas the English expression "from the bottom of my heart" suggests something entirely different. In a sense, she actually places herself in two different stories, one Chinese, the other American. Starting from a study of Rose's language, write an essay in which you explain her problems in terms of those two stories. Think also of real-life examples where people you know have been caught between versions of a story, such as when they had to report events to somebody foreign or older, or in a restricted language, like in a court of law. Use your examples to support a more general conclusion about the way in which we all represent ourselves in stories.

Connections

In "Introduction to *The Second Sex*" (p. 150), Simone de Beauvoir constructs a general theory that she uses to explain the distribution of power between men and women in relationships. Write an essay in which you make use of Beauvoir's theory to interpret Rose's story. Think about what Beauvoir's analysis might be, which aspects of the story it would highlight, and which aspects of the story it might not take into consideration. What does her analysis add to your understanding of the story, particularly in relation to the other characters' interpretations of Rose's behavior?

PAULA GUNN ALLEN

Where I Come from Is Like This

Born in 1939 in Cubero, New Mexico, Paula Gunn Allen is one of the foremost contemporary American Indian writers and scholars. Her mother's family is Laguna Pueblo–Sioux Indian; her father's family is Lebanese. She has written seven books of poetry, including *Shadow Country* (1982) and *Skins and Bones* (1988). Her novel, *The Woman Who Owned the Shadows,* was published in 1983. Her critical works on American Indian literature and culture include *Studies in Native American Literature* (1983) and *The Sacred Hoop* (1986). In her critical essays, Allen defines the themes and issues related to American Indian life. Allen is a strong feminist who traces her beliefs back to the heritage of Pueblo society. She believes that American Indian tribal culture traditionally is gynocratic, or women-centered. In *Spider Woman's Granddaughter* (1989), Allen collected traditional tales and works by American Indian women to show the continuity of themes and traditions from the past to the present. Allen has taught at the University of New Mexico and currently is a professor of Native American Studies at the University of California at Berkeley. She has received numerous grants and awards, including those from the National Endowment for the Arts and the Ford Foundation.

The following essay is an excerpt from *The Sacred Hoop,* in which Allen discusses the plight of American Indian women, who find themselves confronted with the dilemma of choosing between tribal notions of femininity and the mainstream image of womanhood. Allen finds that the tribal tradition offers more varied images for women, as well as greater dignity and importance for women in society.

I

MODERN AMERICAN INDIAN WOMEN, like their non-Indian sisters, are deeply engaged in the struggle to redefine themselves. In their struggle they must reconcile traditional tribal definitions of women with industrial and postindustrial non-Indian definitions. Yet while these definitions seem to be more or less mutually exclusive, Indian women must somehow harmonize and integrate both in their own lives.

An American Indian woman is primarily defined by her tribal identity. In her eyes, her destiny is necessarily that of her people, and her sense of herself as a woman is first and foremost prescribed by her tribe. The definitions of woman's roles are as diverse as tribal cultures in the Americas. In some she is devalued, in others she wields considerable power. In some she is a familial/clan adjunct, in some she is as close to autonomous as her economic circumstances and psychological traits permit. But in no tribal definitions is she perceived in the same way as are women in Western industrial and postindustrial cultures.

In the West, few images of women form part of the cultural mythos, and these are largely sexually charged. Among Christians, the madonna is the female prototype, and she is portrayed as essentially passive: Her contribution is simply that of birthing. Little else is attributed to her and she certainly possesses few of the characteristics that are attributed to mythic figures among Indian tribes. This image is countered (rather than balanced) by the witch-goddess/whore characteristics designed to reinforce cultural beliefs about women, as well as Western adversarial and dualistic perceptions of reality.

The tribes see women variously, but they do not question the power of femininity. Sometimes they see women as fearful, sometimes peaceful, sometimes omnipotent and omniscient, but they never portray women as mindless, helpless, simple, or oppressed. And while the women in a given tribe, clan, or band may be all these things, the individual woman is provided with a variety of images of women from the interconnected supernatural, natural, and social worlds she lives in.

As a half-breed American Indian woman, I cast about in my mind for negative images of Indian women, and I find none that are directed to Indian women alone. The negative images I do have are of Indians in general and in fact are more often of males than of females. All these images come to me from non-Indian sources, and they are always balanced by a positive image. My ideas of womanhood, passed on largely by my mother and grandmothers, Laguna Pueblo women, are about practicality, strength, reasonableness, intelligence, wit, and competence. I also remember vividly the women who came to my father's store, the women who held me and sang to me, the women at Feast Day, at Grab Days, the women in the kitchen of my Cubero home, the women I grew up with; none of them appeared weak or helpless, none of them presented herself tentatively. I remember a certain reserve on those lovely brown faces; I remember the direct gaze of eyes framed by bright-colored shawls draped over their heads and cascading down their backs. I remember the clean cotton dresses and carefully pressed hand-embroidered aprons they always wore; I remember laughter and good food, especially the sweet bread and the oven bread they gave us. Nowhere in my mind is there a foolish woman, a dumb woman, a vain woman, or a plastic woman, though the Indian women I have known have shown a wide range of personal style and demeanor.

My memory includes the Navajo woman who was badly beaten by her Sioux husband; but I also remember that my grandmother abandoned her Sioux husband long ago. I recall the stories about the Laguna woman beaten regularly by her husband in the presence of her children so that the children would not believe in the strength and power of femininity. And I remember the women who drank, who got into fights with other women and with the men, and who often won those battles. I have memories of tired women, partying women, stubborn women, sullen women, amicable women, selfish women, shy women, and aggressive women. Most of all I remember the women who laugh and scold and sit uncomplaining in the long sun on feast days and who cook wonderful food on wood stoves, in beehive mud ovens, and over open fires outdoors.

Among the images of women that come to me from various tribes as well as my own are White Buffalo Woman, who came to the Lakota long ago and brought them the religion of the Sacred Pipe which they still practice; Tinotzin the goddess who came to Juan Diego to remind him that she still walked the hills of her people and sent him with her message, her demand, and her proof to the Catholic bishop in the city nearby. And from Laguna I take the images of Yellow Woman, Coyote Woman, Grandmother Spider (Spider Old Woman), who brought the light, who gave us weaving and medicine, who gave us life. Among the Keres she is known as Thought Woman who created us all and who keeps us in creation even now. I remember Iyatiku, Earth Woman, Corn Woman, who guides and counsels the people to peace and who welcomes us home when we cast off this coil of flesh as huskers cast off the leaves that wrap the corn. I remember Iyatiku's sister, Sun Woman, who held metals and cattle, pigs and sheep, highways and engines and so many things in her bundle, who went away to the east saying that one day she would return.

II

Since the coming of the Anglo-Europeans beginning in the fifteenth century, the fragile web of identity that long held tribal people secure has gradually been weakened and torn. But the oral tradition has prevented the complete destruction of the web, the ultimate disruption of tribal ways. The oral tradition is vital; it heals itself and the tribal web by adapting to the flow of the present while never relinquishing its connection to the past. Its adaptability has always been required, as many generations have experienced. Certainly the modern American Indian woman bears slight resemblance to her forebears—at least on superficial examination—but she is still a tribal woman in her deepest being. Her tribal sense of relationship to all that is continues to flourish. And though she is at times beset by her knowledge of the enormous gap between the life she lives and the life she was raised to live, and while she adapts her mind and being to the circumstances of her present life, she does so in tribal ways, mending the tears in the web of being from which she takes her existence as she goes.

My mother told me stories all the time, though I often did not recognize them as that. My mother told me stories about cooking and childbearing; she told me stories about menstruation and pregnancy; she told me stories about gods and heroes, about fairies and elves, about goddesses and spirits; she told me stories about the land and the sky, about cats and dogs, about snakes and spiders; she told me stories about climbing trees and exploring the mesas; she told me stories about going to dances and getting married; she told me stories about dressing and undressing, about sleeping and waking; she told me stories about herself, about her mother, about her grandmother. She told me stories about grieving and laughing, about thinking and doing; she told me stories about school and about people; about darning and mending; she told me stories about turquoise and about gold; she told me European stories and Laguna stories; she told me Catholic stories and Presbyterian stories; she told me city stories and country stories; she told me political stories and religious stories. She told me stories about living and stories about dying. And in all of those stories she told me who I was, who I was supposed to be, whom I came from, and who would follow me. In this way she taught me the meaning of the words she said, that all life is a circle and everything has a place within it. That's what she said and what she showed me in the things she did and the way she lives.

Of course, through my formal, white, Christian education, I discovered   10
that other people had stories of their own—about women, about Indians, about fact, about reality—and I was amazed by a number of startling suppositions that others made about tribal customs and beliefs. According to the un-Indian, non-Indian view, for instance, Indians barred menstruating women from ceremonies and indeed segregated them from the rest of the people, consigning them to some space specially designed for them. This showed that Indians considered menstruating women unclean and not fit to enjoy the company of decent (nonmenstruating) people, that is, men. I was surprised and confused to hear this because my mother had taught me that white people had strange attitudes toward menstruation: They thought something was bad about it, that it meant you were sick, cursed, sinful, and weak and that you had to be very careful during that time. She taught me that menstruation was a normal occurrence, that I could go swimming or hiking or whatever else I wanted to do during my period. She actively scorned women who took to their beds, who were incapacitated by cramps, who "got the blues."

As I struggled to reconcile these very contradictory interpretations of

American Indians' traditional beliefs concerning menstruation, I realized that the menstrual taboos were about power, not about sin or filth. My conclusion was later borne out by some tribes' own explanations, which, as you may well imagine, came as quite a relief to me.

The truth of the matter as many Indians see it is that women who are at the peak of their fecundity are believed to possess power that throws male power totally out of kilter. They emit such force that, in their presence, any male-owned or -dominated ritual or sacred object cannot do its usual task. For instance, the Lakota say that a menstruating woman anywhere near a yuwipi man, who is a special sort of psychic, spirit-empowered healer, for a day or so before he is to do his ceremony will effectively disempower him. Conversely, among many if not most tribes, important ceremonies cannot be held without the presence of women. Sometimes the ritual woman who empowers the ceremony must be unmarried and virginal so that the power she channels is unalloyed, unweakened by sexual arousal and penetration by a male. Other ceremonies require tumescent women, others the presence of mature women who have borne children, and still others depend for empowerment on postmenopausal women. Women may be segregated from the company of the whole band or village on certain occasions, but on certain occasions men are also segregated. In short, each ritual depends on a certain balance of power, and the positions of women within the phases of womanhood are used by tribal people to empower certain rites. This does not derive from a male-dominant view; it is not a ritual observance imposed on women by men. It derives from a tribal view of reality that distinguishes tribal people from feudal and industrial people.

Among the tribes, the occult power of women, inextricably bound to our hormonal life, is thought to be very great; many hold that we possess innately the blood-given power to kill—with a glance, with a step, or with a judicious mixing of menstrual blood into somebody's soup. Medicine women among the Pomo of California cannot practice until they are sufficiently mature; when they are immature, their power is diffuse and is likely to interfere with their practice until time and experience have it under control. So women of the tribes are not especially inclined to see themselves as poor helpless victims of male domination. Even in those tribes where something akin to male domination was present, women are perceived as powerful, socially, physically, and metaphysically. In times past, as in times present, women carried enormous burdens with aplomb. We were far indeed from the "weaker sex," the designation that white aristocratic sisters unhappily earned for us all.

I remember my mother moving furniture all over the house when she wanted it changed. She didn't wait for my father to come home and help—she just went ahead and moved the piano, a huge upright from the old days, the couch, the refrigerator. Nobody had told her she was too weak to do such things. In imitation of her, I would delight in loading trucks at my father's store with cases of pop or fifty-pound sacks of flour. Even when I was quite small I could do it, and it gave me a belief in my own physical strength that advancing middle age can't quite erase. My mother used to tell me about the Acoma Pueblo women she had seen as a child carrying huge ollas (water pots) on their heads as they wound their way up the tortuous stairwell carved into the face of the "Sky City" mesa, a feat I tried to imitate with books and tin buckets. ("Sky City" is the term used by the Chamber of Commerce for the mother village of Acoma, which is situated atop a high sandstone table mountain.) I was never very successful, but even the attempt reminded me that I was supposed to be strong and balanced to be a proper girl.

Of course, my mother's Laguna people are Keres Indian, reputed to be the 15 last extreme mother-right people on earth. So it is no wonder that I got notably nonwhite notions about the natural strength and prowess of women. Indeed, it is only when I am trying to get non-Indian approval, recognition, or acknowledgment that my "weak sister" emotional and intellectual ploys get the better of my tribal woman's good sense. At such times I forget that I just moved the piano or just wrote a competent paper or just completed a financial transaction satisfactorily or have supported myself and my children for most of my adult life.

Nor is my contradictory behavior atypical. Most Indian women I know are in the same bicultural bind: We vacillate between being dependent and strong, self-reliant and powerless, strongly motivated and hopelessly insecure. We resolve the dilemma in various ways: Some of us party all the time; some of us drink to excess; some of us travel and move around a lot; some of us land good jobs and then quit them; some of us engage in violent exchanges; some of us blow our brains out. We act in these destructive ways because we suffer from the societal conflicts caused by having to identify with two hopelessly opposed cultural definitions of women. Through this destructive dissonance we are unhappy prey to the self-disparagement common to, indeed demanded of, Indians living in the United States today. Our situation is caused by the exigencies of a history of invasion, conquest, and colonization whose searing marks are probably ineradicable. A popular bumper sticker on many Indian cars proclaims: "If You're Indian You're In," to which I always find myself adding under my breath, "Trouble."

III

No Indian can grow to any age without being informed that her people were "savages" who interfered with the march of progress pursued by respectable, loving, civilized white people. We are the villains of the scenario when we are mentioned at all. We are absent from much of white history except when we are calmly, rationally, succinctly, and systematically dehumanized. On the few occasions we are noticed in any way other than as howling, bloodthirsty beings, we are acclaimed for our noble quaintness. In this definition, we are exotic curios. Our ancient arts and customs are used to draw tourist money to state coffers, into the pocketbooks and bank accounts of scholars, and into support of the American-in-Disneyland promoters' dream.

As a Roman Catholic child I was treated to bloody tales of how the savage Indians martyred the hapless priests and missionaries who went among them in an attempt to lead them to the one true path. By the time I was through high school I had the idea that Indians were people who had benefited mightily from the advanced knowledge and superior morality of the Anglo-Europeans. At least I had, perforce, that idea to lay beside the other one that derived from my daily experience of Indian life, an idea less dehumanizing and more accurate because it came from my mother and the other Indian people who raised me. That idea was that Indians are a people who don't tell lies, who care for their children and their old people. You never see an Indian orphan, they said. You always know when you're old that someone will take care of you—one of your children will. Then they'd list the old folks who were being taken care of by this child or that. No child is ever considered illegitimate among the Indians, they said. If a girl gets pregnant, the baby is still part of the family, and the mother is too. That's what they said, and they showed me real people who lived according to those principles.

Of course the ravages of colonization have taken their toll; there are orphans in Indian country now, and abandoned, brutalized old folks; there are even illegitimate children, though the very concept still strikes me as absurd. There are battered children and neglected children, and there are battered wives and women who have been raped by Indian men. Proximity to the "civilizing" effects of white Christians has not improved the moral quality of life in Indian country, though each group, Indian and white, explains the situation differently. Nor is there much yet in the oral tradition that can enable us to adapt to these inhuman changes. But a force is growing in that direction, and it is helping Indian women reclaim their lives. Their power, their sense of direction and of self will soon be visible. It is the force of the women who speak and work and write, and it is formidable.

Through all the centuries of war and death and cultural and psychic destruction have endured the women who raise the children and tend the fires, who pass along the tales and the traditions, who weep and bury the dead, who are the dead, and who never forget. There are always the women, who make pots and weave baskets, who fashion clothes and cheer their children on at powwow, who make fry bread and piki bread, and corn soup and chili stew, who dance and sing and remember and hold within their hearts the dream of their ancient peoples—that one day the woman who thinks will speak to us again, and everywhere there will be peace. Meanwhile we tell the stories and write the books and trade tales of anger and woe and stories of fun and scandal and laugh over all manner of things that happen every day. We watch and we wait.

20

My great-grandmother told my mother: Never forget you are Indian. And my mother told me the same thing. This, then, is how I have gone about remembering, so that my children will remember too.

Considerations

1. In this essay, Allen credits the power of the oral tradition with helping preserve a distinct American Indian identity and culture. How do the American Indian stories she presents help her define her own identity?

2. Allen seems to suffer stereotyping both as an American Indian and as a woman. What negative images of American Indians and of women does she encounter in mainstream American society? How do these two sets of images relate to each other?

3. Allen stresses that a key feature of the oral tradition is the way it preserves traditional values while adapting to change. What processes of adaptation does she exemplify in her essay and how useful are they in developing her argument?

Invitation to Write

As an American Indian, Paula Gunn Allen has been exposed to two different cultures at the same time, both of which have specific ways of transmitting values. Write an essay in which you discuss the way values are handed down to the new generation in Allen's text, and extend the argument to include the ways in which mainstream American culture perpetuates its values. Determine how the transmission of old values and the process of adaptation, both in the American Indian tribes and society at large, work together to create a living tradition.

Connections

Allen places a great deal of emphasis on the stories various members of her family tell her because she realizes that stories carry moral and cultural values. In Ellen Gilchrist's "Music" (p. 357), Rhoda's parents also do their best to convey their values to her, but she rejects them. Rhoda seems to value her personal experience more than what her parents have to say. What is the reason for the difference between the attitudes of these two women toward their families' values?

Write an essay in which you compare Allen's and Rhoda's respective attitudes in order to explore the advantages and disadvantages of learning from both personal experience and older generations. Consider the different cultural contexts to which the two women belong, as well as the notions of "learning" and "experience" each of these cultures entertains.

GARRETT HONGO

Kubota

Garrett Kaoru Hongo was born in Volcano, Hawaii, in 1951 and returns frequently to his native village, a place he finds propitious for the writing of his memoir, *Volcano Journal*. After graduating with honors from Pomona College, he spent a year touring Japan and writing poetry. Later he studied Japanese language and literature at the University of Michigan and received an M.F.A. in English and critical theory from the University of California at Irvine. Hongo has taught poetry writing at the University of Southern California, the University of California at Irvine, and the University of Missouri, where he also edited *The Missouri Review*. He currently teaches English at the University of Oregon, where he directs the creative writing program. Hongo has published several books of poetry, including *Yellow Light* (1982) and *The River of Heaven* (1989), which was a finalist for the 1989 Pulitzer Prize in poetry. Before being collected in these volumes, his poems were published in such magazines as *Antaeus, The New Yorker, The Nation, The American Poetry Review,* and *Ploughshares*. In 1993, he edited a collection of poetry by Asian-American poets called *The Open Boat: Poems from Asian America*. He has won two fellowships from the National Endowment for the Arts and is currently a fellow of the John Simon Guggenheim Foundation.

"Kubota" was first published in *Ploughshares* in 1990 and reprinted in *The Best American Essays 1991*. The essay is part of his memoir and recalls the stories of his grandfather, whose life experience teaches Hongo a valuable lesson in history.

ON DECEMBER 8, 1941, the day after the Japanese attack on Pearl Harbor in Hawaii, my grandfather barricaded himself with his family—my grandmother, my teenage mother, her two sisters and two brothers—inside of his home in La'ie, a sugar plantation village on Oahu's North Shore. This was my maternal grandfather, a man most villagers called by his last name—Kubota. It could mean either "Wayside Field" or else "Broken Dreams," depending on which ideograms he used. Kubota ran La'ie's general store, and the previous night, after a long day of bad news on the radio, some locals had come by, pounded on the front door, and made threats. One was said to have brandished a machete. They were angry and shocked, as the whole nation was in the aftermath of the surprise attack. Kubota was one of the few Japanese Americans in the village and president of the local Japanese language school. He had become a target for their rage and suspicion. A wise man, he locked all his doors and windows and did not open his store the next day, but stayed closed and waited for news from some official.

He was a *kibei,* a Japanese American born in Hawaii (a U.S. Territory then, so he was thus a citizen) but who was subsequently sent back by his father for formal education in Hiroshima, Japan—their home province. *Kibei* is written with two ideograms in Japanese—one is the word for "return" and the other is the word for "rice." Poetically, it means one who returns from America, known as the Land of Rice in Japanese (by contrast, Chinese immigrants called their new home Mountain of Gold).

Kubota was graduated from a Japanese high school and then came back to Hawaii as a teenager. He spoke English—and a Hawaiian Creole version of it at that—with a Japanese accent. But he was well-liked and good at numbers, scrupulous and hard-working like so many immigrants and children of immigrants. Castle & Cook, a grower's company that ran the sugar cane business along the North Shore, hired him on as first a stock boy and then appointed him to run one of its company stores. He did well, had the trust of management and labor—not an easy accomplishment in any day—married, had children, and had begun to exert himself in community affairs and excel in his own recreations. He put together a Japanese community organization that backed a Japanese language school for children and sponsored teachers from Japan. Kubota boarded many of them, in succession, in his own home. This made dinners a silent affair for his talkative, Hawaiian-bred children, as their stern *sensei,* or teacher, was nearly always at table and their own abilities in the Japanese language were as delinquent as their attendance. While Kubota and the *sensei* rattled on about things Japanese, speaking Japanese, his children hurried through their suppers and tried to run off early to listen to the radio shows.

After dinner, while the *sensei* graded exams seated in a wicker chair in the spare room and his wife and children gathered around the radio in the front parlor, Kubota sat on the screened porch outside, reading the local Japanese newspapers. He finished reading about the same time as he finished the tea he drank for his digestion—a habit he'd learned in Japan—and then he'd get out his fishing gear and spread it out on the plank floors. The wraps on his rods needed to be redone, gears in his reels needed oil, and, once through with those tasks, he'd painstakingly wind on hundreds of yards of new line. Fishing was his hobby and his passion. He spent weekends camping along the North Shore beaches with his children, setting up umbrella tents, packing a rice pot and hibachi along for meals. And he caught fish. *Ulu'a* mostly, the huge surf-feeding fish known as the Jack Crevalle on the Mainland, but he'd go after almost anything in its season. In Kawela, a plantation-owned bay nearby, he fished for mullet Hawaiian-style with a throw net, stalking the bottom-hugging, gray-backed schools as they gathered at the stream mouths and in the freshwater springs. In an outrigger out beyond the reef, he'd try for *aku*— the skipjack tuna prized for steaks and, sliced raw and mixed with fresh seaweed and cut onions, for *sashimi* salad. In Kahaluu and Ka'awa and on an offshore rock locals called Goat Island, he loved to go torching, stringing lanterns on bamboo poles stuck in the sand to attract *kumu'u*, the red goatfish, as they schooled at night just inside the reef. But in La'ie on Laniloa Point near Kahuku, the northernmost tip of Oahu, he cast twelve- and fourteen-foot surf rods for the huge, varicolored, and fast-running *ulu'a* as they ran for schools of squid and baitfish just beyond the biggest breakers and past the low sand flats wadable from the shore to nearly a half-mile out. At sunset, against the western light, he looked as if he walked on water as he came back, fish and rods slung over his shoulders, stepping along the rock and coral path just inches under the surface of a running tide.

When it was torching season, in December or January, he'd drive out the   5 afternoon before and stay with old friends, the Tanakas or Yoshikawas, shopkeepers like him who ran stores near the fishing grounds. They'd have been preparing for weeks, selecting and cutting their bamboo poles, cleaning the hurricane lanterns, tearing up burlap sacks for the cloths they'd soak with kerosene and tie onto sticks they'd poke into the soft sand of the shallows. Once lit, touched off with a Zippo lighter, these would be the torches they'd use as beacons to attract the schooling fish. In another time, they might have made up a dozen paper lanterns of the kind mostly used for decorating the summer folk dances outdoors on the grounds of the Buddhist church during *O-Bon,* the Festival for the Dead. But now, wealthy and modern and efficient killers of fish, Tanaka and Kubota used rag-torches and Colemans and cast rods with tips made of Tonkin bamboo and butts of American-spun fiberglass. After just one good night, they might bring back a prize bounty of a dozen burlap bags filled with scores of bloody, rigid fish delicious to eat and even better to give away as gifts to friends, family, and special customers.

It was a Monday night, the day after Pearl Harbor, and there was a rattling knock at the front door. Two FBI agents presented themselves, showed identification, and took my grandfather in for questioning in Honolulu. He didn't return home for days. No one knew what had happened or what was wrong. But there was a roundup going on of all those in the Japanese-American community suspected of sympathizing with the enemy and worse. My grandfather was suspected of espionage, of communicating with offshore Japanese submarines launched from the attack fleet days before war began. Torpedo planes and escort fighters, decorated with the insignia of the Rising Sun, had taken an approach route from northwest of Oahu directly across

Kahuku Point and on towards Pearl. They had strafed an auxiliary air station near the fishing grounds my grandfather loved and destroyed a small gun battery there, killing three men. Kubota was known to have sponsored and harbored Japanese nationals in his own home. He had a radio. He had wholesale access to firearms. Circumstances and an undertone of racial resentment had combined with wartime hysteria in the aftermath of the tragic naval battle to cast suspicion on the loyalties of my grandfather and all other Japanese Americans. The FBI reached out and pulled hundreds of them in for questioning in dragnets cast throughout the West Coast and Hawaii.

My grandfather was lucky, he'd somehow been let go after only a few days. Others were not as fortunate. Hundreds, from small communities in Washington, California, Oregon, and Hawaii, were rounded up and, after what appeared to be routine questioning, shipped off under Justice Department orders to holding centers in Leuppe on the Navaho Reservation in Arizona, in Fort Missoula in Montana, and on Sand Island in Honolulu Harbor. There were other special camps on Maui in Ha'iku and on Hawaii—the "Big Island"—in my own home village of Volcano.

Many of these men—it was exclusively the Japanese-American men suspected of ties to Japan who were initially rounded up—did not see their families again for over four years. Under a suspension of due process that was only after the fact ruled as warranted by military necessity, they were, if only temporarily, "disappeared" in Justice Department prison camps scattered in particularly desolate areas of the United States designated as militarily "safe." These were grim forerunners to the assembly centers and concentration camps for the 120,000 Japanese-American evacuees that were to come later.

I am Kubota's eldest grandchild, and I remember him as a lonely, habitually silent old man who lived with us in our home near Los Angeles for most of my childhood and adolescence. It was the '50s, and my parents had emigrated from Hawaii to the Mainland on the hope of a better life away from the old sugar plantation. After some success, they had sent back for my grandparents and taken them in. And it was my grandparents who did the work of the household while my mother and father worked their salaried city jobs. My grandmother cooked and sewed, washed our clothes, and knitted in the front room under the light of a huge lamp with a bright three-way bulb. Kubota raised a flower garden, read up on soils and grasses in gardening books, and planted a zoysia lawn in front and a dichondra one in back. He planted a small patch near the rear block wall with green onions, eggplant, white Japanese radishes, and cucumber. While he hoed and spaded the loamless, clayey earth of Los Angeles, he sang particularly plangent songs in Japanese about plum blossoms and bamboo groves.

Once, in the mid-'60s, after a dinner during which, as always, he had been silent while he worked away at a meal of fish and rice spiced with dabs of Chinese mustard and catsup thinned with soy sauce, Kubota took his own

10

dishes to the kitchen sink and washed them up. He took a clean jelly jar out of the cupboard—the glass was thick and its shape squatty like an old-fashioned. He reached around to the hutch below where he kept his bourbon. He made himself a drink and retired to the living room where I was expected to join him for "talk story"—the Hawaiian idiom for chewing the fat.

I was a teenager and, though I was bored listening to stories I'd heard often enough before at holiday dinners, I was dutiful. I took my spot on the couch next to Kubota and heard him out. Usually, he'd tell me about his schooling in Japan where he learned *judo* along with mathematics and literature. He'd learned the *soroban* there—the abacus which was the original pocket calculator of the Far East—and that, along with his strong, *judo*-trained back, got him his first job in Hawaii. This was the moral. "Study *ha-ahd*," he'd say with pidgin emphasis. "Learn read good. Learn speak da kine *good* English." The message is the familiar one taught to any children of immigrants—succeed through education. And imitation. But this time, Kubota reached down into his past and told me a different story. I was thirteen by then, and I suppose he thought me ready for it. He told me about Pearl Harbor, how the planes flew in wing after wing of formations over his old house in La'ie in Hawaii, and how, the next day, after Roosevelt had made his famous "Day of Infamy" speech about the treachery of the Japanese, the FBI agents had come to his door and taken him in, hauled him off to Honolulu for questioning and held him without charge for several days. I thought he was lying. I thought he was making up a kind of horror story to shock me and give his moral that much more starch. But it was true. I asked around. I brought it up during History class in junior high school, and my teacher, after silencing me and stepping me off to the back of the room told me that it was indeed so. I asked my mother and she said it was true. I asked my schoolmates, who laughed and ridiculed me for being so ignorant. We lived in a Japanese-American community and the parents of most of my classmates were the *nisei* who had been interned as teenagers all through the war. But there was a strange silence around all of this. There was a hush, as if one were invoking the ill powers of the dead when one brought it up. No one cared to speak about the evacuation and relocation for very long. It wasn't in our history books, though we were studying World War II at the time. It wasn't in the family albums of the people I knew and whom I'd visit staying over weekends with friends. And it wasn't anything that the family talked about or allowed me to keep bringing up either. I was given the facts, told sternly and pointedly that "it was war" and that "nothing could be done." *"Shikatta ga nai"* is the phrase in Japanese, a kind of resolute and determinist pronouncement on how to deal with inexplicable tragedy. I was to know it but not to dwell on it. Japanese Americans were busy trying to forget it ever happened and were having a hard enough time building their new lives after "camp." It was as if we had no history for four years and the relocation was something unspeakable.

But Kubota would not let it go. In session after session for months it seemed, he pounded away at his story. He wanted to tell me the names of the FBI agents. He went over their questions and his responses again and again. He'd tell me how one would try to act friendly towards him, offering him cigarettes while the other, who hounded him with accusations and threats, left the interrogation room. Good cop/bad cop, I thought to myself, already superficially streetwise from stories black classmates told of the Watts riots and from myself having watched too many episodes of *Dragnet* and *The Mod Squad*. But Kubota was not interested in my experiences. I was not made yet and he was determined that his stories be part of my making. He spoke quietly at first, mildly, but once into his narrative and after his drink was down, his voice would rise and quaver with resentment and he'd make his accusations. He gave his testimony to me and I held it at first cautiously in my conscience like it was an heirloom too delicate to expose to strangers and anyone outside of the world Kubota made with his words. "I give you story now," he once said, "and you learn speak good, eh?" It was my job, as the disciple of his preaching I had then become, Ananda to his Buddha, to reassure him with a promise. "You learn speak good like the Dillingham," he'd say another time, referring to the wealthy scion of the grower family who had once run, unsuccessfully, for one of Hawaii's first senatorial seats. Or he'd then invoke a magical name, the name of one of his heroes, a man he thought particularly exemplary and righteous. "Learn speak dah good Ing-rish like *Mistah Inouye*," Kubota shouted. "He *lick* dah Dillingham even in debate. I saw on *terre-bision* myself." He was remembering the debates before the first senatorial election just before Hawaii was admitted to the Union as its 50th state. "You *tell* story," Kubota would end. And I had my injunction.

The town we settled in after the move from Hawaii is called Gardena, the independently incorporated city south of Los Angeles and north of San Pedro harbor. At its northern limit, it borders on Watts and Compton—black towns. To the southwest are Torrance and Redondo Beach—white towns. To the rest of L.A., Gardena is primarily famous for having legalized five-card draw poker after the war. On Vermont Boulevard, its eastern border, there is a dingy little Vegas-like strip of card clubs with huge parking lots and flickering neon signs that spell out "The Rainbow" and "The Horseshoe" in timed sequences of varicolored lights. The town is only secondarily famous as the largest community of Japanese Americans in the United States outside of Honolulu, Hawaii. When I was in high school there, it seemed to me that every *sansei* kid I knew wanted to be a doctor, an engineer, or a pharmacist. Our fathers were gardeners or electricians or nurserymen or ran small businesses catering to other Japanese Americans. Our mothers worked in civil service for the city or as cashiers for Thrifty Drug. What the kids wanted was a good job, good pay, a fine home, and no troubles. No one wanted to mess with the law—from either side—and no one wanted to mess with language or art. They all talked about getting into the right clubs so that they could go to the right schools. There was a certain kind of sameness, an intensely enforced system of conformity. Style was all. Boys wore moccasin-sewn shoes from Flagg Brothers, black A-1 slacks, and Kensington shirts with high collars. Girls wore their hair up in stiff bouffants solidified in hairspray and knew all the latest dances from the Slauson to the Funky Chicken. We did well in chemistry and in math, no one who was Japanese but me spoke in English class or in History unless called upon, and no one talked about World War II. The day after Robert Kennedy was assassinated after winning the California Democratic Primary, we worked on calculus and elected class coordinators for the prom, featuring The 5th Dimension. We avoided grief. We avoided government. We avoided strong feelings and dangers of any kind. Once punished, we tried to maintain a concerted emotional and social discipline and would not willingly seek to fall out of the narrow margin of protective favor again.

But when I was thirteen, in junior high, I'd not understood why it was so difficult for my classmates, those who were themselves Japanese American, to talk about the relocation. They had cringed, too, when I tried to bring it up during our discussions of World War II. I was Hawaiian-born. They were Mainland-born. Their parents had been in camp, had been the ones to suffer the complicated experience of having to distance themselves from their own history and all things Japanese in order to make their way back and into the American social and economic mainstream. It was out of this sense of shame and a fear of stigma I was only beginning to understand that the *nisei* had silenced themselves. And, for their children, among whom I grew up, they wanted no heritage, no culture, no contact with a defiled history. I recall the silence very well. The Japanese-American children around me were burdened in a way I was not. Their injunction was silence. Mine was to speak.

Away at college, in another protected world in its own way as magical to   15
me as the Hawaii of my childhood, I dreamed about my grandfather. Tired from studying languages, practicing German conjugations, or scripting an army's worth of Chinese ideograms on a single sheet of paper, Kubota would come to me as I drifted off into sleep. Or, I would walk across the newly mown ballfield in back of my dormitory, cutting through a streetside phalanx of ancient eucalyptus trees on my way to visit friends off-campus, and I would think of him, his anger, and his sadness.

I don't know myself what makes someone feel that kind of need to have a story they've lived through be deposited somewhere, but I can guess. I think about *The Illiad, The Odyssey, The Peloponnesian Wars* of Thucydides, and a myriad of the works of literature I've studied. A character, almost a *topoi* he occurs so often, is frequently the witness who gives personal testimony about an event the rest of his community cannot even imagine. The Sibyl is such a character. And Procne, the maid whose tongue is cut out so that she will not tell that she has been raped by her own brother-in-law, king of Thebes. There are the dime novels, the epic blockbusters Hollywood makes into mini-series, and then there are the plain, relentless stories of witnesses who have suffered through horrors major and minor that have marked and changed their lives. I haven't myself talked to Holocaust victims. But I've read their survival stories and their stories of witness and been revolted and moved by them. My father-in-law, Al Thiessen, tells me his war stories again and again and I listen. A Mennonite who set aside the strictures of his own church in order to serve, he was a Marine codeman in the Pacific during World War II, in the Signal Corps on Guadalcanal, Morotai, and Bougainville. He was part of the island-hopping maneuver MacArthur had devised to win the war in the Pacific. He saw friends die from bombs which exploded not ten yards away. When he was with the 298th Signal Corps attached to the Thirteenth Air Force, he saw plane after plane come in and crash, just short of the runway, killing their crews, setting the jungle ablaze with oil and gas fires. Emergency wagons would scramble, bouncing over newly bulldozed land men used just the afternoon before for a football game. Every time we go fishing together, whether it's in a McKenzie boat drifting for salmon in Tillamook Bay or taking a lunch break from wading the riffles of a stream in the Cascades, he tells me about what happened to him and the young men in his unit. One was a Jewish boy from Brooklyn. One was a foul-mouthed kid from Kansas. They died. And he *has* to tell me. And I *have* to listen. It's a ritual payment the young owe their elders who have survived. The evacuation and relocation is something like that.

Kubota, my grandfather, had been ill with Alzheimer's disease for some time before he died. At the house he'd built on Kamehameha Highway in Hau'ula, a seacoast village just down the road from La'ie where he had his store, he'd wander out from the garage or greenhouse where he'd set up a workbench, and trudge down to the beach or up towards the line of pines he'd planted while employed by the Works Project Administration during the '30s. Kubota thought he was going fishing. Or he thought he was back at work for Roosevelt planting pines as a wind or soilbreak on the windward flank of the Ko'olau mountains, emerald monoliths rising out of sea and cane fields from Waialua to Kaneohe. When I visited, my grandmother would send me down to the beach to fetch him. Or I'd run down Kam Highway a quarter mile or so and find him hiding in the cane field by the roadside, counting stalks, measuring circumferences in the claw of his thumb and forefinger. The look on his face was confused or concentrated—I didn't know which. But I guessed he was going fishing again. I'd grab him and walk him back to his house on the highway. My grandmother would shut him in a room.

Within a few years, Kubota had a stroke and survived it, then he had another one and was completely debilitated. The family decided to put him in a nursing home in Kahuku, just set back from the highway, within a mile or so of Kahuku Point and the Tanaka Store where he had his first job as a stock boy. He lived there three years, and I visited him once with my aunt. He was like a potato that had been worn down by cooking. Everything on him—his eyes, his teeth, his legs and torso—seemed like it had been sloughed away. What he had been was mostly gone now and I was looking at the nub of a man. In a wheelchair, he grasped my hands and tugged on them—violently. His hands were still thick, and, I believed, strong enough to lift me out of my own seat into his lap. He murmured something in Japanese—he'd long ago ceased to speak any English. My aunt and I cried a little, and we left him.

I remember walking out on the black asphalt of the parking lot of the nursing home. It was heat-cracked and eroded already, and grass had veined itself into the interstices. There were coconut trees around, a cane field I could see across the street, and the ocean I knew was pitching a surf just beyond it. The green Ko'olaus came up behind us. Somewhere nearby, alongside the beach, there was an abandoned airfield in the middle of the canes. As a child, I'd come upon it playing one day, and my friends and I kept returning to it, day after day, playing war or sprinting games or coming to fly kites. I recognize it even now when I see it on TV—it's used as a site for action scenes in the detective shows Hollywood always sets in the Islands: a helicopter chasing the hero racing away in a Ferrari, or gun dealers making a clandestine rendezvous on the abandoned runway. It was the old airfield strafed by Japanese planes the day the major flight attacked Pearl Harbor. It was the airfield the FBI thought my grandfather had targeted in his night-fishing and signaling with the long surf-poles he'd stuck in the sandy bays near Kahuku Point.

Kubota died a short while after I visited him, but not, I thought, without giving me a final message. I was on the Mainland, in California studying for Ph.D. exams, when my grandmother called me with the news. It was a relief. He'd suffered from his debilitation a long time and I was grateful he'd gone. I went home for the funeral and gave the eulogy. My grandmother and I took his ashes home in a small, heavy metal box wrapped in a black *furoshiki*—a large, silk scarf. She showed me the name the priest had given to him on his death, scripted with a calligraphy brush on a long, narrow talent of plain wood. Buddhist commoners, at death, are given priestly names, received symbolically into the clergy. The idea is that, in their next life, one of scholarship and leisure, they might meditate and attain the enlightenment the religion is aimed at. *"Shaku Shūchi,"* the ideograms read. It was Kubota's Buddhist name, incorporating characters from his family and given names. It meant "Shining Wisdom of the Law." He died on Pearl Harbor Day, December 7, 1983.

After years, after I'd finally come back to live in Hawaii again, only once did I dream of Kubota, my grandfather. It was the same night I'd heard HR

442, the redress bill for Japanese Americans, had been signed into law. In my dream that night Kubota was "torching," and he sang a Japanese song, a querulous and wavery folk ballad, as he hung paper lanterns on bamboo poles stuck into the sand in the shallow water of the lagoon behind the reef near Kahuku Point. Then he was at a worktable, smoking a hand-rolled cigarette, letting it dangle from his lips Bogart-style as he drew, daintily and skillfully, with a narrow trim brush, ideogram after ideogram on a score of paper lanterns he had hung in a dark shed to dry. He had painted a talismanic mantra onto each lantern, the ideogram for the word "red" in Japanese, a bit of art blended with some superstition, a piece of sympathetic magic appealing to the magenta coloring on the rough skins of the schooling, night-feeding fish he wanted to attract to his baited hooks. He strung them from pole to pole in the dream then, hiking up his khaki worker's pants so his white ankles showed and wading through the shimmering black waters of the sand flats and then the reef. "The moon is leaving, leaving," he sang in Japanese. "Take me deeper in the savage sea." He turned and crouched like an ice-racer then, leaning forward so that his unshaven face almost touched the light film of water. I could see the light stubble of beard like a fine, gray ash covering the lower half of his face. I could see his gold-rimmed spectacles. He held a small wooden boat in his cupped hands and placed it lightly on the sea and pushed it away. One of his lanterns was on it and, written in small neat rows like a sutra-scroll, it had been decorated with the silvery names of all our dead.

Considerations

1. Hongo writes, "Japanese-American children around me were burdened in a way I was not. Their injunction was silence. Mine was to speak" (para. 14). Most Japanese Americans seemed to want to forget the tragic humiliation they were subjected to after Pearl Harbor. From the history Hongo presents in this essay, how do you account for Kubota's very different reaction to the indignities he suffered?

2. When Hongo is thirteen, Kubota tells him, "I give you story now" (para. 12). Why does the grandfather choose this particular age for his grandson to hear his story? How ready is Hongo to accept his grandfather's story? When does it become his story also?

Invitation to Write

As the oldest grandson, Hongo inherited Kubota's stories. Hongo makes it clear that the process of story-telling was part of his education: "But Kubota was not interested in my experiences. I was not made yet and he was determined that his stories be part of my making. . . . He gave his testimony to me and I held it at first cautiously in my conscience like it was an heirloom" (para. 12). Write an essay in which you explore the role of family stories in the education of the younger generation in Hongo's narrative. Think also about family stories that may have been passed down to you or of events that you will be able to recount to the next generation in the future, and use them as examples in your discussion. Focus particularly on the parts of the stories or events that are part of history but not recorded.

Connections

Hongo's essay reveals how his grandfather's stories made him retrieve history from silence. In the preceding essay, "Where I Come from Is Like This," Paula Gunn Allen also contrasts family stories to the stories she learns from the outside world. Both writers are people who grew up with two sets of stories that present different views of their cultures. Using examples from both texts, write an essay in which you explore the idea of a double cultural heritage as manifested by the different representations of world events in stories. Focus on the dilemma of the younger generation, which must face its dual heritage, and think about the integrative story the younger generation must write.

ASSIGNMENT SEQUENCE

Stories That Shape Our Lives

This sequence first asks you to narrate and reflect upon a story that has been important to you and that has influenced your self-conception. In the next assignment, you will consider how successfully Ellen Gilchrist captures the process of being influenced by stories in her short story "Music." You will turn next to the task of examining the way women use story-telling to counteract weak images of themselves, using as evidence the mothers in Amy Tan's "Without Wood" and Paula Gunn Allen's "Where I Come from Is Like This." These mothers tell their daughters stories that empower them, that give them a sense of belonging. In the next assignment, you will use Garrett Hongo's essay "Kubota," as well as Gilchrist's and Tan's stories, to extend your analysis of the ways stories create a sense of belonging. To understand this process, you will examine the way stories help people bridge gaps between their traditional culture and American culture. The concluding assignment then asks you to use all the texts to discuss the role of stories in reshaping identities and to define the resulting consequences.

Assignment 1: Exploring Experience

Think about your life and identify a story that has been particularly important to you. It should be one that has gripped your imagination in a profound way and worked itself into your life as a reference point. It can be a story you have heard about your family's history or your own life, a story you read or saw on television or in the movies, a story about another individual whom you admire or pity, or a story of a historical event. You can identify stories from other sources as well. Then write the story that has been important to you, evaluate the nature of its importance, and discuss how it has influenced your life on one or two occasions. You could include the circumstances surrounding your introduction to the story, if you remember them. Most importantly, consider why you think this story attracted you and how you have used it to define a sense of your identity.

Assignment 2

The jacket was thrown carelessly over her shoulder like Gene Tierney in Leave Her to Heaven. *I look great in red, she was thinking, catching a glimpse of herself in a store window. It isn't true that redheaded people can't wear red.*

—ELLEN GILCHRIST, *Music*

409

Write a paper in which you examine Ellen Gilchrist's presentation of the effect stories have upon the character of Rhoda, drawing upon your own experience to determine if the process she describes seems realistic or not. Evaluate how the stories influence Rhoda, her behavior, and her ideas of herself. Consider stories from books, poems, and stories about her relatives. To evaluate her response, use your knowledge of your own response to stories, which you described for the previous assignment.

To write this paper, you need to reread the story to pinpoint moments when Rhoda turns to her imagination to define herself. As you read, you can find many examples of different types of stories that Rhoda draws upon. Some are family stories about her relatives; some come from literary texts; some are stories that she invents. Select several examples that you feel are key to understanding Rhoda. Analyze how these stories influence her immediate behavior and her vision of herself as an adult. Use your own knowledge of the way stories influence people to decide how well Gilchrist has captured the way stories shape our lives.

Assignment 3

She said that if I listened to her, later I would know what she knew: where true words came from, always from up high, above everything else. And if I didn't listen to her, she said my ear would bend too easily to other people, all saying words that had no lasting meaning, because they came from the bottom of their hearts, where their own desires lived, a place where I could not belong.

—AMY TAN, *Without Wood*

Both Rose Hsu Jordan, in Amy Tan's story "Without Wood," and Paula Gunn Allen, in her essay "Where I Come from Is Like This," refer to many stories that are particular to their own lives and cultures. Many of these stories are told to them by their mothers to prepare them for their lives. Write an essay in which you examine the effect these stories have in the lives of both women.

To begin your essay, reflect upon the importance of the quotation above in Rose Hsu Jordan's life. Consider especially the way her mother's belief becomes incorporated into the stories that Rose remembers and relives in her dreams. Then consider Allen's narrative in light of the same quotation. Show the role that the mothers' words—their stories—play in the lives of their daughters, and discuss how stories create mother-daughter relationships that empower women.

ASSIGNMENT SEQUENCE

Assignment 4

But Kubota was not interested in my experiences. I was not made yet, and he was determined that his stories be part of my making. He spoke quietly at first, mildly, but once into his narrative and after his drink was down, his voice would rise and quaver with resentment and he'd make his accusations. He gave his testimony to me and I held it at first cautiously in my conscience like it was an heirloom.
—GARRETT HONGO, *Kubota*

In the narratives written by Amy Tan, Paula Gunn Allen, and Garrett Hongo, the stories the narrators inherit help them mediate between the cultural traditions of their families and the culture of the surrounding society. Write an essay that examines the role of stories, within particular cultural traditions, in helping people preserve their cultural heritages and find their own places in American society.

In each case, decide how Rose Hsu Jordan, Paula Gunn Allen, and Garrett Hongo turn to their family stories to preserve important values of their families' cultures. Then, examine the way they think about these stories as they integrate their lives into American society. Looking at a particular example from each text, show how their stories help them resolve differences between their dual identities without making them relinquish their heritages.

Assignment 5

For your final paper, consider the way stories cause people to redefine themselves. For each text in this chapter and in the case of your own experience, decide how identity has been reshaped in response to knowing a story. In order to decide this, look at how an individual's awareness has been broadened or enriched by knowledge of a story. If you see negative consequences instead, explore the circumstances that lead to this result.

Begin your paper by thinking about the way the central person in each text has changed and ask yourself what role the story had in effecting this change. Decide what the characters would be like if they had not heard and integrated a particular story into their lives. For example, what would Rhoda be like if she didn't read books? What would Rose be like if she never learned to listen to the true words of her mother? How would Allen react to non–American Indian stories if she didn't have American Indian stories to counter them? Finally, how would Hongo fill in the unspoken passages of history? These are questions to think about, although you may decide to pick different moments in each text to write about.

Lives in Transition

I don't believe her. She's not the Chief's type. She wants to goad me into confessing that I love her.
—BHARATI MUKHERJEE, *Fighting for the Rebound*

Now I realized, in what amounted to a conversion experience, that I was going to violate the code of my forefathers. I wouldn't tell myself anymore I was tough enough for any hazard, could endure anything because, as my father's old friend had said, "she was born in the right country." I wasn't nearly tough enough to stay around in an emotional climate more desolate than any drought I'd ever seen.
—JILL KER CONWAY, *The Right Country*

A few weeks later, I told my mother that I had no intention of being crazy like the rest of the family. I had found a therapist. I was willing to pay for it myself if she wouldn't.
—ITABARI NJERI, *Bag Lady*

Periods of upheaval can be both frightening and liberating. Not all transitions have positive outcomes, but often growth occurs. In periods of transition, people recognize the possibility and necessity of change, but they also realize

413

that as they face new situations, they leave familiar ones behind. If they are to grow, individuals must make difficult choices, reach important decisions, and start out in new directions. Sometimes they look back to see how far they have come, how much they have changed, and to gauge the impact of their decisions. Adolescence marks a major turning point in individuals' lives, but most psychologists now believe that human lives are marked by passage through many developmental stages. While the three readings in this chapter reveal that transitions include painful moments, they also reveal that such moments provide opportunities for growth and self-exploration. Individuals here have different attitudes toward the possibility of change: Some embrace the chance to redefine themselves, others fight any alteration in routine, and the rest find themselves confused and ambivalent about the changes that lie ahead.

In Bharati Mukherjee's story "Fighting for the Rebound," two individuals—one Filipina, one American—explore the effect a new relationship will have in reshaping their lives. In her autobiographical essay "The Right Country," Jill Ker Conway discusses her decision to leave Australia, exploring the cultural values that once inhibited her from breaking ties to her family and country of birth. When she leaves, she is able to reshape her life according to her desires instead of in response to demands for sacrifice and duty. In Itabari Njeri's essay "Bag Lady," she recounts a definitive confrontation with her mother. In her narration of the memories of childhood and adolescence that culminate in that event, she makes quite clear the psychological distance she has traveled—from a vulnerable child to a young woman in control of her life.

BHARATI MUKHERJEE

Fighting for the Rebound

Bharati Mukherjee was born in Calcutta, India, in 1940. She earned her B.A. from the University of Calcutta, an M.A. in English from the University of Baroda in Gujurat, and her Ph.D. from the University of Iowa. Before moving to the United States, she lived in Canada. Mukherjee has written several novels, including *The Tiger's Daughter* (1972), *Wife* (1975), *Jasmine* (1990), and *The Holder of the World* (1993), and numerous short story collections, including *Darkness* (1985) and *The Middleman and Other Stories,* which won the National Book Critics Circle Award for 1989. Her nonfiction books include *Kautilya's Concept of Diplomacy: A New Interpretation* (1976), *Days and Nights in Calcutta* (1977, with Clark Blaise), and *The Sorrow and the Terror: The Haunting Legacy of the Air India Tragedy* (1987, also with Clark Blaise). Her awards include grants from the Canada Arts Council and the Guggenheim Foundation as well as the National Book Critics Circle Award. Her story "The Management of Grief" was selected for *The Best American Short Stories 1989*. Mukherjee has taught creative writing at Columbia, New York University, and Queens College and currently holds a distinguished professorship at the University of California at Berkeley.

Mukherjee is doubly classified as an Anglo-Indian and American writer, although she definitely prefers the latter designation. In her work, she moves from depicting the inner conflicts of Indian characters who suffer postcolonial identity crises to the equally complicated portrayal of immigrant life in the United States. This change in focus is typified by the character of Jasmine, who evolves from an Indian peasant woman dislodged from her environment into a struggling immigrant consumed by the desire to fulfill her American dream.

The story "Fighting for the Rebound" is reprinted from *The Middleman and Other Stories*. Here, Mukherjee's preoccupation with immigrant life and its dilemmas becomes evident through her heroine, who comes from the Philippines. Mukherjee is especially skillful in presenting both the way Americans see Blanquita and the way Blanquita sees herself through Western eyes.

I'M IN BED WATCHING the Vanilla Gorilla stick it to the Abilene Christians on some really obscure cable channel when Blanquita comes through the door wearing lavender sweats, and over them a frilly see-through apron. It's a November Thursday, a chilly fifty-three, but she's hibachiing butterfly lamb on the balcony.

"Face it, Griff," Blanquita says, wielding the barbecue fork the way empresses wield scepters.

"Face what?"

"That's what I mean," she says. "You're so insensitive, it's awesome."

"Nobody says awesome anymore," I tease. Blanquita speaks six languages, her best being Tagalog, Spanish, and American. 5

"Why not?" she says. Back in Manila, she took a crash course in making nice to Americans, before her father sent her over. In her family they called her Baby. "Bite him, Marcos," she orders her cat. "Spit on him." But Marcos chooses to stay behind the harpsichord and leggy ficus. Marcos knows I am not a cat person; he's known me to sneak in a kick. He takes out his hostilities on the ficus. What he does is chew up a pale, new leaf. I get my greenery for free because the office I work in throws out all browning, scraggly plants and trees. I have an arboretum of rejects.

"Let's start this conversation over," I plead. I'm tentative at the start of relationships, but this time I'm not throwing it away.

"Let's," she says.

"You're beautiful," I say.

"Do you mean that?" 10

I hate it when she goes intense on me. She starts to lift off the Press-On Nails from her thumbs. Her own nails are roundish and ridged, which might be her only imperfection.

"Blanquita the Beautiful." I shoot it through with melody. If I were a songwriter I'd write her a million lyrics. About frangipani blooms and crescent moons. But what I am is a low-level money manager, a solid, decent guy in white shirt and maroon tie and thinning, sandy hair over which hangs the sword of Damocles. The Dow Jones crowds my chest like an implant. I unlist my telephone every six weeks, and still they find me, the widows and orthodontists into the money-market. I feel the sword's point every minute. Get me in futures! In Globals, in Aggressive Growth, in bonds! I try to tell them, for every loser there's a winner, somewhere. Someone's always profiting, just give me time and I'll find it, I'll lock you in it.

Blanquita scoops Marcos off the broadloom and holds him on her hip as she might a baby. "I should never have left Manila," she says. She does some very heavy, very effective sighing. "Pappy was right. The East is East and the West is West and never the twain shall meet."

I get these nuggets from Kipling at least once a week. "But, baby," I object, "you did leave. Atlanta is halfway around the world from the Philippines."

"Poor Pappy," Blanquita moons. "Poor Joker."   15

She doesn't give me much on her family other than that Pappy—Joker Rosario—a one-time big-shot publisher tight with the Marcos crew, is stuck in California stocking shelves in a liquor store. Living like a peon, serving winos in some hotbox *barrio*. Mother runs a beauty shop out of her kitchen in West Hartford, Connecticut. His politics, and those of his daughter, are— to understate it—vile. She'd gotten to America long before his fall, when he still had loot and power and loved to spread it around. She likes to act as though real life began for her at JFK when she got past the customs and im- migration on the seventeenth of October, 1980. That's fine with me. The less I know about growing up in Manila, rich or any other way, the less foreign she feels. Dear old redneck Atlanta is a thing of the past, no need to feel for- eign here. Just wheel your shopping cart through aisles of bok choy and twenty kinds of Jamaican spices at the Farmers' Market, and you'll see that the US of A is still a pioneer country.

She relaxes, and Marcos leaps off the sexy, shallow shelf of her left hip. "You're a racist, patronizing jerk if you think I'm beautiful. I'm just different, that's all."

"Different from whom?"

"All your others."

It's in her interest, somehow, to imagine me as Buckhead's primo   20 swinger, maybe because—I can't be sure—she needs the buzz of perpetual jealousy. She needs to feel herself a temp. For all the rotten things she says about the Philippines, or the mistiness she reserves for the Stars and Stripes, she's kept her old citizenship.

"Baby, Baby, don't do this to me. Please?"

I crank up the Kraftmatic. My knees, drawn up and tense, push against my forehead. Okay, so maybe what I meant was that she isn't a looker in the blondhair-smalltits-greatlegs way that Wendi was. Or Emilou, for that mat- ter. But beautiful is how she makes me feel. Wendi was slow-growth. Emilou was strictly Chapter Eleven.

I can't tell her that. I can't tell her I've been trading on rumor, selling on news, for years. Your smart pinstriper aims for the short-term profit. My track record for pickin 'em is just a little better than blindfold darts. It's as hard to lose big these days as it is to make a killing. I understand those inside traders—it's not the money, it's the rush. I'm hanging in for the balance of the quarter.

But.

If there's a shot, I'll take it.   25

Meantime, the barbecue fork in Blanquita's hand describes circles of such inner distress that I have to take my eyes off the slaughter of the Abilene Christians.

"You don't love me, Griff."

It's hard to know where she learns her lines. They're all so tragically sincere. Maybe they go back to the instant-marriage emporiums in Manila. Or the magazines she reads. Or a series of married, misunderstood men that she must have introduced to emotional chaos. Her tastes in everything are, invariably, unspeakable. She rests a kneecap on the twisted Kraftmatic and weeps. Even her kneecaps . . . well, even the kneecaps get my attention. It's not fair. Behind her, the Vanilla Gorilla is going man-to-man. Marcos is about to strangle himself with orange wool he's pawed out of a dusty wicker yarn basket. Wendi was a knitter. Love flees, but we're stuck with love's debris.

"I'm not saying you don't *like* me, Griff. I'm saying you don't love me, okay?"

Why do I think she's said it all before? Why do I hear "sailor" instead of my name? "Don't spoil what we have." I am begging. 30

She believes me. Her face goes radiant. "What do we have, Griff?" Then she backs away from my hug. She believes me not.

All I get to squeeze are hands adorned with the glamour-length Press-On Nails. She could make a fortune as a hands model if she wanted to. That skin of hers is an evolutionary leap. Holding hands on the bed, we listen for a bit to the lamb spit fat. Anyone can suffer a cold shooting spell. I'm thirty-three and a vet of Club Med vacations; I can still ballhandle, but one-on-one is a younger man's game.

"All right, we'll drop the subject," Blanquita says. "I can be a good sport."

"That's my girl," I say. But I can tell from the angle of her chin and the new stiffness of her posture that she's turning prim and well-brought-up on me. Then she lobs devastation. "I won't be seeing you this weekend."

"It's *ciao* because I haven't bought you a ring?" 35

"No," she says, haughtily. "The Chief's asked me out, that's why. We're going up to his cabin."

I don't believe her. She's not the Chief's type. She wants to goad me into confessing that I love her.

"You're a fast little worker." The Chief, a jowly fifty-five, is rumored to enjoy exotic tastes. But, Christ, there's a difference between exotic and *foreign,* isn't there? Exotic means you know how to use your foreignness, or you make yourself a little foreign in order to appear exotic. Real foreign is a little scary, believe me. The fact is, the Chief brought Blanquita and me together in his office. That was nearly six months ago. I was there to prep him, and she was hustled in, tools of the trade stuffed into a Lancôme tote sack, to make him look good on TV. Blanquita's a makeup artist on the way up and up, and Atlanta is Executives City, where every Chief wants to look terrific before he throws himself to the corporate lions. I watched her operate. She pumped him up a dozen ways. And I just sat there, stunned. The Chief still had moves.

"You sound jealous, Griff." She turns her wicked, bottomless blacks on me and I feel myself squirm.

"Go up to the cabin if you want to. I don't do jealousy, hon." 40

She starts trapping on defense herself now. "You don't do jealousy! Well, you don't have the right to be jealous! You don't have any rights, period! You can't change the ground rules!"

Maybe Wendi wasn't all that certifiable a disaster. Come to think of it, Wendi had her moments. She could be a warm, nurturing person. We talked, we did things together. The summer we were breaking up, I built her kid a treehouse, which might be the only unselfish good I've accomplished in my life. Blanquita's a Third World aristocrat, a hothouse orchid you worship but don't dare touch. I wouldn't dare ask her to help me knock together a bookcase or scrub the grout around the bathroom tiles. But Wendi, alas, never made me feel this special, this loved.

"I'm serious, Griff." She closes her eyes and rams her fists in eyelids that are as delicately mauve as her sweatshirt. "You keep me in limbo. I need to know where we stand."

"I don't want you to go," I say. I'm not myself. I'm a romantic in red suspenders.

"What do you want me to do?" 45

"Whatever you want to do, hon."

Her body sags inside her oversized sweatshirt. She gets off the mattress, strokes Marcos with the toes of her Reeboks, checks a shredded ficus leaf, tosses the skein of orange wool from the balcony down to the parking lot.

"Hullo," I say. "Hey, Baby." I really want to reach her. "Hey, watch him!" Wendi was a big basketball fan, a refugee from Hoosierland, and she was the first and so far the only woman I've known who could sit through a Braves or Falcons game. If I could get Miss Bataan to watch the Gorilla stuff it, we'd be okay, but she doesn't even pretend to watch.

"I'm going to make myself a cup of tea," she says.

We say nothing while she brews herself a pot of cherry almond. Then she 50 sits on my bed and drinks a slow cup, fiddling with the remote control and putting to flight all ten sweaty goons. F. Lee Bailey comes on and talks up the Bhopal tragedy. I can't believe it's been a year. I must have been seeing Emilou on the side when it happened. Yes, in fact Emilou cried, and Wendi had made a fuss about the mascara on my sixty-buck shirt. An auditorium packed with Herbalifers comes on the screen. The Herbalifers are very upbeat and very free enterprise. They perk her up.

"We don't need that," I plead.

"You don't know what you need," she snaps. "You're so narcissistic you don't need anyone. You don't know how to love."

Sailor, I think. It thrills me.

"That's not fair."

But Blanquita the Beautiful races on to bigger issues. "Not just you, Griff," 55
she scolds in that eerily well-bred, Asian convent-schooled voice. "You're all
emotional cripples. All you Americans. You just worry about your own measly
little relationships. You don't care how much you hurt the world."

In changing gears, she's right up there with Mario Andretti. I envy her her
freedom, her Green Card politics. It's love, not justice, that powers her.
Emilou and Wendi would have died if I caught them in an inconsistency.

She jabs at more buttons on the remote control doodad. Herbalifers scuttle into permanent blackness, and a Soweto funeral procession comes on. Big
guys in black boots come at pallbearers with whips and clubs. Blanquita lays
her teacup on the top sheet. These are serious designer sheets, debris from my
months with Emilou. When Joker Rosario went to South Africa back in the
long, long ago, he was treated very, very white. He wrote pleasant things
about South Africa in his paper. Yesterday's statesman is today's purveyor of
Muscatel. South Africa is making her morose, and I dare not ask why. I suddenly remember that the neighborhood dry cleaner doesn't know how to take
tea stains off but does a good job with Kahlúa. Blanquita flashes the black
inscrutables one more time and says, "I can't stand it anymore, Griff. It's got
to stop."

South Africa? I wonder, but dare not hope. I carefully remove her teacup
and take hold of her fingertips, which are still warm from holding the cup,
and pull them up to my beard. "We have each other," I say.

"Do we?"

It's time to take charge, to force the good times to roll. Some nations were 60
built to take charge. It's okay for a nation of pioneers to bully the rest of the
world as long as the cause is just. My heart is pure, my head is clear. I retrieve
the doodad from Blanquita's perfect hand. I want to show her the funtimes of
TV-land. I slice through a Mexican variety show on SIN. Any time of the day
or night, those Mexicans are in tuxedos. All those blow-dried Mexican em-
cees in soccer stadiums, looking like Ricardo Montalbans who never made it.

I know she's a secret fan.

On cue, my trusty nineteen-incher serves up the right stuff. It's National
Cheerleading Contest time. A squad in skimpy skirts, Oceanside High's cut-
est, synchronizes cartwheels and handstands, and starts to dust the competition. I feel godly powers surge through my body as Blanquita relaxes. Soon
she relaxes enough to laugh.

"Did you ever try out as a cheerleader?" I ask. I can sense the imminence
of terrific times.

Blanquita the Beautiful watches the kids on the screen with gratifying
intensity. Then she thrusts a hesitant leg in the air. It's the fault of the French
maid's apron that she's wearing over her baggy sweats; my saucy exotic's
turned a schoolgirl routine into something alien and absurd. Oh, Blanquita,
not so fast!

"I'm too good for you, Griff," she pants, twirling an invisible baton and high-stepping across the condo's wall-to-wall. "Pappy would call you illiterate scum." 65

"And so I am. But Joker's selling rotgut through a retractable grate and Mama's perming Koreans in her living room. Ferdie and Imelda they're not." If People Power hadn't cut them down, if Joker's own reporters hadn't locked him out, Blanquita was promised a place in the Miss Universe contest. That's why she kept her citizenship.

"That's needlessly cruel."

"Baby, you've got to stop living in the past."

"Okay." She stops the twirling and marching. She turns the TV off without the doodad though I've begged her not to many times. Without the light from the screen, the condo room seems as dull and impersonal as a room in a Holiday Inn.

Without Blanquita I'd be just another Joe Blow Buckhead yuppie in his Reeboks. It's she who brings me to bed each night and wakes me up each morning, big as a house and hard as a sidewalk. 70

"Okay," she goes again. "Who needs a crummy tropical past?"

We're out of the woods. I start to relax.

"Two cheers for cable sleaze." I shout. She plucks Marcos from his hidey hole behind the ficus and babies him. "I'm saying yes to the Chief, Griff. Hip, Hip!"

"What?"

"He says I make him look like a million dollars and make him feel like even more." 75

"Get it in writing. That's a low-rent come-on. He wouldn't dare try it on the office girls."

"Of course not."

She's not been getting my point.

"I have to get on with my life. And anyway, you said you weren't jealous so what's to hold me up?"

I check out her pulse rate with my lips. I'm not verbal. Maybe I don't love Blanquita. Because I don't know what love is. I'm not ready for one-on-one. 80

Baby Blanquita is too agitated to smell the charred lamb whooshing off the hibachi, so it's up to me, the narcissist, to rescue the rescue-worthy. The balcony that holds the smoking hibachi is eighteen floors up. Standing between the high gray sky and the pocket-sized pool, I feel omnipotent. Everything's in place.

While I poke the ruined meat with the barbecue fork, an uncommonly handsome blond woman in a ponytail and a cherry-red tracksuit comes out of the building's back door. She hurls a bashed pizza box, like a Frisbee, into the dumpster. Excess energy floats toward me, connecting us. She can't stand still. She tightens a shoelace. We're a community of toned, conditioned athletes.

Use it or lose it. Hands pressed down on somebody's Firebird, she does warm-up routines. I've seen her run in the Lullwater Estate close by, but I've never felt connected enough to her to nod. I heave the meat from the rack to a platter. The woman's still hanging around in that hyper, fidgety way of hers. She's waiting. She's waiting for someone. When a man in a matching tracksuit jogs out the back door, I get depressed. She used to run alone.

Blanquita doesn't say anything about the state of our dinner. It's already stuffed away conveniently in the past. She's got the TV going again. The latest news, hot from Mexico City. "They had this news analyst chap on a minute ago," she says. "They were talking about Vitaly Yurchenko."

I put the butterfly lamb in the kitchen sink. "Why don't you watch about Vitaly Yurchenko on an American station?" I ask. Usually, that steams her. Mexican *is* American! she'll squeal. But instead she says, "He could have had it all if he'd stayed. What's so great about Moscow?"

"Sometimes you blow it for love. It can happen." 85

She runs to me, lavender arms going like wings. Her face—the skin so tight-pored that in the dark I feel I'm stroking petals—glows with new hope. "What are you saying, Griff? Are you saying what I think you're saying?"

I know what I would say if I weren't the solid corporate guy in maroon tie and dark suit. I buy and sell with other people's money and skim enough to just get by. It's worked so far.

"Griff?"

Sailor?

"Let's go for a run, Blanquita." 90

The woman of many men's dreams doesn't wrench herself free from my kissing hold. I don't deserve her.

"Just a short run. To clear our heads. Please?"

Before I met her I used to pump iron. I was pumping so hard I could feel a vein nearly pop in the back of my head. I was a candidate for a stroke. Self-love may be too much like self-hate, who knows? Blanquita got me running. We started out real easy, staying inside the Lullwater Estate like that woman in the red tracksuit. We ran the Peachtree 10K. We could run a marathon if we wanted to. Our weightless feet beat perfect time through city streets and wooded ravines. The daily run is the second best thing we do together, I like to think.

"All right," she says. She gives me one of her demure, convent smiles. "But what'll we do with dinner?"

I point at the shrivelled, carbonized thing in the stainless steel sink. "We 95 could mail it to Africa."

"Biafra?" she asks.

"Baby, Baby . . . Ethiopia, Mozambique. Biafra was gone a long time ago," I tell her. She's very selective with her news. Emilou was a news hound, and I took to watching CNN for a solid winter.

Blanquita pins my condo key to her elasticized waistband and goes out the front door ahead of me. The lawyer from 1403 is waiting by the elevator. I am far enough behind Blanquita to catch the quickie gleam in his eyes before he resumes his cool Duke demeanor and holds the elevator for us. In your face, Blue Devil.

That night Blanquita whips up some green nutritive complexion cream in the Cuisinart. She slaps the green sludge on her face with a rubber spatula. Her face is unequivocally mournful. The sludge in the Cuisinart fills the condo with smells I remember from nature trails of my childhood. Woodsy growths. Mosses. Ferns. I tracked game as a kid; I fished creeks. Atlanta wasn't always this archipelago of developments.

"Better make tonight memorable," she advises. The mask is starting to   100
stiffen, especially around the lips. She has full, pouty, brownish lips. "It's our last night."

How many times has she said that? I've never said it, never had to. The women of my life always got the idea in plenty of time, they made it a mutual-consent, too-bad, and so-long kind of thing. Wendi was really looking for a stepfather to her kids. Emilou was looking for full-time business advice to manage her settlement.

"What's that supposed to mean?"

The lips make a whistling noise from, inside the mask's cutout. "Anyway," she says, "it wasn't all cherry bombs and rockets for me either. Just sparklers."

Sex, intimacy, love. I can't keep any of it straight anymore.

"You're not going to the Chief's cabin in the north woods, period. He's   105
Jack the Ripper."

"You think I can't handle the situation, right? You think I'm just a dumb, naive foreigner you have to protect, right?"

"Yeah."

Then she leaps on me, green face, glamour-length nails, Dior robe and all. I don't know about Baby, but for me those rockets explode.

All day Sunday it rains. The raindrops are of the big, splashy variety, complete with whiffs of wild winds and churned seas. Our winter is starting. I don't do much; I stay in, play Bach on the earphones and vacuum the broadloom. Marcos seems here to stay because I can't bring myself to call the ASPCA.

When the hour for the daily run rolls around, I start out as usual in the   110
doctors' wing of the VA Hospital parking lot, pick my way around Mazdas, Audis, Volvos—they don't have too many station wagons in this neighborhood—keep pace with fit groups in running shoes for as long as it feels good, then shoot ahead, past the serious runners who don't look back when they

hear you coming, past the dogs with Frisbees in their jaws, past the pros who scorn designer tracksuits and the Emory runners with fraternity gizmos on their shirts, pick up more speed until the Reeboks sheathe feet as light as cotton. Then it's time to race. Really race. After Emilou and just before Baby I did wind sprints for a spring at the Atlanta Track Club, ran the three-minute half, ran four of them. I can let it out.

Today in the rain and the changing weather, colder tomorrow, I run longer, pushing harder, than any afternoon in my life. Running is here to stay, even if Baby is gone.

Today I run until a vein in the back of my head feels ready to pop. The stopgap remedy is Fiorinal, and so I pop one while I slump in the shower. It feels so good, the exhaustion, the pile of heavy, cold, sweaty clothes, the whole paraphernalia of deliberate self-depletion. At the track club they had a sign from William Butler Yeats: Torture Body to Pleasure Soul. I believe it.

What to do now? The rain is over, the Falcons are dying on the tube, the sun is staging a comeback. Already, my arms and legs are lightening, I'm re-surging, I'm pink and healthy as a baby.

The nearby mall is so upscale that even the Vendoland janitor is dressed in a bright red blazer. The mall's got the requisite atriums, tinted skylights, fountains, and indoor neo-sidewalk cafés. It's a world-within-the-world; perfect peace and humidity, totally phony, and I love it. The Fiorinal's done its job. My head is vacant and painless.

It must still be raining on the Chief's woodsy acres. 115

I walk into an art framer's. It's the only empty store and the woman behind the counter, a Buckhead version of Liv Ullmann, with a wide sympathetic face, doesn't seem to mind that I don't look like a serious shopper. I give her my toothiest.

"Just looking," I apologize.

"Why?"

"That's a very reasonable question," I say. She is neatly and expensively dressed; at least, everything looks color coordinated and natural fiberish. She seems many cuts above mall sales assistant.

Besides, Blanquita thinks she's too good for me. 120

"Don't tell me you have something to frame," she says, laughing. "And I know you wouldn't buy the junk on these walls." She's really a great sales-lady. She's narrowed my choices in about ten seconds. She's flattered my tastes. Her eyes are the same greenish blue as her paisley sweater vest.

She's intuitive. It's closing time and it's Sunday, and she opens late on Monday. "But you knew that, didn't you?" she smiles. She helps me out in her amused, laid-back way. Her name is Maura. Thirty-four, divorced, no kids; she gets the statistics out of the way. She's established an easy ground-work. In an hour or two she'll ask those leading questions that are part, more and more, of doing love in the eighties. I check automatically for wedding and friendship rings. The flesh on her ring finger isn't blanched and fluted so I know she's been divorced a while. That's a definite plus. The newly single are to be avoided.

Maura came down from Portland, Oregon, three winters ago. "I don't know why I stay." We're having a pitcher of sangría, still in the mall. I like her voice; it's rueful and teasing. I think I even like her big, sensible hands, so unlike Blanquita's. I spot slivers, chewed nails, nothing glazed or pasted on. Hands that frame the art of Atlanta, such as it is. "Let's see, there's Farmers' Market and the International Airport. What else?"

"The CDC," I protest. The doctors and researchers at the Centers for Disease Control may all be aliens but this is no time to diminish the city's glory. "I'm betting on AIDS to put us on the map." There, I've made it easy, no sweat.

She laughs. I feel witty. I malinger, making small talk. Hard to tell what real time it is, out there in the world, but it must be dark. She suggests we go on to Appleby's on the other side of the mall. Appleby's is perfect for what we have going: relaxed fun and zero sentiment. I've struck gold.

No, I've lost my claim.

We have to drive around to the back of the mall. Her car's a banged-up blue Subaru. Not her fault, she explains; an Oriental sideswiped her just outside Farmers' Market on her first week in Atlanta. She kept the dent and let it rust. Her anti-sunbelt statement.

We order ten-cent oysters for her and Buffalo wings for me and a dollar pitcher. We don't feed each other forkfuls as we might have in a prevenereal era. Afterwards we have to walk around some in the parking lot before finding our way back to her Subaru. I haven't oriented myself to her car yet. It's these little things, first moves, losing the first step, that become so tiring, make me feel I'm slowing down. We've had a pleasant time and what I really want is to let her go.

"Want to hear me play the harpsichord?"

She locates her car key inside her pocketbook. That's very original," she says. "Should I believe you?"

"Only one way to find out." The harpsichord was part of love's debris. Wendi was musically inclined.

"It's the best line to date," Maura says as she unlocks the door on the passenger side for me.

Sunday night eases into the dark, cozy A.M. of Monday. Maura and I are having ourselves perfect times. The world's a vale of tears only if you keep peering six weeks into the future.

"You're good for me," she keeps whispering, and makes me believe it. "Griff and the Farmers' Market. You're a whole new reason for me to stay."

"We make a good team," I say, knowing I've said it before. I'm already
slipping back. I never used a line on Baby, and she never got my jokes anyway.
Maura's hair, silvery blond in the condo's dimness, falls over my face. "Partner."

"But we shouldn't talk about it," she says. "That's one of my superstitions."

I feel a small, icy twinge around my heart. I've swallowed too many superstitions these past few months.

Then the phone rings. I lift the phone off the night table and shove it
under the bed.

"Oh, Christ, I just knew it," Maura says. "It's too good to be true, isn't
it?" I can feel her body tremble. It's the first panic she's displayed.

"Look, I'm ignoring it."

"No you're not."

The ringing stops, waits a while, and starts up again.

"I don't have to answer it." I squeeze her rough hand, then splay the palm
flat over my beard. "Give me a smile, pardner."

"It's all right with me," she says in her frank, Northwest way. "You have
a life. Your life doesn't begin and end with me." She's already out of bed,
already fishing through clothes for the simple things she dropped. "But if you
ever need anything framed, do me a big favor, okay?"

The phone keeps up its stop-and-start ringing. It's the Muzak of Purga-
tory. Maura's dressed in an instant.

"There's no reason why you shouldn't be involved with someone."

Because I can't bear to hear it ring anymore, I shout into the mouthpiece,
"What's with you, anyway? You're the one who left!"

But Blanquita the Brave, the giver of two cheers for a new life in a new
continent, the pineapple of Joker Rosario's eyes, his Baby, sounds hysterical.
I make out phrases. The Chief's into games. The Chief doesn't love her. Oh,
Blanquita, you're breaking my heart: Don't you know, didn't anyone ever tell
you about us? Under it all, you still trust us, you still love. She's calling me
from a diner. She's babbling route numbers, gas stations, how to find her.
Can't I hear the semis? I'm all she's got.

I hear my voice, loud and insistent. *"Amoco?"* I'm shouting. "There's a
hundred Amocos between the perimeter and Chatanooga."

"I don't want to know," I hear Maura tell Marcos as I rush the front door,
warm-ups pulled over my pajamas. "I don't want to start anything complicated."

Considerations

1. Griff's comments about his life and his relationship with Blanquita
contain many allusions to sports. Have a closer look at some of these allusions. What do they reveal about Griff's character? To what extent is he the
"typical American male"?

2. Whenever Blanquita tries to make Griff admit he loves her, he backs away from making a commitment. He says at one point, "I'm not ready for one-on-one" (para. 80). How convincing are his reasons for being unable to settle down? How do you think Blanquita would describe their relationship?

Invitation to Write

At a certain point in the story, Griff says, "There's a difference between exotic and *foreign,* isn't there? Exotic means you know how to use your foreignness, or you make yourself a little foreign in order to appear exotic" (para. 38). To what extent does Griff consider Blanquita exotic, and to what extent is she foreign to him? Write an essay in which you examine the notions of "foreign" and "exotic" as Griff defines them, and compare them to the way they are usually presented to us. In order to get a general idea of how "foreign" and "exotic" are perceived in our culture, look at travel brochures or advertisements for vacations abroad.

Connections

In many ways, the tension between Griff and Blanquita is similar to that between American and Third World cultures described by Pico Iyer in "Love Match" (p. 535). To what extent is Griff and Blanquita's relationship influenced by the differences between their cultures? Write an essay about the causes for Griff and Blanquita's failure to communicate using Pico Iyer's insights into the causes of cultural imperialism. Look closely at Griff's observations of Blanquita, and at the way he talks to her and explains America to her to establish whether his attitude is comparable to that of the Western tourists described by Iyer. Use Iyer also to interpret the mutual dependence of the two characters, which becomes apparent at the story's end.

JILL KER CONWAY

The Right Country

Jill Ker Conway was born in Australia in 1934. After her father and one of her brothers died in quick succession, Conway's relationship with her increasingly disturbed mother became oppressive. Her need to escape her mother's demands and her desire to study cultural history eventually led to her decision to immigrate to the United States. After receiving her Ph.D. from Harvard University, Conway became a noted historian. She specializes in the history of American women and was the first woman president of Smith College. Among her many publications are *Merchants and Merinos* (1960), *The Female Experience in Eighteenth- and Nineteenth-Century America* (1982), *The First Generation of American Women Graduates* (1987), *Learning About Women: Gender, Politics, and Power* (1987), and the anthology *Written by Herself: Autobiographies of American Women* (1992).

In *The Road from Coorain* (1989), she recalls her experience of growing up on the western plains of New South Wales with her parents and two brothers. The book begins with the story of her parents' romance and marriage and their heroic struggle to turn their homestead into a thriving sheep ranch. The meditative narrative that follows is the final chapter in *The Road from Coorain*. In this chapter, Conway evokes the landscape of her youth and examines the conditions that determined her decision to leave her home and settle in the United States.

ALTHOUGH I'D PROMISED MYSELF I would make the break with my mother as soon as she was settled after our return to Sydney, I kept backsliding. For one thing, it took a long time to get her settled. No house seemed to suit her exactly. We were no sooner home than she needed treatment for gallstones, and the prospect of surgery loomed in the future. The house and garden she finally liked wasn't available for another six months.

At Coorain, a much-needed new breeding strategy required introduction. Our flocks had been developed to produce long, fine combing wool for the British market. Now the bulk of Australian wool was sold to Japan, where new technologies made it possible to comb and spin high-quality woolen thread from a shorter-stapled fleece. It was a touchy business convincing my mother that higher earnings would come from breeding larger-bodied sheep with denser, shorter fleeces, but she eventually seemed persuaded. She agreed to the expensive purchase of a new line of rams and the culling of the existing flock for sale, provided I would supervise the operation. Telling myself that I would get her through one set of changes at a time, I temporized about my departure. It would be foolish to bring on the possible break in our relationship before I'd got the economic future of Coorain on a solid base.

Within weeks of our return I made the first step toward the eventual break by taking a teaching assistantship in the History Department at the University of Sydney and enrolling as a student for an M.A. in Australian history. The teaching assignments which secured my economic independence were simple and enjoyable. I gave tutorials in European and British history to groups of ten to twelve students, gave occasional lectures in the Australian history course, and graded large piles of essays and examinations. There was no course work for the M.A. degree at the University of Sydney. One simply found one's own thesis topic, persuaded someone to direct one's research, and wrote the dissertation. I wasn't sure there was anyone in the Department of History who would want to direct the kind of study I wanted to write, but to get myself started I signed up with John Ward, the head of the department and the occupant of its only chair. Before I embarked on more research it seemed sensible to turn my undergraduate honors thesis into a series of articles for publication, an exercise which kept me happily at work for the first three or four months after my return. On publication, the essays were well received. They cast new light on the early phases of colonial economic development, and earned me a reputation as a likely future contributor to Australian history.

My occupation introduced me at once to a new society. The people who had previously taught me now became colleagues. It was the custom of the department to ignore generational differences on all social occasions, and different as our places were in the academic hierarchy, we all sat round the same lunch table, or gossiped together over coffee as though we were more or less contemporaries. It was a heady experience to shift gears and begin to call Alan Shaw, my former instructor in British history, whose wit and learning I relished, by his first name. Ernst Bramstedt, the *echt* German scholar who had taught me European history, now consulted with me about the course and pressed offprints of articles in German on me. Duncan MacCallum, the impossible but lovable eccentric who taught Australian history and had trouble moving the class beyond the midnineteenth century in the course of an entire year, was suddenly eating his vegetarian diet of raisins and carrots at my side, and offering bizarre but often brilliant comments about Australian politics. Bruce Mansfield, the warm and gentle humanist, who persevered in believing one could study Erasmus in Sydney even though no library resources were available, gave me a new sense of what it meant to be a scholar. Marjorie Jacobs, already a friend, delighted me by her capacity to cut laughingly through the petty detail of her colleagues' discussions and get the conversation to the point in minutes. They were a wonderful group of friends, encouraging about my teaching, interested in my career. My one problem was that they had very little interest in intellectual and cultural history. I couldn't make them understand the kinds of events I thought interesting. Our department was strong on techniques of research, but no one could understand the kinds of cultural documents I wanted to study. They weren't in archives, but in people's minds and imaginations. Marjorie Jacobs, the most sensitive observer, noticed my frustration, and kept urging me to go abroad to study. "If you don't like England, go to the Sorbonne. Go somewhere where you can see things from another perspective. Whatever you do, don't just stay here." I knew she was right. The question was where.

The pretense of equality masked the fact that the academic structure of Australian universities was inordinately hierarchical, with a single professorial position dominating each discipline, and more junior readers, senior lecturers, and lecturers filling out the ranks of the faculty. Whoever held the chaired position dominated appointments and could virtually build the junior ranks as he pleased. I was fortunate that John Ward had liked my honors dissertation, and was an encouraging friend and mentor. Through my appointment I acquired at least a portion of a room of my own. I was assigned to share a spacious second-floor office, looking out on the tranquil green Quadrangle, with a young Englishwoman who worked in medieval history. She was in Sydney because of the posting of her naval officer husband on an assignment to the Australian navy, and was an intelligent and cultivated observer of Australian society and academic life. I hadn't known many intellectual women before, let alone one close in age to me, so that my friendship with Ruth Chavasse was important.

Early in the 1959 academic year, I was taken aback to be called into John Ward's office and asked if I would pinch-hit for him by giving the lectures in the American history survey course for the next term, since he'd been advised to have medical treatment requiring a term's absence. As my face registered astonishment he said, sensibly and practically, "Come now, Jill, you know much more about this field than the students, and just about what I did when I first began to teach it, so I'm sure you will do it very well, and without too much difficulty." John was Cambridge-trained, but an innovator in his day for his insistence that an educated Australian must know the broad outlines of the history of the United States. I gulped and agreed to give the lectures. It was one thing to give a few lectures on my own particular area of knowledge in Australian history, but quite another to be asked to get up a course at short notice, and do all the lecturing myself. When I asked if there was a syllabus I should follow, John Ward said airily, "Why don't you make up your own. It's always more effective teaching about what interests you. You're interested in the West and the settlement of Australia. Teach them Turner and his critics. It will help you think about your own work."

Suddenly I was as busy as I liked to be. In Sydney some part of each day went into reading nineteenth- and twentieth-century American history. On many weekends, I drove the five hundred-odd miles to Coorain to review the expenditures planned for the next year's maintenance, the sheep sales which went with redirecting the flock to produce the new type of wool favored by Japanese buyers. The two new demands on my time were mutually stimulating. John Ward had given me a nudge in the direction of reading American history, just at a time when I was spending long hours traveling back and forth to the bush, free to speculate about the differences between Australian and American society. My reading about Frederick Jackson Turner's frontier thesis, Oscar Handlin's studies of immigration as a factor in shaping American society, and Perry Miller's analysis of the way the physical environment of North America began to shape the mind and imagination of American colonists introduced major themes for reflection as I made my regular car journeys through several climate zones out to the western plains.

On those journeys I liked to leave Sydney about 4:30 or 5:00 A.M. so that I was away from the heavy traffic on the main routes over the coastal mountains by breakfast time, and ready to settle down to maintain a steady eighty miles an hour west and southwest along the straight dirt roads of the bush, until after about ten hours' driving I arrived in a cloud of red dust by the front gate of Coorain.

In springtime the road west to Bathurst across the mountains was a wonderful passage of extended views across valleys and early morning mist. On the western side the mountains' gentler hills sloped down to rolling countryside; valleys covered with rich black soil sheltered streams winding westward. The gentle slopes rising from each watercourse were crowned with orchards in blossom, while below the contoured patterns of spring crops burst in brilliant green from the dark earth. I liked looking at this scenery with the dew still on it, well before the heat of the day. I always brought breakfast with me: strong tea, brown bread and butter, hard-boiled eggs, and fruit. These I ate at favorite spots: in the middle of a deserted pear orchard alive with bees, or on the roadside at the brow of a hill where the patterns of agriculture—green, brown, gold, and red—could be looked at with half-closed eyes to produce an instant impressionist painting.

Here where the farming was intensive, each curve of the land had its plume of smoke rising from a homestead, nestling beside its accompanying silos and dairy barns. My new interest in American history prompted reflection on how this land had been settled, and on the political heritage of the nineteenth-century battles to wrest it from the hands of the squatter pastoralists, to make it available for small family farms.

Several hours later, one hundred and fifty miles or so beyond the eastern slopes of the mountains, I entered what we called the scrub country. Its bright scarlet earth nourished stunted mallee trees, four to five feet high, twisted by wind and drought, supported by huge gnarled roots. Much of it had been cleared, the roots painfully grubbed and burned, to make way for dry wheat farms, which throve in good seasons and produced relentless red, dusty heartbreak when the rains did not come. These farmhouses were poorer, the outbuildings shabbier, and the children and dogs playing about skinnier than one saw closer to the coast. The red earth, the blazing sun, and the broken hearts of these settlers were the recurring subjects of great Australian painting. It had never occurred to me before to wonder why we didn't celebrate the plenty and lyrical beauty of the fertile slopes beyond the mountains. Now I occupied hours musing about why it was that this experience of the marginal wheat farmers shaped Australian imagery about landscape, as did the figure of the drover and the drover's wife silhouetted against the emptiness of the western plains my journey would bring me to about one or two in the afternoon, when the sun dominated the sky, and the mirages were shimmering on the horizon.

Why was my mind full of images of exhausted, marginal people, or outlaws like Ned Kelly, rather than triumphant frontier figures like Daniel Boone or Buffalo Bill? I knew that somehow it had to do with our relationship to nature, and with the way in which the first settlers' encounter with this environment had formed the inner landscape of the mind, the unspoken, unanalyzed relationship to the order of creation which governs our psyches at the deepest level. Australians saw that relationship as cruel and harsh, and focused the mind's eye on the recurring droughts rather than the images of plenty I could recall from the rich seasons at Coorain. It startled me to realize that although I was now running the enterprise at Coorain to produce an income that was handsome by any but the most plutocratic standards, my emotional life was dominated by images of the great drought. I wished there were a clear way to understand the process by which a people's dominant myths and mental imagery took shape. Now I had seen England and Europe, these myths seemed more important to me than any study of the politics of Federation, or of the precise details of nineteenth-century land policy. I could see that there were models for thinking about such questions in the writing of American history. There was so much to learn I could barely fall asleep at night because my mind raced on at fever pitch about a set of questions I felt no one else understood, or even cared about much.

The actual experience of delivering my first course of lectures was daunting. I had surmounted my shyness in most social settings, but standing up before several hundred people and talking connectedly for fifty minutes was a grueling test. Because university education was virtually free, many students were just putting in time in university study, and lacking motivation, could be raucous.

The morning of each lecturing day, I woke up with a hollow feeling in the pit of my stomach and set out for the University like a prisoner headed for the guillotine. I was beset by a sudden new set of worries about my appearance. I didn't want to hide my anomalous female self under the conventional black academic gown. People must accept or reject me for what I really am, I thought. I'm a woman standing here teaching, not some apologetic, sexually neutral person. I didn't have the powers of analysis to understand that my tenseness and anxiety came from crossing social boundaries, but I did have a visceral sense that if I gave in and muted my female appearance I was lost. At night I had nightmares of standing naked before laughing audiences, or of losing my notes and standing on the platform in terrified silence. In the mornings I taught the day students, all a year or so younger than I. In the evenings I lectured to an older, more thoughtful and diverse group of evening students. They were from every walk of life: taxi drivers, schoolteachers, civil servants, construction laborers. Slowly, cured by exhaustion and frequent exposure, I began to be able to walk toward the lecture hall without my knees knocking together, or becoming sick to my stomach with nervous anxiety. My students mostly listened attentively, and some of the older ones even became friends. I began trying out some of my ideas on the parallels and differences between Australian and American culture on them. People began to ask questions. I started to enjoy teaching.

Outside the University, my new role set me apart from most of my own generation. On the round of Sydney cocktail parties I learned not to volunteer what I did for a living. If I did, most men my age looked at me in astonishment and turned to talk to someone less formidable. Most women were puzzled and didn't know what to talk to me about, assuming, mistakenly, that I wouldn't be interested in talking about the usual women's subjects: clothes, parties, the latest films. Someone doing what I was doing was a real anomaly in the Sydney of the 1950s, and no one in my generation knew what to make of me. In strange company I often told people I was a secretary, just to see how they would react to me if they were not perceiving me through the stereotype of a professional woman. It was hard to drum up much interest in the usual round of Sydney charity parties. My London model days had cured me of wanting to cut a swath as an exponent of fashion, and my daily occupation did make it hard to manage standard party small talk.

It wasn't any more satisfactory to spend time in real intellectual circles. The history department at the University of Sydney was the model of solid respectability, and not noted for its intellectual daring. The most interesting circle at the University revolved around the philosophy and political science departments, and a small coterie of gifted faculty and students who were iconoclasts, cultural rebels, and radical critics of Australian society. I liked their ideas, and enjoyed the fact that their circle also contained journalists and serious writers about Australian politics. The trouble was that their intellectual

15

originality went along with a stultifying conformity to what were considered "advanced" sexual mores. Everyone regarded marriage and monogamy as bourgeois conventions, and it was more or less de rigueur to join in the sexual couplings of the group to share its intellectual life. At their parties, the men dressed colorfully, were lively talkers, and laughed a lot. The women, having rejected bourgeois fashion, often seemed rather drab. They talked intensely about ideas, but their eyes were watchful because it required close attention to sort out the shifting amatory relationships of the group. When I rejected the inevitable sexual advances, I was looked at with pained tolerance, told to overcome my father fixation, and urged to become less bourgeois. It was a bore to have to spend my time with this group rebuffing people's sexual propositions when what I really wanted to do was to explore new ideas and to clarify my thoughts by explaining them to others. I didn't know then that I was encountering the standard Australian left view of women, but I could see that the so-called sexual liberation had asymmetrical results. The women of the group, often brilliant, worked as librarians or journalists, and came home to care for the children in the evening, while their men friends retired to the study. I needed their irreverence about Australian academic life and their clear-eyed analysis of the Australian universities as guardians of a colonial establishment. But in time I came to see that their position of isolation from the mainstream of Australian society was an unhappy and paralyzing one. There *was* no social group on which cultural radicals could base a program of action in Australia. Nothing could be more straitlaced and conservative than the traditional Australian Labor Party. People who were radical and avant-garde in the arts could not have been more comfortably wedded to middle-class mores in other aspects. That left my friends living the life of the mind with no audience to whom they could communicate. We might spend all the time we liked discussing McCarthyism in the United States and the anti-democratic tendencies of Catholic Action in Australia, but there was no one waiting for our pronouncements on either subject. My radical friends were isolated and alienated, more like a religious sect within an uncaring secular society than their models, the European intelligentsia who labored intellectually in a world where ideas *mattered*.

The place I was most at home in was the bush. The older I grew the more I liked backcountry people. I enjoyed the slow and stylized way conversations with strangers developed—the weather, the state of the roads, where the kangaroos were swarming this year, whose yearling had run well at the picnic races. It was as easy as wearing old clothes to arrive at the ram sales, lean on a fence, gaze attentively at the pen of animals, and argue with Geoff Coghlan about which ones would be best for the Coorain flocks.

On my weekends at Coorain I sometimes took an extra day and drove over to spend the night at Clare. I loved Angus Waugh just as much now as I had as a child. It was just plain comfortable to sit by the fire in the evening at

Clare, beneath the paintings of highland cattle, and listen to Angus tell stories. His tales were full of close observation of people, psychological insight, and a wonderful sense of the absurd. He would tease me for being "a bloody intellectual," but underneath the laughter was an old-fashioned Scottish respect for learning. When he came to Sydney for the annual agricultural show, we always made a date to spend the day there, looking at sheep and cattle, agricultural equipment and sheepdog trials, and talking about the wool business. We stayed away from the subject of my mother, because the Australian code didn't permit complaining about life's difficulties, but there was an unspoken understanding between us about why I was spending so much time at Coorain, and about how difficult she had become. After the ceremonial dinner in Sydney's best hotel dining room which finished the day, I always left smiling to myself over his unique and pungent personality. He never failed solemnly to tip the headwaiter sixpence, out of a combination of tightfistedness and the desire to watch the pained expression on the man's face. "Doesn't he ever give you a hard time getting a table?" I asked once after observing this transaction. "No, the poor bugger can't do that," Angus replied. "He knows I've been staying here for forty years, and my father before me."

I sometimes toyed with the idea of settling on Coorain myself, but much as I loved it, I knew I would become a hermitlike female eccentric if I settled into that isolation alone, with no company but the odd stockman and a few sheepdogs. Most backcountry boys never finished high school, or, if they did finish, quickly set about forgetting the book learning they'd been forced to acquire. So if I chose the bush, I would be choosing life alone, and that I didn't want. Moreover, I had a nagging sense that slipping too easily back into the bush code might be my undoing. These ambiguities came into focus for me on one of my drives out to Coorain, in hot November weather. I'd promised to be out by a set day to help with crutching, only to find the night before I was to leave that two dangerously violent prisoners had broken out of jail near Sydney and were reported to be traveling west to Booligal, the next town to Hillston, on my route. I thought briefly about putting things off for a day, but knew that I would never hear the last of "that time you were late coming out because those two jailbirds were on the road." In the backcountry only cowards were cautious. Deciding that any backcountry felon would be too bushwise to be caught by the police on the main road, I set out, not made any more relaxed by the news that two people had been killed by the escapees, at points along the route I was to follow.

My journey was routine in blistering summer heat until on an isolated 20 stretch of road between West Wyalong and Rankins Springs I felt a rear tire blow out. I was out of the car almost before it had stopped and underneath it fixing the jack to the rear axle when a car drove up from the opposite direction, and from my prone position I could see two solid pairs of working boots approaching. Shortly two upside-down but genial faces hove into view as the new arrivals bent down to look under my car, inquiring whether I needed a hand. I slithered out and said, "Yes. I need to change a wheel fast. I'm trying to get to the other side of Hillston by dusk." My helpers were both familiar types. The elder, wrinkled and burned deep brown by the sun, wore the usual broad-brimmed backcountry felt hat and spoke in a characteristically laconic bush fashion. The younger man was a Scot, clearly recently arrived, his face burned scarlet, his gingery eyebrows seeming blond question marks on a sea of crimson. "Where're you headed beyond Hillston?" the elder asked. "I'm going to Coorain, Mossgiel way," I replied. "Coorain? You're not Bill Ker's daughter, are you?" the elder questioned. I nodded. "I was with your father on the Menin Road, a long time ago now," he said. "I always remember what a great horseman he was. Now I look at you, I think you look a bit like him." The Scot, meanwhile, had changed the back wheel and, kneeling to screw on the bolts, looked up to me to say, "Lassie, you're crazy. Don't you know there's a pair of murderers on this road?" Before I could speak my father's old A.I.F. friend answered for me. "She was born in the right country, Jock. She doesn't stop home for any bugger." Jock was unimpressed. "You need air in this tire. Make sure you stop in Rankins Springs and get the other tire mended. You've got a long way to go before you're home tonight." Thanking them for their help, I thought privately, Jock's right. It is silly, what I'm doing. Only someone not part of this culture would have the sense to point it out. It wouldn't do to slide too comfortably back into this world.

I was puzzling about my future and what world I really belonged in when, in early 1959, I went to spend a week with my brother and sister-in-law after the birth of their first child, a strapping son, to be named David, whose god-mother I was to be. They seemed so happy in their tiny house in Charleville that my own life seemed rather empty. Its fulfillments all seemed to lie in the direction of work, because there was no one in any of the variety of circles in which I moved who could participate with me in all the various worlds I liked to inhabit.

The first night of my stay we went to dinner with a visiting American, Alec Merton, whose company was one of the best clients of my brother's air charter business. I remembered that, during his bachelor days, Barry had in-troduced me to a lively and amusing new American friend who was the mobilizer of venture capital for what then seemed a hopeless search for ura-nium in western Queensland and the Northern Territory. Now, several years later, the search had been vindicated, and the geological team hired by the American speculators had located exploitable deposits in what we had grown up learning was barren, resource-poor desert. The dinner was by way of celebration of the discovery, and of the birth of Barry and Roslyn's two-week-old son.

In the Charleville heat our host looked mildly incongruous, dressed as he was in an American seersucker suit and bow tie, while everyone else was in shirtsleeves. In all other respects it was plain to see that this mid-thirtyish, mild-mannered man was at home in this world of cattle ranchers and back-country types. I learned that he was from Arizona, had been educated in the East, had learned his financial skills in New York, but now worked from Phoenix on financing mineral exploration around the world. I was amused that he was able to tell tall tales that were equal to any of the Queensland variety told by the other guests with great gusto and attention to elaborate detail as the party warmed up. It also emerged that when he had first arrived in town he had quickly established his credentials with most of the heavy hitters in the local bar who had planned a cheerful hazing for the visiting Yank. Invited on a bibulous hunting trip which involved heavy rum consumption in the early hours of the morning, while waiting for the dawn and the first flight of ducks, he had acquitted himself with considerable style. While his hosts showed signs of wear and tear and missed many of their shots, each one of his knocked a bird from the air. He had made a point of ostentatiously delivering his lion's share of the plump wild ducks to the wives of each of his hosts, to drive home just who was the best shot, and who had been sober.

It wasn't until one of the cattle-rancher guests suggested a game of poker that our host openly took charge of the evening. Poker was out of the question. He wanted to learn two-up, so that he'd be ready for his future visits to Australian mining camps. A suitable place was found, pennies were produced, and a team of hardy gamblers gathered in a circle. Alec Merton produced a wad of notes and set them in front of me. "Here, Jill, honey. You play for me as well." The game was fast and furious, the stakes high, and his pithy commentary on this Australian game, only half as good as craps, was uproariously funny. By the time Barry and Roslyn left to relieve their babysitter I was one of the half-dozen people left playing, now as hooked as any of the compulsive gamblers at my side. Around midnight I began to have a winning streak. After the third win I started to pick up some of the winnings. "Don't stop now, for God's sake, hang in there," my backer, who was losing heavily, said in my ear. I did as instructed and cleaned out the remaining players after the spinner did his job three more times. "This bloody game's no good," one of the losers said cheerfully. "Good Lord, Barry's sister's beat the pants off us all. Come on, Jill, you're the winner. You've got to shout for everyone." Shouting involved sending for more bottles of Scotch from the bar, the closing of which at 1:00 A.M. was never more than a surface legal formality in Charleville. It was 2:00 A.M. when Alec Merton drove me back to my brother's house during one of the sudden thunderstorms of the Queensland interior. Although I was a little tipsy and still flushed with my winnings, my driver seemed perfectly sober. The high-spirited gambler was gone now and in his place was a man with a startling command of the English language and a more profound view of life than I would have imagined from seeing him egging the game on a few hours before. He talked about the uncertainty of human affairs and the emptiness of success, recited some lines from the Old Testament apropos the setting forth in life of Barry's child, said he'd long remember watching my eyes fixed on the spinning pennies, kissed me soundly good-night, and was gone.

Alec later said he was attracted to me by my reckless gambling, my looks, and my brains. Every intellectual woman wants to be loved for her whole self, to be found attractive for mind as well as body, and I fell deeply in love with Alec in return. I hadn't realized I was looking for an educated male companion who understood my university world, yet was at home in the outback I loved so profoundly. When he came to Sydney to visit me I was astonished to discover that he respected my work and didn't want his presence to detract from it. When I began hesitantly to explain that I would be teaching an evening class the following night and would not be available till after 10:30, he stopped me in mid-sentence. "Why, Jill, you are a busy professional woman, and must turn in your best performance without worrying about me. I'll be waiting for you, when you can get to me." I couldn't believe it; I'd found a man who respected my work and shared my exacting standards about it.

Like all people whose business involves speculative risk, Alec had a talent for living completely in the moment and letting tomorrow's worries wait. He made no secret of his intention to marry within his faith. I made no secret of my plans for an independent career. Meanwhile we took the time to be happy, to savor the pleasure we took in one another's company. In many respects he was the first really sane, thoughtful, and mature person I'd known, and as a result he began to set me straight about many of my approaches to life. When I asked him to meet me in a rundown old bush hotel on the route back from Coorain to Sydney, he came, cheerfully uncomplaining about the battered bedrooms and the marginal plumbing. He was curious about what I was doing out there. "Just why are you fussing about this mother of yours, and spending time running a ranch when you ought to be writing history?" he asked. When I mentioned duty and responsibility to the family, he just shook his head. "Your duty's to your talents," he said. "Never forget it. You can pay someone to run that ranch almost as well as you'll do it. But no one else can develop your gifts."

He had no patience for Australian stoicism. "You mean you weren't allowed to cry when your father died?" he exclaimed, when I tried to explain my lack of emotional expressiveness. "Well, cry right now. I'll sit here and cry with you. It's a tragic story, and you shouldn't try to behave as if it hadn't happened." I found that once I gave in to tears there was no stopping them, and that I was suddenly sobbing about past sorrows I'd scarcely allowed myself to think about. My upbringing had been based on the rule that one didn't intrude one's feelings on anyone else. That was selfishness. Certainly, showing one's feelings was the worst possible breach of taste. Alec was interested in all of my feelings, whether they were sad or happy, and ready to share intensely in them. I hadn't known it was possible to be so happy, or so certain that I was loved in every dimension of my being. This knowledge gave me new kinds of courage. The next time I was in Hillston, I didn't drive right by the cemetery. It was a dry season, the topsoil lifting in a persistent red cloud as I stopped and began my search. It took me a long time to find my father's grave in a lonely, unkempt corner of the graveyard. I pulled the dry weeds away, dusted off the headstone, polished by fifteen years of blowing sand, and wept over it for a long time.

Alec didn't approve of my saturnine worldview and my belief that what was important was to manage one's comportment in life well in the face of inevitable tragedy. "You should read a little less economics and try some theology," he said. "We were created to be happy on this earth." I told him I thought the pursuit of happiness not a very noble purpose for the creation. He said there wasn't a better one, and that I should try to cultivate faith in a benevolent creator.

Whether serious or playful, we were euphorically happy. Alec's business brought him to Australia for a month at a time four or five times a year. We came to know our special places in Sydney and its surrounding countryside in every season of the year. Our favorite spot was a small restaurant, set in a tiny garden, perched high on a cliff above one of Sydney's loveliest beaches. It was a remote, out-of-the-way place, surrounded by eucalyptus forest so untouched that, sitting in the garden, one could sometimes find oneself overlooked by a solitary koala bear, solemnly munching gum tips. On sunny days, the sound of the sea, the smell of ocean mingled with eucalyptus, and the brilliant colors of the garden were intoxicating before one ever sampled the host's well-chosen cellar. On stormy days, it was just as pleasant to sit inside by the fire, look out at the raging ocean, and eat platefuls of sweet Sydney oysters. Sometimes I would look up from daydreaming, gazing into the fire, to find Alec shaking with laughter. "A professor," he would repeat unbelievingly. "I'm having an affair with a history professor." We often lazed away a whole afternoon in the garden, leaving reluctantly as the dust thickened and the lights of yachts began to twinkle on the ocean.

By the time of our second winter it was clear that we two highly emotional people were in danger of losing control of the situation. We each came to our sickeningly final and sensible judgment at about the same time. It was time to part before our feelings for one another became too deep. We had started out playfully enough but had gotten into something more powerful than we'd bargained for.

When I saw him off for the last time, we were both distraught, speechless with suppressed emotion. We stood by the Pan American departure gate in Sydney Airport in floods of tears. "And you're the woman who didn't know how to cry," he finally got out lovingly before embracing me and then walking very slowly out to the plane, stopping to look back just once.

We were both much stronger people for the beautiful sixteen months. It seemed as though I had been loved enough for a lifetime, and as a result, I was less needy, more able to see and hear others, more confident about my own feelings. Alec, for his part, had been a little jaded by wealth and success when he met me. Like most men and women who are successful at a relatively young age, he needed a new purpose and a surer grasp on the important commitments of his life.

Without the new emotional strength and confidence Alec had given me I might have dealt differently with the challenges which erupted in my life at home. Life with my mother was increasingly stormy. About a year after our return from England she sank into a deeper state of paranoia. The change in her behavior came on so slowly that at first I thought I must be imagining it. The seriousness of the problem hit home after I found her white-faced and quivering, clutching one of the quarterly statements from our land and finance agent. The statement showed the price paid to purchase new rams for breeding the Coorain sheep. We had discussed the change endlessly, repetitively, and she had finally sat down reluctantly to write the necessary authorizations. Six months after the fact, she had no recollection of agreeing, and accused me of plotting to make the changes behind her back. "I'll cancel all this at once," she shouted. "Your father would be turning in his grave." When I explained that it was too late to reverse the plan because the new rams had been delivered and already bred, she simmered angrily for weeks, but did no more than call her bankers to complain about my behavior and to insist that in future only she, in person, could authorize expenditures. There were other terrible explosions, which I became inured to, intent on completing the assignments I'd given myself before moving on.

I hoped the excitement of Roslyn's first visit with my mother's first grandson would focus her mind on more positive things. David was a handsome, healthy baby, and his pretty young mother was justly proud of him. I didn't see too much of the daily interaction between my mother, her daughter-in-law, and her new grandson, because the visit coincided with my busiest time of year at the University. My dealings with David consisted of giving him his late-night formula and dandling him on my knee while I worked feverishly at lectures. When Barry joined his wife and child, I thought sentimentally about how splendid it was that our now enlarged family was all under one roof. I should have warned my brother and his wife about my mother's sudden terrible, irrational outbursts, but it was the kind of subject Australians don't discuss, especially when the family was supposed to be putting its best foot forward to welcome a recent bride and a brand-new mother.

Just as Barry and Roslyn were packing at the end of the visit I heard my mother, upstairs, shouting at Roslyn, in the high, excited voice which went with her wildest accusations. I knew she was launched on one of her irrational, angry outbursts, but to my brother and his wife the unprovoked scene was monstrous. My brother and sister-in-law were told to leave the house

35

instantly, my mother, in her madness, claiming that Roslyn had damaged some insignificant piece of furniture. I hurried to tell them to pay no heed to this craziness, that she was often like this these days, that I had endured many worse tongue-lashings—but the damage was done. The outrage was too great. It was heartbreaking to see them depart, shocked, wounded, literally reeling from the unjust and unwarranted attack. The incident and its aftermath would do them both incalculable harm, and I was powerless to do anything about it.

After their departure my mother was in a high state of excitement. She kept on and on like a fugue demanding that I agree with her that her actions had been warranted. When I told her they weren't, that she had behaved unforgivably, the whole cycle was repeated again and again. It was after midnight before I could retreat to my study and assess the events of the day. Because the explosion had not been directed at me, I could see it more clearly for what it was. My mother was now an angry and vindictive woman, her rages out of all proportion to any real or imagined slight. She was most destructive toward her own children, especially where she had the power to damage their relationships with others.

In a moment of weary illumination I saw that she was as impregnably entrenched in her quest for self-immolation as if she occupied the fortified heights of Gallipoli. I'd made many forays to breach those defenses in recent years, incurring some not insignificant wounds in the process. Now I realized, in what amounted to a conversion experience, that I was going to violate the code of my forefathers, I wouldn't tell myself anymore I was tough enough for any hazard, could endure anything because, as my father's old friend had said, "she was born in the right country." I wasn't nearly tough enough to stay around in an emotional climate more desolate than any drought I'd ever seen. I wasn't going to fight anymore. I was going to admit defeat; turn tail; run for cover. My parents, each in his or her own way, had spent the good things in their lives prodigally and had not been careful about harvesting and cherishing the experiences that nourish hope. I was going to be different. I was going to be life-affirming from now on, grateful to have been born, not profligate in risking my life for the sake of the panache of it, not all-too-ready to embrace a hostile fate.

I had set things in good order at Coorain, but that was the last thing I would do for my mother. The woman I knew now was a far cry from the one my father had made me promise to care for. I'd postponed facing what she was really like in the present, but now there was no escaping it. She jeered at psychiatry and mocked the clergy, so there was no way to seek healing for her sick spirit, and hers was very sick. Perhaps, if I got far enough away, I'd be able to see the causes of her undoing. I knew I wasn't without fault in her decline, and that there were parts I was going to have to atone for.

It was dawn when I went to bed, but I wasn't tired. The light was coming up on the day I began my departure. I wasn't exactly elated about it. I felt more like an early Christian convert who had died to the old ways and lives under a new law. Mine was going to be a law of affirming life regardless of past training. It was true I could not look at paintings like Sydney Nolan's Ned Kelly series without total identification with the view of the human predicament they expressed. I resonated totally to Nolan's Kelly, the outlaw, facing corrupt and hostile authority, triumphing existentially even as he is destroyed. When presented with a challenge or a chance to serve a lost cause my spine straightened and my psychic jaw stuck out ready for defiance. But I could use my reason to live by another set of rules. As a historian I knew how few free choices ever face us in life, but this choice of mine now was unquestionably one.

On my way to my first class in the morning, I stopped by the Registrar's Office to pick up the address of the Harvard History Department and the Radcliffe College Graduate School. By the time I went to my evening class, I'd already mailed my request for the necessary application forms. Once I'd surrendered adherence to lost causes I realized that my plans to write a new kind of Australian history couldn't be fulfilled at the University of Sydney. There really was no graduate program in the humanities at Sydney, and I needed professional training and a group of intellectual peers to progress much beyond my current level of historical understanding. I didn't want to join my radical friends in railing against a heedless society. I didn't want to write old-style institutional history of the British Empire and Commonwealth. I wanted to study in the Harvard History Department, where most of the American historians I admired were on the faculty. They seemed to know how to explain the development of a new culture, and I was ready to learn from them. It helped clinch the decision that Boston and Cambridge were about as far away from Sydney as one can get on this planet, and that I'd be totally safe from family visits.

When the forms arrived I was amused to discover that the applicant was asked to write a short biographical essay describing for the Admissions Committee the reasons why he or she had chosen to study at Harvard. What would the hapless committee chairman do if I wrote the truth, I wondered? That I had come to an intellectual dead end in Australia; that I had rejected the cultural values of the country, and wanted to escape while there was still emotional life in me; that I needed to be somewhere where one could look at the history of empires truthfully; that life had been so trying recently that I had taken to drinking far too much, and hoped that life on a modest graduate student's stipend would help sober me up; that Cambridge was halfway round the world from Sydney, and that was a comfortable distance; that I was looking for a more congenial emotional environment, where ideas and feelings completed rather than denied one another.

Chuckling about the plight of the Admissions Committee if I and the other applicants told the truth, I wrote dutifully, to the Renaissance scholar who chaired the committee, "Dear Professor Gilmore, For the last eighteen months I have been teaching Australian history at the University of Sydney, and reading American history as best I can here. I want to enroll in the doctoral program in American history at Harvard, for the 1960–1961 academic year, so that I can develop a deeper understanding of American history and explore the parallels and differences between the Australian and American experiences."

When the acceptance came, my mood changed, though not my resolve. I was haunted by my knowledge of the silence that would enfold the house when I left. I could see my mother, already aged beyond her years, becoming more stooped and skeletal as she forgot to eat and lapsed into greater eccentricity. I had to avert my eyes from the emaciated and frail older women I saw on the street, or in the train, portents of what was to come. I told her my plans just before the arrival of guests, so that she could think of the news as something to boast about. We had lived in a state of armed truce since Barry and Roslyn's unhappy visit, so that the communication was a little like a communiqué between nation-states. She didn't falter. By telling her my decision as I did I established that we were going to act out these events by the script she followed in public, the one in which she was the strong woman urging her children to range far and wide. She knew our relationship had changed and that my resolve was firm. But it never entered her mind that I was not coming back, and I never told her. I dreaded the parting but after some rough moments I learned that time manages the most painful partings for us. One has only to set the date, buy the ticket, and let the earth, sun, and moon make their passages through the sky, until inexorable time carries us with it to the moment of parting.

The hardest leave-taking by far was with Coorain. I made a last visit there, in early September, just a week before I was to leave. I hoped it would be drought-stricken and barren, but there had been good winter rains, and the plains were ablaze with wildflowers, the air heavy with pollen. There was a spring lambing in process, with enough short new shoots of grass to make the lambs feisty, ready for the wild swoops and dashes that young lambs make on a mild sunny day when comfortable and well fed. The house at Coorain was shabbier than ever, and the only trace left of my mother's garden was the citrus grove in fragrant bloom. I looked at it all hungrily. "People will grow old and die; the house will decay, but the desert peas and saltbush will always renew themselves. That's the way to remember it. Even if I never see it again, I'll know just how they look, and the places where they grow."

On my last Sunday, we went over to Clare for lunch. Angus, spry and cheerful, was playing host to a large group of red-haired Waugh nieces and nephews. Much of the lunch was taken up with laughing stories of the early days of Coorain, my parents when young, my brothers and me as children.

45

When it came time to leave, Angus gave us all a small shot of straight Scotch to drink my health. "Take a good look at her," he said. "She's leaving for America tomorrow, and you may not see her again for a long time." As we were downing our toast I wondered whether he knew I wasn't coming back. The question must have passed across my face because as I caught his eye across the room he winked at me, the exaggerated stage wink he'd always given me as a child, when we had a secret we weren't going to tell my parents. It was a benediction.

Having already sold my car in preparation for leaving, I'd made my way out to Coorain by flying to an airport one hundred miles south of Mossgiel. Since I was making farewells I arranged to go back to Sydney by train, to make the familiar journey one last time. As the Diesel gathered speed away from the Ivanhoe station, I remembered my forty-seven-year-old mother and my eleven-year-old self setting out fifteen years ago. That had been an expulsion from Eden and a release from hell. The journey I was about to take didn't fit so neatly into any literary categories I knew. It was certainly no romantic quest. I had had my great romantic experience and sought no other. And there was no way to see it as an odyssey, for I wasn't setting out to conquer anything and there would be no triumphant return. I was leaving because I didn't fit in, never had, and wasn't likely to. I didn't belong for many reasons. I was a woman who wanted to do serious work and have it make a difference. I wanted to think about Australia in a way that made everyone else uncomfortable. I loved my native earth passionately and was going into emotional exile, but there was no turn of political or military fortune which could bring me back in triumph. I was going to another country, to begin all over again. I searched my mind for narratives that dealt with such thorough and all-encompassing defeats, but could come up with none. Then calling on my newly acquired sense of allowing time and events to carry me along, I settled down at the window to watch the familiar scenes go racing by.

Considerations

1. One of Conway's colleagues urged her early on to leave Australia and go abroad to study, saying, "Go somewhere where you can see things from another perspective" (para. 4). Conway eventually heeds her advice, but even before she leaves, she begins to view her experience in a new way. What factors mentioned in her essay help her begin to see her own life and culture from a different point of view?

2. What words and phrases does Conway use to suggest that this period of her life was one of significant change and growth? How did some of the events she viewed as defeats also contribute to a sense of her personal growth?

Invitation to Write

Conway's interest in history is mingled with her desire to find a new way of writing it. She wants to understand why Australians focus on marginal figures like outlaw Ned Kelly, instead of "triumphant frontier figures" like Daniel Boone or Buffalo Bill (para. 12). Write an essay in which you examine her ideas about American history and explain why she is attracted to it. Judging by your own experience in learning American history, establish whether her enthusiasm is indeed justified by the way American history is written and taught. You may also want to argue your own opinions the way history should be written.

Connections

In this autobiographical meditation, Conway describes an increasingly strained relationship with her mother. Marianna De Marco Torgovnick's essay "On Being White, Female, and Born in Bensonhurst" (p. 138) also explores her relationship with her mother, but in a quite different way. In both cases, however, the writers reject many of the values their mothers continue to hold. Write an essay in which you examine the effect of the writers' cultural backgrounds on family relationships. Analyzing at least one example from each text, try also to arrive at more general conclusions about how the relations between mothers and daughters are determined by changing cultural factors.

ITABARI NJERI

Bag Lady

Itabari Njeri was born in New York City and is a graduate of the New York City High School for Music and the Performing Arts, where she studied voice. After deciding not to become a singer, she went to Boston University and the Columbia University Graduate School of Journalism. She has worked as a reporter and producer for National Public Radio in Boston, as an arts critic and essayist for the *Miami Herald,* and as a reporter for the *Los Angeles Times,* where she currently works. She has received numerous fellowships and awards, including the American Book Award, the National Association for Black Journalists Award, and the National Endowment for the Humanities Fellowship for Outstanding Journalists.

The selection "Bag Lady" is a chapter from Njeri's autobiography, *Every Good-Bye Ain't Gone: Family Portraits and Personal Escapades* (1990). The book began as a novel but became nonfiction as she wrote. She combines her experience growing up with a series of portraits of individuals who are members of her extended family. Although as a child she was caught between her Marxist-intellectual father and her less educated mother, who was a nurse, Njeri, in a characteristic move, changes difficulties into strengths. In her preface she writes that, through her family, she "learned early to see and hear the complexity and grand drama that underlay the simplest of human actions." "Bag Lady" is a touching portrait of her mother, and with the benefit of hindsight, Njeri probes deeply into the mother-daughter relationship.

I HAVE LOCKED MY MOTHER in the bathroom. I am in there with her. I am blocking the door and refusing to let her leave not just because she wanted me to transport twenty pounds of Carolina Rice from New York to Lakeland, Florida—where she now lives and can't get her favorite grain—on my way to Miami, where I live. Nor have I bolted the door simply because she now wants me to take a new, soft-sided weekender—just big enough to *not* fit under the seat of a plane or in a compartment above it—back to Miami for my brother who will visit me there soon. I haven't prevented her exit from the can merely for these things, despite the careful logistics of my own travel:

446

carry-on luggage only, each piece weighted not to stress my increasingly bad back, also allowing me to bypass baggage claim, where suitcases are sure to be late or lost, and giving me a carefully timed hour and fifteen minutes to dash through the airport, get through expressway traffic, and reach my office for an appointment in Miami.

That she would prefer to turn me into a personal cargo carrier, rather than put the bag in a box and mail it directly to my brother, is no reason to imprison one's mother. Besides, this is not unusual behavior for her.

No distance between points was ever too great, no occasion too grand for my mother to dump a load of freight in my hands. "Jill," I recall her saying one Easter Sunday, as I stood dressed for the rotogravure—kelly green coat with an empire waist; black patent leather bag; high, black patent leather pumps; short white gloves and a white, high-domed, jockey-style hat Audrey Hepburn would have died for—"I want you to go up to 116th Street and drop this off for your grandmother, then take this to your aunt in the Bronx." Then she handed me a plain brown shopping bag and said, "Good-bye, enjoy yourself."

We lived in Flatbush and I had to ride several trains through several boroughs to make the demanded deliveries. I swore that when I grew up I'd never be dressed to kill and stuck with a plain brown shopping bag again.

My mother is yelling. "Let me out. Girl, if you don't let me out of here . . . 5 move, move . . ." She moves right, I move right. She moves left, I move left. If she backs up, she'll fall into the tub, the bathroom is so small. "I mean it, let me, let me, let me." She is sputtering mad now, and my mother doesn't anger easily. When she does, she is rarely verbal about it.

"You just want to walk around and look cute with that doggone Gucci-Gucci bag you bought here," she fumes at me.

"It's not a Gucci bag," I reply. "It's a Mitsukoshi shopping bag I brought back from Japan." And if they'd had shopping bags as pretty as Mitsukoshi's when I was growing up—bands of yellow, blue, white, red, black, and green on glossy paper with beautiful yellow handles—maybe we wouldn't have had so many arguments about my having to haul cargo over the years. But this is not about the bags, this is not about my life as the family freight hauler.

"No, you can't leave," I shout, trying to suppress a laugh, because our argument is over no laughing matter. But I tend to laugh when I'm angry. Just as I tend to giggle at funerals. My mother doesn't laugh to conceal her feelings. She gets high blood pressure and ulcers.

Thump, thump, thump. That's the sound I heard on the ceiling in our Brooklyn house when I was younger and my mother was bedridden with an ulcer attack. *Thump,* she'd strike with her bedroom slipper again. Translation: "Some cream of pea soup, please."

Sometimes her heavy slippers seemed like Gregory Hines's dancing shoes, 10 convulsed by an epileptic fit: *da-dat, da-dat, da dat-dat-dat-dat, da-dat . . . dat,* signaling one of us to pick up the phone. A simple *dat-dat, da-da* on the kitchen radiator meant "Come and eat."

Sometimes events would warrant a wild rhythmic variation on this theme. As when I was fifteen. *Dat . . . da-da-da-da-da-da-da-da-da dat, da-dat, da-dat . . . da-da . . . da dat,* and so on, meant: "Send that boy home. It's after midnight." Fearing that this had not quelled any suspected adolescent lust, Ma thought reinforcement necessary. A noisy flip-flopping of slippered feet came down the creaky stairs of our eighty-year-old brownstone. My mother, in her infamous slippers, marched past the living room, where my boyfriend and I sat, into the downstairs bathroom, flushed the toilet, banged down the toilet seat, high-stepped past the living room and lingered in the hall opposite us, where she switched the light on and off twice before stomping up-stairs to her bedroom. I often wondered if my mother secretly wanted to be a signalman in the army. Anyway, romance was killed for the night, the boy left, and my mother—master of nonverbal communication—triumphed again.

My mother's personality extended beyond her feet. She was a statuesque beauty of West Indian parentage who longed to live in a house like those in *Better Homes and Gardens.* She had, however, a proclivity for knickknacks everywhere, cluttering too small a room in our Brooklyn brownstone with enormous mahogany furniture, and forcibly integrating a two-and-one-half-by-four-foot portrait of a Spanish matador with modernistic mirror tiles and a wood-and-bronze plaque of Dr. Martin Luther King, Jr., in the same room.

It was a big house, however, giving my mother space to experiment, and she managed to create a few rooms of well-balanced elegance—at least we had no plastic slipcovers in the house.

She still has the house in Brooklyn but moved to Lakeland with my step-father when they both retired. The size of their two-bedroom apartment frustrates her *Better Homes and Gardens* imagination. She has again stuffed the place with too much furniture that is too big. And in a fit of manic energy— "When things get tough, the tough move furniture, vacuum floors, and deco-rate" is her motto—she has turned parts of the apartment into a surreal gar-den. She has hung floral poster art and planted butterfly replicas—butterfly knickknacks for the coffee table, magnetized ones for the refrigerator, and as you enter the apartment, a winged, three-dimensional, blue-hued, bulging-eyed creature about a foot square protruding from a wall. Its grotesque size must be the result of the same genetic engineering that created the two-inch-in-diameter blue glass grapes that sat in a bunch on my mother's Brooklyn dining table for years.

But I haven't incarcerated my mother for these lapses of taste.   15

My mother thinks she is a tightly held secret. She does not believe, for instance, in committing things to paper. And once one does, "you should never keep it," she once told me, explaining why she had no letters from the past. "Everything you need to remember, you will."

But my mother suffers from protectively self-induced amnesia. She cannot or will not connect the dots. Her failure to connect the dots is why I've locked her in, the reason her hot breath is in my face. We have rarely been this close since the womb. I would like to have been closer, but my mother is not a kisser, is not a hugger. I am supposed to know that she loves me because my teeth are straight and my legs aren't bowed.

"Look at that girl's legs," my mother once said, disgusted with the young woman's parents. "They should have had her legs straightened when she was a child."

My mother is a retired nurse. In her forty-year career she has been a bed-side nurse, a public health nurse, and a hospital administrator. She was very good at what she did, and no nurse looked better in uniform. I loved to go to work with her when she was a visiting nurse. When we walked down the street holding hands, it was obvious from all the turned heads that she was impressive in her sharply tailored blue uniform and field cap. At age five, I thought all the stares were simply because of the uniform, the great work it symbolized—and that my mother was pretty. I know now, she was stacked.

Patients were happy to see her; the women too. Some were invalids, others temporarily bedridden. I could see they really needed her. She was gentle, efficient, and gave good injections: Eyes on an alcohol-swabbed section of buttock, she sized the target, then made a quick hit. Her lightning swiftness made it seem almost painless. I know, 'cause she gave me plenty.

I didn't realize until I was grown that she cast a clinical eye on everyone. Of one boyfriend she said: "Very handsome . . . has a slight scoliosis." On my last trip to Lakeland, she looked down at my feet. "You're getting a bunion," she observed.

"Is that a bunion?" I asked. "I thought my foot always curved out like that." She shook her head. She was intimately familiar with my feet, she said, and assured me my foot had not always been that way. Then wagging her finger, she warned me to stop wearing tight, pointed-toe shoes.

With such powers of observation, I wondered, why didn't she comprehend that something was seriously amiss when at the age of sixteen I came to the dinner table nodding; landing, nose first, in my mashed potatoes.

When she asked what was wrong, I told her I was having a migraine attack. Then I went to my bedroom and slept for seventeen hours.

Such behavior was not normal for a healthy sixteen-year-old, she later admitted a friend warned. The friend asked her if I was taking drugs. My mother couldn't conceive of my doing such a thing.

I'd been popping Thorazine for weeks. I'd discovered it among the samples in the doctor's office where I worked after school. When I looked up the indications for the drug in the *Physicians' Desk Reference,* I knew the super-tranquilizer was my kind of chemical. I was not interested in getting high. I wanted to feel nothing—ever.

Why I should have suffered this psychic implosion at sixteen instead of nine, ten, or eleven can be attributed, I guess, to the exacerbating confusion of adolescence. I'd been ripe for it for years, but I was a very controlled child. My seventh-grade homeroom teacher had her suspicions, though: "I find so much maturity in a twelve-year-old extremely disconcerting," she wrote. My behavior was not unusual for the child of an alcoholic, I would learn.

As a teenager, I felt as though I was the only adult in the house. My father was out of control and abusing my mother. For reasons I have never fully fathomed, she endured it for years. Because my mother worked, I was responsible for my little brother most of the time. I had adult responsibilities, and I had to keep adult secrets.

"No, I have no idea why she's so upset," my mother told my junior high school guidance counselor. I had come into school one morning the week before sobbing convulsively. The day I did, I told my counselor what had happened: My father had decided to settle an argument with my mother by raising a hot iron to her face. I'd always been paralyzed by his violence before. But not that morning.

"Don't you touch my mother," I screamed, running at him. I knocked   30
him to the floor and told my mother to "run, run."

I didn't understand someone who didn't know to run.

My father lay on the floor in shock. I discovered years later that he told a judge that I attacked him. The judge didn't go for it. My father thought I'd gone crazy. He stared at me and chuckled meanly. When he got up, he went after my mother, banging on the bathroom door with the iron. I wanted to call the police. But I was afraid of what my father might do to me if I did.

I got my seven-year-old brother. "Peter, I'm going to dial the police. When they answer, you tell them your name and address and to come right away. Your father is trying to kill your mother." This, of course, was not funny. But you don't know my brother. He's an innocent, just like my mother. A man with a dry wit and an easygoing, live-and-let-live manner. That's just the kind of kid he was, too.

"Hello," he said into the phone, lackadaisical and wide-eyed, failing to grasp the urgency of the situation.

"Tell 'em where you live, tell 'em where you live," I whispered frantically,   35
afraid my father would appear at any moment. I said the address and he repeated it into the phone. "And tell them to hurry."

"Hurry, my sister said."

My mother had locked herself in the bathroom and my father was still banging on the door when the police came. My brother let them in. My father was furious. He'd never been exposed before. "Did you call the police?" he demanded.

"No," I said.

"You're a liar, just like your mother."

My mother had to leave the house she bought, because my father 40
wouldn't. I had to beg the police to stay until my mother could safely gather
our things and get out. It was a little before six in the morning, and I remember
her saying how grateful she was that the police had come before our
neighbors were up.

My mother says she does not remember the conversation with my guidance
counselor the week after I'd called the police. Nor does she remember a
meeting, several years before that one, with my doctor. I was a sickly child but
increasingly plagued by psychosomatic illnesses. "Is everything all right at
home?" the doctor asked. My mother was silent. I was eleven, looked at her
stone face and decided to be silent, too. On this visit to Lakeland, when I have
not brought the Carolina Rice, she has repeated that she does not remember
these meetings. That is why she's a captive in the powder room.

At sixteen, when I took my nose out of the mashed potatoes, I was walking
into the walls at school because of the Thorazine. I attended the school
that inspired the movie *Fame*, and had to perform in solo voice class that day.
But I could not hold my head up to sing, and there was something wrong with
my voice. Singing was the the focus of all my energy, it muffled all the dissonance
in my life. But I thought I was losing it.

In the kitchen where my father raised the iron to my mother's face, I was
alone and it was after midnight. She had gotten rid of him, finally filed for
divorce. But the weight of all those years seemed to press against my throat.
My head was on the kitchen table, the knife was near my heart.

"What stopped you?" the doctor asked, years later.

"I tried to do it. I had the point of the knife against my bare chest. And 45
then I thought what my death would mean. What would happen if I never
sang again? That's when I decided I couldn't, the loss to the world would be
too great." The doctor nodded slowly, as I said, "I guess my ego was always
strong. I was a fundamentally healthy child."

"Well," he said, "it is unusual for a sixteen-year-old to have quite that
strong a sense of their global importance."

I put down the knife and called my cousin Karen. She had recently been
released from the mental hospital. She would understand. She had a parent
who was an alcoholic, too.

A few weeks later, I told my mother that I had no intention of being crazy
like the rest of the family. I had found a therapist. I was willing to pay for it
myself if she wouldn't.

She puffed up, then said nothing.

Ten years later, my father was gravely ill. I was twenty-six. I had not seen 50
or talked to him for several years. My parents were divorced, but my mother
had gone to check on him at his Jersey City apartment. She begged me to visit
him.

My mother did not seem to grasp how I felt about my father. She would send birthday and Father's Day cards and gifts to him in my name. She would have my brother take gifts to him, which she bought.

On one of his birthdays, she made my brother deliver a fish dinner to him. My brother got verbally abused as a thank-you. He called me from a phone booth afterward to tell me about it. He was in tears.

I called my mother. "Your children are old enough to decide for themselves if they want to give their father presents or not. You finally divorced him. If we don't want to deal with him, stop trying to ram him down our throats."

That she loved my father was apparent. Something more than love, however, compelled my mother to keep us together when logic dictated she do otherwise. Perhaps it was her conventional notion of "The Family." She didn't get to live it with her own family, maybe that's why she wanted it so much for her children.

She says little about her own childhood. "Slept on a trunk . . ." she once let slip. It seems that happened during the Depression in Harlem. As the oldest, she was responsible for her brother and two sisters while Ruby worked. 55

"The lesser of two evils . . ." is how she described her decision to move south and live with her father and her stepmother. The weather was better for her poor health (she'd had rheumatic fever) and her father would pay for her college education—if she became a nurse. She wanted to be a social worker, but my granddaddy Lord brooked no opposition.

It's hard for me to believe sometimes that Granddaddy was often as unkind to my mother during her childhood as my father was to me during mine. Granddaddy refused to buy my mother a dress for her high school graduation, and only a last-minute gift from Aunt Rene, Ruby's cousin, saved the day. "It was a beautiful dress," my mother recalled once, her lower lip trembling. She caught herself and pressed her lips, then sat more stiffly in her chair. "It was handmade, all lace and white."

Sometimes, my mother told me without rancor, she had to sleep on the hard cot in Granddaddy's infirmary instead of the house.

In the past, I'd heard Aunt Rae say that my stepgrandmother Madelyn, just a few years older than my exceptionally pretty mother, was jealous of her. But my mother would never confirm this. She never had an unkind word to say about Madelyn, who she raised me to think of as a second grandmother. Nonetheless, life with her father and stepmother seems to have been a Cinderella replay.

I guess my father was supposed to be Prince Charming. 60

She had definite ideas about who the father of her children should be, and my daddy seemed to fit: a brilliant scholar, witty, not bad to look at, and "he could waltz fabulously. Your father was light on his feet," she told me. Her role in the marriage was to provide firm but enlightened guidance—something, she complained, her mother never did.

The happy-family plan might have worked if my father had just sat around and been brilliant and witty. My mother certainly tried to fulfill her role. She talked to her children, for instance. She didn't believe in spanking. That she actually did spank—no, beat—me once indicates the seriousness of my crime.

I was about five. My parents were separated and my father had come to visit. My grandmother was taking care of me while my mother was at work. Daddy had bought ice cream and asked me to go to the store to get some cones—the soft kind. He put a five-dollar bill in my hand and off I went. I couldn't find the soft cones at any of the supermarkets in the neighborhood, but I certainly tried. I was gone for two hours. Finally, I went to the candy store. Think of what you could buy with five dollars at a candy store during the Eisenhower years.

I returned home with two brown paper bags filled with toy watches, candy lipsticks, bubble gum, swizzle sticks, spearmint leaves, and Juicy Fruit gum. My mother, dressed in her visiting nurse uniform, grabbed me as I sauntered over the apartment threshold. "Where have you been? Your father sent you to the store hours ago."

I cast a glance over my shoulder at my father. He had a look I'd see again, 65 the one time I told him I loved him. I was sixteen. "You'd be different if I had raised you," was his response to my declaration. It was my first and last offer of affection. But when I was five, he simply had the look without the words.

As if to vindicate herself, my mother whipped me all the way to the candy store, where she told the owner: "You know I would never allow my child to come in here and buy all this junk. Take this and give her the money back." He did. Then she beat me the full three blocks back home.

As I sat in my little red rocking chair whimpering, I blamed it all on my father.

"Please," my mother begged twenty years later, "just go over to Jersey and see your father. Just check on him."

"Why don't you go?" I asked. Then she said my future stepfather thought it best she have nothing more to do with my father. I agreed with that, so I relented.

I rang his doorbell, but he was too weak to come to the door. The apart- 70 ment manager was bowling. I waited two hours for his return. When I finally got in the apartment, my father was lying on the floor naked and bloated. When the ambulance attendants came, he refused to go to the hospital. He knew his name; he knew the date. He was considered mentally competent and could not be taken against his will.

My mother knew all this. She had tried to get him to the hospital the day before, I found out. I was furious that she had let me stumble onto such a scene.

With the help of my father's friend, a city councilman, I got a court order to have him hospitalized. It took two days. By then, my father was so ill he wanted to be taken away.

A student of his—a young man my father had convinced to stay in high school and tutored—called me. The young man was home from college visiting. He was already at the hospital when I arrived. "I'm so sorry, your father is dead," he said tearfully.

No, I told the nurse, I did not want to see his body.

Hours later, I walked into my mother's kitchen in Brooklyn. My brother was sitting at the table eating. "Daddy died today," I told him. He was seventeen at the time. He said nothing. A few minutes later he left the room. I never heard him speak of our father again.

My father wanted to be cremated in a plain pine box without ceremony. He was an atheist. His high school students—many of them Irish-American and Hispanic Catholics—didn't understand this. My mother, though a lapsed Catholic, couldn't accept it either.

"But those were his wishes," I told her, standing in my father's apartment, packing his belongings. As I boxed his vast collection of books, bills from the liquor store fell from the pages. My mother had dumped the funeral arrangements on me and now wanted to direct things. I looked at her disgustedly. "When I die, I certainly hope people carry out my wishes," which were quite explicit. I intended to be mummified and placed in a crypt.

My father was cremated but there was a funeral as my mother wished. "That was your husband," I told her. "Things went on between you that I will never know about. If that's what you want, we'll have a funeral."

Of course my father couldn't just die and leave us in peace. He fancied himself a legal expert after studying the subject at Harvard. He left a substantial amount of money and multiple wills, all of them ruled invalid by a court. I was his oldest living heir, but I had been disinherited. My brother, who had never done him any wrong I know of, had been too. Since my mother divorced him, she got nothing either. What he had was going to go to strangers. I went to court to straighten out his estate.

My attorney—a middle-aged Irish-American who took objection to my African name—didn't like me. My father's friend, the city councilman, had recommended him and assured me he was one of the best attorneys in town. I was sick, about to have major surgery, and didn't have the energy to look for another lawyer. He called me at home.

"Why," the lawyer demanded, "did your father disinherit you?" I was in bed, a television commercial had just ended and *The Gong Show* was coming on. I'd never seen the show before.

"Because my father battered my mother, I hated him for it and he knew it. What else do you want to know?"

"What had you done that caused the rift between you?" the lawyer pressed. I stared at the receiver. I heard the Unknown Comic introduced. "Did you and Dr. Morgan—"

"My father's name was Moreland, not Morgan," I snapped, "and I've answered your question." I hung up and lay in bed facing the white wall. A chipped piece of plaster had been smoothed with spackling compound and painted over. I ran my fingers over the slightly raised surface, then began to pick at it. I remember hearing someone gonged . . . the room darkening . . . a squirrel on my windowsill . . . night. I was still picking at the wall when my cousin Karen, with whom I lived, called my mother.

She was sitting in the kitchen, still in her nurse's uniform, when I finally   85
got out of bed. "Is there anything I can do for you?" she asked. She was seated at the kitchen table, her hands tightly clasped. "Is there anything you need?" Her eyes examined me. I said nothing.

Finally, she rose and walked toward me, held my shoulders, looked into my eyes. "Is there anything I can do?" We tumbled into the long silence, fell through the space of years when questions went unasked, when answers were forbidden. When I'd circled time and returned, I sought my voice. It came out husky, and my words were slowed by the burden of their indictment.

"Why . . . did you make me live with that man?" It was easy being angry with my father. The rage I felt toward my mother was rooted in a sense of betrayal. I would have protected her against anything and everything. Why had she not protected me?

"I did not know you felt so strongly," she said that night in the kitchen.

"I hated him," I said, my eyes fixing her.

"You never said anything," she told me lamely.   90

"I was a child," I said.

That she could finally bring herself to say that night, "I should have left sooner; we all suffered because I stayed with your father," was the best I could expect. And it might have sufficed if the denial hadn't become a permanent aspect of my mother's personality.

When I told her I still went to a therapist, years after that night in the kitchen, she'd purse her lips and say nothing. My cousin Karen is also in therapy, partly because of an alcoholic parent—my mother's sister. She is also involved with Al-Anon and ACOA, Adult Children of Alcoholics. When she tries to discuss these things with my mother, the response is: "Well, if that's what you need." Then my mother cuts her off impatiently.

My mother still does not say my father was an alcoholic. That's one reason she's still in the lavatory. And now her sister is dying of the disease. My mother is in deep pain over this, unable to do anything to save her sister's life. Except to tell my cousin Karen she should be guarding her mother and locking up the gin.

Because alcoholism has destroyed the lives of people she loved and af-   95
fected her, my cousin and I have suggested that my mother attend meetings of

Al-Anon, a support group for the family and loved ones of alcoholics, or talk to a therapist about her feelings.

But my mother is clearly with those Americans who think the weak, the inadequate seek psychological counseling. She would deny this, of course, and just say she doesn't need it.

But her nerves are bad. I'm sure she'd say that's because she has a writer as a daughter. I know in some ways she's happier than she's ever been. Marrying my stepfather, a kind and intelligent person, helped. But just below the surface, I sense a constant anxiety. Her ulcer is under control, but oh, that hypertension.

I have let her out of the jane. She has to finish Thanksgiving dinner. Old friends from New York, who now live near Lakeland, are coming to dinner. The man in the couple is a recovering alcoholic, deeply involved with Alcoholics Anonymous.

Over dessert, my mother mentions that she knows someone with a drinking problem. It is obvious she would like some advice, but doesn't want to get too specific. No one should know her sister has the disease.

I am grinding my teeth. I ask the man about the effects of alcoholism on the family of the drinker. My mother has switched channels. It's time to clear the table.

I know my mother is the product of a generation that did what it had to do without whining, without running to shrinks every time there was a problem. She's a do-it-by-your-bootstraps woman if there ever was one. "Cast down your buckets . . ." she still likes to say, quoting Booker T. Even though she is a nurse, the daughter of a medical doctor—or perhaps because of it— the psyche is still undiscovered territory for her; that, or just too frightening to explore.

Fortunately for our relationship, I can and do connect the dots.

In a past life, I once was told, I lived in feudal Japan. My brother in this life had been my father then. He was a scholar, and against tradition, taught me all he knew, more than most men then ever knew. When he died, I was forced to marry a cruel man who abused me. My husband then was my father in this lifetime. At night, an old nursemaid would secretly come to my room and put salve on the wounds my husband had inflicted. "Your mother in this life was that woman," the psychic claimed.

Hmmmmmmmm.

My mother still thinks I locked her in the bathroom because of the bag.

"I don't think I've ever been so mad," she recalled months after I freed her. She was watching me pack the suitcase my brother never got. I took it, so I kept it.

"And when I think of all the grief you gave me over that bag," she said smugly.

At times, I still entertain the ridiculous notion that one can alter the pattern of another human being's life, that after six decades, my mother will change. Then I come to my senses and only hope my children will have teeth as perfect and legs as straight as mine.

Considerations

1. Njeri begins her narrative with a description of her mother's attempt to turn her into "the family freight hauler" (para. 7). Why do you think she objects so much to this task? How is the role of "cargo carrier" related to her family history?

2. When she tries to analyze her relationship with her parents, Njeri realizes that "it was easy being angry with my father. The rage I felt toward my mother was rooted in a sense of betrayal" (para. 87). What other feelings does Njeri's narrative suggest she held toward her parents?

Invitation to Write

When she recalls her drug use, Njeri confesses: "I was not interested in getting high. I wanted to feel nothing—ever" (para. 26). How can you explain her desire to feel nothing at an age when most adolescents discover and experiment with their feelings? Write an essay in which you try to determine the causes of Njeri's drug use as an adolescent. Examine closely her relationship with both her parents as well as the social and cultural environment in which her family lives. Think also about other possible reasons why young people may resort to drugs.

Connections

At the start of her autobiographical narrative "The Looking-Glass Shame" (p. 97), Judith Ortiz Cofer speaks of a "cultural schizophrenia" that "was undoing many others around [her] at different stages of their lives" (para. 2). In some ways, Itabari Njeri shares the same burden as a first-generation American. Write an essay in which you explore Ortiz Cofer's notion of "cultural schizophrenia" in both narratives. Examine the ways in which the two writers observe and judge their parents' choices and decisions, and identify the causes of the two daughters' alienation from their families.

Assignment Sequence
Lives in Transition

This assignment sequence encourages you to think about the process of growth by first examining a moment of transition in your own life. The next assignment, on Bharati Mukherjee's "Fighting for the Rebound," asks you to identify some of the reasons transitions are difficult. In the third paper, you will look at Mukherjee's story from Blanquita's perspective, comparing her view of American society and the opportunities it offers her with Jill Ker Conway's expectations as an immigrant scholar. Then, using Conway's and Itabari Njeri's experiences, you will explore the role of memory in the process of transition, thinking about how it encourages people to change even while it makes the past harder to leave behind. In your final paper, you will conclude your reflections about transitions by thinking about people's responses to change and the conditions necessary to make transitions into positive experiences.

Assignment 1: Exploring Experience

The title of this chapter, "Lives in Transition," suggests lives in the process of change—entering a new state, leaving a familiar set of circumstances, exploring new territory. Write a paper that describes college as a period of transition in your life.

In your paper, focus on a particular event or a series of changes that made it clear to you that life in college is very different from life in high school or in the work force. As you write about the experience of coming to college, pay particular attention to the changes in your social and academic life, the responsibility you now assume in making decisions, and your relationships to family and friends. In your paper, evaluate the positive and negative consequences of these changes.

Assignment 2

F. Lee Bailey comes on and talks up the Bhopal tragedy. I can't believe it's been a year. I must have been seeing Emilou on the side when it happened. Yes, in fact Emilou cried, and Wendi had made a fuss about the mascara on my sixty-buck shirt.
— BHARATI MUKHERJEE, *Fighting for the Rebound*

458

Use Griff's experience in Bharati Mukherjee's "Fighting for the Rebound" and your own experience of coming to college to evaluate some of the difficulties individuals face in making major changes in their lives. Griff's behavior in his personal life is the same as his professional behavior. Think about the types of changes Griff is afraid to face and how they compare with the changes you described in your previous paper. Then write a paper that examines Griff's behavior and your own; discuss what motivates people to change, and why people do not always want to change.

Griff's repetitious behavior demonstrates that he resists change, but more importantly provides you with clues as to why he fears it. Think about the repetitions in his relationships with women and with his choice of career. Pay particular attention to the language that he uses to ward off unexpected and unfamiliar complications. Use your college experience to identify some of the difficulties college students face in making adjustments. Using these two investigations of the process of change, draw some general conclusions about why people often resist making changes in their lives. Be sure to identify the possible consequences of refusing to change.

Assignment 3

And there was no way to see it as an odyssey, for I wasn't setting out to conquer anything and there would be no triumphant return. I was leaving because I didn't fit in, never had, and wasn't likely to. I didn't belong for many reasons. I was a woman who wanted to do serious work and have it make a difference.
—JILL KER CONWAY, *The Right Country*

Both Jill Ker Conway and Blanquita the Beautiful (in Bharati Mukherjee's short story) arrive in the United States preparing to make major changes in their lives. From your examination of their views and experiences, write a paper that investigates the relationship between the perception of opportunity and an individual's ability to find new possibilities for her life.

Conway comments rather directly on her reasons for leaving home. She arrives to study history from a new approach—at least the approach was new to an Australian historian of her time. Find the statements that suggest her personal and professional reasons for leaving. From them, you can deduce her hopes and expectations for her new life at Harvard. Since Blanquita never directly discusses her own circumstances, her motivations are less clear. According to Griff, Blanquita arrived to conquer the Miss Universe title. Perhaps this is fantasy, a way of paying tribute to her beauty. But you can infer her attitude and expectations through her speech and actions. In both cases, define the possibilities both women see and the effect their vision has on their behavior.

Assignment 4

My mother still thinks I locked her in the bathroom because of the bag.
—ITABARI NJERI, *Bag Lady*

Njeri refers to her role in the family as a deliverer of packages through the term "bag lady." But the term also describes homeless women who stuff all their possessions in bags, who carry everything they value or need with them at all times. Njeri plays on both connotations of the term as she reflects on her role as the keeper of memory for her family, a role her mother rejects. Similarly, Jill Ker Conway writes in "The Right Country" about her vivid memories of her family history and life in the outback. Using both women's stories, write a paper in which you analyze the role of memory in their decisions to make major changes in their lives.

Basing your observations on Njeri's and Conway's experiences, use your paper to examine the role of memory in the process of transition. Using these two autobiographical accounts, explain how memory can be both a powerful instigator and inhibitor of change. Identify the negative experiences that each author wants to avoid repeating. Also identify the rewards they see in making a major change.

Assignment 5

"Don't you touch my mother," I screamed, running at him. I knocked him to the floor and told my mother to "run, run."
I didn't understand someone who didn't know to run.
—ITABARI NJERI, *Bag Lady*

All the readings in this chapter center on individuals whose lives have undergone or are undergoing transitions at the time of writing. While some of the individuals concerned have a strong internal desire to seek new experiences, they also receive a strong external stimulus to change. Write a paper in which you examine the way people change in response to other individuals they encounter.

While it obviously makes sense to look at individuals who encourage change, equally important are individuals who unconsciously inspire change. Escape can be as powerful a motivator as opportunity. For each reading, point out the individuals who are supportive, as well as the individuals who are not. Examine the roles of family, love, and professional relationships in creating a desire for change.

Assignment 6

All the readings in this chapter either directly or indirectly examine the circumstances that accompany change. You have been writing about some of these circumstances in your previous papers, especially in your initial paper, which examined your college experience. For your final paper, use your knowledge of these texts and the knowledge of your own experiences to identify the circumstances that push individuals to make major changes. Furthermore, identify the elements that make it likely that the effects of change will have positive circumstances.

In the previous paper, you discussed the role individual relationships have in pushing people toward change. This time, also discuss other factors, expressed by the individuals in the readings, that effect change. A few of these are ambition, motivation, emotional well-being, love, or deprivation. If it appears difficult to see what makes some individuals undertake change, reflect briefly on other individuals in the text who seem "stuck" and unable to change.

10

Language and Perception

At home I was quiet, so perhaps I seemed formal *to my relations and other Spanish-speaking visitors to the house. But outside the house— my God!—I talked.*

—RICHARD RODRIGUEZ, *Complexion*

Ways of talking associated with masculinity are also associated with leadership and authority. But ways of talking that are considered feminine are not. Whatever a man does to enhance his authority also enhances his masculinity. But if a woman adapts her style to a position of authority that she has achieved or to which she aspires, she risks compromsing her femininity, in the eyes of others.

—DEBORAH TANNEN, *Damned If You Do*

In Winnebago, Minnesota, at least, talking doesn't mean analyzing. It doesn't mean taking a problem and dissecting it, then examining it through a series of lenses, philosophical, emotional, economic, socio-logical, and historical. Talking doesn't mean engaging in repartee, rationalizing, casting off guilt, blame, or insecurities, the way we might shed coats and sweaters on a warm spring day.

—JANE STAW and MARY SWANDER, *If You Can Talk to a Guy*

The written word is weak. Many people prefer life to it. Life gets your blood going, and it smells good. Writing is mere writing, litera-ture is mere.

—ANNIE DILLARD, *The Writing Life*

We live in close intimacy with language, yet most often we take it for granted. Because the capacity to speak is natural to humans, we tend to think that understanding each other by means of a language is natural. Usually, we do not consider language an important factor in our daily activities unless we are confronted with situations where misunderstandings and total incomprehension oblige us to look at the medium that carries the message.

Although language is usually defined as a means of communication, it can perform a number of other functions, which, because they are related to other social activities, are not normally attributed to linguistic performance. For example, some experts argue that the language a person speaks influences that person's perception of the world. Similarly, the way a person speaks can influence how others perceive him or her. Any close look at the linguistic phenomenon demonstrates that it is much more complicated than most people realize. In fact, "the meaning of meaning" has preoccupied linguists and language philosophers for ages. The texts that follow, although not directly involved in that debate, offer a good sample of the ways in which the function of language goes beyond communication, and suggest that meaning has to be understood as more than a reference to a thing or even to an idea.

Richard Rodriguez's essay "Complexion" deals with a situation where people have to communicate across a language barrier. In such cases, language becomes an obstacle to communication rather than its medium, revealing that it is not only the translatable meaning of words that makes it possible for people to understand each other, but also the cultural background they share. In "Damned If You Do," Deborah Tannen explores the question of meaning determined by cultural environment and the importance of gendered speaking styles, drawing attention to the different purposes for which men and women use language. The fact that strict communication is not always the purpose of speaking is clearly shown in Jane Staw and Mary Swander's essay "If You Can Talk to a Guy": In Winnebago, Minnesota, meaning is generated by gesture or silence as much as by the literal sense of the words spoken. Conversation here functions to affirm bonds between people and between people and their communal past. Finally, Annie Dillard's meditations on the art of writing put language in yet another perspective; from the point of view of a writer, language is a material out of which art is created.

All the texts in this chapter reveal aspects of language and of meaning that habitually pass unnoticed. In their separate ways, the authors gesture toward a more complex understanding of the linguistic phenomenon and of its social and cultural dimensions. Whether used to convey messages or to reveal attitudes, to establish class and gender relations or to create a work of art, language is never simply individual expression but a bond between the people who share it.

RICHARD RODRIGUEZ

Complexion

Richard Rodriguez was born in San Francisco in 1944, the third of four children of Mexican immigrant parents. He attended parochial schools in Sacramento, where he grew up, and received his undergraduate degree from Stanford. After graduate work at Columbia University, the Warburg Institute in London, and the University of California at Berkeley, Rodriguez earned a Ph.D. in English Renaissance literature. Originally, Rodriguez had planned a teaching career, but he decided to become a writer instead. One of the foremost critics of bilingual education, he has written frequently on this issue, as well as on the experience of being Mexican-American. His articles have been published in *Harper's* magazine, *The American Scholar, The New York Times Magazine,* and elsewhere.

"Complexion" is the fourth chapter of Rodriguez's autobiographical work *Hunger of Memory: The Education of Richard Rodriguez* (1982). The chapter focuses on a period of time when Rodriguez took a summer job as a construction worker. Rodriguez's feeling of being caught "in-between" the experience of Mexican Americans and the mainstream culture appears here in his description of himself as an interpreter between his boss and the Mexican day workers. He feels further alienated by the fact that, unlike his co-workers and his father, he is not permanently committed to his work. The hard and sometimes dehumanizing tasks he has to perform during a summer vacation give him only a superficial feel for his father's lifetime hardship.

VISITING THE EAST COAST or the gray capitals of Europe during the long months of winter, I often meet people at deluxe hotels who comment on my complexion. (In such hotels it appears nowadays a mark of leisure and wealth to have a complexion like mine.) Have I been skiing? In the Swiss Alps? Have I just returned from a Caribbean vacation? No. I say no softly but in a firm voice that intends to explain: My complexion is dark. (My skin is brown. More exactly, terra-cotta in sunlight, tawny in shade. I do not redden in sunlight. Instead, my skin becomes progressively dark; the sun singes the flesh.)

When I was a boy, the white summer sun of Sacramento would darken me so my T-shirt would seem bleached against my slender dark arms. My mother would see me come up the front steps. She'd wait for the screen door to slam at my back. "You look like a *negrito*," she'd say, angry, sorry to be angry, frustrated almost to laughing, scorn. "You know how important looks are in this country. With *los gringos* looks are all that they judge on. But you! Look at you! You're so careless!" Then she'd start in all over again. "You won't be satisfied till you end up looking like *los pobres* who work in the fields, *los braceros*."

(*Los braceros:* those men who work with their *brazos*, their arms; Mexican nationals who were licensed to work for American farmers in the 1950s. They worked very hard for very little money, my father would tell me. And what money they earned they sent back to Mexico to support their families, my mother would add. *Los pobres*—the poor, the pitiful, the powerless ones. But paradoxically also powerful men. They were the men with brown-muscled arms I stared at in awe on Saturday mornings when they showed up downtown like gypsies to shop at Woolworth's or Penney's. On Monday nights they would gather hours early on the steps of the Memorial Auditorium for the wrestling matches. Passing by on my bicycle in summer, I would spy them there, clustered in small groups, talking—frightening and fascinating men— some wearing Texas *sombreros* and T-shirts which shone fluorescent in the twilight. I would sit forward in the back seat of our family's '48 Chevy to see them, working alongside Valley highways: dark men on an even horizon, loading a truck amid rows of straight green. Powerful, powerless men. Their fascinating darkness—like mine—to be feared.)

"You'll end up looking just like them."

I

Regarding my family, I see faces that do not closely resemble my own. Like some other Mexican families, my family suggests Mexico's confused colonial past. Gathered around a table, we appear to be from separate continents. My father's face recalls faces I have seen in France. His complexion is white—he does not tan; he does not burn. Over the years, his dark wavy hair has grayed handsomely. But with time his face has sagged to a perpetual sigh. My mother, whose surname is inexplicably Irish—Moran—has an olive complexion. People have frequently wondered if, perhaps, she is Italian or Portuguese. And, in fact, she looks as though she could be from southern Europe. My mother's face has not aged as quickly as the rest of her body; it remains smooth and glowing—a cool tan—which her gray hair cleanly accentuates. My older brother has inherited her good looks. When he was a boy, people would tell him that he looked like Mario Lanza, and hearing it he would smile with dimpled assurance. He would come home from high school with girlfriends who seemed to me glamorous (because they were) blonds. And during those years I envied him his skin that burned red and peeled like the skin of the *gringos.* His complexion never darkened like mine. My youngest sister is exotically pale, almost ashen. She is delicately featured, Near Eastern, people have said. Only my older sister has a complexion as dark as mine, though her facial features are much less harshly defined than my own. To many people meeting her, she seems (they say) Polynesian. I am the only one in the family whose face is severely cut to the line of ancient Indian ancestors. My face is mournfully long, in the classical Indian manner; my profile suggests one of those beak-nosed Mayan sculptures—the eaglelike face upturned, open-mouthed, against the deserted, primitive sky.

"We are Mexicans," my mother and father would say, and taught their four children to say whenever we (often) were asked about our ancestry. My mother and father scorned those "white" Mexican Americans who tried to pass themselves off as Spanish. My parents would never have thought of denying their ancestry. I never denied it: My ancestry is Mexican, I told strangers mechanically. But I never forgot that only my older sister's complexion was as dark as mine.

My older sister never spoke to me about her complexion when she was a girl. But I guessed that she found her dark skin a burden. I knew that she suffered for being a "nigger." As she came home from grammar school, little boys came up behind her and pushed her down to the sidewalk. In high school, she struggled in the adolescent competition for boyfriends in a world of football games and proms, a world where her looks were plainly uncommon. In college, she was afraid and scornful when dark-skinned foreign students from countries like Turkey and India found her attractive. She revealed her fear of dark skin to me only in adulthood when, regarding her own three children, she quietly admitted relief that they were all light.

That is the kind of remark women in my family have often made before. As a boy, I'd stay in the kitchen (never seeming to attract any notice), listening while my aunts spoke of their pleasure at having light children. (The men, some of whom were dark-skinned from years of working out of doors, would be in another part of the house.) It was the woman's spoken concern: the fear of having a dark-skinned son or daughter. Remedies were exchanged. One aunt prescribed to her sisters the elixir of large doses of castor oil during the last weeks of pregnancy. (The remedy risked an abortion.) Children born dark grew up to have their faces treated regularly with a mixture of egg white and lemon juice concentrate. (In my case, the solution never would take.) One Mexican-American friend of my mother's, who regarded it a special blessing that she had a measure of English blood, spoke disparagingly of her husband, a construction worker, for being so dark. "He doesn't take care of himself," she complained. But the remark, I noticed, annoyed my mother, who sat tracing an invisible design with her finger on the tablecloth.

There was affection too and a kind of humor about these matters. With daring tenderness, one of my uncles would refer to his wife as *mi negra*. An aunt regularly called her dark child *mi feito* (my little ugly one), her smile only partially hidden as she bent down to dig her mouth under his ticklish chin. And at times relatives spoke scornfully of pale, white skin. A *gringo's* skin resembled *masa*—baker's dough—someone remarked. Everyone laughed. Voices chuckled over the fact that the *gringos* spent so many hours in summer sunning themselves. ("They need to get sun because they look like *los muertos*.")

I heard the laughing but remembered what the women had said, with unsmiling voices, concerning dark skin. Nothing I heard outside the house, regarding my skin, was so impressive to me. 10

In public I occasionally heard racial slurs. Complete strangers would yell out at me. A teenager drove past, shouting, "Hey, Greaser! Hey, Pancho!" Over his shoulder I saw the giggling face of his girlfriend. A boy pedaled by and announced matter-of-factly, "I pee on dirty Mexicans." Such remarks would be said so casually that I wouldn't quickly realize that they were being addressed to me. When I did, I would be paralyzed with embarrassment, unable to return the insult. (Those times I happened to be with white grammar school friends, *they* shouted back. Imbued with the mysterious kindness of children, my friends would never ask later why I hadn't yelled out in my own defense.)

In all, there could not have been more than a dozen incidents of name-calling. That there were so few suggests that I was not a primary victim of racial abuse. But that, even today, I can clearly remember particular incidents is proof of their impact. Because of such incidents, I listened when my parents remarked that Mexicans were often mistreated in California border towns. And in Texas. I listened carefully when I heard that two of my cousins had been refused admittance to an "all-white" swimming pool. And that an uncle had been told by some man to go back to Africa. I followed the progress of the southern black civil rights movement, which was gaining prominent notice in Sacramento's afternoon newspaper. But what most intrigued me was the connection between dark skin and poverty. Because I heard my mother speak so often about the relegation of dark people to menial labor, I considered the great victims of racism to be those who were poor and forced to do menial work. People like the farmworkers whose skin was dark from the sun.

After meeting a black grammar school friend of my sister's, I remember thinking that she wasn't really "black." What interested me was the fact that she wasn't poor. (Her well-dressed parents would come by after work to pick her up in a shiny green Oldsmobile.) By contrast, the garbage men who appeared every Friday morning seemed to me unmistakably black. (I didn't bother to ask my parents why Sacramento garbage men always were black. I thought I knew.) One morning I was in the backyard when a man opened the gate. He was an ugly, square-faced black man with popping red eyes, a pail slung over his shoulder. As he approached, I stood up. And in a voice that seemed to me very weak, I piped, "Hi." But the man paid me no heed. He strode past to the can by the garage. In a single broad movement, he overturned its contents into his larger pail. Our can came crashing down as he turned and left me watching, in awe.

"*Pobres negros,*" my mother remarked when she'd notice a headline in the paper about a civil rights demonstration in the South. "How the *gringos* mistreat them." In the same tone of voice she'd tell me about the mistreatment her brother endured years before. (After my grandfather's death, my grandmother had come to America with her son and five daughters.) "My sisters, we were still all just teenagers. And since *mi pápa* was dead, my brother had to be the head of the family. He had to support us, to find work. But what skills did he have! Twenty years old. *Pobre.* He was tall, like your grandfather. And strong. He did construction work. 'Construction!' The *gringos* kept him digging all day, doing the dirtiest jobs. And they would pay him next to nothing. Sometimes they promised him one salary and paid him less when he finished. But what could he do? Report them? We weren't citizens then. He didn't even know English. And he was dark. What chances could he have? As soon as we sisters got older, he went right back to Mexico. He hated this country. He looked so tired when he left. Already with a hunchback. Still in his twenties. But old-looking. No life for him here. *Pobre.*"

Dark skin was for my mother the most important symbol of a life of oppressive labor and poverty. But both my parents recognized other symbols as well. 15

My father noticed the feel of every hand he shook. (He'd smile sometimes—marvel more than scorn—remembering a man he'd met who had soft, uncalloused hands.)

My mother would grab a towel in the kitchen and rub my oily face sore when I came in from playing outside. "Clean the *graza* off of your face!" (*Greaser!*)

Symbols: When my older sister, then in high school, asked my mother if she could do light housework in the afternoons for a rich lady we knew, my mother was frightened by the idea. For several weeks she troubled over it before granting conditional permission: "Just remember, you're not a maid. I don't want you wearing a uniform." My father echoed the same warning. Walking with him past a hotel, I watched as he stared at a doorman dressed like a Beefeater. "How can anyone let himself be dressed up like that? Like a clown. Don't you ever get a job where you have to put on a uniform." In summertime neighbors would ask me if I wanted to earn extra money by mowing their lawns. Again and again my mother worried: "Why did they ask *you*? Can't you find anything better?" Inevitably, she'd relent. She knew I needed the money. But I was instructed to work after dinner. ("When the sun's not so hot.") Even then, I'd have to wear a hat. *Un sombrero de* baseball.

(*Sombrero*. Watching gray cowboy movies, I'd brood over the meaning of the broad-rimmed hat—that troubling symbol—which comically distinguished a Mexican cowboy from real cowboys.)

From my father came no warnings concerning the sun. His fear was of dark factory jobs. He remembered too well his first jobs when he came to this country, not intending to stay, just to earn money enough to sail on to Australia. (In Mexico he had heard too many stories of discrimination in *los Estados Unidos*. So it was Australia, that distant island-continent, that loomed in his imagination as his "America.") The work my father found in San Francisco was work for the unskilled. A factory job. Then a cannery job. (He'd remember the noise and the heat.) Then a job at a warehouse. (He'd remember the dark stench of old urine.) At one place there were fistfights; at another a supervisor who hated Chinese and Mexicans. Nowhere a union.

His memory of himself in those years is held by those jobs. Never making money enough for passage to Australia; slowly giving up the plan of returning to school to resume his third-grade education—to become an engineer. My memory of him in those years, however, is lifted from photographs in the family album which show him on his honeymoon with my mother—the woman who had convinced him to stay in America. I have studied their photographs often, seeking to find in those figures some clear resemblance to the man and the woman I've known as my parents. But the youthful faces in the photos remain, behind dark glasses, shadowy figures anticipating my mother and father.

They are pictured on the grounds of the Coronado Hotel near San Diego, standing in the pale light of a winter afternoon. She is wearing slacks. Her hair falls seductively over one side of her face. He appears wearing a double-breasted suit, an unneeded raincoat draped over his arm. Another shows them standing together, solemnly staring ahead. Their shoulders barely are touching. There is to their pose an aristocratic formality, an elegant Latin hauteur.

The man in those pictures is the same man who was fascinated by Italian grand opera. I have never known just what my father saw in the spectacle, but he has told me that he would take my mother to the Opera House every Friday night—if he had money enough for orchestra seats. ("Why go to sit in the balcony?") On Sundays he'd don Italian silk scarves and a camel's hair coat to take his new wife to the polo matches in Golden Gate Park. But one weekend my father stopped going to the opera and polo matches. He would blame the change in his life on one job—a warehouse job, working for a large corporation which today advertises its products with the smiling faces of children. "They made me an old man before my time," he'd say to me many years later. Afterward, jobs got easier and cleaner. Eventually, in middle age, he got a job making false teeth. But his youth was spent at the warehouse. "Everything changed," his wife remembers. The dapper young man in the old photographs yielded to the man I saw after dinner: haggard, asleep on the sofa.

During "The Ed Sullivan Show" on Sunday nights, when Roberta Peters or Licia Albanese would appear on the tiny blue screen, his head would jerk up alert. He'd sit forward while the notes of Puccini sounded before him. ("Un bel dí.")

By the time they had a family, my parents no longer dressed in very fine clothes. Those symbols of great wealth and the reality of their lives too noisily clashed. No longer did they try to fit themselves, like paper-doll figures, behind trappings so foreign to their actual lives. My father no longer wore silk scarves or expensive wool suits. He sold his tuxedo to a second-hand store for five dollars. My mother sold her rabbit fur coat to the wife of a Spanish radio station disc jockey. ("It looks better on you than it does on me," she kept telling the lady until the sale was completed.) I was six years old at the time, but I recall watching the transaction with complete understanding. The woman I knew as my mother was already physically unlike the woman in her honeymoon photos. My mother's hair was short. Her shoulders were thick from carrying children. Her fingers were swollen red, toughened by house-cleaning. Already my mother would admit to foreseeing herself in her own mother, a woman grown old, bald, and bowlegged, after a hard lifetime of working.

In their manner, both my parents continued to respect the symbols of 25 what they considered to be upper-class life. Very early, they taught me the *propria* way of eating *como los ricos*. And I was carefully taught elaborate formulas of polite greeting and parting. The dark little boy would be invited by classmates to the rich houses on Forty-fourth and Forty-fifth streets. "How do you do?" or "I am very pleased to meet you," I would say, bowing slightly to the amused mothers of classmates. "Thank you very much for the dinner; it was very delicious."

I made an impression. I intended to make an impression, to be invited back. (I soon realized that the trick was to get the mother or father to notice me.) From those early days began my association with rich people, my fascination with their secret. My mother worried. She warned me not to come home expecting to have the things my friends possessed. But she needn't have said anything. When I went to the big houses, I remembered that I was, at best, a visitor to the world I saw there. For that reason, I was an especially watchful guest. I was my parents' child. Things most middle-class children wouldn't trouble to notice, I studied. Remembered to see: the starched black and white uniform worn by the maid who opened the door; the Mexican gardeners—their complexions as dark as my own. (One gardener's face, glassed by sweat, looked up to see me going inside.)

"Take Richard upstairs and show him your electric train," the mother said. But it was really the vast polished dining room table I'd come to appraise. Those nights when I was invited to stay for dinner, I'd notice that my friend's mother rang a small silver bell to tell the black woman when to bring in the food. The father, at his end of the table, ate while wearing his tie. When I was not required to speak, I'd skate the icy cut of crystal with my eye; my gaze would follow the golden threads etched onto the rim of china. With my mother's eyes I'd see my hostess's manicured nails and judge them to be marks of her leisure. Later, when my schoolmate's father would bid me goodnight, I would feel his soft fingers and palm when we shook hands. And turning to leave, I'd see my dark self, lit by chandelier light, in a tall hallway mirror.

2

Complexion. My first conscious experience of sexual excitement concerns my complexion. One summer weekend, when I was around seven years old, I was at a public swimming pool with the whole family. I remember sitting on the damp pavement next to the pool and seeing my mother, in the spectators' bleachers, holding my younger sister on her lap. My mother, I noticed, was watching my father as he stood on a diving board, waving to her. I watched her wave back. Then saw her radiant, bashful, astonishing smile. In that second I sensed that my mother and father had a relationship I knew nothing about. A nervous excitement encircled my stomach as I saw my mother's eyes follow my father's figure curving into the water. A second or two later, he emerged. I heard him call out. Smiling, his voice sounded, buoyant, calling me to swim to him. But turning to see him, I caught my mother's eye. I heard her shout over to me. In Spanish she called through the crowd: "Put a towel on over your shoulders." In public, she didn't want to say why. I knew.

The incident anticipates the shame and sexual inferiority I was to feel in later years because of my dark complexion. I was to grow up an ugly child. Or one who thought himself ugly. (*Feo.*) One night when I was eleven or twelve years old, I locked myself in the bathroom and carefully regarded my reflection in the mirror over the sink. Without any pleasure I studied my skin. I turned on the faucet. (In my mind I heard the swirling voices of aunts, and even my mother's voice, whispering, whispering incessantly about lemon juice solutions and dark, *feo* children.) With a bar of soap, I fashioned a thick ball of lather. I began soaping my arms. I took my father's straight razor out of the medicine cabinet. Slowly, with steady deliberateness, I put the blade against my flesh, pressed it as close as I could without cutting, and moved it up and down across my skin to see if I could get out, somehow lessen, the dark. All I succeeded in doing, however, was in shaving my arms bare of their hair. For as I noted with disappointment, the dark would not come out. It remained. Trapped. Deep in the cells of my skin.

Throughout adolescence, I felt myself mysteriously marked. Nothing else 30 about my appearance would concern me so much as the fact that my complexion was dark. My mother would say how sorry she was that there was not money enough to get braces to straighten my teeth. But I never bothered about my teeth. In three-way mirrors at department stores, I'd see my profile dramatically defined by a long nose, but it was really only the color of my skin that caught my attention.

I wasn't afraid that I would become a menial laborer because of my skin. Nor did my complexion make me feel especially vulnerable to racial abuse. (I didn't really consider my dark skin to be a racial characteristic. I would have been only too happy to look as Mexican as my light-skinned older brother.) Simply, I judged myself ugly. And, since the women in my family had been the ones who discussed it in such worried tones, I felt my dark skin made me unattractive to women.

Thirteen years old. Fourteen. In a grammar school art class, when the assignment was to draw a self-portrait, I tried and I tried but could not bring myself to shade in the face on the paper to anything like my actual tone. With disgust then I would come face to face with myself in mirrors. With disappointment I located myself in class photographs—my dark face undefined by the camera which had clearly described the white faces of classmates. Or I'd see my dark wrist against my long-sleeved white shirt.

I grew divorced from my body. Insecure, overweight, listless. On hot summer days when my rubber-soled shoes soaked up the heat from the sidewalk, I kept my head down. Or walked in the shade. My mother didn't need anymore to tell me to watch out for the sun. I denied myself a sensational life. The normal, extraordinary, animal excitement of feeling my body alive— riding shirtless on a bicycle in the warm wind created by furious self-propelled motion—the sensations that first had excited in me a sense of my maleness, I denied. I was too ashamed of my body. I wanted to forget that I had a body because I had a brown body. I was grateful that none of my classmates ever mentioned the fact.

I continued to see the *braceros,* those men I resembled in one way and, in another way, didn't resemble at all. On the watery horizon of a Valley afternoon, I'd see them. And though I feared looking like them, it was with silent envy that I regarded them still. I envied them their physical lives, their freedom to violate the taboo of the sun. Closer to home I would notice the shirtless construction workers, the roofers, the sweating men tarring the street in front of the house. And I'd see the Mexican gardeners. I was unwilling to admit the attraction of their lives. I tried to deny it by looking away. But what was denied became strongly desired.

In high school physical education classes, I withdrew, in the regular company of five or six classmates, to a distant corner of a football field where we smoked and talked. Our company was composed of bodies too short or too tall, all graceless and all—except mine—pale. Our conversation was usually witty. (In fact we were intelligent.) If we referred to the athletic contests around us, it was with sarcasm. With savage scorn I'd refer to the "animals" playing football or baseball. It would have been important for me to have 35

joined them. Or for me to have taken off my shirt, to have let the sun burn
dark on my skin, and to have run barefoot on the warm wet grass. It would
have been very important. Too important. It would have been too telling a
gesture—to admit the desire for sensation, the body, my body.

Fifteen, sixteen. I was a teenager shy in the presence of girls. Never dated.
Barely could talk to a girl without stammering. In high school I went to several dances, but I never managed to ask a girl to dance. So I stopped going. I
cannot remember high school years now with the parade of typical images:
bright drive-ins or gliding blue shadows of a Junior Prom. At home most weekend nights, I would pass evenings reading. Like those hidden, precocious adolescents who have no real-life sexual experiences, I read a great deal of romantic
fiction. "You won't find it in your books," my brother would playfully taunt me
as he prepared to go to a party by freezing the crest of the wave in his hair with
sticky pomade. Through my reading, however, I developed a fabulous and sophisticated sexual imagination. At seventeen, I may not have known how to engage a girl in small talk, but I had read *Lady Chatterley's Lover.*

It annoyed me to hear my father's teasing: that I would never know what
"real work" is; that my hands were so soft. I think I knew it was his way of
admitting pleasure and pride in my academic success. But I didn't smile. My
mother said she was glad her children were getting their educations and
would not be pushed around like *los pobres.* I heard the remark ironically as
a reminder of my separation from *los braceros.* At such times I suspected that
education was making me effeminate. The odd thing, however, was that I did
not judge my classmates so harshly. Nor did I consider my male teachers in
high school effeminate. It was only myself I judged against some shadowy,
mythical Mexican laborer—dark like me, yet very different.

Language was crucial. I knew that I had violated the ideal of the *macho*
by becoming such a dedicated student of language and literature. *Machismo*
was a word never exactly defined by the persons who used it. (It was best
described in the "proper" behavior of men.) Women at home, nevertheless,
would repeat the old Mexican dictum that a man should be *feo, fuerte, y
formal.* "The three F's," my mother called them, smiling slyly. *Feo* I took to
mean not literally ugly so much as ruggedly handsome. (When my mother and
her sisters spent a loud, laughing afternoon determining ideal male good
looks, they finally settled on the actor Gilbert Roland, who was neither too
pretty nor ugly but had looks "like a man.") *Fuerte,* "strong," seemed to
mean not physical strength as much as inner strength, character. A depend-
able man is *fuerte. Fuerte* for that reason was a characteristic subsumed by the
last of the three qualities, and the one I most often considered—*formal.* To be
formal is to be steady. A man of responsibility, a good provider. Someone
formal is also constant. A person to be relied upon in adversity. A sober man,
a man of high seriousness.

I learned a great deal about being *formal* just by listening to the way my father and other male relatives of his generation spoke. A man was not silent necessarily. Nor was he limited in the tones he could sound. For example, he could tell a long, involved, humorous story and laugh at his own humor with high-pitched giggling. But a man was not talkative the way a woman could be. It was permitted a woman to be gossipy and chatty. (When one heard many voices in a room, it was usually women who were talking.) Men spoke much less rapidly. And often men spoke in monologues. (When one voice sounded in a crowded room, it was most often a man's voice one heard.) More important than any of this was the fact that a man never verbally revealed his emotions. Men did not speak about their unease in moments of crisis or danger. It was the woman who worried aloud when her husband got laid off from work. At times of illness or death in the family, a man was usually quiet, even silent. Women spoke up to voice prayers. In distress, women always sounded quick ejaculations to God or the Virgin; women prayed in clearly audible voices at a wake held in a funeral parlor. And on the subject of love, a woman was verbally expansive. She spoke of her yearning and delight. A married man, if he spoke publicly about love, usually did so with playful, mischievous irony. Younger, unmarried men more often were quiet. (The *macho* is a silent suitor. *Formal.*)

At home I was quiet, so perhaps I seemed *formal* to my relations and other Spanish-speaking visitors to the house. But outside the house—my God!—I talked. Particularly in class or alone with my teachers, I chattered. (Talking seemed to make teachers think I was bright.) I often was proud of my way with words. Though, on other occasions, for example, when I would hear my mother busily speaking to women, it would occur to me that my attachment to words made me like her. Her son. Not *formal* like my father. At such times I even suspected that my nostalgia for sounds—the noisy, intimate Spanish sounds of my past—was nothing more than effeminate yearning.

High school English teachers encouraged me to describe very personal feelings in words. Poems and short stories I wrote, expressing sorrow and loneliness, were awarded high grades. In my bedroom were books by poets and novelists—books that I loved—in which male writers published feelings the men in my family never revealed or acknowledged in words. And it seemed to me that there was something unmanly about my attachment to literature. Even today, when so much about the myth of the macho no longer concerns me, I cannot altogether evade such notions. Writing these pages, admitting my embarrassment or my guilt, admitting my sexual anxieties and my physical insecurity, I have not been able to forget that I am not being *formal.*

So be it.

40

3

I went to college at Stanford, attracted partly by its academic reputation, partly because it was the school rich people went to. I found myself on a campus with golden children of western America's upper middle class. Many were students both ambitious for academic success *and* accustomed to leisured life in the sun. In the afternoon, they lay spread out, sunbathing in front of the library, reading Swift or Engels or Beckett. Others went by in convertibles, off to play tennis or ride horses or sail. Beach boys dressed in tank-tops and shorts were my classmates in undergraduate seminars. Tall tan girls wearing white strapless dresses sat directly in front of me in lecture rooms. I'd study them, their physical confidence. I was still recognizably kin to the boy I had been. Less tortured perhaps. But still kin. At Stanford, it's true, I began to have something like a conventional sexual life. I don't think, however, that I really believed that the women I knew found me physically appealing. I continued to stay out of the sun. I didn't linger in mirrors. And I was the student at Stanford who remembered to notice the Mexican-American janitors and gardeners working on campus.

It was at Stanford, one day near the end of my senior year, that a friend told me about a summer construction job he knew was available. I was quickly alert. Desire uncoiled within me. My friend said that he knew I had been looking for summer employment. He knew I needed some money. Almost apologetically he explained: It was something I probably wouldn't be interested in, but a friend of his, a contractor, needed someone for the summer to do menial jobs. There would be lots of shoveling and raking and sweeping. Nothing too hard. But nothing more interesting either. Still, the pay would be good. Did I want it? Or did I know someone who did?

I did. Yes, I said, surprised to hear myself say it.   45

In the weeks following, friends cautioned that I had no idea how hard physical labor really is. ("You only *think* you know what it is like to shovel for eight hours straight.") Their objections seemed to me challenges. They resolved the issue. I became happy with my plan. I decided, however, not to tell my parents. I wouldn't tell my mother because I could guess her worried reaction. I would tell my father only after the summer was over, when I could announce that, after all, I did know what "real work" is like.

The day I met the contractor (a Princeton graduate, it turned out), he asked me whether I had done any physical labor before. "In high school, during the summer," I lied. And although he seemed to regard me with skepticism, he decided to give me a try. Several days later, expectant, I arrived at my first construction site. I would take off my shirt to the sun. And at last grasp desired sensation. No longer afraid. At last become like a *bracero*. "We need those tree stumps out of here by tomorrow," the contractor said. I started to work.

I labored with excitement that first morning—and all the days after. The work was harder than I could have expected. But it was never as tedious as my friends had warned me it would be. There was too much physical pleasure in the labor. Especially early in the day, I would be most alert to the sensations of movement and straining. Beginning around seven each morning (when the air was still damp but the scent of weeds and dry earth anticipated the heat of the sun), I would feel my body resist the first thrusts of the shovel. My arms, tightened by sleep, would gradually loosen; after only several minutes, sweat would gather in beads on my forehead and then—a short while later—I would feel my chest silky with sweat in the breeze. I would return to my work. A nervous spark of pain would fly up my arm and settle to burn like an ember in the thick of my shoulder. An hour, two passed. Three. My whole body would assume regular movements; my shoveling would be described by identical, even movements. Even later in the day, my enthusiasm for primitive sensation would survive the heat and the dust and the insects pricking my back. I would strain wildly for sensation as the day came to a close. At three-thirty, quitting time, I would stand upright and slowly let my head fall back, luxuriating in the feeling of tightness relieved.

Some of the men working nearby would watch me and laugh. Two or three of the older men took the trouble to teach me the right way to use a pick, the correct way to shovel. "You're doing it wrong, too fucking hard," one man scolded. Then proceeded to show me—what persons who work with their bodies all their lives quickly learn—the most economical way to use one's body in labor.

"Don't make your back do so much work," he instructed. I stood impatiently listening, half listening, vaguely watching, then noticed his work-thickened fingers clutching the shovel. I was annoyed. I wanted to tell him that I enjoyed shoveling the wrong way. And I didn't want to learn the right way. I wasn't afraid of back pain. I liked the way my body felt sore at the end of the day. 50

I was about to, but, as it turned out, I didn't say a thing. Rather it was at that moment I realized that I was fooling myself if I expected a few weeks of labor to gain me admission to the world of the laborer. I would not learn in three months what my father had meant by "real work." I was not bound to this job; I could imagine its rapid conclusion. For me the sensations of exertion and fatigue could be savored. For my father or uncle, working at comparable jobs when they were my age, such sensations were to be feared. Fatigue took a different toll on their bodies—and minds.

It was, I know, a simple insight. But it was with this realization that I took my first step that summer toward realizing something even more important about the "worker." In the company of carpenters, electricians, plumbers, and painters at lunch, I would often sit quietly, observant. I was not shy in such company. I felt easy, pleased by the knowledge that I was casually accepted, my presence taken for granted by men (exotics) who worked with their hands. Some days the younger men would talk and talk about sex, and they would howl at women who drove by in cars. Other days the talk at lunchtime was subdued; men gathered in separate groups. It depended on who was around. There were rough, good-natured workers. Others were quiet. The more I remember that summer, the more I realize that there was no single *type* of worker. I am embarrassed to say I had not expected such diversity. I certainly had not expected to meet, for example, a plumber who was an abstract painter in his off hours and admired the work of Mark Rothko. Nor did I expect to meet so many workers with college diplomas. (They were the ones who were not surprised that I intended to enter graduate school in the fall.) I suppose what I really want to say here is painfully obvious, but I must say it nevertheless: The men of that summer were middle-class Americans. They certainly didn't constitute an oppressed society. Carefully completing their work sheets; talking about the fortunes of local football teams; planning Las Vegas vacations; comparing the gas mileage of various makes of campers—they were not *los pobres* my mother had spoken about.

On two occasions, the contractor hired a group of Mexican aliens. They were employed to cut down some trees and haul off debris. In all, there were six men of varying age. The youngest in his late twenties; the oldest (his father?) perhaps sixty years old. They came and they left in a single old truck. Anonymous men. They were never introduced to the other men at the site. Immediately upon their arrival, they would follow the contractor's directions, start working—rarely resting—seemingly driven by a fatalistic sense that work which had to be done was best done as quickly as possible.

I watched them sometimes. Perhaps they watched me. The only time I saw them pay me much notice was one day at lunchtime when I was laughing with the other men. The Mexicans sat apart when they ate, just as they worked by themselves. Quiet. I rarely heard them say much to each other. All I could hear were their voices calling out sharply to one another, giving directions. Otherwise, when they stood briefly resting, they talked among themselves in voices too hard to overhear.

The contractor knew enough Spanish, and the Mexicans—or at least the oldest of them, their spokesman—seemed to know enough English to communicate. But because I was around, the contractor decided one day to make me his translator. (He assumed I could speak Spanish.) I did what I was told. Shyly I went over to tell the Mexicans that the *patrón* wanted them to do something else before they left for the day. As I started to speak, I was afraid with my old fear that I would be unable to pronounce the Spanish words. But it was a simple instruction I had to convey. I could say it in phrases.

The dark sweating faces turned toward me as I spoke. They stopped their work to hear me. Each nodded in response. I stood there. I wanted to say something more. But what could I say in Spanish, even if I could have pronounced the words right? Perhaps I just wanted to engage them in small talk, to be assured of their confidence, our familiarity. I thought for a moment to ask them where in Mexico they were from. Something like that. And maybe I wanted to tell them (a lie, if need be) that my parents were from the same part of Mexico.

I stood there.

Their faces watched me. The eyes of the man directly in front of me moved slowly over my shoulder, and I turned to follow his glance toward *el patrón* some distance away. For a moment I felt swept up by that glance into the Mexicans' company. But then I heard one of them returning to work. And then the others went back to work. I left them without saying anything more.

When they had finished, the contractor went over to pay them in cash. (He later told me that he paid them collectively—"for the job," though he wouldn't tell me their wages. He said something quickly about the good rate of exchange "in their own country.") I can still hear the loudly confident voice he used with the Mexicans. It was the sound of the *gringo* I had heard as a very young boy. And I can still hear the quiet, indistinct sounds of the Mexican, the oldest, who replied. At hearing that voice I was sad for the Mexicans. Depressed by their vulnerability. Angry at myself. The adventure of the summer seemed suddenly ludicrous. I would not shorten the distance I felt from *los pobres* with a few weeks of physical labor. I would not become like them. They were different from me.

After that summer, a great deal—and not very much really—changed in my 60 life. The curse of physical shame was broken by the sun; I was no longer ashamed of my body. No longer would I deny myself the pleasing sensations of my maleness. During those years when middle-class black Americans began to assert with pride, "Black is beautiful," I was able to regard my complexion without shame. I am today darker than I ever was as a boy. I have taken up the middle-class sport of long-distance running. Nearly every day now I run ten or fifteen miles, barely clothed, my skin exposed to the California winter rain and wind or the summer sun of late afternoon. The torso, the soccer player's calves and thighs, the arms of the twenty-year-old I never was, I possess now in my thirties. I study the youthful parody shape in the mirror: the stomach lipped tight by muscle; the shoulders rounded by chin-ups; the arms veined strong. This man. A man. I meet him. He laughs to see me, what I have become.

The dandy. I wear double-breasted Italian suits and custom-made English shoes. I resemble no one so much as my father—the man pictured in those honeymoon photos. At that point in life when he abandoned the dandy's posture, I assume it. At the point when my parents would not consider going on vacation, I register at the Hotel Carlyle in New York and the Plaza Athenée in Paris. I am as taken by the symbols of leisure and wealth as they were. For my parents, however, those symbols became taunts, reminders of all they could not achieve in one lifetime. For me those same symbols are reassuring reminders of public success. I tempt vulgarity to be reassured. I am filled with the gaudy delight, the monstrous grace of the *nouveau riche.*

In recent years I have had occasion to lecture in ghetto high schools. There I see students of remarkable style and physical grace. (One can see more dandies in such schools than one ever will find in middle-class high schools.) There is not the look of casual assurance I saw students at Stanford display. Ghetto girls mimic high-fashion models. Their dresses are of bold, forceful color; their figures elegant, long; the stance theatrical. Boys wear shirts that grip at their overdeveloped muscular bodies. (Against a powerless future, they engage images of strength.) Bad nutrition does not yet tell. Great disappointment, fatal to youth, awaits them still. For the moment, movements in school hallways are dancelike, a procession of postures in a sexual masque. Watching them, I feel a kind of envy. I wonder how different my adolescence would have been had I been free. . . . But no, it is my parents I see—their optimism during those years when they were entertained by Italian grand opera.

The registration clerk in London wonders if I have just been to Switzerland. And the man who carries my luggage in New York guesses the Caribbean. My complexion becomes a mark of my leisure. Yet no one would regard my complexion the same way if I entered such hotels through the service entrance. That is only to say that my complexion assumes its significance from the context of my life. My skin, in itself, means nothing. I stress the point because I know there are people who would label me "disadvantaged" because of my color. They make the same mistake I made as a boy, when I thought a disadvantaged life was circumscribed by particular occupations. That summer I worked in the sun may have made me physically indistinguishable from the Mexicans working nearby. (My skin was actually darker because, unlike them, I worked without wearing a shirt. By late August my hands were probably as tough as theirs.) But I was not one of *los pobres.* What made me different from them was an attitude of *mind,* my imagination of myself.

I do not blame my mother for warning me away from the sun when I was young. In a world where her brother had become an old man in his twenties because he was dark, my complexion was something to worry about. "Don't run in the sun," she warns me today. I run. In the end, my father was right—though perhaps he did not know how right or why—to say that I would never know what real work is. I will never know what he felt at his last factory job. If tomorrow I worked at some kind of factory, it would go differently for me. My long education would favor me. I could act as a public person—able to defend my interests, to unionize, to petition, to speak up—to challenge and demand. (I will never know what real work is.) I will never know what the Mexicans knew, gathering their shovels and ladders and saws.

Their silence stays with me now. The wages those Mexicans received for 65 their labor were only a measure of their disadvantaged condition. Their silence is more telling. They lack a public identity. They remain profoundly alien. Persons apart. People lacking a union obviously, people without grounds. They depend upon the relative good will or fairness of their employers each day. For such people, lacking a better alternative, it is not such an unreasonable risk.

Their silence stays with me. I have taken these many words to describe its impact. Only: the quiet. Something uncanny about it. Its compliance. Vulnerability. Pathos. As I heard their truck rumbling away, I shuddered, my face mirrored with sweat. I had finally come face to face with *los pobres*.

Considerations

1. Early in the essay, Rodriguez's mother warns him that "you won't be satisfied till you end up looking like *los pobres* who work in the fields, *los braceros*" (para. 2). What role do the conversations heard by Rodriguez during his childhood play in the development of his attitudes toward and his relationships with Mexican day workers? How prophetic do his mother's words prove to be?

2. Rodriguez ends this part of his narrative by sharing his father's conclusion that he will never know what real work is. Given his comments and experiences here, how is Rodriguez defining the word *work*? How do his ideas about gender, education, and race shape his definition?

Invitation to Write

Apart from the complications related to his dual cultural heritage, Rodriguez's experience with a summer job is common to most American adolescents. Write an essay in which you examine the role of first work experiences in shaping the character of young Americans. Follow the development of Rodriguez's new attitude toward work and compare it with your own similar experiences. Consider also the influence his parents' work experience exerted on his way of thinking about work. Based on his example and the other examples you have discussed, draw a more general conclusion about the role of work in forming one's identity.

Connections

In his essay "The Global Elite" (p. 290), Robert Reich suggests that the elitism in today's society is generated by those people who are basically employed to analyze and manipulate symbols. As a literature student among the regular construction workers, Rodriguez may also appear to be a member of the elite. How does his background as a student of literature affect the way he looks at his summer experiences?

Write an essay in which you evaluate Rodriguez's view of his work experience. First determine the extent to which a writer falls into the category of symbolic analysts, which was described by Reich. Weigh the difficulty of each job against its usefulness. After carefully examining all the aspects of the various kinds of work, decide whether you share Rodriguez's antielitism or Reich's theory that symbolic analysts are useful to society.

JANE STAW
MARY SWANDER

If You Can Talk to a Guy

Jane Anne Staw received a Ph.D. in French literature from the University of Michigan and an M.F.A. from the Writers' Workshop at the University of Iowa. She has taught at Stanford and at the University of California at Berkeley. Her poetry has been published in *Columbia, The Agnii Review,* and *The Iowa Review.* She has also translated *A Day in the Strait* (1985) by the French poet Emmanuel Hocquard.

Mary Swander holds a B.A. and an M.F.A. from the University of Iowa. She has taught at several midwestern colleges and has published essays, short stories, and two books of poems, *Succession* (1979) and *Driving the Body Back* (1986). She has received the Discovery/*Nation* Award and the Carl Sandburg Award, as well as two Ingram Merrill Foundation Awards for poetry. In 1987 she was awarded a National Endowment for the Arts fellowship. Currently, she teaches at Iowa State University. Mary Swander's first collaboration with Jane Staw was *Parsnips in the Snow* (1990), a collection of interviews with gardeners across several midwestern states published by the University of Iowa Press.

"If You Can Talk to a Guy" appeared in *A Place of Sense: Essays in Search of the Midwest* (1988), an anthology of essays and photographs about the Midwest. Although written by several different authors, these essays share a sense of daily life and its unexpected surprises in an area extending from Nebraska to Ohio. Many of the essays reflect upon the importance of small-town rituals and rhythms, of personal and communal memories, of a life-style inextricably linked to the existence of family farms, and of the values that have emerged from geography and history. "If You Can Talk to a Guy" is no exception in this respect: In conversations between the two authors and local men and women, it reveals the profound connection between the place, the way of life, and the imaginations of the people living in the Midwest. The encounters at the small inn in Winnebago, Minnesota, teach the two traveling academics how much you can achieve "if you can talk to a guy."

THE WAITRESS AT THE VILLAGE INN CAFÉ in Winnebago, Minnesota, bounces back and forth between our booth in the very back of the café and a round table in the front window occupied by three women and two men, all nursing their coffee. It is four o'clock and the Village Inn is almost empty, its regulars back home, cooling off in front of fans—their morning and afternoon coffees, their gossip of adultery, cancers, trips to Arizona, and farm foreclosures behind them. It might have been on a day like this, around two o'clock in the afternoon, that Harold Golly met up with Henry Dauner at the counter of the Village Inn, over coffee and lemon meringue pie. They were neighbors, Henry's farm just across the fields from Harold's, and had worked together often, combining one or the other's corn in the fall. For several years, as Harold tells the story, Henry's health had been bad. Then his wife had died of breast cancer. After that, Henry had decided to sell his farm. And he was planning to sell it to Harold's daughter and son-in-law. Everything had been agreed on since January.

Henry had first talked about selling the farm a year and a half earlier. One morning, as soon as he got the crops in that spring, Henry had stopped over at Harold's. "I just don't feel like farming anymore," he said. Then he drove away. That was on a Friday, Harold remembers, and as usual his daughter Mary and her husband, Duane, were due in from Minneapolis, where they were both teachers. That night at supper, while the family passed the corn from Harold's garden and the beef from his herd of Angus, Harold stopped chewing for a moment and looked around the table, from his wife, Helen, to Mary, and then to Duane. "Henry says he's going to sell his farm," he told them. "He doesn't feel like farming anymore."

Mary put down her fork and looked straight at her father. "You go back and tell Henry we'd like to buy it."

That fall, probably on a late-October morning, the air papery cool, Harold drove down the lane away from his house—past the grove of bur oaks and the apple orchard, over the small creek, down the county road, so windy even the natives give directions in left and right, rather than the traditional north and south, and finally across the one-lane bridge that had collapsed several times the winter before—to help Henry harvest his last crop of feed corn. Neither man mentioned the imminent sale of the farm.

A few months later, in December, Harold noticed Henry in his driveway one morning and went out to meet him. "Do you think Mary and Duane still want the farm?" Henry asked, the window on his pick-up cranked down halfway, his breath pluming up in front of his face. "I think so," Harold answered. "I'll call them tonight."

"Well," Henry said, "if they want it, tell them to meet me at the attorney's office in Truman on Saturday."

So they met in Truman—Henry, Duane, Mary, and the attorney—and they agreed on everything. That Monday, Mary and Duane returned to finish out their year in Minneapolis and Harold and Henry chatted, as usual, over coffee at the Village Inn. Outside, the snow drifted in the ditches, and the windows of the café frosted up so that you could no longer see across the street to the filling station. Over the next few months, the bridge leading to Harold's house collapsed two more times. The pipes in Henry's barn burst. And just outside of town, a couple from Joplin, Missouri, lost their orientation during a blizzard and froze to death in their car.

But by June, the county had begun work on a new bridge and Duane and Mary were getting ready to move, packing up their books and organizing a garage sale to clear out their daughter's old toys, the green easy chair the cat had shredded with its claws, and kitchen odds and ends—old jelly glasses, an extra grater or two, a one-legged colander, their first set of dishes.

One day that June, right before Mary and Duane were due in town, Harold stopped at the Village Inn after a round of golf. When he walked in, he saw Henry sitting at the counter. Harold tipped his seed cap to Kathy the waitress, then walked over to where Henry was sitting and straddled the stool next to him. They talked as usual—about Harold's golf game, about last week's storm that had knocked over half of Jim Nelson's corn. But Harold noticed that Henry was very quiet. "It was a beautiful June day," Harold recalls. "And when we finished our coffee, we walked out and stopped at one of our pickups. Tears began to roll down Henry's cheeks and off his nose."

"I can't sell Duane and Mary the farm the way I want to," Henry said. "I gotta have more money down or the judge won't approve the sale."   10

"Well," Harold said, "Henry, now don't get downhearted about this. Let me go home and talk to Helen. We'll help buy it, I think."

Harold and Helen did help Duane and Mary buy the farm. And when we visited Harold's place, last summer, sent there by some friends in neighboring Blue Earth who thought we might enjoy both Harold and the view, Harold told us the story of the sale. "So, you see," he said, when he had finished, his hoarse voice rising, "that's the advantage of being able to talk to a guy face-to-face." Then, Harold lifted his head and raised his arm nose-high, his index finger pointing across acres of corn that wound their way up and down the hills and around the Blue Earth River banked on both sides by cottonwoods. "See that stand of trees over there, right at the end of my finger?" he asked, indicating a blur of green. "Well, that's Mary and Duane's farm, right behind those trees. And right over here," he pivoted his body ninety degrees to the east, "is my son Tom's farm. He farms that big corn field. Oh, he taught school for a while. But then his father-in-law decided to sell. And all Tom ever wanted to do was farm, anyway. I can show you his drill and planter. They're just out in the shed here."

When Harold Golly told Henry not to get downhearted on that beautiful June morning, when he told him he'd talk to Helen about helping to buy the farm, it's not likely that he planned to stop off at his lawyer's, or consult the

Minneapolis Star's farm section to check on the price of land. Nor is it likely that he rushed home, and finding Helen in the kitchen icing his favorite chocolate cake, asked her to put down her wooden spoon and listen. More likely, Harold went out and worked in his garden on that beautiful summer day, running his hoe up and down the rows of corn and tomatoes, bending over the cucumbers to weed, setting the hose next to the beets and letting the water seep into the blue-black earth as he worked. And once he had finished in the garden, pinching back several tomato plants, gathering the last of the summer's peas, he had probably gone back into the house and taken a shower. Then, he probably sat down with the newspaper, in his easy chair by the front door, to wait for Helen to call him to supper. And once they were sitting at the square table in the kitchen, with its plastic flowered cloth, his fork full of mashed potatoes, Harold probably said to Helen, "Ran into Henry at the Village Inn today."

"Oh," Helen might have replied, continuing to chew on her pork chop.

"Henry seemed sort of quiet."   15

"Well, he's had it kind of rough."

"The judge wants more money down for the farm. I told him we might help," Harold may finally have said, his fork clicking against the plate as he set it down.

People like Harold, Henry, and Helen communicate important things with few words. They act in the same way. And it's understandable. Their economy of gesture, paradoxically, conforms to the way they make their living. The scale of their lives is enormous—hundreds of acres, thousands of bushels of corn or soy. But once they prepare the fields and plant, they must step aside, leaving their fates to nature and the U.S. government. Even the way they plant signals economy. Harold and Henry don't broadcast their seed by the fistful. Instead, in the old days walking along the rows with a horse and drill, or today mounted atop twenty-four-row planters, they deposit at the most three kernels to a hill. And if later in the season the weather turns against them, bringing in enough lashing rain and wind to knock over entire sections of adolescent corn, they don't—like a vegetable gardener—throw on their boots and slickers and dash through the fields hammering in stakes and tying up the stalks. They sit by their radios and listen. And then, when the winds have subsided and the rains tapered off, they might go and stand at the top of a rise, one hand shading their eyes to survey the damage. And even then, even if they see half their corn lying on its side, the tassels buried in mud, they don't run to the barn for twine. Instead, they go back into the house and turn the radio on again, listening to the news, assessing the extent of the damage in the area, waiting. Any other response—hurried calls to neighbors, graphic descriptions of the storm, or the state of the fields to family—would be an excess, not unlike the ten inches of rain and the sixty MPH winds of the recent storm.

By necessity, then, farmers are conservers; they save everything—seeds, old crates, junk cars down by the creek, string, buckets, work shoes. Words are no exception.

"Can I get you anything else?" the waitress at the Village Inn asks, ap- 20 proaching our table, her blond hair fanning out from her head as she walks. "Well, at least have another cup of coffee. I'm not used to people just having one cup," she urges, already leaning over to pick up our mugs and refill them from the glass pot steaming in her hands. We thank her and she smiles at us, displaying a set of teeth that look like kernels of white sweet corn. Then she twirls around and bounces back toward the cash register—just in case one of her two tables should suddenly ask for the bill. As she passes the group at the round table in the front, the thin, hollow-chested man with the hearing aid calls her over. The rest of the café is still empty, its newly Naugahyded booths shiny, the front counter, where Harold and Henry used to sit, updated to a series of tables for two, making the café feel truncated and incomplete.

"Do you play sports in school?" the man asks the waitress.

"Yes. I played volleyball last year," she answers, flexing the muscles in her arms. "And this year I'm planning to go out for cheerleading."

"I thought so," the skinny man replies, and everybody at the table nods in agreement.

"Why don't you try basketball?" the second man asks, shifting his weight in the chair so that his belly rests on his left instead of his right knee. "That's a good sport these days. Always has been, of course."

The conversation at the front table gradually peters out and the waitress 25 busies herself behind the counter. A while later, a raspy voice drifts toward us: "You're from out of town, aren't you?" We look up and the skinny man, his glasses too large for his face, beckons us over. "Well, so are we. We come from Bricelyn, the next town over. Population 285. We're out for the afternoon," he explains.

"Yes," a high, quavering voice joins in. "Our sister's at the home here and we come once a week to take her out and give her a little break. We always come to the Village Inn."

"Yes, we always come to the Village Inn," the woman in the middle, the oldest, whispers. "And they've just remodeled this past year."

We look around at the straight-back metal and plastic chairs, the chandelier at the entrance, the indoor-outdoor carpet on the floor, green with yellow diamonds, the same green as Harold Golly's carpet, but his covered a living room floor that had been laid in 1900.

Of course, Harold's house hadn't always stood on the crest of the hill, next to the grove of bur oaks, Harold had told us that afternoon. The original farm house had burned down, and this one, built by the White brothers, two carpenters living on an adjacent farm, had been moved all the way from Huntley in 1911. One of Harold's friends, a neighbor on another adjacent farm, had seen it all happen. In fact, he had helped. The man's name was Bob Hope, and he had been seventeen years old at the time. He was the person responsible for moving the plank from behind the rollers every two hundred feet, when the cable the horses had been winding in ran out.

"It was quite an operation," Harold said. "They attached cables to the house, and a team would go round and round and round, winding the cable until they got the house up to this jack. Then they had to unstake that and take it out another two hundred feet. It took them a few days, what with the rain and the cables breaking. And I think one of the horses even collapsed."

When Harold finished telling the story, we looked over the fields in the direction of Huntley, west of Winnebago, up and down five miles of sinewy road, and imagined the two-story, white-frame house with its front porch being towed across the prairie. It would have been in the fall—the winter field snowed in, the spring field mud, the summer field full of corn—in the fall, after the corn was picked, the wind slapping the leaves in the trees, the cows gleaning the stubble. But as Harold told the story that afternoon, we could tell that for him, the house was moved again and again, whenever he looked out over his fields toward Huntley—Bob Hope, the White brothers, the team of horses, their driver, Harold's in-laws who had lived in the house first, all still present, too.

Each time Harold Golly steps out of his house and looks across his land, east to his son Tom's, west to Mary and Duane's, all of these people assemble there, on the crest where he stands. And that afternoon as he told us his stories, we had felt a part of that assembly also, looking out over the fields with Harold and Helen and their granddaughter Kristen, their pasts and presents coming together on a piece of land and at a time that transcended last year's winter blizzards, the spring floods, the summer's oats ripening next to Harold's garden, to create an eternal moment, outside of time and space.

"Why don't you pull up a chair?" the skinny man in the Village Inn invites. And before we have even scooted into place, he asks, "Where did you say you were from again? We're from Bricelyn."

"Yes, they come and take me out every week," the oldest woman whispers, "my two sisters and my brothers-in-law."

"Yes," a third female voice adds, "We used to be five sisters. Two died, so now there's just the three of us. We come up from Bricelyn. We all live there. Well, except for my sister, here, who's in the home. See," she continues, pulling a pin the size of a half-dollar out from her dress and craning her neck down to read the "I love Bricelyn" logo.

"What are you girls doing here?" the skinny man asks.

We tell him we are there to interview gardeners for a book we are writing.

"Then you oughta go talk to my next-door neighbor, Leroy Nelson. Everyone calls him Doc. He's a retired veterinarian. He's a real gardener."

"Boy, does he have melons!" the youngest sister smacks her lips.

"Oh, yeah. And he even raises his seedlings inside in the winter," says the   40
skinny man, shoving his glasses back up his nose. "But the funniest thing is, Doc just raises the stuff to give away. He has another huge garden somewhere out in the country, and you should see him in August. He loads up his pickup with melons and drives up and down the streets of Bricelyn giving them away. And then he takes another load up to his daughter in Winona. And another to his son in the Cities. My God, he even gives his seedlings away. He raises a thousand of them in his basement and gives a lot of those to Harold Beckman in the spring. And Harold's another one. He goes around Bricelyn planting trees. He used to manage the canning factory over there and when he retired he decided to beautify the town. Made a planter for petunias at the entrance to our city park. And a few years back, he put in a whole row of Austrian pines. And then last year, he had a big barbeque for the town, a fund-raiser (he raised $975.00), so he could plant another row of pines at the north edge of town as a snow break. And Maureen—she owns the beauty shop—is quite a gardener herself. Of course, I garden some. Mostly tomatoes. But this year's been a bad year. You're welcome to stop by, though."

The three sisters and the one brother-in-law nod their agreement.

"Maybe we'll give Leroy a call," we say, and ask the waitress for the pay phone.

"When you call Doc, just tell him Leon Lora sent you. He's my neighbor. Lives right next door to me. Right on Fifth and Elm. Just across from the funeral home." Again everybody at the table nods and smiles, the oldest sister wiping her mouth with a lipstick-smeared napkin.

Back at our booth, we discuss whether or not to call Leroy Nelson. If we do call, we'll have to see him and his garden immediately, since we are planning to head back home that evening. And we are tired. We left Ames, Iowa, at 7:00 in the morning, driving straight north to Blue Earth, where we had an appointment with a woman who gardened and raised rabbits. Her garden turned out to be full of weeds, but she was very eager to brew up some Lipton tea and model her angora toe-warmers, mittens, and berets, the whole time telling us about her three sons' electronics business in San Diego and her daughters' recipes for rabbit and onion pies. After that, we barely had time to gulp down a cartonful of yogurt, sitting on the tailgate in front of the Blue Earth County Courthouse, before rolling up and down the tree-lined lane to Harold Golly's where he, his wife, Helen, and granddaughter Kristen waited for us on the swing set in front of the house.

But somehow, we hate to let Leon Lora down. In the first place, he lis-   45
tened to us when we spoke. Not just politely or perfunctorily, but attentively. And then he responded, not with his own expertise, but with a list of people

he thought might help us out. We don't always encounter listeners like that, our everyday lives populated by people from universities. And it feels good to be listened to. It's the way a red-tailed hawk must feel when the temperature is just right and it catches a thermal, and wings outstretched, it glides and glides, over a canopy of willows by the river, past a field of beans, over some pastureland where a few herefords loll around the watering tank, their tails swishing. A friend of ours from New York said he had never finished a sentence until he went to Iowa to study. "It was the first time anybody ever listened to me," he told us.

We also can't bear to let Leon down because he offered us small-town hospitality, inviting us into the web of social relationships that make up his world: his tomatoes, Doc Nelson's melons, his sister-in-law's illness, Bricelyn's history. And he would certainly learn if we ignored his invitation. All he'd have to do is walk next door. So, we open the *Rand McNally Road Atlas,* locating Winnebago, on the south-central border of Iowa and Minnesota, then, tracing our way back through Blue Earth over Interstate 90, we follow Highway 253 to Bricelyn. It's right on our way home.

We finger the map and calculate the mileage on the most direct route down the Faribault County roads. Harold Golly had been a county commissioner once, when he was sixty-two years old. For only one term, though, since the job had kept him away from home two-thirds of the time and—more important, he chuckled—it had interfered with his golf. During the four years he had served, there were the usual problems with welfare and pay raises, but Harold had boasted that afternoon that in all those four years, only one man had ever gotten mad at him. It was over a ditch. In the northeast part of the county, the land is flat and the ditches fill up with trees and dirt, creating a drainage problem, Harold explained. After several nights of open discussion, the commission had taken a vote on cleaning up some of those ditches.

Harold's had been the deciding vote. But according to Harold, he had been cornered. "One commissioner lived along the ditch in question, so he couldn't vote. And another sat talking in the back of the room all night and didn't come up and take care of his job. So, that left three of us to handle it—the chairman and two others. There were about one hundred seventy-five people there, and the other commissioner made the motion to clean the ditch. Well, I seconded it. And the chairman called for the vote. And there were just the two of us, so it passed!"

That was on a Tuesday night, and the man who got mad at Harold wasn't at the meeting. But on Thursday night, as Harold told it, when he went bowling, "Boy, that guy jumped all over me."

"You're gonna flood the ditch I'm on."

"Were you at the meeting the other night?" Harold asked.

"No. But I heard what you did. You're gonna clean out number three and that'll flood nine."

50

So Harold looked hard at the man—past the smoke from the man's cigarette curling up in front of his face, past the angry brown eyes and the scar
stretching from his eyebrow to temple, where a scythe had caught him when
he was just a kid—and asked, "Well, were you satisfied with what they did in
1948?"

"Yeah, that was fine," the man answered.

"Well, if you'd have been to the meeting, you'd know that all we're doing   55
is cleaning the ditch to the same depth it was back in 1948, with the same
slant on the bank."

"Well," the other man said, stubbing his cigarette out on the floor, "that's
all right."

"So you see," Harold paused, adjusting his seed cap on his head, "if you can
talk to a guy, you can generally take care of anything."

And by now, we think we understand what Harold meant by talking. In
Winnebago, Minnesota, at least, talking doesn't mean analyzing. It doesn't
mean taking a problem and dissecting it, then examining it through a series of
lenses, philosophical, emotional, economic, sociological, and historical. Talking doesn't mean engaging in repartee, rationalizing, casting off guilt, blame,
or insecurities, the way we might shed coats and sweaters on a warm spring
day. For Harold Golly, and for the rest of the rural Midwest, talking means
telling stories—stories about hailstorms and tornadoes, about stomach cancer
and repossessions, about hired hands and chocolate cakes, about church potluck socials and college degrees.

So Harold Golly recalled the incident with his accuser as a story, as an
event that became much larger than the five minutes they had spent together
and the several sentences they had exchanged. Instead, it was a plot, set both
in the bowling alley and the county courthouse, a plot that began with the
first of three public discussions and ended in the Winnebago Bowling Alley,
against the hum of the balls down the lanes and the crash of the pins onto the
slick floor.

And if Harold recalls his life as a fabric of stories, with its warp and woof   60
of family, farm, and town, and not as a yellowish, narrow band of ticker tape
announcing a parade of achievements, he recounts his life as a story also. Any
particular happening or sight—an ear of corn, a year-old steer attempting to
mount its mother, a dead limb on an oak tree—may spark Harold, leading
him and his listeners away from the moment, away from the green crest where
his house sits looking over Elm Creek, away from the fields of corn, their
tassels spraying out pollen in the wind, to the time his son Tom got trapped
inside the corn bin, or to his own wedding day in the Presbyterian church next
to the Interstate Building, the gladiolas around the pulpit from his mother-in-
law's garden.

"Here's your bill," the waitress at the Village Inn says, ripping a piece of green paper from her pad. "No hurry, though. I'm just getting organized for the dinner crowd."

But it's time for us to be going if we're to stop and visit with Leroy Nelson, so we gather our money and equipment up and go to the register to pay, stopping to chat for a few more minutes with the Bricelyn crowd. Then we're rolling down Main Street, through Winnebago, and on to Highway 169. The day is just cooling down and the rising wind rushes through the truck and whisks the maps off the dash. We roll the windows up partway, our skin unbracing in the moist evening after an hour of air conditioning.

A half hour later we're driving through Bricelyn's downtown. A few children ride bicycles up and down the sidewalk, on the east. And one block of boarded-up buildings stands on the west. There's a beauty shop, Maureen's Curling Corner, a lumberyard, a post office of blond brick with an American flag flapping out front, and a pink stucco veterinary office. But Regis Implement has gone out of business, as have the Variety Store, the grocery store, and the filling station at the end of the block. Bricelyn is clearly on its way down, and yet when we get out of the truck and walk over to the park to inspect Harold Beckman's petunia planter, we wonder if its citizens see the town the way we do. A new flower planter and a row of three-foot Austrian pines are the town's way of throwing a line out to the future. And the past is still present also, surfacing whenever anybody looks at Maureen's Curling Corner and remembers Trudy Oster, the first owner, with her tight blond curls, her rose-red Revlon shaping her lips into a heart, and her stories, told while her fingers wound the plastic rollers up the women's hair, then repeated by her customers at the supper table that night, and again over the backyard cannas the following afternoon.

In years to come, the stories in Bricelyn will likely be about Harold Beckman, and how the former canning-plant manager finished his life beautifying the town. And Harold Golly's descendants are likely to tell stories about how he combined until he was ninety years old, driving the machine one fall for twelve days straight. With their stories, the people of south-central Minnesota live in a fluid time and place, which allows them to see through boarded-up buildings to their future city park, splashed pink and red with petunias and set off by a grove of fifty-foot Austrian pines, their needles glossy, their dark gray bark cracked into deep hollows. It allows their worlds to be peopled not only by their husbands and wives, children and grandchildren, but also by the hired hand who lived on the farm twenty years earlier, or by an elementary-school friend who went off to live in the Twin Cities. And it allows their space to expand, almost indefinitely, to encompass their daughter's farm, three miles away, where their granddaughter is riding her bike up and down the gravel drive, to encompass even Japan, home of the exchange student who lived with their son the past year and graduated from Winnebago High School that spring.

Harold Golly and his friends live a kind of paradox. They are people of   65
few words and gestures, their speech like the act of shucking peas, as they slip
their planters' thumbs up the pod until four or five peas pop out. But many of
them are also tellers of stories, twentieth-century bards, who feel equally at
home with grander gestures—harvesting one thousand bushels of corn in one
day, or inviting you into their homes for lemonade and an afternoon of stories, which can lead you anywhere, from the creek running along the farm to
the hailstorm of 1907. Tall tales, if you didn't know them to be true. These are
Harold Golly and his friends' conversation. Their form of recreation. They are
what enables them to make it through the hail and the rain, the cancer and the
senility, the bankruptcy and repossession. They are their blessing.

Considerations

1. The first story the two authors hear at the Village Inn Café in Winnebago concerns the sale of a farm, which takes place over several months. This
does not seem to be a long time by local standards. What gives local people their
sense of time? What kind of rhythm do they seem to follow in their daily lives?

2. The authors set the opening scene of their essay at the Village Inn and
return to it frequently throughout the essay. What role does the setting play in
helping the authors tell the story of the sale of the farm? Why do they switch
back and forth between the story about the farm and the story about the
people in the café talking about gardening?

3. As they describe life in two small midwestern towns, the authors examine the forces that create a sense of community. From their comments, what conditions do you think Staw and Swander would say must be present to create a
sense of community? What conditions do they imply might weaken it?

Invitation to Write

The beauty of the landscape and the gentleness of the people make the midwestern towns described by Staw and Swander seem especially attractive. Although the authors speak exclusively in positive terms, this celebrated way of
life is not without a downside. Reread the text and try to pinpoint what the
negative aspects of the farmers' lives might be. Look, for instance, at the way
women are treated, or try to imagine how such a community would react to
an immigrant or minority presence. What is the relation between the positive
and the negative aspects of this kind of life? Write an essay in which you
outline the characteristics of community life in the midwestern towns described by Staw and Swander. Develop a general concept of community based
on Staw and Swander's text, and explain its positive and negative aspects.

Connections

Since Staw and Swander and William Least Heat-Moon are writing about small towns in the Midwest, it is not surprising that the two essays focus on such similar images of community life as, for instance, the downtown café, where people gather to talk. However, in Least Heat-Moon's *Emma Chase* (p. 282), the café is run by a "radical feminist" who has just returned to town, and Staw and Swander's café is run by a longtime inhabitant of the community. How does this difference affect the atmosphere and the conversations that take place in the two cafés? Write an essay in which you compare the perception of community life by the people belonging to the community and an outsider's perceptions. Consider the differences between Linda Thurston's perspective and the Winnebago inhabitants' perspective. Decide which perspective gives a better sense of the place talked about.

Deborah Tannen

Damned If You Do

Born in 1945, Deborah Tannen is the author of many scholarly works on linguistics, including *Talking Voices: Repetition, Dialogue, and Imagery in Conversational Discourse* (1989), *Spoken and Written Language: Exploring Orality and Literacy* (1982), *Lilika Nakos* (1983), and *Conversational Style: Analyzing Talk Among Friends* (1984). She has also published two best-selling books on linguistics for a more general audience: *That's Not What I Meant: How Conversational Style Makes or Breaks Your Relationships* (1986) and *You Just Don't Understand: Women and Men in Conversation* (1990). Her articles on linguistics have appeared in the *New York Times*, *New York* magazine, the *Washington Post*, the *Boston Globe*, and *McCall's*. She has made television appearances on "Today," "Donahue," "Oprah," and "The McLaughlin Group." Currently a professor of linguistics at Georgetown University, Tannen has received grants from the National Endowment for the Humanities, the Rockefeller Foundation, and the National Science Foundation.

You Just Don't Understand examines the patterns of language use according to gender and the difficulties resulting from the stylistic differences between men's and women's speech. Tannen adopts a sociolinguistic approach, which considers language within the social context of its usage. According to the sociolinguistic theory of language, success of communication depends not only on a correct decoding of the message but also on familiarity with cultural and social contexts, patterns of behavior, and gender-determined attitudes. "Damned If You Do" occupies a special place in Tannen's book, as it reveals the way communication is hindered by prejudices against women.

Morton, a psychologist on the staff of a private clinic, has a problem with the clinic director, Roberta. At staff meetings, Roberta generally opens discussion of issues by asking all staff members for their opinions. She invites debate about the pros and cons of proposals, but somehow, when the meeting ends, they always end up deciding—by consensus—to do what Roberta thinks best. The women on the staff are happy with Roberta as a director.

495

They feel she listens to their points of view, and they like the rule by consensus rather than fiat. But Morton feels Roberta is manipulative. If they are going to do what she wants anyway, why does she make them waste their breath expressing opinions? He would prefer she just lay down the law, since she is the boss.

Morton's impression that Roberta does not act like a boss is the result of style differences. She *is* acting like a boss—a woman boss. She prefers to rule by consensus, and the women on her staff like it that way. But he is frustrated by her indirectness; he thinks she should rule by fiat.

Style differences may also be partly responsible for the observation that some women who have achieved high status or positions of authority do not behave in ways appropriate to their positions. But there may be another factor at work too. Since Matina Horner's pioneering research, many psychologists have observed that women seem to fear success. Again, the research on children's play sheds light.

Take Marjorie Harness Goodwin's research on verbal routines by which the preteen and teenage girls in her study criticized each other behind their backs. Significantly, and sadly, the examples Goodwin mentions are based on success: Girls are criticized for appearing better than the others in the group. Of two disputes that Goodwin describes, one girl's offense was to skip a grade in school and get straight A's on her report card; the other girl incurred the wrath of her peers by wearing newer and more expensive clothes than they.

In my own study of videotaped conversations among friends, a similar 5
complaint is lodged by the sixth-grade girls against another girl:

Shannon: She's gotta wear a Polo every *day.*
Julia: I know, well I like *Polo,* but *God*!
Shannon: Every *day!*?
Julia: Really!
Shannon: Just think how much—and sh-she's putting herself *up.*

Appearing better than others is a violation of the girls' egalitarian ethic: People are supposed to stress their connections and similarity.

In light of these and many other studies of girls' real conversations, it is no wonder that girls fear rejection by their peers if they appear too successful and boys don't. Boys, from the earliest age, learn that they can get what they want—higher status—by displaying superiority. Girls learn that displaying superiority will not get them what they want—affiliation with their peers. For this, they have to appear the same as, not better than, their friends.

The appearance of similarity does not mean actual sameness. Penelope Eckert, who spent several years with high school students in a midwestern city, explains how complex the girls' system of masked status can be. For example, the popular girls are the ones who must determine when to switch from the clothes of one season to the clothes of the next—for example, from winter to spring clothing. If less popular girls show up wearing cotton clothes while the popular girls are still wearing wool, they have committed a gaffe, shown themselves to be outsiders. If they switch after the popular girls have appeared in cotton, they mark themselves as followers, limited to public information. The goal is to dress in unison: If they make the switch on the same day as the popular girls, they are gloriously the same—and have subtly proven that they are in the know.

Never Boast or Brag

Another aspect of the pressure on girls not to appear better than their peers is the injunction not to boast. Gender differences in attitudes toward boasting are the cause of much mutual judgment and misjudgment between women and men—and some odd verbal behavior on the part of women.

For example, a college student named Connie was telling her friends that a high school adviser had tried to talk her out of applying to the college they were all now attending. The adviser had felt that Connie's applying would hurt the chances of another girl from the same high school, Sylvia. In explaining the adviser's thinking, Connie said, "Sylvia's grades weren't—I mean—it sounds so pompous of me, but Sylvia's grades weren't as good as mine." Connie could barely bring herself to make a simple factual statement about her grades, because it smacked of boasting.

Margaret and Charles are both successful lawyers. Though they get along 10 perfectly well when alone, they occasionally find themselves arguing after dinner engagements with new acquaintances, especially people who have status and connections in tax law, Charles's specialty. Margaret feels that Charles boasts: He lets it be known how important he is by mentioning recognition he has received, cases he has won, and important people he knows (in Margaret's view, name-dropping). In his eagerness to impress, he sometimes embellishes what he has done and implies that he knows people he has actually met only once or twice. For her part, Margaret tries to hide her success. She deliberately avoids letting on if she knows important people whose names arise in the conversation, and she never alludes to her many accomplishments.

Charles is as frustrated by Margaret's behavior as she is by his. If she will not let on how important she is, he does it for her. This upsets her even more. She feels his boasting for her is as impolite as her doing it herself, and all the alternatives she can imagine are unappealing: She can ignore or disrupt Charles's attempts to speak for her, which seems rude to him and violates what she feels is an obligation to support him; she can let him talk for her, which frames her as a child who cannot speak for herself; or she can participate, and speak in a way she does not want to speak—boasting.

Margaret feels people will not like her if she boasts; she would rather they learn from others how successful she is, and she feels they will approve of her modesty when they do. She also fears people will not like Charles if he boasts, and this is upsetting to her because she is affiliated with Charles, so what people think of him is a reflection on her. Charles, on the other hand, feels that people will not respect him unless he lets them know he merits respect. He also feels they will respect Margaret more if they know that she is an accomplished attorney, not just his wife.

Both Margaret and Charles judge each other's ways of talking in terms of personality characteristics—and each also places moral value on style. Margaret assumes that a good person is modest and self-effacing. Charles considers displaying accomplishments to be a requirement, not a liability, and he regards Margaret's (to him, false) modesty as foolishly self-denigrating, evidence of insecurity. Each one thinks he or she is simply expecting the other to be a good person, but their definitions of a good person vary because of the differing expectations for a good girl and a good boy.

The reluctance of girls and women to boast in certain situations shows up in two strikingly similar examples that I encountered in vastly different contexts. Ingmar Bergman's *Scenes from a Marriage* opens with a couple being interviewed for a magazine by a woman named Mrs. Palm. Marianne and Johan respond very differently to Mrs. Palm's question "How would you describe yourselves in a few words?" This is Johan's answer:

> It might sound conceited if I described myself as extremely intelligent, successful, youthful, well-balanced, and sexy. A man with a world conscience, cultivated, well-read, popular, and a good mixer. Let me see, what else can I think of . . . friendly. Friendly in a nice way even to people who are worse off. I like sports. I'm a good family man. A good son. I have no debts and I pay my taxes. I respect our government whatever it does, and I love our royal family. I've left the state church. Is this enough or do you want more details? I'm a splendid lover. Aren't I, Marianne?

This is Marianne's answer:

> Hmm, what can I say . . . I'm married to Johan and have two daughters.

Even with prodding Marianne doesn't add much information:

> *Marianne:* That's all I can think of for the moment.
> *Mrs. Palm:* There must be something . . .
> *Marianne:* I think Johan is rather nice.
> *Johan:* Kind of you, I'm sure.
> *Marianne:* We've been married for ten years.
> *Johan:* I've just renewed the contract.
> *Marianne:* I doubt if I have the same natural appreciation of my own

excellence as Johan. But to tell the truth, I'm glad I can live the life I do. It's a good life, if you know what I mean. Well, what else can I say . . . Oh dear, this is difficult!

Johan: She has a nice figure.

Marianne: You're joking. I'm trying to take this thing seriously. I have two daughters, Karin and Eva.

Johan: You've already said that.

I was reminded of this fictional conversation when I read the following   15
real-life dialogue in Carol Gilligan's *In a Different Voice.* As part of her research exploring children's moral development, Gilligan interviewed two
eleven-year-old children named Amy and Jake. Among the questions she
asked them was "How would you describe yourself to yourself?" I heard loud
echoes of Johan and Marianne in Jake's and Amy's responses. First, here is
how Jake answered:

Perfect. That's my conceited side. What do you want—any way that
I choose to describe myself? (*Interviewer: If you had to describe the
person you are in a way that you yourself would know it was you,
what would you say?*) I'd start off with eleven years old. Jake [last
name]. I'd have to add that I live in [town], because that is a big part
of me, and also that my father is a doctor, because I think that does
change me a little bit, and that I don't believe in crime, except for
when your name is Heinz [a reference to a previous question Jake
was asked]; that I think school is boring, because I think that kind of
changes your character a little bit. I don't sort of know how to describe myself, because I don't know how to read my personality. (*If
you had to describe the way you actually would describe yourself,
what would you say?*) I like corny jokes. I don't really like to get
down to work, but I can do all the stuff in school. Every single problem that I have seen in school I have been able to do, except for ones
that take knowledge, and after I do the reading, I have been able to
do them, but sometimes I don't want to waste my time on easy homework. And also I'm crazy about sports. I think, unlike a lot of people,
that the world still has hope . . . Most people that I know I like, and
I have the good life, pretty much as good as any I have seen, and I am
tall for my age.

This is how the girl, Amy, answered the question:

You mean my character? (*What do you think?*) Well, I don't know.
I'd describe myself as, well, what do you mean? (*If you had to describe the person you are in a way that you yourself would know it
was you, what would you say?*) Well, I'd say that I was someone who
likes school and studying, and that's what I want to do with my life.

I want to be some kind of a scientist or something, and I want to do things, and I want to help people. And I think that's what kind of person I am, or what kind of person I try to be. And that's probably how I'd describe myself. And I want to do something to help other people. (*Why is that?*) Well, because I think that this world has a lot of problems, and I think that everybody should try to help somebody else in some way, and the way I'm choosing is through science.

What struck me about these two children's answers to the same question was, first, how much longer Jake's was (and I assume the ellipsis after "hope" indicates even more words are omitted), and how boastful it was—in contrast to Amy's statement, which was not boastful at all. Jake says he's perfect, his father is a doctor, he can solve "every single problem" at school even though he finds school boring, he has the best life he has seen, and he's tall. It is possible that his comment "sometimes I don't want to waste my time on easy homework" might be a defense of less-than-superior achievement at school. In contrast, Amy says she likes school and studying but doesn't say if she does well at it, and that she wants to help people through science.

Both Johan in Bergman's screenplay and Jake in Gilligan's interview are aware that they sound "conceited" and make a joke of it. Indeed, Johan's entire answer seems tongue-in-cheek, like his comments interspersed in Marianne's answer. But Johan and Jake say what they do nonetheless. Though Amy has a bit more to say than Marianne, it isn't that much more. Both Amy and Marianne repeat themselves rather than fulfill the request in a way that might sound like bragging. Marianne does not mention that she is a lawyer. Amy says she plans to be a scientist, but she emphasizes that her purpose will be to help others rather than to achieve money, fame, or status.

Women's feelings that they should not boast come from explicit training as well as peer pressure in childhood. Such training is described in the alumnae newsletter of one of the most academically challenging girls' high schools in the country. In this newsletter a woman wrote an epitaph to her sister, who had been the very top student in her graduating class and who had recently died. A brilliant woman, her sister had had a moderately successful career that did not reflect her spectacular ability. The writer comments that her sister "took too much to heart her mother's admonitions: Stay in the background; never brag; always do your best."

These examples demonstrate that women are expected not to boast in relatively public situations, but it would be misleading to imply that women never boast at all. I return to the couple I dubbed Margaret and Charles for an example of a context in which she boasted but he felt he would not have. In the situation described earlier, Margaret felt Charles should not "show off" to new acquaintances. On another occasion, Charles felt that Margaret was inappropriately boasting. In complaining to close friends that she had not been promoted to partner as quickly as men in her firm who had brought in much less business and had far fewer billable hours, Margaret enumerated her early successes. Charles told her later that he thought this had been insensitive, since one of their listening friends was a young lawyer who was not advancing quickly at all. To Charles, self-aggrandizing information is to be used in public to achieve status, appropriately displayed when first meeting people or with people who have, or seem to be claiming, superior status. But to Margaret, self-aggrandizing information is to be used only in private, appropriately revealed in rapport-talk—conversations with people she knows and trusts, who will not judge her for her pride. When dealing with close friends, she forgets about their relative status—an aspect of relationships that Charles never forgets.

The different lenses of status and connection may once more work against women. Women are reluctant to display their achievements in public in order to be likable, but regarded through the lens of status, they are systematically underestimated, and thought self-deprecating and insecure. It is tempting to recommend that women learn to display their accomplishments in public, to ensure that they receive the respect they have earned. Unfortunately, however, women are judged by the standards of women's behavior.

This was evident, for example, at a faculty meeting devoted to promotions, at which a woman professor's success was described: She was extremely well published and well known in the field. A man commented with approval, "She wears it well." In other words, she was praised for not acting as successful as she was. By implication, if she had acted in a way consonant with her achievement, she would not have been praised—and perhaps would not have been liked.

His Politeness Is Her Powerlessness

There are many kinds of evidence that women and men are judged differently even if they talk the same way. This tendency makes mischief in discussions of women, men, and power. If a linguistic strategy is used by a woman, it is seen as powerless; if it is done by a man, it is seen as powerful. Often, the labeling of "women's language" as "powerless language" reflects the view of women's behavior through the lens of men's.

Because they are not struggling to be one-up, women often find themselves framed as one-down. Any situation is ripe for misinterpretation, because status and connections are displayed by the same moves. This ambiguity accounts for much misinterpretation, by experts as well as nonexperts, by which women's ways of talking, uttered in a spirit of rapport, are branded powerless. Nowhere is this inherent ambiguity clearer than in a brief comment in a newspaper article in which a couple, both psychologists, were jointly interviewed. The journalist asked them the meaning of "being very polite." The two experts responded simultaneously, giving different answers. The man said, "Subservience." The woman said, "Sensitivity." Both experts were right, but each was describing the view of a different gender.

Experts and nonexperts alike tend to see anything women do as evidence of powerlessness. The same newspaper article quotes another psychologist as saying, "A man might ask a woman, 'Will you please go to the store?' where a woman might say, 'Gee, I really need a few things from the store, but I'm so tired.'" The woman's style is called "covert," a term suggesting negative qualities like being "sneaky" and "underhanded." The reason offered for this is power: The woman doesn't feel she has a right to ask directly.

Granted, women have lower status than men in our society. But this is not necessarily why they prefer not to make outright demands. The explanation for a woman's indirectness could just as well be her seeking connection. If you get your way as a result of having demanded it, the payoff is satisfying in terms of status: You're one-up because others are doing as you told them. But if you get your way because others happened to want the same thing, or because they offered freely, the payoff is in rapport. You're neither one-up nor one-down but happily connected to others whose wants are the same as yours. Furthermore, if indirectness is understood by both parties, then there is nothing covert about it: That a request is being made is clear. Calling an indirect communication covert reflects the view of someone for whom the direct style seems "natural" and "logical"—a view more common among men.

Indirectness itself does not reflect powerlessness. It is easy to think of situations where indirectness is the prerogative of those in power. For example, a wealthy couple who know that their servants will do their bidding need not give direct orders, but can simply state wishes: The woman of the house says, "It's chilly in here," and the servant sets about raising the temperature. The man of the house says, "It's dinner time," and the servant sees about having dinner served. Perhaps the ultimate indirectness is getting someone to do something without saying anything at all: The hostess rings a bell and the maid brings the next course; or a parent enters the room where children are misbehaving and stands with hands on hips, and the children immediately stop what they're doing.

Entire cultures operate on elaborate systems of indirectness. For example, I discovered in a small research project that most Greeks assumed that a wife who asked, "Would you like to go to the party?" was hinting that she wanted to go. They felt that she wouldn't bring it up if she didn't want to go. Furthermore, they felt, she would not state her preference outright because that would sound like a demand. Indirectness was the appropriate means for communicating her preference.

Japanese culture has developed indirectness to a fine art. For example, a

Japanese anthropologist, Harumi Befu, explains the delicate exchange of indirectness required by a simple invitation to lunch. When her friend extended the invitation, Befu first had to determine whether it was meant literally or just *pro forma,* much as an American might say, "We'll have to have you over for dinner some time" but would not expect you to turn up at the door. Having decided the invitation was meant literally and having accepted, Befu was then asked what she would like to eat. Following custom, she said anything would do, but her friend, also following custom, pressed her to specify. Host and guest repeated this exchange an appropriate number of times, until Befu deemed it polite to answer the question—politely—by saying that tea over rice would be fine. When she arrived for lunch, she was indeed served tea over rice—as the last course of a sumptuous meal. Befu was not surprised by the feast, because she knew that protocol required it. Had she been given what she had asked for, she would have been insulted. But protocol also required that she make a great show of being surprised.

This account of mutual indirectness in a lunch invitation may strike Americans as excessive. But far more cultures in the world use elaborate systems of indirectness than value directness. Only modern Western societies place a priority on direct communication, and even for us it is more a value than a practice.

Evidence from other cultures also makes it clear that indirectness does not in itself reflect low status. Rather, our assumptions about the status of women compel us to interpret anything they do as reflecting low status. Anthropologist Elinor Keenan, for example, found that in a Malagasy-speaking village on the island of Madagascar, it is women who are direct and men who are indirect. And the villagers see the men's indirect way of speaking, using metaphors and proverbs, as the better way. For them, indirectness, like the men who use it, has high status. They regard women's direct style as clumsy and crude, debasing the beautiful subtlety of men's language. Whether women or men are direct or indirect differs; what remains constant is that the women's style is negatively evaluated—seen as lower in status than the men's.

It's Different Coming from a Man

Research from our own culture provides many examples of the same behavior being interpreted differently depending on whether it's done by women or men. Take, for example, the case of "tag questions"—statements with little questions added onto the end, as in "It's a nice day, isn't it?" Linguist Robin Lakoff first pointed out that many women use more tag questions than men. Though studies seeking to test Lakoff's observation have had somewhat mixed results, most support it. Jacqueline Sachs, observing the language of children as young as two to five, found that girls used more than twice as many tag questions as boys. And research has shown that people *expect* women to use tags. Psychologists David and Robert Siegler conducted an experiment asking adults to guess the sex of speakers. Sure enough, the stereotype held: Subjects guessed a woman was speaking when tags were used, a man when they weren't. The stereotype can actually be more compelling than reality: In another experiment, psychologists Nora Newcombe and Diane Arnkoff presented adults with communications in which women and men used equal numbers of tag questions, and found that their subjects thought the women had used more.

Most troubling of all, women and men are judged differently even if they speak the same way. Communications researcher Patricia Hayes Bradley found that when women used tag questions and disclaimers, subjects judged them as less intelligent and knowledgeable *than men who also used them.* When women did not give support for their arguments, they were judged less intelligent and knowledgeable, *but men who advanced arguments without support were not.* In other words, talking in ways that are associated with women causes women to be judged negatively, but talking the same way does not have this effect on men. So it is not the ways of talking that are having the effect so much as people's attitudes toward women and men.

Many other studies have similar results. Psychologists John and Sandra Condry asked subjects to interpret why an infant was crying. If they had been told the baby was a boy, subjects thought he was angry, but if they had been told it was a girl, they thought she was afraid. Anne Macke and Laurel Richardson, with Judith Cook, discovered that when students judged professors, generating more class discussion was taken to be a sign of incompetence—only if the professor was female.

Silence Is Golden—or Leaden

Research itself has fallen prey to this double standard. In studies claiming that men exert power by talking more than women, women's silence is cited as evidence that they have no power. At the same time, other studies claim that men's use of silence and refusing to speak is a show of their power. A theme running through Mirra Komarovsky's classic study *Blue Collar Marriage* is that many of the wives interviewed said they talked more than their husbands ("He's tongue-tied," one woman said of her husband; "My husband has a great habit of not talking," said another). More of the wives want to talk, and have their husbands talk, about problems. In contrast, more husbands withdraw in the face of troubles ("When I don't feel good, I light out and don't dump my load on them"), emotional stress, or a wife's "demands." Yet there is no question but that these husbands are "dominant" in their marriages. Taciturnity itself can be an instrument of power. Komarovsky quotes a mother who says of her husband, "He doesn't say much but he means what he says and the children mind him."

Jack Sattel believes men use silence to exercise power over women, and he illustrates with the following scene from Erica Jong's novel *Fear of Flying*. The first line of dialogue is spoken by Isadora, the second by her husband, Bennett.

"Why do you always have to do this to me? You make me feel so lonely.

"That comes from you."

"What do you mean it comes from me? Tonight I wanted to be happy. It's Christmas Eve. Why do you turn on me? What did I do?"

Silence.

"What did I do?"

He looks at her as if her not knowing were another injury.

"Look, let's just go to sleep now. Let's just forget it."

Forget what?"

He says nothing.

"Forget the fact that you turned on me? Forget the fact that you're punishing me for nothing? Forget the fact that I'm lonely and cold, that it's Christmas Eve and again you've ruined it for me? Is that what you want me to forget?"

"I won't discuss it."

"Discuss what? *What* won't you discuss?"

"Shut up! I won't have you screaming in the hotel."

"I don't give a fuck what you won't have me do. I'd like to be treated civilly. I'd like you to at least do me the courtesy of telling me why you're in such a funk. And don't look at me that way . . ."

"What way?"

"As if my not being able to read your mind were my greatest sin. I *can't* read your mind. I *don't* know why you're so mad. I *can't* intuit your every wish. If that's what you want in a wife you don't have it in me."

"I certainly don't."

"Then what is it? Please tell me."

"I shouldn't have to."

"Good God! Do you mean to tell me I'm expected to be a mind reader? Is that the kind of mothering you want?"

"If you had any empathy for me . . ."

"But I *do*. My God, you don't give me a chance."

"You tune out. You don't listen."

"It was something in the movie, wasn't it?"

"What, in the movie?"

"The quiz again. Do you have to quiz me like some kind of criminal? Do you have to *cross-examine* me? . . . It was the funeral scene. . . . The little boy looking at his dead mother. Something got you there. That was when you got depressed."

Silence.

"Well, *wasn't* it?"

Silence.

"Oh come on, Bennett, you're making me *furious*. Please tell me. Please."

(He gives the words singly like little gifts. Like hard little turds.) "What was it about that scene that got me?"

"Don't quiz me. Tell me! (She puts her arms around him. He pulls away. She falls to the floor holding onto his pajama leg. It looks less like an embrace than like a rescue scene, she sinking, he reluctantly allowing her to cling to his leg for support.)

"Get up!"

(Crying) "Only if you tell me."

(He jerks his leg away.) "I'm going to bed."

This painful scene does seem to support Sattel's claim that Bennett uses silence as a weapon against his wife. Each successive refusal to tell her what's bothering him is like a blow laying her lower and lower—until she is literally on the floor. But would our interpretation change if we reversed the genders in this scene?

With genders reversed, the scene seems impossible. It is hard to imagine a 35 man begging his wife to tell him what he did wrong. What leaped to my mind, when I tried to reverse genders, was a scene in which the man withdraws, disabling her silence as a weapon. What makes Bennett's silence so punishing is Isadora's insistence on making him talk to her. It is the interaction of the two styles—his withdrawal and her insistence that he tell her what she did wrong—that is devastating to both. If Bennett shared Isadora's belief that problems should be talked out, or she shared his practice of withdrawing when problems arise, they would not have found themselves in this devastating scene.

"I'm Sorry, I'm Not Apologizing"

There are many ways that women talk that make sense and are effective in conversations with women but appear powerless and self-deprecating in conversations with men. One such pattern is that many women seem to apologize all the time. An apology is a move that frames the apologizer as one-down. This might seem obvious. But the following example shows that an apparent apology may not be intended in that spirit at all.

A teacher was having trouble with a student widely known to be incorrigible. Finally, she sent the boy to the principal's office. Later the principal approached her in the teachers' lounge and told her the student had been suspended. The teacher replied, "I'm sorry," and the principal reassured her, "It's not your fault." The teacher was taken aback by the principal's reassurance, because it had not occurred to her that the student's suspension might be her fault until he said it. To her, "I'm sorry" did not mean "I apologize"; it meant "I'm sorry to hear that." "I'm sorry" was intended to establish a connection to the principal by implying, "I know you must feel bad about this; I do too." She was framing herself as connected to him by similar feelings. By interpreting her words of shared feeling as an apology, the principal introduced the notion that she might be at fault, and framed himself as one-up, in a position to absolve her of guilt.

The continuation of this story indicates that these different points of view may be associated with gender. When this teacher told her grown daughter about the incident, the daughter agreed that the principal's reaction had been strange. But when she told her son and husband, they upbraided her for apologizing when she had not been at fault. They too interpreted "I'm sorry" as an apology.

There are several dynamics that make women appear to apologize too much. For one thing, women may be more likely to apologize because they do not instinctively balk at risking a one-down position. This is not to say that they relish it, just that it is less likely to set off automatic alarms in their heads. Yet another factor is that women are heard as apologizing when they do not intend to do so. Women frequently say "I'm sorry" to express sympathy and concern, not apology.

This confusion is rooted in the double meaning of the word *sorry*. This double meaning is highlighted in the following anecdote. A twelve-year-old Japanese girl living in the United States was writing a letter of condolence to her grandmother in Japan because her grandfather had died. The girl was writing in Japanese, but she was more accustomed to English. She began in the appropriate way: "I'm so sorry that Grandfather died." But then she stopped and looked at what she had written. "That doesn't sound right," she said to her mother. "I didn't kill him." Because she was writing in a language that was not second nature to her, this girl realized that an expression most people use automatically had a different meaning when interpreted literally. "I'm sorry," used figuratively to express regret, could be interpreted literally to mean "I apologize."

The difference between ritual and literal uses of language is also at play in the following example. A businesswoman named Beverly returned from an out-of-town trip to find a phone message on her answering machine from her division head. The message explained that he had found an enormous number of errors in a report written by her assistant. He told her that he had indicated the errors, returned the report to the assistant, and arranged for the deadline to be extended while she typed in the corrections. Beverly was surprised, since she had read and approved the report before leaving on vacation, but she said, "I'm sorry"—and was offended when he said, "I'm not blaming anyone." This seemed to imply that he *was* blaming her, since he introduced the idea.

"Please Don't Accept My Apology"

Beverly asked her assistant to show her the lengthy corrected report and became angry when she saw that half the pages had "errors" marked, but few were actually errors. Nearly all involved punctuation, and most were matters of stylistic preference, such as adding commas after brief introductory phrases or before the conjunction and. In a large number of cases, she felt that her division head had introduced punctuation errors into sentences that were grammatically correct as they stood.

Later that day she encountered the division head at an office party and announced as soon as she saw him that she was angry at him and told him why. She realized by his reaction that she had offended his sensibilities by raising the matter in front of someone else. She immediately apologized for having blurted out her anger rather than expressing it more diplomatically, and she later visited him in his office to apologize again. She was sure that if she apologized for having confronted him in the wrong way at the wrong time, he would counterapologize for having overcorrected the report and for going directly to the assistant instead of through her. Instead, he generously said, "I accept your apology," and affably changed the subject to office politics.

Now accepting an apology is arguably quite rude. From the point of view of connection, an apology should be matched. And from the perspective of status, an apology should be deflected. In this view, a person who apologizes takes a one-down position, and accepting the apology preserves that asymmetry, whereas deflecting the apology restores balance. Although she felt immediately uncomfortable, Beverly did not realize until after she had left the office, all smiles and goodwill, that not only had her division head rudely accepted her apology, but he had not offered a balancing one.

Women's and men's differential awareness of status may have been the cause of Beverly's problem in a more fundamental way too. She felt quite friendly with her division head; she liked him; she had come to think of him as a friend. For her, as for many women, being friends means downplaying if not obliterating status differences. When she blurted out her anger, she was not thinking of herself as upbraiding a superior in front of others. To the extent that he remained aware of the difference in their status despite their friendly relationship, to accept her criticism would have amounted to public humiliation. Had she focused on their status differ-

45

ences rather than their friendship, she would not have approached him as she did. She would not, for example, have taken that tack with the company president.

Women Adapt to Men's Norms

In all these examples, the styles more typical of men are generally evaluated more positively and are taken as the norm. In a related and perhaps even more distressing asymmetry, when women and men are in groups together, the very games they play are more likely to be men's games than women's.

In Ursula Le Guin's story "In and Out," a former secretary recalls an all-women meeting:

> Like when the group of secretaries met to plan a meeting to talk about women in the city government, and the meeting had been so terrific, people saying things they didn't even know they thought, and ideas coming up, and nobody pushing anybody around.

By implication, an interchange in which people got to say what they were thinking and nobody was pushing anybody around was not the norm for meetings she had participated in or observed, but a quality that distinguished this meeting, in which only women participated.

A professor commented on how pleasant she found it to work on all-women committees, as compared to the mixed-gender committees she was more used to. But when she made this observation at a mixed-gender dinner party, a man strenuously objected. He said he had noticed no difference between all-male committees and those that included women. This man was surely telling the truth as he experienced it, because when women and men get together they interact according to men's, not women's, norms. So being in a mixed rather than a same-gender meeting makes less difference to men than to women.

Research in a range of disciplines shows that women make more adjustments than men in mixed groups. Elizabeth Aries found, in comparing the body postures of young men and women in all-male, all-female, and mixed discussion groups, that the men sat more or less the same way whether or not there were women present: They sprawled out in "relaxed" positions, taking up a large amount of space around them. The women in her study, however, drew themselves in, assuming "ladylike" postures, when there were men in the group, but relaxed and sprawled out when there weren't. In other words, the men took the same physical positions whether or not there were women present, but the women seemed to feel they were onstage when men were there, backstage when they found themselves with women only.

A similar point emerges from a study by Alice Deakins of the topics that women and men talk about. Deakins did what is called an eavesdropping 50 study: While seated alone in a dining room where bank officers had lunch, she noted what people at adjacent tables were talking about. This was not a situation where the men were executives and the women their wives and secretaries. The men and women in Deakins's study were all bank officers, meeting as equals at work. Deakins found that when there were no women present, the men talked mostly about business and never about people, not even people at work. Their next most often discussed topic was food. Another common topic was sports and recreation. When women talked alone, their most frequent topic was people—not people at work so much as friends, children, and partners in personal relationships. The women discussed business next, and third, health, which included weight control.

When women and men got together, they tended to avoid the topics that each group liked best and settle on topics of interest to both. But in discussing those topics, *they followed the style of the men alone.* They talked about food the way men did, focusing on the food they were eating and about restaurants rather than diet and health. They talked about recreation the way men did, focusing on sports and vacations rather than exercising for diet or health, as the women did when they were alone. And they talked about housing in the way men did, focusing on location, property values, and commuting time, rather than the way women did, focusing on the interiors of houses (for example, layout and insulation) and what goes on among people inside houses (for example, finding cleaning help).

In analyzing tape recordings of private conversations among teenagers, Deborah Lange found a similar pattern. When the girls were alone, they talked about problems in their relationships with friends; when boys were alone, they talked about activities and plans and made comments about friends. When boys and girls were together, they talked about activities and plans and made comments about friends. In other words, when boys and girls talked together, they talked more or less the way boys talked when there were no girls present. But when girls got together with no boys present, they talked very differently.

All these (and many other) studies show that male-female conversations are more like men's conversations than they are like women's. So when women and men talk to each other, both make adjustments, but the women make more. Women are at a disadvantage in mixed-sex groups, because they have had less practice in conducting conversation the way it is being conducted in these groups. This may help to explain why girls do better at single-sex schools, whereas boys do about the same whether they go to boys' schools or coeducational ones. It may also explain why the women, but not the men, in Aries's study of college discussion groups said they preferred the same-gender group. All of these studies help to answer the question of why women are dissatisfied with communication in their relationships with men, while men who are parties to the same conversations express less dissatisfaction with them.

The talk that takes place at meetings and discussion groups is relatively more public, more like report-talk. Considering their preference for rapport-talk, it is not surprising that many women find it hard to get the floor at meetings, even though many men have a hard time getting the floor in conversations with women who are overlapping to build rapport. One reason many women find it difficult to get and keep the floor at meetings with men is that they won't compete for it. However, this chapter has presented only a few of many studies showing that even when women do behave the same as men, they get different responses. This raises the question of how much women's difficulty in getting heard at meetings results from their ways of talking, and how much from their being women. This question also throws into relief the asymmetry of options available to women and men.

Equal Discrimination

Many women tell of having made a comment at a meeting or conference that 55 is ignored. Later a man makes the same comment and it is picked up, approved or discussed, attributed to him rather than to her. Most women feel that this happens because people are less likely to pay attention to an idea that is raised by a woman, and the studies mentioned above indicate that there is truth to that. But the *way* ideas are raised may be a factor too. The following experience indicates this, but it also indicates that women and men do not have the same options available.

Professor A, a biochemist who teaches at a major university and is well known in his field, told me of the following experience. Having a diffident style, and being timid about speaking in public, he geared up his courage to speak following a public lecture in the biology department. He phrased his observation as a question: "Have you considered this chemical influence on the biological process you just described?" The lecturer responded, in effect, "No, I haven't," and the point was dropped. Soon after, however, another man, Professor B, spoke up. He began, "I would like to return to the point made by my colleague Professor A, because I think it is very important." He then repeated the point in a long-winded way. The idea then became the focus of extended discussion, and everyone who spoke to the issue began by saying, "I'd like to comment further on the important point raised by Professor B."

Had Professor A been a woman, it would have been natural to assume that the idea was first ignored because it was expressed by a woman, and later taken up because it was expressed by a man. But in this case, both speakers were men, so their gender could not have been the cause of the different responses they received. What was different was the way the two men expressed the "same" idea. Perhaps Professor A had not explained his idea in enough detail to allow others to see its importance. More likely, the way he spoke—diffidently, briefly, and phrasing his point as a question—framed his idea as not important, whereas the way Professor B spoke—at length and in a loud, declamatory voice—framed the same idea with a different metamessage: "This is important. Take note!"

This example is important because it sheds light on the role played by *how* people speak, regardless of their gender. But it also shows that women are at a disadvantage, since women are more likely than men to phrase their ideas as questions, take up less time with their questions, and speak at lower volume and higher pitch. The example shows that men who do not use the forceful strategies associated with masculinity are also at a disadvantage. In this sense, Professor A was in the same position as a woman who speaks in the same way.

Unequal Remedies

But in another sense, Professor A's position is very different from that of a woman who has a similar conversational style. If Professor A decided to adjust his style to be more like Professor B's, he would find himself commanding more attention in public, if that is what he wants. And in the process, he would better fit the model of masculinity in our culture. But women who attempt to adjust their styles by speaking louder, longer, and with more self-assertion will also better fit the model of masculinity. They may command more attention and be more respected, but they may also be disliked and disparaged as aggressive and unfeminine.

Indeed, a woman need not be particularly aggressive to be criticized. A   60
professor who invited a prominent woman researcher to speak to his students was shocked to hear some of his students—both female and male—comment later that they had found her arrogant. He had seen nothing arrogant about her at all. She simply hadn't engaged in any of the womanly behavior they had come to expect, such as continually smiling, qualifying her statements, or cocking her head in a charming way.

Ways of talking associated with masculinity are also associated with leadership and authority. But ways of talking that are considered feminine are not. Whatever a man does to enhance his authority also enhances his masculinity. But if a woman adapts her style to a position of authority that she has achieved or to which she aspires, she risks compromising her femininity, in the eyes of others.

As a woman who has achieved a high level of status in my profession, I grapple with this contradiction daily. When I go to academic conferences, I often meet colleagues from other universities who know me only by my scholarly publications and reputation. Not infrequently, new acquaintances say that they are surprised that I am so nice or so feminine. "You're not what I expected," I have repeatedly been told. "You're not aggressive at all." Others have remarked, "I thought you'd be cold," or "hard," or "competitive."

When I press them about why they expected that of me, I am told, "I just figured that any woman who is as successful as you would have to be that way."

Just such assumptions emerge from a study by Harriet Wall and Anita Barry of college students' expectations about male and female professors. The researchers gave students identical materials on prospective professors—information about their academic backgrounds, publications, and letters of recommendation—and asked the students to predict how well the candidates would do if hired, including their chances to win a distinguished teaching award. Some who read the materials under a woman's name predicted that she would not win the award because, as one writer put it, "Too much business, not enough personality." No one made inferences like this when exactly the same "file" was read under a man's name.

Another reason women professors may be judged more harshly than men, Wall and Barry found, is that students expect more of women. Those who thought they were evaluating a woman expected her to be more nurturing and to devote more time to her students outside of class than those who thought they were evaluating a man. The researchers point out that in evaluating real professors, students might have more praise for a male professor than for a female who actually devotes more time to them, because the woman is, after all, just doing what's expected, while the man is doing more than expected. In reading this study, I was, of course, reminded of the graduate student who had called me at home on Sunday because she didn't want to bother her dissertation director at home.

Language Keeps Women in Their Place

Nowhere is the conflict between femininity and authority more crucial than with women in politics. The characteristics of a good man and a good candidate are the same, but a woman has to choose between coming across as a strong leader *or* a good woman. If a man appears forceful, logical, direct, masterful, and powerful, he enhances his value as a man. If a woman appears forceful, logical, direct, masterful, or powerful, she risks undercutting her value as a woman.

As Robin Lakoff shows in *Language and Woman's Place,* language comes at women from two angles: the words they speak, and the words spoken about them. If I wrote, "After delivering the acceptance speech, the candidate fainted," you would know I was talking about a woman. Men do not faint; they pass out. And these terms have vastly different connotations that both reflect and affect our images of women and men. *Fainting* conjures up a frail figure crumpling into a man's rescuing arms, the back of her hand pressed to her forehead—probably for little reason, maybe just for dramatic effect. *Passing out* suggests a straightforward fall to the floor.

An article in *Newsweek* during the 1984 presidential campaign quoted a Reagan aide who called Ferraro "a nasty woman" who would "claw Ronald Reagan's eyes out." Never mind the nastiness of the remark and of the newsmagazine's using it to open its article. Applied to a man, *nasty* would be so tame as to seem harmless. Furthermore, men don't claw; they punch and sock, with correspondingly more forceful results. The verb *claw* both reflects and reinforces the stereotypical metaphor of women as cats. Each time someone uses an expression associated with this metaphor, it reinforces it, suggesting a general "cattiness" in women's character.

Even when seeming to praise Ferraro, the article used terms drenched in gender. She was credited with "a striking gift for tart political rhetoric, needling Ronald Reagan on the fairness issue and twitting the Reagan-Bush campaign for its reluctance to let Bush debate her." If we reversed subject and object, *needling* and *twitting* would not sound like praise for Reagan's verbal ability—or any man's. (I will refrain from commenting on the connotations of *tart*, assuming the word's double meaning was at least consciously unintended.)

In his book *The Language of Politics*, Michael Geis gives several examples of words used to describe Ferraro that undercut her. One headline called her "spunky," another "feisty." As Geis observes, *spunky* and *feisty* are used only for creatures that are small and lacking in real power; they could be said of a Pekingese but not a Great Dane, perhaps of Mickey Rooney but not of John Wayne—in other words, of any average-size woman, but not of an average-size man.

I am sure that the journalists who wrote these descriptions of Ferraro 70 came to praise her, not to bury her. Perhaps they felt they were choosing snappy, eye-catching phrases. But their words bent back and trivialized the vice presidential candidate, highlighting, even if unintentionally, the incongruity between her images as a woman and as a political leader. When we think we are using language, our language is using us.

It's not that journalists, other writers, or everyday speakers are deliberately, or even unintentionally, "sexist" in their use of language. The important point is that gender distinctions are built into language. The words available to us to describe women and men are not the same words. And, most damaging of all, through language, our images and attitudes are buttressed and shaped. Simply by understanding and using the words of our language, we all absorb and pass on different, asymmetrical assumptions about men and women.

Bound by Body Language

Body language is eloquent too. Political candidates necessarily circulate photographs of their families. In the typical family photograph, the candidate looks straight out at the camera, while his wife gazes up at him. This leads the viewer's eye to the candidate as the center of interest. In a well-publicized family photograph, Ferraro was looking up at her husband and he was looking straight out. It is an appealing photo, which shows her as a good woman, but makes him the inappropriate center of interest, just as his finances became the center of interest in candidate Ferraro's financial disclosure. Had the family photograph shown Ferraro looking straight out, with her husband gazing adoringly at her, it would not have been an effective campaign photo, because she would have looked like a domineering wife with a namby-pamby for a husband.

Ironically, it is probably more difficult for a woman to hold a position of authority in a relatively egalitarian society like that of the United States than in more hierarchical ones. An American woman who owned and edited an English-language magazine in Athens told me that when Greeks came to the magazine to do business, as soon as they realized that she was the boss, they focused their attention on her. But if her male assistant editor was in the room, Americans were irresistibly drawn to address themselves to him. It seems that Greeks' sensitivity to the publisher's status overrode their awareness of her gender, but Americans, who are less intimated by status than Greeks, could not rise above their awareness of gender.

Much of this book has shown that women's and men's style differences are symmetrically misleading. Men and women learn to use language in the different worlds of boys and girls, and each group interprets the other's ways of talking in terms of its own. But in many ways, differences between women's and men's styles are not symmetrical. When men and women get together in groups, they are likely to talk in ways more familiar and comfortable to the men. And both women's and men's ways of talking are typically judged by the standards of men's styles, which are regarded as the norm. Most distressing in a society where equality is the agreed-upon goal, and where more and more women are entering high-status positions, women in authority find themselves in a double bind. If they speak in ways expected of women, they are seen as inadequate leaders. If they speak in ways expected of leaders, they are seen as inadequate women. The road to authority is tough for women, and once they get there it's a bed of thorns.

Considerations

1. Tannen opens her essay with an anecdote about the unhappiness of Morton, a staff psychologist. How would you explain Morton's complaints, given the analyses that Tannen presents later on?

2. Tannen often uses the passive voice. For example, she says: "Unfortunately, however, women *are judged* by the standards of women's behavior" (para. 19; emphasis added). Find two or three other examples where Tannen

uses the passive voice to make a general statement. Who or what is the agent implied in the passive voice? Who, for instance, judges the women by the standards of women's behavior?

Invitation to Write

Tannen's focus is linguistics, but her argument has many social and political implications. As the title of the chapter suggests, Tannen is aware of the women's movement and of women's struggle to be recognized as equal partners in American society. That struggle is rooted, in part, in historical notions of gender roles, which were derived from social and economic conditions that are different from our own. In an essay of your own, explore the implicit historical dimension of Tannen's argument. Look at examples in the text that clearly indicate a historical evolution. For instance, the attitudes of the professional couple may be explained by the tradition of marriage where only the husband was employed.

Connections

In Amy Tan's story "Without Wood" (p. 379) the narrator and main character, Rose, declares that whatever her mother said "seemed true to [her]. The power of her words was that strong" (para. 2). Deborah Tannen also gives examples of situations where power is expressed and even obtained through language. Working with examples from Tan's story and Tannen's essay, write an essay in which you explore the connections between power, status, and gender on the one hand and language on the other. Use Tannen's insights into the use of language to analyze and interpret the relationships Rose has with her husband, her mother, and her friends.

ANNIE DILLARD

The Writing Life

Born in 1945, Annie Dillard grew up in Pittsburgh and was educated at Hollins College in Virginia. Books are an important part of her life, as she reveals in her autobiography, *An American Childhood* (1987). Her father's favorite book, *Life on the Mississippi* by Mark Twain, may have inspired him to leave his family and make a six-month voyage down the Ohio River, provoking a small family crisis for his wife and daughters. Dillard has written eight books, including a volume of poetry and a collection of essays, and edited *The Best American Essays 1988*. Her second book, *Pilgrim at Tinker Creek* (1974), written when she was twenty-nine, won a Pulitzer Prize and gained her wide recognition as an important new writer. Since then, she has won many awards for her writing, including a National Endowment for the Arts grant, a Guggenheim Foundation grant, and a National Book Critics Circle Award nomination for her autobiography. She has recently published a novel entitled *The Living* (1992). Dillard is writer in-residence and adjunct professor at Wesleyan University in Connecticut.

Dillard's books are frequently described as "nature writing." She often focuses on apparently insignificant natural phenomena, discussing them in language that reveals not only their significance but also their potential as metaphors for human life. Her attention to detail and her capacity to make surprising revelations are present also in the following selection, which is the first chapter of *The Writing Life*. In this book, Dillard appeals to her readers' imaginations to make them understand how she conceptualizes the writing process.

No one suspects the days to be gods.
—EMERSON

When you write, you lay out a line of words. The line of words is a miner's pick, a wood-carver's gouge, a surgeon's probe. You wield it, and it digs a path you follow. Soon you find yourself deep in new territory. Is it a dead end, or have you located the real subject? You will know tomorrow, or this time next year.

You make the path boldly and follow it fearfully. You go where the path leads. At the end of the path, you find a box canyon. You hammer out reports, dispatch bulletins.

The writing has changed, in your hands, and in a twinkling, from an expression of your notions to an epistemological tool. The new place interests you because it is not clear. You attend. In your humility, you lay down the words carefully, watching all the angles. Now the earlier writing looks soft and careless. Process is nothing; erase your tracks. The path is not the work. I hope your tracks have grown over; I hope birds ate the crumbs; I hope you will toss it all and not look back.

The line of words is a hammer. You hammer against the walls of your house. You tap the walls, lightly, everywhere. After giving many years' attention to these things, you know what to listen for. Some of the walls are bearing walls; they have to stay, or everything will fall down. Other walls can go with impunity; you can hear the difference. Unfortunately, it is often a bearing wall that has to go. It cannot be helped. There is only one solution, which appalls you, but there it is. Knock it out. Duck.

Courage utterly opposes the bold hope that this is such fine stuff the work 5 needs it, or the world. Courage, exhausted, stands on bare reality: This writing weakens the work. You must demolish the work and start over. You can save some of the sentences, like bricks. It will be a miracle if you can save some of the paragraphs, no matter how excellent in themselves or hard-won. You can waste a year worrying about it, or you can get it over with now. (Are you a woman, or a mouse?)

The part you must jettison is not only the best-written part; it is also, oddly, that part which was to have been the very point. It is the original key passage, the passage on which the rest was to hang, and from which you yourself drew the courage to begin. Henry James knew it well, and said it best. In his preface to *The Spoils of Poynton*, he pities the writer, in a comical pair of sentences that rises to a howl: "Which is the work in which he hasn't surrendered, under dire difficulty, the best thing he meant to have kept? In which indeed, before the dreadful *done*, doesn't he ask himself what has become of the thing all for the sweet sake of which it was to proceed to that extremity?"

So it is that a writer writes many books. In each book, he intended several urgent and vivid points, many of which he sacrificed as the book's form hardened. "The youth gets together his materials to build a bridge to the moon," Thoreau noted mournfully, "or perchance a palace or temple on the earth, and at length the middle-aged man concludes to build a wood-shed with them." The writer returns to these materials, these passionate subjects, as to unfinished business, for they are his life's work.

It is the beginning of a work that the writer throws away.

A painting covers its tracks. Painters work from the ground up. The latest version of a painting overlays earlier versions, and obliterates them. Writers, on the other hand, work from left to right. The discardable chapters are on the left. The latest version of a literary work begins somewhere in the work's middle, and hardens toward the end. The earlier version remains lumpishly on the left; the work's beginning greets the reader with the wrong hand. In those early pages and chapters anyone may find bold leaps to nowhere, read the brave beginnings of dropped themes, hear a tone since abandoned, discover blind alleys, track red herrings, and laboriously learn a setting now false.

Several delusions weaken the writer's resolve to throw away work. If he   10
has read his pages too often, those pages will have a necessary quality, the ring of the inevitable, like poetry known by heart; they will perfectly answer their own familiar rhythms. He will retain them. He may retain those pages if they possess some virtues, such as power in themselves, though they lack the cardinal virtue, which is pertinence to, and unity with, the book's thrust. Sometimes the writer leaves his early chapters in place from gratitude; he cannot contemplate them or read them without feeling again the blessed relief that exalted him when the words first appeared—relief that he was writing anything at all. That beginning served to get him where he was going, after all; surely the reader needs it, too, as groundwork. But no.

Every year the aspiring photographer brought a stack of his best prints to an old, honored photographer, seeking his judgment. Every year the old man studied the prints and painstakingly ordered them into two piles, bad and good. Every year the old man moved a certain landscape print into the bad stack. At length he turned to the young man: "You submit this same landscape every year, and every year I put it on the bad stack. Why do you like it so much?" The young photographer said, "Because I had to climb a mountain to get it."

A cabdriver sang his songs to me, in New York. Some we sang together. He had turned the meter off; he drove around midtown, singing. One long song he sang twice; it was the only dull one. I said, You already sang that one; let's sing something else. And he said, "You don't know how long it took me to get that one together."

How many books do we read from which the writer lacked courage to tie off the umbilical cord? How many gifts do we open from which the writer neglected to remove the price tag? Is it pertinent, is it courteous, for us to learn what it cost the writer personally?

You write it all, discovering it at the end of the line of words. The line of words is a fiber optic, flexible as wire; it illumines the path just before its fragile tip. You probe with it, delicate as a worm.

Few sights are so absurd as that of an inchworm leading its dimwit life. Inch-   15
worms are the caterpillar larvae of several moths or butterflies. The cabbage

looper, for example, is an inchworm. I often see an inchworm: It is a skinny bright green thing, pale and thin as a vein, an inch long, and apparently totally unfit for life in this world. It wears out its days in constant panic.

Every inchworm I have seen was stuck in long grasses. The wretched inchworm hangs from the side of a grassblade and throws its head around from side to side, seeming to wail. What! No further? Its back pair of nubby feet clasps the grass stem; its front three pairs of nubs rear back and flail in the air, apparently in search of a footing. What! No further? What? It searches everywhere in the wide world for the rest of the grass, which is right under its nose. By dumb luck it touches the grass. Its front legs hang on; it lifts and buckles its green inch, and places its hind legs just behind its front legs. Its body makes a loop, a bight. All it has to do now is slide its front legs up the grass stem. Instead it gets lost. It throws up its head and front legs, flings its upper body out into the void, and panics again. What! No further? End of world? And so forth, until it actually reaches the grasshead's tip. By then its wee weight may be bending the grass toward some other grass plant. Its davening, apocalyptic prayers sway the grasshead and bump it into something. I have seen it many times. The blind and frantic numbskull makes it off one grassblade and onto another one, which it will climb in virtual hysteria for several hours. Every step brings it to the universe's rim. And now—What! No further? End of world? Ah, here's ground. What! No further? Yike!

"Why don't you just jump?" I tell it, disgusted. "Put yourself out of your misery."

I admire those eighteenth-century Hasids who understood the risk of prayer. Rabbi Uri of Strelisk took sorrowful leave of his household every morning because he was setting off to his prayers. He told his family how to dispose of his manuscripts if praying should kill him. A ritual slaughterer, similarly, every morning bade goodbye to his wife and children and wept as if he would never see them again. His friend asked him why. Because, he answered, when I begin I call out to the Lord. Then I pray, "Have mercy on us." Who knows what the Lord's power will do to me in that moment after I have invoked it and before I beg for mercy?

When you are stuck in a book; when you are well into writing it, and know what comes next, and yet cannot go on; when every morning for a week or a month you enter its room and turn your back on it; then the trouble is either of two things. Either the structure has forked, so the narrative, or the logic, has developed a hairline fracture that will shortly split it up the middle—or you are approaching a fatal mistake. What you had planned will not do. If you pursue your present course, the book will explode or collapse, and you do not know about it yet, quite.

In Bridgeport, Connecticut, one morning in April 1987, a six-story   20 concrete-slab building under construction collapsed, and killed twenty-eight men. Just before it collapsed, a woman across the street leaned from her window and said to a passerby, "That building is starting to shake." "Lady," he said, according to the Hartford *Courant*, "you got rocks in your head."

You notice only this: Your worker—your one and only, your prized, coddled, and driven worker—is not going out on that job. Will not budge, not even for you, boss. Has been at it long enough to know when the air smells wrong; can sense a tremor through boot soles. Nonsense, you say; it is perfectly safe. But the worker will not go. Will not even look at the site. Just developed heart trouble. Would rather starve. Sorry.

What do you do? Acknowledge, first, that you cannot do nothing. Lay out the structure you already have, x-ray it for a hairline fracture, find it, and think about it for a week or a year; solve the insoluble problem. Or subject the next part, the part at which the worker balks, to harsh tests. It harbors an unexamined and wrong premise. Something completely necessary is false or fatal. Once you find it, and if you can accept the finding, of course it will mean starting again. This is why many experienced writers urge young men and women to learn a useful trade.

Every morning you climb several flights of stairs, enter your study, open the French doors, and slide your desk and chair out into the middle of the air. The desk and chair float thirty feet from the ground, between the crowns of maple trees. The furniture is in place; you go back for your thermos of coffee. Then, wincing, you step out again through the French doors and sit down on the chair and look over the desktop. You can see clear to the river from here in winter. You pour yourself a cup of coffee.

Birds fly under your chair. In spring, when the leaves open in the maples' crowns, your view stops in the treetops just beyond the desk; yellow warblers hiss and whisper on the high twigs, and catch flies. Get to work. Your work is to keep cranking the flywheel that turns the gears that spin the belt in the engine of belief that keeps you and your desk in midair.

Putting a book together is interesting and exhilarating. It is sufficiently   25
difficult and complex that it engages all your intelligence. It is life at its most free. Your freedom as a writer is not freedom of expression in the sense of wild blurting; you may not let rip. It is life at its most free, if you are fortunate enough to be able to try it, because you select your materials, invent your task, and pace yourself. In the democracies, you may even write and publish anything you please about any governments or institutions, even if what you write is demonstrably false.

The obverse of this freedom, of course, is that your work is so meaningless, so fully for yourself alone, and so worthless to the world, that no one except you cares whether you do it well, or ever. You are free to make several thousand close judgment calls a day. Your freedom is a by-product of your days' triviality. A shoe salesman—who is doing others' tasks, who must answer to two or three bosses, who must do his job their way, and must put himself in their hands, at their place, during their hours—is nevertheless working usefully. Further, if the shoe salesman fails to appear one morning, someone will notice and miss him. Your manuscript, on which you lavish such care, has no needs or wishes; it knows you not. Nor does anyone need your manuscript; everyone needs shoes more. There are many manuscripts already—worthy ones, most edifying and moving ones, intelligent and powerful ones. If you believed *Paradise Lost* to be excellent, would you buy it? Why not shoot yourself, actually, rather than finish one more excellent manuscript on which to gag the world?

To find a honey tree, first catch a bee. Catch a bee when its legs are heavy with pollen; then it is ready for home. It is simple enough to catch a bee on a flower: Hold a cup or glass above the bee, and when it flies up, cap the cup with a piece of cardboard. Carry the bee to a nearby open spot—best an elevated one—release it, and watch where it goes. Keep your eyes on it as long as you can see it, and hie you to that last known place. Wait there until you see another bee; catch it, release it, and watch. Bee after bee will lead toward the honey tree, until you see the final bee enter the tree. Thoreau describes this process in his journals. So a book leads its writer.

You may wonder how you start, how you catch the first one. What do you use for bait?

You have no choice. One bad winter in the Arctic, and not too long ago, an Algonquin woman and her baby were left alone after everyone else in their winter camp had starved. Ernest Thompson Seton tells it. The woman walked from the camp where everyone had died, and found at a lake a cache. The cache contained one small fishhook. It was simple to rig a line, but she had no bait, and no hope of bait. The baby cried. She took a knife and cut a strip from her own thigh. She fished with the worm of her own flesh and caught a jackfish; she fed the child and herself. Of course she saved the fish gut for bait. She lived alone at the lake, on fish, until spring, when she walked out again and found people. Seton's informant had seen the scar on her thigh.

It takes years to write a book—between two and ten years. Less is so rare as to be statistically insignificant. One American writer has written a dozen major books over six decades. He wrote one of those books, a perfect novel, in three months. He speaks of it, still, with awe, almost whispering. Who wants to offend the spirit that hands out such books?

Faulkner wrote *As I Lay Dying* in six weeks; he claimed he knocked it off in his spare time from a twelve-hour-a-day job performing manual labor. There are other examples from other continents and centuries, just as albinos,

30

assassins, saints, big people, and little people show up from time to time in large populations. Out of a human population on earth of four and a half billion, perhaps twenty people can write a book in a year. Some people lift cars, too. Some people enter week-long sled-dog races, go over Niagara Falls in barrels, fly planes through the Arc de Triomphe. Some people feel no pain in childbirth. Some people eat cars. There is no call to take human extremes as norms.

Writing a book, full time, takes between two and ten years. The long poem, John Berryman said, takes between five and ten years. Thomas Mann was a prodigy of production. Working full time, he wrote a page a day. That is 365 pages a year, for he did write every day—a good-sized book a year. At a page a day, he was one of the most prolific writers who ever lived. Flaubert wrote steadily, with only the usual, appalling, strains. For twenty-five years he finished a big book every five to seven years. My guess is that full-time writers average a book every five years: seventy-three usable pages a year, or a usable fifth of a page a day. The years that biographers and other nonfiction writers spend amassing and mastering materials are well matched by the years novelists and short-story writers spend fabricating solid worlds that answer to immaterial truths. On plenty of days the writer can write three or four pages, and on plenty of other days he concludes he must throw them away.

Octavio Paz cites the example of "Saint-Pol-Roux, who used to hang the inscription 'The poet is working' from his door while he slept."

The notion that one can write better during one season of the year than another Samuel Johnson labeled, "Imagination operating upon luxury." Another luxury for an idle imagination is the writer's own feeling about the work. There is neither a proportional relationship, nor an inverse one, between a writer's estimation of a work in progress and its actual quality. The feeling that the work is magnificent, and the feeling that it is abominable, are both mosquitoes to be repelled, ignored, or killed, but not indulged.

The reason to perfect a piece of prose as it progresses—to secure each sentence before building on it—is that original writing fashions a form. It unrolls out into nothingness. It grows cell to cell, bole to bough to twig to leaf; any careful word may suggest a route, may begin a strand of metaphor or event out of which much, or all, will develop. Perfecting the work inch by inch, writing from the first word toward the last, displays the courage and fear this method induces. The strain, like Giacometti's penciled search for precision and honesty, enlivens the work and impels it toward its truest end. A pile of decent work behind him, no matter how small, fuels the writer's hope, too; his pride emboldens and impels him. One Washington writer—Charlie Butts—so prizes momentum, and so fears self-consciousness, that he writes fiction in a

35

rush of his own devising. He leaves his house on distracting errands, hurries in the door, and without taking off his coat, sits at a typewriter and retypes in a blur of speed all of the story he has written to date. Impetus propels him to add another sentence or two before he notices he is writing and seizes up. Then he leaves the house and repeats the process; he runs in the door and retypes the entire story, hoping to squeeze out another sentence the way some car engines turn over after the ignition is off, or the way Warner Bros.' Wile E. Coyote continues running for several yards beyond the edge of a cliff, until he notices.

The reason not to perfect a work as it progresses is that, concomitantly, original work fashions a form the true shape of which it discovers only as it proceeds, so the early strokes are useless, however fine their sheen. Only when a paragraph's role in the context of the whole work is clear can the envisioning writer direct its complexity of detail to strengthen the work's ends.

Fiction writers who toss up their arms helplessly because their characters "take over"—powerful rascals, what is a god to do?—refer, I think, to these structural mysteries that seize any serious work, whether or not it possesses fifth-column characters who wreak havoc from within. Sometimes part of a book simply gets up and walks away. The writer cannot force it back in place. It wanders off to die. It is like the astonishing—and common—starfish called the sea star. A sea star is a starfish with many arms; each arm is called a ray. From time to time a sea star breaks itself, and no one knows why. One of the rays twists itself off and walks away. Dr. S. P. Monks describes one species, which lives on rocky Pacific shores:

"I am inclined to think that *Phataria* . . . always breaks itself, no matter what may be the impulse. They make breaks when conditions are changed, sometimes within a few hours after being placed in jars. . . . Whatever may be the stimulus, the animal can and does break of itself. . . . The ordinary method is for the main portion of the starfish to remain fixed and passive with the tube feet set on the side of the departing ray, and for this ray to walk slowly away at right angles to the body, to change position, twist, and do all the active labor necessary to the breakage." Marine biologist Ed Ricketts comments on this: "It would seem that in an animal that deliberately pulls itself apart we have the very acme of something or other."

The written word is weak. Many people prefer life to it. Life gets your blood going, and it smells good. Writing is mere writing, literature is mere. It appeals only to the subtlest senses—the imagination's vision, and the imagination's hearing—and the moral sense, and the intellect. This writing that you do, that so thrills you, that so rocks and exhilarates you, as if you were dancing next to the band, is barely audible to anyone else. The reader's ear must adjust down from loud life to the subtle, imaginary sounds of the written word. An ordinary reader picking up a book can't yet hear a thing; it will take half an hour to pick up the writing's modulations, its ups and downs and louds and softs.

An intriguing entomological experiment shows that a male butterfly will ignore a living female butterfly of his own species in favor of a painted cardboard one, if the cardboard one is big. If the cardboard one is bigger than he is, bigger than any female butterfly ever could be. He jumps the piece of cardboard. Over and over again, he jumps the piece of cardboard. Nearby, the real, living female butterfly opens and closes her wings in vain. 40

Films and television stimulate the body's senses too, in big ways. A nine-foot handsome face, and its three-foot-wide smile, are irresistible. Look at the long legs on that man, as high as a wall, and coming straight toward you. The music builds. The moving, lighted screen fills your brain. You do not like filmed car chases? See if you can turn away. Try not to watch. Even knowing you are manipulated, you are still as helpless as the male butterfly drawn to painted cardboard.

That is the movies. That is their ground. The printed word cannot compete with the movies on their ground, and should not. You can describe beautiful faces, car chases, or valleys full of Indians on horseback until you run out of words, and you will not approach the movies' spectacle. Novels written with film contracts in mind have a faint but unmistakable, and ruinous, odor. I cannot name what, in the text, alerts the reader to suspect the writer of mixed motives; I cannot specify which sentences, in several books, have caused me to read on with increasing dismay, and finally close the books because I smelled a rat. Such books seem uneasy being books; they seem eager to fling off their disguises and jump onto screens.

Why would anyone read a book instead of watching big people move on a screen? Because a book can be literature. It is a subtle thing—a poor thing, but our own. In my view, the more literary the book—the more purely verbal, crafted sentence by sentence, the more imaginative, reasoned, and deep—the more likely people are to read it. The people who read are the people who like literature, after all, whatever that might be. They like, or require, what books alone have. If they want to see films that evening, they will find films. If they do not like to read, they will not. People who read are not too lazy to flip on the television; they prefer books. I cannot imagine a sorrier pursuit than struggling for years a write a book that attempts to appeal to people who do not read in the first place.

You climb a long ladder until you can see over the roof, or over the clouds. You are writing a book. You watch your shod feet step on each round rung, one at a time; you do not hurry and do not rest. Your feet feel the steep ladder's balance; the long muscles in your thighs check its sway. You climb steadily, doing your job in the dark. When you reach the end, there is nothing more to climb. The sun hits you. The bright wideness surprises you; you had forgotten there was an end. You look back at the ladder's two feet on the distant grass, astonished.

The line of words fingers your own heart. It invades arteries, and enters the   45
heart on a flood of breath; it presses the moving rims of thick valves; it palpates the dark muscle strong as horses, feeling for something, it knows not what. A queer picture beds in the muscle like a worm encysted—some film of feeling, some song forgotten, a scene in a dark bedroom, a corner of the woodlot, a terrible dining room, that exalting sidewalk; these fragments are heavy with meaning. The line of words peels them back, dissects them out. Will the bared tissue burn? Do you want to expose these scenes to the light? You may locate them and leave them, or poke the spot hard till the sore bleeds on your finger, and write with that blood. If the sore spot is not fatal, if it does not grow and block something, you can use its power for many years, until the heart resorbs it.

The line of words feels for cracks in the firmament.

The line of words is heading out past Jupiter this morning. Traveling 150 kilometers a second, it makes no sound. The big yellow planet and its white moons spin. The line of words speeds past Jupiter and its cumbrous, dizzying orbit; it looks neither to the right nor to the left. It will be leaving the solar system soon, single-minded, rapt, rushing heaven like a soul. You are in Houston, Texas, watching the monitor. You saw a simulation: The line of words waited still, hushed, pointed with longing. The big yellow planet spun toward it like a pitched ball and passed beside it, low and outside. Jupiter was so large, the arc of its edge at the screen's bottom looked flat. The probe twined on; its wild path passed between white suns small as dots; these stars fell away on either side, like the lights on a tunnel's walls.

Now you watch symbols move on your monitor; you stare at the signals the probe sends back, transmits in your own tongue, numbers. Maybe later you can guess at what they mean—what they might mean about space at the edge of the solar system, or about your instruments. Right now, you are flying. Right now, your job is to hold your breath.

Considerations

1. Dillard agrees with Samuel Johnson's view that the season of the year has absolutely no effect on an author's ability to write. What other myths about writing does she implicitly confront and demolish? What concept of writing does she oppose to popular notions about the creative process?

2. Dillard uses a number of anecdotes and descriptions of natural phe-

nomena to give us an idea of a writer's dilemmas. Study a couple of these metaphors. How do they define her concept of writing?

3. In *An American Childhood,* Dillard explains that the early motivation to read about insects came from the feeling that "here between some book's front and back covers . . . was another map to the neighborhood I had explored all my life, and fancied I knew, a map depicting hitherto invisible landmarks" (165). Which of the metaphors she uses to describe writing also describe making the invisible visible?

Invitation to Write

Although Dillard writes specifically about the work involved in writing, underlying her statements is a philosophy of work in general. Write an essay in which you try to define Dillard's concept of work. Consider the drawbacks and struggles but also the rewards that are implied in this concept. Think also about our common notion of work and compare it to Dillard's in order to decide whether most Americans would share her ideas.

Connections

In "Scott Myers, Entrepreneur" (p. 242), Bruce Tucker and Paul Leinberger include many of Myers's reflections about the jobs he has held and the type of work he wanted to do. They end with the description of the ideal job he has found for himself. Write an essay in which you explore the role of self-expression in the definitions of work that emerge from Dillard's writing and Tucker and Leinberger's interview. Reread both essays and underline the passages where work is related to self-expression. Study these examples before you proceed to reveal the connections between the way both Dillard, as a writer, and Scott Myers, as an entrepreneur, define themselves and the way they regard their work.

ASSIGNMENT SEQUENCE
Language and Perception

This assignment sequence groups four essays that deal either explicitly or implicitly with language. Through them, you will have the chance to explore different facets of the linguistic phenomenon.

In your first essay, you will explore several familiar situations in which language makes a difference and determine the assumptions that underlie the use of language. You will continue these explorations in the second assignment, where you will take a closer look at the conversational situations depicted by Richard Rodriguez in his autobiographical essay "Complexion." In your third assignment, you will examine Rodriguez's essay again, this time in order to verify or disprove Deborah Tannen's theory about gender-specific language. In your fourth assignment you will be given the opportunity to study Tannen's notion of "rapport" language and, again, give a wider scope to her theory by relating it to Jane Staw and Mary Swander's account of life in the Midwest. Your fifth assignment will ask you to compare the ideas about literature and language voiced or implied by both Annie Dillard and Richard Rodriguez. And in the sixth assignment, you will consider Dillard together with Staw and Swander in order to explore narrative language and its characteristics. Finally, in the last assignment, you will pull together all the discussions you have built around language and its various usages in order to explore the complex notion of linguistic meaning.

Assignment 1: Exploring Experience

Besides communicating meaning, language can mark a person's social class, status, or gender, define the relationship between subordinate and superior in a work situation, include or exclude a person from a group, connect or separate people, entertain or deceive the speakers, and enable or disable a person. In this assignment you are invited to think about the many functions of language that are not covered by the standard "means of communication" definition. Write an essay in which you formulate a new and more comprehensive definition of language that includes the social and cultural factors that intervene in the process of communication.

Think about three or four situations where language—the way we express ourselves, our choice of vocabulary, or the tone we use—counts, such as in job interviewing, letter writing, poetry or literature writing, political campaigning, getting acquainted, joining a group, or traveling abroad. Make a list of examples and determine how important language is in each case. Establish also what other factors are involved in the success or failure of communication. Then analyze your examples in order to reveal the assumptions that underlie our use of language. Be sure to compare the results of your analyses to the basic definition of language as a means of communication.

Assignment 2

I can still hear the loudly confident voice he used with the Mexicans. It was the sound of the gringo *I had heard as a very young boy. And I can still hear the quiet, indistinct sounds of the Mexican, the oldest, who replied. At hearing that voice I was sad for the Mexicans.*
—RICHARD RODRIGUEZ, *Complexion*

In the quotation above, Richard Rodriguez describes linguistics that are related to social status, to employer/employee relations, and to the peculiar situation of a foreigner who does not completely master a new language. The situation suggests that being able to communicate in another language is not simply a matter of speaking the words, but also of being familiar with and able to function in a different culture. Write an essay in which you develop an analysis of Rodriguez's examples and observations to establish the value and significance of language in the bilingual environment where he grew up.

Review the essay and locate the instances where Rodriguez comments on language. Make an inventory of all the aspects of the linguistic phenomenon covered by Rodriguez in his commentaries. Pay particular attention to the instances where language marks a social or cultural division: the immigrant workers and their boss, the men and the women in the family, etc. Think also of the significance that playing the role of translator has for Rodriguez.

Assignment 3

Most troubling of all, women and men are judged differently even if they speak the same way.
—DEBORAH TANNEN, *Damned If You Do*

In her essay, Deborah Tannen discusses the stylistic differences between the ways men and women talk. Richard Rodriguez, in "Complexion," actually provides some examples of the ways men and women speak. How might these examples enhance Tannen's theory? Based on the examples provided by these two authors, write an essay in which you evaluate the importance of speaking style in relationships between people who belong to different social or gender groups.

Study the examples Tannen discusses and locate similar examples in Rodriguez's essay. Look also at the examples you used in your previous paper and find other stylistic differences that are not necessarily determined by gender. Discuss both gender and social divisions marked by style and consider closely the coexistence of such styles. You may also give some thought to the factors that enable people to communicate in spite of blunders and misunderstandings.

Assignment 4

Only modern Western societies place a priority on direct communication, and even for us it is more a value than a practice.
—DEBORAH TANNEN, *Damned If You Do*

As they are described by Jane Staw and Mary Swander in "If You Can Talk to a Guy," the inhabitants of Winnebago, Minnesota, have a special view of language, which is reflected in its local usage. In her essay "Damned If You Do," Deborah Tannen alerts us to the relation between language, socialization, and gender. Both essays challenge the common view that language serves simply to communicate ideas. Write an essay in which you determine to what extent language in Winnebago functions as "rapport" and to what extent it serves as a means of communication.

Study the conversations rendered by Staw and Swander in their essay and compare them to Tannen's examples of conversational situations. Determine whether the purpose of the exchanges that take place between the Winnebago people aims at conveying a message or at establishing a rapport. Think about how the relations between people affect the way they talk to each other; think also about talk that apparently says nothing yet communicates something; and think about the way people express their feelings in the examples offered by the authors.

Assignment 5

You can save some of the sentences, like bricks.
—ANNIE DILLARD, *The Writing Life*

Annie Dillard sometimes uses the act of building as a metaphor for the art of writing. Curiously enough, Richard Rodriguez, who experienced actual construction work, does not think about the literary process as similar to building. Using Dillard's and Rodriguez's views about writing as a reference point, write an essay in which you explore the relation between written language and the creative process.

First, study not only the authors' explicit statements, but their implications concerning language and writing. Note that Rodriguez does not speak directly about writing, while Dillard does not speak directly about language. After you have determined what views are implied in the essays, compare the two author's opinions about language, as well as their views of the writing process. Progress toward an evaluation of the relation between language and the creative process. To clarify that relation, you might also consider the notions about work and about the notions of freedom that the two authors entertain.

Assignment 6

With their stories, the people of south-central Minnesota live in a fluid time and place.
—JANE STAW AND MARY SWANDER, *If You Can Talk to a Guy*

Theorizing about writing, Annie Dillard argues that a story is born and grows during the creative process and eventually acquires a life of its own. Much of the writer's efforts are turned toward producing this "living" quality of a story. In Jane Staw and Mary Swander's "If You Can Talk to a Guy," however, the making of a story does not seem to require so much effort. On the contrary, it is a natural and simple process, a manifestation of ordinary speech. Write an essay in which you explore the assumptions about language in these texts in order to establish those characteristics that distinguish storytelling from pure communication.

Establish what the definition of a story is for Dillard and what it would be for the Minnesota people who talk to Staw and Swander. Determine both the differences and the similarities of the two definitions and explain what assumptions about language are implied in both. For instance, Dillard thinks writing—that is, using language—is a way to acquire knowledge, whereas the inhabitants of Winnebago assume that language is a way to reach other people and establish relationships. Find other contradictions of this sort and use them to find your own definition of narrative language.

Assignment 7

The writing has changed, in your hands, and in a twinkling, from an expression of your notions to an epistemological tool.
—ANNIE DILLARD, *The Writing Life*

In the papers you have written so far, several aspects of language have emerged as attendant to the act of communication: language as class or gender marker, language as rapport, language as material for the art of writing. In this final assignment of the sequence, think of all these aspects as part of the same whole. An ensemble view of them all can lead you to a more complex definition of language. With each redefinition of language, we also redefine our notion of meaning and we go further and further away from the idea that language is an "expression of [our] notions." Write an essay in which you use all your previous discussions about language in order to determine the nature of linguistic meaning.

Take a look at the definitions of language which have resulted from your previous essays. Consider the way meaning is produced in each situation as well as the agents who participate in its production. Determine whether language has intrinsic meaning or whether it acquires meaning according to the situations in which it is used.

11

Cultures in Contact

*F*or often, the denizens of the place we call paradise long for nothing so much as news of that "real paradise" across the seas—the concrete metropolis of skyscrapers and burger joints. And often what we call corruption, they might be inclined to call progress or profit. As tourists, we have reason to hope that the quaint anachronism we have discovered will always remain "unspoiled," as fixed as a museum piece for our inspection. It is perilous, however, to assume that its inhabitants will long for the same.

—PICO IYER, *Love Match*

Western life-styles, products, and approaches . . . generate the wrong kind of development in the context of poor nations. The Western middle-class way of life is so far above the conditions of the bulk of the population in these countries that the elites can enjoy it only at the cost of grotesque inequalities and exploitation.
—PAUL HARRISON, *The Westernization of the World*

One of our worst defects, our best fictions, is to believe that our miseries have been imposed on us from abroad, that others, for example, the conquistadores, have always been responsible for our problems.
—MARIO VARGAS LLOSA, *Questions of Conquest*

Cultural contact between Western civilizations and those in other parts of the world has a long historical tradition. Non-European cultures have contributed much to European civilization. Egyptian artistic motifs reappeared in the stone decoration of early medieval Christian churches in Europe. The Arabs ruled Spain as part of their empire after the fall of the Roman Empire; being more advanced in philosophy, medicine, and science than the Spanish, Arabic culture had a strong influence on the Christian and Jewish cultures that coexisted on the Iberian Peninsula. Eventually, Europeans traveled to distant destinations. The Crusaders left their European homelands for the Holy Lands. Leaving Venice, Marco Polo traveled to China in the twelfth century. Evidence now credits the Norsemen, led by Leif Eriksson, with establishing and abandoning settlements in North America several centuries before Christopher Columbus's "discovery" of the New World. However, Westerners had little effect on the cultures of the lands they visited in that era. Instead, the knowledge that they brought back had a deeper impact upon their own cultures.

Most of the current discussion about the dissemination of culture focuses on the influence of the West upon the rest of the world. Because modern technology has decreased the distance between different countries, any cultural impact is more immediate and occurs at a faster rate. When change occurs at such an accelerated rate, the result is a disruption of traditional worlds. Western values supplant the values of indigenous cultures instead of being slowly assimilated by those cultures. Modern technology brought by Westerners radically changes the economic structure of indigenous cultures. It also makes possible the media networks that replace non-Western cultural images with Western ones as familiar as more traditional images. The difference between past and present intercultural dialogues lies in the one-sided nature of the conversation. It is feared that developing cultures could lose their distinguishing characteristics if they accept the Western model as the only one to follow.

The authors of the readings in this sequence all discuss the effects of westernization, but they look at it from different angles. Pico Iyer, in "Love Match," suggests that the relationship between East and West is two-sided. Westerners both exploit undeveloped countries and lament their exploitation. Iyer points out that denizens of undeveloped countries see their own situation and choices quite differently than he does. Mario Vargas Llosa goes further, with "Questions of Conquest," to argue that the seeds of destruction of indigenous cultures are buried in those cultures themselves. He sees no way of preserving them in Peru: Either the indigenous inhabitants adapt to the Western model to survive or they will die out. In "The Westernization of the World," Paul Harrison terms the process of westernization a source of poverty and problems. Yet Harrison does not suggest rejecting all results of westernization. These three authors' different analyses of and approaches to the discussion of westernization serve as a point of departure for contemporary exploration.

PICO IYER

Love Match

Pico Iyer was born in Oxford, England, in 1957 to Indian parents. He received his education at Eton, Oxford, and Harvard. He writes on world affairs for *Time* magazine, which he credits for generous support for his ventures. Although he is a full-time employee, *Time* gave him lengthy leaves of absence to travel, enabling him to gather material for *Video Night in Kathmandu and Other Reports from the Not-So-Far East* (1988). "Love Match" is the introductory chapter to that book. Unlike traditional travel writing, the chapters in his book are essays, and they record the impressions of more than a single visit. By approaching each subject from several points in time, he is able to assess continuing processes of cultural diffusion and confusion. The travels he describes began in 1985 and covered a period of several years. Iyer has also contributed to to *Partisan Review, Smithsonian Magazine,* the *Village Voice,* the *Times Literary Supplement,* and many other publications. He has published a number of books based on his travels, among them *The Recovery of Innocence* (1984), *The Lady and the Monk: Four Seasons in Kyoto* (1991), and *Falling off the Map: Some Lonely Places of the World* (1993).

In "Love Match," Iyer considers not only the image the West has of the non-Western countries but also the ideas these countries entertain about the West. He clearly sees the relationship between Western and non-Western countries as equally balanced, whether they are founded on mutual appreciation or hatred.

W*ind in the west,*
fallen leaves
gathering in the east.
　　　　　—BUSON

All tourist people are my bread and butter. So I need to help everything as I could. If I do not help them, they will never forgive me because I fully understand their love or sincerity. I don't have enough money, but I need to pay their gratitude at one day.
　　　　　—*The credo of* MAUNG-MAUNG, *trishaw driver,*
　　　　　chalked up on a blackboard inside his hut in Mandalay

Rambo had conquered Asia. In China, a million people raced to see *First Blood* within ten days of its Beijing opening, and black marketeers were hawking tickets at seven times the official price. In India, five separate remakes of the American hit went instantly into production, one of them recasting the macho superman as a sari-clad woman. In Thailand, fifteen-foot cutouts of the avenging demon towered over the lobbies of some of the ten Bangkok cinemas in which the movie was playing, training their machine guns on all who passed. And in Indonesia, the Rambo Amusement Arcade was going great guns, while vendors along the streets offered posters of no one but the nation's three leading deities: President Suharto, Siva, and Stallone.

As I crisscrossed Asia in the fall of 1985, every cinema that I visited for ten straight weeks featured a Stallone extravaganza. In Chengdu, I heard John Rambo mumble his *First Blood* truisms in sullen, machine-gun Mandarin and saw the audience break into tut-tuts of headshaking admiration as our hero kerpowed seven cops in a single scene. In Jogjakarta, I went to *Rambo* on the same night as the *Ramayana* (though the modern divinity was watched by hosts of young couples, stately ladies in sarongs, and bright-eyed little scamps, many of whom had paid the equivalent of two months' salary for their seats, while, on the other side of town, the replaying of the ancient myth remained virtually unvisited). Just five days later, I took an overnight bus across Java, and, soon enough, the video screen next to the driver crackled into life and there—who else?—was the Italian Stallion, reasserting his Dionysian beliefs against Apollo Creed. As the final credits began to roll, my neighbor, a soldier just returned from putting down rebels in the jungles of East Timor, sat back with a satisfied sigh. "That," he pronounced aptly, "was very fantastic."

Silencing soldiers, toppling systems, conquering millions, and making money fist over fist across the continent, Rambo was unrivaled as the most powerful force in Asia that autumn. "No man, no law, no woman can stop him," gasped the ads in the Bangkok papers. "Everyone Is Applauding Screen's Most Invincible Hero," agreed one of the three ads on a single page of India's respected *Statesman*. "The Second Greatest U.S. Box Office Hit in History," roared the marquee in faraway Sabah. "I think he's very beautiful," cooed a twenty-three-year-old Chinese girl to a foreign reporter. "So vigorous and so graceful. Is he married?"

Rambo had also, I knew, shattered box-office records everywhere from Beirut to San Salvador. But there seemed a particular justice in his capturing of Asian hearts and minds. For Rambo's great mission, after all, was to reverse the course of history and, single-fisted, to redress America's military losses in the theaters of Asia. And in a way, of course, the movie's revisionism had done exactly that, succeeding where the American army had failed, and winning over an entire continent. Some of the appeal of the blockhead-buster lay, no doubt, in its presentation of a kung fu spectacular more professional than the local efforts and more polished than the competing displays of Norris and Bronson. Some might just have reflected the after-tremors of its earth-shaking reception in the States. But whatever the cause of the drama's success, the effect was undeniable: Millions of Asians were taking as their role model an All-American mercenary. When William Broyles returned to his old battle-grounds in Vietnam in 1984, he found the locals jiving along to "Born in the U.S.A.," Bruce Springsteen's anthem for the disenfranchised Vietnam vet, and greeting him with cries of "America Number One!" "America," concluded Broyles, "is going to be much more difficult to defeat in this battle than we were in the others. Our clothes, our language, our movies, and our music—our way of life—are far more powerful than our bombs."

The prospect of witnessing that low-intensity conflict was one of the impulses that took me first to Asia. Over the course of two years, I spent a total of seven months crisscrossing the continent on four separate trips, mostly in order to see its sights, but also in order to visit the front lines of this cultural campaign. I was interested to find out how America's pop-cultural imperialism spread through the world's most ancient civilizations. I wanted to see what kind of resistance had been put up against the Coca-Colonizing forces and what kind of counter-strategies were planned. And I hoped to discover which Americas got through to the other side of the world, and which got lost in translation.

This contest for cultural sovereignty was nothing new, of course. Colonel Sanders and General Motors had first set up base camps across the global village years ago, and America's Ambassador-at-Large throughout the world had long been the retired World War I flying ace Snoopy. Fifteen years before the first American troops showed up, Norman Lewis described families in Saigon listening respectfully to a local rendition of "When Irish Eyes Are Smiling." And fully a quarter century ago, Arthur Koestler had stated as a given that the world was moving toward "a uniform, mechanized, stereo-typed culture," a mass culture that struck him as a form of mass suicide. The syllogism was old enough now to be almost an axiom: Pop culture ruled the world, and America ruled pop culture. Thus America ruled the waves—or at the very least, the airwaves.

In recent years, however, the takeover had radically intensified and rapidly accelerated. For one thing, satellites were now beaming images of America across the globe faster than a speeding bullet; the explosion of video had sent history spinning like the wheels of an overturned bicycle. For another, as the world grew smaller and ever smaller, so too did its props: Not only had distances in time and space been shrunk, but the latest weapons of cultural warfare—videos, cassettes, and computer disks—were far more portable than the big screens and heavy instruments of a decade before. They could be smuggled through border checkpoints, under barbed-wire fences and into distant homes as easily, almost, as a whim. In the cultural campaign, the equivalent of germ warfare had replaced that of heavy-tank assaults.

Suddenly, then, America could be found uncensored in even the world's most closed societies, intact in even its most distant corners. Peasants in China or the Soviet Union could now enjoy images of swimming pools, shopping malls, and the other star-spangled pleasures of the Affluent Society inside their own living rooms; remote villagers in rural Burma could now applaud Rambo's larger-than-life heroics only days after they hit the screens of Wisconsin; and the Little House on the Prairie was now a part of the neighborhood in 108 countries around the world.

More important, the video revolution was bringing home the power of the Pax Americana with greater allure and immediacy than even the most cunning propaganda. Already, the ruling mullahs in Iran were fretting that their capital's newly formed clandestine Michael Jackson clubs could easily turn into revolutionary cells. And I once heard one of Washington's most senior foreign policy veterans privately maintain that the single issue that most exercised the Soviets was not the nuclear arms race, or the war of espionage, or Afghanistan or Nicaragua or Cuba, or even the rising confidence of China, but simply the resistless penetration of video.

In 1985, another influence was also carrying American dollars and dreams to every corner of the world with more force and more urgency than ever before: people. Tourists were the great foot soldiers of the new invasion; tourists, in a sense, were the terrorists of cultural expansionism, what Sartre once called "the cool invaders." Scarcely forty years ago, most of the world's secret places were known only to adventurers, soldiers, missionaries, and a few enterprising traders; in recent years, however, the secrets were open, and so too was the world—anyone with a credit card could become a lay colonialist. Nepal, which had never seen a tourist until 1955, now welcomed 200,000 foreign visitors each year; China, which had rigidly closed its doors for decades, had 11,000 tourists a day clambering along the Great Wall by 1985. The road to Mandalay and even the road to Xanadu were crowded now with Westerners—men in search of women, dreamers in search of enlightenment, traders in search of riches. In 1985, many Asians considered the single great import from the West, after Rambo, to be AIDS.

Not all the incoming forces, of course, were American. Mick Jagger was as much the poet laureate of the modern world as Michael Jackson, and Sophie Marceau vied with Phoebe Cates as the poster queen of Southeast Asia. If Springsteen turned out to be my unexpected traveling companion across the continent, so too did the British group Dire Straits: Their latest album greeted me in a tiny inn in Hiroshima, then blasted my eardrums from a car in Beijing, then wafted over me in the soft tropical night of a Balinese guesthouse, then serenaded me once more in the Kathmandu home of a local Lothario. And the back roads of Asia were far more crowded with Canadians and Germans and

10

Australians than with Americans. But still, when it came to movies and TV, the United States remained the Great Communicator. And if pop culture was, in effect, just a shorthand for all that was young and modern and rich and free, it was also a virtual synonym for America.

Everywhere, in fact, dreams of pleasure and profit were stamped "Made in America." Cities from San Salvador to Singapore turned themselves into bright imitations of Californian, not Parisian or Liverpudlian, suburbs; Garfield, not Tintin, had become the alter ego of millions of Germans and Japanese; and it was not the yen or the Deutschemark that had become the universal currency, but the dollar, even—no, especially—in the Communist bloc. The hymn of the East Side, as well as the West, was still "I Want to Live in America."

This kind of influence was not by any means stronger or more pervasive in Asia than elsewhere in the developing world. Yet of all the fronts on which the battle was being waged, Asia seemed to be the fiercest and most complex. Asia, after all, had been the site of the world's most vexed and various colonial struggles, and Asia was also the theater for most of America's recent military confrontations. Asia was also increasingly mounting a formidable counterattack upon the long-unquestioned economic domination of the West, and Asia now included three out of four of all the world's souls. Asia, above all, seemed home to most of history's oldest and subtlest cultures. How, I wondered, would proud, traditionalist societies founded on a sense of family and community respond to the Fighting Machine's grunting individualism and back-to-basics primitivism? How would developing nations deal with refugees from affluence, voluntary dropouts from the Promised Land? And what would decorous Buddhists make of the crucifix-swinging Madonna?

Asia also appealed to me because it was unmatched in its heterogeneity; in China, Japan, and India alone, the continent had three great traditions as deep as they were diverse. Texts read us as much as we do them, and in the different ways that different cultures responded to forces from the West, I hoped to see something of their different characters and priorities.

Rambo again proved illustrative. In China, the very showing of the film 15 had advertised a new cultural openness to the West, even as the black-market chicanery it set off betrayed some of the less happy foreign influences streaming in through the open door; ideologically, the movie served both as political propaganda (confirming the Chinese in their belief that the Vietnamese were devious swine) and as a subject for earnest self-criticism, dialectically worked out in the letter columns of the *China Daily*. In India, the movie had been seized upon by the quick-witted moguls of the world's largest film industry and swiftly redesigned to fit the mythic contours of Indian formula fantasy; yet its heroic success had also set off bouts of typical Indian philosophizing—even a newspaper ad couched its come-on in a kind of marveling rumination:

"No sex, no romance, no lady character, yet constantly patronized by Male and Female. The RAMBO syndrome."

In the Philippines, the movie had passed, like so much American cultural debris, into the very language and mythology of the country, blurring even further the country's always uncertain division between politics and show biz: Onetime Defense Minister Juan Ponce Enrile was wont to represent himself, on posters and in threats, as a kind of homegrown Rambo. And in Vietnam, to complete the circle, this latest version of the war had, inevitably, become an instrument of propaganda: The Vietnamese accused Ronald Reagan of trying to "Ramboize" the youth of America, hardly mentioning the more unsettling fact that Rambo was "Reaganizing" the youth of all the world.

As I drifted out of the theater where I had seen *Rambo,* and into the warm Indonesian night, only one line from the movie really stayed with me. The hero's boss, Colonel Trautman, had been discussing the maverick naked ape with the heartless Washington bureaucrat Murdock. "What you choose to call hell," he had said of his explosive charge, "he calls home." However inadvertently, that sentence suggested many of the other ideas that first sent me East: that home has nothing to do with hearth, and everything to do with a state of mind; that one man's home may be his compatriot's exile; that home is, finally, not the physical place, but the role and the self we choose to occupy.

I went to Asia, then, not only to see Asia, but also to see America, from a different vantage point and with new eyes. I left one kind of home to find another: to discover what resided in me and where I resided most fully, and so to better appreciate—in both senses of the word—the home I had left. The point was made best by one great traveler who saw the world without ever leaving home, and, indeed, created a home that was a world within—Thoreau: "Our journeying is a great-circle sailing."

To travel across the globe simply to locate the facilities of the place one has quit would, of course, be an elaborate exercise in perversity. Only those who travel for business, and nothing more, would really wish to ask the questions addressed by Anne Tyler's Accidental Tourist: "What restaurants in Tokyo offered Sweet 'n Low? Did Amsterdam have a McDonald's? Did Mexico City have a Taco Bell? Did any place in Rome serve Chef Boyardee ravioli? Other travelers hoped to discover distinctive local wines; Macon's readers searched for pasteurized and homogenized milk." Pasteurized and homogenized cultures are not what take us abroad. Yet, at the same time, many a traveler knows that the Temple of the Golden Arches and the Palace of the Burger King never seem so appealing as when one is searching for a regular meal in the back streets of Kyoto. And Father *Time* never seems so authoritative, or so agreeably familiar, as when one is yearning for news in the mountains of Tibet.

If the great horror of traveling is that the foreign can come to seem drearily familiar, the happy surprise of traveling is that the familiar can come to seem wondrously exotic. Abroad, we are not ourselves; and as the normal and the novel are transposed, the very things that we might shun at home are touched with the glamour of the exotic. I had never seen, or wished to see, a Burt Reynolds movie until I found myself stuck in a miserable guest-house in Bandar Sari Begawan; I had never been to a Dunkin' Donuts parlor until I decided to treat myself after a hard day's work in Bangkok. I enjoyed my first ever Yorkie bar in Surabaya (and my second there too, a few minutes later). And my first experience of the Emmy Awards came in the darkened lobby of a run-down hotel in Singapore, where the ceremonies were annotated, with beery profanities, by a gang of tattooed European and Australian sailors who broke off from their lusty commentary only when a French or Filipina trollop drifted barefoot through the room and out into the monsoony night. [20]

While I was in Asia, I made ritual pilgrimages to the Taj Mahal, Pagan, and Borobudur; I climbed live volcanoes in the dead of the Javanese night and rode elephants through the jungles of Nepal. I spent nights in an Indonesian hut, where my roommates consisted of two pack rats, a lizard, and a family-size cockroach, and other nights in a Mogul palace on a lake, where I sat for hours on the marbled roof, watching the silver of moon on water. In Bali, I witnessed a rare and sumptuous cremation, and in Kyoto, I saw the unearthly Daimonji Festival, when all the town is lit with lanterns to guide departed spirits home. None of this, however, is recorded in the pages that follow, partly because all of it has gone on, and will go on, one hopes, for centuries, and partly because such familiar marvels may be better described by travelers more observant than myself.

More than such postcard wonders, however, what interested me were the brand-new kinds of exotica thrown up by our synthetic age, the novel cultural hybrids peculiar to the tag end of the twentieth century. "Travel itself," observes Paul Fussell in *Abroad,* "even the most commonplace, is an implicit quest for anomaly," and the most remarkable anomalies in the global village today are surely those created by willy-nilly collisions and collusions between East and West: the local bands in socialist Burma that play note-perfect version of the Doors' "L.A. Woman," in Burmese; the American tenpin bowling alley that is the latest nighttime hot spot in Beijing; the Baskin-Robbins imitation in Hiroshima that sells "vegetable" ice cream in such flavors as mugwort, soy milk, sweet potato, and "marron"; or the bespectacled transvestite in Singapore who, when asked to name the best restaurant in a town justly celebrated for its unique combination of Chinese, Indian, and Malaysian delicacies, answers, without a moment's hesitation, "Denny's."

I wanted also, while I was in Asia, to see how America was regarded and reconstituted abroad, to measure the country by the shadow it casts. Much of the world, inevitably, looks to its richest industrial nation for promiscuous images of power and affluence; abroad, as at home, the land of Chuck Bronson and Harold Robbins will always command a greater following than that of Emerson and Terrence Malick. Often, in fact, the America one sees around the globe seems as loud and crass and overweight as the caricatured American tourist. And just as celebrities pander to the images they foster, acting out our dreams of what they ought to be, so America often caters to the world's image of America, cranking out slick and inexpensive products made almost exclusively for foreign consumption—in Jogjakarta, the cinema that was not showing *Rambo* offered *The Earthling,* with Ricky Schroder and William Holden, and *Dead and Buried,* starring Melody Anderson and James Farentino.

Yet America also projects a more promising and more hopeful image around the world, as a culture of success stories and of the youthful excesses that may accompany them. Lee Iaocca's memoirs are devoured far more eagerly from Rio to Riyadh than those of Akio Morita or Giovanni Agnelli, and George Washington is a folk hero in many Asian classrooms in a way that George III will never be. The most popular contemporary American writer in the very different markets of France and West Germany is Charles Bukowski, the disheveled boho laureate of booze and broads in low-life L.A. In the world's collective popular imagination, America the Beautiful stands next to America the Technicolor Dreamcoast.

This division in itself is hardly unique: Every culture casts conflicting images before the world. We associate India with desperate poverty and maharajah opulence, Britain with punks and patricians. But in the case of America, subject of so many daydreams and ideals, so intensely felt and so eagerly pursued, the contradictions are even more pronounced: For not only is the country's political power enormous, but it is matched—and sometimes opposed—by its cultural influence. When Reagan speaks, the world listens; yet Springsteen is shouting the opposite message in the other ear. While Congress sends money to the contras, the global village tunes in to Jackson Browne. 25

And if the image of America is perplexingly double-edged, the responses it provokes in many parts of the globe are appropriately fork-tongued: With one breath, they shout, "Yankee Go Home," and with the next, "America Number One!" "In the Third World," writes Michael Howard, "anti-Americanism is almost a *lingua franca.*" Yet in the Third World, a hunger for American culture is almost taken for granted, and "making it" often means nothing more than making it to the Land of the Free. The Communist guerrillas in the Philippines fight capitalism while wearing UCLA T-shirts. The Sandinista leaders in Nicaragua wage war against "U.S. Imperialism" while watching prime-time American TV on private satellite dishes. And many whites in South Africa cling to apartheid, yet cannot get enough of Bill Cosby, Eddie Murphy, and Mr. T.

All these contradictions are further exacerbated by one simple but inevitable fact: the disproportion between America's formidable power around the globe and the much more modest presence of individual Americans abroad. "We think of the United States," writes Octavio Paz, on behalf of all Latin Americans, "simultaneously, and without contradiction, as Goliath, Polyphemus, and Pantagruel." Yet that daunting weight falls upon the shoulders of the small and decidedly unmythic traveler, tourist or expatriate. Around the world, S. J. Perelman noted, the American occupies "the curious dual role of skinflint and sucker, the usurer bent on exacting his pound of flesh and the hapless pigeon whose poke was a challenge to any smart grifter." The incongruity applies equally, of course, to the Russians abroad, as it did to the Englishman, the Chinese, and all the other imperialists of the past. But in the case of America, at once so ubiquitous and so many-headed throughout the world, the schizophrenia seems especially charged. If Bruce Springsteen is not Reagan, still less is that backpacking social worker from Tacoma. Again and again in my travels, I had been asked, by Greeks, Nicaraguans, and Moroccans, how the American government could be such a ruthless bully, while the American people seemed so friendly, good-natured, and warm. I went to Asia in part to find out.

II

To mention, however faintly, the West's cultural assault on the East is, inevitably, to draw dangerously close to the fashionable belief that the First World is corrupting the Third. And to accept that AIDS and Rambo are the two great "Western" exports of 1985 is to encourage some all too easy conclusions: that the West's main contributions to the rest of the world are sex and violence, a cureless disease and a killer cure; that America is exporting nothing but a literal kind of infection and a bloody sort of indoctrination. In place of physical imperialism, we often assert a kind of sentimental colonialism that would replace Rambo myths with Sambo myths and conclude that because the First World feels guilty, the Third World must be innocent—what Pascal Bruckner refers to as "compassion as contempt."

This, however, I find simplistic—both because corruption often says most about those who detect it and because the developing world may often have good reason to assent in its own transformation.

This is not to deny that the First World has indeed inflicted much damage   30
on the Third, especially through the inhuman calculations of geopolitics. If power corrupts, superpowers are super-corrupting, and the past decade alone has seen each of the major powers destroy a self-contained Asian culture by dragging it into the cross fire of the Real World: Tibet was invaded for strategic reasons by the Chinese, and now the dreamed-of Shangri-La is almost lost forever; Afghanistan was overrun by Soviet tanks, and now the Michauds' photographic record of its fugitive beauties must be subtitled, with appropriate melancholy, "Paradise Lost"; Cambodia, once so gentle a land that cyclo

drivers were said to tip their passengers, fell into the sights of Washington and is now just a land of corpses.

On an individual level too, Western tourists invariably visit destruction on the places they visit, descending in droves on some "authentic Eastern village" until only two things are certain: It is neither Eastern nor authentic. Each passing season (and each passing tourist) brings new developments to the forgotten places of the world—and in a never-never land, every development is a change for the worse. In search of a lovely simplicity, Westerners saddle the East with complexities; in search of peace, they bring agitation. As soon as Arcadia is seen as a potential commodity, amenities spring up on every side to meet outsiders' needs, and paradise is not so much lost as remaindered. In Asia alone, Bali, Tahiti, Sri Lanka, and Nepal have already been so taken over by Paradise stores, Paradise hotels, and Paradise cafés that they sometimes seem less like utopias than packaged imitations of utopia; Ladakh, Tibet, and Ko Samui may one day follow. No man, they say, is an island; in the age of international travel, not even an island can remain an island for long.

Like every tourist, moreover, I found myself spreading corruption even as I decried it. In northern Thailand, I joined a friend in giving hill tribesmen tutorials in the songs of Sam Cooke until a young Thai girl was breaking the silence of the jungle with a piercing refrain of "She was sixteen, too young to love, and I was too young to know." In China, I gave a local boy eager for some English-language reading matter a copy of the only novel I had on hand—Gore Vidal's strenuously perverse *Duluth*. And in a faraway hill station in Burma, a group of cheery black marketeers treated me to tea and I, in return, taught them the words "lesbian" and "skin flicks," with which they seemed much pleased.

Yet that in itself betrays some of the paradoxes that haunt our talk of corruption. For often, the denizens of the place we call paradise long for nothing so much as news of that "real paradise" across the seas—the concrete metropolis of skyscrapers and burger joints. And often what we call corruption, they might be inclined to call progress or profit. As tourists, we have reason to hope that the quaint anachronism we have discovered will always remain "unspoiled," as fixed as a museum piece for our inspection. It is perilous, however, to assume that its inhabitants will long for the same. Indeed, a kind of imperial arrogance underlies the very assumption that the people of the developing world should be happier without the TVs and motorbikes that we find so indispensable ourselves. If money does not buy happiness, neither does poverty.

In other ways too, our laments for lost paradises may really have much more to do with our own state of mind than with the state of the place whose decline we mourn. Whenever we recall the places we have seen, we tend to observe them in the late afternoon glow of nostalgia, after memory, the mind's great cosmetician, has softened out rough edges, smoothed out imperfections, and removed the whole to a lovely abstract distance. Just as a good man, once dead, is remembered as a saint, so a pleasant place, once quit, is recalled as a utopia. Nothing is ever what it used to be.

If the First World is not invariably corrupting the Third, we are sometimes apt   35
to leap to the opposite conclusion: that the Third World, in fact, is hustling the First. As tourists, moreover, we are so bombarded with importunities from a variety of locals—girls who live off their bodies and touts who live off their wits, merchants who use friendship to lure us into their stores, and "students" who attach themselves to us in order to improve their English—that we begin to regard ourselves as beleaguered innocents and those we meet as shameless predators.

To do so, however, is to ignore the great asymmetry that governs every meeting between tourist and local: that we are there by choice and they largely by circumstance; that we are traveling in the spirit of pleasure, adventure, and romance, while they are mired in the more urgent business of trying to survive; and that we, often courted by the government, enjoy a kind of unofficial diplomatic immunity, which gives us all the perks of authority and none of the perils of responsibility, while they must stake their hopes on every potential transaction.

Descending upon native lands quite literally from the heavens, *dei ex machinae* from an alien world of affluence, we understandably strike many locals in much the same way that movie stars strike us. And just as some of us are wont to accost a celebrity glimpsed by chance at a restaurant, so many people in developing countries may be tempted to do anything and everything possible to come into contact with the free-moving visitors from abroad and their world of distant glamour. They have nothing to lose in approaching a foreigner—at worst, they will merely be insulted or pushed away. And they have everything to gain: a memory, a conversation, an old copy of *Paris Match,* perhaps even a friendship or a job opportunity. Every foreigner is a messenger from a world of dreams.

"Do you know Beverly Hills?" I was once asked by a young Burmese boy who had just spent nine months in jail for trying to escape his closed motherland. "Do you know Hollywood? Las Vegas? The Potomac, I think, is very famous. Am I right? Detroit, Michigan, is where they make cars. Ford. General Motors. Chevrolet. Do you know Howard Hughes? There are many Jewish people in New York. Am I right? And also at *Time* magazine? Am I right?" Tell us about life behind the scenes, we ask the star, and which is the best place in the whole wide world, and what is Liz Taylor really like.

The touts that accost us are nearly always, to be sure, worldly pragmatists. But they are also, in many cases, wistful dreamers, whose hopes are not so different from the ones our culture encourages: to slough off straitened circumstances and set up a new life and a new self abroad, underwritten by hard work and dedication. American dreams are strongest in the hearts of those who have seen America only in their dreams.

I first met Maung-Maung as I stumbled off a sixteen-hour third-class 40 overnight train from Rangoon to Mandalay. He was standing outside the station, waiting to pick up tourists; a scrawny fellow in his late twenties, with a sailor's cap, a beard, a torn white shirt above his *longyi,* and an open, rough-hewn face—a typical tout, in short. Beside him stood his bicycle trishaw. On one side was painted the legend "My Life"; on the other, "B.Sc. (Maths)."

We haggled for a few minutes. Then Maung-Maung smilingly persuaded me to part with a somewhat inflated fare—twenty cents—for the trip across town, and together we began cruising through the wide, sunny boulevards of the city of kings. As we set off, we began to exchange the usual questions— age, place of birth, marital status, and education—and before long we found that our answers often jibed. Soon, indeed, the conversation was proceeding swimmingly. A little while into our talk, my driver, while carefully steering his trishaw with one hand, sank the other into his pocket and handed back to me a piece of jade. I admired it dutifully, then extended it back in his direction. "No," he said. "This is present."

Where, I instantly wondered, was the catch—was he framing me, or bribing me, or cunningly putting me in his debt? What was the small print? What did he want?

"I want you," said Maung-Maung, "to have something so you can always remember me. Also, so you can always have happy memories of Mandalay." I did not know how to respond. "You see," he went on, "if I love other people, they will love me. It is like Newton's law, or Archimedes."

This was not what I had expected. "I think," he added, "it is always good to apply physics to life."

That I did not doubt. But still I was somewhat taken aback. "Did you 45 study physics at school?"

"No, I study physics in college. You see, I am graduate from University of Mandalay—B.Sc. Mathematics." He waved with pride at the inscription on the side of his trishaw.

"And you completed all your studies."

"Yes. B.Sc. Mathematics."

"Then why are you working in this kind of job?"

"Other jobs are difficult. You see, here in Burma, a teacher earns only 50 two hundred fifty kyats [$30] in a month. Managing director has only one thousand kyats [$125]. Even President makes only four thousand kyats [$500]. For me, I do not make much money. But in this job, I can meet tourist and improve my English. Experience, I believe, is the best teacher."

"But surely you could earn much more just by driving a horse cart?"

"I am Buddhist," Maung-Maung reminded me gently, as he went pedaling calmly through the streets. "I do not want to inflict harm on any living creature. If I hit horse in this life, in next life I come back as horse."

"So"—I was still skeptical—"you live off tourists instead?"

"Yes," he said, turning around to give me a smile. My irony, it seems, was wasted. "Until two years ago, in my village in Shan States, I had never seen a tourist."

"Never?"

"Only in movies." Again he smiled back at me.

I was still trying to puzzle out why a university graduate would be content with such a humble job when Maung-Maung, as he pedaled, reached into the basket perched in front of his handlebars and pulled out a thick leather book. Looking ahead as he steered, he handed it back to me to read. Reluctantly, I opened it, bracing myself for porno postcards or other illicit souvenirs. Inside, however, was nothing but a series of black-and-white snapshots. Every one of them had been painstakingly annotated in English: "My Headmaster," "My Monk," "My Brothers and Sisters," "My Friend's Girlfriend." And his own girlfriend? "I had picture before. But after she broke my heart, and fall in love with other people, I tear it out."

At the very back of his book, in textbook English, Maung-Maung had carefully inscribed the principles by which he lived.

1. Abstain from violence.
2. Abstain from illicit sexual intercourse.
3. Abstain from intoxicants of all kinds.
4. Always be helpful.
5. Always be kind.

"It must be hard," I said dryly, "to stick to all these rules."

"Yes. It is not always easy," he confessed. "But I must try. If people ask me for food, my monk tell me, I must always give them money. But if they want money for playing cards, I must give them no help. My monk also explain I must always give forgiveness—even to people who hurt me. If you put air into volleyball and throw it against wall, it bounces back. But if you do not put in air, what happens? It collapses against wall."

Faith, in short, was its own vindication.

I was now beginning to suspect that I would find no more engaging guide to Mandalay than Maung-Maung, so I asked him if he would agree to show me around. "Yes, thank you very much. But first, please, I would like you to see my home."

Ah, I thought, here comes the setup. Once I'm in his house, far from the center of a city I don't know, he will drop a drug in my tea or pull out a knife or even bring in a few accomplices. I will find out too late that his friendliness is only a means to an end.

Maung-Maung did nothing to dispel these suspicions as he pedaled the trishaw off the main street and we began to pass through dirty alleyways, down narrow lanes of run-down shacks. At last we pulled up before a hut, fronted with weeds. Smiling proudly, he got off and asked me to enter.

There was not much to see inside his tiny room. There was a cot, on which sat a young man, his head buried in his hands. There was another cot, on which Maung-Maung invited me to sit as he introduced me to his roommate. The only other piece of furniture was a blackboard in a corner on which my host had written out the statement reproduced in the epigraph to this book, expressing his lifelong pledge to be of service to tourists.

I sat down, not sure what was meant to happen next. For a few minutes, we made desultory conversation. His home, Maung-Maung explained, cost thirty kyats [$4] a month. This other man was also a university graduate, but he had no job: Every night, he got drunk. Then, after a few moments of reflection, my host reached down to the floor next to his bed and picked up what I took to be his two most valuable belongings.

Solemnly, he handed the first of them to me. It was a sociology textbook from Australia. Its title was *Life in Modern America*. Then, as gently as if it were his Bible, Maung-Maung passed across the other volume, a dusty old English-Burmese dictionary, its yellowed pages falling from their covers. "Every night," he explained, "after I am finished on trishaw, I come here and read this. Also, every word I do not know I look up." Inside the front cover, he had copied out a few specimen sentences. *If you do this, you may end up in jail. My heart is lacerated by what you said. What a lark.*

I was touched by his show of trust. But I also felt as uncertain as an actor walking through a play he hasn't read. Perhaps, I said a little uneasily, we should go now, so we can be sure of seeing all the sights of Mandalay before sundown. "Do not worry," Maung-Maung assured me with a quiet smile, "we will see everything. I know how long the trip will take. But first, please, I would like you to see this."

Reaching under his bed, he pulled out what was clearly his most precious treasure of all. With a mixture of shyness and pride, he handed over a thick black notebook. I looked at the cover for markings and, finding none, opened it up. Inside, placed in alphabetical order, was every single letter he had ever received from a foreign visitor. Every one was meticulously dated and annotated; many were accompanied by handwritten testimonials or reminiscences from the tourists Maung-Maung had met. On some pages, he had affixed wrinkled passport photos of his foreign visitors by which he could remember them.

Toward the end of the book, Maung-Maung had composed a two-page essay, laboriously inscribed in neat and grammatical English, called "Guide to Jewelry." It was followed by two further monographs,"For You" and "For the Tourists." In them, Maung-Maung warned visitors against "twisty characters," explained something of the history and beauty of Mandalay, and told his readers not to trust him until he had proved worthy of their trust.

Made quiet by this labor of love, I looked up. "This must have taken you a long time to write."

"Yes," he replied with a bashful smile. "I have to look many times at dictionary. But it is my pleasure to help tourists."

I went back to flipping through the book. At the very end of the volume, carefully copied out, was a final four-page essay, entitled "My Life."

He had grown up, Maung-Maung wrote, in a small village, the eldest of ten children. His mother had never learned to read, and feeling that her disability made her "blind," she was determined that her children go to school. It was not easy, because his father was a farmer and earned only three-hundred kyats a month. Still, Maung-Maung, as the eldest, was able to complete his education at the local school.

When he finished, he told his parents that he wanted to go to university. Sorrowfully, they told him that they could not afford it—they had given him all they had for his schooling. He knew that was true, but still he was set on continuing his studies. "I have hand. I have head. I have legs," he told them. "I wish to stand on my own legs." With that, he left his village and went to Mandalay. Deeply wounded by his desertion, his parents did not speak to him for a year.

In Mandalay, Maung-Maung's narrative continued, he had begun to finance his studies by digging holes—he got four kyats for every hole. Then he got a job cleaning clothes. Then he went to a monastery and washed dishes and clothes in exchange for board and lodging. Finally, he took a night job as a trishaw driver.

When they heard of that, his parents were shocked. "They think I go with prostitutes. Everyone looks down on trishaw driver. Also other trishaw drivers hate me because I am a student. I do not want to quarrel with them. But I do not like it when they say dirty things or go with prostitutes." Nevertheless, after graduation Maung-Maung decided to pay seven kyats a day to rent a trishaw full-time. Sometimes, he wrote, he made less than one kyat a day, and many nights he slept in his vehicle in the hope of catching the first tourists of the day. He was a poor man, he went on, but he made more money than his father. Most important, he made many friends. And through riding his trishaw he had begun to learn English.

His dream, Maung-Maung's essay concluded, was to buy his own trishaw. But that cost four hundred dollars. And his greatest dream was, one day, to get a "Further Certificate" in mathematics. He had already planned the details of that far-off moment when he could invite his parents to his graduation. "I must hire taxi. I must buy English suit. I must pay for my parents to come to Mandalay. I know that it is expensive, but I want to express my gratitude to my parents. They are my lovers."

75

When I finished the essay, Maung-Maung smiled back his gratitude, and gave me a tour of the city as he had promised.

The American Empire in the East: That was my grand theme as I set forth. But as soon as I left the realm of abstract labels and generalized forces, and came down to individuals—to myself, Maung-Maung, and many others like him— the easy contrasts began to grow confused. If cultures are only individuals writ large, as Salman Rushdie and Gabriel García Márquez have suggested, individuals are small cultures in themselves. Everyone is familiar with the slogan of Kipling's "Oh, East is East, and West is West, and never the twain shall meet." But few recall that the lines that conclude the refrain, just a few syllables later, exclaim, "But there is neither East nor West, border, nor breed, nor birth, / When two strong men stand face to face, though they come from the ends of the earth!" 80

On a grand collective level, the encounters between East and West might well be interpreted as a battle; but on the human level, the meeting more closely resembled a mating dance (even Rambo, while waging war against the Vietnamese, had fallen in love with a Vietnamese girl). Whenever a Westerner meets an Easterner, each is to some extent confronted with the unknown. And the unknown is at once an enticement and a challenge; it awakens in us both the lover and the would-be conqueror. When Westerner meets Easterner, therefore, each finds himself often drawn to the other, yet mystified; each projects his romantic hopes on the stranger, as well as his designs; and each pursues both his illusions and his vested interests with a curious mix of innocence and calculation that shifts with every step.

Everywhere I went in Asia, I came upon variations on this same uncertain pattern: in the streets of China, where locals half woo, half recoil from Westerners whose ways remain alien but whose goods are now irresistible; in the country-and-western bars of Manila, where former conqueror and former conquest slow-dance cheek to cheek with an affection, and a guilt, born of longtime familiarity; in the high places of the Himalayas, where affluent Westerners eager to slough off their riches in order to find religion meet local wise men so poor that they have made of riches a religion; and, most vividly of all, in the darkened bars of Bangkok, where a Western man and a Thai girl exchange shy questions and tentative glances, neither knowing whether either is after love or something else. Sometimes, the romance seemed like a blind date, sometimes like a passionate attachment; sometimes like a back-street coupling, sometimes like the rhyme of kindred spirits. Always, though, it made any talk of winners and losers irrelevant.

Usually, too, the cross-cultural affairs developed with all the contradictory twists and turns of any romance in which opposites attract and then retract and then don't know exactly where they stand. The Westerner is drawn to the tradition of the Easterner, and almost covets his knowledge of suffering, but what attracts the Easterner to the West is exactly the opposite—his future, and his freedom from all hardship. After a while, each starts to become more like the other, and somewhat less like the person the other seeks. The New Yorker disappoints the locals by turning into a barefoot ascetic dressed in bangles and beads, while the Nepali peasant frustrates his foreign supplicants by turning out to be a traveling salesman in Levi's and Madonna T-shirt. Soon, neither is quite the person he was, or the one the other wanted. The upshot is confusion. "You cannot have pineapple for breakfast," a Thai waitress once admonished me. "Why?" I asked. "What do *you* have for breakfast?" "Hot dog."

It is never hard, in such skewed exchanges, to find silliness and self-delusion. "Everybody thought that everybody else was ridiculously exotic," writes Gita Mehta of East-West relations in *Karma Cola,* "and everybody got it wrong." Yet Mehta's cold-eyed perspective does justice to only one aspect of this encounter. For the rest, I prefer to listen to her wise and very different compatriot, R. K. Narayan, whose typical tale "God and the Cobbler" describes a chance meeting in a crowded Indian street between a Western hippie and a village cobbler. Each, absurdly, takes the other to be a god. Yet the beauty of their folly is that each, lifted by the other's faith, surprises himself, and us, by somehow rising to the challenge and proving worthy of the trust he has mistakenly inspired: Each, taken out of himself, becomes, not a god perhaps, but something better than a dupe or fraud. Faith becomes its own vindication. And at the story's end, each leaves the other with a kind of benediction, the more valuable because untypical.

Every trip we take deposits us at the same forking of the paths: It can be a shortcut to alienation—removed from our home and distanced from our immediate surroundings, we can afford to be contemptuous of both; or it can be a voyage into renewal, as, leaving our selves and pasts at home and traveling light, we recover our innocence abroad. Abroad, we are all Titanias, so bedazzled by strangeness that we comically mistake asses for beauties; but away from home, we can also be Mirandas, so new to the world that our blind faith can become a kind of higher sight. "After living in Asia," John Krich quotes an old hand as saying. "You trust nobody, but you believe everything." At the same time, as Edmond Taylor wrote, Asia is "the school of doubt in which one learns faith in man." If every journey makes us wiser about the world, it also returns us to a sort of childhood. In alien parts, we speak more simply, in our own or some other language, move more freely, unencumbered by the histories that we carry around at home, and look more excitedly, with eyes of wonder. And if every trip worth taking is both a tragedy and a comedy, rich with melodrama and farce, it is also, at its heart, a love story. The romance with the foreign must certainly be leavened with a spirit of keen and unillusioned realism; but it must also be observed with a measure of faith.

Considerations

1. One of the first individuals Iyer encounters in his journey through Malaysia is Maung-Maung from Mandalay. Looking at this particular encounter, evaluate Maung-Maung's response to Western influences. How has his life been changed by contact with Western ideas? In what ways has he resisted the influence of Western values?

2. Since Iyer is always present as a figure in his essays, we have a dual view of his interactions with the people he encounters. We see his comments about those he meets as well as their responses to him. What portrait of Iyer emerges from the way he presents his impressions about the people he meets? What do the locals think about him? How can you explain the difference between these two portrayals of the author?

Invitation to Write

"Texts read us as much as we do them," remarks Iyer when speaking about his traveling experience in the Far East (para. 14). Therefore, when traveling, not only can we "read" other cultures but we can also learn about how our culture is "read" by others. Write an essay in which you explore the "reading" of the U.S. culture and its representatives in the countries Pico Iyer visited. Look at the different images of America these Eastern countries have created and determine what they have in common as well as the extent to which they are encouraged by Americans themselves. Compare such images with the image you have of America in order to arrive at a more general conclusion about how the image of a culture is generated within and outside of itself.

Connections

Iyer writes about other cultures as a visitor. In "The Spider's Web" (p. 180), Leonard Kibera presents an insider's view of the effects of westernization on an African country. Write an essay in which you explore westernization in postcolonial cultures as reflected in these two texts. Compare the effects the contact with Western culture has had on the lives of the indigenous populations both in the story and in the essay. Think about what Western penetration signifies in both cases and find a definition of westernization based on what the two perceptions of Western influence have in common.

PAUL HARRISON

The Westernization of the World

Paul Harrison, born in 1923 in England, is an economist by training and a writer by profession. He attended Manchester Grammar School and earned master's degrees at Cambridge University and the London School of Economics. In 1968, Harrison began teaching in French at the University of Ife in Nigeria, a position that led to his interest in the development of the Third World. Since then, he has traveled throughout Asia, Africa, and Latin America in order to gather material for his studies. He writes on the effects of development and poverty upon the lives of people in developing countries. His books include *Inside the Third World: The Anatomy of Poverty* (1980), *The Third World Tomorrow: A Report from the Battlefront in the War Against Poverty* (1983), *The Greening of Africa: Breaking Through in the Battle for Land and Food* (1987), and *The Third Revolution: Environment, Population, and a Sustainable World* (1992). Harrison has contributed numerous articles to publications of major United Nations agencies such as the World Health Organization, the Food and Agriculture Organization, UNICEF, and the International Labour Office. He has also been a frequent contributor to the *Guardian, New Society, New Scientist,* and the *Encyclopedia Britannica.* Currently, Harrison is a freelance writer and journalist based in London.

"The Westernization of the World" is the third chapter of the second edition of *Inside the Third World,* a book that explores the interrelationships between politics, culture, economic development, and poverty. The essay deals with the spreading of Western culture and its values among countries that are not only geographically but also culturally remote.

The bourgeoisie has, through its exploitation of the world market, given a cosmopolitan character to production and consumption in every country.

—KARL MARX

In Singapore, Peking opera still lives, in the backstreets. On Boat Quay, where great barges moor to unload rice from Thailand, raw rubber from Malaysia, or timber from Sumatra, I watched a troupe of travelling actors throw up a canvas-and-wood booth stage, paint on their white faces and lozenge eyes, and don their resplendent vermilion, ultramarine, and gold robes. Then, to raptured audiences of bent old women and little children with perfect circle faces, they enacted tales of feudal princes and magic birds and wars and tragic love affairs, sweeping their sleeves and singing in strange metallic voices.

The performance had been paid for by a local cultural society as part of a religious festival. A purple cloth temple had been erected on the quayside, painted papier-mâché sculptures were burning down like giant joss ticks, and middle-aged men were sharing out gifts to be distributed among members' families: red buckets, roast ducks, candies, and moon cakes. The son of the organizer, a fashionable young man in Italian shirt and gold-rimmed glasses, was looking on with amused benevolence. I asked him why only old people and children were watching the show.

"Young people don't like these operas," he said. "They are too old-fashioned. We would prefer to see a high-quality Western variety show, something like that."

He spoke for a whole generation. Go to almost any village in the Third World and you will find youths who scorn traditional dress and sport denims and T-shirts. Go into any bank and the tellers will be dressed as would their European counterparts; at night the manager will climb into his car and go home to watch TV in a home that would not stick out on a European or North American estate. Every capital city in the world is getting to look like every other; it is Marshall McLuhan's global village, but the style is exclusively Western. And not just in consumer fashions: The mimicry extends to architecture, industrial technology, approaches to health care, education, and housing.

To the ethnocentric Westerner or the westernized local, that may seem the most natural thing in the world. That is modern life, they might think. That is the way it will all be one day. That is what development and economic growth are all about. $\quad$ 5

Yet the dispassionate observer can only be puzzled by this growing world uniformity. Surely one should expect more diversity, more indigenous styles and models of development? Why is almost everyone following virtually the same European road? The Third World's obsession with the Western way of life has perverted development and is rapidly destroying good and bad in traditional cultures, flinging the baby out with the bath water. It is the most totally pervasive example of what historians call cultural diffusion in the history of mankind.

Its origins, of course, lie in the colonial experience. European rule was something quite different from the general run of conquests. Previous invaders more often than not settled down in their new territories, interbred and assimilated a good deal of local culture. Not so the Europeans. Some, like the Iberians or the Dutch, were not averse to cohabitation with native women:

unlike the British, they seemed free of purely racial prejudice. But all the Europeans suffered from the same cultural arrogance. Perhaps it is the peculiar self-righteousness of Pauline Christianity that accounts for this trait. Whatever the cause, never a doubt entered their minds that native cultures could be in any way, materially, morally, or spiritually, superior to their own, and that the supposedly benighted inhabitants of the darker continents needed enlightening.

And so there grew up, alongside political and economic imperialism, that more insidious form of control—cultural imperialism. It conquered not just the bodies, but the souls of its victims, turning them into willing accomplices.

Cultural imperialism began its conquest of the Third World with the indoctrination of an elite of local collaborators. The missionary schools sought to produce converts to Christianity who would go out and proselytize among their own people, helping to eradicate traditional culture. Later the government schools aimed to turn out a class of junior bureaucrats and lower military officers who would help to exploit and repress their own people. The British were subtle about this, since they wanted the natives, even the Anglicized among them, to keep their distance. The French, and the Portuguese in Africa, explicitly aimed at the "assimilation" of gifted natives, by which was meant their metamorphosis into model Frenchmen and Lusitanians, distinguishable only by the tint of their skin.

The second channel of transmission was more indirect and voluntary. It   10
worked by what sociologists call reference-group behaviour, found when someone copies the habits and life-style of a social group he wishes to belong to, or to be classed with, and abandons those of his own group. This happened in the West when the new rich of early commerce and industry aped the nobility they secretly aspired to join. Not surprisingly the social climbers in the colonies started to mimic their conquerors. The returned slaves who carried the first wave of westernization in West Africa wore black woolen suits and starched collars in the heat of the dry season. The new officer corps of India were moulded into what the Indian writer Nirad Chaudhuri has called "imitation, polo-playing English subalterns," complete with waxed moustaches and peacock chests. The elite of Indians, adding their own caste-consciousness to the class-consciousness of their rulers, became more British than the British (and still are).

There was another psychological motive for adopting Western ways, deriving from the arrogance and haughtiness of the colonialists. As the Martiniquan political philosopher, Frantz Fanon, remarked, colonial rule was an experience in racial humiliation. Practically every leader of a newly independent state could recall some experience such as being turned out of a club or manhandled on the street by whites, often of low status. The local elite were made to feel ashamed of their colour and of their culture. "I begin to suffer from not being a white man," Fanon wrote, "to the degree that the white man imposes discrimination on me, makes me a colonized native, robs me of all worth, all individuality. . . . Then I will quite simply try to make myself white: That is, I will compel the white man to acknowledge that I am human." To this complex Fanon attributes the colonized natives' constant preoccupation with attracting the attention of the white man, becoming powerful like the white man, proving at all costs that blacks too can be civilized. Given the racism and culturism of the whites, this could only be done by succeeding in their terms, and by adopting their ways.

This desire to prove equality surely helps to explain why Ghana's Nkrumah built the huge stadium and triumphal arch of Black Star Square in Accra. Why the tiny native village of Ivory Coast president Houphouët-Boigny has been graced with a four-lane motorway starting and ending nowhere, a five-star hotel and ultra-modern conference centre. Why Sukarno transformed Indonesia's capital, Jakarta, into an exercise in gigantism, scarred with six-lane highways and neo-fascist monuments in the most hideous taste. The aim was not only to show the old imperialists, but to impress other Third World leaders in the only way everyone would recognize: the Western way.

The influence of Western life-styles spread even to those few nations who escaped the colonial yoke. By the end of the nineteenth century, the elites of the entire non-Western world were taking Europe as their reference group. The progress of the virus can be followed visibly in a room of Topkapi, the Ottoman palace in Istanbul, where a sequence of showcases display the costumes worn by each successive sultan. They begin with kaftans and turbans. Slowly elements of Western military uniform creep in, until the last sultans are decked out in brocade, epaulettes, and cocked hats.

The root of the problem with nations that were never colonized, like Turkey, China, and Japan, was probably their consciousness of Western military superiority. The beating of these three powerful nations at the hands of the West was a humiliating, traumatic experience. For China and Japan, the encounter with the advanced military technology of the industrialized nations was as terrifying as an invasion of extraterrestrials. Europe's earlier discovery of the rest of the world had delivered a mild culture shock to her ethnocentric attitudes. The Orient's contact with Europe shook nations to the foundations, calling into question the roots of their civilizations and all the assumptions and institutions on which their lives were based.

In all three nations groups of Young Turks grew up, believing that their countries could successfully take on the West only if they adopted Western culture, institutions, and even clothing, for all these ingredients were somehow involved in the production of Western technology. As early as the 1840s, Chinese intellectuals were beginning to modify the ancient view that China was in all respects the greatest civilization in the world. The administrator Wei Yüan urged his countrymen to "learn the superior technology of the barbarians in order to control them." But the required changes could not be confined to the technical realm. Effectiveness in technology is the outcome of an entire social system. "Since we were knocked out by cannon balls," wrote M. Chiang, "naturally we became interested in them, thinking that by learning to make them we could strike back. From studying cannon balls we came to mechanical inventions which in turn lead to political reforms, which lead us again to the political philosophies of the West." The republican revolution of 1911 attempted to modernize China, but her subjection to the West continued until another Young Turk, Mao Tse-tung, applied that alternative brand of westernization: communism, though in a unique adaptation.

The Japanese were forced to open their borders to Western goods in 1853, after a couple of centuries of total isolation. They had to rethink fast in order to survive. From 1867, the Meiji rulers westernized Japan with astonishing speed, adopting Western science, technology, and even manners: Short haircuts became the rule, ballroom dancing caught on, and *moningku* with *haikara* (morning coats and high collars) were worn. The transformation was so successful that by the 1970s the Japanese were trouncing the West at its own game. But they had won their economic independence at the cost of losing their cultural autonomy.

Turkey, defeated in the First World War, her immense empire in fragments, set about transforming herself under that compulsive and ruthless westernizer, Kemal Atatürk. The Arabic script was abolished and replaced with the Roman alphabet. Kemal's strange exploits as a hatter will probably stand as the symbol of westernization carried to absurd lengths. His biographer, Lord Kinross, relates that while travelling in the West as a young man, the future president had smarted under Western insults and condescension about the Turkish national hat, the fez. Later, he made the wearing of the fez a criminal offence. "The people of the Turkish republic," he said in a speech launching the new policy, "must prove that they are civilized and advanced persons in their outward respect also. . . . A civilized, international dress is worthy and appropriate for our nation and we will wear it. Boots or shoes on our feet, trousers on our legs, shirt and tie, jacket and waistcoat—and, of course, to complete these, a cover with a brim on our heads. I want to make this clear. This head covering is called a hat."

The Home-grown Colonialists

The fixation with the West did not end at independence. The elites who took power in Latin America were Europeans and imposed European ways on their subjects. Those who assumed office in Africa and Asia were scions of the Western-educated class who had turned sour on their rulers: Indeed, their demands for independence were often backed up with quotes from the Western political writers they had pored over in their student garrets in Oxbridge,

London, or Paris. As Nehru wrote, with unconscious reference to himself: "The British had created a new caste or class in India, the English-educated class, which lived in a world of its own, cut off from the mass of the population, and looked always, even when protesting, towards its rulers." And even in independence, he might have added, towards its former rulers.

On reflection, it is obvious why few of the new ruling elites developed an indigenous model of development. Most were not themselves members of traditional ruling elites. If they owed their new-found power to anything, it was to their literacy, their Western education, the familiarity with Western ideas, and the Western-style institutions of government that they had inherited. In so far as they had clear goals, these were to transform their countries, in the shortest possible time, into Western societies complete with all mod cons. And so they started building miniature Western societies in the centre of their biggest cities and went on building out from there, hoping to cover their whole national territory, little realizing that it would take centuries, following this path, before the majority began to benefit.

The departure of the colonial powers had created a status vacuum, the filling of which gave a further boost to westernization. The old sources of status in ceremony, ritual, and traditional power were dying. The new power strata, politicians, bureaucrats, businessmen, sought to define their status against each other by the only method all of them recognized: the flaunting of material goods of a Western kind. India's political elite moved into tasteful colonial town houses—furnished in a style long dead in Britain—in the tree-lined avenues of New Delhi, while the *nouveaux riches* of younger states built themselves palatial Beverly Hills–style mansions.

The growth of the modern state and economy undermined status and values at local levels, and the westernized elite now became the reference group that social climbers lower down the ladder would ape. Everyone in a position to do so tried to gain status by the conspicuous consumption of a modern life-style, and to acquire the necessary funds they were ready to abrogate all the bonds of traditional obligations.

In many countries the new rulers practised a brand of internal colonialism over their own people. This was, and is, at its most blatant in Latin America, where it still has a racial aspect. The new rulers who assumed power in the early nineteenth century were of European stock, and their descendants still dominate the elites. People from native Indian, or African slave backgrounds, were treated as a subject group, discriminated against, restricted to lowly jobs, forced to adopt European culture, religion, and language.

The situation in Africa and Asia was not all that different. In a few countries the internal colonialism was racial too: the creoles of Liberia and Sierra Leone, the Tutsi of Burundi. In most of the rest it was cultural. The "colonizers" were the westernized elite, whom Nirad Chaudhuri has compared to "a separate ethnic entity with its own collective psychology." The "colonized" are all those groups who do not belong to the modern westernized sector. They too, as we shall see, have been discriminated against, neglected in government spending, and now show signs of becoming a sort of hereditary caste just as surely as if they really were a subject race.

Today westernization has spread into every nook and cranny in the Third World, and because of the discrimination practised against the nonwesternized, it is proceeding with accelerating pace. It creeps down key arteries of indigenous society, poisoning it from within. From the top, it is disseminated through the activities and example of the local hierarchy and squirarchy. From the bottom, the young in particular have become its carriers: For them, adopting Western dress and life-styles is something like becoming a hippie or a punk rocker. It gives them a symbol of supposed superiority and an excuse to hold their parents in contempt. It is their own form of youth rebellion, but one from which, unlike Western adolescents, they are unlikely to recover. The schools have been potent instruments of westernization among the young: They often impose Western uniforms on pupils, and teach syllabuses emphasizing modern, urban activities and values. Young people emerge dazed and uprooted, despising their own culture.

The Six-million-dollar Cultural Imperialist

The educational message is reinforced by adult media, which are, as communications sociologist Jeremy Tunstall has remarked, Anglo-American all over the world. 25

In Indonesia, and in Pakistan, Thailand, Malaysia, Nigeria, Ghana, Kenya, Colombia, Peru, the largest advertising agency is American. Three out of five top agencies are American in India, Mexico, and Argentina. They use Western methods, often Western images. In Europe, Martini is sold with shots of rich playboys and debutantes, skiing, air ballooning, racing in light aeroplanes: If you buy the product, it is implied, you pick up some of the aura. The reference group most frequently chosen in Third World advertising is the affluent, westernized elite, and even government campaigns use the same approach. One Iranian family-planning poster I have collected contrasts a poor family, in traditional clothing, in a rundown, bare mud hut, with a vast and screaming brood, with a small family with two children in a plush suburban house with radio and TV, husband in city suit, shirt, collar, and tie, wife in skirt and blouse and pinafore. Have only two children, the hidden message reads, and you too can enjoy this desirable Western life-style. Indigenous ways are held up to scorn and ridicule—indeed, throughout the Third World traditional culture has become a negative reference group, a group that all ambitious, go-ahead people seek to escape and deny all connection with.

Not only are marketing methods Western: The products they are selling are often Western too—Levi's, pop cassettes, mopeds are all marketed hard.

A person who uses any one of them is already assuming an element of the desired image and is more receptive to others. So the big multinationals can benefit from economies of scale, products are almost identical the world over. In November 1976 William Bourke, then vice-president of Ford's North American Automotive Operations, predicted the emergence of a single world market with a single world style: "The day is not far off when manufacturers ... will be producing the same line of products for sale everywhere in the world, with only the most minor of variations." This would come about through the "homogenizing of consumer tastes" through modern communications. If the product is not made to suit the market, the market has to be moulded to suit the product. The multinationals join forces with the national elites as agents of westernization.

Western life-styles are also promoted through the entertainment media. Western-made films penetrate into every large city in the Third World. Ouagadougou, Upper Volta's capital deep in the Sahel, has a cinema where Western thrillers and disaster movies are shown. Their influence is immediately visible, for the whole street outside is thronged every night with Western-dressed office clerks, market porters, and shop assistants, their mobilettes parked in dense rows.

Television plays a similar role. Poor countries who decide to set up their own TV service (whether to foster national integration or to pander to the aspirations of the elite) almost always find themselves forced, once they start broadcasting for entertainment and not merely for education, to use large amounts of foreign material, chiefly American, to fill their schedules. The American networks can make extra copies of TV videotapes at a negligible cost compared to the original cost of production. The vast economies of scale enable them to sell "quality" products more cheaply than countries could produce their own programmes.

So programming throughout much of the Third World broadcasts the American way of life of rugged consumerist individualism. CBS programmes are distributed in a hundred countries. *Hawaii Five-O* sells in forty-seven countries and is dubbed into six languages. *Bonanza* attracts a world audience of 350 million. In a survey of TV programming in 1970–71, media expert Tapio Varis found that 84 percent of Guatemala's TV time was taken up with imported programmes, 62 percent of Uruguay's, 55 percent of Chile's, 50 percent of the Dominican Republic's (compare the USA ratio of only 1 or 2 percent, and Britain's of 12 percent). In Asia, 71 percent of Malaysia's programmes were imported, 35 percent of Pakistan's, 31 percent of Korea's, 29 percent of the Philippines, and 22 percent of Taiwan's. In Africa and the Arab world, Zambia imported 64 percent of her programmes, Iraq 52 percent, Egypt 41 percent, and Lebanon 40 percent. Singapore is one of the most dominated, devoting some 78 percent of TV schedules to alien matter. It is instructive to quote a typical week's TV highlights selected by Bailyne Sung for

30

readers of the *Straits Times: M'Liss, a Comedy of the Old West, Best Sellers, Jalna, Charlie's Angels, Cher, Mary Tyler Moore, Donny and Marie* (all American); *The World at War, Shoulder to Shoulder, Sykes, Play Soccer Jack Charlton's Way, The Explorers* (all British). On the film pages, advertisements for the week's shows: *Airport '77, Eagles over London, A Star is Born, The Deep,* along, it is true, with such authentic Chinese thrillers as *Bionic Boy* and *Shaolin Killing Machine.* And, if all that is not enough, you can turn to the paper's comic strip page where you will find not a single Chinese or Malay series, but the nuclear family problems and consumer behaviour of *The Gambols, Bugs Bunny, Blondie,* and *Bringing up Father* ("You're supposed to be on your way to work," says daughter. "Ssh ... this is a good TV programme," grunts father.)

Over the Malacca straits in Indonesia, and you can witness an even more curious spectacle. There, American TV serials are not even dubbed or subtitled into the national language, Bahasa Indonesia. A commentator introduces them, like an Italian opera, with a summary of the plot, then off you go with *The Six Million Dollar Man,* and all non-English-speaking viewers can do is to watch the kicks, leaps, and knockouts. Indonesian TV does run authentic Javanese comedies and cultural programmes of regional dances. But they also run locally made programmes in which Western-dressed Indonesian crooners sing perfect imitations of American songs, squatting on motorbikes and wearing racy caps: The style and slickness of the imported programmes has to be imitated by national production too, if they are not to look naive and wooden. Television has begun to penetrate even the remote areas of Java, where there may be just one or two sets per village, mounted on a post outside the local government offices or on the wall of an enterprising bar owner. It is a depressing sight to see these people, who are supreme artists of dance and theatre, gaping wide-eyed at Western soap operas. One evening I noticed enormous crowds thronging round the public sets and spilling out of bars, and inquired what they were watching. It was a Muhammad Ali fight.

The final channel of cultural imperialism is tourism. Westerners, sick of the empty, smothering materialism of their own civilization, trek east and south on dream holidays and youthful odysseys, perhaps looking for a simplicity that Europe lost many centuries ago, and which the Third World itself is fast losing.

Destinations are attractive in the measure that they are unspoiled. Yet the very act of going to them spoils them and despoils them. The Westerner goes to find somewhere uncontaminated by westernization. His visit, in itself, contaminates. He carries the virus with him. He has the Midas touch. As soon as Westerners start arriving in numbers, governments, multinationals, and even international development agencies rush up five-star hotels. The Western tourist is unable to escape his own shadow, and a protective wall of Western comforts and debased imitations of local culture grow up around him.

The contrasts are pitiful. It is a charmless sight to see fat American widows heaved up onto a camel's back in idyllic Tunisian oases or African vendors clustering like flies around topless Swedes on Gambian beaches. Gradually the village economy is distorted; the primary aim is no longer to see to its own needs, but rather to cater for the consumerist whims of foreigners. Locals leave their fields and fishing boats and become touts, flunkeys, or donkey-guides. Thieves and whores arrive.

National culture is not immune. The visual and performing arts tend to   35
degenerate from the sacred and symbolic into vulgar, commercialized spectacles and stereotyped products. The moneychangers take over the temple. As economist Jacques Bugnicourt has pointed out, tourism grows into an incitement to the pillage and plundering of local art and archaeology and the desecration of religious sites. In Nigeria, traders used to come knocking on my door at all hours of the evening and spread out their wares: the factitious side by side with the authentic, ebony-smooth heads along with rough-hewn dance masks. Traders were scouring the villages for family treasures: carved drums and granary doors, ornate spears and idols. And, because the people were poor, they risked the wrath of their gods and sold them.

Under this barrage of onslaughts, traditional cultures and social structures are diseased, dying; in many places dead. This trend has to be lamented, not just for nostalgic reasons. Just as the dwindling of animal species threatens the balance and diversity of nature, the genetic bank upon which the continuing vitality of life depends, so the disappearance of whole groups of societies reduces the cultural diversity of mankind.

The Islamic revival that swept the Moslem world in the late seventies represented an understandable rebellion against the imposition of alien cultural forms, but it was partly reactionary in character and aimed at maintaining some of the least equitable features of traditional culture: Similar movements of cultural reaction exist in India. Restoration of the old ways, good and bad, is no better a solution than their total eradication. Some features of traditional life deserve to go, because they conflict with justice and equity: the low status of women everywhere and of untouchables in India and so on. New paths must be found that can combine the best indigenous values with social justice, as some countries, at some periods, have succeeded in doing.

What the Third World needs now, for rapid development benefiting all, is redistribution, cooperation, emphasis on production, autonomy, self-help, participation. The lure of westernization has perverted development goals, making the isolated individual consumer the goal of most efforts. Western life-styles, products, and approaches . . . generate the wrong kind of development in the context of poor nations. The Western middle-class way of life is so far above the conditions of the bulk of the population in these countries that the elites can enjoy it only at the cost of grotesque inequalities and exploitation.

Western technologies of housing, industry, health, are expensive, too, and poor countries are short of funds. The choice of Western approaches has meant, of necessity, that government spending was concentrated in small, high-quality packets which benefited only the few. Meanwhile, the majority languished in neglected poverty.

Considerations

1. Harrison sees the westernization of the world as the result of the unlikely, but evident, cooperation between colonizer and colonized. How do Western cultures disseminate their values?

2. What part does Harrison think is played by the indigenous populations in the devaluation and loss of their own cultures?

3. The results of westernization are, by and large, tragic, since many cultures are destroyed in the process. Nevertheless, the mixture of cultures gives rise to comic incongruities in some cases. Examine one or two of Harrison's examples of the westernization phenomenon. What is comic and what is tragic about the situations he describes?

Invitation to Write

According to Harrison, the spread of Western values among Third World countries has resulted in damage to their cultures. Not only colonialism but also the less-aggressive phenomenon of tourism contributes to the transformation of the non-Western cultures. The process of change due to the intervention, in whatever form, of another culture is not, however, a purely Third World occurrence. Consider the United States and the successive waves of immigration, which have changed not only the ethnic composition of the population but also American culture as a whole. Write an essay in which you explore the idea of intercultural influence on the basis of Harrison's examples. Also consider examples of changes in American culture under the influence of ethnic or minority cultures. Compare them to the "westernization" described by Harrison in order to decide whether intercultural influence is indeed a negative phenomenon.

Connections

Both Paul Harrison and Pico Iyer ("Love Match," p. 535) reflect on the influence of tourism on indigenous cultures. Write an essay in which you decide whether they would agree on the effects of tourism in underdeveloped countries.

One way to do this would be to think about whether Iyer would feel his experiences in Bail justify Harrison's observations. Consider how he would respond to Harrison's belief that "Westerners, sick of the empty, smothering materialism of their own civilization, trek east and south on dream holidays and youthful odysseys, perhaps looking for a simplicity that Europe lost many centuries ago, and which the Third World itself is fast losing" (para. 32).

Questions of Conquest

Mario Vargas Llosa, a well-known South American author and politician, was born in 1936 in Arequipa, Peru, in a relatively rich family with aristocratic connections. Because his parents were separated for a long period of time, he spent most of his childhood with his maternal grandparents. He got his early education in Bolivia before being sent to a Peruvian military school. Later, Vargas Llosa went to study in Spain and began a journalistic career in France. His first novel, *La ciudad y los perros* (1962), translated into English as *The Time of the Hero,* depicts the corruption and violence he encountered in the military academy. His other works include *The Green House* (1966), *Conversation in the Cathedral* (1969), *Captain Pantoja and the Special Service* (1973), *Aunt Julia and the Scriptwriter* (1977), *The War of the End of the World* (1981), *The Real Life of Alejandro Mayta* (1984), *The Storyteller* (1988), and *In Praise of the Stepmother* (1990). In all of them, Vargas Llosa explores themes related to his culture: exaggerated masculinity, violence, and sensuality, as well as the fascinating life of the Peruvian jungle. His stylistic innovations, similar to those of James Joyce and William Faulkner, are closely related to the themes he explores, as well as to his vision of a fabulous world rich in uncertainty and paradox.

Besides fiction, Vargas Llosa has written literary criticism and political essays. "Questions of Conquest" began as a lecture he delivered at Syracuse University and published, in a slightly different form, in *A Writer's Reality* (1991). The following version was published in *Harper's* magazine and was later included in *The Best American Essays 1990.* The essay expresses Vargas Llosa's political views on the important and controversial issue of the Spanish conquest, which began to be fiercely debated preceding the five-hundredth anniversary of Columbus's voyage to America. Unlike many of his peers, Vargas Llosa argues that rather than assigning blame for the conquest, one should study it in order to discover the causes of South America's present predicament.

IN MADRID NOT LONG AGO, a shadowy group calling itself the Association of Indian Cultures held a press conference to announce that its members (it was not clear who these men and women might be) were preparing to undertake, in Spain and also throughout Latin America, a number of acts of "sabotage." It is, of course, a sad fact of life that in a number of Latin American countries—in Spain as well—the planting of bombs and the destruction of property continue to be perceived by some as a means of achieving justice, or self-determination, or, as in my country, Peru, the realization of a revolutionary utopia. But the Association of Indian Cultures did not seem interested in seizing the future. Their battle was with the past.

What are to be sabotaged by this group are the numerous quincentennial ceremonies and festivities scheduled for 1992 to commemorate the epochal voyage nearly 500 years ago of Columbus's three small caravels. The Association of Indian Cultures believes that the momentous events of 1492 should in no way be celebrated; and although I have yet to hear of other persons willing to make the point through subversion, I do know that the group will not lack for sympathizers.

The question most crucial to these individuals is the oldest one: Was the discovery and conquest of America by Europeans the greatest feat of the Christian West or one of history's monumental crimes? It is a question they ask rhetorically and perhaps will answer with violence. This is not to say that to discuss what could have happened as opposed to what did happen is a useless undertaking: Historians and thinkers have pondered the question since the seventeenth century, producing wonderful books and speculations. But to me the debate serves no practical purpose, and I intend to stay out of it. What would America be like in the 1990s if the dominant cultures were those of the Aztecs and Incas? The one answer, ultimately, is that there is no way to know.

I have two other questions, both having to do with the conquest, and I happen to think that an honest and thoughtful discussion of them is as timely and urgent as any others one could pose just now about Latin America. First: How was it possible that cultures as powerful and sophisticated as those of the ancient Mexicans and Peruvians—huge imperial cultures, as opposed to the scattered tribes of North America—so easily crumbled when encountered by infinitesimally small bands of Spanish adventurers? This question is itself centuries old, but not academic. In its answer may lie the basis for an understanding of the world the conquest engendered, a chronically "underdeveloped" world that has, for the most part, remained incapable of realizing its goals and visions.

The second question is this: Why have the postcolonial republics of the Americas—republics that might have been expected to have deeper and broader notions of liberty, equality, and fraternity—failed so miserably to improve the lives of their Indian citizens? Even as I write, not only the Amazonian rain forests but the small tribes who have managed for so long to survive there are being barbarously exterminated in the name of progress.

To begin to answer these questions, we must put down our newspapers and open the pages of the books that allow us to see close up the era when the

Europeans dared to venture to sea in search of a new route to India and its spices, and happened instead on an unspoiled continent with its own peoples, customs, and civilizations. The chronicles of the conquest form an astonishingly rich literature—a literature at once fantastical and true. Through these books we can rediscover a period and a place, much as the readers of contemporary Latin American fiction discover the contemporary life of a continent. In their own way, the early chroniclers were the first Magical Realists.

The historian who mastered the subject of the discovery and conquest of Peru by the Spaniards better than anyone else had a tragic story. He died without having written the book for which he had prepared himself his whole life and whose theme he knew so well that he almost gave the impression of being omniscient. His name was Raúl Porras Barrenechea. He was a small, pot-bellied man with a large forehead and a pair of blue eyes that became impregnated with malice every time he mocked someone. He was the most brilliant teacher I have ever had.

In the big old house of San Marcos, the first university founded by the Spaniards in the New World, a place that had already begun to fall into an irreparable process of decay when I passed through it in the 1950s, Porras Barrenechea's lectures on historical sources attracted such a vast number of listeners that it was necessary to arrive well in advance so as not to be left outside the classroom listening together with dozens of students literally hanging from the doors and windows.

Whenever Porras Barrenechea spoke, history became anecdote, gesture, adventure, color, psychology. He depicted history as a series of mirrors that had the magnificence of a Renaissance painting and in which the determining factor of events was never the impersonal forces, the geographical imperative, the economic relations of divine providence, but a cast of certain outstanding individuals whose audacity, genius, charisma, or contagious insanity had imposed on each era and society a certain orientation and shape. As well as this concept of history, which the scientific historians had already named as romantic in an effort to discredit it, Porras Barrenechea demanded knowledge and documentary precision, which none of his colleagues and critics at San Marcos had at that time been able to equal. Those historians who dismissed Porras Barrenechea because he was interested in simple, narrated history instead of a social or economic interpretation had been less effective than he was in explaining to us that crucial event in the destiny of Europe and America—the destruction of the Inca Empire and the linking of its vast territories and peoples to the Western world. This was because for Porras Barrenechea, although history had to have a dramatic quality, architectonic beauty, suspense, richness, and a wide range of human types and excellence in the style of a great fiction, everything in it also had to be scrupulously true, proven time after time.

In order to be able to narrate the discovery and conquest of Peru in this   10
way, Porras Barrenechea first had to evaluate very carefully all the witnesses
and documents so as to establish the degree of credibility of each one of them.
And in the numerous cases of deceitful testimonies, Porras Barrenechea had to
find out the reasons that led the authors to conceal, misrepresent, or over-
claim the facts; knowing their peculiar limitations, those sources had a double
meaning—what they revealed and what they distorted.

For forty years Porras Barrenechea dedicated all his powerful intellectual
energy to this heroic hermeneutics. All the works he published while he was
alive constitute the preliminary work for what should have been his magnum
opus. When he was perfectly ready to embark upon it, pressing on with assurance through the labyrinthine jungle of chronicles, letters, testaments, rhymes,
and ballads of the discovery and conquest that he had read, cleansed, confronted, and almost memorized, sudden death put an end to his encyclopedic
information. As a result, all those interested in that era and in the men who
lived in it have had to keep on reading the old but so far unsurpassed history
of the conquest written by an American who never set foot in the country but
who sketched it with extraordinary skill—William Prescott.

Dazzled by Porras Barrenechea's lectures, at one time I seriously considered the possibility of putting literature aside so as to dedicate myself to history. Porras Barrenechea had asked me to work with him as an assistant in an
ambitious project on the general history of Peru under the auspices of the
Lima bookseller and publisher Juan Mejía Baca. It was Porras Barrenechea's
task to write the volumes devoted to the conquest and emancipation. For four
years I spent three hours a day, five days a week, in that dusty house on Col-
ina Street in Lima, where the books, the card indexes, and the notebooks had
slowly invaded and devoured everything except Porras Barrenechea's bed and
the dining table. My job was to read and take notes on the chronicles' various
themes, but principally the myths and legends that preceded and followed the
discovery and conquest of Peru. That experience has become an unforgettable
memory for me. Whoever is familiar with the chronicles of the discovery and
conquest of America will understand why. They represent for us Latin Americans what the novels of chivalry represent for Europe, the beginning of literary fiction as we understand it today. The tradition from which sprang books
like *One Hundred Years of Solitude,* Julio Cortázar's short stories, and the
works of the Paraguayan novelist Augusto Roa Bastos, books in which we are
exposed to a world totally reconstructed and subverted by fantasy, started
without doubt in those chronicles of the conquest and discovery that I read
and annotated under the guidance of Porras Barrenechea.

The chronicle, a hermaphrodite genre, is distilling fiction into life all the
time, as in Jorge Luis Borges's tale "Tlon, Uqbar, Orbis Tertius." Does this
mean that its testimony must be challenged from a historical point of view
and accepted only as literature? Not at all. Its exaggerations and fantasies

often reveal more about the reality of the era than its truths. Astonishing miracles from time to time enliven the tedious pages of the *Crónica moralizada,* the exemplary chronicle of Father Calancha; sulfurous outrages come from the male and female demons, fastidiously catechized in the Indian villages by the extirpators of idolatries like Father Arriaga, to justify the devastations of idols, amulets, ornaments, handicrafts, and tombs. This teaches more about the innocence, fanaticism, and stupidity of the time than the wisest of treatises.

As long as one knows how to read them, everything is contained in these pages written sometimes by men who hardly knew how to write and who were impelled by the unusual nature of contemporary events to try to communicate and register them for posterity, thanks to an intuition of the privilege they enjoyed, that of being the witnesses of and actors in events that were changing the history of the world. Because they narrated these events under the passion of recently lived experience, they often related things that to us seem like naive or cynical fantasies. For the people of the time, this was not so; they were phantoms that credulity, surprise, fear, and hatred had endowed with a solidity and vitality often more powerful than beings made of flesh and blood.

The conquest of the Tawantinsuyu—the name given to the Inca Empire in its 15 totality—by a handful of Spaniards is a fact of history that even now, after having digested and ruminated over all the explanations, we find hard to unravel. The first wave of conquistadores, Francisco Pizarro and his companions, was fewer than 200, not counting the black slaves and the collaborating Indians. When the reinforcements started to arrive, this first wave had already dealt a mortal blow and taken over an empire that had ruled over at least twenty million people. This was not a primitive society made up of barbaric tribes, like the ones the Spaniards had found in the Caribbean or in Darién, but a civilization that had reached a high level of social, military, agricultural, and handicraft development that in many ways Spain itself had not reached.

The most remarkable aspects of this civilization, however, were not the paths that crossed the four *suyus,* or regions, of the vast territory, the temples and fortresses, the irrigation systems, or the complex administrative organizations, but something about which all the testimonies of the chronicles agree. This civilization managed to eradicate hunger in that immense region. It was able to distribute all that was produced in such a way that all its subjects had enough to eat. Only a very small number of empires throughout the whole world have succeeded in achieving this feat. Are the conquistadores' firearms, horses, and armor enough to explain the immediate collapse of this Inca civilization at the first clash with the Spaniards? It is true the gunpowder, the bullets, and the charging of beasts that were unknown to them paralyzed the Indians with a religious terror and provoked in them the feeling that they were fighting not against men but against gods who were invulnerable to the arrows and slings with which they fought. Even so, the numerical difference was such that the Quechua ocean would have had simply to shake in order to drown the invader.

What prevented this from happening? What is the profound explanation for that defeat from which the Inca population never recovered? The answer may perhaps lie hidden in the moving account that appears in the chronicles of what happened in the Cajamarca Square the day Pizarro captured the last ruler of the empire, Inca Atahualpa. We must, above all, read the accounts of those who were there, those who lived through the event or had direct testimony of it.

At the precise moment the Inca emperor is captured, before the battle begins, his armies give up the fight as if manacled by a magic force. The slaughter is indescribable, but only from one of the two sides. The Spaniards discharged their harquebuses, thrust their pikes and swords, and charged their horses against a bewildered mass, which, having witnessed the capture of their god and master, seemed unable to defend itself or even to run away. In the space of a few minutes, the army, which defeated Prince Huáscar, the emperor's half brother, in a battle for rule, and which dominated all the northern provinces of the empire, disintegrated like ice in warm water.

The vertical and totalitarian structure of the Tawantinsuyu was without doubt more harmful to its survival than all the conquistadores' firearms and iron weapons. As soon as the Inca, that figure who was the vortex toward which all the wills converged searching for inspiration and vitality, the axis around which the entire society was organized and upon which depended the life and death of every person, from the richest to the poorest, was captured, no one knew how to act. And so they did the only thing they could do with heroism, we must admit, but without breaking the 1,001 taboos and precepts that regulated their existence. They let themselves get killed. And that was the fate of dozens and perhaps hundreds of Indians stultified by the confusion and the loss of leadership they suffered when the Inca emperor, the life force of their universe, was captured right before their eyes. Those Indians who let themselves be knifed or blown up into pieces that somber afternoon in Cajamarca Square lacked the ability to make their own decisions either with the sanction of authority or indeed against it and were incapable of taking individual initiative, of acting with a certain degree of independence according to the changing circumstances.

Those 180 Spaniards who had placed the Indians in ambush and were now slaughtering them did possess this ability. It was this difference, more than the numerical one or the weapons, that created an immense inequality between those civilizations. The individual had no importance and virtually no existence in that pyramidal and theocratic society whose achievements had always been collective and anonymous—carrying the gigantic stones of the

Machu Picchu citadel or of the Ollantay fortress up the steepest of peaks, directing water to all the slopes of the cordillera hills by building terraces that even today enable irrigation to take place in the most desolate places, and making paths to unite regions separated by infernal geographies.

A state religion that took away the individual's free will and crowned the authority's decision with the aura of a divine mandate turned the Tawantin-suyu into a beehive—laborious, efficient, stoic. But its immense power was, in fact, very fragile. It rested completely on the sovereign god's shoulders, the man whom the Indian had to serve and to whom he owed a total and selfless obedience. It was religion rather than force that preserved the people's meta-physical docility toward the Inca. It was an essentially political religion, which on the one hand turned the Indians into diligent servants and on the other was capable of receiving into its bosom as minor gods all the deities of the peoples that had been conquered, whose idols were moved to Cuzco and enthroned by the Inca himself. The Inca religion was less cruel than the Aztec one, for it performed human sacrifices with a certain degree of moderation, if this can be said, making use only of the necessary cruelty to ensure hypnosis and fear of the subjects toward the divine power incarnated in the temporary power of the Inca.

We cannot call into question the organizing genius of the Inca. The speed with which the empire, in the short period of a century, grew from its nucleus in Cuzco high in the Andes to become a civilization that embraced three quarters of South America is incredible. And this was the result not only of the Quechua's military efficiency but also of the Inca's ability to persuade the neighboring peoples and cultures to join the Tawantinsuyu. Once these other peoples and cultures became part of the empire, the bureaucratic mechanism was immediately set in motion, enrolling the new servants in that system that dissolves individual life into a series of tasks and gregarious duties carefully programmed and supervised by the gigantic network of administrators whom the Inca sent to the farthest borders. Either to prevent or to extinguish rebel-liousness, there was a system called *mitimaes,* by which villages and people were removed en masse to faraway places where, feeling misplaced and lost, these exiles naturally assumed an attitude of passivity and absolute respect, which of course represented the Inca system's ideal citizen.

Such a civilization was capable of fighting against the natural elements and defeating them. It was capable of consuming rationally what it produced, heaping together reserves for future times of poverty or disaster. And it was also able to evolve slowly and with care in the field of knowledge, inventing only that which could support it and deterring all that which in some way or another could undermine its foundation—as, for example, writing or any other form of expression likely to develop individual pride or a rebellious imagination.

It was not capable, however, of facing the unexpected, that absolute novelty presented by the balance of armored men on horseback who assaulted the Incas with weapons transgressing all the war-and-peace patterns known to them. When, after the initial confusion, attempts to resist started breaking out here and there, it was too late. The complicated machinery regulating the empire had entered a process of decomposition. Leaderless with the murder of Inca Huayna Capac's two sons, Huáscar and Atahualpa, the Inca system seems to fall into a monumental state of confusion and cosmic deviation, similar to the chaos that, according to the Cuzcan sages, the Amautas, had prevailed in the world before the Tawantinsuyu was founded by the mythical Manco Capac and Mama Ocllo.

While on the one hand caravans of Indians loaded with gold and silver   25
continued to offer treasures to the conquistadores to pay for the Inca's rescue, on the other hand a group of Quechua generals, attempting to organize a resistance, fired at the wrong target, for they were venting their fury on the Indian cultures that had begun to collaborate with the Spaniards because of all their grudges against their ancient masters. At any rate, Spain had already won the game. Rebellious outbreaks were always localized and counter-checked by the servile obedience that great sectors of the Inca system transferred automatically from the Incas to the new masters.

Those who destroyed the Inca Empire and created that country called Peru, a country that four and a half centuries later has not yet managed to heal the bleeding wounds of its birth, were men whom we can hardly admire. They were, it is true, uncommonly courageous, but, contrary to what the edifying stories teach us, most of them lacked any idealism or higher purpose. They possessed only greed, hunger, and in the best of cases a certain vocation for adventure. The cruelty in which the Spaniards took pride, and the chronicles depict to the point of making us shiver, was inscribed in the ferocious customs of the times and was without doubt equivalent to that of the people they subdued and almost extinguished. Three centuries later, the Inca population had been reduced from twenty million to only six.

But these semiliterate, implacable, and greedy swordsmen, who even before having completely conquered the Inca Empire were already savagely fighting among themselves or fighting the pacifiers sent against them by the faraway monarch to whom they had given a continent, represented a culture in which, we will never know whether for the benefit or the disgrace of mankind, something new and exotic had germinated in the history of man. In this culture, although injustice and abuse often favored by religion had proliferated, by the alliance of multiple factors—among them chance—a social space of human activities had evolved that was neither legislated nor controlled by those in power. This evolution would produce the most extraordinary economic, scientific, and technical development human civilization has ever known since the times of the cavemen with their clubs. Moreover, this new society would give way to the creation of the individual as the sovereign source of values by which society would be judged.

Those who, rightly, are shocked by the abuses and crimes of the conquest must bear in mind that the first men to condemn them and ask that they be brought to an end were men, like Father Bartolomé de Las Casas, who came to America with the conquistadores and abandoned the ranks in order to collaborate with the vanquished, whose suffering they divulged with an indignation and virulence that still move us today.

Father Las Casas was the most active, although not the only one, of those nonconformists who rebelled against the abuses inflicted upon the Indians. They fought against their fellow men and against the policies of their own country in the name of a moral principle that to them was higher than any principle of nation or state. This self-determination could not have been possible among the Incas or any of the other pre-Hispanic cultures. In these cultures, as in the other great civilizations of history foreign to the West, the individual could not morally question the social organism of which he was a part, because he existed only as an integral atom of that organism and because for him the dictates of the state could not be separated from morality. The first culture to interrogate and question itself, the first to break up the masses into individual beings who with time gradually gained the right to think and act for themselves, was to become, thanks to that unknown exercise, freedom, the most powerful civilization in our world.

It seems to me useless to ask oneself whether it was good that it happened   30
in this manner or whether it would have been better for humanity if the individual had never been born and the tradition of the antlike societies had continued forever. The pages of the chronicles of the conquest and discovery depict that crucial, bloody moment, full of phantasmagoria, when—disguised as a handful of invading treasure hunters, killing and destroying—the Judeo-Christian tradition, the Spanish language, Greece, Rome, the Renaissance, the notion of individual sovereignty, and the chance of living in freedom reached the shores of the Empire of the Sun. So it was that we as Peruvians were born. And, of course, the Bolivians, Chileans, Ecuadoreans, Colombians, and others.

Almost five centuries later, this notion of individual sovereignty is still an unfinished business. We have not yet, properly speaking, seen the light. We in Latin America do not yet constitute real nations. Our contemporary reality is still impregnated with the violence and marvels that those first texts of our literature, those novels disguised as history or historical books corrupted by fiction, told us about.

At least one basic problem is the same. Two cultures, one Western and modern, the other aboriginal and archaic, hardly coexist, separated from each other because of the exploitation and discrimination that the former exercises over the latter. Our country, our countries, are in a deep sense more a fiction than a reality. In the eighteenth century, in France, the name of Peru rang with a golden echo. And an expression was then born: *Ce n'est pas le Pérou,* which is used when something is not as rich and extraordinary as its legendary name suggests. Well, *Le Pérou n'est pas le Pérou.* It never was, at least for the majority of its inhabitants, that fabulous country of legends and fictions but rather an artificial gathering of men from different languages, customs, and traditions whose only common denominator was having been condemned by history to live together without knowing or loving one another.

Immense opportunities brought by the civilization that discovered and conquered America have been beneficial only to a minority, sometimes a very small one; whereas the great majority managed to have only the negative share of the conquest—that is, contributing in their serfdom and sacrifice, in their misery and neglect, to the prosperity and refinement of the westernized elites. One of our worst defects, our best fictions, is to believe that our miseries have been imposed on us from abroad, that others, for example, the conquistadores, have always been responsible for our problems. There are countries in Latin America—Mexico is the best example—in which the Spaniards are even now severely indicted for what they did to the Indians. Did they really do it? We did it; we are the conquistadores.

They were our parents and grandparents who came to our shores and gave us the names we have and the language we speak. They also gave us the habit of passing to the devil the responsibility for any evil we do. Instead of making amends for what they did, by improving and correcting our relations with our indigenous compatriots, mixing with them and amalgamating ourselves to form a new culture that would have been a kind of synthesis of the best of both, we, the westernized Latin Americans, have persevered in the worst habits of our forebears, behaving toward the Indians during the nineteenth and twentieth centuries as the Spaniards behaved toward the Aztecs and the Incas, and sometimes even worse. We must remember that in countries like Chile and Argentina, it was during the republic (in the nineteenth century), not during the colony, that the native cultures were systematically exterminated. In the Amazon jungle, and in the mountains of Guatemala, the exterminating continues.

It is a fact that in many of our countries, as in Peru, we share, in spite of the pious and hypocritical indigenous rhetoric of our men of letters and our politicians, the mentality of the conquistadores. Only in countries where the native population was small or nonexistent, or where the aboriginals were practically liquidated, can we talk of integrated societies. In the others, discreet, sometimes unconscious, but very effective apartheid prevails. Important as integration is, the obstacle to achieving it lies in the huge economic gap between the two communities. Indian peasants live in such a primitive way that communication is practically impossible. It is only when they move to the cities that they have the opportunity to mingle with the other Peru. The price they must pay for integration is high—renunciation of their culture, their language, their beliefs, their traditions and customs, and the adoption of the culture of their ancient masters. After one generation they become mestizos. They are no longer Indians.

Perhaps there is no realistic way to integrate our societies other than by asking the Indians to pay that price. Perhaps the ideal—that is, the preservation of the primitive cultures of America—is a utopia incompatible with this other and more urgent goal—the establishment of societies in which social and economic inequalities among citizens be reduced to human, reasonable limits and where everybody can enjoy at least a decent and free life. In any case, we have been unable to reach any of those ideals and are still, as when we had just entered Western history, trying to find out what we are and what our future will be.

If forced to choose between the preservation of Indian cultures and their complete assimilation, with great sadness I would choose modernization of the Indian population, because there are priorities; and the first priority is, of course, to fight hunger and misery. My novel *The Storyteller* is about a very small tribe in the Amazon called the Machiguengas. Their culture is alive in spite of the fact that it has been repressed and persecuted since Inca times. It should be respected. The Machiguengas are still resisting change, but their world is now so fragile that they cannot resist much longer. They have been reduced to practically nothing. It is tragic to destroy what is still living, still a driving cultural possibility, even if it is archaic; but I am afraid we shall have to make a choice. For I know of no case in which it has been possible to have both things at the same time, except in those countries in which two different cultures have evolved more or less simultaneously. But where there is such an economic and social gap, modernization is possible only with the sacrifice of the Indian cultures.

One of the saddest aspects of the Latin American culture is that, in countries like Argentina, there were men of great intelligence, real idealists, who gave moral and philosophical reasons to continue the destruction of Indian cultures that began with the conquistadores. The case of Domingo F. Sarmiento is particularly sad to me, for I admire him very much. He was a great writer and also a great idealist. He was totally convinced that the only way in which Argentina could become modern was through westernization; that is, through the elimination of everything that was non-Western. He considered the Indian tradition, which was still present in the countryside of Argentina, a major obstacle for the progress and modernization of the country. He gave the moral and intellectual arguments in favor of what proved to be the decimation of the native population. That tragic mistake still looms in the Argentine psyche. In Argentine literature there is an emptiness that Argentine writers have been trying to fill by importing everything. The Argentines are the most curious and cosmopolitan people in Latin America, but they are still trying to fill the void caused by the destruction of their past.

This is why it is useful for us to review the literature that gives testimony to the discovery and the conquest. In the chronicles we not only dream about the time in which our fantasy and our realities seem to be incestuously confused. In them there is an extraordinary mixture of reality and fantasy, of reality and fiction in a united work. It is a literature that is totalizing, in the sense that it is a literature that embraces not only objective reality but also subjective reality in a new synthesis. The difference, of course, is that the chronicles accomplished that synthesis out of ignorance and naivete and that modern writers have accomplished it through sophistication. But a link can be established. There are chronicles that are especially imaginative and even fantastic in the deeds they describe. For instance, the description of the first journey to the Amazon in the chronicle of Gaspar de Carvajal. It is exceptional, like a fantastic novel. And, of course, Gabriel García Máquez has used themes from the chronicles in his fiction.

In the chronicles we also learn about the roots of our problems and the challenges that are still there unanswered. And in these half-literary, half-historical pages we also perceive—formless, mysterious, fascinating—the promise of something new and formidable, something that if it ever turned into reality would enrich the world and improve civilization. Of this promise we have only had until now sporadic manifestations—in our literature and in our art, for example. But it is not only in our fiction that we must strive to achieve. We must not stop until our promise passes from our dreams and words into our daily lives and becomes objective reality. We must not permit our countries to disappear, as did my dear teacher, the historian Porras Barrenechea, without writing in real life the definite masterwork we have been preparing ourselves to accomplish since the three caravels stumbled onto our coast.

Considerations

1. At the start of his essay, Vargas Llosa raises two questions, one relative to the conquest and another about the present day treatment of the "Indians." He seems to have a ready answer for the first one. Why is he less precise about the answer to the second? What is, in fact, the relation between the two questions?

2. Vargas Llosa suggests, at several points in his essay, that it seems useless to him to either regret or glorify the history he describes. Locate and explain other ideas about history and its utility in the text. What do you think is his overall conception of history? How does it compare with your ideas on the subject?

Invitation to Write

Vargas Llosa explains that his essay was written in response to questions posed by the Association of Indian Cultures, a group that did not want to celebrate the arrival of Christopher Columbus in the western hemisphere. Traditionally, the United States has celebrated Columbus Day in a way that suggests "the discovery and conquest of America by Europeans [was] the greatest feat of the Christian West" (para. 3). Why is Columbus now viewed as a villain?

Write an essay in which you place Vargas Llosa's view of the conquest in the context of other perspectives on that event. If you are not familiar with the controversy, consult other articles on the subject. Any local library should be able to offer quite a number of them, especially from 1990 and 1991 newspapers or magazines.

Connections

In her essay "A Small Place" (p. 342), Jamaica Kincaid concludes, "As for what we were like before we met you, I no longer care. No periods of time over which my ancestors held sway, no documentation of complex civilisations, is any comfort to me. Even if I really come from people who were living like monkeys in trees, it was better to be that than what happened to me, what I became after I met you" (para. 6). Vargas Llosa states: "It seems to me useless to ask oneself whether it was good that it happened in this manner or whether it would have been better for humanity if the individual had never been born and the tradition of the antlike societies had continued forever" (para. 30). Write an essay in which you compare their opposed positions and determine what makes each of these writers adopt such a position. Consider the political implications of the two opinions, as well as the different styles in which the essays are written.

ASSIGNMENT SEQUENCE
Cultures in Contact

This assignment sequence will give you a chance to explore the several views of westernization held by the three authors, and to arrive at a statement of your own opinion. You will begin by remembering your early ideas about America's image in the world. The second assignment will ask you to look at the responses to America as described by Pico Iyer and relate them to your own sense of the views of America in Third World countries. The third assignment will ask you to explore the views of tourism that appear in the essays of Iyer and Paul Harrison. Their different approaches to the subject, personal and theoretical, will influence your own response to their essays. For your fourth paper, you will return to the subject of tourists to decide if they are conquerors in disguise. You will consider whether their influence on the process of change parallels the influence of the conquistadores. For your final paper in the sequence, you will consider the possible responses of Iyer and Harrison to Mario Vargas Llosa's analysis of the inevitability of westernization. After you do so, you will present your own conclusions about the relationship between Western ideas and native cultures.

Assignment 1: Exploring Experience

Children necessarily have an incomplete view of the world they live in. Still, at a very young age, children begin gathering information and composing a frame of reference, building the beginning of a complex system of knowledge. Think about your earliest impressions of people living in other countries and cultures. Then write a paper that explores several examples of your early impressions regarding the relationship of Americans to people of other countries, comparing them to your current ideas on the subject.

To begin your paper, think about several specific instances in which you have come into contact with other cultures. Examples of these experiences shouldn't be hard to find; children often study other countries in elementary school, collect donations for UNICEF, for church, or for synagogue to send to people abroad. They meet people from abroad: relatives, teachers, and classmates. Children read books and newspapers that have stories designed to increase their awareness of world events. Find some specific examples of these kinds of experiences from your own past. Describe them and decide how you thought America appeared to other people and the way those other people appeared to you. Explain if you still find those early images valid, or if you have modified them.

Assignment 2

I went to Asia, then, not only to see Asia, but also to see America, from a different vantage point and with new eyes.
—PICO IYER, *Love Match*

Pico Iyer's travels gave him a new image of America. As he traveled, he found that inhabitants of foreign countries saw selected aspects of American experience as representative of the whole. Using Iyer's experience and your first paper, write a paper about the different images of America abroad. Decide if the individuals encountered by Iyer see America according to the way you, as a child or today, imagined America's image abroad.

Before you begin, go through Iyer's essay and underline several passages that describe his meetings with people abroad. Maung-Maung's story is the most fully recounted meeting, but there are others. Also look at several of his discussions of the reaction of people to American media, televisions shows, movies, or music. From these moments in his essay, note Iyer's main points about the image of America held by people abroad. As you compare them to your own, explain why people are likely to see America in any of these ways.

Assignment 3

The final channel of cultural imperialism is tourism. Westerners, sick of the empty, smothering materialism of their own civilization, trek east and south on dream holidays and youthful odysseys, perhaps looking for a simplicity that Europe lost many centuries ago, and which the Third World itself is fast losing.
—PAUL HARRISON, *The Westernization of the World*

Tourism is a topic in the essays of both Pico Iyer and Paul Harrison. Iyer is himself a traveler and tourist analyzing his own participation in the process of cultural change. Harrison looks at tourism as one of several Western influences on the Third World. Write a paper that compares the views of the two authors on the role tourism plays in promoting the westernization of Third World countries.

Tourism is a central concern in Iyer's essay, so you should have no difficulty finding two or three examples of his meetings with individuals living in the different places he visits. In his reflections about his interactions, he discusses his own role in the process of change and the effects of that change. Also be alert to other examples he gives of the influence of tourism. Harrison writes much less about tourism as such. However, since he classifies it as one form of westernization, many of his remarks about westernization in general can be applied to this specific aspect of it.

Assignment 4

These semiliterate, implacable, and greedy swordsmen, who even before having completely conquered the Inca Empire were already savagely fighting among themselves or fighting the pacifiers sent against them by the faraway monarch to whom they had given a continent, represented a culture in which, we will never know whether for the benefit or the disgrace of mankind, something new and exotic had germinated in the history of man.
— MARIO VARGAS LLOSA, *Questions of Conquest*

In his essay, Mario Vargas Llosa describes the arrival of conquistadores in Peru and its impact on the culture. But in "Love Match," Pico Iyer reflects upon the influence of another type of traveler, the tourist. Both types of foreigners—warriors and world travelers—change the shape of the societies they visit. Write a paper in which you examine the consequences to non-Western societies of both kinds of visitors. Discuss how the processes initiated by each bring about westernization. How different are these two routes to westernization in process and end result?

As you reread the essays by Iyer and Vargas Llosa, think about the circumstances surrounding the initial contacts, the types of changes initiated, and the long-term effects. Think about the inhabitants' responses to change. Also look at the long-term effect of westernization on the original culture as it exists today.

Assignment 5

If forced to choose between the preservation of Indian cultures and their complete assimilation, with great sadness I would choose modernization of the Indian population, because there are priorities; and the first priority is, of course, to fight hunger and misery.
— MARIO VARGAS LLOSA, *Questions of Conquest*

As he writes about the current position of the descendants of the preconquest cultures of Latin America, Mario Vargas Llosa suggests that they must abandon their traditional way of life in order to escape poverty. Write a paper in which you explain how Pico Iyer and Paul Harrison would respond to Mario Vargas Llosa's position. After you examine their positions, present your own conclusion. Decide if the loss of non-Western cultures is an inescapable condition of westernization.

Look beyond the quotation by Mario Vargas Llosa to understand the reasons he gives for arriving at this conclusion. Then see if Pico Iyer's experiences and Paul Harrison's argument suggest other ways of responding to

Western ideas. In each case, look at the author's background and his relationship to the societies he writes about as a means of understanding his perspective. This relationship probably helps shape his argument and provides clues to his point of view.

Acknowledgments (continued from page iv)

Louise Erdrich, "American Horse." Copyright © 1983 by Louise Erdrich. Reprinted by permission of the author.

Erika Friedl, "A Betrothal, a Rape, and a Guess About Turan's Fate." From *Women of Deh Koh: Lives in an Iranian Village* by Erika Friedl. Published by Smithsonian Press 1989, copyright Smithsonian Institution, pp. 110–119.

Ernest J. Gaines, "Just Like a Tree." From *Bloodline* by Ernest J. Gaines. Copyright © 1963, 1964, 1968 by Ernest J. Gaines. Used by permission of Doubleday, a division of Bantam Doubleday Dell Publishing Group, Inc.

Ellen Gilchrist, "Music." From *Victory over Japan* by Ellen Gilchrist. Copyright © 1983, 1984 by Ellen Gilchrist. By permission of Little, Brown and Company.

David Gilmore, "Performative Excellence: Circum-Mediterranean." From *Manhood in the Making* by David D. Gilmore. Copyright © 1990 by Yale University Press. Reprinted by permission of Yale University Press.

Paul Harrison, "The Westernization of the World." From *Inside the Third World: An Anatomy of Poverty*, Second Edition, by Paul Harrison. Copyright © 1982. Reprinted by permission of the author.

Garrett Hongo, "Kubota." "Kubota" first appeared in *Ploughshares,* vol. 16, nos. 2 and 3. Reprinted by permission of the author.

Pico Iyer, "Love Match." From *Video Night in Kathmandu and Other Reports from the Not-So-Far East* by Pico Iyer. Copyright © 1988 by Pico Iyer. Reprinted by permission of Alfred A. Knopf, Inc.

David Jackson, "One of the Boys." From *Unmasking Masculinity* by David Jackson. Copyright © 1990. Reprinted by permission of Unwin Hyman, division of Routledge.

Louise J. Kaplan, "Adolescence: The Farewell to Childhood." From *Adolescence: The Farewell to Childhood* by Louise J. Kaplan (New York: Simon & Schuster, 1984). Copyright © 1984 by Louise J. Kaplan. Reprinted by permission of Louise J. Kaplan, Ph.D.

Leonard Kibera, "The Spider's Web." From *Potent Ash* by Leonard Kibera (Nairobi: East African Publishing House, 1968).

Jamaica Kincaid, "A Small Place." Excerpted from *A Small Place* by Jamaica Kincaid. Copyright © 1988 by Jamaica Kincaid. Reprinted by permission of Farrar, Straus & Giroux, Inc.

William Least Heat-Moon, "The Emma Chase." From *PrairyErth: A Deepmap* by William Least Heat-Moon. Copyright © 1991 by William Least Heat-Moon. Reprinted by permission of Houghton Mifflin Company. All rights reserved.

Karl Marx, "Alienated Labor," trans. T. B. Bottomore. From *Marx's Concept of Man* by Erich Fromm. Copyright © 1966 by Erich Fromm. Reprinted by permission of the Continuum Publishing Company.

Neil Miller, "A Time of Change." From *In Search of Gay America* by Neil Miller. Copyright © 1989 by Neil Miller. Used by permission of Atlantic Monthly Press.

Bharati Mukherjee, "Fighting for the Rebound." From *The Middleman and Other Stories* by Bharati Mukherjee (Grove: New York). Copyright © 1988. Reprinted by permission of The Elaine Markson Literary Agency, Bharati Mukherjee, and Grove Press, Inc.

Itabari Njeri, "Bag Lady." From *Every Good-Bye Ain't Gone* by Itabari Njeri. Copyright © 1990 by Itabari Njeri. Reprinted by permission of Times Books, a division of Random House, Inc.

Edna O'Brien, "The Widow." From *Lantern Slides* by Edna O'Brien. First appeared in *The New Yorker*, Jan. 23, 1989. Copyright © 1989, 1990 by Edna O'Brien. Reprinted by permission of Farrar, Straus & Giroux, Inc.

Judith Ortiz Cofer, "The Looking-Glass Shame." From *Silent Dancing: A Partial Remembrance of a Puerto Rican Childhood* by Judith Ortiz Cofer. Copyright © 1990 by Arte Publico Press. Permission granted by Arte Publico Press of the University of Houston.

Robert Reich, "The Global Elite." From the *New York Times*, January 20, 1991. Copyright © 1991 by The New York Times Company. Reprinted by permission of the *New York Times*, Raphael Sagalyn, Inc., and Robert B. Reich.

Richard Rodriguez, "Complexion." From *Hunger of Memory* by Richard Rodriguez. Copyright © 1982 by Richard Rodriguez. Reprinted by permission of David R. Godine, Publisher.

Philip Roth, "His Roth." From the prologue to *The Facts* by Philip Roth. Copyright © 1988 by Philip Roth. Reprinted by permission of Farrar, Straus & Giroux, Inc.

Index of
Authors and Titles

MAKING CULTURAL CONNECTIONS

Readings for Critical Analysis

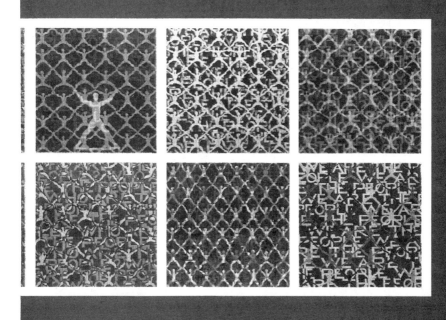

MARILYN RYE

For information, write: St. Martin's Press, Inc.
175 Fifth Avenue, New York, NY 10010

Editorial Offices: Bedford Books *of* St. Martin's Press
29 Winchester Street, Boston, MA 02116

ISBN: 0–312–07505–7

Preface

The purpose of this manual is to provide teachers with a brief description of the pedagogy behind *Making Cultural Connections* as well as with some insights on the readings contained in the book. I would like to emphasize here, at the outset, that my interpretation of these readings is not meant to be definitive. I have not attempted to give direct answers to the questions following the readings, since they have been conceived so as to elicit a variety of responses. The insights I provide here, as well as some of my suggestions on how to use the book, aim only to help teachers establish their own pedagogy and make their own choices as far as the form their class is going to take. Ultimately, I think, the direction the class will take depends on the responses and commentaries the students raise in discussion and in their writing.

Besides the comments on the individual assignments, the manual contains some reflections on the benefits of using a multicultural reader, an overview of the readings contained in the textbook, a description of the apparatus, and tips about using it. In the interest of flexibility, some alternate tables of contents are provided to help reorganize the material according to alternate thematic groupings, connections between selections, and rhetorical divisions. A sample syllabus suggests one way in which a semester's work can be organized. Brief commentaries on each assignment sequence include suggestions of novels that can be read to enhance the sequence. Since I have experimented with some of the texts in my own class, I have also included a modified assignment sequence that shows how the readings from *Making Cultural Connections* can be combined with novels to give students a more complete foundation for writing. One of my students, who responded particularly well to the assignments, is profiled, and his papers are offered as samples of student work.

Contents

3. Defining Women's Lives 26

4. Defining Men's Lives 30

5. Working in the World 35

6. Individuals in Communities 40

7. Environments of Prejudice 45

8. Stories That Shape Our Lives 50

Teaching with
Making Cultural Connections

Making Cultural Connections can be described as a multicultural reader. Perhaps the most distinctive feature of what is known as multicultural teaching is a curriculum that includes writers representing Western culture as well as authors from cultures traditionally ignored or marginalized. Marilyn Rye's reader features a combination of both canonical and noncanonical authors whose writings are at once challenging and exciting. Although the book does not attempt to represent all cultures, its emphasis on diversity fosters an understanding that multiculturalism means more than exposure to other cultures. Since the values, customs, symbols, and behavior of other peoples are different from ours, and such differences are among the main sources of misunderstandings and hostilities between cultures, learning how to deal with cultural differences is, perhaps, one of the most urgent tasks of an educated person.

The struggle against prejudice and bigotry has taught most of us to look beyond differences and search for the basic humanity in all of us. Sometimes, however, this enthusiasm for finding the common denominator of all humankind makes us overlook cultural diversity and its important manifestations. Value systems from other cultures can contradict ours, and sometimes these systems seem unacceptable. Raymonde Carroll's anthropological research, for instance, demonstrates how even similar cultures, such as French and American, can be at odds about such an important matter as child-rearing. The almost violent reactions of French people to the behavior of American children, as well as the Americans' bitter disapproval of French parents, show that more is at stake than the children's education. Each party seems to feel threatened by the rules the other finds correct, and the sense of identity of each seems to be challenged. In most cultures, we are taught to distinguish right from wrong. The possible existence of two different but right choices is often threatening. In accepting the choices of cultures other than our own, we learn to redefine our identity in relation to the identities of others.

Rye's collection helps us realize that dealing with differences begins for many in a multicultural classroom. Differences surface in writing. When students come to our classes, they already know how to write, but their ways of writing can be different from the one we are trying to teach. In criticizing their work, we challenge their ideas of good writing, and thus threaten their senses of identity. In the writing class, therefore, we already have to negotiate our differences.

But as these selections demonstrate, the necessity of being able to deal with differences extends beyond the classroom. It applies to the adolescent in search of an identity and in conflict with a parent; the individual who tries to belong to a community and finds his beliefs at odds with those of others; and men and women who enter relationships, whether romantic or professional. Differences surface not only in principles but also in language, behavior, and feelings.

The process of writing itself can be conceived of as an effort toward self-discovery in the midst of differences. Most students coming into college encounter a culture that is not yet their own, and writing can be their main tool not only in adjusting to a new environment but also in establishing their own place in it. Rather than force them to adhere to our norms, we have to help them appropriate our knowledge. In this case, appropriating means not only accepting our knowledge as their own; it means participating in the making of that knowledge and changing it in essential ways. Students usually hesitate to take such initiative in traditional learning environments where, to paraphrase Paulo Freire's metaphor, knowledge is deposited in their minds as if in a bank. They have to be encouraged to understand education as a cultural exchange, and multicultural material is ideal for such a purpose. An understanding of what is at stake in other cultures' values and beliefs is an essential companion to the study of writing. In the multicultural context, writing itself should lead students to acquire a new sense of identity and find their place among others.

In addition to helping students see themselves as explorers of unfamiliar experience, the multicultural textbook offers an ideal frame for critical thinking. While students are often content to repeat clichés instead of developing original ideas, the combination of canonical and noncanonical readings in *Making Cultural Connections* does not allow much room for standard interpretations. When reading a classic like Karl Marx's "Alienated Labor" together with the beautiful, but little-known story "Maybe" by Wakako Yamauchi, students will have to come to an original understanding of the concepts involved. When he was writing *Das Kapital*, Marx had little idea that more than a hundred years later, workers in America, particularly those from other cultures, would be alienated in more ways than one. In working with these two readings, the student has the opportunity to take Marx's ideas a step further.

Different combinations of readings may also reveal different possibilities for critical interpretation and will cultivate students' analytical skills. Kibera's disgruntled hero in "The Spider's Web," for instance, illustrates Paul Harrison's view of westernization as a force that resulted in the devastation of other cultures; yet, Kibera's image of manhood also strikingly resembles the one held by Philip Roth in his nostalgic evocation of his father. The multicultural context makes possible a questioning of established truths, a critical confrontation of values and opinions from which a student will eventually emerge an informed and thorough critic of any ideology presenting itself for his or her acceptance.

About the Readings

Making Cultural Connections offers a selection of readings that challenge students both through cultural diversity and academic or literary sophistication. Being longer than readings normally found in other composition readers, the essays and short stories presented in this collection demand sustained reading of the kind students are normally confronted with in most disciplines during their college career. They introduce students to an academic discourse that is of a high quality and free of jargon, and prepare them for their future work in college. Although the scholarly level of the essays—some of which are chapters in books or studies—is quite high, the texts are not intimidating. They present complex concepts in an accessible form.

The essays in this reader range from classics like Karl Marx's "Alienated Labor" and Simone de Beauvoir's "Introduction to *The Second Sex*," to contemporary and controversial arguments such as Mario Vargas Llosa's "Questions of Conquest" and Marianna De Marco Torgovnick's "On Being White, Female, and Born in Bensonhurst." Scholarly pieces such as "Is There a Family? New Anthropological Views" by Collier, Rosaldo, and Yanagisako and "Performative Excellence: Circum-Mediterranean" by David Gilmore expose the students to the kind of writing they might have to do as researchers. Confessional narratives, like Richard Rodriguez's "Complexion" and Judith Ortiz Cofer's "The Looking-Glass Shame," can motivate students to search for meaning in their own experience. Stories rich in symbols and metaphors, like Louise Erdrich's "American Horse" and Leonard Kibera's "The Spider's Web," can inspire students to analyze and interpret literature and to connect the literary phenomenon to its cultural context. Interview-based pieces, like Neil Miller's "A Time of Change" and William Least Heat-Moon's "The Emma Chase," may lead students to experiment with interviewing.

In *Making Cultural Connections*, the readings have been grouped thematically, but it should be observed that it is not always the central theme of a particular text that has determined its place in a certain chapter. Often a secondary issue debated by the author places a piece in its group. The grouping has been determined by the possibility of using one reading (or more) in order to reflect on the others. For instance, reading "If You Can Talk to a Guy" by Jane Staw and Mary Swander together with Deborah Tannen's "Damned If You Do" can reveal the former essay's profound meditation on language. At the same time it will show that Tannen's theory has more than one application. Texts can be made to reflect upon each other in many ways, and the organization of *Making Cultural Connections* reveals some of the possibilities. Rye's principle has been to encourage students to look beyond the obvious similarities between texts to find the implied and, in many cases, richer connections.

In the text, every group of readings is preceded by an introduction to the theme of the chapter. The themes include family, adolescence, gender roles, work, community, prejudice, the role of stories, life transitions, language, and westernization. While some of the themes are subjects of current public debate, others are less familiar and in need of more exploration. Each reading is also preceded by informative notes about the author's life and work, which can help students place the author both geographically and historically.

Every chapter contains a sequence of assignments. The theme of a sequence reflects the theme of its chapter, and the connections between the respective texts are made apparent in the assignments. Every chapter begins with selected quotations from the texts, which suggest the ideas to be in the chapter discussions and assignments. The juxtaposition of quotations reflects how the readings relate to each other and how they can enhance each other's meaning. For instance the chapter called "Growing Into Adulthood" starts with several quotations that suggest, each in a different way, that to grow up actually means to live up to expectations set by one's culture. It also becomes clear that such expectations are related to one's gender. The definition of adolescence and its relation to gender is, in fact, the topic of many of the assignments contained in this chapter and in the sequence of assignments that follows it.

A class discussion of the quotations might pique the students' interest in the subject, while teaching the students to pay attention to details, to form expectations while reading, and to anticipate the outcome of an argument. The quotations can be the subject of repeated discussion during the time dedicated to the respective chapter. They certainly will be spotted by the students when they read the entire text from which the quotation was taken. At that point students will have to think about each quotation in its original context. The quotations reappear at the beginning of the assignments of each sequence.

About Questions and Assignments

The idea that encountering other cultures is a crucial experience in the formative process of young people dominates not only the themes of the readings but also the pedagogy promoted by *Making Cultural Connections*. Requiring the student to focus on issues that cannot easily be dismissed is the basic principle of the questions and assignments in *Making Cultural Connections*. Every text is followed by two or three "Considerations" questions which ask students to do a second reading of the text and which prepare them for writing. The first writing assignment is called "Invitation to Write" and stresses the connection to personal experience. The second writing assignment, called "Connections," requires students to read two texts and discuss them together in an essay of their own. The sequence of assignments placed at the end of the chapter obliges students to approach the same topic from different angles. These different types of assignments can be used in combination or separately. In what follows, I shall explain the purpose of each type of assignment.

Considerations. The "Considerations" questions focus on problematic aspects of the texts with a view to inspiring students to go beyond a simple understanding of the text's main point. Sometimes, these questions bring up difficulties in the reading that cannot be attributed solely to the students' lack of initiation in a certain field. For instance, students will be puzzled by Simone de Beauvoir's subtle changes of voice in "Introduction to *The Second Sex.*" A teacher might be inclined to lecture about the possibility of multiple voices in a text and thus provide students with a standard way of reading. However, a longer class discussion might bring to light a genuine problem that the writer herself was faced with. Beauvoir wrote her essay against patriarchal domination at a time when she was not in possession of a feminist (or at least feminine) discourse. She practically lacked the language to oppose male domination and had to resort to ironic voicing in order to make her points. By discussing her problems, students will become aware that the difficulties they encounter in their writing may derive from the necessity to adjust their own voices to the accepted discourse.

Focusing on such problematic aspects of the readings can inspire the students to analyze and become critical about the text. Not all of the questions deal with the authors' response to his or her cultural context. Quite a number of questions address the presence of symbols or metaphors, especially in fiction. They encourage the students to discover layers of meaning, as well as verbal patterns of rich significance, as in Dillard's "The Writing Life," for instance.

The "Considerations" questions may be used as starting points for class discussions, as the basis for work in peer groups, or as journal writing assignments. Class discussion gives students their chance to say what they think about their readings, to formulate questions, and to express their opinions about various issues. Discussion may be hard to start, especially at the beginning of the semester, when students are not acquainted with each other and may be shy about speaking in front of the class. I have found that working in peer groups is quite useful in getting the students to know each other and to exchange ideas. The class can be divided in groups of three or four students which are then given a "Considerations" question to discuss. They are allowed to debate the question among themselves for ten or fifteen minutes, and then one representative of the group will present the group's conclusions to the class. Assigning a different question to each group helps students feel that their work benefits the whole class. The answers to the "Considerations" questions may also be written at home in journal form and brought to class for review in the peer groups. These questions can be an occasion for free writing, which gets students involved with their reading.

Invitation to Write. "Invitation to Write" aims at relating a text to the students' life experiences. The questions under this title address the kind of knowledge students naturally bring to the text in the process of reading. In this way, they are given an opportunity to link the readings to what they know about the topic in question. "Invitation to Write" implies a thorough understanding of the text and the capacity to extend the text's arguments. Working on these assignments may require a second reading and some practice in analyzing examples from real life. For instance, if they are writing about Paula Gunn Allen's "Where I Come from Is Like This," the students need to understand her view on the transmission of values in American Indian tribes. It is only after analyzing her arguments that they can compare the American Indian perpetuation of customs and wisdom to the transmission of values in mainstream American society. This may involve prewriting in journal form or a class discussion. The same activities may be used to test examples of values and their transmission. Students may want to discuss TV shows or movies in which certain values are emphasized, or they may share their family experience. In this way their knowledge becomes relevant to the understanding of the reading.

Connections. The process of integrating different kinds of knowledge is further encouraged by the "Connections" questions, which help students perceive a continuity in reading. Having read a text, we incorporate it into our experience, and we bring it to bear on all our following readings. Sometimes, the connected readings may be quite similar in theme and argument. Most of the time, however, the texts brought together under "Connections" are different from each other: One may be theoretical, the other fictional; one may be old, the other new. The ways in which texts reflect upon each other may also vary: Sometimes a theoretical argument is brought to bear upon the understanding of a narrative; sometimes a comparison brings to light unexpected similarities or differences; at other times, the implications of a metaphor from one reading are extended into another. To complete this kind of assignment, students will have to reread the texts and keep confronting them in their minutest details.

Assignment Sequences. In addition to the questions pertaining to individual texts, *Making Cultural Connections* offers a sequence of assignments at the end of each chapter. The purpose of sequencing assignments is to give students the opportunity to reflect upon a topic from various angles. Sequencing obliges them to delve deeper into a certain field of study. The readings are recontextualized several times, demonstrating to students how their own interpretations can evolve.

Teaching with
Assignment Sequences

An assignment sequence allows concentrated, long-term focus on a specific topic. When writing on a subject that is never going to be discussed again, students may not realize how important it is to reflect on all its aspects and to connect it with other issues. When the subject under discussion remains the same for a longer period of time, however, students acquire a sense of how texts can be linked to each other, how the reading of one text can enhance the reading of another, or more practically, how reading one text can help us say (write) something about another. For instance, read by itself, Erika Friedl's "A Betrothal, a Rape, and a Guess About Turan's Fate" can appear as a window into the lives of women in a small Iranian village. We may notice that the women know where they are allowed to go and where they cannot go, that they have a sense of what their territory is. The significance of this perception of space division becomes apparent when we think of Friedl's piece in relation to Torgovnick's essay about Bensonhurst. Discovering the similarities may lead us to the conclusion that social, racial, and gender divisions are reflected in the way people share space. This conclusion becomes even more significant when we enlarge the pool of texts by including Simone de Beauvoir's "Introduction to *The Second Sex.*" Through sequencing, students will be able to reuse, reevaluate, and build upon their own ideas and conclusions.

The sequences offered by *Making Cultural Connections* almost always start by asking the students to tackle the topic without referring to the selections in the chapter. Because such an assignment appeals to the students' background, to their previous knowledge, it stimulates their curiosity and lays the foundation of their future interest in the topic. Naturally, they will get more involved with the assigned readings after having approached the topic on their own. From the outset, the students are thus encouraged to think of themselves as authors, to defend their opinions, and to question the readings rather than receive them passively. In addition to setting forth the question to be considered, the assignment gives students tips about tackling the topic: what orientation to give it, what kind of examples to look for and where they can find them, and so on. Such hints are helpful in starting the paper. Of course, students can use their own approach and examples. The hints are designed to help them, not to restrict their efforts.

The second assignment in a sequence usually refers to just one text whose exploration can become relevant to the following assignments. Sometimes, when a particularly difficult piece (Marx or Beauvoir, for instance) is included in the sequence, even a later assignment might ask the students to deal with only one reading. But the majority of the assignments ask the students to read one text (or two) within the frame of another. For instance, in the assignment sequence from chapter 5, "Working in the World," Robert C. Christopher's "The Fruits of Industry," with its evaluation of Japanese methods of management, becomes the frame within which the work conditions in America, as presented in Yamauchi's "Maybe" and Tucker and Leinberger's "Scott Myers, Entrepreneur," can be discussed.

In the last assignment of the sequence, all texts are integrated, which may add a new twist to the previous interpretations. Take, for instance, the assignment sequence from chapter 10, "Language and Perception," which asks students to develop a definition of language by looking at it from different angles. The last assignment in the sequence, however, asks them to work toward a definition of linguistic meaning. The question of meaning is there all along, but in the final paper, it becomes the main concern. In this way, students are obliged to reconsider what they have said, test the validity of their previous conclusions, and reuse the pool of examples they have already analyzed.

When working with assignment sequences, certain adjustments will have to be made to the syllabus. Some of the texts may be discussed several times. Some time should be allotted to reading and discussing student papers. This can be done either within peer groups or by distributing photocopies of one or more papers to the entire class. It is important for students to begin to think of themselves as writers whose work has an audience and whose statements count in the general discussion on the topic. Revision is also an important component of a writing class, and working with sequences can give new meaning to this activity. Students need to review their work by putting it in different contexts. This will make them understand that when revising an individual assignment, they have to deal with more than just cosmetic changes: They need to re-think and re-see their subject.

It is perhaps at this point that I should emphasize the flexibility of *Making Cultural Connections*. There are many options for the teacher who uses this reader. If a teacher decides not to use sequences, the questions following each reading offer enough material for the class. The "Considerations" questions may be used as journal writing assignments, "Invitation to Write" can be used after the reading of one text as a first step toward its exploration, and the "Connections" questions as more complex writing assignments. These categories of questions can be nicely adjusted to a class focusing on various rhetorical forms. Not only do the readings illustrate the forms, as shown in the rhetorical index (p. 113 of this manual), but many assignments encourage the adoption of one rhetorical form or another. For instance, the connection between David Gilmore's essay "Performative Excellence: Circum-Mediterranean" and David Jackson's autobiographical account "One of the Boys" invites a comparison/contrast type of treatment. The "Invitation to Write" following James Baldwin's "Whose Child Are You?" may be executed as a narrative. Needless to say, all assignments can be modified so that they serve as practice for various rhetorical forms.

Using sequences is, to my mind, one of the most interesting options because it gives students a sense of purpose for a long period of time. Sequences involve them in writing projects that last more than one week and give them the opportunity to study a specific topic in depth. Depending on the number of assignments contained in the sequence and on the number of readings included, two or three sequences can be used in a semester. If the number of assignments is unusually high, one can combine one sequence with the assignments that follow the readings (see the sample syllabus on p. 13 of this manual). To increase the number of readings, the titles included in the "Connections" assignments can be added to the reading list.

Sequences can be "customized," that is, changed to suit other purposes. (See the example of a customized sequence on p. 71 of this manual.) They can be enlarged by adding readings that fall under different headings but are thematically close to the topic at hand. For instance, the sequence from chapter 5, "Working in the World" can be enriched by adding Annie Dillard's "The Writing Life" and Richard Rodriguez's "Complexion." Naturally, assignments should be modified to include the extra readings, or some new assignments can be added. A sequence can also be used in combination with a novel, and the assignments can be reformulated to include the extra material. I have suggested novels that can be used in this way when commenting on each sequence. New sequences can also be created by regrouping the texts, and the thematic index (p. 109 of this manual) can help in selecting readings for such a purpose.

Tips on Teaching with Multicultural Material in a Writing Class

Here, I would like to go into some detail on the way students react to the pedagogy suggested by *Making Cultural Connections*. The concentration on themes and the scholarly aspect of the readings may lead some students to believe that the writing class is no different than other subject courses they take. This misapprehension should be dispelled from the start. Although the writing instructor should be prepared to guide students through their experience of self-discovery, she or he need not be an expert in all the domains of knowledge or in the different cultures that the texts represent. Rather, the teacher should consider him- or herself a slightly more experienced student who can show the others how one finds one's way in a new field of study or in a difficult text. This position should be made clear to the students, because they often expect the teacher to be an expert who has answers to all the questions. In the writing class, one does not learn answers; one learns to question. Although it has an apparent topic, the writing class is not about the topic as much as it is about questioning and debate.

One other point worth making here is that the assignments in *Making Cultural Connections* will never elicit a uniform response from the students. Although the purpose of each assignment is quite clear, the assignments allow the students to take their own perspective on the material. The diverse personal experiences of the students can lead to a great diversity in their responses. I have also been surprised by the variety of details from the texts which they choose to bring up in their arguments. This variety of responses is stimulating and offers wonderful material for working in peer groups.

A successful writing class, especially one that focuses on multicultural or cross-cultural material, may prompt the students to express ideas that can be, from a teacher's perspective, downright offensive. Students do not come to class innocent of opinion. They have been educated, and they have absorbed opinions, ideas, and beliefs from their parents, teachers, literature, or the media. They are quite convinced that the ideology that has been fed to them is their own and are always ready to defend it. I worked a long time with students before I realized what they mean by their "opinion." Every time I encouraged them to write something original they would translate my request with "So, you want my opinion!" and then would flood the paper with a slew of clichés. It was necessary to introduce the concept of forming an opinion and to work on understanding its deep meaning.

Yet, the matter of discussing opinions is more complex than accepting a variety of responses. Should a teacher, for instance, accept racist or sexist remarks as original opinion? One should first doubt whether such opinions are indeed original. Looking at them closely, I found that they were not "personal" opinions at all. They were most often coming from somewhere in the student's past and were the result of some indoctrination. However, I never tell students they have said something offensive to me. That would make the whole argument too personal. Instead, I encourage the students not to generalize before they have examined the evidence. Once they start that process, I scrutinize their logical connections and suggest other pieces of evidence to examine. Of course, one cannot always hope to change a student's convictions if they are very strong. Once I had an Islamic student who was faced with reading and analyzing a story about the exploitation of women in an Iranian village. Forced to examine the evidence, he managed to produce a grim picture of an abusive and corrupt environment. He added, however, several paragraphs saying that the author is a liar and that actually the Muslim religion protects women. I had to be satisfied with the first part of the paper and ignore the second. One can only hope that once they have learned to examine evidence, most students will apply their skills beyond readings, to the world around them.

There is another aspect of the problem I have just described. Obviously, my student's reaction was emotional rather than rational. Emotional involvement is not necessarily bad. I think that students should be allowed to get emotionally engaged with the material they read and learn about. That kind of participation ensures that they connect with their readings and are interested in what they write. Emotions can, however, produce bad writing. When I comment on some of the questions in *Making Cultural Connections*, I warn against an emotional response to issues currently under public debate. It is difficult to analyze these issues objectively when one is on one side or another, and I urge students to look for the reason behind the disputes rather than try to settle them. Yet, the classroom should provide a forum for talking about how the students feel, and it should, at the same time, be a place where emotions are brought under analysis. Self-reflection can be the first step toward analyzing the reading material.

Getting the students to think on their own is not an easy task. Most often, the mental clichés are also linguistic clichés, neatly formulated in beautiful words and correct grammar. When students get away from the clichés, they are on their own. Language gets out of control, grammar collapses. In most of my classes this happens in the second paper. I give most attention to this paper, and I assign more revisions than one for it. I also tell the students that the problems they are encountering are genuine, that anyone trying to think independently is faced with them—Ph.D. candidates on the first chapters of their dissertations may have the same kind of problems. It is important that students not get discouraged or believe that it is some

11

deficiency of theirs that prevents them from writing successful essays. I wish also to give a word of encouragement to beginning teachers: It does get better!

What I most appreciate in the papers at this stage are the leaps that students' logic makes. I remember a particular paper about rape, in which the student (a woman) started with some clichés about women's own contribution to their becoming victims of rape. During the revision process, she was pressed to analyze the evidence. In so doing, she began to understand that culturally constructed notions of romance encourage violence and that rape is an extreme manifestation of aggressive courtship. Between the beginning and the end of the paper there was a glaring inconsistency, but what a delight to see a student starting to think! At this early stage, such a paper deserves a high grade in spite of its contradictions.

Usually by the third paper, the students are able to formulate their own ideas, to work with a text, and have only to practice working with more than one text at a time. We also work on issues of refinement: how to introduce a quotation and comment on it; how to make transitions from one part of the argument to another; how to organize the material so that the transitions appear natural; how to write an effective thesis paragraph; and how to write a conclusion that is not merely a repetition of the thesis.

All in all, teaching with multicultural material is an exciting adventure that can be renewed with each semester and each new group of students. Each class of students is different, and it is the students' diversity that makes the classes interesting and stimulating. Contrary to popular opinion, the writing class is a place where a dedicated teacher can never get bored.

Sample Syllabus

The following brief course description and sample syllabus for a class that meets twice a week is one I have given my students.

Brief Course Description

The aim of the class is to help you think critically, develop your ideas, learn to examine evidence, and draw conclusions on the basis of evidence, in short, to construct a sound argument. You are also expected to learn to edit your writing, avoid grammar and spelling errors, and present your papers in a professional manner (that is, correctly typed and following an accepted style). The amount of writing done during the class may vary if one counts journal assignments, revisions, and in-class writing. However, the idea is to produce five or six papers, totaling approximately twenty to twenty-five pages of finished writing.

Grading is something of a problem in the writing class. On the one hand, grades may be irrelevant in the earlier stages of the class. I want you to realize that you will be engaged in a long-term project and that you will be actually learning how to write, not just showing that you already know how to write. A high grade on the first paper reflects what you bring to class, not what you have learned in the class. On the other hand, you may feel uneasy about not having your work graded, and you might want to know where you stand. Therefore, I have opted for a middle path: I grade all (finished) papers, but in establishing the final grade, I give more weight to the papers written in the second half of the semester.

The class also includes two exams, which are meant to demonstrate your capacity to work independently with a text. Before the exam, you will be asked to read one text. Each exam takes place in two class sessions in order to give you the opportunity to revise your work. In the first session, you will receive the question of the assignment and write your first draft, which I will collect at the end of the class. You may look back on the text, but you will not be allowed to bring notes to class or to write on the margins in the book. During the second session, you will be given your draft and asked to revise it.

Materials: Marilyn Rye, *Making Cultural Connections*
a guide to grammar and style
a folder to keep writings in

Texts: Ellen Gilchrist, "Music" (chapter 8, "Stories That Shape Our Lives")
Amy Tan, "Without Wood" (chapter 8)
Simone de Beauvoir, "Introduction to *The Second Sex*" (chapter 3, "Defining Women's Lives")

Deborah Tannen, "Damned If You Do" (chapter 10, "Language and Perception")

Paula Gunn Allen, "Where I Come from Is Like This" (chapter 8)

Garrett Hongo, "Kubota" (chapter 8)

Itabari Njeri, "Bag Lady" (chapter 9, "Lives in Transition")

Judith Ortiz Cofer, "The Looking-Glass Shame" (chapter 2, "Growing Into Adulthood")

Two more texts of my choice will be used for the exams.

Weekly Schedule

Week 1: a. First meeting: Writing sample. Read quotations at the beginning of chapter 8, "Stories That Shape Our Lives," and write about the significance of the combination. *Homework:* Read the introduction to chapter 8.

b. Class discussion on the introduction and on fiction in general. *Homework:* Read Ellen Gilchrist, "Music."

Week 2: a. Discuss "Considerations" questions following Gilchrist in peer groups and in the larger class. Raise additional questions about Gilchrist. *Homework:* Respond to the "Invitation to Write" following Gilchrist.

b. Discuss papers in peer groups, and give suggestions for revision. *Homework:* Read Amy Tan, "Without Wood." Write a journal entry in response to the "Considerations" questions following Tan.

Week 3: a. Discuss Tan and review journals. *Homework:* Complete assignment 1 in the sequence.

b. Discuss papers and exchange ideas on stories. *Homework:* Read Simone de Beauvoir, "Introduction to *The Second Sex*." Respond in your journal to the "Invitation to Write" following Beauvoir.

Week 4: a. Discuss Beauvoir in peer groups and review journals. *Homework:* Write an answer to the "Connections" question following Tan (linking Tan with Beauvoir).

b. Review answer to the "Connections" question. Discuss Tan in relation to Beauvoir. *Homework:* Complete assignment 2 in the sequence.

Week 5: a. Discuss papers in peer groups and recommend revisions. *Homework:* Read Deborah Tannen, "Damned If You Do."

b. Discuss Tannen together with Beauvoir and Tan. *Homework:* Write an answer to the "Connections" question following Tannen (linking Tannen with Tan).

Week 6:   **a.** Review answer to the "Connections" question. Revise assignment 2 in the sequence. *Homework:* Read Paula Gunn Allen, "Where I Come from Is Like This."

                   b. Compare Tan, Gilchrist, and Allen. *Homework:* Write an answer to the "Connections" question following Allen (linking Allen with Gilchrist).

Week 7:   *Reserved for midterm exam.*

Week 8:   **a.** Review answer to the "Connections" question linking Allen and Gilchrist. *Homework:* Complete assignment 3 in the sequence.

                   b. Review assignment 3 in peer groups and recommend revisions.

Week 9:   **a.** Work on revisions of assignment 3 in the sequence. *Homework:* Read Garrett Hongo, "Kubota."

                   b. Discuss the "Considerations" questions for Hongo. *Homework:* Respond in your journal to the "Connections" question following Gilchrist (linking Gilchrist with Hongo).

Week 10:   **a.** Review answer to the "Connections" question. *Homework:* Complete assignment 4 in the sequence.

                   b. Review assignment 4 in peer groups and recommend revisions. *Homework:* Read Itabari Njeri's "Bag Lady" and Judith Ortiz Cofer's "The Looking-Glass Shame."

Week 11:   **a.** Discuss "Considerations" questions for Njeri. *Homework:* Revise assignment 4.

                   b. Discuss Njeri and Ortiz Cofer. *Homework:* Write an answer to the "Connections" question following Njeri (linking Njeri with Ortiz Cofer).

Week 12:   **a.** Review answers to the "Connections" question. *Homework:* Complete assignment 5 in the sequence.

                   b. Review assignment 5 and recommend revisions.

Week 13:   **a.** In-class writing in response to the "Invitation to Write" following Hongo.

                   b. Revise assignment 5 of the sequence.

Week 14:   *Reserved for final exam.*

1

Functions of the Family

ERNEST J. GAINES
Just Like a Tree (p. 5)

Considerations

1. Gaines's narrative contains numerous instances where ordinary events are given symbolic value. The discussion of the title and a brief analysis of the poem standing as a motto will lead the students to discover symbolic connections in the story. They could focus on the stubbornness of the mule—Mr. Bascom—which, like Aunt Fe, does not want to be moved; Leola's exclamation that "the name's [Aunt Fe's] been 'mongst us just like us own family name. Just like the name o' God" (p. 9); Aunt Clo's elaboration on the title metaphor; Aunt Fe's death at the end. They might also give some thought to the derivative "roots" metaphor, which is reinforced by references to slavery. This, in turn, could open up the question of how important it is for African Americans to have a sense of community.

2. "Just Like a Tree" is narrated in a complex manner, reminiscent of Faulkner's style. Yet, in this particular story, the technique of multiple narrators may serve a different purpose from Faulkner's, since it is not the point of view, but the voice of the character that is given primary importance. Once alerted to the presence of many voices in the narrative, the students can explore differences between male and female voices, child and adult voices, or discover the city slicker voice of James and the "white" voice of Anne-Marie Duvall. A class discussion may also explore the overall effect of the voices, which overlap in their accounts of the events.

Invitation to Write

Although this sequence deals with family, the assignments referring to Gaines's text deal with community and may be easily integrated in that sequence. The community focus opens up questions about various racial and cultural issues and may serve to show students that there are different angles from which they can regard the text. If suburbanites, the students have probably never pondered much on the notion of community. The discussion of the community's significance in the story may lead them to reconsider their own ties to people around them, inside and outside the family. Perhaps the fact that we do not consider such ties "communal" signals a need to redefine the notion of community. Attempting such a problematic definition makes excellent material for a student paper.

Connections

This assignment could also be profitably used as a second question in a sequence on community. In preparation for this paper, the class should perhaps discuss cultural symbolism. Usually students are familiar with the notion of symbol in relation to literature, but they will need to be alerted to the manner in which a community (or group of people with common interests) tends to give significance to certain objects or landmarks. Such objects acquire value as symbols simply because they have been invested with the emotions and ideals of the people who see them as symbols.

NEIL MILLER
A Time of Change (p. 25)

Considerations

1. Miller's essay is likely to spark more controversy in the classroom than any other selection in this book. From the beginning, I would direct the discussion away from the controversy itself and toward a deeper understanding of the cultural circumstances which generate it. Miller's examples, Mo and Ellen, are in many ways creating a new homosexual controversy. As the material about Florida shows, homosexuals who are also parents encounter bitter disapproval. Becoming parents and being ordinary parents are gay people's newest challenges to societal norms.

2. A more detailed look at the responses of the community to gay parenting will make clear what is at stake in the controversy. The community's responses should be carefully analyzed here; a thorough understanding of these attitudes is very important.

3. After analyzing the particular instances of opposition to homosexual parenting, students can generalize and consider the problem in our society at large. Examples from the news may be available to make the discussion current.

Invitation to Write

If used as a writing assignment, this question will give the students an opportunity to think about the controversy surrounding homosexuality in terms different from the general debate in the press or other media. They should perhaps reflect on the new possibility—offered to homosexuals by medical technology—to become parents. Homosexuality has been traditionally marginalized and considered deviant in part because it does not produce children. Without the responsibility of children, folk wisdom has it, there is no guarantee of a stable family, hence the questionable assumption on the part of many heterosexuals that gays are promiscuous. Gay parenting puts the controversy in a whole new perspective. Society can no longer exclude homosexuals as non-procreative (therefore useless) members, but has to deal with the complex task of redefining notions of family and parenthood.

Connections

"Is There a Family? New Anthropological Views" will give students several theoretical positions that can help them conceptualize their responses to the questions above. Once the basic definition of family comes into question, the reasons for the controversy surrounding gays become clearer. Following Collier, Rosaldo, and Yanagisako, students will be able to see that culturally developed notions are not immutable and that new social realities demand the revision of old norms.

In all the preceding assignments, the worst danger is for students to react emotionally and to feel their own identities threatened if they admit that homosexuality is acceptable. If gay, the students might also react emotionally and try to defend the agenda of gay liberation. For all students, it is important to realize that an expository essay is not a debate that can settle a public dispute, but a work that focuses on the underlying causes of events or attitudes. In this particular case, students might discover that the homosexual controversy is not easily settled because the cultural stakes involved refuel it periodically.

JANE COLLIER, MICHELLE Z. ROSALDO, AND SYLVIA YANAGISAKO
Is There a Family?
New Anthropological Views (p. 38)

Considerations

1. The authors of the essay point out repeatedly that most assumptions about family are based on or go together with assumptions about the role of women in both family and society at large. The discussion of this question can range from an analysis of the examples found in the text—Malinowski's idea that "love" is essential to family ties, for instance—to examples in our society. Discussing such examples will prepare the students for writing, especially if the assignment sequence for this unit is used.

2. The ideology behind theories about the family should become evident in the comparison between the nineteenth-century views, Malinowski's views, and our views today. The concept of ideology may have to be explained to students, who might be ready to accept an ideology, rather than define the concept. The discussion of ideology might lead to other questions about

culture and its component systems. Their interrelations should perhaps be emphasized at this point. For instance, ideas about family cannot be separated from ideas about state, property, gender roles, and so on. The examples from other cultures provided by the authors should help to point out such relations.

3. The feminist position of the authors is perhaps one of the essay's most interesting features. Their own ideology can be debated in the same way the ideologies of the other "family" theorists were in responses to the previous question. There is also a vague implication that the concepts about family coming from people like Malinowski are oriented against the emancipation of women. If this implication is mentioned in class discussion, it should provoke a very interesting debate among the students.

Invitation to Write

Students are here asked to do what Collier, Rosaldo, and Yanagisako declare to be beyond their scope. The paper or journal entry need not attempt to solve all the problems that the authors foresee or to cover all the possible perspectives on the "American family." Rather, this assignment should be used to alert students to the fact that a term normally taken for granted may become problematic when concrete examples are considered. The numerous "family" shows on television should be an excellent source of examples. What is important for the students here is to begin to see these examples in the conceptual framework offered by the essay.

Connections

This assignment sends students to another text in which the "family" question is not explicitly raised. They will have to do some critical reading in order to discover the implications present in Scott Myers's story. In addition they will have to reconsider other conceptual aspects of "Is There a Family? New Anthropological Views." A preliminary discussion should perhaps emphasize the opposition between the concept of family and that of the state or the marketplace. Many of Scott Myers's problems derive from the fact that he does not accept the opposition and wants to establish a continuity between these two spheres of his life. One can also explore the significance of his success and consider whether or not he is an example to follow.

ASSIGNMENT SEQUENCE
Functions of the Family (p. 54)

This sequence brings together the essays in ways that will help students find new angles from which to consider the "family" question. Beyond the social function of the family, students will have the opportunity to rethink the concept from the individual's point of view. If the family serves social

19

purposes, how does it serve the individual? The student will also have the opportunity to look deeper into the opposition between public and private and question its validity.

The sequence could well be used in combination with the assignments following each text as well as with a novel. An excellent novel to accompany the material in this chapter would be *The Family* by Buchi Emecheta (Braziller, 1990). This novel deals with a loose family unit in need of definition because it exists at an intersection of different cultures. It also deals with a case of child abuse, quite interesting to discuss in relation with Malinowski's ideas about "love" in the family. In the same line, Toni Morrison's *The Bluest Eye* (WSP, 1972) could be of use to enrich the sequence. Besides exploring a distorted notion of love that manifests itself as rape, Morrison's novel invites us to perceive the cultural differences between the white middle-class "family" and the African-American families living under exploitation.

2

Growing Into Adulthood

DAVID JACKSON
One of the Boys (p. 63)

Considerations

1. The interesting thing about Jackson's autobiography is the fact that he analyzes his experience and interprets it with the help of theoretical material concerned with gender. By looking at the way he endows the incidents of his adolescence with meaning, students may be encouraged to appreciate the relation between theory and experience. The initial quotations can serve as a starting point for discovering this relation. If one teaches the "narrative" as rhetorical form, this is an excellent opportunity to discuss the value of narrating one's personal experience.

2. Although the boarding-school system is not part of American culture, students may relate to Jackson's experience on the basis of milder incidents from their own lives. This question may lead to a generalization about the way boys and girls learn how to be men and women in society. A variety of examples volunteered by students should provide good material for analysis.

If students are shy about their own experience, you can always use characters from television shows or movies in order to bring the discussion home, so to speak.

3. This question touches on a subtle point in Jackson's argument. The contradictory character of most cultural injunctions is one of the most puzzling phenomena of any society. Once they discover the contradiction shown by the author, students may think of other examples in which the same kind of contradiction occurs: For instance, each gender is supposed to be attracted to the opposite one, but segregation of men and women seems to be the rule in most societies.

Invitation to Write

Some of the discussions based on the "Considerations" questions should help the students tackle this assignment. The point here is to become more aware of the culturally enforced ideas about gender roles within our own society. Students may respond differently to this assignment depending on their gender and the kind of family they grew up in. Again, they may be encouraged to debate the issue if they use examples from current sitcoms, commercials, or movies. They may also bring up the issue of how different cultures deal with gender education: Various immigrant or minority groups may have different ideas regarding gender and child-rearing methods.

Connections

This assignment may require a rereading of Jackson's analytical narrative with a special attention to language. One might also have to consult a British dictionary for the meaning of certain words and phrases less common in America. It will be interesting to see how students differentiate between Jackson and Tannen. Although these two writers think along the same lines, Jackson's point of view is definitely masculine, whereas Tannen's is definitely feminine. In preparation for the assignment you could role-play the two authors in a class discussion to discover their subtle differences.

RAYMONDE CARROLL
Parents and Children (p. 80)

Considerations

1. Carroll mentions that in French culture it is usually the behavior of parents that is under scrutiny, rather than that of children. Indeed, in her examples one can see that the Americans criticize the French parents and hardly say anything at all about the children. Their judgment of the children is nevertheless implied. A discussion of several examples should bring up the

21

implications, especially the comments made by American students about French children's clothes.

2. Carroll tells a number of anecdotes, the significance of which is not immediately revealed. Going back to these examples after the students have finished reading her essay will help them understand not only the purpose of the examples but also her more theoretical conclusions.

3. To answer this question, students will have to draw out the implications of Carroll's argument. She never says—although she implies it—that Americans prize individualism over the good of the community, that they avoid controlling other people's lives, that they have a notion of freedom hard to understand for the more collectively oriented European societies. It would also be interesting to compare her appraisal of American attitudes to Kaplan's, who seems to be too much of an insider to see them as clearly as Carroll does. Kaplan thinks, for instance, that parents are neglected in their old age because American culture values youth more than age, whereas Carroll sees the same attitude as stemming from the respect for the parents' capacity to manage their lives without help.

Invitation to Write

Students may get easily excited by the topic of child-rearing, which is implied in this question. Even if they do not have children, they have definite ideas about what they like and what they do not like in a child or in a parent. They should probably be steered toward exploring the reasons behind their own judgments. What is a good child is determined to a large extent by what is a good adult. Carroll's observations might show students how to approach the topic as a question related to cultural identity. They should be able to use her approach in discussing examples from their own experience. Maybe a period of observation should be allowed so that students can gather their own material.

Connections

By the time they arrive at this assignment, students may already have noticed and debated Carroll's limitations. Most observers of American culture have in view the white, Anglo-Saxon middle class rather than the mosaic of all ethnic groups. Ortiz Cofer's childhood resembles in some respects that of middle-class Americans, but in others her education at home is quite similar to the French. This combination should elicit many interpretations. It might also lead to the exploration of another issue: cultural schizophrenia. Ortiz Cofer is actually brought up in one culture and has to live in another.

JUDITH ORTIZ COFER
The Looking-Glass Shame (p. 97)

Considerations

1. Ortiz Cofer is not explicit about the purpose Virginia Woolf's quotation serves. The metaphor alludes to more than the relation with one's body during adolescence, since it refers not only to young Judith but also to her mother and father. A close look at the passages that contain references to the mirror will help students focus on the complexities of Ortiz Cofer's self-discovery, which she cannot separate from her condition as an immigrant.

2. The last remark in the narrative is interesting because it makes one reconsider the whole story. Although she never mentions invisibility, she implies it all along, and those implications could be related to the "mirror" metaphor borrowed from Woolf. I would steer the students away from facile generalizations about the person within and the person without. Ortiz Cofer's imagery points rather toward bringing together one's self with one's body; she is concerned about growing into one's self.

Invitation to Write

It would be easy to conclude that, as a child, Ortiz Cofer felt isolated because her family and her home were different from those of her peers. However, Ortiz Cofer's narrative is more complex because her condition as an immigrant is inextricable from her adolescence. She does not arrive in the United States with an existing sense of identity, but has to create it by negotiating between the values of her family and the values of the society. It will be useful for students to analyze her problems by thinking up examples that coincide only partially with hers. The desire to be accepted is common to adolescents and immigrants, but its source and consequences might be different. The responses to this assignment may offer a variety of examples and modes of pursuing the analogy between somebody foreign to a culture and the adolescent, who also has to be initiated in the ways of a culture not yet his or her own.

Connections

This assignment should take the students from a stereotypical view of an immigrant's problem to more probing questions about how a culture establishes itself as dominant. If they observe the similarities between the American Indian family in Erdrich's story and Ortiz Cofer's family, they will be able to analyze in depth the relations of domination. They will also be able to discover that such relations, usually determined by economic factors, have important cultural components: the way the values of one culture are imposed upon another leading to unfair judgments.

A related issue is that of the individual and his or her transition or adaptation from one culture to another. The achievement of one's potential is conditioned by the degree of adaptation to one's culture. In the cases of the characters portrayed by Ortiz Cofer or Erdrich, a tremendous amount of that potential is wasted in the very process of adjustment. In Erdrich, one can even see how the whole potential is wasted. Either treatment of the topic should produce an interesting result.

LOUISE J. KAPLAN
Adolescence:
The Farewell to Childhood (p. 107)

Considerations

1. This question, as well as those following, is meant to help students pursue Kaplan's argument to its logical conclusions. Kaplan's essay raises many issues that it does not pursue, and these issues can make excellent topics of discussion in class. One might even start by locating the points of Kaplan's argument that need more development or probing into.

2. The gender issues are in need of clarification within the context of Kaplan's argument on adolescence. They may be discussed by appealing to examples from the other texts or from the students' own experience with gendered socialization.

3. Kaplan's conclusions are not among the most obvious. She is probably arguing against other theories current in psychology, and it is difficult for a reader ignorant of those to see what she wants. Kaplan seems also rather undecided on whether adolescence is perceived differently by different cultures or whether it has some universal traits. The question needs to be thoroughly debated in preparation for writing. A discussion of how difficult it is to define Kaplan's purpose will offer the students an example of how we (as nonspecialists) can find our way in a specialized text.

Invitation to Write

Puberty rites or rites of passage are likely to fascinate students, and they will certainly be interested in exploring their significance. They should be encouraged to discover the symbolic meaning of each ritual that is not completely explained by Kaplan. The other equally attractive aspect of this topic is the possible analogy between modern adolescent behavior and the rituals of older cultures. Students might even be able to discover the symbolic value of their own contemporary substitutes for the ancient rites.

Connections

This assignment should lead to a clarification of Kaplan's position concerning the universality of adolescent experience. Carroll's greater attention to cultural differences should enable students to see where Kaplan hesitates to commit herself to the idea that the very concept of adolescence may be culturally determined. There should be occasion here also for an exploration of the American ideas about youth (adolescence) and old age. Since both Kaplan and Carroll offer an approach as well as many examples, the two texts can be used interchangeably as theoretical models and sources of examples. Examples from the students' own experience are also acceptable.

ASSIGNMENT SEQUENCE
Growing Into Adulthood (p. 123)

This sequence gives students the opportunity to engage in a longer project and to think about the questions related to adolescence from different perspectives. Bringing the texts together, it may become clear that, from the point of view of the individual, adolescence is related, most of the time, to pain. Jackson's and Ortiz Cofer's autobiographical analyses of adolescence both explore the feelings of inadequacy and isolation, from the male and female point of view, respectively. The cultural diversity of authors represented in the selections should also shed some light on how different cultures handle adolescent problems and how they conceptualize this difficult period of life. With all its shortcomings, Kaplan's argument offers a theoretical frame for all other texts.

The sequence could be used in combination with a novel like Tsitsi Dangarembga's *Nervous Conditions* (Seal Press–Feminist, 1989) which focuses on the choices of a young woman growing up in the newly decolonized—but still culturally enslaved—Kenya. Dangarembga's insights into the problems of female adolescence are as poignant as her indictment of colonialism, and in this respect her book would tally well with Ortiz Cofer, Jackson, and Carroll. The trials and tribulations of adolescence from the male point of view are vividly illustrated by Timothy Wangusa's *Upon This Mountain* (Heinemann Educational Books, 1989) which is situated in a Uganda still dominated by tribal values and customs. The rituals described here will be a nice complement to Kaplan's more generalized account of puberty rites. I guess the difficulty here would be in choosing one novel or the other, because the choice will give a certain gender orientation to the class.

3

Defining Women's Lives

ERIKA FRIEDL

A Betrothal, a Rape, and
a Guess About Turan's Fate (p. 129)

Considerations

1. Friedl represents a trend in current anthropology arguing that the anthropological study should be a dialogue with the people under study rather than an argument about them. This minimizes interpretation of the "native" cultures by avoiding the imposition of the researcher's own cultural values upon his or her subjects. The proponents of interpretive anthropology, on the other hand, think that such impositions are inevitable and that one need only be aware that, when interpreting the other, one is actually defining oneself. Friedl's style of reporting should, however, be interesting even without an awareness of the debates surrounding anthropological studies. She gives us maximum access to the women's thinking but also leaves us with the task of interpretation. One should note that Friedl's own account is not totally free of interpretation: The word *rape* in the title is not part of the Iranian women's vocabulary, and the very concept of rape seems foreign to them.

2. This is an interesting question to discuss because the sharing of space is not so evident, and the text will have to be perused repeatedly in order to find the passages where the divisions of space are clear. The discussion might also lead to noticing that violence on the part of men is almost taken for granted and that women seem to live in fear. Their space is protected, but it resembles in many ways a prison.

Invitation to Write

Rape is one of the topics of social debate in American culture today, and it should be particularly interesting to students. Again, the danger is that students might adopt one side or the other of the public debate and forget to analyze the reasons behind the controversy. Working with Friedl's text might help students recognize masculine and feminine attitudes that, in a milder form, exist in our society too. The obvious difficulty the women have in separating masculine desire for women from violent behavior, which becomes apparent in their remarks, should lead the students to perform a deeper analysis of the phenomenon of courtship and romantic love.

Connections

This question might be easily integrated in the assignment sequence about men (p. 212). It also plays a necessary role in this chapter where the main emphasis is on women and where male students might feel that they are being unduly subjected to a feminist approach. The assignment has another, more technical interest. Since Friedl's text seems to deal exclusively with women, unearthing the assumptions about male behavior in it will be interesting work. A good starting point for connecting the two readings is the observation that Abbas appears attractively masculine in spite of his immorality. Gilmore's more theoretical formulations should offer the concepts necessary to explain the ideal of masculinity implicit in Deh Koh culture.

MARIANNA DE MARCO TORGOVNICK
On Being White, Female, and Born in Bensonhurst (p. 138)

Considerations

1. Torgovnick is aware that she has never cut her ties to the neighborhood, in spite of all her rebellion. Beyond the uneasy feeling that Bensonhurst is perhaps not the most generous and liberal environment to have grown up in, she still feels connected to it. Sometimes, her connection to the provincial atmosphere of the place becomes apparent even against her will. For instance, when she says "My father is not a racist" and follows with her father's obviously racist remarks, it is rather hard to believe that this comes from the author of *Gone Primitive*, which indicts racism in its most elusive forms. Perhaps the discussion of such remarks can lead to more general questions like "What is racism, after all?"

2. Torgovnick offers a spatial metaphor to describe the invisible social barriers that people raise among themselves. The concrete examples can easily become symbolic of cultural divisions not only between ethnicities and races but also between genders. The discussion of this question can easily be related to Friedl's text. It is the question that brings these texts together in the assignment sequence.

3. This question should not be difficult to answer after an attentive second reading of the essay. It is perhaps one of the things that Torgovnick hesitates to admit even to herself, that the reach of her parents' prejudices determined nearly *all* her decisions. The discussion may inspire students to ask themselves how and by whom their own decisions are determined.

Invitation to Write

This assignment should stir up questions about individuality, sense of identity, and the necessity to belong to a family, a community, and a tradition. It may also inspire students to look into social mobility and observe the dislocations that take place when one moves up in society. When she talks with a new acquaintance who shares with her a Bensonhurst past, Torgovnick relates his lapse into what he calls a "werewolf" transformation (p. 144). The incident is worth discussing in preparation for the paper, since it can bring up questions about the authenticity of one who has crossed class barriers. Other students may focus on the ambivalence of Torgovnick's feelings toward her past and explore their own feelings about the environment where they grew up.

Connections

The comparison between the communities portrayed by Torgovnick and Gaines is sure to raise controversy in the classroom. It should help students understand the issue of racism in a deeper and more meaningful way than either old prejudices or new liberalisms portray it. Torgovnick's reference to her roots, with their "simultaneously choking and nutritive power" should inspire students to search for both the positive values that the group to which we belong instills in us and to the negative consequences of overvaluing our own characteristics at the expense of others. A closer look at the community depicted by Gaines in "Just Like a Tree" may also reveal tendencies toward prejudice among Aunt Fe's friends.

SIMONE DE BEAUVOIR
Introduction to The Second Sex (p. 150)

Considerations

1. As I pointed out in my introductory remarks, it is better to pose this as a question rather than explaining to the students the concept of voicing, that is, taking on the persona of someone and quoting him or her without using quotation marks. The debates will surely lead to interesting conclusions, since the students should feel that this is a question they themselves would ask. They will probably engage readily in the exploration of an issue that is important to them.

2. This is a restatement of the first question and will probably lead students to continue the same debate. It will be interesting to figure out why Beauvoir cannot simply overthrow the bonds of masculine discourse. A similarity with Torgovnick's situation may be noted here, and it is worth discussing how much of Beauvoir's upbringing according to French methods of education (see Carroll, p. 80) still persists in her writing.

3. It is interesting for students to trace how the concept of "other" evolves in Beauvoir's essay. First, this process will help them develop their own concepts, and second, it will spare them the trouble of using the word in the way she does without having really understood its meaning.

Invitation to Write

Female students will probably be eager to start exploring the topic of feminism, but this kind of assignment may get negative reactions from the male students. How to deal with such problems? As in the case of any controversial issue, the students should first be guided toward an understanding of the concepts involved in Beauvoir's argument. Once they approach the "woman" question conceptually, male students can be spared the emotional reactions that the subject could otherwise bring up. Emotional reactions by the female students are also to be avoided. Feelings do not have to be repressed during class discussion, where the students' emotional responses could lead to a lively debate. In writing, however, students should be encouraged to analyze what they feel and come to a deeper understanding of what is at stake in gender definitions.

Connections

This assignment should bring forth most of the implication of Deborah Tannen's essay. Tannen is obviously writing from a feminist perspective, but she assumes, perhaps too much, that everybody is familiar with general feminist theory. This kind of assumption glosses over different orientations in feminism and sometimes even obscures her argument. Beauvoir's more explicit theoretical position should help students uncover Tannen's underlying assumptions and make explicit issues that she only implies. The emphasis on Beauvoir could well be reversed, and Tannen could be used to explain, from a linguistic standpoint, Beauvoir's difficulty in finding the right voice for her essay. Either way, the effort to read Tannen and Beauvoir together is likely to produce interesting arguments in student papers.

ASSIGNMENT SEQUENCE
Defining Women's Lives (p. 166)

The questions following each text in this chapter are especially suited to preparing the students for writing the assignment sequence. The sequence itself focuses attention on details that might be overlooked in a first reading and thus forces the students to deepen their interpretation of the texts. One strong point of this sequence is the quality of Beauvoir's argument, which offers many possibilities for both theoretical exploration and interpretation of concrete examples. It is advisable to use this chapter and sequence in combination with the sequence on men in order to achieve a gender balance.

29

There are quite a number of novels that could be used to complement the texts in this chapter. Buchi Emecheta's *The Joys of Motherhood* (Heinemann Educational Books, 1989) is especially interesting in this context not only because it deals with women from an African culture (a culture not represented in the chapter) but also because it deals with changes in the social norms regarding women, changes brought about by westernization and modernization. It also raises the issue of motherhood, which is not dealt with extensively in the chapter. At the other end of the spectrum of women's issues stands Nawal El Saadawi's *Woman at Point Zero* (Humanities Press International, 1983). Saadawi explores questions related to prostitution, another issue that is not debated in the texts included here.

4

Defining Men's Lives

PHILIP ROTH
His Roth (p. 173)

Considerations

1. "His Roth" is basically a nostalgic piece, and the way it actually deals with questions of masculinity will not be immediately evident to students. They will need to work through Roth's essay in order to discover the assumptions about family, masculinity, and other notions normally taken for granted.

2. Here again, students will have to read through Roth's description of pain in order to discover the masculinist assumptions implied in it. One of the most striking occasions to discover such implications is the description of the father's physical transformation: Unmanned by the disease, the senior Roth begins to look like his own mother, a resemblance that Philip ordinarily does not perceive.

3. Roth is a crafty writer and the little details of his descriptions or the peculiarities of his language are quite interesting to explore. The cultural bias that relegates the care of little boys to mothers and leaves the initiation into adulthood to fathers creeps into his names: "To be at all is to be her Philip, but in the embroilment with the buffeting world, my history still takes its

spin from beginning as his Roth (para. 19)." In fact, the whole of the last paragraph needs special attention and a very close reading.

Invitation to Write

Roth's essay could easily be included in a modified sequence concerning the family. His family is very typical of a traditional way of life that he identifies as Jewish, but that can be easily extrapolated to all America of the first half of the century. "His Roth" could compare nicely with Torgovnick's description of her family. The traditional family structure represented by the Roths will give excellent material for comparisons with our own contemporary ideas on the matter. Social developments that were already appearing during Roth's childhood have forced a substantial change in the way a family is defined.

Connections

This is another assignment that could be used in a sequence about family. Roth and Rodriguez are interesting to compare because they are both accomplished writers who search for significance in the events of their lives. In writing about their past experiences, both are more obviously nostalgic than Torgovnick, for instance. Strangely enough, they also seem less aware than she is that they are being nostalgic. The assignment may elicit different responses from students. They could emphasize the idea of fatherhood and discuss issues of masculinity and initiation into manhood. On the other hand, they could treat the topic at a more abstract level and focus on the dynamic of the relation between the individual and his or her environment or family. Another way to look at this pair of autobiographic writings is to consider the ethnic background of the authors. Perceiving themselves as minorities, certain ethnic groups give more importance to family ties than people in the mainstream are inclined to do.

LEONARD KIBERA
The Spider's Web (p. 180)

Considerations

1. The dreams of Kibera's hero are likely to attract symbolic interpretations. Some knowledge of psychoanalytic interpretations of dreams applied here might give interesting results. The students do not, however, need to rely on such knowledge in order to notice that the changes taking place in Ngotho's society have affected him at an unconscious level. Guessing about his unconscious may also lead to interpretations of his reactions to the events taking place in his life. Ngotho does not know what actually happens to him or why what happens affects him in such a negative way.

2. One has to attribute to Ngotho a rather superstitious mind in order to understand his fear of Lois. This question should lead to a discussion about the society of Kenya depicted by Kibera. Limited information about the country may be available in dictionaries, but it is more important for the students to make inferences from the story itself. The imagination in which Lois acquires monstrous and supernatural proportions has, as Wallace Stevens would put it, "itself to be imagined."

3. I think the symbols in the story have to be given particular attention. They are very powerful in isolation, but they are even more interesting to consider together as they form a symbolic network that vividly renders Ngotho's dream world, or his unconscious. Some obvious symbols to discuss are the image of Lois as a queen bee, the coffin in Ngotho's dream, and the fragile but entangling spider's web mentioned in the title. These symbols suggest the helpless and inferior position of Ngotho.

Invitation to Write

The exploration of gender issues crossed with issues of class and race should lead to interesting arguments. Gender is one of the most controversial issues of the developing African countries. In spite of all its ill effects, colonialism has benefited women and other groups oppressed under tribal rule. Lois is an example of an individual who has gotten the upper hand as a consequence of the country's transformations under colonialism. With the British gone, Ngotho hopes for a return to old tribal rule, under which a man can be a man, and Lois makes that dream impossible for him. The dilemma of African nationalism is that a return to native culture also means a return to various traditional forms of oppression.

Connections

Harrison's theory about the vestiges of colonialism offers an ideal framework for treating the most obvious issue in the story. Both texts can be better interpreted if read together. Harrison generalizes rather quickly sometimes, and a confrontation between his ideas and the concrete example of Ngotho will certainly raise the right questions about his argument. The blind spots of Ngotho's frustrations are, in turn, likely to become clearer when a historical outlook like that of Harrison's is taken into consideration.

DAVID GILMORE
Performative Excellence: Circum-Mediterranean (p. 190)

Considerations

1. Students will likely be attracted to Lorenzo's story because it gives the reader pause from the more theoretical and abstract part of Gilmore's argument. Lorenzo is, in many ways, the wrong man in the wrong culture. His intellectual pursuits make him quite similar to Gilmore himself, and a comparison between the author and his example should be quite interesting. The fact that Lorenzo could be successful in another culture should be discussed at some length in order to avoid the understanding of masculinity as an exclusively nonintellectual achievement.

2. Gilmore implies, but does not say, that masculinity as a cultural construct is an ideal and that in practice no man can actually live up to it. This implication should become clear in analyzing the author's propensity for negative rather than positive examples. The criticisms of Lorenzo and Alfredo actually make up a good assessment of the ideal characteristics of masculinity. One can also observe that the only perfect men that Gilmore mentions are mythological heroes, not human beings.

Invitation to Write

This assignment should get the students excited about examples of the American ideal of masculinity. There should be plenty of examples from the older western movies (John Wayne's roles in particular), other types of tough guy movies (Humphrey Bogart's), as well as older family movies (*It's a Wonderful Life*, for instance). From among the more recent heroes, they could pick the ideals of manhood portrayed by Arnold Schwarzenegger, or the more sensitive type portrayed by Kevin Costner. It would be interesting to compare older portrayals of manhood with the newer ones and to notice the changes. Students could also follow Gilmore's example and look for cases of inadequacy. The examples, if carefully analyzed, should enrich the students' understanding of Gilmore's theory and should enable them to make cross-cultural comparisons.

Connections

Jackson's argument is the ideal counterpart for Gilmore's from the points of view of method and cultural variety. Reading their arguments together should illuminate both, for Gilmore's breadth should enrich and be enriched by Jackson's depth. If they focus more on Gilmore, the students will be able to question his detachment from the whole matter. He speaks as if his identity as a man were not at stake at all. One may wonder whether that is possible. As for Jackson, the exclusively personal concern may make one wonder about the validity of his argument. Another way to orient the essay would be to focus on the differences in the ways the two cultures conceptualize masculinity.

ASSIGNMENT SEQUENCE
Defining Men's Lives (p. 212)

Aside from Gilmore's clearly oriented argument, the readings in this chapter do not deal with masculinity in obvious ways. This will oblige the students to go back to the texts with increased attention. The sequence should also lead students to observe cultural differences, since gender definitions are among the most evident cultural constructs. The connection with the students' personal experience should also arouse their interest. As in the case of the chapter about women, I would recommend either taking the two chapters together, or emphasizing the possibilities of applying the theory about one gender to the other gender.

Many novels are candidates for companions to the texts in this chapter. Practically, all canonical American novels (from Mark Twain's to Ernest Hemingway's) reveal the authors' preoccupation with masculinity. Noncanonical works from other cultures would be better, however, both because they do not come with the baggage of traditional interpretation and because they will increase the variety of examples. *Chronicle of a Death Foretold* (Ballantine, 1984), by Gabriel García Márquez, portrays machismo in action—violent action, I might add—and could elicit discussion about the relation between the demands of manhood and violence. Timothy Wangusa's *Upon This Mountain* (Heinemann Educational Books, 1989) deals with initiation to manhood and offers models of masculinity from an African culture. The novel is also interesting because it depicts masculinity in a time of change when the old ideals are displaced by the new.

5

Working in the World

WAKAKO YAMAUCHI
Maybe (p. 219)

Considerations

1. This question may prompt the students to make connections between the situations of minorities and immigrants and to find out what they have in common. There are, of course, racial implications too: Florence is perceived as "not American" mainly because of her race. The Pearl Harbor incidents mentioned by Yamauchi are also evoked by Garrett Hongo in "Kubota."

2. Students might find different answers to this question. Obviously Zenobia perceives Florence as a rival. The workers relate to Florence in a way they never could with Zenobia, who has power over them. Perhaps at the bottom of Zenobia's hatred is her envy of Florence's native-born status.

Invitation to Write

Yamauchi deals with working conditions that are not likely to be familiar to most students. This assignment should be an occasion to think about the way relations of domination are generated in a work situation. Economic inequality is not always the key factor. A good way to begin might be to explore the cultural values implied in the relations between employers and employees. American culture tends to reduce such relations between people to an economic level, but as in the case of Zenobia's jealousy, education may also be a factor. Because she is educated, Florence does not feel dependent on her employer. One may also think of other cultures (Japan happens to be one) in which age is regarded with reverence.

Connections

Two approaches to this question are possible. The first is to start with the theory and verify it by analyzing the examples. The second is to start from analyzing the examples and then reach conclusions that can be compared to the theory. The play upon the word *alien* should inspire the students to probe deeper into Marx's concept of alienation. Like Beauvoir's "other," this is not an easy concept to digest and the word runs the risk of losing its meaning by being overused. If alerted to gender issues, students might also notice how Marx refers only to "man." What would he have to say about working women or women's work?

ROBERT C. CHRISTOPHER
The Fruits of Industry (p. 228)

Considerations

1. In this and the other questions, I think it is important to emphasize that the attitude toward work is formed within a culture and reflects the culture's other values as well. Americans prize a spirit of independence in relation to work. The Japanese, in contrast, emphasize loyalty to their employer and a commitment to the common good. Christopher cites Japanese management expert Jiro Tokuyama, who believes that "the differences between Japanese and American managerial techniques are merely symptoms of a far deeper and probably ineradicable difference" (para. 48). Christopher quotes another Japanese executive, Yoshiya Ariyoshi, who asks: "How can anyone reasonably expect Americans—individualistic and independent-minded Americans—to behave like group-oriented Japanese?" (para. 48).

2. The Japanese corporate system has attracted much praise due to its enormous success. While analyzing the merits of the system, students may be alerted to the fact that success is not only the product of efficiency. There is also an element of chance. Among the factors Christopher did not consider is the oil crisis which made the compact Japanese cars an instant success in the United States. As for the disadvantages of the Japanese system, the mainstream press is beginning to discuss them. Students might research this question of the downside of the Japanese economic miracle and share information with each other in peer groups.

Invitation to Write

This assignment is asking the students to approach the questions debated by Christopher from the individual's point of view. Implied here is actually a comparison between the Japanese and American cultures not only as far as work is concerned but also with regard to their views on the relation between individual and community, the concept of freedom, the very notion of happiness. American culture is one of the few that tend to see work as personal fulfillment or at least as a partial source of satisfaction. It should be clear to students that in principle the types of methods used by the Japanese are unacceptable to Americans. Asking why may lead, however, to a more interesting discussion.

TUCKER AND LEINBERGER, *Scott Myers, Entrepreneur* (TEXT PP. 242–253)

Connections

Here the students will again have to compare two different cultures. From the start, they should avoid the mistake of considering Zodiac Prints a typically American company. In fact it is more Latin American than anything else. Evidently, Zenobia's erratic style of management would horrify the Japanese, but her taco picnics might also be interpreted as caring for her workers as members of a family, a principle germane to the one that guides Japanese companies' treatment of their workers. One other interesting thing to consider here is Florence's point of view. Is she representative of mainstream America or are her Japanese roots influencing her perceptions?

BRUCE TUCKER AND PAUL LEINBERGER
Scott Myers, Entrepreneur (p. 242)

Considerations

1. Scott Myers's personality is interesting to discuss, because the issue of the whole essay is, in fact, individualism. On the one hand, Scott represents an entire generation of Americans who became uncomfortable with being part of an organization. On the other, his discontent has to be seen as an expression of his individuality.

2. This question is obviously leading to Marx. What happens to the individual under the pressure of the organization? There should be ample opportunity here for the students to bring into discussion their own attitudes toward work.

3. If they think of this question in relation to the previous readings, the students will be able to debate the relation between family and work. They could compare the family-like organization of Japanese companies to Myers's workplaces. They might find that the Japanese companies are more like Memorex than like Scott's new business; the hours are long and demanding and the companies expect complete loyalty from the employees. Maybe Scott has in mind a different kind of family. After all, the concept of family is just about as complicated as the concept of work.

Invitation to Write

Here is an opportunity to develop two concepts and to analyze their relation. This may look difficult, at first, but students might have plenty of examples from their own experience. They could consider how tasks are distributed in the family and relate the division of work to gender roles. The authors of the essay argue that the changes in family structure are determined by social and economic changes. They do not go into much detail about them and the students have ample opportunity to figure out what kind of changes

37

are involved. One such change regards the roles played by men and women both in the family and in society at large.

Connections

The comparison between the Japanese and American ways of organizing work haunts this chapter. However, this question reorients the discussion toward the needs of the individual. A new reading of Christopher's essay might be necessary, since his main focus is precisely not the individual, but the organization. Scott Myers's dilemmas may have to be reconsidered too. Students should also observe the dialectic between organizational efficiency and individual satisfaction in work. In theory, the maximum efficiency of the company and its success should lead to the worker's satisfaction: The more money the company makes, the more it pays its workers. Also, happy workers should be more productive and increase the company's success. In practice, the company's efficiency restrains the worker's freedom and can eventually make him or her unhappy. The more highly organized the company is, the more it restricts the individual's freedom and creativity. Reflecting on the relation between work and personal happiness in this paper will prepare the students for reading Marx.

KARL MARX
Alienated Labor (p. 254)

Considerations

1. Marx's criticism of capitalist labor relations is based on close observations of the nineteenth-century reality in Europe. One should not forget, however, that Marx is also the product of that culture and therefore may be burdened with its prejudices. One can recognize here a kind of Rousseauistic "back to nature" urgency. Marx is obviously trying to shape the future on the model of a shadowy past, the golden age, that we always imagine to have preceded us. It will probably be hard for students to notice such echoes, but they might be able to identify the nature-industry opposition and to wonder whether such opposition really holds. One interesting way to appraise Marx's projections would be to suggest a comparison to some other imagined futures, such as those produced by science fiction novels or movies.

2. Alienation is not an easy concept here and the students will have to look closely at all the examples Marx uses to build it up. They might want to think of their own examples of alienation and also discuss the other possible senses of the word.

3. In *The Sacred and the Profane: The Nature of Religions* (HBJ, 1959), Mircea Eliade argues that the success of Marxism is due to its close similarity to religion: "Marx takes over and continues one of the great eschatological myths of the Asiatico-Mediterranean world—the redeeming role of the Just

(the 'chosen,' the 'anointed,' the 'innocent,' the 'messenger'; in our day, the proletariat), whose sufferings are destined to change the ontological status of the world" (206). The abundance of the religious analogies in the text offered here not only confirms this assessment, but also shows how deeply Marx was entrenched in the ideology he was trying to overturn. As with Beauvoir, one can make a case that the author lacks the language and the conceptual means to oppose the culture that has practically created him or her.

Invitation to Write

The starting point here should perhaps be the underlying distaste for technology that pervades Marx's essay. If they are at all familiar with the American literature of the nineteenth century, students might be able to recognize anxieties of the kind Hawthorne or Poe magnified in terrifying metaphors of science gone amok. But even in the absence of such background, students would probably react to Marx's implied phobia of technology. Today technology is so much a part of our lives, that we cannot even imagine the world without it. Far from having destroyed our humanity, technology has helped us become more human. In many cases, it makes work easier, more pleasant; it makes leisure possible and also enables us to communicate. If they do not start thinking along these lines, however, students will have ample opportunity to bring Marx up to date and argue against the alienating effect of computers, cellular phones, and remote controls.

Connections

One could hardly describe Scott Myers as a Marxist; yet, on a certain level his concerns are similar to Marx's. This essay could be written as an exploration of the concept of alienation with Myers as an example. Naturally, the concept needs to be brought up to date. On the other hand, students may focus on the differences between Myers's case and what Marx describes as alienation of labor. Marx is basically concerned with the relation between the worker and production. Myers gives up his job at Memorex out of concern for his personal growth and for his relationship with his family. For Marx, the family is never explicitly in the picture.

ASSIGNMENT SEQUENCE
Working in the World (p. 264)

The assignments in this sequence will give students the opportunity to think theoretically about a topic they might have discussed only informally before. Ideas about work are central to American culture, and work is certainly an experience most of us share. There are types of work that are not brought up in the texts included in this chapter, for instance, artistic work. The point of view of a self-employed person is also not considered. Annie

Dillard's essay "The Writing Life" (p. 517) and Robert Reich's "The Global Elite" (p. 290) would be interesting additions to this sequence.

Some novels could also add new dimensions to the debate around work. Chinua Achebe's *Things Fall Apart* (Knopf, 1992), although ostensibly dealing with colonialism, offers a rich insight into the attitudes of a tribal society about work. The closeness to nature and the obviously intimate relation between human beings and their work would perhaps illuminate Marx's concept of alienation. On the other hand, the deep connection between work and religion in the tribe may prove that work is never a natural but a cultural concept. Another aspect of the question of work emerges in James Welch's *The Indian Lawyer* (Viking Penguin, 1991), which takes us into the world of underprivileged groups. For Welch's hero, work—his profession—is a means of obtaining a better social status. It is also alienated and alienating work, since it separates the individual from his culture.

6

Individuals in Communities

EDNA O'BRIEN
The Widow (p. 271)

Considerations

1. This should generate an interesting debate in a class discussion. In many ways, Biddy is offensive, even to us: She drinks (and drives), and she does not seem eager to make friends in the neighborhood. But is that all there is to her behavior? Students should be directed to consider how the community defines its rules through the point of view adopted in the narrative. We do not know anything about Bridget's motivations, and that makes it hard for us to take her side. It should be noticed, however, that her infractions consist of doing what men usually do. She is basically violating the taboos of femininity.

2. The answer to this question will draw upon information and analysis developed in response to the previous question. The attitudes of the town are easy to infer from the way Bridget is criticized. Students should be able to notice that sometimes there is a dissenting voice in the chorus of the

neighborhood: The reports of the shopkeeper, for instance, are not always negative.

3. The relative novelty of the automobile should be a clue here. But this question should lead beyond the simple guess of the time period to a discussion of the changes that are visible not only in the aspect of the town but also in the behavior of people. Bridget's independent behavior is one of those changes greeted with suspicion and mistrust by the conservative little town.

Invitation to Write

Perhaps the most striking feature of the community in this story is its need to control the lives of individuals. The rules of good behavior are firmly established, and everyone watches everyone else to see that they are respected. The students may be repelled by this kind of control, but they may also be able to make connections with contemporary environments in which this kind of attention to another's behavior is in force. The community also plays the role of interpreter of the events. The accidents happening in Bridget's life are considered to be the consequences of her unacceptable behavior. Bridget's death becomes symbolic proof of the evil represented by novelty (whether in technology or behavior): She dies in the car that she drove in defiance of everybody in the community. The community is thus not only a group of people with common interests but also the enforcer of values and beliefs inherited from the past.

Connections

This assignment should attract the students' attention to the fact that gender roles are, in fact, decided upon by the community in which we live. Reading Gilmore will enable students to identify the traits of masculine behavior in Bridget's case. On the other hand, reading "The Widow" will allow students to notice that the communities described in Gilmore's case studies are quite similar to the town in the story. The community's control over the individual is perhaps the most prominent feature of them all. Maybe in a second draft, students should be encouraged to think about the reason behind this form of control. Usually, a cultural feature that appears to be negative may have developed out of a good intention: The community may want to take control because it feels responsible for its members. An analogy with parent-child relationships may be helpful.

WILLIAM LEAST HEAT-MOON
The Emma Chase (p. 282)

Considerations

1. It is important to differentiate between the community's values and the values of one individual. Linda Thurston seems to subscribe to the view that traditional values can be changed and old customs can be replaced by new ones. She also seems to have a clear idea of what makes a custom a custom and promotes her new values by creating traditions of her own: Serving a particular type of food and digging out an old picture to employ it as a symbol are only a few of the things she does to change the people's way of seeing and thinking about things.

2. Least Heat-Moon has a journalistic style that gives the illusion of total objectivity. However, total objectivity is hard to reach. A good feature article, even one based on an interview, has a shape and a theme. By calling Thurston's project a fantasy (if it was Least Heat-Moon who introduced the term), he adds the allure of a fulfilled dream to his story.

If Thurston was the one to describe her project as a "fantasy," her use of the word underscores her desire to return to roots and work out her political philosophy in relation to the environment that influenced her earliest thoughts. The word also reveals the ephemerality of the project: Thurston knows all along that this would be just an interlude in her life as a feminist and an activist.

Invitation to Write

This assignment could easily start with a discussion of the symbol that Linda Thurston has chosen for her café. Her awareness of the importance of symbols for creating a spirit of community needs some attention too. It is interesting to notice that, as in her phrase "going forward to my roots," Linda does not think of the community as something given and accepted. She thinks of community as something to be made, constructed through the wills of individuals like her. Paradoxically, it is her confidence in the power of individuals that gives her a basis for the community. Unlike Bridget's townspeople, she is not interested in what people do. She does not aspire to control them, but she offers them an opportunity to do something else. Her ideas may be inspiring for students involved in college organizations who want to make these organizations channels for their beliefs. Compared to a traditional idea of a community, Thurston's vision is quite unorthodox.

Connections

Robert Reich offers the ideal context in which the ideas promoted by Linda Thurston can be discussed. He talks about sweeping changes in our society that have put the very notion of "community" to the test. One of the weaknesses of his analysis is that he sees all changes taking place as a result of technological and urban development. He does not even look for an individual, human factor in what is going on. People with their beliefs and ideas seem to be engulfed by industrial conglomerates and their social by-products, such as the class of symbolic analysts. Thurston would probably argue powerfully against that kind of attitude, and students should be able to compare the two attitudes and the causes behind them.

ROBERT REICH
The Global Elite (p. 290)

Considerations

1. It is important for students to understand that "community" is not a clearly defined concept but rather a cultural construct that changes not only geographically but also historically. Reich presents a version of "community" different from the ones that have emerged in the previous texts. He does seem to have in mind space as the defining factor for community, but there are other factors involved. Social stratification and economic inequality seem to drive together groups within the same range of income. This is why certain areas are wealthy, while others are poor. When people are driven together only because of their income, they are not likely to develop community ties.

2. The word *secession* might remind students of the Civil War, and they could start the exploration of its meaning from there. Reich implies that the symbolic analysts willingly separate from the rest of the population and that there is a war going on between them and the less economically advantaged.

Invitation to Write

In many ways, an analysis of the mall phenomenon may be an argument against Reich. Unlike the elite clubs he describes, the mall is a democratic place, where people come not only to shop but also to relax and eat out. Teenagers in particular feel that a mall is a communal place where they can meet other people and make friends. Yet, to some extent, malls do tend to segregate by income level. Although the spectrum of incomes of people who shop at the mall is wider, the mall will not attract very high income people, and it is also out of reach for people with low and no income at all. Malls are also private places, in the legal sense, and foster no stable relationships, relying entirely on economic associations.

43

Connections

Here is another way to attack Reich's argument about elite groups and the segregation of communities by income. Reich seems to be concerned solely with big cities and their suburbs. He neglects vast areas of the country that are still rural and traditional.

Students should be alerted to the difficulty of constructing an argument about a contemporary social trend. They could also draw out the implications of an essay like that of Staw and Swander which, under the guise of reporting, actually presents the quiet community life of Minnesota's villages as an alternative to the noise and impersonal coldness of modern life.

ASSIGNMENT SEQUENCE
Individuals in Communities (p. 300)

The sequence will help students bring together all the issues related to the notion of community. The task of defining community will lead them to explore the notion historically, noticing the changes through which it evolves. They can also think of the factors that contribute to the development of certain ideas about the community such as economic conditions, technological advances, changes in population patterns. They should be encouraged to inquire into the reasons why definitions of community fluctuate. Another aspect of the community question is that of its relation to the individual and its role in shaping an individual's sense of identity. Here, students should pay particular attention to the dynamic of the relation between private and public interests, and perhaps consider the individual's contribution to the community's dictates.

A nice complement to this sequence would be Buchi Emecheta's novel *The Bride Price* (Braziller, 1976), which portrays two star-crossed lovers who defy the rules of their tribal community. Because of their daring, they are haunted by misfortune, and the tragic ending of the book shows the rules of the community malignantly triumphant. Emecheta's book, which gives almost supernatural dimension to the power of communal prejudice, compares interestingly to O'Brien's story. Equally interesting is Toni Morrison's *Sula* (NAL-Dutton, 1987), which should create a lot of discussion around the idea of assertive individuality as opposed to communal conformity. In Morrison's novel the role of community as interpreter of events and individual actions is also quite evident.

7

Environments of Prejudice

JAMES BALDWIN
Whose Child Are You? (p. 309)

Considerations

1. Baldwin's narrative is quite complex, and reducing its meaning to either its message about racism or to its portrayal of adolescence would be a mistake. He deals with the psychological phenomenon of adolescence from the particular point of view of an underprivileged and persecuted group. Baldwin focuses on his feelings and thoughts, but his descriptions of other adolescents are equally revealing of the dilemmas they all face. The passage on p. 313 where Baldwin talks about a "gimmick" that an African-American youth has to find—"And it does not matter what the gimmick is"—is full of suggestions that can be related to present-day situations.

2. Baldwin's text is rich in implications. The beginning offers some clues to the kind of religious belief Baldwin might be holding at the time he writes. I would also direct the students to look for the way he describes the church and its representatives. There might be a suggestion in the text that the kind of surrogate parental care offered by the church to the young is also offered to the whole African-American population as a substitute for real dignity and a place in society. The seductive lure of the church also needs to be discussed in detail.

Invitation to Write

This assignment will probably be interpreted differently according to the students' backgrounds. Even if they do not belong to an underprivileged group, students will be able to examine their own choices after they have analyzed Baldwin's. The fact that the author is African American serves to emphasize the role of the environment in the choices he makes. Students should also be directed to relate the choices made in adolescence to the growth of their personality. Making choices is part of the process by which our identity is formed.

Connections

The psychological aspect of Baldwin's narrative is perhaps the most interesting to discuss, since his childhood and adolescence are not typical of the mainstream. His case is complicated by the fact that the very culture to which he belongs has developed under oppression and in the shadow of a dominant (white) culture. A good way to approach this topic would be to start from a comparison of the parents rather than of the children described in both texts. While the parents represent authority in Kaplan, in Baldwin the parental role is distorted by the father's own insecurities deriving from his position in society: Baldwin talks about the fear he could hear in his father's voice. Baldwin's rebellion against his father thus acquires a different significance. With practically no parental authority to fight against, Baldwin is looking for some basic dignity for himself as a person as well as for his race. What he cannot accept is his father's submission to whites, and therefore he is rebelling against society's rule more than he is rebelling against his father. Such rebellion might result in a social change with positive consequences.

HARUHIKO YOSHIMEKI
Learning the Language (p. 317)

Considerations

1. The meaning of the word *racism* fluctuates historically. Students may begin with the basic definition they know and progress toward a deeper understanding of the word's significance. Yoshimeki's narrative offers numerous situations that can serve as a basis for discussion. His examples become more interesting as they enlighten students to the fact that there are more than two human races, and that anyone can discriminate or be discriminated against. The relative racial innocence of little Harry is shattered when Carl's brother-in-law tells him that he has to choose between being white and being black. The ultimatum that Harry faces reveals the belief that blacks and whites are completely different, so that relations with both are impossible. This kind of thinking is the product of racism and also perpetuates it.

2. There are at least two issues to discuss here: One is the relation between language and culture. Besides the principal's advice to Harry, one can also look at the case of the Japanese war bride who refuses to learn or remember English, because she never feels at home in the United States. The second issue is that of the complexity of the cultural environment in Louisiana. To reveal its paradoxes one may look at the passage where an army officer comes to school to talk about Vietnam (paras. 14–31), or at the reactions of Carl's family when Harry comes to visit (paras. 88–108).

Invitation to Write

How we learn about racism, or, more precisely, how we learn to become racist, is an interesting topic to debate, because we are rarely aware of when and how our attitudes are formed. Yoshimeki's self-analysis provides a good model for students to explore their own experience with racial attitudes and prejudices. If this is to become a paper, I think it would be a good idea to have a class discussion in preparation for writing where students can all bring their examples and discuss them with their classmates. Harry's experiences (the advice he receives from his father's colleagues or from Carl's brother-in-law) will also have to be examined. One can also examine Harry's own observations made in innocence (and ignorance) of the racial environment in Louisiana.

Connections

Baldwin's experience of adolescence as an African American might enlighten Yoshimeki about the attitudes and behaviors of the students in his class. A rereading of Baldwin will certainly be necessary in order to establish the psychological conditions under which the African-American children develop. Once those have been established, "Learning the Language" should also be reread. One might be able to find in Yoshimeki's own text the explanations for the children's behavior: the park rules, the integration of the school, the constant harassment to which the African Americans are subjected. Baldwin's search for ways to achieve dignity might enlighten Yoshimeki about why the first two black children he meets wear suits at school. The description of the African-American girls coming of age in Harlem, their sudden maturity, could also explain to young Harry the behavior of the girls in his class.

LOUISE ERDRICH
American Horse (p. 330)

Considerations

1. Considering the role played by the tribal police in the life of the reservation will enable students to familiarize themselves with the setting in which Albertine's and Buddy's drama unfolds. They might be able to gather information about the life of American Indians from a library or other sources. The kind of prejudice and racism portrayed in this story is not as well known as the discrimination against African Americans, and it needs some study. The most horrible aspect of it is perhaps the fact that the crushing of the tribal culture is being performed in the name of good intentions, and the members of the tribe are expected to participate in their own destruction. Harmony's actions may also remind students of historical situations and of the notion of "good Indians" who cooperated with the whites in the destruction of the other nations.

2. The visions offer a glimpse into the mind-set of a culture with rich and meaningful imagination. "The giant potato peeler," dreamed by Buddy, appears only once but somehow acquires symbolic value throughout the story. The machine-like efficiency of Vicki Koob, the brutality of the policeman, and the futility of Albertine's resistance could all be reflected in

47

Buddy's dream. The butterfly image is even richer in significance and should be followed closely throughout the story. Albertine's sense of identity and her strength are related to the memory of her father rubbing her with the colors of the dead butterfly "for grace." She literally attacks Harmony with the buckle in the shape of a butterfly. But although the buckle is solid turquoise, she might as well have hit him with the fragile wings of the real butterfly. Her grace cannot save her from the brute force that snatches her child away from her.

Invitation to Write

By exploring the notion of family in this story, the students can understand how different cultural concepts lead to misunderstandings between cultures. They will also see how a dominant culture imposes its ideology. Because mainstream American culture dominates, it can impose its values on the most intimate relationships of an American Indian family. Because Albertine's living arrangements do not meet the standard deemed proper for raising a child, Vicki Koob considers herself entitled to act on the child's behalf. Students will probably volunteer a lot of ideas about what a family is or should be and might even have difficulty understanding Albertine's point of view. An attentive analysis of the loving relation between her and Buddy would, I think, help them in that direction.

Connections

Paula Gunn Allen's analysis of American Indian common sense and wisdom should help students understand the subtlest points of Erdrich's story. In many respects, American Indian cultures offer more choices to the individuals than the mainstream does. However, American Indian women are in a double bind since they have to live up to both tribal and mainstream standards. Such contradictory standards may explain Albertine's attitudes as well as her misfortune. Allen's analysis of the perceptions that lead to stereotypes of American Indians can find a concrete illustration in Vicki's attitude.

JAMAICA KINCAID
A Small Place (p. 342)

Considerations

1. Kincaid, like Yoshimeki, vacillates between a child's perspective—which is ignorant because innocent—and the adult's educated view. The shifts from one attitude to another are interesting to study because they can explain the emotional reactions that accompany the more balanced analytical perspective. One can debate here another question: Are racism, prejudice, and humiliation things we can talk about without emotion? If we can, should we?

2. The characterization of the English as criminals needs a lot of debate here. It is an accusation made in hindsight, and it attributes malignant intentions without leaving any room for an answer from the other side. Of course, this blindness to the other culture's values and motives is what characterized the English when they colonized not only Antigua, but also other countries. Somewhere, between anger and justified frustration, Kincaid shares in both the ignorance and the violence of those whom she accuses, but she is the victim of oppression, and her position is, therefore, different.

Invitation to Write

If they are young, the students may not have a personal experience that resulted for them in a change of perspective. If that is the case, they might look at current revisions of history. The "Columbus" controversy—a related topic to Kincaid's—may give the students enough material to compare with Kincaid's double perspective. Much was written about this controversy in 1992 during the celebration of his landing 500 years before. Students might also consider the way the former colonial powers, like England, regard their previous deeds. In fact, the attitude of professing guilt for the deeds of the past is present in America too.

Connections

Tourism seems such an innocent activity and so far from evil intentions that one might be surprised to find it on the list of Western crimes against the rest of the world. The two texts should open the students' eyes to the fact that no contact between cultures can be innocent of interference or intrusion. A cultural exchange can be positive only when the two cultures respect each other equally. Students might observe that it is the relation of domination between the two cultures involved which brings about the negative effects of tourism.

ASSIGNMENT SEQUENCE
Environments of Prejudice (p. 350)

The assignment sequence will help students go beyond the elementary understanding of prejudice and will enable them to look at its roots. The texts in this chapter are not conventional condemnations of racism, but complex accounts of complex experiences. Seeing oneself from the "other's" point of view is the main objective here, and it might lead students to analyze their own racial attitudes. We are all potential racists and have a good chance to become racist if we do not do anything about it. The readings demonstrate amply that neither innocence nor ignorance protect us against racism and that learning about it is the only way to prevent it. The sequence aims at helping students to define a way to live without hating or hurting the other.

As companion novels one may use Maya Angelou's *I Know Why the Caged Bird Sings* (Bantam, 1983), which would tally well with Baldwin's autobiographical account and will offer the African-American female's point of view on the matter of prejudice. An alternative is Bharati Mukherjee's *The Tiger's Daughter* (Fawcett, 1991) which takes us to contemporary India where a complicated network of prejudices separates the Indians not only from the English but also from Americans and African Americans.

8

Stories That Shape Our Lives

ELLEN GILCHRIST
Music (p. 357)

Considerations

1. It is hard to decide who is responsible for Rhoda's never ending quarrels with her parents. The story does not give a clear point of view: There are times when readers would take the parents' side, others when they would agree with Rhoda. Trying to find out the ways in which Rhoda takes after her father will probably clarify the perspective of the story. The discussion about the dinosaurs is quite revealing. Both Rhoda and her father seem to have strong convictions and defend them ferociously. Following in the steps of Flannery O'Connor, Gilchrist seems to find single-mindedness common to all human beings, irrespective of age and of the differences between their convictions.

2. It will probably not be difficult for students to identify the role models whose glamorous ways Rhoda is trying to emulate. One interesting thing to notice here is that she chooses them from outside her family, even outside her social class. It might even be argued that she goes outside her own culture for role models. The world of movie stars and poets together with the world of teen magazines is so far from her own reality as to seem completely foreign, and her parents probably think of it that way. It is also an idealized world where nothing could possibly be wrong.

Invitation to Write

Students are likely to be attracted to this topic because they all will have had misunderstandings with their parents. A good place to start is perhaps to examine the way Rhoda and her parents communicate, or fail to communicate. The possibility of negotiating opinions or respecting a divergent point of view does not occur to either Rhoda or her parents. Another issue to focus on is the contribution of adolescent rebellion to social change. Rhoda carries some of her convictions into her mature years. Some careful discriminations have to be made here, because Rhoda belongs not only to another generation but also to another class: Having fulfilled her dream to become a writer she has risen above the social status of her parents.

Connections

The comparison between Hongo's meditative narrative and Rhoda's story should bring to the surface aspects that would remain hidden when reading the texts separately. The relationship between Kubota and his grandson is never antagonistic, although the two might have reasons to disagree: Hongo grows up American, while the grandfather continues to uphold the values of the Japanese culture. Rhoda's story, on the other hand, seems so typically a teenager's story that the cultural implications of her behavior might escape even an experienced reader. Rhoda is animated by such a strong desire to identify with upscale culture that she bluntly opposes everything that comes from her family. Hongo, on the other hand, feels much more connected to his family and is ready to accept its heritage, perhaps because the mainstream culture does not completely accept him. One interesting point for the students to explore may be the fact that both Rhoda and Hongo think of writing as their vocation.

AMY TAN
Without Wood (p. 379)

Considerations

1. Students might speculate first about the symbolic value of Mr. Chou in Chinese culture and about a possible correspondence to Mr. Sandman. But Rose has invented a private and more complicated symbolism for the man who is supposed to help children go to sleep: He is a keeper of nightmares rather than the guardian of dreams. Since she seems to see herself as a rebel against maternal authority, Rose feels threatened by the promise of good sleep that her mother offers to her unconditionally. Likewise, when she grows up, she acts against her mother's wisdom and loses the magical strength that respect for motherly advice could have given her. She loses the good Mr. Chou and has a nightmare. Another subject for speculation is the fact that,

when she dreams of Mr. Chou as an adult, Rose's sleep is drug induced and self-destructive.

2. There might be seeds for controversy here. Students will find it difficult to believe that someone could be burdened by too many choices. But having the choices is not enough: One must also assume the responsibility of a decision. In a curious way, by returning to her mother for advice and counsel, Rose acquires that capacity, although her mother comes from a world without many choices. The capacity to make decisions has to do with her sense of identity, and following the logic of the story, one would say that she has become more American by remembering that she was Chinese.

3. A case-by-case discussion might lead to interesting debates about Rose's motives in changing her story. The story is different partly because she wants to make her interlocutor understand it and partly because she wants to appear in a certain light to her family and friends. Another reason may be that she herself changes every time she tells it, and the story reflects her new identity.

Invitation to Write

This assignment can make the students think about stories as much as it will make them think about language. The idea that stories shape our lives has some currency in post-modern criticism. French philosopher François Lyotard, for instance, talks about master narratives—stories in which the models and values of a culture are reflected. Linguist Jerome Bruner conducted research leading to the conclusion that story-telling is the basic mode we use to make sense of our lives. And Hayden White shows how history, which in its own way shapes culture, is conceived almost exclusively in a narrative mode. These authors might offer interesting reading for the teacher who would like to guide his or her students through this particular chapter. Rose, who literally changes her story according to the audience, is an interesting case to examine. Her different stories mirror her indecision about the world she wants to live in.

As far as language is concerned, in Rose's case, it adjusts to interlocutors just as easily as her stories do. It will be interesting for students to think about how certain restrictions posed on language can change the meaning of a story. They can also reflect on how the language in which we tell our story affects our sense of identity.

Connections

This is another occasion to make use of a rich concept. The balance of power between men and women is an implicit rather than explicit topic in Beauvoir. The students will thus have an opportunity to analyze her text from a new angle. Tan's story should also appear enriched by the introduction of Beauvoir's ideas. It would be interesting to debate Rose's case from a feminist point of view in the context of her cultural confusion. The kind of strength Rose acquires from her mother would probably please Beauvoir, but one has to point out that its source is in a culture where women are anything but emancipated.

PAULA GUNN ALLEN
Where I Come from Is Like This (p. 390)

Considerations

1. Although she strongly asserts American Indian culture, Allen recognizes the cultural duality at the basis of her own identity. Students should be invited to examine that duality in both its negative and positive aspects. Although inheriting more than one culture may cause confusion and disorientation, it can also present more choices, and with them more responsibility. Allen is especially interested in choices for women, and this is what she finds in the American Indian stories. She feels that, inspired by them, she can really choose who she wants to be.

2. It is important for students to make connections between different kinds of discrimination and to understand that they have a common root. It is also important to point out the differences, and to understand that every attitude acquires its meaning in its context. Discrimination against American Indians and sexism are generated by the same desire to dominate another. However, sexism functions in the American Indian cultural environment as well as in the mainstream. An American Indian woman is doubly discriminated against in the mainstream.

3. The adaptability of American Indian tradition is indeed emphasized by Allen. This may, however, reflect the author's political position. There is no question that any culture can change; as a matter of fact, all cultures change under the influence of various factors whether internal or external. For a conquered culture, however, change may represent a surrender to the dominant culture. The particular situation of American Indians in this respect has to be seen from a more general point of view. While the perpetuation of the old traditions is essential to preserve a sense of identity, the social and economic conditions demand adjustment to life in the mainstream. Like Leslie Marmon Silko in *Ceremony* (Viking Penguin, 1986), Allen seems to opt for an adaptation of the traditions themselves to the new conditions. A look at Allen's examples of adaptation may clarify her position on this matter.

Invitation to Write

In considering other cultures students should also reflect upon mainstream American culture. Many of its aspects are obscure to most of us who live within it. Comparisons with other cultures may be quite revealing. As far as the transmission of cultural values is concerned, students will have a number of sources to draw upon. They can think of education, parental advice, religion, the media, and the arts as modes of perpetuating culture. Although the means by which our society preserves and transmits its values are far more complex than telling stories, narratives offer a clear example of the way a tradition is handed down. Students could explore analogies between story-telling and other means of transmitting culture with interesting results.

Connections

The topic of this essay is interesting even as an abstract question: What is better and more useful, to learn from others or to learn from one's own experience? I feel certain that most students will answer that both modes are useful, even necessary. They will have to notice, however, that certain cultures emphasize one mode over another. In more traditional cultures, such as the American Indian one exemplified by Allen, even personal experience may be conceived of as an initiation, a test designed by the elders to teach the beginner a lesson. The individual experience is subordinated to cultural control. Rhoda, on the other hand, wants to have absolute control over her experiences. It would be interesting to find out whether her experiences are indeed genuinely individual and original. Also one can debate whether her desire to cut her own path does indeed bring her fulfillment.

GARRETT HONGO
Kubota (p. 398)

Considerations

1. The attitude of his fellow Japanese Americans and the behavior of his grandfather represent for Hongo the two options of the immigrant: to adjust to the mainstream and to ignore one's past, or to define one's identity in the complex context of one's history. The dismissal of the past is complicated in the case of Japanese Americans by the racial factor, which makes Kubota's way the logical choice. No matter how well adjusted and successful they are, Japanese Americans will be identified by the mainstream as Japanese. It can be argued that Hongo himself follows in his grandfather's footsteps by choosing to write, that is, to tell the story, and thus to preserve history.

2. Students are likely to identify here a rite of passage, especially if they have read Kaplan or some similar material. They should also be encouraged to analyze Hongo's own narrative as an offshoot of Kubota's education of

young Hongo. They should notice that Hongo listens to his grandfather with a certain reluctance, just to humor him, and it is not until later that he understands the significance of the story-telling and treasures it.

Invitation to Write

Students may not be aware that story-telling plays an important role in their lives. Hongo's narrative may motivate them to discover such stories in their own experience. They should be encouraged to extend the meaning of the word *story* in order to include the many ways in which their identity is shaped by various narratives. They may, for instance, think of the turbulent sixties, which may have been described by their parents or the media. The way Woodstock is remembered, for instance, is the stuff of legend. They could also think of the memory of the Vietnam war as it emerges from books, movies, and television shows, or about such famous people as Elvis Presley or Marilyn Monroe, whose lives are an inexhaustible source of stories. Thinking about contemporary events important enough to remember twenty years from now should also be fun: How are we going to tell the story? What have we learned from it?

Connections

The two texts combined in this assignment converge in their outlook on history and especially in their revelation of alternative history, history as seen from an unofficial point of view. Comparison is easy, and that is why students should be urged to look beyond it, at the effect of story-telling. Most of the time, one's identity is connected to a story: We conceive of ourselves as characters in a narrative. We feel happy if we can see ourselves as positive characters and may become neurotic if we cannot. Much psychotherapy is dedicated to helping patients construct stories in which they appear as positive characters. But having to live in two stories at once is a complication of another kind. At times, what makes one a positive character in one story may make him or her negative in the other, especially if the stories belong to groups in a relation of domination. Both Allen and Hongo are in search of the ideal situation where one is a positive character in both stories.

ASSIGNMENT SEQUENCE
Stories That Shape Our Lives (p. 409)

This sequence brings the students closer to personal experience than any other in the book. It may be successfully used in a creative writing class focused on autobiographical writing. Besides focusing on interpreting personal experience and discovering its significance for others, the texts highlight the interaction between the individual and his or her culture, between parents and children, and between minority groups and mainstream. To regard all these issues in terms of stories is a new and different angle for the students who may have already discussed them in other contexts. The focus of the students' papers may vary. They might place more emphasis on narrative and its possibilities of creating a sense of identity, or they may think of stories as ways of transmitting cultural values and stress the latter. In any case, the material offered by the texts in this chapter is rich in implications.

Among the novels that could usefully accompany this sequence, Maxine Hong Kingston's *The Woman Warrior* (Random House, 1989) presents itself as an obvious choice. Its kinship with the writings of Amy Tan may create an interest in the plight of Chinese immigrant women and the stories that shape their lives. On the other hand, Toni Morrison's *Song of Solomon* (NAL-Dutton, 1989) might add an African American to the series of characters whose identities originate in stories. The novel's hero, Macon (Milkman) Dead is the perfect example of a man who literally discovers his identity in a story. The fact that this story is at once a legend and a repressed history relates well to Hongo's and Allen's points of view.

9

Lives in Transition

BHARATI MUKHERJEE
Fighting for the Rebound (p. 415)

Considerations

1. Griff's references to sports make him typical of an entire category of American men that the students will have no difficulty in identifying. They should, however, be asked to look at the implications of his allusions. There is a very poignant scene where Griff asks Blanquita whether she had tried cheerleading. When Blanquita attempts a move and proves quite clumsy at it, Griff thinks she has "turned a schoolgirl routine into something alien and absurd" (p. 420). One may wonder what is more absurd: Blanquita's attempt at the routine, or Griff's request that she do it. Griff's tastes are defined by this incongruity: He likes things to be all-American, but being all-American includes an enormous appetite for the exotic and the non-American.

2. Griff's indecision may have to do with his general immaturity: In many ways he is a typical bachelor never ready for commitment. He may also be undecided because he does not understand much about Blanquita. He is attracted to her and admires her beauty, but his fear of her mysterious past is reflected in the way he tries to trivialize it. As for Blanquita, it is hard to know how she feels about her relationship with Griff. One may examine closely what she says and interpret her gestures as described by Griff. Judging by those, she seems a helpless romantic trying to appear emancipated and detached.

Invitation to Write

The notion of exoticism should interest students. The main thing they have to understand here is that "exotic" is one way of viewing the foreign. And while perceiving the foreign as exotic may look like the positive alternative, it can be as damaging to intercultural relationships as bigotry. One good way to start would be with the question of foreign travel: Why do people go to visit other countries? What are they looking for? Another basic observation is that the same people who seem entranced with foreign countries may be repelled by the foreigners who live in this country. Probing into such questions will lead the students to understand what is implied in the relationship between Griff and Blanquita: Like the distant landscapes in the travel agency brochures, Blanquita appears colorful, glossy, and one-dimensional.

Connections

This is not going to be an easy assignment. It is easier to look at the relations between cultures when we consider them collectively and not personally. However, Pico Iyer's examples should make comparisons easier. His generalizations may also help the students to see the complexities of the relationship between Griff and Blanquita. There is more than romance between them, for each of them is quite aware that they belong in two different camps. Although they are both cultural hybrids in many ways—Griff due to his openness to the exotic, Blanquita because she is an immigrant—they remain separated by a feeling of maladjustment.

JILL KER CONWAY
The Right Country (p. 428)

Considerations

1. Conway is one of those people who do not feel at home in their own culture. Of course, her history studies and the American boyfriend help her see things in a different way, but there is more to her transformation than a

superficial contact with America. Students should be encouraged to examine closely the way she interprets her life and her decisions. In many ways, she is prepared to become an American by her unease with her own culture and by her desire to take care of her individual needs in spite of conventions and norms that bind her to her family or to her class.

2. It is always interesting for students to discover patterns of imagery or meaningful repetitions in a text. In this particular one, the vocabulary reflects the author's state of mind better than she explicitly describes it. "To change" and "to break" appear frequently, expressing her desire to make her life anew. Likewise, "ambiguity" and "puzzle" mark her confusion and her difficulty in implementing the changes.

Invitation to Write

This assignment might fit in nicely with the sequence on stories and history because it will again raise the question of how history is written. What is important to tell about the past is an interesting question in many ways. In connection to Conway's autobiographical account, it is particularly significant because it relates to questions about cultures. Clearly, American culture with its emphasis on individualism and its democratic inclinations will favor a history focused on marginal figures. It also favors the outlook on life that Conway had arrived at. Even though she knows Australian history better, her American-influenced approach does not fit with the more conservative and hierarchical view of life dominant in Australia. Students will probably have a lot to say about the way they learned history and the way it should be taught. They may also find that what Conway sees as the American approach may exist only at a scholarly level and may not be the practice in schools.

Connections

The similarities between Conway's and Torgovnick's situations should be clear to the students from the start, but they should be encouraged to go beyond a simple comparison. They should attempt to define the cultural factors that are involved in the conflicts between mothers and daughters. One may also notice that, due to their education, both women break away not only from their family's environment but also from their class. This assignment might lead the students to give some thought to the question of the individual's relation to his or her culture. One may ask, in such a context, to what extent the breaking away from the family changes the individual's identity. Another question might focus on whether such individual initiatives ultimately can change the culture itself.

ITABARI NJERI
Bag Lady (p. 446)

Considerations

1. Since the family history is given in the story, students will quickly make the connection between the times of poverty and the habit of carrying bags. They might also want to think about the sentimental attachments people can form to things or routines related to certain periods in their lives. Usually, one forms such attachments when one gets older, and the younger generation simply does not understand them. Students can analyze the text to find out what significance the bag carrying has for the mother and how the daughter interprets the gesture. Students may decide that, like the bag ladies who carry all their belongings with them, Njeri carries a lot of "psychological baggage," including a sense of being responsible for her family's decisions.

2. Njeri's relation with her parents is complicated by hindsight. There are obviously two ways in which she sees and judges her parents: through the anger of her childhood, due to their inability to attend to her needs, and through a more compassionate and sympathetic view as an adult, when she begins to understand their problems. In examining Njeri's feelings, students should also be directed to pay some attention to gender roles and to the expectations related to such roles.

Invitation to Write

The topic of drug addiction should engage students since there is so much talk about it in the media. As in the case of any controversial subject, they should be directed to understand and interpret the text rather than resort to official opinions. The complexity of the family relations in Njeri's story should inspire the students to explore the deeper cause of drug addiction, what drugs stand for, and the symbolic dimension of resorting to drugs. Students may also think about the social environments where the use of drugs is more frequent.

Connections

Ortiz Cofer's and Njeri's narratives are quite similar, and it will not be difficult for students to notice the resemblances between their situations. Yet, they will probably have to work out the similarity between the two families, which is not immediately evident. Ortiz Cofer's immigrant family is clearly culturally different, and this is the main source of her embarrassment as an adolescent. In Njeri's case, the cultural difference is more subtle, but through analysis it should become apparent that her African-American parents are not quite in the mainstream and that their problems with each other cannot give Njeri the feeling that her life is "normal." Although Njeri and Ortiz Cofer seem both to have been embarrassed by their families as children, one should also notice that they are both nostalgic for their childhood and both show more sympathy toward their parents in adulthood. They may share the realization that, in spite of their disadvantages, their parents essentially contributed to their sense of identity.

ASSIGNMENT SEQUENCE
Lives in Transition (p. 458)

The sequence will bring out additional aspects of the texts included in the chapter. Besides being able to study the environments between which people move when their lives are in transition, students will have the opportunity to give some thought to the role played by memory in interpreting the past and shaping the future. Conway's and Njeri's accounts are both recollections and interpretations of certain periods in their lives. Students should be directed to analyze the work of interpretation. They also need to focus on how people react to change and on the personal growth involved in it. Transitions of the kind described in the texts are not necessarily part of everyone's experience, but they should not be regarded as exceptional. Students might also wonder what determines such transitions, whether they are decided upon by the person (Conway, for instance, wants and plans the change) or forced upon people (Blanquita's case).

As a companion novel for this sequence I would recommend Leslie Marmon Silko's *Ceremony* (Viking Penguin, 1986) whose hero, a mixed breed American Indian, undergoes a profound spiritual transformation in which he learns how to reconcile the past and the present, as well as to live at peace with his double heritage. Bharati Mukherjee's *Jasmine* (Fawcett, 1990) may also be a good choice, since her heroine goes through several transitions in search of her identity.

10

Language and Perception

RICHARD RODRIGUEZ
Complexion (p. 465)

Considerations

1. Richard Rodriguez's dilemma regarding his relation with the Mexican workers is one faced by many members of a minority who have achieved middle-class status. It is essentially a situation where a person's identity is in crisis, since class no longer coincides with race or ethnicity. The discrimination against him by the "Anglos" would demand that he identify with the "braceros," but his education and his command of English put him miles ahead of them. This advantage is probably perceived by his mother when she advises him to stay away from the sun.

2. This question will oblige students to probe deep into Rodriguez's text to discover all the intricacies of his motives. He obviously defines work as physical labor, and according to his mother, he should be glad that he will never know what it is. On the other hand, his culture identifies that kind of work with masculinity. His father's assessment actually means "You will never be a man." The anxiety that he cannot live up to this standard of masculinity explains Richard's reaction to his father's words, and it is the reason he chooses these particular events to recount. He speaks not only about his lack of aptitude for physical work but also about his ability (and desire) to speak well—a quality relegated to women.

Invitation to Write

This assignment could be easily included in the sequence about work where Rodriguez's interpretation of his work experience could be a welcome addition. The students may respond enthusiastically to the opportunity to share their summer job experiences. One has to watch here for the danger of transforming the assignment into a trivial narrative. Work experiences can be quite meaningful, and an attentive reading of Rodriguez should enable the students to analyze their own work experiences by highlighting issues of class, gender, education, and race. They might also give special attention to the relation between parents and children when their lines of work differ.

Connections

In this assignment students will have the opportunity to evaluate Reich's terminology. A good place to start is by analyzing his term and applying it to a traditional profession like writing or teaching literature. This might prompt some students to probe into the relation between the utility of the work and the pay. A close scrutiny can show that some of the work most useful to society does not necessarily receive the highest pay. The students might also want to determine whether Rodriguez is indeed antielitist or whether he simply feels guilty for having advantages his family did not have. It is important that students feel free to argue either way, for the assignment is not meant to restrict their thinking.

JANE STAW AND MARY SWANDER
If You Can Talk to a Guy (p. 483)

Considerations

1. The local sense of time in this story is part of a world view, which in turn is determined by the geographical conditions. Rural communities are closer to the rhythms of nature than industrial areas. Obviously, the people in Winnebago feel time according to the season, that is, in cycles.

2. Staw and Swander are very keen on stories, and the way the locals nest one story in another probably influenced the style of their own narrative. You may wish to discuss different characteristics of the oral tradition—for example, the use of repetitions and interruptions. Students could also be encouraged to analyze how they tell their own stories.

3. The authors' admiration for rural communities seems to be rather uncritical. The slow rhythm of life and the homogeneity of the population, the unquestioning attitude with which women obey men and children obey parents, and the unbounded confidence that one can solve all problems by talking are all fostered by the special situation of an agrarian society.

Invitation to Write

The previous "Considerations" question may help students with this assignment. Staw and Swander aren't very critical of what is going on in the midwestern communities they visit. However, from their stories one can perceive the limited horizon that determines the local views and attitudes. If integrated with the sequence on community, this assignment might lead to interesting comparisons between the notions of community that prevail in various geographical regions and different economic conditions. Of course, the community in Winnebago appears ideal, but only for that place and for that time. Any intrusion into it would probably upset the balance of calm and goodwill.

Connections

The students may start by considering the similarities between the communities described in the two texts and then go on to point out the differences. The concept of point of view needs to be introduced in order to make finer distinctions. Linda Thurston's feminism is perhaps the best way to stir controversy in the class about the rural communities of the Midwest. An interesting exercise would be to imagine Thurston speaking about the communities described by Staw and Swander. She would probably be quick to notice that the division of labor between men and women is very clear-cut, that women are quite submissive to men and do not even talk unless they are addressed. Likewise, students could imagine Linda's community as described by Staw and Swander. Would they approve of her café? And what would they think of her?

DEBORAH TANNEN
Damned If You Do (p. 495)

Considerations

1. Tannen's analysis of the differences between the way men and women talk (and behave) should give the students enough clues about what is going on in the first anecdote she tells. A deeper analysis might also uncover the fact that the way Roberta conducts the business of making decisions is quite similar to the way many American mothers negotiate with their children. These mothers do not say no to the child; instead, they steer him or her toward the decision they think is the right one. This would be quite in tune with Tannen, since she argues that the way women speak and behave is determined by their education to be mothers and caretakers.

2. Tannen's syntactic habits may spring from the same source as Beauvoir's. It is clear that the agent here is society; yet, society includes not only men but also women. It should be pointed out that women do sometimes agree with the society's view of them and participate in passing judgment on other women. This does not happen because women are by nature critical of each other but because they think in the way culture has taught them to think. A return to Beauvoir's argument might be useful here.

Invitation to Write

To work on this assignment, students will have to deal with the implications of Tannen's argument, and this might require a thorough rereading of the text. Students might debate whether Tannen's argument is feminist or not, and readers might disagree about the kind of feminism it promotes. The notion that women speak differently from men may actually encourage antifeminist views. A historical perspective on Tannen's material will help the students clarify some of the most obscure points in this essay. They might decide in the end that the linguistic differences derive from natural differences or that language is one other area in which women are trained to become second-class citizens in this society.

Connections

This assignment encourages students to discover the power relations reflected in the language in Tan's story. Tannen will be helpful for this task, but her argument need not be accepted uncritically. Because Tannen focuses on gender, she is not always explicit about the fact that she is describing power relations. There are excellent examples of such power play in the language of Tan's story, but one should not forget that Ted's power derives not only from the fact that he is a man but also that he is a white American. Rose's mother may also be an interesting example to discuss from the point of view of language, since she manages to wield some power of her own in spite of a linguistic handicap.

ANNIE DILLARD
The Writing Life (p. 517)

Considerations

1. Dillard seems to reject the idea that writing can be outlined and pre-planned. In this respect, she seems to subscribe to the theory that language acquires its meaning in use as opposed to the view that words have intrinsic meaning. While opposing various misconceptions about writing, Dillard forges a myth of her own. Her way of letting language carry her wherever it must go generates in language a kind of metaphysical power. Students might want to debate this question in the context of their own writing: Dillard may inspire them to use writing for the purpose of discovery as long as they are vigilant and not careless in following language's lead.

2. Dillard's analogies complicate rather than simplify the concept of writing. It will be interesting for students to study several such metaphors and analyze the analogies for their deeper implications. The question at that point will be whether the analogies are indeed doing the job of defining writing. The fact that she uses more than one analogy may indicate that she does not find any of them satisfactory. Students should also notice that the terms of the analogies are related to various crafts, suggesting that writing is itself a craft.

3. The fact that writing can reveal hidden things supports the idea that writing cannot be planned too carefully in advance; it becomes meaningful only as it happens. Students could speculate on the nature of the invisible reality that writing makes visible.

Invitation to Write

This assignment could also fit in the sequence about work. It relates work to creativity and to the individual's fulfillment. Work of the kind Dillard describes would indeed be most satisfying, but one must ask whether we all have the chance to develop and valorize our creativity. But if work of the creative kind is satisfactory, an analysis of Dillard's description of the writing process can show us that it is not easy. In creating something, one assumes responsibility for the thing created. Students should debate here questions about the utility of work, whether work should be directed to practical purposes or simply performed for personal satisfaction. There are plenty of opportunities here for students to draw upon their own experience with work in general and writing in particular.

Connections

Scott Myers is another advocate of personal satisfaction in work. Although his work is quite different from Dillard's, he would probably agree with the implications of her description of writing. It would be an interesting exercise for students to imagine creative writing as an organized production that is judged by its output. They might also take the contrary point of view and argue that personal satisfaction in work is a luxury most of us cannot afford. Can society as a whole afford it?

ASSIGNMENT SEQUENCE
Language and Perception (p. 528)

Although frequently raised by philosophers, questions about language are not often raised in public debates. This is why the topic is likely to stir interest in students and stimulate them to write interesting papers. The initial questions about language may be raised in a class debate. Then students can discover many of the complexities involved in the act of speech as they appear in the texts. It would be interesting for students to do experiments of their own in order to verify the hypotheses of Deborah Tannen, for instance, or to try to experiment with writing in the way Dillard does. Oral story-telling could be another line of experimentation. They could also raise questions about accents and what they represent in American culture.

As a companion text for the sequence, Richard Rodriguez's *Hunger of Memory* (Bantam, 1983) seems an obvious choice. The language question, which appears by implication in "Complexion," is the central question of his book. Another interesting autobiographical account with a focus on language is Eva Hoffman's *Lost in Translation* (Viking Penguin, 1990), which also reveals the complicated relations between language, culture, and individuality.

11

Cultures in Contact

PICO IYER

Love Match (p. 535)

Considerations

1. Maung-Maung's view of the West gives us a glimpse into how non-Western societies might perceive the world. Whereas from America and western Europe one can regard the world as an extension of one's own culture, with interesting differences, from the non-Western point of view, the world might look like a pyramid with the West at the top. As a non-Westerner, Maung-Maung is aware of his culture and cherishes his values, but he cannot ignore Western values. Maung-Maung's collection of souvenirs from his Western customers is a shrine dedicated to the West. In Iyer's essay, one can observe quite closely the way Western culture extends its domination over the rest of the world.

2. It will be interesting for students to figure out Iyer's point of view. Although in the essay he appears as the spokesperson of the West and of America, his Indian descent may explain his rather critical attitude. In his criticism of the culture he represents, there is a certain detachment—intellectual Westerners are usually more guilt-ridden than critical, as Harrison's essay can prove. Iyer does not completely identify with Western values; yet, in his role as a tourist, he represents the West to the locals. He is viewed as a precious source of information about what is perceived to be the center of the world.

Invitation to Write

A discussion of the extended meaning of "reading" could precede the writing of this paper or be included in it. Students should become aware that one can regard anything—from a play or movie to a person or a culture—as a text. Once this notion of reading has been established they could practice with several examples before they study Iyer's essay. As far as the images foreigners have of America are concerned, it is always interesting to compare them with what we think about ourselves. Sometimes our image in the other's eyes may be unflattering, but it might also promote deeper self-reflection. There is also the question of how deep one can go in understanding or portraying another. In reading Iyer's account, one gets the feeling that both sides are superficial and quick in their judgment of each other. There are certain passages in which some tourists deliberately create a distorted image of their country. Those would be interesting to analyze: One could get the feeling that the whole relation between cultures is a sort of game of mutual deception.

Connections

Iyer understands that the process of westernization is not unilateral and that certain tendencies in non-Western countries lead to the adoption of the Western model. There is, in the cultures he describes, an aspiration for a better place, no doubt generated by poverty and disappointment. Perhaps in other times that place would have been heaven, but these days it is the West. With this assignment students will have the opportunity to read Iyer's examples more closely and to understand their significance. Kibera's story makes an excellent comparison for Iyer's essay, since it shows how the very image of the natives' world is altered. The transformations of the environment and of the society are also reflected in psychological distortions, as in the case of Kibera's character Ngotho. Kibera also makes clear that societies of the kind portrayed in his story needed a change; however, the change resulting from the contact with the West is traumatic and alienating.

PAUL HARRISON
The Westernization of the World (p. 553)

Considerations

1. It should be clear to students that expansionism and imperialism are the main factors in the westernization of the world. They could go further in their commentaries if they think about the Westerners' confidence that the values of their culture are universal. Religion might have something to do with this, since in earlier times especially, Christians preached the uniqueness of their God. Such beliefs account, in part, for the imposition of Western values on other cultures.

2. Non-Western cultures mimic Western styles, fashions, industrial technology, architecture, approaches to education, and other aspects of life in the West in order to participate in the economic and cultural success of the West. Harrison makes the point that when European colonial powers came to the Third World, local collaborators were indoctrinated by missionary and government schools. These collaborators helped carry on the work of cultural imperialism. The Western emphasis on individualism might also have something to do with the West's success in dominating the world. This emphasis appeals to those who find themselves in conflict with the norms of their own culture. Harrison talks a lot about clothes, and an interesting discussion might ensue about whether clothes are related to the idea of individuality and freedom. Many of the traditional costumes are uniform, whereas Western

fashion stresses variety. Of course, one could also argue that jeans are uniform, but the shirts are always different. Additionally, jeans are appreciated by everyone because of their comfortable fit, which comes to stand for freedom.

3. Harrison has several comic moments in his essay: The description of the new elites in former colonial countries, of their exploits and monuments, is comic in an absurd way. Also the incongruity between the Western tourists and the African landscapes can give rise to comic effects. Since the comedy of his descriptions is not intended as such—Harrison discovers the humor of the situations, rather than producing it—the students might want to debate the meaning of "comic" and distinguish between various sorts of comedic effects.

Invitation to Write

This assignment directs students to another aspect of the contact between cultures and lets them explore the phenomenon of cultural change regardless of its negative effects. To perceive this phenomenon as purely negative simplifies it and reduces its magnitude. It is important also to understand that exchanges between cultures can have positive results. The United States can offer much to other cultures and it has received much from other cultures. Students can do research to find examples of positive cultural exchange in addition to looking more closely at Harrison's examples. If they are willing to go further, students might want to look into the tendency, present in Harrison's text and in others, to abhor mixtures of any kind and to label any transformation as destruction. What would the world be like if all cultures were homogeneous and pure?

Connections

A comparison between Harrison and Iyer is interesting to make because the similarity between their essays can be misleading. Only a deeper understanding of their arguments can reveal the points on which they differ. Iyer's is a more recent and more complex experience with tourism: While Harrison sees only the bad attitude of Western tourists, Iyer is quick to observe the profit of local opportunists who have transformed tourism into an industry. The illusion that the unspoiled regions of other continents still preserve the innocence that Europe had lost long ago is shattered by Iyer's revelations of corruption and moral disintegration among the locals.

MARIO VARGAS LLOSA
Questions of Conquest (p. 565)

Considerations

1. Vargas Llosa's first question is one often debated by historians, and his answer to it is in keeping with arguments coming from other intellectuals, like Tzvetan Todorov and Octavio Paz. They all attribute the success of western European civilization in conquering others to its emphasis on individualism. Such emphasis was not some intrinsic characteristic of Western culture but rather the product of the changes that took place during the age of discovery itself. Vargas Llosa's second question is more interesting as it does not receive a direct answer in his essay. Octavio Paz argues that modern South American societies inherit some of the hierarchical structure of the pre-Columbian civilizations. But the more interesting question to debate here is why Vargas Llosa himself tries to find the answer in history while proclaiming that it is not there.

2. Vargas Llosa remains ambiguous about the uses of history, and there may be contradictions in his essay that students will be able to discover. The debate around this question could be expanded to general concepts about history or the relation between history and present-day politics.

Invitation to Write

The Columbus controversy will probably interest students. But this is an assignment that could give rise to clichéd responses of one kind or another, and a preliminary discussion may be necessary. Students should be steered away from the desire to solve the controversy and toward a more academic debate about the way historical perspectives change. Columbus may be seen as a hero or a villain not only according to the interests of a certain group but also according to the needs of a certain age. He becomes the symbol of whatever an age values most: When America is in need of a symbol for its identity, Columbus may be the ideal one; when space travel becomes possible, Columbus becomes a symbol of exploration; when American Indian groups demand their rights, Columbus becomes the symbol of ruthless, illegitimate conquest. How much Columbus had to do with his symbolic status is less interesting than the phenomenon of his becoming a symbol.

As you might expect, Vargas Llosa's controversial article drew heated response. To extend this assignment, you could ask students to find the letters written in response to Vargas Llosa that were published in subsequent issues of *Harper's* magazine. (Many were included in the April 1991 issue.)

Connections

The confrontation of two such different positions should produce interesting arguments in student papers. What is important to understand here is that there are political stakes involved. The interpretation of history is in neither case free from political engagement. Vargas Llosa is oriented toward a solution that would give everyone equal rights and thus erase the sins of the past. According to him, we need to detach ourselves from ancient disputes and build the future together. It is a nice and noble ideal, but can history indeed be forgotten? Jamaica Kincaid thinks that the wounds left by history can never heal and, implicitly, she demands reparation. But what form would that reparation take? Neither position can be taken to a logical conclusion, and it is quite evident that emotions are involved in both. Kincaid's emotional involvement is obvious in her style, but the more academic standpoint of Vargas Llosa does not exempt him from a similar involvement.

ASSIGNMENT SEQUENCE
Cultures in Contact (p. 578)

This topic should become interesting to students once they are directed to discover the theoretical options they have for treating it. They can look at the phenomenon of contact between cultures from a historical or political point of view. The process by which cultures arrive at images of other cultures can be studied starting from a simple exercise in which the students observe and describe each other's behavior. Questions like what determines our self-image and why others see us differently should form a basis for a more sophisticated analysis pertaining to the benefits and the losses resulting from contacts between cultures. While the essays seem to emphasize the idea of invasion or conquest, the students could also think of the more positive aspects of encountering other cultures. Another question to consider is why, when cultures meet, they seem to establish a negative rather than a positive relationship. Or is it that we only see it that way?

As a companion novel for this sequence, Chinua Achebe's *No Longer at Ease* (Fawcett, 1985), which deals with the consequences of westernization in Nigeria, would be an excellent choice, since it illustrates the theme quite well, and adds an African culture to those already represented in the essays. Another interesting choice would be Vargas Llosa's own novel *The Storyteller* (Viking Penguin, 1990), which illustrates the assimilation of a modern Westerner by an indigenous tribe in the Amazon jungle. Metaphorically, this novel asks us to speculate about what would have happened if the indigenous cultures of South America had put their stamp on the Europeans instead of being assimilated by them.

Customizing Sequences

What follows is a customized sequence, which I have used in my class while experimenting with texts from *Making Cultural Connections*. The texts are from chapter 3, "Defining Women's Lives"; chapter 4, "Defining Men's Lives"; and chapter 8, "Stories That Shape Our Lives." In addition to Leonard Kibera's "The Spider's Web," David Gilmore's "Performative Excellence: Circum-Mediterranean," and Simone de Beauvoir's "Introduction to *The Second Sex*," we read the novel *The Joys of Motherhood* by Buchi Emecheta. For exams, I used Philip Roth's "His Roth" and Paula Gunn Allen's "Where I Come from Is Like This." The assignments for writing have been modified to include the novel.

The class worked on computers, a practice especially suited to assignment sequences. As I mentioned before, sequencing demands revisions, and revisions are best done on screen rather than on hard copy. New and sophisticated writing programs offer the writer a large number of options for editing, cutting and pasting, and restructuring sentences. Such possibilities, literally at one's fingertips, encourage students to review and improve their work. They may also become more adventurous writers knowing that what they compose can easily be erased without a trace.

The first assignment in the sequence below is a modification of the "Invitation to Write" that follows "The Spider's Web," by Leonard Kibera. Rather than linking it to personal experience I directed the students to produce a sophisticated analysis of the story. This analysis led to increased interest in the roles of men and women in society. The second assignment asks for a comparative treatment of gender roles in the African societies portrayed by Kibera and Emecheta. The authors' points of view also represent the two genders, and there is room for interpretation of their treatment of that issue.

For a third paper I assign Philip Roth's "His Roth," directing students to analyze the concept of masculinity implicit in Roth's nostalgic piece. This assignment is used for an in-class midterm exam which takes place in two sessions. In the first, students draft their papers, and in the second they revise them on the computer.

The fourth assignment asks students to use Gilmore's conceptual frame in order to analyze the roles of men in the societies presented in the fiction they have read up to that point. The fifth assignment, a modified version of one of the "Considerations" questions following Beauvoir's "Introduction to *The Second Sex*," essentially asks them to do the same with her essay. I should mention here that we read the novel several chapters at a time, not all at once. Some novels may be difficult to divide this way, but I think it is useful for students to learn to read in depth and to stop and analyze certain passages before they write. If the novel is read all at once, students find it a chore to return to the book and select material for their papers.

The sixth assignment asks the students to bring together all their previous arguments in a complex comparative analysis of gender roles in different cultures. This is their final project and it resulted in longer papers. As far as the length of the papers is concerned, I like to increase the required number of pages with every new assignment. We start at three pages and end at seven.

The last assignment is actually another in-class writing sample serving as final exam. Students are assigned the text to read in advance and given the text of the assignment in the first session when they draft their papers. In the second session allotted to the exam, they revise their work. Given the time limits, this is a shorter paper, testing the student's capacity to deal with a new reading and writing assignment independently.

Sample Student Papers

To illustrate the results one can get when working with a sequence, I include in this section the papers of one of my students whose response to the assignments was close to ideal. While not typical for all students in a writing class, his papers illustrate the possibilities open to students by the type of assignments included in *Making Cultural Connections*.

Tae Woo Lee is an intelligent and vivacious person, and he became quite involved with the materials we were reading. This involvement may partly be due to his handicap, which he identifies as his difference from others: Tae Woo is blind and relies on the help of a talking computer in order to write his papers. His strong motivation in the writing class may also have to do with the fact that English is his second language. I asked for a revision of each paper in this class, and the papers presented here are revised versions. I would like to stress again the fact that these papers are the result of sustained work from an exceptionally motivated student.

What Tae Woo's papers best illustrate is the development of a student's ability to think critically. In the first paper, he seems simply to follow instructions and is rather puzzled by the twist the assignment has put on the story. He cannot easily combine the issue of gender with the issue of power relations between master and servant when the woman and not the man is dominant. He gets a better grip on this issue in the second paper, and by the fourth he is able to refine it and use it in a different context. Another hesitation occurs in his fourth paper, in which he grapples with theoretical material for the first time. By the fifth assignment, he is able to handle theoretical concepts with ease.

Of course, even at the end of the semester, Tae Woo stumbles from time to time, not always finding the right word, struggling with syntax, and occasionally extending a paragraph out of bounds. But these are difficulties all writers encounter and, in time, overcome. As far as content is concerned, Tae Woo seems to have become entangled in the riddle of local versus universal gender definitions, a problem he never manages to solve. But who does? In grading the papers, I was not looking for perfection, but for the effort that went into them and for his progress as a writer. I think his endeavor was successful because he has learned to think on his own, to handle difficult concepts, to draw his conclusions from the evidence examined. He is now equipped to read and write in any of the difficult subjects he will study in college.

In addition to marginal comments on specific points of style and content (a few of which are reproduced below), I usually write a final comment in the form of a letter to the student in which I try to analyze his or her work and to figure out the reasons why he or she has or has not succeeded in producing a good paper. I have included my comments to Tae Woo after each paper.

ASSIGNMENT SEQUENCE
Defining Men's and Women's Lives

Assignment 1

Kibera's story "The Spider's Web" depicts Ngotho's confusion and feelings of helplessness. Because it is told from his point of view, we tend to sympathize with him and to see him as a victim of the lingering colonial spirit embodied by Lois, the "Queen." However, his hate and frustration are determined not only by his position as a servant but also by the fact that his exploiter is a woman. Write an essay in which you explore the complexity of the relationship between Ngotho and Lois. Determine how much of Ngotho's frustration derives from the fact that he is socially inferior and how much of it is due to his bruised masculine pride.

Reread the story and look closely at all the passages where Ngotho complains about Lois and her husband. From those you can determine the nature of his complaints. Examine also the nature of his nostalgia for older times. Finally, try to imagine Lois from the inside: What would the story look like if told from her point of view?

```
Tae Woo Lee
Basic Composition 350:100
Professor Anca Rosu
Assignment 1
```

Servants are often frustrated by their position in the master-slave hierarchy. They are usually bothered by the fact that they are culturally inferior and mistreated by the people they work for. In "The Spider's Web," Ngotho is frustrated not only because he is a servant, but also because his "master" is a woman. The social conditions of his culture make him feel hurt to be ruled and mistreated by a woman of his own race. Throughout the story we see examples of how he is angered by the relationship that he has with Lois and her husband.

Ngotho has many reasons to be frustrated. He understands the position he holds in his life considering his social status: "He knew that there would always be masters and servants" (p. 185). He is even more concerned with the fact that Lois is a woman who had once belonged to his social class. In fact, Lois used to be friends with his daughter. Now she is similar to every white person whom Ngotho was accustomed to working for. The narrator expresses this: "Was this the girl he once knew as Lois back in his home village?" (p. 183).

Women in Ngotho's society were normally placed in inferior roles. Lois is different from other women because she is strong and has a domineering personality. When she is younger, we are shown Lois's aggressive personality. Ngotho considered this, at the time, to be a positive personal quality. However, as her social status rises above his, Lois, from Ngotho's view, starts abusing her social position with her aggressiveness. Thus, when Lois becomes Ngotho's master, her personality seems threatening to him. Ngotho ceases to respect this quality, and that eventually causes him to hate her. His frustration also comes from the fact that a woman of his own race is in charge of him. He had expected to be mistreated by a white master; however, when he is mistreated by other blacks, he is greatly offended. He had thought that if a black man or woman was able to get a good social position, he or she would do something that would benefit blacks in general. His frustration is increased when he realizes that this is not a reality.

Ngotho remarks quite often about how the roles of men and women had become reversed. Whenever he complains, we can see how he felt women should be treated: "Where was the old warrior who at the end of the battle would go home to his wife and make her moan under his heavy sweat?" (p. 186). He believes that women are there to serve the husband, not the other way around. Mr. Njogu angers him because of his lack of authority in the marriage, and "Once or twice he would have liked to kick Mr Njogu. He looked all so sensibly handsome and clean as he buzzed after his wife on a broken wing and--a spot of jam on his tie--said he wanted the key to the car" (p. 186).

Lois was given the title "Queen" because she was a heroine to the people in her village. Her being called queen shows her strength of character and her authority. Her servants are afraid of her because of her strong characteristics. Ngotho feels uncomfortable even walking in front of her: "As she approached Mrs Njogu, he seemed to sweep a tactful curve off the path, as if to move up the wall first and then try to back in slowly towards the master's door and hope memsahib would make way" (p. 183).

Lois is a very proud and courageous woman. She is not afraid to speak out for what she believes in. This is apparent in her days as a schoolteacher: "Slowly, the lady supervisor measured out light taps down the class and having eliminated the gap that came between master and servant, stood face to face with Lois" (p. 184). This scene shows that Lois is not intimidated by her supervisor, because she knows that she is right. However, after her social status is improved, she uses her aggressiveness to control her servants. She is helping herself instead of helping the people of her own race who are oppressed. In fact, she is in the position of oppressing other blacks, her servants.

If the story had been written from Lois's point of view, the reader would probably feel more sympathetic toward her. She might relate negative things about Ngotho that we are not told about. Lois probably does not see herself the way Ngotho sees her. She probably feels she owes nothing to the people of her own race. Instead, she may think she deserves to enjoy her prosperity. It is difficult to determine how the story would change, were it told from Lois's point of view, because we know little about Lois's character besides what Ngotho has related to us. In order to fully determine how the story would change, we must put our feet into Lois's shoes. Ngotho and Lois have a complex relationship due to the differences in their social class and gender. The frustrations that Ngotho feels throughout the story are taken out finally on Mr. Njogu. From Lois's point of view, it probably looks like Ngotho stabbed her husband due to jealousy he has for the status his masters were able to achieve, a status he is unable to obtain.

Tae Woo,

You have executed the assignment quite well, following the instructions carefully. Sometimes your desire to conform to the instructions seems even to restrict your moves, so to speak. In your third paragraph, for instance, your sentences come too quickly one after another, as if in answer to some questions. Meanwhile, you seem to have forgotten that the paragraph itself has to have its own coherence, and that generalizations have to derive from some evidence. How do you know, for instance, that women in Ngotho's society are normally placed in inferior roles? When did you find out that Lois is aggressive? The desire to conform to the assignment may also account for some abrupt transitions from one paragraph to another in the first half of your paper.

One thing that makes your paper a little inconclusive is the fact that you try to keep a balance between two interpretations of the story: one that seems to emphasize the neocolonial relation and another that stresses the gender roles. In fact, if you look at the way these two issues are linked, you may come up with a very sophisticated argument. So far, the possibility of that argument is reflected only by the tension between the two aspects of the relationship between Ngotho and Lois.

The observations above are meant to show you how the paper can be improved. The paper is quite good as it is and responds well to the assignment. In the future, you may take more liberty with the assignment. My hints are designed to help you start the paper, but you do not need to follow them to the letter.

Grade assigned: B

Assignment 2

In this assignment you are asked to pursue the issue of men's and women's roles in society based on examples from Emecheta's novel *The Joys of Motherhood* and Kibera's story "The Spider's Web." These roles are interesting to observe because the societies depicted by these authors are in transition from a traditional tribal life to modern life. Beliefs and rules of conduct are in a state of change, and confusion often dominates. Write an essay explaining the expectations society has of men and women as represented in the texts mentioned above.

Consider Ngotho's dissatisfaction in his role as the servant of a woman. From Ngotho's experience draw some conclusions about what society (and Ngotho himself) expects from a man. Think also about the way other men like Lois's husband in "The Spider's Web" or Agbadi, Amatokwu, and Nnaife in *The Joys of Motherhood* fulfill the role of "man." The expectations society has of them are reflected in the way they act, in their satisfaction or dissatisfaction with their achievements, in the criticisms voiced by others about them. Think also about the women in the two narratives. Why, for instance, are Lois ("The Spider's Web") and Ona (*The Joys of Motherhood*) considered unnatural rebels in their respective societies? Consider the uses of conformity as exemplified by Nnu Ego: Why isn't she successful as a woman in spite of her willingness to conform to expectations?

Tae Woo Lee
Basic Composition 350:100
Professor Anca Rosu
Assignment 2

In the African societies which are discussed in the readings there are defining expectations for men and women. Both Buchi Emecheta and Leonard Kibera deal with this issue of gender roles assigned for men and women. In the novel The Joys of Motherhood, Emecheta explores the lives of members of the Ibuza and Ogboli societies, particularly women, who are considered property by men and can be sold at any time. In the short story "The Spider's Web," Kibera chooses to deal with the issue through the life of a man who works for a woman, thereby switching the traditional gender roles. Each story shows how the society's expectations define the lives of the characters.

The characters in both readings are expected to follow the roles assigned to their gender by the society. Those who do not are considered "weak men" or "bad women." Ona, a character in The Joys of Mother-hood, is a strong example. She does not conform to her society's expectations of women. One example of her nonconformity is her refusal to marry her lover, Agbadi. Ona is, therefore, described by Agbadi as "a young woman who managed to combine stubbornness with arrogance" (Emecheta 11). He believes that she "enjoyed humiliating him by refusing to be his wife" and "Agbadi was not supposed to be the kind of man women should say such things to" (Emecheta 11). Unlike the "other women who were willing to worship and serve him in all things" as was expected, Ona is considered "a rude, egocentric woman who had been spoilt by her father" (Emecheta 12). The attitudes which Agbadi expresses are characteristic of the way of thinking in the society. Since Ona refuses to follow the assigned roles, she is looked upon negatively.

Ngotho in "The Spider's Web" also criticizes the manhood of Mr. Njogu since he also does not follow the assigned gender roles. He finds himself wondering, "Where was the old warrior who at the end of the battle would go home to his wife and make her moan under his heavy sweat?" (Kibera 186). Ngotho mentions warriors because they symbolize the power of men: Men, not women, fought battles. Because of Mr. Njogu's lack of "power" over his wife, Ngotho sees him as "a male weakling in a fat queen bee's hive, slowly being milked dry and sapless, dying" (Kibera 186). Ngotho criti-cizes Mr. Njogu for allowing his wife to act against her gender role. Ngotho believes that Mrs. Njogu should act according to society's expectations, being subservient and obedient, and Mr. Njogu should be the one in power in the household.

Inconsistency with society's assigned gender roles also affects the way in which characters view themselves. For example, in "The Spider's Web," Ngotho expresses dissatisfaction with his life as a servant for Mrs. Njogu. In this short story, the traditional roles of men and women have been reversed. A female is in a position of power over a male, treating him like property. Ngotho says that "he had even caught himself looking at her from an angle where formerly he had stared her straight in the face" (Kibera 183). Ngotho expresses a discomfort with being a servant to a woman that is not present in his attitude towards his male master. In Ngotho's eyes "everything had become crooked, subtle, and he had to watch his step" (Kibera 186). He wonders "why he should have swept a curve off the path that morning, as memsahib filled the door" (Kibera 186). He is clearly uncomfortable with his actions of subservience towards Mrs. Njogu. He sees them as a weakness. Ngotho defies Mrs. Njogu's power by "eating more of her meals whenever she was not in sight" (Kibera 183). However, "he had come to hate himself for it and felt it was a coward's way out" (Kibera 183). He hates to hide his actions from his master because he feels that a man should be able to do what he wants to. The reader can speculate that Ngotho would not have the same reactions if it were a man who treated him as Mrs. Njogu does. By reversing the traditional gender roles in the short story, Kibera shows how strongly they are felt by the society. Had the expectations of men and women not been so clearly assigned, Ngotho's feelings of inadequacy and doubts in himself would not have been the same.

In The Joys of Motherhood, the character Nnu Ego also has feelings of inadequacy, like Ngotho, when she does not fulfill the expectations society has for her gender. Pregnancy is valued by the people, and women who do not produce heirs are looked on with dissatisfaction. Childbearing acts as proof of womanhood. Nnu Ego does fulfill one expectation which is important for women in the society: virginity, or virtue. It is believed that if "a woman is virtuous, it is easy for her to conceive" (Emecheta 31). However, Nnu Ego is

79

unable to have a child in the first few months and feels that she is "failing everybody" (Emecheta 31). Her husband takes a second wife who becomes pregnant in the first month. This situation increases Nnu Ego's feelings of inadequacy, and she shrinks "more and more into herself" (Emecheta 32). So important is childbearing in womanhood that it has the effect of destroying Nnu Ego's worth in her eyes and the eyes of others. Her husband ignores her, saying, "I have no time to waste my precious male seed on a woman who is infertile" (Emecheta 32). Womanhood, and manhood to a certain extent, is defined by the ability to produce heirs. So desperate is Nnu Ego to have this feeling of completion, possible only through pregnancy, that she begins to treat the second wife's son as her own. This situation acts as further proof of how strongly some characters strive to adhere to the expectations society assigns to their gender.

The idea of women as property or objects is another issue that the authors explore. In The Joys of Motherhood, it is interesting to note the names that are given to the women. The name Ona has the meaning "a priceless jewel" (Emecheta 11). When naming Nnu Ego, Agbadi says, "This child is priceless, more than twenty bags of cowries. I think that should really be her name because she is a beauty and she is mine" (Emecheta 26). The names given to the women are signs of the attitudes which men have towards them and the objectifying view that is held in this society. Ngotho refers to Mrs. Njogu as the "Queen" (Kibera 182). This could be a reference to the Queen of England who ruled the entire country as Ngotho points out. It is also an allusion to the queen bee image which he uses to describe Mrs. Njogu. The way in which it is used shows that Ngotho sees women with some power over men as sole rulers or imperious women. Clearly, he does not refer to Mr. Njogu as the King.

Both authors explore gender roles in African societies. Each shows what the expectations are for

both men and women. The authors explore the attitudes
characters have about themselves and others according
to the assigned gender roles. In this way, the reader
is brought into the experience of the African society
and is allowed to decide whether the gender roles are
acceptable.

Tae Woo,

*I see that you have become more free and imaginative in the
execution of the assignment. That is a step in the right direction: Take
control of your argument. You have given the paper a nice pattern pro-
gressing from society's perceptions of men's and women's roles toward
self-perceptions determined by those roles.*

*I cannot help but notice that you have given priority to women over
men here. Agbadi, for instance, who is a "man's man," receives little attention. You have a good point when you say that women's position as
property is reflected in their names. I have also noticed that your indecision in the interpretation of Kibera's story has disappeared, and now you
have a firm grip on this reading.*

Grade assigned: B+

Assignment 3

In "His Roth," Philip Roth highlights the moments when he
fears losing his father: a dangerous appendectomy, the time when the
father is about to die. Remembering such occasions, Roth also evokes
the qualities that made his father a "man" under normal circumstances. In fact, the occasions are sad because his father seems to be
"unmanned" by disease.

Write an essay in which you define the role of the father in the
family as Roth presents it and explain the connections between fatherhood, family structure, and masculinity. To make your point,
you may have to take into account not only the portrayal of the father but also the presentation of women, which defines men by contrast.

Tae Woo Lee
Basic Composition 350:100
Professor Anca Rosu
Assignment 3

        In the story "His Roth," Philip Roth uses his own
experiences to deal with the importance of the family
and the role of the father within the family structure.

The author presents fatherhood as a very important part of the family structure. He explores his idea of what the duties of fatherhood are. Roth presents fatherhood, the family structure, and masculinity as three connected things which are dependent on one another. Without a father, the family structure breaks down. Without masculinity, a man's role as a father is weakened.

Roth considers fatherhood a strong part of the family structure, and this can be seen in the way he views the two boys whose father is dead. The author says that he "thought of them as no less blighted than the blind girl who attended our school" (175). He feels that a father is necessary to a "normal" family structure. He compares fatherless families to a girl who has a physical handicap. This shows that he considers being without a father a handicap as well. Furthermore, the father is so important in Roth's eyes that even his absence has an effect on the family. He says about the two boys that "everything either of them did or said seemed determined by his being a boy with a dead father" (175). Without a man performing the duties of fatherhood, the family is abnormal in Roth's eyes. The family structure is broken.

Because of his illness, the author's father loses many of the qualities that are considered masculine. Prior to the sickness, Roth sees his father as hard working and strong, both physically and mentally. When the author thinks about his father, these are the things that come to mind. When his father comes home from the hospital in his weakened state, the author says: "He'd lost nearly thirty pounds, his shrunken face disclosed itself to us as a replica of my elderly grandmother's" (174). When his father is in his weakened condition, Roth associates him with a woman. The author's father has lost much of his physical strength, and this has affected his mental strength as well. The author uses words like "self-sufficiency" and "determination" to describe his father's past strength.

However, after his father's return from the hospital, Roth says he is "stunned by how helpless he appeared seated weakly in a chair" (175). He is stunned because his father no longer possesses any of the masculine qualities he associated with him. Most important, his father did not have physical strength. Before he became ill, he was able to work hard and support himself and his family. Now he is barely able to walk and eat on his own. This lack of strength makes him upset: He "could no longer control himself" (175). This incident shows how the father himself considered masculinity to be part of fatherhood. In his illness, he feels and appears almost powerless.

Roth believes maintaining the family structure is a duty of fatherhood. The author quotes a biblical reference, saying, "The family is God, the family is One" (175). Furthermore, Roth considers family "indi-visibility, the first commandment" (175). He explains the view of his people, saying that despite "internal friction and strife, [the family] was assumed to be an indissoluble consolidation" (175). It is a duty of fa-therhood to keep the family structure in place. With-out him it is considered to be broken down. He says that "Jews didn't get divorced" (175). Except for "the movie magazines and the tabloid headlines, [divorce] didn't exist" (175). A father who divorces his wife is considered to have made a transgression, "a breach of faith with his wife, his children, his entire clan" (175-76). When his Uncle Bernie divorces his wife, Roth says that "Bernie encountered virtually universal condemnation" (176). The author says that his parents probably would have been more supportive of the uncle if he had committed a crime.

This shows how highly the family structure was valued and how seriously the role of the father was taken. In Roth's view, the father has a definite in-fluence on a child's development by being a role model in his family or by being absent. The influence might not be visible at first, but as time goes on the child eventually realizes that his father contributed a lot to his personal development. Roth looks back on his past and realizes the influence of his father. He realizes the connection between fatherhood, family structure, and masculinity. It is when he finally looks beyond his father's physical strength and other characteristics that he is able to have a closer relationship with him.

Tae Woo,

This is a good analysis of Roth's narrative. You have made a lot of progress in both reading and writing. I notice that you have organized your ideas well and that your transitions are smooth. As far as content is concerned, you made some very interesting observations. I particularly like the passage in which you notice that not having a father is perceived as a handicap by Roth.

One thing that is missing from the paper is perhaps an attempt to evaluate Roth's attitude. Is he in tune with what we believe about families today? Or is his view rather old-fashioned?

Grade assigned: A

Assignment 4

At the start of his essay "Performative Excellence: Circum-Mediterranean," David Gilmore states that "the male image as it exists in many Mediterranean societies...is not so different in effect from masculine imagery elsewhere" (191). Using the ideas you have developed in the previous paper with regard to the role of men in the societies depicted by Kibera and Emecheta, you are in a position to test Gilmore's statement. Write an essay in which you decide whether we can develop a concept of masculinity that would be valid in more than one culture.

Start by defining masculinity in Gilmore's terms. Look at his examples and at the way he deduces the male ideal from the criticisms received by the males he has chosen as his examples. Notice that all of them actually fail the test of manhood. This might lead you to examples of men who fail in Kibera and Emecheta (Ngotho, Mr. Njogu, Nnaife). Think also of counterexamples of men who are successful at the task of "being a man," in both Gilmore and Emecheta. What is the price of their success?

Tae Woo Lee
Basic Composition 350:100
Professor Anca Rosu
Assignment 4

One cannot deny that maleness or manhood is something that is established at birth. However, in a discussion of manhood in terms of masculinity, one must factor in the criteria or conditions dictated by a particular culture or society. These criteria might vary in their specificity from culture to culture, but there is found a common concept of masculinity. Masculinity or manhood involves such things as being physically strong, having a family, and being able to provide for it. Using the manhood requirements of the cultures of the Mediterranean which are outlined in the essay "Performative Excellence: Circum-Mediterranean," by David Gilmore, this can be proven. A comparison with the criteria found in the African cultures in The Joys of Motherhood by Buchi Emecheta and "The Spider's Web" by Leonard Kibera provides evidence of this common concept.

An important factor in determining manhood or masculinity is the ability to produce heirs, or what Gilmore refers to as "impregnating one's wife" (198). The primary responsibility for pregnancy is placed on the man. Gilmore uses the example of the culture of Italy where "only a wife's pregnancy could sustain her husband's masculinity" (198). When a man and woman are unsuccessful in producing heirs, "the blame of barrenness is placed squarely on him, not his wife, for it is always the man who is expected to initiate (and accomplish) things" (Gilmore 199). The use of this criterion to determine masculinity can also be found in The Joys of Motherhood. The character Amatokwu has to deal with the consequences of not fulfilling this criterion. When his wife Nnu Ego does not become pregnant in the first few months, he complains, "My father is beginning to look at me in a strange way" (Emecheta 31). He realizes that, unless he produces an heir soon, he will be considered a failure at being a man. In order to protect his manhood, Amatokwu has to take another wife, who becomes pregnant within the first few months. He does so because, as Gilmore states in his essay, the responsibility of producing heirs is the man's (197-99). If his first wife did not become pregnant, it was his duty to find someone who would. Not to do so is to fail his people and fail in his role as a man.

Personal income is another characteristic of manhood or masculinity, according to Gilmore's essay. It is believed that "the husband, to be a real man, must contribute the lion's share of income to support wife and family" (Gilmore 199). One reason why the example Lorenzo was considered a failure at being a man was his lack of income or the inability to provide for his family. Lorenzo "had no discernible job, and as he earned no money, he contributed nothing concrete to his family's impoverished larder" (Gilmore 192). A good man is able to put the greatest amount of money into the family, whether or not other members work. A man who does not do this is not a real man. This is an attitude that is present in the cultures of the other readings as well. In The Joys of Motherhood, Agbadi, who is very wealthy, is considered a good man in the community. This is shown by the community's reaction to the size of the dowry he provides for his daughter when she marries. When Amatokwu and his people come for Nnu Ego, it is described as a night the "people of Ibuza were never to forget" (Emecheta 30). The narrator states that Agbadi "excelled himself" then goes on to list the many things that he sent with his daughter including "seven hefty men and seven young girls, . . . seven goats, baskets and baskets of yams" (Emecheta 30). The narrator lists all of these things because they are signs of Agbadi's wealth and his ability to provide for his daughter. It influences the way the people measure his manhood. As the author states, "If a new bride is too mouthy about her people, she will effectively be challenged: 'But are your people more generous than Nwokocha Agbadi of Ogboli?'" (Emecheta 30). The people pay tribute to Agbadi's wealth and manhood by using his name in this proverbial saying.

In "The Spider's Web," personal income also determines masculinity or manhood. The character Ngotho is a servant in this story and by being such is not as good a man as one who can provide for himself. Being without personal income forces him to take on a position of subservience to a woman, which is very unmasculine. As Gilmore states in his essay, "To be dependent upon another man is bad enough, but to acknowledge dependence upon a woman is worse" (204). Furthermore, he writes that "there is indeed no greater fear among men than the loss of this personal autonomy to a dominant woman" (205). This is an inversion of the traditional roles of men and women and "destroys the formal basis for manhood" (Gilmore 204). Because of his status as a servant to a woman, Ngotho is dependent on a woman and, therefore, according to the criteria of his society, he lacks masculinity or manhood.

One reason why great emphasis is placed on personal income is because of its effect on the relationship between a man and a woman, primarily the wife. A man must have a dominant and independent role in his relationship with a woman in order to be considered masculine. He must be able to protect his wife and family. Lack of dominance is an immediate weakening of one's manhood. Gilmore writes, "a man must gain full and total independence from women as a necessary criterion of manhood" (205). These feelings are echoed in the other cultures discussed in the readings. In Kibera's "The Spider's Web," the characters Ngotho, Kago, and Mr. Njogu are not considered manly enough because of their lack of domination in their relationships with women. Ngotho is a servant controlled by a female master. Ngotho struggles with his feelings of subservience and notes that "he had even caught himself looking at her from an angle where formerly he had stared her straight in her face" (Kibera 183). Ngotho, as a man, sees the acts of subservience towards a woman as weak. He considers Mr. Njogu less of a man because he does not dominate his wife, Mrs. Njogu. He refers to Mr. Njogu as "a male weakling in a fat queen bee's hive, slowly being milked dry and sapless, dying" (Kibera 186). He sees Mrs. Njogu as the head of the household; she has the position of dominance. Ngotho asks, "Where was the old warrior who at the end of the battle would go home to his wife and make her moan under his heavy sweat?" (Kibera 186). In Ngotho's eyes, it is the man who should hold a position of dominance or control in the relationship. The attitude that Ngotho holds about manhood or masculinity is very similar to what is expressed in Gilmore's essay. A "good" or "real" man must be dominant in his relationship with a woman. Perhaps a simple way of summing up the concept of manhood is: A male is born and a man is made. In order to possess what society labels manhood or masculinity, a male must fulfill the criteria or requirements that society considers necessary. By comparing the cultures in the three readings, it becomes clear that this is true in almost every society. If a man is not capable of fulfilling these duties, he will be criticized in the society and will not be considered a "good" or "real" man. As time goes on, perhaps this type of judgment will disappear. Males will be considered men regardless of whether or not they fulfill these standards and, as a result, the attitudes held toward women will change as well.

Tae Woo,
You have written a well-organized argument supported by both theory and examples. Some syntactic difficulties have occurred, I presume, because this is the first time you have dealt with a scholarly essay full of complicated concepts. In fact, given that it is indeed the first time, I must say you handled it rather well.

One thing that should have emerged more clearly in the paper is whether cultural differences qualify or invalidate Gilmore's claim that the criteria for masculinity are universal.
Grade assigned: B+

Assignment 5

In her "Introduction to *The Second Sex*," Simone de Beauvoir takes the simple word *other* and transforms it into a concept which she applies not only to women as a distinct social group but to all kinds of groups which may be considered as deviating from mainstream society. Write an essay in which you develop the idea of "otherness" and apply it to the narratives we have studied.

Locate the passages where Beauvoir develops the concept. Look at her examples and think of some examples of your own gathered from the narratives. For the purpose, reread Emecheta's novel and Kibera's story to find passages where you can identify cases where a dominant group treats the dominated group as "other." Naturally, women will appear as "other" in relation to men, but there will also be cases where the colonized Africans are cast as "other" by the colonizers. Create a connection between these two categories of examples and consider the relations between dominant and dominated groups. Notice that in some cases there is a double otherness, that of being an African and that of being a woman.

Tae Woo Lee
Basic Composition 350:100
Professor Anca Rosu
Assignment 5

In the "Introduction to The Second Sex," Simone de Beauvoir uses the word other as an effective way of summing up the position of women in society. "Otherness" implies, as the title itself states, the secondary status of the female sex. Beauvoir strengthens this concept using examples of additional groups that have been placed in a position of Otherness: Africans, Jews, etc. However, she is careful to maintain the distinction between the domination of these groups and the domination of women. The texts of The Joys of Motherhood by Buchi Emecheta and "The Spider's Web" by Leonard Kibera provide useful examples to explore this concept of Otherness in different contexts. Using them, one can explore the relationship of the dominant and the dominated in its different forms.

Before applying Beauvoir's concept of Otherness to the two pieces of literature, it is useful to test its validity by applying it to other circumstances. In part of her "Introduction to The Second Sex," Beauvoir says that "a man is in the right in being a man; it is the woman who is in the wrong" (152). She also goes on to say that "there is an absolute human type, the masculine" (153). These statements point to the conditions of society in which man is considered the norm or the standard. However, the relationship between man and woman is not the only instance where the concept of Otherness can be applied. It is possible to observe in society other labels or adjectives that indicate this "absolute human type." White, heterosexual, rich, healthy, American, etc. In almost every category—economic, physical, or sexual—a norm is set up against which everything else is defined as the Other. This way of thinking leads to the breakdown of groups into the dominant and the dominated. It is an inevitable consequence. This is the case with almost every label used by society to categorize human beings. Furthermore, out of each set of labels there is one that is considered the absolute, the norm, or at the very least, the most desirable. For instance out of the set of economic labels—poor, middle class, rich—rich is what society holds up as the most desirable condition. In terms of sexuality, heterosexuals are considered the norm and anything outside of that realm is the Other. Physical characteristics can also be categorized as Absolute and Other. For example, a healthy person is the Absolute, while someone with a physical handicap is the Other and is subjected to dominance. One can even go so far as to examine the realm of living things in which human beings are the Absolute and the rest are the Others. As Beauvoir states, "Thus it is that no group ever sets itself up as the One without at once setting up the Other over against itself" (154). In almost every facet of existence, Beauvoir's concept of Otherness can be applied.

It is also important to compare and contrast the Otherness of women, which is Beauvoir's primary focus, and the Otherness of other dominated groups. If man is in the position of Absolute and dominant in terms of sex, women are automatically pushed into the position of Other. This places women in an inevitable predicament because there are only two sexes, a fact that makes the role of Other for women unique. This uniqueness is further established by the fact that being female is determined by biology. Unlike the Otherness that exists for certain groups defined by religion or sexual-orientation, womanhood is a genetic fact that cannot be hidden. Although racial groups that experience Otherness and domination are also biologically determined, they are not alone in this category of Otherness. It is a position that racially oppressed groups share. White may be considered the Absolute, but there are several different racial groups that occupy the position of Other, unlike women who are the sole Other in relation to men. Racially oppressed groups, in contrast to women, have a cultural identity which they can use to define themselves as the One, thus turning the tables. Historically, no one has identified a culture of women which can be used for this sort of empowerment. Persons in economic groups that are dominated have a certain amount of control over changing their economic status. Beauvoir correctly writes, "A condition brought about . . . can be abolished . . . , it might seem that a natural condition is beyond the possibility of change" (155). It is important to recognize these differences when applying the concept of Otherness to different groups. Though there are some similarities, the differences for women pose other obstacles to overcome.

Beauvoir deals with Otherness in terms of the relationship between men and women. This type of Otherness is very prominent in Buchi Emecheta's novel The

Joys of Motherhood. In the African culture of this particular novel, women as the Other are defined in terms of their relationship to men, the One. They are primarily sexual objects or valued for their ability to produce offspring which brings manhood to the male. Among the people in the African cultures in the novel, "all agreed that a woman without a child for her husband was a failed woman" (Emecheta 62). Another example of this attitude is when the character Ubani expresses the belief that a "woman may be ugly and grow old, but a man is never ugly and never old. He matures with age and is dignified" (Emecheta 71). This is a belief that is present in every society in which men are in a position of dominance. Particularly damaging is the fact that women define themselves in terms of these rules created by men. When Nnu Ego loses her child she is so desperate that she attempts to commit suicide. She asks, "How would people understand that she had wanted so desperately to be a woman like every-body else, but had now failed again?" (Emecheta 61). As Beauvoir states in her essay, "Every female human being is not necessarily a woman; to be so considered she must share in that mysterious and threatened reality known as femininity" (151). In the case of the society in Emecheta's novel, a woman's femininity is determined by her ability to provide children for her husband.

In "The Spider's Web" by Leonard Kibera, another form of Otherness is present. It deals with an economic or social situation in which the One or dominant is the master and the Other is the servant. Ngotho and Kago fall into this category of Otherness. The evidence of Otherness and dominance is present in the actions of the characters. In describing Kago, Kibera writes that he was as "subservient as a child" (182). He possessed "ready aggressiveness where men of his class were concerned . . . but when it came to Mrs Njogu he wound tail between his legs and stammered" (Kibera 182). Ngotho too is stripped of his "manhood"

because he is a servant, and therefore, the Other.
This is something he deals with inside. Kibera writes
that "Ngotho seemed to tread carefully the fifty violent paces between the two doors, the irreconcilable
gap between the classes" (183). This passage effectively symbolizes the breakdown of people into master
as Absolute and servant as Other.

The condition of servant as Other is also present
in The Joys of Motherhood. Nnaife must deal with this
kind of dominance. When his master approaches, "his
heart [begins] to beat faster . . . he pulls himself up
straighter" (Emecheta 83). He kept "his head bowed in
submission" when speaking to his master (Emecheta 84).
Emecheta describes him as "one of those Africans who
were so used to being told they were stupid in those
days that they started to believe in their own imperfections" (83). Like the women in the novel, they begin to define themselves according to the terms their
dominator uses. The twist on this Otherness is that
the individual who is the master is a woman, an Other
in terms of the two sexes. The question is which Absolute is the more powerful of the two: the male servant
or the female master. This issue is explored in both
"The Spider's Web" and The Joys of Motherhood, for both
characters must deal with being submissive to women
whom they consider inferior.

Some characters in the novel fall into what can
be referred to as "double Otherness." The African
women in the novel are the Other because of their sex
and because they are colonized. Men like Nnaife are
subjected to double Otherness because they are both
colonized and impoverished. The African men in the
novel who are wealthy dominate those who are not. This
is also the case in "The Spider's Web" in which
Ngotho's master is an African female. Double Otherness
is present whenever a person falls into more than one
group that is considered Other. If the American,
white, heterosexual, young, healthy, rich male is considered the Absolute, then any person who falls outside

of this description is an Other of sorts. Therefore, a better term may be "multiple Otherness" as opposed to double Otherness.

It seems that the groups which fall into the category of Other have no real power in society. The Absolute is the group that provides the standard for the Other. However, one group cannot exist without the other. If everyone were of one economic class, there would be no need for the breakdown into poor, middle class, or rich. The Absolute uses the Other as a background against which they see themselves. In <u>The Joys of Motherhood</u>, women are necessary if men are to experience manhood. There would not be such a thing as a master without a servant. The colonizer would not exist without someone to colonize. Each group perpetuates the other's existence.

Society is dominated by certain types of people. Those who are not part of this group are dominated. People such as white Americans or the wealthy or men are examples of people who dominate our society. Although this has not been emphasized as greatly, even the handicapped can be considered an Other. Beauvoir's concept of Otherness can be applied to any group that is dominated. The novel by Emecheta and Kibera's short story are good sources for illustrating this concept of Otherness. However, society in general provides even more instances where this breakdown takes place.

Tae Woo,
I think that now you have managed to handle a theoretical reading quite well. That may be partly because you clarified Beauvoir's concepts first and illustrated them with examples from your own experience. The examples from the literary pieces are quite relevant and well integrated as well. I also notice that now you have brought your argument from your first paper to successful completion.
Grade assigned: A

Assignment 6

In this assignment you will be well advised to bring together all the concepts you have explored so far and all the examples you have analyzed. The main task will be the same as the one in assignment 2: to define gender roles in the societies presented by the authors you have read. This time, however, you will have to take into account the theoretical concepts acquired from Simone de Beauvoir's "Introduction to *The Second Sex*" and David Gilmore's "Performative Excellence: Circum-Mediterranean." Write an essay in which you explain the complexity of gender roles in both traditional and transitional societies. Develop concepts of masculinity and femininity that encompass the complexity.

First, make sure that you explore the ways in which men's and women's roles are socially and culturally determined. Think of men and women in the social context in which they lead their lives. Consider the historical conditions that can affect the expectations imposed on both genders when a society evolves. Men, for instance, who are usually dominant, may become the dominated when their society is colonized. Double domination, as in the case of colonialism, may also change the roles of women, in some cases giving them the courage to reject the domination of men.

Tae Woo Lee
Basic Composition 350:100
Professor Anca Rosu
Assignment 6

In every society, gender raises complex issues. No matter what the society, each one has a certain set of defining criteria assigned to each sex. These criteria reflect what role each sex is expected to play in the society. The issues raised around gender are the subject each of the following authors addresses in different ways. In <u>The Joys of Motherhood</u> Buchi Emecheta uses the novel genre to address the subject. The reader is exposed to these issues through the life experiences of a woman in colonized Africa. Leonard Kibera deals with gender issues as well in the short story "The Spider's Web." His story is told from the perspective of an African male who is the servant of an African female. Kibera uses this situation to explore the complexity of gender and society's expectations for each sex. While Emecheta and Kibera characterize the struggle to be either masculine or feminine, the other authors address gender issues from a theoretical basis.

Simone de Beauvoir deals with the plight of females in "Introduction to The Second Sex," forming her thesis around the idea of man being considered the first sex and women being the Other. David Gilmore's essay "Performative Excellence: Circum-Mediterranean" explores the images of the male and tries to answer the question: What exactly does masculinity or manhood mean? He takes his examples from the cultures of the Mediterranean. All these readings together offer a broad dissection of the worldwide society and give insight into the gender issues raised. Whether in fiction or in essay form, the authors, though unable to give a worldwide look at these problems, offer an interesting exploration of gender roles.

Being male or female is a quality established at birth. Therefore sex is something rather simply defined. The complexity arises when one attempts to define what it means to be masculine or feminine. A man or woman must show evidence of possessing certain qualities which society says are appropriate for a man or a woman. Defining what it means to be a man or a woman, therefore, becomes a complex task.

In "Performative Excellence," David Gilmore attempts to give insight into the question of manhood and, in the process, deals with womanhood as well. It would have been impossible for him to write the essay without any mention of women. The reader finds that masculinity or manhood is not something that can be defined or fathomed completely independently of the female sex. It is very much the man's relationship to women that is the grounds for the criteria. In order to see a male as a man, the relationship between him and his wife is, perhaps, the key factor. Masculinity and femininity are two concepts that must work hand-in-hand in order to be successful. According to society's criteria a masculine man cannot be paired with a woman who lacks feminine qualities. Even statements that seem to exclude the female sex from the definition do, in fact, act as proof of woman's importance. For instance, if a "self-respecting man" must be "a man among men" (Gilmore 205) it is still his relationship to women that is factored in. If "a real man must be out-of-doors among men" (Gilmore 205) it appears again, even in her absence, that she is a factor. In order to be considered a real man he must be independent of the woman with whom he has a relationship. He must have a balance in the amount of time he spends with her and without her. Women are used as the canvas or background against which a man paints a portrait of himself.

A way of illustrating this is the relationship between some of the couples in The Joys of Motherhood by Buchi Emecheta. For this society the production of offspring is the most important characteristic in terms of womanhood and manhood. A barren woman is an outcast in the society. However, a woman's infertility also affects the way in which a man is viewed. Not only is her womanhood called into question; his manhood is also speculated upon. When Nnu Ego has trouble bearing children with her first husband, he complains that his father is beginning to look at him strangely and soon takes another wife (Emecheta 31). This behavior echoes a characteristic of Italian society in which "only a wife's pregnancy could sustain her husband's masculinity" (Gilmore 198). For men "the ultimate test is that of competence in reproduction" (Gilmore 198). The woman is relegated to a position in the background, where everything she does serves as evidence of her husband's manhood. Hardly any of her qualities are self-serving or independent of the man in her life.

It is just this sort of pushing to the background that relegates women to the position of "second sex," as Simone de Beauvoir titles her book. Beauvoir deals with the fact that women are in the position of the defined as opposed to the definer. Furthermore, the distinction made between man as the first sex and woman as the second leads to the ensuing discrimination that takes place in almost every patriarchal society. The ideas that Beauvoir outlines in her introduction are illustrated in the novel The Joys of Motherhood. Beauvoir deals with the question: What is a woman? She writes that one answer offered to the question is that "woman is womb" (Beauvoir 151). This reflects the general sentiment of almost every society that a woman's most compelling quality is her ability to bear children. As discussed earlier, this importance is placed on her because it acts as proof of a man's masculinity, his fertility. In The Joys of Motherhood, the ability to bear children is considered the most important if not the only sign of womanhood. Any other feminine characteristics are overlooked if a woman is barren. The understanding in the society is "that a woman without a child for her husband [is] a failed woman" (Emecheta 62). There is nothing that a woman can do independently of a man. As the other sex, her existence is dependent upon the man.

Any overlap of so-called "masculine" or "feminine" characteristics creates social problems for men and women. One way of illustrating this is in the example of homosexuality. In his essay, Gilmore observes that bachelorhood is "accounted the most lamentable fate outside of blatant homosexuality, which is truly disgusting to them" (193). This is echoed in most societies. Homosexual males and females are ostracized because they are perceived as lacking what society labels masculine or feminine. The gender roles that society has assigned their sex are considered to have been crossed over. This shows that sexuality is directly related to gender roles and what society considers to be masculine or feminine.

Besides the example of homosexuality, the idea can also be illustrated by the adjectives that society assigns to each sex. If one were to make a list of the words one would use to describe a real man one would likely come up with words such as aggressive, strong, courageous, protective, etc. On the other hand, a good woman would likely be described as quiet, soft, weak,

98

obedient, helpful, etc. This goes back to the ideas in
Simone de Beauvoir's essay where women are on, not the
assertive, but the receiving end of almost every activity, the Other. In <u>The Joys of Motherhood</u>, women who
do not have these feminine qualities are looked down on
by the community. For example, Ona is considered a
"bad woman" (Emecheta 21) by other females because she
is described as a "woman who was troublesome and im-
petuous, who had the audacity to fight with her man before letting him have her" (Emecheta 21). Ona takes on
assertive qualities or so-called "masculine" characteristics. Instead of taking the role of Other as described in <u>The Second Sex</u> she attempts to take control
of her body and her sexuality.

Another example in <u>The Joys of Motherhood</u> is when
Nnu Ego and Adaku are described as "rebellious women
chasing and berating their husband" (Emecheta 136) when
in fact they are defending themselves from Nnaife.
When they step outside of the qualities assigned to
their gender role, they are met with negative responses. Even when a woman steps outside of her expected role because of things beyond her control like
infertility, she is looked down on. Recall for instance that a barren woman is considered "a failed
woman" (Emecheta 62).

Gilmore also addresses this crossing over of the
gender roles. He writes that there "is indeed no
greater fear among men than the loss of this personal
autonomy to a dominant woman" (205). This accounts for
the society's belief that being "dependent upon another
man is bad enough, but to acknowledge dependence upon a
woman is worse" (Gilmore 204). Self-determination and
independence are qualities reserved for men. In fact,
to be considered a real man, the male must be the one
"dominating and provisioning rather than being dominated and provisioned by women" (Gilmore 204-05). A
woman who has these "manly" characteristics is not in
possession of femininity or qualities that are considered appropriate for a woman. Indeed an assertive

woman is considered a destructive force. Gilmore writes that the "inversion of sex roles, because it turns wife into mother, subverts both the man and the family unit, sending both down to corruption and defeat" (205). Gilmore's statement makes it appear that a woman is an asset to the family only when she remains in her position of Other. Otherwise, she is considered a threat, especially to a male's manhood. This is the sentiment of Ngotho in "The Spider's Web." This character holds on to the traditional beliefs of his African society in which the man is dominant. His master is a female, and it is obviously a relationship he resents, since in his mind, the male should be in control. He considers her, Mrs. Njogu, to be dominant in her relationship with her husband as well. He calls Mr. Njogu "a male weakling in a fat queen bee's hive, slowly being milked dry and sapless" (Kibera 186). He asks, "Where was the old warrior who at the end of the battle would go home to his wife and make her moan under his heavy sweat?" (Kibera 186). His thoughts echo the sentiments mentioned in Gilmore's essay. Sexuality is directly related to a male's manhood.

Most interesting is the fact that the qualifications that society sets up for men and women to be considered truly masculine or feminine are destined to fail. This is especially true in the case of women who lack the power to define what womanhood means according to themselves. Nnu Ego, more than any other character, exemplifies this. Womanhood is decided by a female's ability to produce heirs. However, when she does finally bear children she does not have the feeling of completion that childbirth was supposed to bring her according to society's criteria. The problem with these qualifications is a rigidity that does not take into account the full gamut of human reactions and emotions. At times Nnu Ego makes decisions that are in her worst interest when following the criteria for femininity. Perhaps it is fitting that those who pray to her shrine are not given children (Emecheta 224). In the later years of her life, when she is all but ignored by her offspring, Nnu Ego finally realizes that the joy of being a woman is something that is born and found within, not in the womb.

The complexities raised by gender issues are not easily resolved. Nor do the readings give any clearcut solutions to the problems they raise. The four authors give insight into society's definition of gender and the ensuing expectations. In <u>The Joys of Motherhood</u>, Emecheta offers the reader an opportunity to understand the experiences of women in a patriarchal society. By focusing on the women in the community, the reader gets a sense of their emotions and inner thoughts. Simone de Beauvoir's "Introduction to <u>The Second Sex</u>" contributes a clarifying way of looking at the positions of men and women in sexist society. By comparing women to other oppressed groups one can see the similarities and better understand the plight of the female sex. By trying to explain the concept of manhood through various examples, Gilmore's "Performative Excellence" shows how it is impossible to judge the worth of every individual according to one set of criteria. "The Spider's Web," by Leonard Kibera, shows the effect that not living up to these criteria has on the male psyche. While the readings do not give solutions, their addressing the complexities serves as the first step. In order to resolve the issues, society must first recognize them and their effects.

Tae Woo,

Here, you have successfully brought together some of the most salient points of the previous papers in a new and more comprehensive framework. This is a nice paper starting from interesting observations and ending with a powerful conclusion. Among its shortcomings is perhaps a tendency to use "big" words which do not always show up in the right context. It's OK to use any kind of words as long as you are sure you know their meaning and usage.

All in all, you have developed a clear understanding of the issues related to gender and you may have disentangled some of their subtlest points. Nevertheless, you have left one point unclear: Can one speak of universal standards of masculinity and femininity, or are such standards local? Some characteristics are undoubtedly cross-cultural, as your comparisons demonstrate, but others seem specific to certain places. This is a question to think about in the future.

Grade assigned: A-

Assignment 7

In her essay "Where I Come from Is Like This," Paula Gunn Allen emphasizes the power of women in the tribal tradition of American Indians. Her emphasis seems to contradict the general idea of the mainstream (white) society that women are "the weaker sex." Why do women appear to be powerful in the tribal context and weak in the society at large?

Write an essay in which you define the concept of power in relation to gender. Compare the concept of power emerging from Allen's essay to the way we normally define power in order to explain the different view of women in tribal and mainstream societies.

Tae Woo Lee
Basic Composition 350:100
Professor Anca Rosu
Final Exam

In "Where I Come from Is Like This," Paula Gunn Allen transforms the traditional meaning of power into one that encompasses more people. In other words, it takes the lives of more people into consideration, more than the mainstream society. Allen defines power in many ways that are different than what is normally used in descriptions of power.

In the mainstream society, power is defined by the control one has over the lives of others. Allen describes it, in terms of the tribal societies, as the control the individual has in his or her own life. The power of women is visible in their self-determination, the level of respect they are given by the tribe, and in short, their ability to be seen as complete individuals and as a diverse, balanced sex.

Even though the American Indian woman is "primarily defined by her tribal identity" (391), one gets a sense that the woman takes part in the defining process. The fact that women are defined by their society echoes the ways of mainstream society. In almost every culture, it is the surrounding society which gives a female "her sense of herself as a woman" (391). This is in some ways inevitable as one is influenced in youth by the people in one's family or by those one comes into contact with. These people, who make up society, offer their opinions and experiences of what womanhood means. The difference, in tribal society, comes from the way in which the woman is perceived in tribal definitions as opposed to Western definitions.

This difference may come largely from the oral tradition which permits the society in which women have the power to pass down definitions of womanhood to each generation of women. This counters Western society, in which the media in all forms are largely controlled by men who, therefore, control the images. Allen equates the power of American Indian women with "their sense of direction and of self" (396). This sense of self stems from the ability to take the greatest part in defining womanhood in general and, in some ways, the individual self.

The power of women can be witnessed when Allen recalls that her "ideas of womanhood" were "passed on largely by [her] mother and grandmothers" (391). This shows that the majority of the images and perceptions she has of what it means to be a woman were influenced by women whom she trusted. One can infer that any additional influence was provided by other women in and outside of the family and by some men. Allen's idea of womanhood involving "practicality, strength, reasonableness, intelligence, wit, and competence" (391) gives her a positive and empowering perception of women. Her images are minus "a foolish woman, a dumb woman, a vain woman, or a plastic woman" (391-92). She is instilled with ideas of women with power, the power of self-determination. The women are not clones of one another but show "a wide range of personal style and demeanor" (392).

Allen recognizes the variety and the balance that exist among women, each one an individual. She gives power the meaning of being seen in one's entirety. When she remembers the Navajo woman who was badly beaten by her Sioux husband, this image is balanced by the memory of her grandmother who "abandoned her Sioux husband long ago" (392). She has a bank of female images: "sullen women, amicable women, selfish women" (392). She realizes that although the "tribes see women variously" they "do not question the power of femininity" (391). Unlike many Western portrayals of women as sexual objects or as breeders, the tribal context gives women a certain power by presenting them completely. Allen contends that "the individual woman is provided with a variety of images of women from the interconnected supernatural, natural, and social worlds she lives in" (391). Therefore she has a wide range of images from which she can draw to see herself.

Allen describes power in a way that is not often found in mainstream society. Instead of giving empowerment the meaning of controlling others, she describes it as determining one's self. In the tribal society, women have the primary control over the images which are associated with them and these images are realistic. They cover the wide range of characteristics embodied by women, no two of whom are the same. Instead of the Western conception of femininity, where sexuality and fertility are considered the most important qualities, the tribal society focuses on the entire woman. This for Allen means empowerment for women: having the power to define themselves and pass these images on to their own daughters.

Tae Woo,

I like the way you have developed the concept of power in this paper as well as some of your observations regarding Allen's examples. At times, however, you seem to idealize her too much—or maybe she idealizes her background (but you could have pointed that out). In your essay, the tribal society among American Indians seems like a paradise for women. But your point about the ability of women to define themselves as a source of power is quite valid.

   Grade assigned: A-

Index of Connections

The following list of works linked by "Connections" questions in the text is organized alphabetically by author. Page citations refer to the page on which the "Connections" question can be found.

Thematic Index

The themes are listed in the order in which they appear in *Makin Cultural Connections*.

Family

Jane Collier, Michelle Z. Rosaldo, and Sylvia Yanagisako, *Is There a Family? New Anthropological Views* (p. 38)
Jill Ker Conway, *The Right Country* (p. 428)
Ernest J. Gaines, *Just Like a Tree* (p. 5)
Ellen Gilchrist, *Music* (p. 357)
Garrett Hongo, *Kubota* (p. 398)
Neil Miller, *A Time of Change* (p. 25)
Itabari Njeri, *Bag Lady* (p. 446)
Philip Roth, *His Roth* (p. 173)
Amy Tan, *Without Wood* (p. 379)
Marianna De Marco Torgovnick, *On Being White, Female, and Born in Bensonhurst* (p. 138)

Adolescence

James Baldwin, *Whose Child Are You?* (p. 309)
Raymonde Carroll, *Parents and Children* (p. 80)
Ellen Gilchrist, *Music* (p. 357)
David Jackson, *One of the Boys* (p. 63)
Louise J. Kaplan, *Adolescence: The Farewell to Childhood* (p. 107)
Judith Ortiz Cofer, *The Looking-Glass Shame* (p. 97)

Women

Paula Gunn Allen, *Where I Come from Is Like This* (p. 390)
Simone de Beauvoir, *Introduction to* The Second Sex (p. 150)
Jill Ker Conway, *The Right Country* (p. 428)
Erika Friedl, *A Betrothal, a Rape, and a Guess About Turan's Fate* (p. 129)
Leonard Kibera, *The Spider's Web* (p. 180)
William Least Heat-Moon, *The Emma Chase* (p. 282)
Edna O'Brien, *The Widow* (p. 271)
Amy Tan, *Without Wood* (p. 379)
Deborah Tannen, *Damned If You Do* (p. 495)

110

Cultures in Contact

Rhetorical Index

Many of the selections listed here employ several rhetorical strategies at once and may be found under several headings.

Analysis

Analogy

Classification

Comparison and Contrast

Definition

Description

Example and Illustration

Exposition